Statistical Techniques
in Business and Economics

The Irwin Series in Quantitative Analysis for Business

Consulting Editor   Robert B. Fetter   Yale University

Statistical Techniques   In Business   Fifth
Techniques   and Economics   Edition

Robert D. Mason
The University of Toledo

1982
RICHARD D. IRWIN, INC. Homewood, Illinois 60430

ISBN 0-256-02656-4

Library of Congress Catalog Card No. 81-82880

Printed in the United States of America

7 8 9 0 MP 9 8 7 6 5

Dow Jones-Irwin, a division of Richard D. Irwin, Inc.,
has developed Personal Learning Aids (PLAIDS)
to accompany texts in this subject area. Copies can
be purchased through your bookstore or by writing
PLAIDS, 1818 Ridge Road, Homewood, IL 60430.

To Dorothy

Preface

This text is designed primarily for a first course in business and economic statistics. However, students majoring in any of the social sciences will find the illustrative material quite familiar. The mathematics can be handled by students who do not have an extensive mathematical background.

The book is divided into 24 chapters, and 16 appendixes are included. There is ample material for a one-year course, but considerable latitude is possible in the selection of topics for shorter courses. A one-semester course, for example, could include Chapters 1–5, 9–15, and 20. The primary objective of this fifth edition remains the same as that of the previous editions. Both descriptive statistics and inferential statistics are covered, but the main emphasis is on inferential statistics. In addition, there are a number of special-interest topics such as quality control, time series analysis, and index numbers.

The text includes a number of new special features.

It is now oriented to the example—solution approach.

At various points in each section there are *self-reviews* designed to give students an opportunity to work problems similar to the examples. Answers and methods of solution are given in the margin adjacent to the self-review problems. This work serves to reinforce the student's understanding of the preceding material.

A *chapter self-review examination* at the end of each chapter covers all the material in the chapter. This test allows the student to evaluate his or her overall comprehension of the subject matter.

A number of applications presented use the Statistical Package for the Social Sciences, Minitab, and Basic to illustrate the computer's potential for problem solving.

Both a *chapter summary* and a *chapter outline* are presented at the end of each chapter. Students can use them to pull together the ideas of the chapter.

New material in this fifth edition also includes exponential smoothing, the moving-average method of smoothing time series, and the normal approximation to the binomial. The material on probability and probability distributions has been revised and expanded to three chapters. The presentation of tests of hypotheses has also been revised and is now contained in three chapters.

A new, 200-page Study Guide now accompanies the text. The chapter organization of this comprehensive study guide is the same as the text's. For each chapter there are:

Chapter objectives.

An extensive summary.

A glossary of terms.

Problems with detailed solutions.

Student practice exercises, with answers.

A two- or four-page tear-out chapter assignment.

A Teacher's Manual contains the full solutions to all the exercises in the textbook and all the chapter assignments in the Study Guide.

I wish to express special thanks to colleagues William G. Marchal and Douglas A. Lind for their many helpful comments in organizing this fifth edition. Special acknowledgment is given to Jeff Hooper, Mesa Community College; Charles N. Keppler, Miami Dade Community College; Charles E. Leitle, Missouri Southern State College; William G. Marchal, University of Toledo; Douglas W. Morrill, Centenary College of Louisiana; John C. Shannon, Suffolk University, Boston, Massachusetts; and Lee C. Wilson, Mason Community College; who made many valuable comments and criticisms in their reviews of the manuscript. I am indebted to the Literary Executor of the late Sir Ronald A. Fisher, F.R.S. Cambridge; to Dr. Frank Yates, F.R.S. Rothamsted; and to Messrs. Oliver and Boyd, Ltd., for permission to reprint Tables III and IV of their book *Statistical Tables for Biological, Agriculture and Medical Research.*

Robert D. Mason

A note to the student

This textbook is constructed to aid you in your study by presenting the subject matter in small, easy-to-take steps with frequent checks to determine whether you fully understood the preceding material.

As you progress through each chapter you will be asked to solve a problem and interpret your findings. The answer to each *self-review* is always given on the left side adjacent to the problem. Cover the answer before starting work. Following is an example.

SELF-REVIEW

---

a. The range is 54.3, found by

b. Highest value − Lowest value
   = 297.9 − 243.6
   = 54.3.

(Cover the answers in the left hand column.)

The consumer price indexes for May in selected cities are: Cleveland, 285.1; Buffalo, 297.9; Denver, 256.7; Atlanta, 284.7; Chicago, 243.6; Dallas, 277.2.

a. What is the range?

b. *Now verify your answer against the one given in the margin.*

There are *exercises* after each section, if you need additional practice. The answers to selected exercises and the methods of solution are given in Appendix A.

Another distinctive feature of this text is the *Chapter Self-Review Examination* with answers and method of solution given in Appendix A. By completing this test you can better evaluate your comprehension of all the material in the chapter.

Contents

4. Describing data—measures of central tendency   59

5. Measures of dispersion and skewness 95

6. Index numbers 133

7. Time series analysis 163

10. Discrete probability distributions 255

11. The normal probability distribution 279

12. An introduction to sampling 301

20. Simple regression and correlation analysis 497

21. Multiple regression and correlation analysis 527

Appendixes 601

Index 677

1

INTRODUCTION

Many television viewers visualize a **statistician** as one who records each yard gained by rushing in the Dallas Cowboys–Denver Broncos Monday night football game, or who records each foul shot attempted and points made in the Boston Celtics–Detroit Piston game. We are constantly bombarded during and after the game with **statistics**: Larry Bird of the Celtics scored a career high of 28 points in the first half, Tony Dorsett gained 103 yards before retiring in the third quarter, Chris Evert Lloyd beat Virginia Ruzici of Romania 7–5 and 6–1, and Gorman Thomas of the Brewers scored two runs, and had one hit in three times at bat.

Likewise, reference to *The Wall Street Journal, Business Week,* annual reports of industry, and other sources of business data revealed that Arvida Realty Sales, Inc.,[1] is handling the sale of a four-bedroom home in the harbor section, priced at $547,500; the average hourly earnings in contract construction are $10.35,[2] Connecticut produced 4,950,000 pounds of tobacco in 1981;[3] and IBM has 341,279 employees, 737,230 stockholders, and an annual gross income from sales, rentals, and services of $26,213,000,000.[4] Fifty-one percent of the millionaires in the United States are women, and 95 percent of the money in the United States is managed by women. A final statistic from Norton Simon: the total compensation of the chairman of the board, David J. Mahoney, was $2,037,000 in 1981.

Statistics has a more precise meaning, however. It is defined as the *science of collecting, organizing, presenting, analyzing, and interpreting numerical data for the purpose of making better decisions in the face of uncertainty.*

Just as lawyers have "rules of evidence" and accountants have "commonly accepted practices," statisticians follow some standard guidelines when dealing with data. The basic techniques employed by statisticians are discussed in the following chapters.

---

[1] *The Sarasota* (Florida) *Herald-Tribune,* April 12, 1981, p. 11D.

[2] *Survey of Current Business,* February 1981, p. S–13.

[3] Department of Agriculture.

[4] 1980 Annual Report, International Business Machines Corporation, p. 1.

What is statistics?

2

**DESCRIPTIVE
STATISTICS**

Note in the foregoing definition that one facet of statistics deals with collection, organization, and presentation, that is, with methods used in *describing* data. For example, NCR Corporation wanted to show its stockholders the rapid growth in earnings per share since 1976. They were portrayed by a descriptive tool called a **bar chart** (see Chart 1–1). NCR also wanted to show the dramatic decreases in long-term debt since 1976. This was described in the form of a **line chart** (Chart 1–2).

Several chapters in this book are devoted to descriptive statistics. Various sources of statistical data and graphic presentation are examined in Chapter 2. Organization of data is explored in Chapter 3. Analysis of statistical data may be accomplished by computing one or more measures of central tendency (Chapter 4) and measuring the dispersion (Chapter 5). Further, it may be appropriate to convert the data to indexes (Chapter 6) or to use the statistical techniques described in other chapters.

CHART 1–1

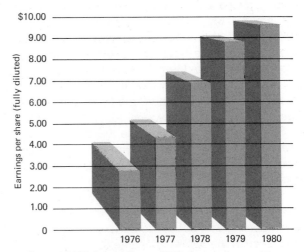

Source: 1980 Annual Report NCR Corporation, p. 43.

**CHART 1–2
Long-term debt,
1976–1980**

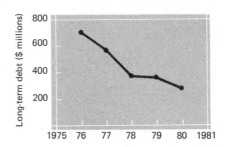

Source: 1980 Annual Report, NCR Corporation, p. 43.

INDUCTIVE STATISTICS

Inductive statistics, which is also called **statistical inference**, is the facet of statistics that goes beyond merely describing the situation. Methods of statistical inference deal with a **sample** taken from a **population**. Examples of a population, alternatively called a **universe**, are: all the persons eligible to vote, the total number of freshmen students at the university, all the fish in a pond, all the wheat in a truck, and the total number of pinion gears manufactured by a machine during a one-hour period. That is, the totality of all the statistics that can be collected on a group of people, fish, machined parts, and so on can be designated as the population. Note that a population in the statistical sense of the word does not necessarily refer to people.

A number of items selected from a population is called a **sample**. Professional polling organizations select less than 3,000 voters out of millions throughout the United States prior to an election. And based on the sample responses, certain inferences are made relative to how all voters will cast their ballots. One automobile manufacturer takes a sample of five pinion gears every hour, and on the basis of the sample results makes a decision on the quality of all pinion gears produced during the hour. A small scoop of wheat is taken from a truck as it is waiting to be unloaded at a local grain elevator. Based on the results of the tests on the grain, a price is established for the whole truckload. In each of the illustrations cited, it was not feasible to study the whole population. The sample of voters was necessary because of the prohibitive cost of contacting all the voters just prior to the election. Testing wheat for moisture content destroys it, thus making a sample imperative.

As further examples of the extensive use of sampling, the U.S. Department of Labor is constantly monitoring employment, unemployment, wages, and so on. Based on the sample surveys, the Department releases such statistics as: 1.1 persons per 100 employed in manufacturing quit in November, the average hourly wage in January was $10.44 in construction and $5.16 in retail trade.[5] The U.S. Bureau of the Census reported that to monitor the youth unemployment problem, the Bureau conducts "a monthly Current Population Survey (CPS) using a national probability sample composed of rotating groups totaling approximately 65,000 households per month. The Census Bureau enumerators contact the households in the sample each month and ask a series of structured questions about the labor force status of each member 16 years of age and over during the preceding week."[6] James A. King and Clagett G. Smith used "systematic random sampling procedures" to select 2,737 professional persons in a study of mental health hospitals.[7]

Statistical inferences, generalizations, forecasts, and predictions all go beyond the realm of descriptive statistics. Predicting about the unknown assumes that there are certain *risks* involved. Five pinion gears, for example,

---

[5] *Monthly Labor Review,* March 1981, pp. 92, 96.

[6] Ibid., p. 3.

[7] *Social Science,* Summer 1976, pp. 161–69.

selected at random from all pinion gears manufactured during the hour might be perfect. It might be inferred from this sample that all gears produced were satisfactory. But since this inference was based on a sample, there is a chance that not all the gears produced are satisfactory. Opinion polling and the test marketing of a new cereal, soap, or toothpaste on a sample basis also assume that there is a risk involved in making inferences about the behavior of the population. The opinion poll or market survey might indicate that candidate X will win in a landslide or that, if marketed, a new cereal will be purchased by a substantial proportion of the population. However, there is a chance that candidate Y might win, and the cereal might be rejected by consumers, resulting in a substantial loss to the manufacturer.

Columnist Philip Wagner emphasizes the dangers inherent in sampling in a critical article on the federal government's unemployment statistics released monthly.[8]

> Some statistics are reliable. That is generally true of sports statistics— batting averages and the like. Thus we learn to trust statistics. But this is not the case with many of the statistics on intrinsically more important matters. Unemployment statistics, for example. First there are the arbitrary definitions of what is or is not unemployment, most of them highly debatable. Then there are samplings which are assumed but not known to be representative of the whole. Then there are the samplers themselves, of variable competence, drawing their samples from sources of variable reliability. Formulas are then applied to this raw amorphous mass. The mixture is fed into a computer which produces a stream of numbers, rates, and ratios. Thus a spurious precision is fabricated out of the most appallingly imprecise material.
>
> If it comes to a choice between the sort of statistics the public is fed day in and day out, and a guarded but well-informed guess, I'll take the guess every time. At least you know it is only a guess, whereas a statistic is too easily taken for the truth.

Descriptive statistics will be considered first. Some important sources of business statistics and the presentation of data in the form of charts will be discussed in Chapter 2.

---

[8] The *Blade,* Toledo, Ohio, January 27, 1977, p. 31.

2

INTRODUCTION

This chapter begins our study of **descriptive statistics.** Recall from Chapter 1 that this facet of statistics is concerned with the collection, presentation, and description of numerical data. Describing data may be as simple as collecting sales data for the past five years from the company files and presenting them in the annual report in the form of a line graph. Another research project by the marketing department of a firm manufacturing personal products for men might involve designing a questionnaire and administering it to 1,600 males through a personal interview, in order to collect information on their use of after-shave lotion, deodorant, and other personal products. The results of the survey might be described to management by means of graphs, averages, and other techniques.

Other investigations may require statistics on money turnover, population, exports, employment, prices, etc. For example, a firm considering establishing several distribution centers in the state might want the population by county. Does this type of information exist? If so, where can it be located? And, a management-union negotiating team concerned with establishing minimum hourly incomes for computer operators, welders, secretaries, and other categories of company employees would no doubt employ information on hourly incomes paid employees in similar jobs in various regions of the country. Are these income figures available? They are. The following section will, therefore, concentrate on some of the standard sources of business and economic data. Then there is a brief discussion of the survey as a source of data. Finally, some of the commonly used techniques used to present numerical data graphically will be examined.

Collection and presentation of data

SOURCES OF
PUBLISHED
DATA

Standard
business and
economic sources

Depending on the problem, a well-known source such as the *Historical Statistics of the United States,* the *Statistical Abstract of the United States,* or one of the many publications listed in the following paragraphs might be consulted. Those listed are merely representative of a large number of publications, and the list is not intended to be all-inclusive. They have been arbitrarily classified into government, private, and international publications. Actual figures have been cited to illustrate the type of statistics included.

Publications of the federal government

Decennial publications. The U.S. government undoubtedly generates more statistics than any other organization or any foreign government. The many departments and bureaus, including the Bureau of the Census, the Department of Labor, and the Federal Trade Commission, publish and distribute data decennially, annually, monthly, weekly, and daily. The Bureau of the Census conducts a census of population and a census of housing every 10th year. A large number of detailed reports on the characteristics of the population (such as age, income, sex) are available. The bureau also makes annual estimates and projections of the population by state, age, sex, and so on. For example:

Year and series	Total population of the United States* (in millions)
1950	152.3
1960	180.7
1970	204.9
1980	222.3
Projections:	
1990–95	254.7
1995–2000	269.4

*As of July 1. Includes Armed Forces abroad.
Source: U.S. Bureau of the Census, *Current Population Reports,* series P–25, nos. 310, 802, and 888.

Annual publications. The U.S. Department of Commerce has published the *Statistical Abstract of the United States* annually since 1878. Most of the statistical information is for the most recent year, but many series contain data for the past four or five years. The table of contents for the 1,000-page publication lists such sections as population, vital statistics, immigration, education, law enforcement, labor prices, elections, power, transportation, manufacturing, fishing, and agriculture.

A few assorted figures:

Last year 20,591 persons were murdered.

In Brazil, 33.8 percent of the dwellings have piped water.

There are 534,000 computer specialists in the United States of whom 26 percent are female.

There are 120,485,000 automobiles (including cabs) in the United States.

Monthly publications. Most of the departments of the federal government also publish statistical data on a monthly basis. The Department of Labor puts out the *Monthly Labor Review*. About 40 pages are devoted to labor turnover, earnings, hours, consumer and wholesale prices, work stoppages, and work injuries. From a recent issue come the following:

Workers in petroleum and coal products have $11.13 gross average hourly earnings.

Among black men aged 20 to 21 years, 23.2 percent are unemployed.

About 1 employee in 15 reported at least one absence during the week.

There were 201 work stoppages in the United States in November involving 51,900 workers.

The Department of Commerce also published the *Survey of Current Business* monthly. It has two main sections. One section is devoted to current business statistics; the other section contains a discussion of business highlights, prices, business failures, and industrial prospects. The half set aside for business statistics includes about 2,500 statistics every month. In most cases, the most recent month and the preceding 11 months are given.

During the week of November 3–8 commercial banks made 72,123 loans to farmers totaling $1,301,641,000. The average maturity date was 7.3 months, and the average interest rate was 15.46 percent. These are but a few of the thousands of financial figures published monthly by the Board of Governors of the Federal Reserve System in the *Federal Reserve Bulletin*. The first 100 pages are devoted to articles of interest to bankers and others in the field of finance. The last 50 pages contain the statistics on business loans, interest rates, assets and liabilities, and demand deposits. Also included are many related series such as the volume of retail sales and indexes of production, housing starts, and exports.

Publications of private organizations

Annual publications. Many trade associations compile and release various types of statistical data. For example, the Motor Vehicle Manufacturers Association publishes annually *Motor Vehicle Facts & Figures*. It gives automobile registrations back to 1900 (4,192), annual production of busses, number of trucks and automobiles registered by state, the number of vehicles produced by General Motors, Ford, and other manufacturers, the number of traffic deaths, and so on.

The *World Almanac and Book of Facts,* and the *Information Please Almanac Atlas and Yearbook* are two publications which contain a variety of statistics on sales, sports, and so on. From the *Information Please Almanac* (published by Simon & Schuster):

> There were 416 males and 19 females in the House of Representatives, 97th Congress.
>
> George Gervin of San Antonio was the N.B.A. scoring champion in 1979–80 with 2,585 points in 78 games, for an average of 33.1 points a game.

Publications of international organizations

Annual publications. The Statistical Office of the United Nations, Department of Economic and Social Affairs, is the leading organization disseminating international information. They publish two volumes annually.

For the *Statistical Yearbook,* over 160 countries or territories submit their national statistics directly by questionnaire, while others make statistics available by means of published documents. The table of contents lists sections on population, agriculture, manufacturing, communications, finance, and education for most of the countries.

In the *Demographic Yearbook,* official population statistics from almost 250 entities of the world are included. Data on nationality, mortality, marriage, divorce, and population by age, sex, and so on are presented.

Monthly publications. The *Monthly Bulletin of Statistics* includes both annual and monthly figures for most countries on such diversified items as production of motor vehicles, population, residential construction, and exports. A few selected figures are:

> The world population is 4,336 million.
>
> The average monthly production of passenger cars in Brazil is 46,100.

Consulting reference aids

If the search of standard reference books containing economic and business data is unproductive, the following reference aids may be consulted: Volume 1 of *The Encyclopedia of Business Sources* by Paul Wasserman is an especially valuable reference guide to sources of information of various industries, from the ice cream industry, to the arsenic industry. In addition, references are listed by topics, such as vitamins or industrial hygiene. H. Webster Johnson's *How to Use the Business Library* is a similar publication.

The *Business Periodicals Index* is somewhat typical of a number of indexes. Over 100 business periodicals are searched every month, including *Business Week, Fortune, Sales Management,* and *Textile World.* As indicated in the prefatory note, it is a "cumulative subject index to English language periodicals in the fields of accounting, advertising and public relations, automation, banking, communications, economics, finance and investments, insurance, labor, management, marketing, taxation, and specific businesses, industries, and trades." A few examples from a monthly issue:

COMPUTER crimes
    See also
    Computers—Access control

Computer crime: low risk for potential criminals; high risk for corporations. R. Bloom. Data Mgt. 18:24–6 D '80

Computer crime: separating the myth from the reality. P. Watkins. CA Mag 114:47–7 Ja '81

Detecting & preventing accounts receivable fraud through computer systems. E. T. Leininger, Credit & Fin Mgt 33:18–20 Ja '81

Proposed Federal Computer Systems Protection Act. L. M. Marquis, CPA J 50:29–32 D '80

Who are the computer criminals? J. Becker. il Sec Mgt 25:22+ Ja '81

Management

Data General's management trouble. Bus W p58 F 9 '81

Memorex tries a turnaround—again. Bus W p78+ Ja 19 '81

In addition to the *Business Periodicals Index,* The *New York Times,* and *The Wall Street Journal* publish indexes which contain information regarding articles of an economic or business nature.

The federal government since 1895 has published a monthly guide to government publications called the *Monthly Catalog of United States Government Publications.*

Many statistical publications also list other sources of data. The Guide to Sources in the appendix of the *Statistical Abstract of the United States* is excellent.

THE SURVEY AS A SOURCE OF DATA

Generally speaking, the purpose of a survey is to gather statistical data which are not available in published or any other form. A number of different methods may be used to collect the needed information. One is a *mail questionnaire.* Recently Merrill Lynch & Co., Inc., sent a questionnaire to each of its shareholders:

Dear Shareholder:

We want to make every effort to know our shareholders better and to communicate with them in the best possible manner. We believe that the answers to the attached questionnaire may help us do both. We'd appreciate your taking a few minutes of your time to fill in the questionnaire and return it to us in the envelope provided. We will be pleased to report to you on the results of the survey.

If you prefer not to be identified, you need not give your name and address. Thank your for your cooperation.

Merrill Lynch & Co., Inc.
Investor Relations

The mail questionnaire is a relatively inexpensive method of collecting data, especially if the respondents are spread over a wide geographic area. The major disadvantage of the mail questionnaire is the rather low percentage of returns. Research firms report a low of 10 to 15 percent response for some surveys they conduct. The response varies, however, depending upon the construction of the questionnaire and the interest the respondents have in the subject. For example, a 15-page questionnaire sent to over 100 major oil companies resulted in a 92 percent response.

Universities and professional survey organizations, such as Roper Polls, conduct *personal interviews* to determine the need for a shopping center, the popularity of a political candidate, and so on. Personal contacts are more expensive than mailing out questionnaires because a competent staff of interviewers must be maintained and given instructions for every survey. The major advantage of the personal interview technique is the high percentage of responses possible.

Many research organizations use a combination of the mail questionnaire and the personal interview approach. A personal call is made on the nonrespondents.

Criteria for questionnaire construction

Certain criteria for conducting a successful survey, based primarily on the experiences of companies, universities, and individuals, have been developed. A few of these criteria follow. (All of the illustrations cited have been taken from actual surveys.)

1. *The person conducting the survey must introduce himself or herself and state the objective of the survey.* (Refer to the Merrill Lynch letter.)

2. *Adequate instructions must be given.* From the Merrill Lynch questionnaire:

    On whose recommendation did you buy the stock? (check one, or several)

☐ Broker	☐ Financial publication
☐ Banker	☐ Friends and relatives
☐ Investment counselor	☐ Own judgment
☐ Financial information service	☐ Other _____

3. *Certain words which can be interpreted differently must be either avoided or defined.*

    Example

    A national magazine asked officer managers: "By about how much could you improve productivity in your company's office operations if you installed the most modern office equipment and systems? $ _____.

    Do you think that the office managers could approximate a figure? What is productivity in an office? What is modern office equipment and systems?

4. *Bias should be avoided.* Superlatives such as "beautiful" often bias answers. Others by inference bias the answer.

    Example

    Now that you know the advantages of this pain reliever, don't you feel you should have it on hand the next time you need pain relief?

_____ 1. Yes, pain is unpleasant enough without risking an upset stomach as well.

_____ 2. Yes, I am interested in a pain reliever that gets into my bloodstream twice as fast as plain aspirin.

_____ 3. Yes, the brand name assures me of consistent high quality.

_____ 4. Yes, as I have to use pain relievers frequently, I think I should be concerned with the stomach upset plain aspirin can cause.

_____ 5. No.

LEVELS OF MEASUREMENT

The statistics presented in the many sources mentioned in the foregoing section can be classified as being either nominal, ordinal, interval, or ratio levels of measurement. The type of graph to use in portraying data depends in part on the level of measurement. It is appropriate, therefore, to briefly identify the four levels.

Nominal level of measurement

The information presented in Table 2–1 is considered to be nominal measurement. This level is considered as being the most "primitive," the "lowest," or the most limited type of measurement.

The words *nominal level of measurement* and *nominal scaled* are commonly used when referring to this type of data which can *only be classified into categories*. In the strict sense of the words, however, there are no measurements and no scales involved. Instead, there are just counts.

The arrangement of the religions could have been changed. Roman Catholic could have been listed first; Jewish, second; and so on. This essentially indicates that for nominal level of measurement *there is no particular order for the groupings*. Further, the categories are considered to be mutually exclusive, meaning, for example, that a person could not be a Protestant and have no religion at the same time.

It should be noted that in order to process data on religious preference, sex, employment by industry, and so forth, the categories are often coded 1, 2, 3, . . . with, say, 1 representing Protestant, 2 representing Roman Catholic, and so on. This facilitates counting when a computer or other counting devices are used. It is not permissible, however, to manipulate

TABLE 2–1
Religion reported by the population of the United States 14 years old and over

Religion	Total
Protestant	78,952,000
Roman Catholic	30,669,000
Jewish	3,868,000
Other religion	1,545,000
No religion	3,195,000
Religion not reported	1,104,000
Total	119,333,000

Source: U.S. Department of Commerce, Bureau of the Census, *Current Population Reports,* series P–20, no. 79.

these numbers algebraically. For example, $1 + 2$ does not equal 3; that is, a Protestant + a Roman Catholic does not equal a person of the Jewish religion.

Tests applied to nominal-scaled data do not make any assumptions regarding the underlying distribution of the population from which the sample was selected. Thus, these tests are called *distribution-free* or *nonparametric* tests. Some of these tests will be discussed in the two chapters devoted to nonparametric methods (Chapters 17 and 18).

Ordinal level of measurement

Table 2–2 is an illustration of ordinal level of measurement. Note that one category is higher than the next one, i.e., "superior" is a higher rating than "good," "good" is higher than "average," and so on.

TABLE 2–2 Student ratings of an instructor

Student rating	Number of ratings
Superior	6
Good	18
Average	15
Poor	7
Inferior	0

Source: Classroom survey.

If 1 is substituted for superior, 2 substituted for good, and so on, a 1 ranking is obviously higher than a 2 ranking, and a 2 ranking is higher than a 3 ranking. However, it cannot be said that (as an example) an instructor rated good is twice as competent as an instructor rated average, and an instructor rated superior is twice as competent as one rated good. It can only be said that a rating of superior is greater than a rating of good, and a good rating is greater than an average rating. This "greater than" concept and the concept of *unequal distances between the categories* is shown schematically using a straight line.

Rating of instructor	Superior	Good	Average	Poor	Inferior
Number representing rating	1	2	3	4	5

In review, the major difference between a nominal and an ordinal level of measurement is the "greater than" relationship between the ordinal-level categories. Otherwise, the ordinal scale of measurement has the same characteristics as the nominal scale.

Interval and ratio levels of measurement

Interval level of measurement is the next *higher* level. The length of service of several employees is used to illustrate the concept of interval scaling. Sam has been with the company five years longer than Joe. Sam has two years less service than Pete. And the number of years between Joe and Sam is the same as between John and Junior. *For interval level of measure, the distances between numbers are of a known, constant size.*

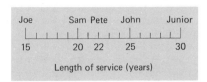

In addition to the equidistant characteristic, interval-scaled measurements have all the features of nominal and ordinal measurements. The lengths of service are mutually exclusive; i.e., Sam could not have exactly 15, 20, 22, 25, and 30 years with the company at the same time. And the "greater-than" feature of ordinal data permits ranking the length of service from the longest (Junior) to the shortest (Joe).

The equal units permit meaningful addition and division. Thus the arithmetic mean length of service (22.4 years) has meaning, and such parametric measures as the variance, standard deviation, and range can be computed.

The distinction between interval and ratio level of measurement is purely academic. Interval-level measurement is the highest level assumed by all of the tests of significance (and measures of correlation). Therefore, ratio-level measurements will not be discussed.

GRAPHICAL PRESENTATION OF DATA

Statistical data, such as annual sales or production data, can be presented in either *chart* or *table* form. Usually, a well-drawn chart (also called a graph) attracts more reader attention. The old Chinese proverb "A picture is worth a thousand words" is endorsed by *Business Week, Forbes, Fortune,* and other business magazines which use charts rather extensively. A chart may be defined loosely as a pictorial form of presenting data.

It is difficult, however, to read *exact* figures from most charts. For example, if the exact closing price of a stock traded on the New York Stock Exchange, or the exact dollar deficit of the company incurred for each of the last four years, is needed, a table is a more logical choice. Only graphic construction will be considered here.

The arithmetic scale

Most economic and business data are plotted on paper having either an arithmetic scale or a ratio scale. The arithmetic scale is the more commonly used and will be considered first.

The divisions on arithmetic graph paper are equidistant. In the following illustration, the distance between each of the divisions on the vertical (*Y*) axis is $10 million. The distance between each of the lines on the horizontal (*X*) axis is one year. *Equal distances on arithmetic paper represent equal amounts.*

Notice in the accompanying illustration that the numbers on the vertical scale (sales) increase in magnitude from the origin of zero. The years progress from left to right on the X-axis.

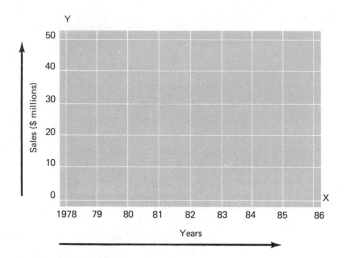

Recall from algebra that there are four quadrants to a grid. Note in the following illustration that both the X values and the Y values are positive in quadrant 1. Since most business data are positive, it is the one most frequently used.

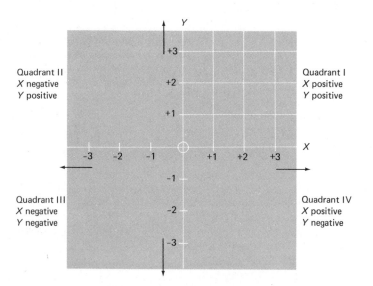

Simple line charts and simple bar charts

Simple line charts are ideal for portraying the trend of sales, exports, and other business series over a period of time. Chart 2–1, for example, shows the general decline in new passenger car sales since 1978.

CHART 2–1
A simple line chart

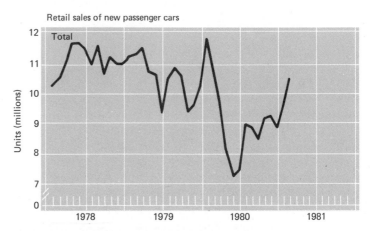

Retail sales of new passenger cars

Source: U.S. Department of Commerce, Bureau of Economic Analysis, *Survey of Current Business,* March 1981, p. 2.

Simple bar charts are equally appropriate for showing a single series over a period of time. Chart 2–2, often referred to as a **vertical bar chart**, depicts the trend in the number of persons in the United States receiving food stamps.

CHART 2–2
A vertical bar chart

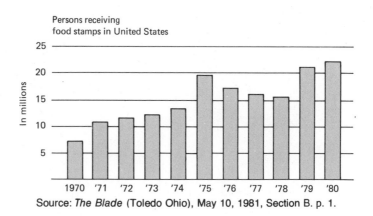

Persons receiving food stamps in United States

Source: *The Blade* (Toledo Ohio), May 10, 1981, Section B. p. 1.

Chart 2–3, often referred to as a **horizontal bar chart,** shows the increase in food prices for selected countries from 1970 through 1979.

CHART 2–3
A horizontal bar chart

Increase in world food prices

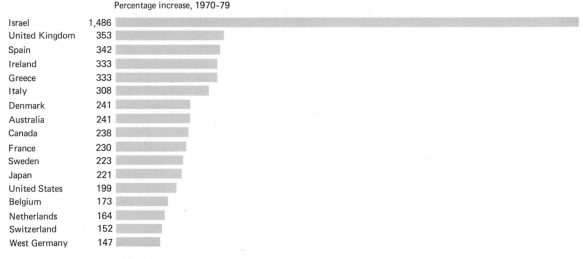

Percentage increase, 1970–79

Israel	1,486
United Kingdom	353
Spain	342
Ireland	333
Greece	333
Italy	308
Denmark	241
Australia	241
Canada	238
France	230
Sweden	223
Japan	221
United States	199
Belgium	173
Netherlands	164
Switzerland	152
West Germany	147

Source: U.S. Department of Commerce, Bureau of the Census, *Social Indicators III,* 1980.

Multiple-line charts and multiple-bar charts

Past enrollments in four-year and two-year institutions of higher education and projections to 1984 are shown in a **multiple-bar chart** (Chart 2–5).

It is readily apparent that enrollment in two-year institutions has been gaining rapidly relative to enrollment in four-year schools. (The actual data show that in 1960 there were seven students enrolled in four-year institutions for every one student in a two-year school. By 1984, however, it is estimated that the ratio will be down to 2.4:1.)

CHART 2–4
A multiple-bar chart

Enrollments in institutions of higher education 1960-1970 and projections to 1984

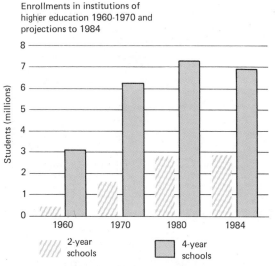

Source: U.S. National Center for Education Statistics, *Projections of Education Statistics,* to 1984–85.

Two or more series are often portrayed on one chart. The life expectancy at birth, by race and sex, since 1900 is portrayed in a **multiple-line chart** (Chart 2-4).

CHART 2-5
A multiple-line chart

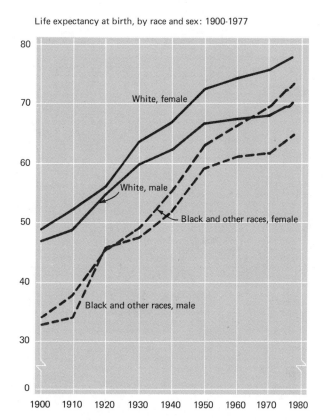

Life expectancy at birth, by race and sex: 1900-1977

Source: U.S. Department of Health, Education, and Welfare, *Vital Statistics of the United States*, vol. 1, various years.

Component bar charts

A department store has three departments—a tie department, a shoe department, and a suit department. Management wants to show graphically the change in total sales for the three years of 1979, 1980, and 1981 and also the change in each department relative to the total. The sales of the three departments were:

Department	Sales ($000,000)		
	1979	1980	1981
Tie	$ 2	$ 3	$ 2
Shoe	10	8	3
Suit	4	8	18
Total	$16	$19	$23

To construct a **component bar chart**, the tie sales of $2 million for 1979 are plotted first (Step 1).

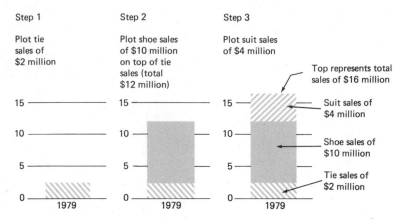

The sales for all three years are shown in Chart 2–6. Note that for each year, tie sales were plotted first at the bottom of the bar, shoe sales were placed on top of tie sales, and suit sales were the last component plotted. The top of each bar represents the total sales for the year.

**CHART 2–6
A component bar chart**

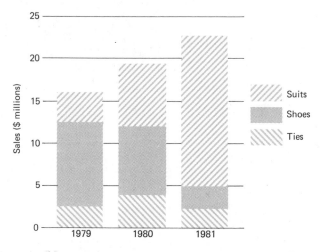

The interpretation of the component bar chart is:

1. Total sales increased during the three years.
2. Tie sales have remained relatively constant over the three-year period.
3. Shoe sales decreased as a component of the total.
4. Suit sales increased rapidly as a component of the total.

Two-directional bar charts

A **two-directional chart** is alternately called a **duo-directional, two-way,** or **bilateral chart.** A two-directional chart can be used to show profit and loss, above-normal and below-normal activity, and percent changes from one period of time to another. To illustrate, suppose that the sales for the first six months of 1982 are to be compared with those for the first six months of 1981. The objective in this problem is to show the *percent change* in sales, *not* the change in the dollar amounts. The sales data are:

	Sales the first six months		Percent change from 1981 to
Department	1981	1982	1982
Girdle	$ 4,000	$ 3,000	−25
Hardware	1,000	1,500	50
Radio	10,000	5,000	−50
TV	100,000	110,000	10
Small appliances	25,000	50,000	100

Note that girdle sales decreased 25 percent from 1981 to 1982, found by [($3,000 − $4,000)/$4,000](100). And hardware sales increased 50 percent during the same period, calculated by [($1,500 − $1,000/$1,000](100).

The percentage changes are divided into two groups. The percentage increases are usually arranged in descending order. The percentage decreases are usually arranged in ascending order.

Percentage increases	Percentage decreases
100 small appliances	−25 Girdle
50 Hardware	−50 Radio
10 TV	

To construct a **two-directional bar chart,** the percent changes are usually plotted in the same ascending and descending order (Chart 2–7). The center

**CHART 2–7
A two-directional bar chart**

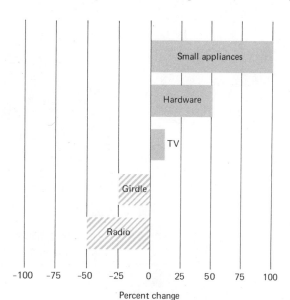

line is the origin for each bar. The most common method is to plot the percent increases to the right of the origin and the percent decreases to the left of the origin as illustrated.

Pie charts

Pie charts are especially useful if the relative sizes of the components of the total are to be emphasized. As shown, commercially printed paper is available containing the precise measurements needed to construct a pie chart. The following problem is used to illustrate the procedure if such paper is not available.

The percent of each tax dollar going to schools, roads, and so on is to be portrayed graphically. The total amount of taxes collected was $2 million, of which $440,000 was spent on supporting the schools, $1,160,000 on roads, $320,000 on administration, and $80,000 for graft. Of the total (100 percent), 22 percent went for schools, found by $440,000/$2,000,000. Likewise, 58 percent of the total was spent on roads, found by $1,160,000/$2,000,000; and 16 percent of each tax dollar went for administration; graft accounted for 4 percent.

As shown in Chart 2–8, to plot the 22 percent going to schools, one line is drawn from 0 to the center of the circle and another straight line from the center to 22 percent on the circle. Adding 22 percent and 58 percent for roads, we get 80 percent. A line is then drawn from the center to 80. The area of the circle between 22 percent and 80 percent shows the percent of the tax dollar going for roads. Adding the 16 percent for administration to 80 percent gives 96 percent, and a line is drawn to 96 percent. The area between 96 percent and 100 percent, or 0, is the percent going for graft (4 percent).

CHART 2–8
A pie chart

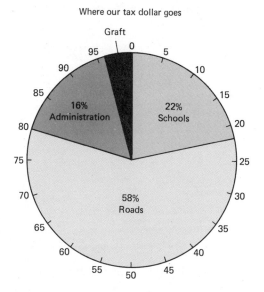

Where our tax dollar goes

Semilogarithmic (ratio) scaling

The previous line and bar charts were drawn on arithmetic paper. Its main feature is that *equal distances represent equal amounts*. There are occasions, however, when the *percent change* in two or more series is to be emphasized. The appropriate paper used to plot these cases is called **semilogarithmic paper**. It is sometimes referred to as ratio paper.

Design of semilogarithmic (ratio) paper

The Y-axis of semilogarithmic paper is constructed by using logarithms. The X-axis is evenly spaced and has an arithmetic scaling. An illustration of one-cycle ratio papers follows (Chart 2–9). Note that the bottom figure on the Y-axis is 1 and the top of the cycle is 10. Thus, the distance from the bottom of a cycle to the top of the cycle on the logarithmic scale represents a *10-fold increase*. Notice too that the distance from 1 to 2 on the Y scale is the same as the distance from 2 to 4. And the distance from 4 to 8 is the same as from 2 to 4. Further, the distance from 1 to 2 is 100 percent, from 2 to 4 is 100 percent, and from 4 to 8 is 100 percent. Thus, *equal distances on ratio paper represent equal percent changes*.

**CHART 2–9
One-cycle
semilogarithmic paper**

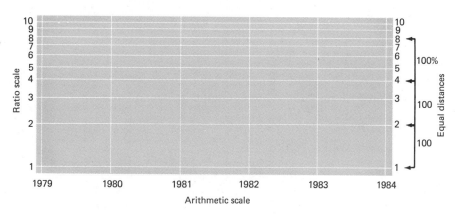

Semilogarithmic paper is very versatile. If, for example, production increased from 18 units in 1976 to 210 units in 1982, two cycles would be needed. (See Chart 2–10.) The first cycle could start at 10 (instead of 1). The top of the cycle is 100 (a 10-fold increase). The 100 is also the beginning of the second cycle. The top of the second cycle is 10 times 100, or 1,000. Had three cycles been needed, the top of the third cycle would be 10,000, the top of the fourth cycle (if needed) would be 100,000, and so on.

**CHART 2–10
Two-cycle
semilogarithmic paper**

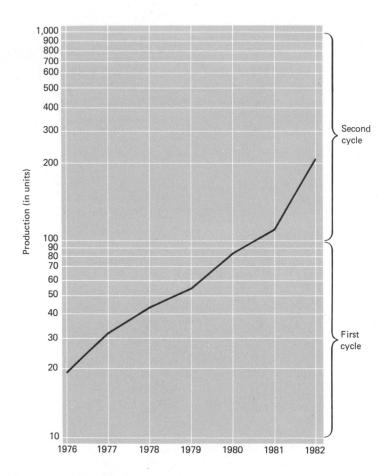

Application of semilogarithmic paper

Arithmetic progression.   Assume that a company wishes to show the rate of change for a sales series. The sales were plotted using an arithmetic scale (Chart 2–11). Have the sales been increasing at a steady rate?

The first impression is that sales did advance at a steady rate. The increase from 1976 to 1977 appears to be the same as from 1977 to 1978, and so

**CHART 2–11
A sales series plotted
on arithmetic paper**

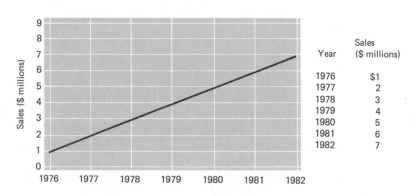

Year	Sales ($ millions)
1976	$1
1977	2
1978	3
1979	4
1980	5
1981	6
1982	7

on. A more thorough study of the actual sales, however, shows that between 1976 and 1977, sales increased 100 percent (from $1 million to $2 million); the second year the sales increased 50 percent (from $2 million to 3 million); the next year, 33 percent; and so on.

The same *arithmetic progression* is plotted on ratio paper in Chart 2–12. Sales are increasing, but at a decreasing rate.

CHART 2–12
A sales series plotted on semilogarithmic paper

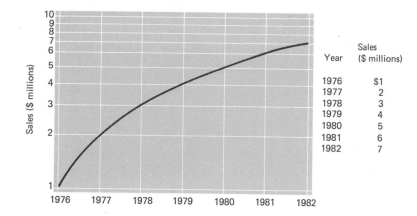

Year	Sales ($ millions)
1976	$1
1977	2
1978	3
1979	4
1980	5
1981	6
1982	7

The answer to the question of which paper to use depends on what the statistician wants to emphasize. If the *amount* of change from year to year is most important, *arithmetic paper* should be used. If the *rate* of growth is more important, *semilog paper* should be used.

Geometric progression. Referring to the production series plotted in Chart 2–13 (arithmetic scale), did production lag from 1974 to about 1977 and then increase rapidly? It appears so.

CHART 2–13
A production series plotted on arithmetic paper

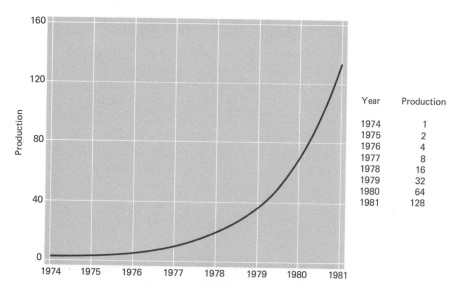

Year	Production
1974	1
1975	2
1976	4
1977	8
1978	16
1979	32
1980	64
1981	128

An examination of the actual figures which accompany the chart, however, reveals that production actually increased 100 percent from 1974 to 1975 and another 100 percent from 1975 to 1976 and so on. When plotted on semilogarithmic paper, the series results in a straight line (Chart 2–14), indicating that production increased at a constant rate from 1974 to 1981.

CHART 2–14
A production series plotted on semilogarithmic paper

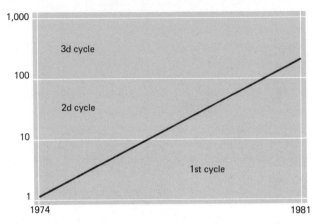

Source: A summary of the White House Conference on the Industrial World Ahead. *A Look at Business in 1990* (Washington, D.C., U.S. Government Printing Office).

As an actual example, the White House Conference on the Industrial World Ahead included in the summary report the following chart on the need for classroom teachers. Note that, in general, the projected demand for all three types of teachers will level off by 1990. Semilogarithmic paper was used because there was interest in emphasizing the rate of change.

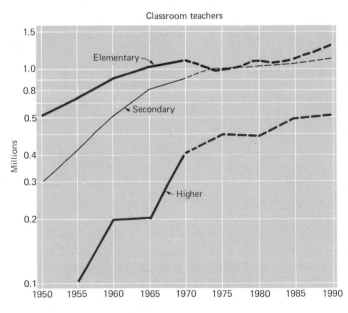

**CHAPTER
SUMMARY**

This chapter introduced descriptive statistics. It encompasses the collection, presentation, and description of numerical data. Data may be available internally, in the company files, or it may be necessary to conduct a survey in order to obtain the needed information. Numerical data of national and international interest are available in such federal publications as the *Monthly Labor Review* and the *Survey of Current Business*. The United Nations releases annual and monthly information in the *Statistical Yearbook* and the *Monthly Bulletin of Statistics*. In addition, there are many trade publications, such as *Ward's Automotive*, which give national statistics. If the data of interest cannot be located, consider consulting a reference aid such as Wasserman's *Encyclopedia of Business Sources*.

It was stressed that if a survey is to be conducted to obtain the needed information, the questionnaire should be constructed so that the respondent can complete it easily. Bias and words with many interpretations should be avoided.

There are four levels of measurement, namely, nominal, ordinal, interval, and ratio. The nominal level of measurement is the "lowest" level, and data on this level can only be classified into categories. As an example, the sex of persons filling out a questionnaire can only be classified into one of two categories, female and male. If the data can be tallied into categories, such as freshman, sophomore, junior, and senior, which imply a ranking from low to high, the level of measurement is ordinal. If the distances between numbers are of a known, constant size, the level of measurement is interval. Ages, weights, incomes, and lengths are a few examples.

Several well-known types of graphs are discussed, including line graphs, bar graphs, and pie graphs. Most graphs are plotted on arithmetic paper because the intent is to show changes in amounts. However, if the percent of change from one time period to another is to be emphasized, semilogarithmic paper should be used.

**CHAPTER
OUTLINE**

**Collection and
presentation of
data**

I. Sources of published data.
   A. Publications of the federal government. (The following is representative of a large number of business and economic publications.)
      1. Decennial publications.
         a. Census of Population. Includes a U.S. summary, population by state, and so on. Age, sex, and income are only a few of the variables.
         b. Census of Housing. Includes the number of one-family and two-family homes by state and by county, age of homes, number of homes with electricity, with baths, and so on.
      2. Annual publications.
         a. Statistical Abstract of the United States. Contains a wide

        variety of data on agriculture, crime, sales, exports, fishing, and so on.

    3. Monthly publications.

       a. Monthly Labor Review. Every issue contains about 40 pages of data on labor, including employment, labor turnover, and hours and wages.

       b. Survey of Current Business. Every issue contains data on the gross national product, prices, imports, exports, sales, and so on.

       c. Federal Reserve Bulletin. Bank debits, consumer debt, and interest rates are just a few of the series in the 50 pages each month devoted to financial statistics.

B. Publications of private organizations.

    1. Annual publications.

       a. Motor Vehicle Facts & Figures. Typical of many publications by automobile, steel, and other industries. Contains automobile registrations by state, production of automobiles, trucks, and other vehicles, accidents, and so on.

       b. World Almanac and *Information Please Almanac* includes business and economic statistics, population data, sports data, and a variety of other information.

C. Publications by international organizations.

    1. United Nations publications.

       a. Annual. *Statistical Yearbook* has sections on world population, agriculture, manufacturing, etc. *Demographic Yearbook* has for most countries data on marriages, divorce, etc. *Yearbook of International Trade Statistics,* as the name implies, has hundreds of pages on imports and exports of all countries.

       b. Monthly. *Monthly Bulletin of Statistics* contains a variety of monthly and annual figures on production of automobiles, population, construction, prices, and so on.

D. Consulting reference aids.

    1. Reference aids. Johnson's *How to Use the Business Library* is typical of several reference guides which list thousands of periodicals and other sources of information in such categories as real estate, foreign trade, and marketing.

    2. Business indexes. *The Business Periodicals Index* is typical of several indexes. More than 100 business periodicals are searched every month and the magazine articles are classified under such topics as aircraft industry, plant security, and football.

II. The survey as a source of data.

A. Mail questionnaire.

    1. Advantages. Inexpensive, especially if respondents are scattered over a wide geographic area. Usually an effective way of obtaining information.

2. Disadvantages. Response may be low, especially if the questionnaire is poorly designed and/or the subject area is of little interest to the respondent.

3. Criteria for questionnaire construction. The following are only a few.

    a. Include a letter explaining the purpose of the survey, enclose a self-addressed envelope, assure the respondent that answers will be kept in strictest confidence.

    b. Adequate instructions must be given. Example: *Check only one answer.*

    c. Certain words which can be interpreted differently, such as *family,* must be either avoided or defined.

    d. Bias should be avoided. Example: *Do you like this magnificent automobile? Yes_____ No_____*

III. Graphic presentation of data.

    A. Arithmetic scale. Equal distances on arithmetic paper represent equal amounts.

    B. Semilogarithmic (ratio) scale. Equal distances on ratio paper represent equal percent changes.

    C. Types of charts.

        1. Simple line charts and simple bar charts.

        2. Multiple-line charts and multiple-bar charts.

        3. Component bar charts.

        4. Two-directional bar charts.

        5. Pie charts.

CHAPTER EXERCISES

1. Cite the title of the book or periodical that contains the following statistical information.

    a. The number of bushels of wheat harvested last year, the average annual temperature in Alabama, the estimated population of the United States in 1990, and the number of murders committed during the past three years are needed. These diversified statistics are contained in a 1,000-page annual publication of the federal government.

    b. A monthly publication of the federal government includes 40 pages of statistics such as "the average number of hours worked last month in mining was 38.1," "the rate of unemployment in December was 6.2 percent," and "the labor turnover for July was 2.9."

    c. An international publication released monthly includes the tonnage of coal mined in Ireland last month, the unemployment rate in France in June, and the population of Samoa.

    d. In addition to releasing monthly statistics on the labor force, the federal government publishes a periodical containing such monthly financial data as total bank deposits in the United States and total installment debt. Another federal publication includes such figures as the gross national product last quarter, the consumer price index last month, and the production of iron ore. Give the title of one, or both, of these periodicals.

2. Graph the sales of department stores for 1980 and January 1981 (shown below in millions of dollars) in the form of a simple line chart.

	Jan.	Feb.	Mar.	Apr.	May	June	July	Aug.	Sept.	Oct.	Nov.	Dec.
1980...	5,488	5,571	6,770	6,975	7,736	7,116	7,023	7,889	7,350	8,255	9,709	14,963
1981...	5,958											

Source: *Survey of Current Business,* March 1981, p. S-10.

3. Depict the number of quits per 100 employees in manufacturing since 1977 in the form of a simple bar chart. Make the chart complete by inserting a table number, a title, and the source.

Year	Number of quits per 100 employees
1977	1.8
1978	2.1
1979	2.0
1980	1.5

Source: *Monthly Labor Review,* March 1981, p. 92.

4. The percentages of the civilian labor force unemployed in 1964–80 were:

Year	Percent unemployed	Year	Percent unemployed
1964	5.2	1972	5.6
1965	4.5	1973	4.9
1966	3.8	1974	5.6
1967	3.8	1975	8.5
1968	3.6	1976	7.7
1969	3.5	1977	7.0
1970	4.9	1978	6.0
1971	5.9	1979	5.8
		1980	7.1

Source: *Monthly Labor Review,* March 1981, p. 83.

Show the unemployment rate since 1964 in either a simple line chart or a simple bar chart.

5. Portray the trend in the weekly earnings since 1975. (This exact problem of years and months was not covered. Use your imagination.)

Gross average weekly earnings

Date	Weekly earnings
1975	$163.53
1976	175.45
1977	189.00
1978	203.70
1979	219.30
1980	
Jan	225.34
Feb	226.75
Mar	229.15
Apr	228.55
May	229.95
June	233.33

Date	Weekly earnings
July	234.39
Aug	237.14
Sept	240.04
Oct	242.16
Nov	244.63
Dec	246.71
1981	
Jan	246.05

Source: *Monthly Labor Review,* March 1981, p. 98.

6. Depict state and federal government employment in the form of either a component bar chart or a pie chart.

Employment	
State	Federal
13,147,000	2,773,000

Source: *Monthly Labor Review,* March 1981, p. 89.

7. The Siesta Key Utility Authority (Sarasota, Florida) released the following information on where its customer dollars go.

Percent	Expenditure
24	Purchased water
21	Wages and benefits
19	Maintenance, Reserves, Extensions
19	Debt service
10	Supplies, insurance fees
7	Power

Source: 1980 *Annual Report,* Siesta Key Authority, Inc., Sarasota, Florida.

Show the data in the form of a pie graph.

8. The Siesta Key Utility Authority also wanted to portray graphically the contaminants in its water compared with amounts permitted by the Wilson-Grizzle Act. The contaminants in milligrams per liter (May–December average 1980) are shown below.

	Milligrams per liter	
Contaminant	SKUA final effluent	Permitted by Wilson-Grizzle Act
Biochemical oxygen demand	1.5	5.0
Suspended solids	0.8	5.0
Nitrogen	2.0	3.0
Phosphorus	0.7	1.0

Source: *1980 Annual Report,* Siesta Key Authority, Inc. Sarasota, Florida.

Portray the information graphically. (You select the type of graph.)

9. The annual sales volume of paper (in thousands of tons) of the Boise Cascade Corporation, by type of paper is:

Type of paper	Sales volume (000 tons)
Printing and publishing papers	1,223
Newsprint	418
Packaging papers and paperboard	139
Speciality paperboard	67
Market pulp	209

Source: 1980 Annual Report, Boise Cascade Corporation, p. 64.

Portray the sales data in one form of a pie chart.

10. There is interest in portraying graphically the percentage change in the operating profit of the Kaiser Aluminum & Chemical Corporation from 1979 to 1980, by type of business (in millions of dollars).

Type of business	1979	1980
Aluminum	$313.0	$254.9
Agricultural chemicals	11.0	25.4
Refractories	25.8	9.8
Industrial chemicals	32.7	27.8
Trading	9.4	14.5

Source: 1980 Annual Report, Kaiser Aluminum & Chemical Corporation, p. 27.

Depict the percentage change in the operating profit from 1979 to 1980 in the form of a two-directional bar chart.

11. The population of the United States, Colorado, and Arizona for the years 1910–80 and the estimated population in 2000 are:

Year	United States	Colorado	Arizona
1910	92,407,000	799,000	204,000
1930	123,077,000	1,036,000	436,000
1950	151,868,000	1,325,000	750,000
1970	203,805,000	2,225,000	1,792,000
1980	222,300,000	2,772,000	2,450,000
2000*	259,869,000	3,183,000	2,913,000

*Series IIC projections.
Source: Current Population Reports, series P-25, nos. 375, 477, and 796.

a. Plot the three series on the same sheet of semilogarithmic paper.
b. Interpret the three trends.

12. As the market research director of a large manufacturer of appliances you are requested to design a questionnaire to be mailed to consumers concerning their buying plans during the forthcoming year with respect to such items as color televisions, refrigerators, microwave ovens, and so on. The manufacturer wants some objective answers, including whether the consumer definitely plans to buy, might buy, or will not buy, and the price range being considered. In addition to buying intentions and price range, include other questions that

would be valuable to the manufacturer. The questionnaire should have a letter of introduction.

13. As the editor of the campus newspaper you want to stimulate more reader interest by publishing a series of articles on the sports program, the adequacy of academic programs, campus security, and the faculty, to mention just a few. Design a questionnaire that could be sent to the students (or included in the campus newspaper), including a letter of introduction.

3

As noted in Chapter 1, one facet of statistics is concerned with describing data. Chapter 2 began our study of **descriptive statistics**. We examined several graphic (pictorial) ways of describing data, including line charts, bar charts, and pie charts.

Statisticians often employ a **frequency distribution** to organize and describe data. Then in order to present the distribution graphically, a **histogram**, a **frequency polygon**, and a **cumulative frequency polygon** may be drawn.

Describing data— frequency distributions

THE FREQUENCY DISTRIBUTION

A frequency distribution is a *grouping of interval-level data into categories showing the number of observations in each category*. The construction of a frequency distribution is illustrated by using the daily commissions of 120 salespersons.

EXAMPLE

To challenge its salespersons, a large department store chain converted from a weekly wage to a commission plan. A study of the effects of the new commission plan was inauguarated by selecting 120 salespersons at random and observing their daily commissions rounded to the nearest dollar (see Table 3–1). The unorganized listing of data in Table 3–1 is referred to as the **raw data**.

TABLE 3–1
Daily commissions earned by 120 salespersons

$52	$59	$46	$61	$46	$50	$41	$53	$58	$38
51	52	51	56	50	53	48	52	52	64
53	38	56	52	66	47	52	56	47	(69) ← high
42	52	42	53	52	47	48	41	51	50
56	57	52	41	35	51	53	51	36	51
50	57	54	51	58	62	45	46	57	46
52	47	50	58	47	33	50	59	53	39
low → (31)	55	59	52	45	50	52	55	42	52
49	52	38	62	62	55	43	55	52	40
68	48	63	48	47	60	57	56	45	53
52	58	57	65	57	56	61	40	63	37
45	57	46	32	49	44	53	52	49	42

How would these daily commissions be grouped into a frequency distribution?

SOLUTION

There are two methods of organizing the raw data in Table 3–1 into a frequency distribution. The first requires setting up an **array**. *An array is an ordering of the observations from the smallest to the largest, or vice versa*. Referring back to Table 3–1, the daily commissions are scanned for the lowest commission ($31) and the highest ($69). Every number from $31 to $69 is listed. (See Table 3–2.)

The next step is **tallying** the daily commissions into the array. The usual practice is to use the tally mark (/) to represent a commission.[1] (See Table 3–2.) Note in the table that $31 appears once, three salespersons had a daily commission of $38, and seven earned $57.

---

[1] In order to assure that each observation is counted, some system such as a check (√) should be used. Example:

$52 √
51 √

**TABLE 3–2
The array and
tallies**

$30		$40	//	$50	𝓗𝓛 //	$60	/
31	/	41	///	51	𝓗𝓛 //	61	//
32	/	42	////	52	𝓗𝓛 //// 𝓗𝓛 //	62	///
33	/	43	/	53	//// ///	63	//
34		44	/	54	/	64	/
35	/	45	////	55	////	65	/
36	/	46	𝓗𝓛	56	𝓗𝓛 /	66	/
37	/	47	𝓗𝓛 /	57	𝓗𝓛 //	67	
38	///	48	////	58	////	68	/
39	/	49	///	59	///	69	/

In order to summarize the information in Table 3–2 into a frequency distribution, a decision must be made regarding the limits of each category. Each category (class) has two limits—a lower class limit and an upper class limit. The usual practice is to let the lower limit of the first class be a number slightly below the lowest observation in the array, and to make all the classes have the same width. In this example it was decided to make the lower class limit of the first class $30 (slightly below $31) and the upper class limit of that class $34. The next class is written $35–$39 and includes the commissions of $35, $36, $37, $38, and $39. In other words, the class limits are included in a particular category.

Note from Table 3–2 that there are three tallies, or **class frequencies**, in the $30–$34 class and seven in the $35–$39 class. The classes and class frequencies are shown in the form of a frequency distribution in Table 3–3.

**TABLE 3–3
Frequency
distribution of the
daily commissions of
120 salespersons**

Daily commissions	Number of salespersons
$30–$34	3
35– 39	7
40– 44	11
45– 49	22
50– 54	40
55– 59	24
60– 64	9
65– 69	4
	120

The second, or alternative, method of organizing raw data into a frequency distribution permits tallying the daily commissions directly into predetermined classes. By doing this, the tedious work of setting up an array is eliminated. (See Table 3–4.)

What observations can the finance director now make about the daily commissions? (1) The lowest daily commission is about $30, the highest about $69. (2) Most of the salespersons earn between $45 and $59 per day. (3) The largest concentration of daily commissions is between $50 and $54.

Forcing the daily commissions into a frequency distribution has caused some loss of information. However, the advantages of condensing the data

TABLE 3-4
Tallying the daily commissions directly into predetermined classes

Daily commissions		Frequencies
$30–34	///	3
35–39	𝑁𝑁 //	7
40–44	𝑁𝑁 𝑁𝑁 /	11
45–49	𝑁𝑁 𝑁𝑁 𝑁𝑁 𝑁𝑁 //	22
50–54	𝑁𝑁 𝑁𝑁 𝑁𝑁 𝑁𝑁 𝑁𝑁 𝑁𝑁 𝑁𝑁 𝑁𝑁	40
55–59	𝑁𝑁 𝑁𝑁 𝑁𝑁 𝑁𝑁 ////	24
60–64	𝑁𝑁 ////	9
65–69	////	4

into a frequency distribution more than offset the disadvantages. From the distribution of the daily commissions we can quickly see a typical value and the variation around that value.

Following is a self-review. Cover the answers on the left-hand side and do the problems. Then uncover the answers and check them.

─────────── **SELF-REVIEW 3-1** ───────────

a. The raw data.

b.

Monthly incomes	Tallies	Number
$1,400–$1,499	//	2
1,500– 1,599	///	3
1,600– 1,699	//	2
1,700– 1,799	/	1
Total		8

c. Class frequencies.
d. The lowest monthly income is about $1,400, the highest $1,799. The largest concentration of incomes is in the $1,500–$1,599 class.

The monthly incomes of a small sample of computer operators are: $1,650, $1,475, $1,760, $1,540, $1,495, $1,590, $1,625, and $1,510.

a. What are the ungrouped numbers $1,650, $1,275, and so on called?
b. Using $1,400–$1,499 as the first class, $1,500–$1,599 as the second class, etc., organize the monthly incomes into a frequency distribution.
c. What are the numbers in the right column of your frequency distribution called?
d. Describe the distribution of monthly incomes.

True class limits

The classes in the daily commission problem were given as $30–$34, $35–$39, $40–$44, and so on. These are called the **stated class limits**. The commissions were rounded to the nearest dollar using conventional rounding rules. A daily commission of $29.50 was rounded *up* to $30. Any amount over $34 but under $34.50 was rounded *down* to $34. Thus, the $30–$34 class actually encompasses all commissions from $29.50 inclusive up to but not including $34.50. Likewise, the next class, $34–$39, contains commissions between $34.50 and $39.50. These class limits ($29.50, $34.50, $39.50, etc.) are called the **true class limits.** The stated class limits and the true class limits for the distribution of daily commissions are shown in Table 3–5.

If the stated limits for a distribution were $2,000–$2,400, $2,500–$2,900, and so on, and if rounding was involved, the original data has apparently been rounded to the nearest $100. The true class limits, therefore, would be

TABLE 3–5
Stated limits and true
limits for the daily
commission
distribution

Stated limits	True limits	Frequencies
$30–$34	$29.50–$34.50	3
35– 39	34.50– 39.50	7
40– 44	39.50– 44.50	11
45– 49	44.50– 49.50	22
50– 54	49.50– 54.50	40
55– 59	54.50– 59.50	24
60– 64	59.50– 64.50	9
65– 69	64.50– 69.50	4

$1,950–$2,450, $2,450–$2,950, and so on. If stated limits are 6.5–6.9, 7.0–7.4, 7.5–7.9, and if rounding was involved, we would assume that the data had been rounded to the nearest tenth and the true limits would be found by "splitting the difference" between the stated limits of adjacent classes. The true limits, therefore, would be 6.45–6.95, 6.95–7.45, 7.45–7.95, and so forth.

True class limits will be used in the next section when we portray the distribution of the daily commissions in the form of a histogram. And, in Chapter 4, the true limits are needed to determine the median commission earned.

Midpoints

The midpoint of a class is determined by going halfway between either the stated class limits or the true class limits. It is obtained by adding the lower and upper limits and dividing the total by two. Halfway between the stated limits of $30–$34 is $32, found by ($30 + $34)/2. The midpoint best represents, or is typical of, the value in that class. The class midpoints are used to construct a frequency polygon in the following section, and to compute the arithmetic mean in Chapter 4.

--- **SELF-REVIEW 3–2** ---

a. Nearest $1,000.
b. The stated class limits.
c. $49,500–$59,500
   59,500– 69,500.
d. $54,500 and $64,500. $54,500 was found by
   ($50,000 + $59,000)/2.

The first two classes for a distribution of annual incomes which were rounded are:

$50,000–$59,000
60,000– 69,000

a. Were the annual incomes rounded to the nearest $1, $10, $100, $1,000, or $10,000?
b. What are these class limits called?
c. What are the true class limits of the first two classes?
d. What are the midpoints of the first two classes?

Class intervals

The **class interval** may be determined by (1)subtracting the lower true limit of a class from its upper true limit or (2) subtracting the lower stated limit of one class from the lower stated limit of the next-higher class. As an illustration:

Ages			
Stated limits	True limits	Class interval	Found by
10-19	9.5-19.5	10	Either 20 − 10 or 19.5 − 9.5
20-24	19.5-24.5	5	Either 25 − 20 or 24.5 − 19.5

If the classes are of equal width, the class interval may also be found by determining the distance between any two successive midpoints.

EXAMPLE

For the daily commissions:

Stated limits	True limits	Midpoints
$30-$34	$29.50-$34.50	$32
35- 39	34.50- 39.50	37
40- 44	39.50- 44.50	42

What is the class interval?

SOLUTION

Subtracting lower true limit of a class from upper true limit:	$34.50 − $29.50 = $5.
Subtracting successive lower stated limits:	$35 − $30 = $5.
Subtracting successive midpoints:	$37 − $32 = $5.

SELF-REVIEW 3-3

a. $10,000, found by $64,450 − $54,450.
b. $10,000, found by $59,950 − $49,950.
c. $10,000, found by $60,000 − $50,000.

Monthly sales are rounded to the nearest $100 and organized into a frequency distribution. The stated limits are:

$50,000-$59,900
60,000- 69,900
70,000- 79,900

a. Using midpoints, what is the class interval?
b. Using the true limits, what is the class interval?
c. Using the stated limits, what is the class interval?

Hints on constructing a frequency distribution

1. Suppose you have a mass of raw data to organize into a frequency distribution. What class interval should be used? The following formula developed by Sturges[2] gives a suggested class interval:

$$\text{Suggested class interval} = \frac{\text{Highest value} - \text{Lowest value}}{1 + 3.322(\text{logarithm of the total frequencies})}$$

Using the daily commissions in Table 3–1, we get a suggested class interval of $4.81.

$$\frac{\$69 - \$31}{1 + 3.322(\log \text{ of } 120)} = \frac{\$38}{1 + 3.322(2.0792)} = \frac{\$38}{1 + 6.9071024} = \$4.81$$

Since the commissions are given in whole dollars, the suggested class interval of $4.81 may not be appropriate. The problem could be resolved by making the size of the class interval either $4 or $5.

Of course, the personal judgment of the statistician can influence the number of classes. Too many or too few classes might not reveal the basic shape of the distribution. A class interval of $22, for example, would not reveal much about the pattern of the daily commissions (see Table 3–6). About all we could say would be that approximately half of the commissions are below $51.50 and half above $51.50.

**TABLE 3–6
Examples of too
few classes**

Daily commissions	Number
$30–$51	57
52– 73	63
Total	120

2. Whenever possible, the widths of the class intervals should be equal. Unequal class intervals present problems if the frequency distribution is portrayed graphically and in computing certain averages and measures of dispersion which will be discussed in Chapters 4 and 5. Unequal class intervals, however, may be necessary in certain situations in order to avoid a large number of empty, or almost empty, classes. The Internal Revenue Service used unequal-size class intervals to give the distribution of adjusted gross incomes of individuals (see Table 3–7). Had the IRS used an equal-size class interval of $1,000, over 1,000 classes would have been required to encompass all the incomes! It would, of course, be almost impossible to analyze this large a frequency distribution.

3. Avoid overlapping class limits such as $1,300–$1,400, $1,400–$1,500, and $1,500–$1,600. It would not be clear where to tally $1,400. Does it belong in the $1,300–$1,400 class or the $1,400–$1,500 class? Rounding in-

---

[2] A. Sturges, *Journal of the American Statistical Association*, March 1926, pp. 65–66.

TABLE 3–7
Adjusted gross income for individuals filing income tax returns

Adjusted gross income class	Number of returns (in thousands)
Under $2,000	135
$ 2,000–$ 2,999	3,399
3,000– 4,999	8,175
5,000– 9,999	19,740
10,000– 14,999	15,539
15,000– 24,999	14,944
25,000– 49,999	4,451
50,000– 99,999	699
100,000– 499,999	162
500,000– 999,999	3
$1,000,000 and over	1

comes to the nearest dollar, so that classes are $1,300–$1,399, $1,400–$1,499, and $1,500–$1,599, avoids this problem.

4. Try not to have **open–end classes**. The classes "Under $2,000" and "$1,000,000 and over" used by the IRS in Table 3–7 are examples of open-end classes. They cause problems in graphing, described in the next section, and in computing certain averages and measures of dispersion, shown in Chapters 4 and 5.

─────────────── SELF-REVIEW 3–4 ───────────────

1. *a.* $202.4716, found by

$$\frac{\$2,548 - \$1,041}{1 + 3.322(\log \text{ of } 87)} = \frac{\$1,507}{7.443019}$$

   b. $200.
   c. 8.
   d. $1,000 – $1,199
       1,200 – 1,399
2. Unequal size class intervals.
   Open-end class.
   Overlapping classes.

1. The monthly salaries of a sample of 87 grocery store managers were rounded to the nearest dollar. They ranged from a low of $1,041 to a high of $2,548.
   a. Using the Sturges formula, determine the suggested class interval.
   b. What would be a simpler class interval?
   c. How many classes would you use?
   d. What are the stated class limits for the first class? The next class?
2. Suppose classes are written as:

      40–60
      60–90
      90–150
      150 and over

These classes illustrate three practices which should be avoided. What are they?

EXERCISES

Answers and method of solution for selected exercises are given in Appendix A.

1. The International Monetary Fund reported these annual percent increases in consumer prices for selected countries.

Country	Increase (in percent)	Country	Increase (in percent)
North America		Europe	
Bahamas	3.3	Austria	5.5
Canada	8.0	Belgium	7.1
Dominican Republic	12.9	Denmark	11.1
El Salvador	11.9	Finland	12.7
Guatemala	12.6	France	9.5
Jamaica	11.4	Germany, West	3.9
Mexico	26.4	Greece	12.2
Trinidad and Tobago	11.9	Ireland	13.6
United States	6.5	Italy	17.0
South America		Netherlands	6.4
Brazil	43.7	Norway	9.2
Colombia	30.0	Portugal	24.3
Ecuador	13.0	Spain	24.5
Peru	38.1	Sweden	11.4
Venezuela	7.7	Switzerland	1.3
Asia		Turkey	27.2
China, Republic of	7.0	United Kingdom	15.8
Egypt	12.7	Yugoslavia	14.6
India	8.5	Africa	
Indonesia	11.0	Cameroons	14.6
Iran	27.3	Ethiopia	16.6
Israel	34.6	Ivory Coast	27.5
Japan	8.1	Kenya	10.4
Jordan	35.2	Madagascar	3.0
Korea, South	10.3	Morocco	12.5
Kuwait	8.2	Nigeria	21.6
Malaysia	4.8	South Africa	11.3
Pakistan	10.1	Tunisia	6.6
Philippines	7.9	Zambia	19.8
Saudi Arabia	11.3	Oceania	
Sri Lanka	1.3	Australia	12.3
Syrian Arab Republic	12.6	New Zealand	14.4
Thailand	8.4		

a. Round the percent increases to the nearest whole percent using the usual rounding procedure. (Example: 10.5 is rounded upt to 11, but 10.4 is rounded down to 10.) Then, using the rounded figures, set up an array and tally.

b. Using the Sturges formula, determine a suggested class interval.

c. Construct a frequency distribution.

d. Interpret your findings.

2. The Department of Commerce, Bureau of Economic Analysis, released the following data on the per capita personal income by states.

State	Per capita income	State	Per capita income
Alabama	$ 6,291	Montana	$6,755
Alaska	10,963	Nebraska	7,582
Arizona	7,372	Nevada	9,439

State	Per capita income	State	Per capita income
Arkansas	$ 5,969	New Hampshire	$ 7,357
California	8,927	New Jersey	8,773
Colorado	8,105	New Mexico	6,574
Connecticut	8,911	New York	8,224
Delaware	8,534	North Carolina	6,575
District of Columbia	9,924	North Dakota	7,174
Florida	7,573	Ohio	7,855
Georgia	6,705	Oklahoma	7,137
Hawaii	8,437	Oregon	8,092
Idaho	7,015	Pennsylvania	7,740
Illinois	8,903	Rhode Island	7,472
Indiana	7,706	South Carolina	6,288
Iowa	8,002	South Dakota	6,864
Kansas	7,882	Tennessee	6,547
Kentucky	6,607	Texas	7,730
Louisiana	6,716	Utah	6,566
Maine	6,292	Vermont	6,566
Maryland	8,363	Virginia	7,671
Massachusetts	7,924	Washington	8,495
Michigan	8,483	West Virginia	6,624
Minnesota	7,910	Wisconsin	7,532
Mississippi	5,529	Wyoming	8,636
Missouri	7,313		

a. Using the Sturges formula, determine a suggested class interval.
b. Construct a frequency distribution.
c. Interpret your findings.

GRAPHICAL REPRESENTATION OF A FREQUENCY DISTRIBUTION

As noted, the frequency distribution is a method for organizing raw data. The usual next step is to portray the frequency distribution of a graph, namely, a **histogram**, a **frequency polygon**, or a **cumulative frequency polygon**. Now let's look at how each of these are constructed.

Histogram

The **histogram** is the most commonly used way of portraying the frequency distribution. It is also the most easily interpreted.

EXAMPLE

The daily commissions of the 120 salespersons is repeated in Table 3–8.

TABLE 3–8
Daily commissions of 120 salespersons

Stated limits	True limits	Class frequencies
$30–$34	$29.50–$34.50	3
35– 39	34.50– 39.50	7
40– 44	39.50– 44.50	11

Stated limits	True limits	Class frequencies
45– 49	44.50– 49.50	22
50– 54	49.50– 54.50	40
55– 59	54.50– 59.50	24
60– 64	59.50– 64.50	9
65– 69	64.50– 69.50	4

How do you portray the commissions in a histogram?

SOLUTION

The class frequencies are scaled on the vertical axis (*Y*-axis). Either the stated limits, the true limits, or the midpoints are scaled on the horizontal axis (*X*-axis). The true limits will be used in this illustration. Referring to Table 3–8, note that three salespersons had commissions between $29.50 and $34.50. To construct a histogram, draw vertical lines from $29.50 and $34.50 to points opposite 3 on the *Y*-axis. The tops of these two lines are connected to form a bar, as shown in Chart 3–1. Also shown is the next step—that is, lines are drawn vertically from $34.50 and $39.50 to 7 on the *Y*-axis and the tops connected to form a bar. That bar represents the seven commissions in the $34.50–$39.50 class.

CHART 3–1

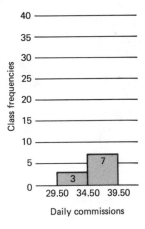

This procedure is continued for all the classes, until the histogram shown in Chart 3–2 is complete.

From the histogram it is easy to see that (1) the lowest daily commission is about $29.50, (2) the highest is about $69.50, (3) most of the commissions are between $44.50 and $59.50, and (4) the largest concentration (40) is between $49.50 and $54.50.

44

CHART 3–2
Histogram showing the commissions of 120 salespersons

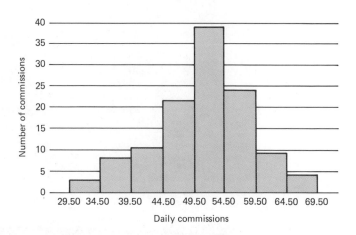

SELF-REVIEW 3–5

a.

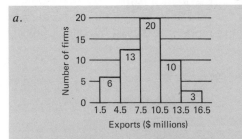

b. None of the chemical firms exported less than $1.5 million or more than $16.5 million. The largest number (20) exported between $7.5 million and $10.5 million in chemicals.

The annual exports of 52 small chemical firms were organized into a frequency distribution.

Exports (in millions)	Number
$2–$ 4	6
5– 7	13
8– 10	20
11– 13	10
14– 16	3

a. Construct a histogram of this frequency distribution using the true class limits.
b. Describe the pattern of exports.

EXERCISES

3. Using the frequency distribution from Exercise 1, portray the price increases in a histogram.

4. Using the frequency distribution from Exercise 2, portray the percapita incomes in a histogram.

Frequency polygon   The **frequency polygon** may be used instead of the histogram to portray the frequency distribution graphically.

EXAMPLE

The *midpoints* of the classes and the corresponding *class frequencies* are used to construct a frequency polygon. The distribution of daily commissions is repeated showing the midpoints.

Commissions	Midpoints	Frequency
$30–$34	$32	3
35– 39	37	7
40– 44	42	11
45– 49	47	22
50– 54	52	40
55– 59	57	24
60– 64	62	9
65– 69	67	4

How is a frequency polygon constructed?

SOLUTION

The class frequencies are again scaled on the vertical axis (Y-axis). The daily commissions are represented on the X-axis by the midpoints of each class. The $30–$34 class, for example, is represented by its midpoint, $32. To make the first plot, move horizontally to $32, the midpoint, and then vertically to 3, the class frequency, and place a dot. The next plot is $X = \$37$, $Y = 7$. This process is continued until all the classes are accounted for. Then the dots are connected *in order*. The point representing the first class is joined to the one representing the second class, and so forth.

Note in Chart 3–3 that, to complete the frequency polygon, midpoints of $27 and $72 were added to the two extremes and the polygon was "anchored" to the horizontal axis at zero frequencies.

CHART 3–3
Frequency polygon showing the commissions of 120 salespersons

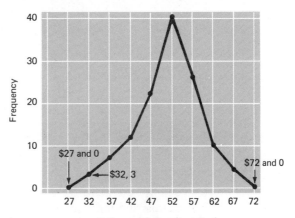

Daily commissions (in dollars)

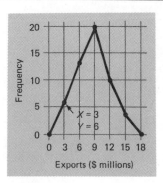

Exports ($ millions)

The annual exports of a group of small chemical firms are repeated from the previous self-review.

Exports (in millions)	Number
$2-$ 4	6
5- 7	13
8- 10	20
11- 13	10
14- 16	3

Portray the frequency distribution in a frequency polygon.

EXERCISES

5. Construct a frequency polygon for the distribution of price increases in Exercise 1.

6. Construct a frequency polygon for the distribution of per capita incomes in Exercise 2.

Percent frequency polygon

A frequency polygon is especially useful in comparing two frequency distributions. If the totals of frequencies in each distribution are about the same, the distributions can be plotted on the same graph and compared directly. Chart 3-4, for example, shows the hourly wage distributions for two firms, one in Arizona and one in New Mexico. It is obvious that the employees in the New Mexico firm have a higher wage level than the employees working for the Arizona firm.

CHART 3-4

Hourly wages

A problem arises when the total of frequencies for one distribution is significantly higher than for the other. Chart 3-5 depicts the wage patterns for a small firm and a large firm. It is almost impossible to find the wage distribution for the small firm!

How can we compare the two wage distributions? The frequencies for each of the distributions can be converted to percents of the total. Then the two sets of percents are plotted in the form of a **percent frequency polygon** on the same graph.

CHART 3–5

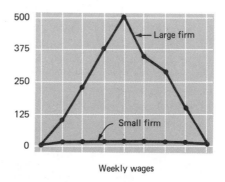

Weekly wages

EXAMPLE

The frequency distribution of the weekly wages for both the large firm and the small firm mentioned above are in Table 3–9.

**TABLE 3–9
Weekly wages
of employees
in two firms**

	Number	
Weekly wages	Small firm	Large firm
$120–$169	1	98
170– 219	6	240
220– 269	7	425
270– 319	9	504
320– 369	7	351
370– 419	6	257
420– 469	4	125
Total	40	2,000

Can the two wage distributions be described in percent frequency polygons?

SOLUTION

Convert each of the class frequencies to a percent of the total. Starting with the small firm, note in Table 3–9 that there are 40 wages. To convert the first class frequency of 1 to a percent of the total, it is divided by 40, thus $1 \div 40 = 0.025 = 2.5$ percent. The next class frequency of 6 was divided by 40 to give 15.0 percent. This process is continued for all class frequencies. The procedure for converting the class frequencies of the large firm is identical to that followed for the small firm except that the divisor is 2,000. For the first class, $98 \div 2,000 = 0.049 = 4.9$ percent, and so on. The two sets of percentages are shown in Table 3–10, and the percent frequency polygons are in Chart 3–6. Note that the percentages for each distribution total 100.0 percent (except for a slight discrepancy due to rounding).

TABLE 3–10
Percent frequency distributions

Weekly wages	Percent of total	
	Small firm	Large firm
$120–$169	2.5	4.9
170– 219	15.0	12.0
220– 269	17.5	21.3
270– 319	22.5	25.2
320– 369	17.5	17.6
370– 419	15.0	12.9
420– 469	10.0	6.3
Total	100.0	100.2

CHART 3–6
Percent frequency polygon

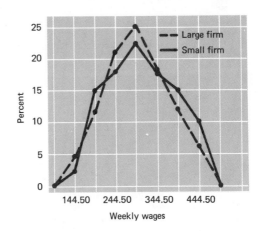

You will no doubt agree that now the two wage patterns are remarkably similar.

─────────────── **SELF-REVIEW 3–7** ───────────────

a.

	Chemical (in percent)	Rug (in percent)
$ 2–$ 4	11.5	0.0
5– 7	25.0	3.0
8– 10	38.5	5.0
11– 13	19.2	15.5
14– 16	5.8	48.0
17– 19	0.0	23.5
20– 22	0.0	5.0
Total	100.0	100.0

The value of the exports of 52 chemical firms in the previous self-review are to be compared with the exports of a group of rug exporters. The two distributions are:

Exports (in millions)	Number of firms	
	Chemical	Rug
$ 2–$ 4	6	0
5– 7	13	6
8– 10	20	10
11– 13	10	31
14– 16	3	96
17– 19	0	47
20– 22	0	10

b.

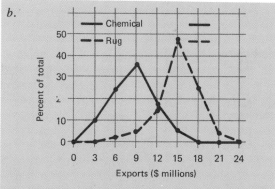

a. Convert each set of frequencies to percents of the total.

b. Portray the two distributions in percent frequency polygons.

c. Interpret your chart.

c. The volume of exports for the rug exporters is much higher than for the chemical firms. The typical values are about $9 million for chemicals, $15 for rugs.

Cumulative frequency polygon

How many salespersons earn over $53 a week in commissions? What percent earn less than $50 a week? The answers to these questions can be approximated by developing a **cumulative frequency distribution** and drawing a **cumulative frequency polygon**. The cumulative frequency polygon is often called an **ogive**. There are two kinds of cumulative frequency distributions, a **less-than-cumulative frequency distribution** and a **more-than-cumulative frequency distribution**.

EXAMPLE

To design a less-than-cumulative frequency distribution, the class frequencies are added, starting with the lowest class and continuing through the highest class. The corresponding cumulative frequency polygon is constructed by plotting the *cumulative frequencies* and their respective *upper true class limits*. Using the distribution of daily commissions in the following table, how are a less-than-cumulative frequency distribution and a cumulative frequency polygon constructed?

SOLUTION

Referring to Table 3–11, note that three salespersons earned less than $34.50, the upper true limit of the lowest class. Those 3, plus the 7 salespersons in the next-lowest class, or a total of 10, earned less than $39.50. The cumulative number of frequencies for the next class is 21, found by 3 + 7 + 11. This process of determining the cumulative frequencies is continued for all the classes.

TABLE 3–11
Daily commissions of
120 salespersons

Stated limits	True limits	Class frequencies		Cumulative frequencies
$30–$34	$29.50–$34.50	3	Add down ↓	3
35– 39	34.50– 39.50	7		10
40– 44	39.50– 44.50	11		21
45– 49	44.50– 49.50	22		43
50– 54	49.50– 54.50	40		83
55– 59	54.50– 59.50	24		107
60– 64	59.50– 64.50	9		116
65– 69	64.50– 69.50	4		120
Total		120		

The accompanying less-than-cumulative frequency polygon can now be constructed by plotting the cumulative frequencies and the corresponding upper true class limits. The first plot is made by moving horizontally to $34.50 and vertically to 3 and placing a dot. The next plot is $39.50 and 10. The completed ogive is illustrated in Chart 3–7. As shown, one common practice is to plot the cumulative frequencies on the left Y-axis and the cumulative percents on the right.

CHART 3–7
A less-than-cumulative frequency polygon

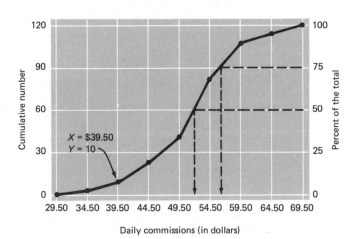

A few approximate figures from the chart are: Fifty percent of the salespersons earn less than $52 daily in commissions (arrived at by drawing a dashed line from 50 percent to the distribution curve and dropping vertically to the X-axis). Three out of every four salespersons (75 percent) earn less than $57 daily.

SELF-REVIEW 3–8

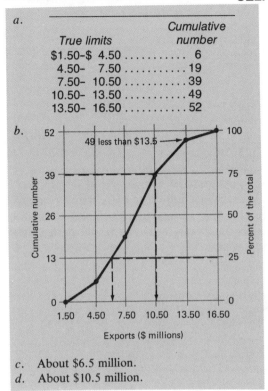

a.

True limits	Cumulative number
$1.50–$ 4.50	6
4.50– 7.50	19
7.50– 10.50	39
10.50– 13.50	49
13.50– 16.50	52

b.

c. About $6.5 million.
d. About $10.5 million.

The annual exports of a group of small chemical firms are again repeated.

Exports (in millions)	Number of firms
$2–$ 4	6
5– 7	13
8– 10	20
11– 13	10
14– 16	3

a. Design a less-than-cumulative frequency distribution showing the true limits and the cumulative frequencies.
b. Draw a less-than-cumulative frequency polygon.
c. Based on the polygon, 25 percent of the firms export less than what amount?
d. Based on the polygon, 39 out of the 52 firms export less than what amount?

A more-than-cumulative frequency distribution is constructed by starting with the highest class and adding the frequencies up to the lowest class. To draw a more-than-cumulative frequency polygon, the *lower* true limits and their corresponding cumulative frequencies are used.

EXAMPLE

The daily commissions of 120 salespersons are again used to show the construction of a more-than-cumulative frequency distribution and its corresponding ogive.

SOLUTION

In Table 3–12 we start with the highest class ($65–$69) and add the class frequencies *up*. The 4 class frequencies in that class plus 9 frequencies in the next class up gives a cumulative number of 13. This process is continued for all classes.

**TABLE 3–12
Daily commissions of
120 salespersons**

Stated limits	True limits	Class frequencies		Cumulative frequencies
$30–$34	$29.50–$34.50	3		120
35– 39	34.50– 39.50	7		117
40– 44	39.50– 44.50	11		110
45– 49	44.50– 49.50	22		99
50– 54	49.50– 54.50	40	↑	77
55– 59	54.50– 59.50	24		37
60– 64	59.50– 64.50	9	Add	13
65– 69	64.50– 69.50	4	up	4

The lower true limits and the cumulative frequencies are plotted to give a more-than-cumulative frequency polygon (see Chart 3–8). If we wanted to determine how many salespersons earned a daily commission more than $52, a line would be drawn vertically from $52, as shown, to the polygon and then left to the Y-axis. The number on the Y-axis is about 57, meaning that 57 salespersons earn more than $52 a day.

**CHART 3–8
A more-than-
cumulative frequency
polygon**

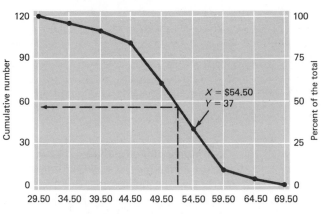

SELF-REVIEW 3–9

a.

True limits	Cumulative number
$1.50–$ 4.50	52
4.50– 7.50	46
7.50– 10.50	33
10.50– 13.50	13
13.50– 16.50	3

The annual exports of a group of small chemical firms are repeated again.

Exports (in millions)	Number of firms
$ 2–$ 4	6
5– 7	13
8– 10	20
11– 13	10
14– 16	3

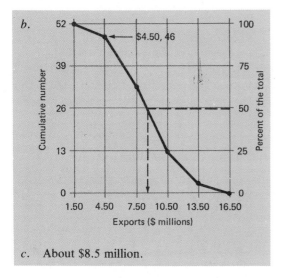

b.

c. About $8.5 million.

a. Design a more-than-cumulative frequency distribution showing the true limits and the cumulative frequencies.
b. Draw a more-than-cumulative frequency polygon.
c. Based on the ogive, 50 percent of the firms export more than what amount?

EXERCISES

7. Using the frequency distribution you constructed in Exercise 1:
   a. Develop a less-than cumulative frequency distribution.
   b. Portray the less-than-cumulative frequency distribution in the form of a polygon. Insert both the cumulative frequencies and percents of the total on the *Y*-axis.
   c. Based on the polygon, half of the countries had an annual increase in consumer prices less than what percent?

8. Using the frequency distribution you constructed in Exercise 2:
   a. Develop a more-than-cumulative frequency distribution.
   b. Portray this distribution in the form of a more-than ogive.
   c. Based on your ogive, one out of every four states have per capita incomes of more than what amount?

CHAPTER SUMMARY

This chapter dealt with organizing raw data into a frequency distribution. To construct one, the data are tallied into categories and the tallies counted. The categories are called classes and the counts, the class frequencies. A frequency distribution reveals such characteristics of the data as the spread, and the region where the observations are concentrated. The data may be further described graphically by drawing a histogram, a frequency polygon, or a cumulative frequency polygon.

CHAPTER OUTLINE

Frequency distributions

I. Frequency distributions.
   A. *Purpose.* To organize ungrouped (raw) data into some meaningful form.
   B. *Definition.* A frequency distribution is a grouping of data into classes and recording the number of cases in each class.

C. *Procedure*.
1. Construct an array. An array is an ordered list of the values from the smallest to the largest, or vice versa.
2. Tally. Tally the data into the array.
3. Decide on width of class interval, number of classes, and class limits. Suggested class interval can be determined by the Sturges formula:

$$\frac{\text{Highest value} - \text{Lowest value}}{1 + 3.322 \text{ (logarithm of the total frequencies)}}$$

4. Transfer tallies from the array into the appropriate classes to construct the frequency distribution. Example:

Age (in years)	Number f
20–24	3
25–29	7
30–34	2

D. Other criteria for constructing a frequency distribution.
1. Avoid having too few or too many classes.
2. Widths of class intervals should be equal, if possible.
3. Open-end classes should be avoided, if possible.

II. Graphic presentation of frequency distributions.
A. Histogram. Scale the lower and upper true class limits on the *X*-axis, and the class frequencies on the *Y*-axis. Example:

Age, stated limits	Age, true limits	Number f
20–24	19.5–24.5	3
25–29	24.5–29.5	7
30–34	29.5–34.5	2

B. Frequency polygon. Scale classes on the *X*-axis and class frequencies on the *Y*-axis. The midpoint of the class represents the class. Plot the midpoints and corresponding frequencies. Same example:

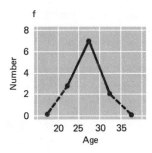

C. Cumulative frequency polygons.
   1. Less-than-cumulative frequency polygon. Accumulate frequencies starting with the *lowest* class. Plot cumulative frequencies and the corresponding upper true class limits. Same example:

Age, true limits (in years)	Number f	Cumulative frequencies CF
19.5–24.5 3		3
24.5–29.5 7		10
29.5–34.5 2		12

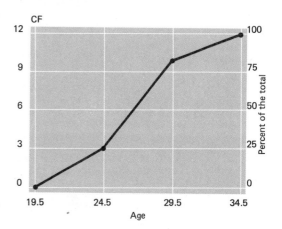

   2. More-than-cumulative frequency polygon. Accumulate frequencies starting with the *highest* class. Plot cumulative frequencies and the corresponding *lower* true class limits. Same example:

Age, true limits (in years)	Number f	Cumulative frequencies CF
19.5–24.5 3		12
24.5–29.5 7		9
29.5–34.5 2		2

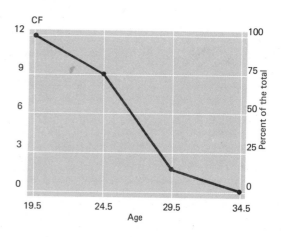

**CHAPTER
EXERCISES**

9. The number of shareholders was included in a study of a selected group of large companies.

Company	Number of shareholders	Company	Number of shareholders
Pan American World Airways	144,000	Northeast Utilities	200,000
General Public Utilities	177,000	Standard Oil (Indiana)	173,000
Occidental Petroleum	266,000	Atlantic Richfield	195,000
Middle South Utilities	133,000	Detroit Edison	220,000
Chrysler Corporation	209,000	Eastman Kodak	251,000
Standard Oil of California	264,000	Dow Chemical	137,000
Bethlehem Steel	160,000	Pennsylvania Power	150,000
Long Island Lighting	143,000	American Electric Power	282,000
RCA	246,000	Ohio Edison	158,000
Greyhound Corporation	151,000	Transamerica Corporation	162,000
Pacific Gas & Electric	239,000	Columbia Gas System	165,000
Niagara Mohawk Power	204,000	International Telephone &	
E. I. du Pont de Nemours	204,000	Telegraph	223,000
Westinghouse Electric	195,000	Union Electric	158,000
Union Carbide	176,000	Virginia Electric and Power	162,000
BankAmerica	175,000	Public Service Electric & Gas	225,000
		Consumers Power	161,000

The numbers of shareholders are to be organized into a frequency distribution and several graphs drawn to portray the distribution.

   a. Determine the class interval. Use the Sturges formula for the suggested size of the class interval as a guide.

   b. Construct a frequency distribution giving both the stated class limits and the true class limits. The numbers of shareholders have been rounded to the nearest thousand.)

   c. Portray the distribution in a histogram.

   d. Portray the distribution in a frequency polygon.

   e. Portray the distribution in a less-than-cumulative frequency polygon.

   f. Portray the distribution in a more-than-cumulative frequency polygon.

   g. Based on the ogive, three out of every four (75 percent) of the companies have less than how many shareholders?

   h. Write a brief analysis of the number of shareholders based on the frequency distribution and graphs.

10. A 100-bed hospital had 18,200 patients during the year for an annual turnover rate of 18.2 patients per bed (18,200/100 = 18.2). The hospital administrator believes turnover is too low—that is, patients are remaining in the hospital beds too long. Other staff members think that the turnover rate is about average compared with those of other hospitals in the United States. In order to compare the turnover rate of 18.2 patients per bed with experience in other states, the following data from the American Hospital Association are to be used.

State	Beds	Admissions during year	State	Beds	Admissions during year
Alabama	25,198	729,240	Missouri	35,667	965,244
Alaska	1,697	57,922	Montana	5,119	144,144
Arizona	11,140	367,737	Nebraska	11,473	302,585
Arkansas	13,589	421,222	Nevada	3,243	105,930
California	115,378	3,345,048	New Hampshire	4,997	136,458
Colorado	15,075	472,423	New Jersey	45,199	1,088,024
Connecticut	19,079	454,950	New Mexico	6,552	186,035
Delaware	4,688	82,848	New York	140,779	2,785,786
District of			North Carolina	34,220	914,892
Columbia	9,850	212,467	North Dakota	5,999	147,096
Florida	54,854	1,570,560	Ohio	67,769	1,859,769
Georgia	31,173	931,583	Oklahoma	17,286	509,052
Hawaii	3,868	118,806	Oregon	12,031	375,034
Idaho	3,697	134,051	Pennsylvania	89,368	1,966,769
Illinois	76,135	2,034,274	Rhode Island	6,841	146,353
Indiana	34,458	872,372	South Carolina	17,337	476,403
Iowa	21,549	567,319	South Dakota	5,978	145,291
Kansas	18,116	464,737	Tennessee	31,235	914,852
Kentucky	18,749	645,344	Texas	77,951	2,386,814
Louisiana	25,016	759,617	Utah	5,036	202,216
Maine	7,326	181,075	Vermont	3,075	78,813
Maryland	24,865	550,578	Virginia	32,212	787,152
Massachusetts	47,635	949,928	Washington	16,250	587,351
Michigan	52,423	1,486,950	West Virginia	15,510	395,269
Minnesota	31,141	726,550	Wisconsin	29,757	782,959
Mississippi	16,930	462,902	Wyoming	2,584	68,988

a. Convert the data for each state to patient turnover per hospital bed. Round the turnover rates to the nearest whole number using conventional rounding rules (31.5 is rounded up to 32, but 31.49 is rounded down to 31).

b. Construct an array.

c. Determine the class interval to be used in constructing a frequency distribution. Hint: Use the Sturges formula for the suggested class interval.

d. Design a frequency distribution giving both the stated limits and the true class limits.

e. Construct a histogram and a frequency polygon.

f. Construct a less-than-cumulative and a more-than-cumulative frequency distribution and portray the data in the form of a less-than and a more-than ogive. Show the cumulative frequencies on the left Y-axis and percents of total on the right.

g. Briefly summarize your findings.

h. What conclusions will the administrator of the 100-bed hospital reach regarding the turnover rate at her hospital?

4

INTRODUCTION

As noted in Chapter 3, raw data can be described by organizing it into a table, called a frequency distribution, and portraying the distribution graphically in a histogram or polygon. This chapter is concerned with another way of summarizing quantitative data, namely, by reporting one or more **measures of central tendency**. As implied, these are measures that locate the center of a set of observations. You are already familiar with measures of central tendency but probably refer to them as averages. No doubt you know your cumulative grade point average (and we hope it is 3.95). If you follow the sports scene you are bombarded with averages—for example, that Earl Campbell of the Houston Oilers averaged 5.3 yards per carry in the first half of the Monday night game against the Tampa Bay Buccaneers. Other examples from current literature: Standard Oil of California reported that the average cost of drilling an oil well is $1,943,000. The average hourly wage in mining is $9.69, and the median family income in the United States is $21,062.

Four measures of central tendency commonly used in business and economics are examined in the following sections. They are the **arithmetic mean**, the **median**, the **mode**, and the **geometric mean**.

The arithmetic mean, median, and mode of ungrouped, or raw data, will be discussed first. Then the computation of the three averages for data grouped into a frequency distribution will be examined.

Describing data—measures
of central tendency

MEAN, MEDIAN, AND MODE OF UNGROUPED DATA

The arithmetic mean

The **arithmetic mean**, often called the **mean**, is the most widely used average. The mean of a group of ungrouped observations is *the sum of all the observations divided by the total number of observations*.

$$\text{Mean} = \frac{\text{Sum of all the observations}}{\text{Total number of observations}}.$$

Instead of writing out in words the full directions for computing the mean (or any other measure), it is more convenient to use the shorthand notation of algebra. At times, we will be concerned with a *sample*, which is part of a population, other times with the entire *population*. The mean of a sample and the mean of a population are computed in the same way, but the shorthand notation used is different. The formula for a *sample* is:

$$\bar{X} = \frac{\Sigma X}{n}$$

where:

$\bar{X}$ stands for the sample mean. It is read "X bar."
X stands for a particular observation.
Σ is the Greek capital sigma and indicates the operation of adding.

So

ΣX stands for the sum of all the Xs.
n is the total number of observations in the sample.

The mean of a population in terms of symbols is:

$$\mu = \frac{\Sigma X}{N}$$

where:

μ stands for the population mean. It is mu, the Greek letter for lower-case m.
N is the total number of observations in the population.

As before, ΣX stands for the sum of all the Xs.

EXAMPLE

The weights of five ball bearings selected at random from the production line are (in grams): 85.4, 85.3, 84.9, 85.4, and 85.0. What is the arithmetic mean weight of the sample observations?

SOLUTION

$$\text{Arithmetic mean} = \frac{\text{Sum of all the observations}}{\text{Total number of observations}}$$

$$\bar{X} = \frac{\Sigma X}{n}$$

$$= \frac{85.4 + 85.3 + 84.9 + 85.4 + 85.0}{5}$$

$$= \frac{426.0}{5}$$

$$= 85.2$$

The arithmetic mean weight is 85.2 grams.

SELF-REVIEW 4–1

1. *a.* $\bar{X} = \frac{\Sigma X}{n}$

   b. $= \frac{\$187,100}{4}$

   $= \$46,775$

   $= \$46,800$ rounded

2. *a.* $\mu = \frac{\Sigma X}{N}$

   b. $= \frac{498}{6}$

   $= 83$

(A reminder: cover the answers in the left-hand column.)

1. The annual incomes of a sample of several middle-management employees are (to the nearest $100): $42,900, $49,100, $38,300, and $56,800.
   a. Give the formula for the sample mean.
   b. Determine the sample mean rounded to the nearest $100.

2. All the students in advanced computer science S411 are considered the population. Their course grades are 92, 96, 61, 86, 79, and 84.
   a. Give the formula for the population mean.
   b. Compute the mean course grade.

The weighted arithmetic mean

If a retail department store pays salespersons either $6.50, $7.50, or $8.50 an hour, it might be concluded that the arithmetic mean hourly wage is $7.50, found by ($6.70 + $7.50 + $8.50)/3. This is true only if there are the *same* number of salespersons earning $6.50, $7.50, and $8.50 an hour. However, suppose 14 salespersons earn $6.50 an hour, 10 are paid $7.50, and 2 get $8.50. To find the mean, $6.50 is **weighted**, or multiplied, by 14, $7.50 is weighted by 10, and $8.50 is weighted by 2. The resulting average is aptly called the **weighted arithmetic mean**.

In general, the weighted mean of a set of numbers designated $X_1, X_2, X_3, \ldots X_n$ with corresponding weights $w_1, w_2, w_3 \ldots, w_n$ is computed by:

$$\bar{X}_w = \frac{w_1 X_1 + w_2 X_2 + w_3 X_3 + \ldots + w_n X_n}{w_1 + w_2 + w_3 + \ldots + w_n}$$

This may be shortened to:

$$\overline{X}_w = \frac{\Sigma w \cdot X}{\Sigma w}$$

For the above problem:

$$\overline{X}_w = \frac{14(\$6.50) + 10(\$7.50) + 2(\$8.50)}{14 + 10 + 2}$$

$$= \frac{\$183}{26}$$

$$= \$7.038$$

The weighted arithmetic mean hourly wage is $7.04.

The arithmetic mean is used extensively to locate the middle of numerical data. The federal government, for example, uses it to report the typical or representative hourly earnings and the average hours worked per week in retail trade and other industries. The mean of a sample is employed in later chapters to draw conclusions about an entire population.

The median

To illustrate the need for a measure of central tendency other than the arithmetic mean, suppose that you were invited to a beach party. The host and hostess informed you that the average age of the persons who had already accepted their invitation was about 35. Would you accept their invitation? If you were in the 18-to-21-year age bracket you might decline, reasoning that those attending would be almost twice your age! However, checking the individual ages of those who said they would attend might change your mind. The ages are: 19, 21, 18, 20, and 95. The arithmetic mean age is about 35, as the host and hostess reported, but one age (95) is pulling the arithmetic mean upward, causing it to be an unrepresentative average. It does seem that an age between 19 and 21 would be a more typical or representative average. The median does exactly that. The median of ungrouped data is *the middle value of the observations after they have been ordered by size.*

The median age of the person who accepted the invitation to the beach party is 20 years.

Ages ordered from low to high		Ages ordered from high to low
18		95
19		21
20	←—— median ——→	20
21		19
95		18

Note that there are the same number of ages below the median of 20 as above it.

The median is, therefore, unaffected by extremely low or extremely high observations.

Had the highest age been 23, or 50, or 110 years, the median age would still have been 20. Likewise, had the lowest age been 2 or 16, the median age would still be 20.

In the previous illustration there are an *odd* number of observations (five). How is the median determined for an *even* number of observations? As before, the observations are ordered. Then the usual practice is to find the arithmetic mean of the two middle observations.

EXAMPLES

1. The hourly wages of several stock boys are: $4.75, $4.05, $3.95, $4.60, $5.15, and $4.40. What is the median hourly wage?

2. The lengths of time it took several production workers to complete a task are (in seconds): 45, 37, 160, and 42. What is the median length of time required to complete the task?

SOLUTIONS

1. Arranging the hourly wages from low to high:

    $3.95
    4.05
    4.40
    4.60 ←— median
    4.75
    5.15

    The median wage is $4.50, found by determining the arithmetic means of the two center observations: ($4.40 + $4.60) ÷ 2 = $4.50.

2. Arranging the times from low to high:

    37
    42
    45 ←— median
    160

    The median time is 43.5 seconds, found by (42 + 45) ÷ 2.

Again, note that there are the same number of observations below the median as above it.

SELF-REVIEW 4–2

1. *a.* $439.
   b. 3, 3.
2. *a.* 7, found by (6 + 8)/2 = 7.
   b. 3, 3.

1. A sample of single persons receiving social security payments revealed these monthly benefits: $426, $299, $290, $687, $480, $439, and $565.

    a. What is the median monthly benefit?

b. How many observations are below the median? Above it?

2. The numbers of work stoppages in a highly industrialized region for selected months are: 6, 0, 10, 14, 8, and 0.

   a. What is the median number of stoppages?

   b. How many observations are below the median? Above it?

There is a minimal amount of work involved in arranging a few ungrouped observations from low to high and selecting the middle value. If there are a large number of observations, a computer greatly reduces the amount of work. As shown in the following exhibit, the median number of years of education is 11.

```
PROBLEM NAME...SAMPLE DATA: EDUCATION OF FACTORY WORKERS, PLANT A

                INPUT DATA

    11.00    12.00    10.00    12.00    10.00    12.00    10.00    12.00
    11.00    12.00    11.00    11.00    12.00    10.00    12.00    13.00
    12.00    12.00    11.00    11.00    11.00    10.00    10.00    11.00
    12.00    10.00    12.00    10.00     9.00    11.00    11.00    11.00
     8.00    11.00    11.00    11.00    10.00    12.00    12.00    12.00
    11.00    10.00    12.00    11.00    12.00    12.00    11.00    12.00
    11.00    11.00    10.00     9.00    12.00    11.00    10.00    10.00
    12.00    11.00     8.00    11.00    12.00    12.00    11.00    12.00
     9.00    12.00    10.00    12.00    11.00    11.00    11.00    11.00
    12.00    10.00    11.00    11.00    11.00    12.00    11.00    11.00
    12.00    11.00    12.00    12.00    12.00    13.00    12.00    11.00


NUMBER OF OBSERVATIONS    88

MEDIAN       11.00
```

The mode

Ungrouped data. The mode is sometimes used to describe the typical member of a set of observations. It is the *value of the observation which appears most frequently*. It is very easy to use because it requires no rearrangement of the data and no arithmetic.

EXAMPLE

The annual salary of the governor for selected states is:

Arizona $35,000	Illinois $58,000	Ohio $50,000
California ... 49,100	Louisiana 50,000	Tennessee 50,000
Colorado ... 50,000	Maryland 60,000	Texas 71,400
Florida 50,000	Massachusetts ... 40,000	West Virginia ... 50,000
Idaho 40,000	New Jersey 65,000	Wyoming 55,000

What is the modal (mode) annual salary?

SOLUTION

A perusal of the salaries reveals that the annual salary of $50,000 appears more often (six times) than any other salary. The mode is, therefore, $50,000.

The mode is especially useful in describing nonquantitative data. For example, a company has developed five bath oils but wants to market just one. Chart 4–1 shows the results of a marketing survey designed to find out which bath oil consumers prefer. The largest number of respondents favored Sexy, as evidenced by the highest bar in Chart 4–1. Thus, Sexy is the mode. You might ponder this question: Why can't the arithmetic mean or median be computed?

CHART 4–1

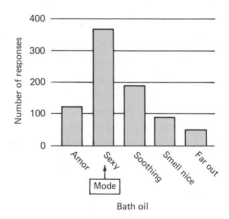

Bath oil

SELF-REVIEW 4–3

1. *a.* 200.
   b. $\bar{X} = 1617/8 = 202.125$.
   c. 202, found by $(200 + 204)/2$.

   Notice that the three averages are different. This usually happens.
2. There is no mode.

1. A machine filling paint cans appears to be operating erratically. A sample of the output for 15-minute periods revealed these figures (in gallons): 207, 200, 191, 200, 205, 204, 210, and 200.
   a. Determine the modal number of gallons filled by the machine during a 15-minute period.
   b. What is the sample mean?
   c. What is the median?
2. What is the mode of these stock prices: 22½, 61¼, 52, 76⅜ and 35⅝?

EXERCISES

(A reminder: The answers and methods of solution for selected exercises are given in Appendix A.)

1. The net income per share for Wells Fargo Mortgage and Equity Trust for the past five years was $0.37, $0.95, $1.34, $1.93, and $2.10 respectively. What is the arithmetic mean net income per share for the five-year period?

2. The cash dividends on the common stocks of 20 firms traded on the New York Stock Exchange are:

$2.90	$1.01	$0.11	$1.38	$1.34
1.34	2.40	2.45	0.78	0.32
0.96	3.90	1.72	2.10	1.46
3.10	1.11	1.34	1.00	2.44

   a. What is the modal dividend?
   b. Find the median dividend.
   c. Determine the arithmetic mean dividend.

3. Refer to Exercise 2. Had each firm given exactly $1 more in cash dividends, how would it affect the
   a. Mode?
   b. Median?
   c. Arithmetic mean?

4. A sample of the hourly production of a small transistor radio, Model 220A, by the day shift revealed these production figures:

290	289	294	305	286	275	280
282	282	277	295	294	290	
290	292	298	300	281	290	
290	279	278	284	290	288	
288	290	283	290	278	280	

   a. What is the modal hourly production?
   b. Determine the median hourly production.
   c. How many observations are there below the median? Above it?
   d. Find the arithmetic mean hourly production.

5. The average annual inflation rates for selected countries during the past six years according to the World Bank are:

Afghanistan	3.1	France	9.3	Panama	11.2
Argentina	88.7	Greece	13.3	Paraguay	13.6
Brazil	26.1	Haiti	13.5	Peru	15.6
Canada	9.2	Hong Kong	8.6	Philippines	15.1
Chile	273.6	Japan	10.1	Spain	12.8
China	11.9	Lebanon	4.4	Sri Lanka	11.5
Costa Rica	13.7	Liberia	10.3	United States	7.9
Denmark	9.8	Mexico	14.2	Uruguay	70.5
Egypt	5.2	Norway	8.6	Yugoslavia	16.3
Finland	13.6	Pakistan	15.2	Zimbabwe	7.5

   Determine:
   a. The arithmetic mean inflation rate for these selected countries.
   b. The median inflation rate.
   c. Which average would you use to represent the typical inflation rate? Why?

6. A stockbroker placed the following order for a customer:

   50 shares of Kaiser Aluminum preferred at $104 a share.
   200 shares of GTE preferred at $25¼ a share.
   10 shares of Boston Edison preferred at $9⅛ a share.

   What is the weighted arithmetic mean price per share?

7. During the past six months, the purchasing agent bought:

    1,200 tons of coal at $28.50 a ton.
    3,000 tons at $87.25 a ton.
      500 tons at $88.00 a ton.

    What is the weighted arithmetic mean price per ton?

8. The sales manager of a shirt manufacturer sold these quantities during the week:

    10 gross at $4.85 a shirt.
    80 gross at $4.30 a shirt.
     3 gross at $5.12 a shirt.

    What is the weighted arithmetic mean price per shirt?

MEAN, MEDIAN, AND MODE OF GROUPED DATA

The arithmetic mean

Quite often such agencies as the federal government release numerical information already grouped in a frequency distribution. For example, census data and the annual incomes of taxpayers are presented in grouped form. It is impractical, or impossible, to secure the original data. The mean, median, and mode therefore must be estimated from the grouped data.

To approximate the arithmetic mean of data organized into a frequency distribution, the observations in each class are treated as if they are concentrated at the *midpoint* of the class. Using the **direct method**, the mean of a sample is computed by:

$$\bar{X} = \frac{\Sigma fX}{n}$$

where:

$\bar{X}$ is the designation for the arithmetic mean.
X is the mid-value, or midpoint, of each class.
f is the frequency in each class.
fX is the frequency in each class times the midpoint of the class.
ΣfX is the sum of these products.
n is the total number of frequencies.

EXAMPLE

Recall from Chapter 3 that the personnel director of a large department store chain embarked on a study of the commissions earned during a day by the company's salespersons. A sample of 120 commissions was organized into the frequency distribution shown in Table 4–1.

68

TABLE 4–1
Daily commissions
earned by 120
salespersons

Daily commission	Number
$30–$34	3
35– 39	7
40– 44	11
45– 49	22
50– 54	40
55– 59	24
60– 64	9
65– 69	4

What is the arithmetic mean commission?

SOLUTION

It is assumed that all three commissions in the $30–$34 class are at the midpoint of $32, all seven commissions in the $35–$39 class fall at the midpoint of $37, and so on. To estimate the mean, the frequency in each class, f, is multiplied by the class midpoint, X, to give fX. These products are summed to arrive at ΣfX. This total is divided by the total number of frequencies, n, to get the arithmetic mean. The calculations needed are illustrated in Table 4–2.

TABLE 4–2
Calculations needed
for the arithmetic
mean

Daily commission	Frequency f	Midpoint X	Frequency × midpoint fX
$30–$34	3	$32	$ 96
35– 39	7	37	259
40– 44	11	42	462
45– 49	22	47	1,034
50– 54	40	52	2,080
55– 59	24	57	1,368
60– 69	9	62	558
65– 69	4	67	268
	120		$ 6125
	↑		↑
	$\boxed{n}$		$\boxed{\Sigma fX}$

$$\bar{X} = \frac{\Sigma fX}{n}$$

$$= \frac{\$6,125}{120}$$

$$= \$51.04$$

The arithmetic mean daily commission is $51.04.

The estimated arithmetic mean based on the daily commissions grouped in this frequency distribution was computed to be $51.04. The arithmetic mean commission based on the original data in Chapter 3 is $50.88. The difference of 16 cents is a result of the grouping. If a different class interval had been selected, the mean would probably be another slightly different value. The sacrifice in accuracy due to grouping is seldom large, and the benefit derived is that masses of data are more easily stored and manipulated in grouped form.

SELF-REVIEW 4–4
---

	f	X	fX
80– 89	5	84.5	422.5
90– 99	9	94.5	850.5
100–109	20	104.5	2,090.0
110–119	8	114.5	916.0
120–129	6	124.5	747.0
130–139	2	134.5	269.0
	50		5,295.0

$$\bar{X} = \frac{\Sigma fX}{n} = \frac{5,295.0}{50} = 105.9$$

A sample of the weekly production of a minicomputer, Model 5600, by the third shift was organized into a frequency distribution.

Weekly production	Frequency
80– 89	5
90– 99	9
100–109	20
110–119	8
120–129	6
130–139	2

Estimate the arithmetic mean weekly production.

If the frequencies and the class midpoints are large and the intervals are all equal, an alternative method of estimating the mean reduces the size of the values to be manipulated. The method is often called the **coded method.** It is sometimes referred to as the "method of false position" because you guess at the true location of the arithmetic mean and then measure how far off you are.

The formula is:

$$\bar{X} = \bar{X}_0 + \frac{i(\Sigma fd)}{n}$$

where, as before,

$\bar{X}$ is the symbol for the arithmetic mean.
$\bar{X}_0$ is the guessed arithmetic mean.
i is the size of the class interval.
f is the class frequency.
d is the coded midpoints.
n is the total number of observations.

The steps are:

1. To reduce the size of the numbers, any class midpoint near the center of the frequency distribution is chosen and designated by $\bar{X}_0$. Usually the class containing the greatest number of frequencies is selected.

2. The midpoint of the class containing the guessed mean is set equal to zero (see the following example). These coded midpoints are represented by the letter d.

3. The midpoint of the class immediately following the class containing the guessed mean is coded as $+1$. The midpoint of the class immediately prior to the class containing the guessed mean is coded as -1. This process is continued until all the class midpoints are coded.

4. The frequency in each class f is multiplied by the coded midpoint d and summed, recognizing that some of the fd's are positive and others negative.

5. The arithmetic mean deviation ($\Sigma fd/n$) is computed and multiplied by the size of the class interval (i). This "correction factor" is added to the original guessed mean ($\bar{X}_0$) to give the arithmetic mean ($\bar{X}$).

EXAMPLE

The frequency distribution giving the daily commissions earned by 120 salespersons is repeated in Table 4–3 below.

TABLE 4–3
Daily commissions earned by 120 salespersons

Daily commission	Number
$30–$34	3
35– 39	7
40– 44	11
45– 49	22
50– 54	40
55– 59	24
60– 64	9
65– 69	4

Estimate the arithmetic mean daily commission using the coded method.

SOLUTION

The procedure is shown in Table 4–4. As a first step, a class midpoint near the center of the distribution is chosen. The midpoint of $52 was chosen in this case. That midpoint ($52) is "coded," or set equal to zero. The midpoint of the $45–$49, class which is immediately prior to the class containing the guessed mean, is coded as -1. (See the column labeled "coded value" in Table 4–4.) This process is continued until all the class midpoints are coded. Then the frequencies are multiplied by the coded values and summed.

The arithmetic mean deviation is then computed ($-23/120$), and multiplied by the size of the class interval ($5). Finally, this "correction factor" is added to the original guessed mean of $52.

TABLE 4–4
Calculations needed for the arithmetic mean commission

Daily commissions	Frequencies f	Coded value d	Frequencies × coded value fd
$30–$34	3	−4	−12 ⎫
35– 39	7	−3	−21 ⎪
40– 44	11	−2	−22 ⎬ −77
45– 49	22	−1	−22 ⎭
50– 54	40	0	0
55– 59	24	+1	+24 ⎫
60– 64	9	+2	+18 ⎬ +54
65– 69	4	+3	+12 ⎭
	120		−23
	↑ n		↑ Σfd

Repeating the formula:

$$\bar{X} = \bar{X}_0 + \frac{i(\Sigma fd)}{n}$$

Inserting the appropriate values:

$$\bar{X} = \$52 + \frac{\$5(-23)}{120} = \$52 - \frac{\$115}{120} = \$51.04$$

which is the same mean as computed by the direct method.

The calculation of the arithmetic mean of the foregoing sample data by the coded method did not materially reduce the computation time. However, if the size of the digits being handled is large, coding reduces their size.

SELF-REVIEW 4–5

Any midpoint can be chosen. We chose 104.5.
a. 105.9.

Weekly production	f	d	fd
80– 89	5	−2	−10
90– 99	9	−1	− 9
100–109	20	0	0
110–119	8	+1	8
120–129	6	+2	12
130–139	2	+3	6
	50		+ 7

$\bar{X} = 104.5 + 10(7)/50 = 104.5 + 1.4 = 105.9.$
b. Yes.

The weekly production figures from self-review 4–4 are repeated below.

Weekly production	Frequencies
80– 89	5
90– 99	9
100–109	20
110–119	8
120–129	6
130–139	2

a. Estimate the arithmetic mean production using the coded method.
b. Does your answer agree with the one for Self-Review 4–4?

EXERCISES

9. A study of the production employees of a firm involved recording their ages. A sample was selected, and the ages were organized into a frequency distribution:

Ages	Number	Ages	Number
20–24	3	45–49	8
25–29	9	50–54	5
30–34	15	55–59	4
35–39	26	60–64	2
40–44	12		

  a. Estimate the arithmetic mean age using the direct method.
  b. Estimate the arithmetic mean age using the coded method.

10. The results from a survey of middle management annual salaries are:

Annual salaries	Number
$30,000–$39,000	16
40,000– 49,000	30
50,000– 59,000	45
60,000– 69,000	80
70,000– 79,000	32
80,000– 89,000	14

  a. Estimate the arithmetic mean annual salary using the direct method.
  b. Estimate the arithmetic mean annual salarly using the coded method.

The median

The median of data organized in a frequency distribution can be estimated by (1) locating the class interval in which the median lies, and then (2) interpolating within that class to arrive at the median. The rationale for this approach is that the members of the median class are uniformly spread throughout the class interval.

The median can also be estimated using the formula

$$\text{Median} = L + \frac{\frac{n}{2} - CF}{f} \quad (i)$$

where:

  L is the lower *true* limit of the class containing the median.
  n is the total number of frequencies.
  CF is the cumulative number of frequencies in all the classes immediately preceeding the class containing the median.
  i is the width of the class in which the median lies.

First, we shall estimate the median by locating the class in which it falls and interpolating to estimate the median. Then the formula for the median will be applied to check our answer.

EXAMPLE

The daily commissions of 120 salespersons are used again to show the procedure for estimating the median (see Table 4–5). The cumulative frequencies in the right column will be used shortly.

**TABLE 4–5
Daily commissions of
120 salespersons**

Daily commissions	Frequencies f	Cumulative frequencies CF
$30–$34	3	3
35– 39	7	10
40– 44	11	21
45– 49	22	43
50– 54	40	83
55– 59	24	107
60– 64	9	116
65– 69	4	120

What is the median daily commission?

SOLUTION

The daily commissions of the 120 salespersons have already been arranged in ascending order from the stated limits of $30 to $69. It is common practice to locate the middle observation by dividing the total number of observations by two. In this case, $n/2 = 120/2 = 60$.[1] The class containing the 60th salesperson is located by referring to the cumulative frequency column in Table 4–5. Notice that 43 salespersons earn $49 or less and 83 earn $54 or less. Hence, the 60th commission amount is in the $50–$54 class. The lower limit of that class is really $49.50 and the upper limit is $54.50. We have, therefore, located the median commission somewhere between $49.50 and $54.50.

To interpolate in that class for the estimated median, it is assumed that the commissions are evenly distributed between the lower and upper true limits. In Chart 4–2, there are 17 salespersons between the 43rd and 60th salespersons, and there are 40 salespersons in the class containing the median. The median is therefore, 17/40 of the distance between $49.50 and $54.50. This distance is $5. Therefore, 17/40 of $5, or $2.125, is added to the lower true limit of $49.50, giving $51.625, the estimated median daily commission.

---

[1] Technically it should be $(n + 1)/2$, but the difference is usually negligible.

CHART 4–2

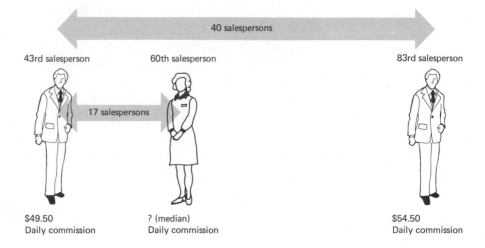

To use the formula given previously, L is $49.50, the lower true limit of the class containing the median. n is 120 salespersons, CF is 43, the cumulative number of commissions preceding the median class, f is 40, the frequency in the median class, and i is $5, the width of the class containing the median.

$$\text{Median} = L + \frac{\frac{n}{2} - CF}{f} \ (i)$$

Substituting we get:

$$= \$49.50 + \frac{\frac{120}{2} - 43}{40} \ (\$5)$$

$$= \$49.50 + \frac{17}{40} \ (\$5)$$

$$= \$49.50 + \$2.125$$
$$= \$51.625 \ (\text{same as determined previously})$$

The estimated median daily commission is $51.625, or $51.63 rounded.

The assumption underlying the approximation of the median—that the frequencies in the median class are distributed evenly between $49.50 and $54.50—may not be correct. Therefore, it is safer to say that *about* half the salespersons earn less than $51.63 and the other half more than $51.63. Again, the median of data grouped in a frequency distribution ($51.63 in this case) and the median of ungrouped data ($52, from Chapter 3) will probably be somewhat different, but such calculations are the best one can do under the circumstances.

A final note: The median is based only on the frequencies and the true class limits of the median class. The open-end classes that occur at the extremes are rarely needed. Therefore, the median of a frequency distribution having open ends can virtually always be determined. The arithmetic mean of a frequency distribution with an open-end class cannot be accurately computed—unless, of course, the midpoints of the open-end classes are estimated. Further, the median can be determined if *percentage frequencies* are given instead of the actual frequencies because it is the value with 50 percent of the distribution above it and 50 percent below it and does not depend on actual counts. The percents are considered as substitutes for the actual frequencies. In a sense, they are actual frequencies with the total being 100.0. Problem 2 in the following self-review has both an open end and percentage frequencies.

SELF-REVIEW 4–6

---

1. 105.0

True class limits	f	CF
79.5– 89.5	5	5
89.5– 99.5	9	14
99.5–109.5	20	34
109.5–119.5	8	42
119.5–129.5	6	48
129.5–139.5	2	50

$n/2 = 50/2 = 25$. The 25th weekly production figures if in the 99.5–109.5 class.

$$99.5 + 11/20 \text{ of } 10 = 99.5 + 5.5 = 105.0$$

or,

$$\text{Median} = 99.5 + \frac{\frac{50}{2} - 14}{20} (10) = 105.0$$

2. $5,050.

Lower true limit	CF
$1,950	5.7
2,950	21.9
3,950	47.0
4,950	77.0
5,950	96.4
6,950	100.0

$$\$4,950 + \frac{\frac{100}{2} - 47.0}{30} (\$1,000)$$

$$= \$4,950 + \frac{3}{30} (\$1,000)$$

$$= \$5,050$$

1. The weekly production figures from the previous self-review are repeated below.

Weekly production	Frequencies
80– 89	5
90– 99	9
100–109	20
110–119	8
120–129	6
130–139	2

Assuming that the true class limits are 79.5–89.5, and so on, estimate the median weekly production.

2. The monthly payroll of staff members of law firms were organized into a percentage distribution.

Monthly payroll		Percent of total
Stated limits	True limits	
$2,000–$2,900	$1,950–$2,950	5.7
3,000– 3,900	2,950– 3,950	16.2
4,000– 4,900	3,950– 4,950	25.1
5,000– 5,900	4,950– 5,950	30.0
6,000– 6,900	5,950– 6,950	19.4
7,000 and over	6,950 and over	3.6

Estimate the median monthly payroll.

EXERCISES

11. The ages of the production employees of a firm from Exercise 9 are repeated. The true lower limits are 19.5, 24.5, and so on.

Ages	Number	Ages	Number
20–24	3	45–49	8
25–29	9	50–54	5
30–34	15	55–59	4
35–39	26	60–64	2
40–44	12		

Estimate the median age.

12. The annual salaries of middle-management personnel from Problem 10 are repeated. The true limits are $29,500–$39,500, etc.

Annual Salaries	Number
$30,000–$39,000	16
40,000– 49,000	30
50,000– 59,000	45
60,000– 69,000	80
70,000– 79,000	32
80,000– 89,000	14

Estimate the median annual salary.

13. The Department of Commerce, Bureau of the Census, reported that 515,600 unmarried women gave birth last year. The age and number of unmarried mothers are presented in a frequency distribution.

Age of mother	Number (in 000)
Under 15 years	10.1
15–19 years	239.7
20–24 years	168.6
25–29 years	62.4
30–34 years	23.7
35–39 years	8.8
40 years and over	2.3

Estimate the median age of the mother.

The mode

If data are grouped into a frequency distribution, the **mode** can be approximated by the *midpoint of the class containing the largest number of class frequencies*. This mode is often referred to as the **observed** or **crude mode**. Again referring to the daily commissions of the salespersons, shown in Table 4–6, note that the greatest number of salespersons earned between $50 and $54 (because 40 is the largest class frequency). The class midpoint of $52 is the crude mode.

Sometimes the **computed mode** is used to approximate the value that appears most frequently. Referring to Table 4–6, the assumption is that the frequencies in the modal class (40) are distributed evenly throughout the class. This condition may not exist, because there are more salespersons in

TABLE 4–6
Daily commissions of
120 salespersons

Daily commissions	Frequencies
$30–$34	3
35– 39	7
40– 44	11
45– 49	22
50– 54	40
55– 59	24
60– 64	9
65– 69	4

the class following the modal class (24) than prior to it (22). Thus, it may be that the mode is above the midpoint ($52). To find the computed mode:

$$\text{Mode} = L + \frac{\Delta_1}{\Delta_1 + \Delta_2} \ (i)$$

where:

L Is the lower true limit of the modal class ($49.50 for the commissions in Table 4–6).

Δ_1 (pronounced delta one) is computed by: frequency in the modal class minus the frequency in the class immediately prior to the modal class ($40 - 22 = 18$).

Δ_2 (pronounced delta two) is computed by: frequency in the modal class minus the frequency in the class following the modal class ($40 - 24 = 16$).

i is the width of the modal class ($5).

Solving:

$$\text{Mode} = L + \frac{\Delta_1}{\Delta_1 + \Delta_2} \ (i)$$

$$= \$49.50 + \frac{18}{18 + 16} \ (\$5)$$

$$= \$49.50 + \$2.65$$

$$= \$52.15$$

═══════════════ **SELF-REVIEW 4–7** ═══════════════

1. 104.5, the midpoint of the 100–109 class.
2. $5,450, the midpoint of the $5,000–$5,900 class.

Refer back to the previous self-review.

1. What is the crude mode for the daily production figures given in Problem 1?
2. What is the crude modal monthly payroll in Problem 2?

Two values may occur a large number of times. The distribution is then called **bimodal**. Suppose that the ages of a sample of workers are 22, 27, 30, 30, 30, 30, 34, 58, 60, 60, 60, 60, and 65. The two modes are 30 years and 60 years. Often the two points of concentration develop because the population being sampled is not homogeneous. In this illustration, the population might be composed of two distinct groups—one a group of relatively young employees who have been recently hired to meet the increased demand for a product, and the other a group of older employees who have been with the company a long time.

If a large number of workers were sampled, the distribution of their ages when plotted might appear as shown in Chart 4–3. Note that the two peaks need not be exactly equal in height in order for us to consider the distribution bimodal.

As shown in the chart, the median age is approximately 45 years. This age would not be a representative age for those just recently hired. Neither would the older group of employees consider it a typical age. Thus, a logical decision would be to divide the employees into two distinct groups before continuing the analysis of the data.

CHART 4–3
A bimodal distribution

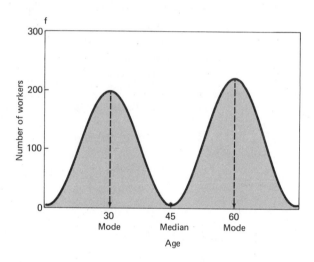

EXERCISES

14. Refer back to Exercise 11.
    a. What is the crude modal age of the production employees?
    b. What is the computed mode?

15. Refer to Exercise 12.
    a. What is the crude modal annual salary?
    b. What is the computed mode?

16. Refer to Exercise 13.
    a. What is the crude modal age of the unmarried mother?
    b. What is the computed mode?

RELATIONSHIP OF THE MEAN, MEDIAN, AND MODE

Refer to the frequency polygon in Chart 4–4. It is **symmetrical**, meaning that *the distribution has the same shape on either side of the center*. If the polygon were folded in half, the two halves would be identical. For a symmetric distribution, the mode, median, and mean are located at the center and are always equal. They are all 20 years in Chart 4–4.

CHART 4–4
Smoothed frequency polygon of the lengths of service for all employees, Nordeen Chemical Company

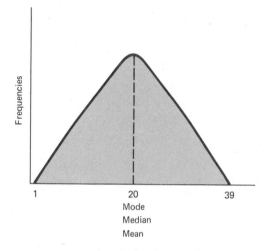

The length of service at the highest point of the curve is the *mode* (20 years). Because the frequency curve is symmetrical, the *median* corresponds to the point where the distribution is cut in half (20 years). The total of the lengths of service for employees with long service with the company is offset by the total service of newer employees, resulting in an *arithmetic mean* of 20 years.

As the distribution becomes asymmetrical, or skewed, this relationship between the three averages changes. In a **positively skewed distribution,** the arithmetic mean is the highest of the three averages. This is so because the

CHART 4–5
A positively skewed distribution

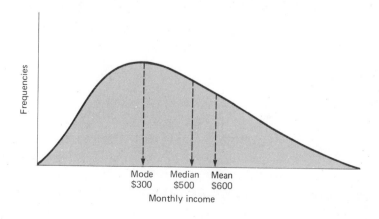

mean is influenced more than the median or mode by a few extremely high values. The median is generally the next-largest average in a positively skewed frequency distribution. The mode is the smallest of the three averages.

Conversely, in a distribution that is **negatively skewed,** the mean is generally the lowest of the three averages. The mean is, of course, influenced by a few extremely low observations. The median is greater than the arithmetic mean. The modal value is the largest of the three averages.

CHART 4–6
A negatively skewed distribution

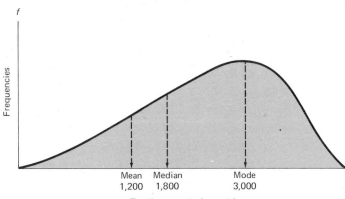

If two averages of a moderately skewed frequency distribution are known, the third can be approximated. The formulas are:

$$\text{Mode} = \text{Mean} - 3(\text{Mean} - \text{Median})$$

$$\text{Mean} = \frac{3(\text{Median}) - \text{Mode}}{2}$$

$$\text{Median} = \frac{2(\text{Mean}) + \text{Mode}}{3}$$

SELF-REVIEW 4–8

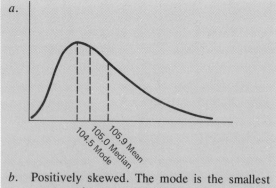

a.

b. Positively skewed. The mode is the smallest average, the mean the largest.

You have already computed the mean weekly production to be 105.9 units, the median to be 105.0 units and the crude mode to be 104.5 units.

a. Sketch the production in the form of a smoothed frequency polygon. Note the location of the mean, median, and mode on the X-axis.

b. Is the distribution symmetrical, positively skewed, or negatively skewed? Explain.

EXERCISES

17. The mean, median, and crude mode of the daily commissions earned by a group of salespersons were computed previously. $\bar{X}$ = \$51.04, median = \$51.63, mode = \$52.00.
    a. Sketch the commissions in the form of a smoothed frequency polygon. Note the location of the mean, median, and mode on the X-axis.
    b. Is the distribution symmetrical, positively skewed, or negatively skewed? Explain.

18. The distribution of the number of hand calculators sold by the bookstore during a month is moderately skewed. The modal number sold is 40, the median 48.
    a. Approximate the mean number sold.
    b. Is the distribution negatively skewed or positively skewed? Explain.

19. The distribution of the prices of a large number of common stocks is moderately skewed. The modal price is \$31.50, the mean \$28.14.
    a. Estimate the median price.
    b. What does the median price indicate?
    c. Describe the skewness in the distribution.

GEOMETRIC MEAN

There are two main uses of the **geometric mean**, namely, (1) to average percents, indexes, and relatives; and (2) to determine the average percent increase in sales, production, or other business or economic series from one time period to another.

The **geometric mean** of a set of n positive numbers is defined as the nth *root of the product of* n *numbers*. Thus, the formula for the geometric mean is written:

$$\text{G.M.} = \sqrt[n]{(X_1)(X_2)(X_3) \ldots (X_n)}$$

EXAMPLE

To illustrate its use in averaging percents, suppose that the profits earned by a construction company on four projects were 3, 2, 4, and 6 percent, respectively. What is the geometric mean profit?

SOLUTION

$$\text{G.M.} = \sqrt[n]{(X_1)(X_2)(X_3) \ldots (X_n)}$$
$$= \sqrt[4]{(3)(2)(4)(6)}$$
$$= \sqrt[4]{144}$$

At this point, logarithms greatly facilitate the computation of the geometric mean. There is a table of common logarithms in Appendix B. To continue:

$$\text{Logarithm of the geometric mean} = \frac{\text{Logarithm of 144}}{4}$$

$$= \frac{2.1584}{4}$$

$$= 0.5396$$

The antilogarithm of 0.5396 is $\simeq$ 3.46. The geometric mean profit is 3.46 percent.

Instead of first determining the product of the four profit figures and then using logarithms to arrive at the geometric mean, logarithms can be used exclusively. After locating the logarithm of each profit figure (see table in Appendix B), the logarithms are summed, and the sum is divided by 4, as follows:

Number X	Logarithms of the numbers log of X
3	0.4771
2	0.3010
4	0.6021
6	0.7782
	2.1584

$$\text{Log of G.M.} = \frac{\Sigma \log X}{n} = \frac{2.1584}{4} = 0.5396$$

Again, the antilog of 0.5396 is 3.46 (same answer).

The arithmetic mean profit is 3.75 percent. Although the profit of 6 percent is not extremely large, it is weighting the arithmetic mean upward. The geometric mean of 3.46 gives a more conservative profit figure because it is not so heavily weighted by extreme values. It will be, in fact, either equal to or less than the arithmetic mean.

EXAMPLE

To cite another example, suppose that the prices of five gold mining stocks increased by 37.1; 1,140.0; 0.927; 2.7; and 842.0 percent, respectively, since 1975. What is the geometric mean percent increase in the price of the five stocks?

SOLUTION

It would be rather awkward to compute the geometric mean increase by first finding the product of the five numbers. Instead, the logarithm of each percent increase is summed and the sum divided by five.

Company	Percent increase X	Logarithm of X characteristic and mantissa
A	37.100	1.5694
B	1,140.000	3.0569
C	0.927	9.9671 − 10
D	2.700	0.4314
E	842.000	2.9253
	2,022.727	17.9501 − 10, or 7.9501

$$\text{Log of G.M.} = \frac{\Sigma \log X}{n} = \frac{7.9501}{5} = 1.5900$$

The antilogarithm of the quotient (1.5900) is the geometric mean increase (38.9 percent).

Contrast the geometric mean of 38.9 percent with the arithmetic mean of 404.5 percent, found by 2,022.727/5. Again, it is evident that the geometric mean is not so highly influenced by extreme values as is the arithmetic mean.

Now to explore the second application of the geometric mean—determining the average percent increase in sales, exports, or other business series from one time period to another.

The formula for the geometric mean as applied to this type of problem is:

$$\text{G.M.} = \left[\sqrt[n-1]{\frac{\text{Value at end of period}}{\text{Value at beginning of period}}} \right] - 1$$

EXAMPLE

Suppose that the population of Podunk Hollow in 1980 was 2 persons and the estimated number for 1990 is 22. What is the estimated average annual percentage increase?

SOLUTION

Note that there are 11 years. Thus, $n = 11$. To explain, the 11 years are 1980, 1981, 1982, 1983, 1984, 1985, 1986, 1987, 1988, 1989, and 1990. Even though there are 11 years involved, there are only 10 annual rates of change, namely, from 1980 to 1981, from 1981 to 1982 and so forth up to the change from 1989 to 1990.

The formula for the geometric mean as applied to this type of problem is:

$$\text{G.M.} = \left[\sqrt[n-1]{\frac{\text{Population at end of period}}{\text{Population at beginning of period}}} \right] - 1$$

$$= \left[\sqrt[11-1]{\frac{22}{2}} \right] - 1$$

$$= \left[\sqrt[10]{11} \right] - 1$$

To find the 10th root of 11:

$$\frac{\text{Log of 11}}{10} = \frac{1.0414}{10}$$

$$= 0.10414$$

The antilog of 0.10414 is approximately 1.27. One (1) is then subtracted from this number to give the geometric mean percent increase.

$$1.27 - 1 = 0.27$$

0.27 is multiplied by 100 to express it as a percent.

The geometric mean annual increase in population is 27 percent. The interpretation, is that the estimated average annual increase in the population of Podunk Hollow between 1980 and 1990 is 27 percent.

SELF-REVIEW 4–9

1. *a.* 8.39 percent.

X	log of X
4.91	0.6911
5.75	0.7597
8.12	0.9096
21.60	1.3345
	3.6949

3.6949/4
= 0.923725
Antilog of 0.923725
= 8.39%

   b. 10.1 percent, found by 40.38/4.
2. About 9 percent, found by log of 5.24/20 = 0.7193/20 = 0.03597. Antilog of 0.03597 ≅ 1.09. Then, $(1.09 - 1)(100) = (0.09)(100) = 9$ percent.

1. The annual yield, in percent, of four stocks are: 4.91, 5.75, 8.12, and 21.60.
   a. Find the geometric mean yield.
   b. Find the arithmetic mean yield.
2. Production increased from 23,000 units in 1961 to 120,520 units in 1981. Find the geometric mean annual percent increase.

EXERCISES

20. The Department of Commerce, Bureau of Economic Analysis, reported these rates of personal saving by Americans for the past seven years: 6.3 percent, 5.4 percent, 4.9 percent, 6.4 percent, 8.1 percent, 7.7 percent and 5.4 percent. Find the geometric mean rate of saving.

21. The Department of Labor, Bureau of Labor Statistics, reported that in a five-year period during the depression of the 1930s the annual unemployment rates were: 23.6 percent, 21.7 percent, 16.9 percent, 19.0 percent and 14.6 percent. What was the geometric mean annual unemployment rate?

22. Monsanto Company had net sales of $1.972 billion in 1970 and $6.193 billion in 1979. Determine the average (geometric mean) annual percent increase.

23. Boise Cascade Corporation declared a cash dividend per common share of $0.4375 in 1974 and $1.50 in 1979. What is the geometric mean annual increase from 1974 to 1979?

**CHAPTER
SUMMARY**

Four measures of central tendency are discussed in this chapter. They describe the "center," or typical value of a set of data. The **arithmetic mean** is the most widely used average. It is computed by *summing the observations and dividing the total by the number of observations*. The value of every observation is used in its computation. Thus, for a set of data containing extreme values, the arithmetic mean may not be the most representative average.

The **median** is less sensitive to extremely large or extremely small observations. It is the *value of the middle observation after the data set has been arranged in ascending order*. The **mode** is the *value of the most frequently observed item*.

The relationships among the mode, median, and arithmetic mean gives us information about skewness. If the mean is the largest measure of central tendency, the median the next largest, and the mode the smallest, the distribution is **positively skewed.** If the mode is the largest of the three measures and the mean the smallest, the distribution is **negatively skewed**. If the three averages are identical, the distribution is referred to as **symmetrical**.

The **geometric mean** is especially useful for averaging percents, ratios, and index numbers, and finding the average annual rate of change from one time period (say 1970) to another time period (say 1982). It is computed by finding the nth root of the product of n numbers.

**CHAPTER
OUTLINE**

**Measures of
central tendency**

I. Measures of central tendency.
    A. *Purpose*. To arrive at one value around which the observations tend to cluster, and which is typical of their magnitude. This one value is often called an *average*. It might be the arithmetic mean, median, mode, or geometric mean.
II. Arithmetic mean.
    A. *Definition*.

$$\text{Mean} = \frac{\text{Sum of all the values}}{\text{Number of values}}$$

    B. *Formulas*. For ungrouped data:

If a sample:

$$\bar{X} = \frac{\Sigma X}{n}$$

If a population:

$$\mu = \frac{\Sigma X}{N}$$

where ΣX directs one to sum all the values and n or N represents the total number of values. For sample data grouped into a frequency table, use either:

$$\bar{X} = \frac{\Sigma fX}{n} \quad \text{(direct method)}$$

or

$$\bar{X} = \bar{X}_0 = \frac{i(\Sigma fd)}{n} \quad \text{(coded method)}$$

   C. *Use.* It is the most commonly used measure of central tendency. A few examples are: the mean test score for an examination, the mean monthly sales, and the mean age of welfare recipients.

   D. *Limitations.* Since all values are used in its computation, the mean cannot be computed if the frequency distribution has open-end classes (unless, of course, the midpoints of the open-end classes are estimated). It is affected by extremely high or low values. The mean, therefore, is an inappropriate average to use when the distribution is highly skewed.

III. Median.

   A. *Defintion.* It is the value corresponding to the point above which and below which half of the values fall.

   B. *Computation.* Ungrouped data: For an *odd-numbered* set of values, arrange them in order and select the middle value. For an *even-numbered* set, first arrange the values in order. The median is halfway between the two center values.

   C. *Formula.* For data grouped in a frequency table:

$$\text{Median} = L + \frac{\frac{n}{2} - CF}{f}(i)$$

   D. *Use.* Used extensively by the federal government in reporting a typical starting salary, the average number of hours worked in coal mining during the week, and so on. It is not affected by extreme values as is the mean. It is, therefore, an appropriate average to represent the typical observation in a skewed distribution. The median is also the recommended measure of central tendency to use if the distribution has open ends and/or unequal class widths.

   E. *Limitations.* It cannot be manipulated algebraically. For example, the median wage of a skewed distribution times the number of workers will not give the total payroll.

IV. Mode.

   A. *Definition.* For ungrouped data it is the value of the item that appears most frequently. For data in a frequency distribution, the mode can be represented by the midpoint of the class containing the largest number of class frequencies.

   B. *Formula.* For the *computed* mode:

$$\text{Mode} = L + \frac{\Delta_1}{\Delta_1 + \Delta_2} \; (i)$$

C. *Use.* It is not used as often as the mean or median but might have priority if one class has an unusually large frequency or the data are nominal level. The mode is not affected by a few extreme values. It can be computed if the frequency distribution has open ends or the classes are of unequal width.

D. *Limitations.* The mode cannot be manipulated algebraically.

V. Relationship of the arithmetic mean, median, and mode.

A. A *symmetrical* distribution. The arithmetic mean, median, and mode are equal.

B. A *positively skewed* distribution. The arithmetic mean is the highest of the three averages (because it is influenced more than the median or mode by a few extremely high values). The median is the next-largest measure of central tendency and the mode, which is at the apex of the curve, is the smallest of the three averages.

C. A *negatively skewed* distribution. The mean is the lowest of the three averages, being unduly influenced by a few extremely low values. The median is greater than the arithmetic mean and the mode is the largest of the three averages.

D. An approximate relationship among the three averages. If there is a sufficiently large number of observations to suggest a smoothed distribution and if the shape of the curve is only moderately skewed, the *median is approximately one third of the distance* from the arithmetic mean toward the mode.

E. If two averages of a moderately skewed frequency distribution are known, the third can be approximated. The formulas are:

$$\text{Mode} = \text{Mean} - 3(\text{Mean} - \text{Median})$$

$$\text{Mean} = \frac{3(\text{Median}) - \text{Mode}}{2}$$

$$\text{Median} = \frac{2(\text{Mean}) + \text{Mode}}{3}$$

VI. Geometric mean.

A. *Formulas.*

$$\text{Geometric mean} = \sqrt[n]{(X_1)(X_2)(X_3) \ldots (X_n)}$$

$$\text{Geometric mean} = \left[\sqrt[n-1]{\frac{\text{Value of end of period}}{\text{Value of beginning of period}}} \right] - 1$$

B. *Use.* To average percents, indexes, and relatives. To determine the average percent increase in sales, production, or other business or economic series from one time period to another.

C. *Limitations*. The geometric mean cannot be computed if one of the numbers is negative or zero (as there is no logarithm of a negative number or zero).

24. Nonresident annual tuition charges for a sample of accredited U.S. senior colleges and universities are:

Adelphi University (N.Y.) $3,510	University of Detroit (Mich.) $3,450
University of Alabama (Ala.) 1,543	Eastern Kentucky University (Ky.) ... 1,200
Alcorn State University (Miss.) ... 784	University of Florida (Fla.) 1,710
Bates College (Maine) 4,850	Knox College (Ill.) 3,795
Brigham Young University (Utah) 1,350	New Hampshire College (N.H.) 3,692
Carleton College (Minn.) 5,725	University of Rhode Island (R.I.) 2,125

 a. Determine the mean annual tuition.
 b. Determine the median annual tuition.
 c. Determine the modal annual tuition.

25. The Interstate Commerce Commission released these domestic freight figures representing the amount of freight carried by major carriers (in millions of ton miles):

Year	Railroads	Inland waterways	Motor trucks	Oil pipelines	Air carriers
1976	799,876	372,865	510,000	515,000	3,900
1977	832,000	368,275	555,000	546,000	4,181
1978	870,000	389,250	602,000	568,000	4,632
1979	851,000	360,240	580,000	550,000	4,490
1980*	848,000	355,000	572,000	542,000	3,800

 *Preliminary.

 a. What is the arithmetic mean annual ton miles (in millions of ton miles) carried by railroads during the five-year period?
 b. What is the median annual ton miles (in millions of ton miles) carried on inland waterways for the five-year period?

26. An automatic machine filling containers appears to be performing erratically. A check of the weights of the contents of a number of cans revealed:

Weights (in grams)	Number of cans
130–139	2
140–149	8
150–159	20
160–169	15
170–179	9
180–189	7
190–199	3
200–209	2

 a. To the nearest 10th of a gram (such as 161.3), estimate the arithmetic mean weight of the contents of a can.
 b. To the nearest 10th of a gram, estimate the median weight of the contents of a can.

    c.   What is the modal weight?

    d.   Is the distribution of the weights symmetrical, positively skewed, or negatively skewed? Cite evidence.

27.   The Bureau of the Census, in *Current Population Reports,* series P-20, gives the ages of divorced males and females (in thousands of persons 18 years old and over):

Age	Males	Females
18–19	5	9
20–24	80	210
25–29	174	303
30–34	210	315
35–44	385	656
45–54	450	656
55–64	295	409
65–74	174	200
75 and over	56	69

    a.   Estimate the median age of divorced males. Interpret.

    b.   Estimate the median age of divorced females. Interpret.

    c.   Estimate the modal age for the males. For the females.

28.   The Department of Commerce, Bureau of the Census, reported on the number of income earners in American families:

Number of earners	Number (in thousands)
0	7,083
1	18,621
2	22,414
3	5,533
4 or more	2,797

What is the modal number of income earners in a typical American family? Explain what this indicates.

29.

Measures of central tendency	Shapes of distribution
Arithmetic mean	Symmetrical
Median	Positively skewed
Mode	Negatively skewed

    a.   Which measure of central tendency is defined as the value of the item that appears most frequently?

    b.   Which two measures of central tendency are not affected by extremely small or extremely large values?

    c.   Which measure (not listed) must be used to determine the average annual percent increase in sales, for example, from 1962 to 1982?

    d.   How is the shape of a frequency distribution described if the three measures of central tendency are equal?

    e.   How is the shape of a frequency distribution described if the mean is the largest of the three measures of central tendency?

    f.   Which measure of central tendency is determined by summing all of the values and dividing the sum by the number of values?

g. Which measure of central tendency is defined as the point above which half of the values lie and below which the other half lie?

h. In a negatively skewed frequency distribution, which measure of central tendency is the largest?

30. An auctioneer specializes in selling late-model used cars. The selling prices of a large number of automobiles were grouped into a frequency distribution, and a smoothed frequency polygon was drawn.

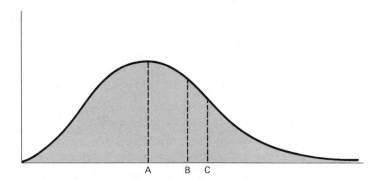

The average represented by the letter *A* was computed to be $3,000, and the average represented by *B* is $3,220.

a. Approximate the average represented by the letter *C*.

b. What is this average called, and why is it larger than than the other two averages?

31. Each employee is given a production rating which represents his efficiency on the job. The ratings were organized into a frequency distribution and then portrayed in the form of a less-than-cumulative frequency polygon.

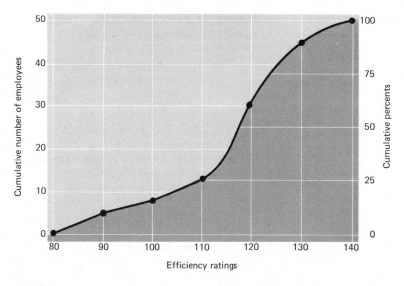

Based on the chart, what is the approximate median rating?

32. The median price of a single-family home in 1977 was $45,000. According to a Princeton University economist in a report to the U.S. Senate Banking Committee, the price of the same home will be $90,000 by 1986. If this becomes a reality, what will be the average annual precent increase from 1977 to 1986 (to the nearest 10th of a percent, such as 15.6 percent)?

33. The highs for the week of selected stocks listed on the New York Stock Exchange are:

Goodyear	17⅜
Haliburton	150
Helene Curtis	9½
Ginos	11⅛
King Dept. Stores	16¼

   a. What is the arithmetic mean high price for the week?
   b. What is the geometric mean high price?
   c. What is the median high price?
   d. What is the modal high price?
   e. Which measure would you use to represent the high prices? Why?

CHAPTER SELF-REVIEW EXAMINATION

Do all of the problems, and then check your answers against those given in Appendix A.

Score each problem five points.

In questions 1–10, for each question choose the letter appearing before the correct answer.

Questions	*Answers*

1. Which measure of central tendency is found by arranging the data from low to high and selecting the middle value?

A. Arithmetic mean.

B. Median.

C. Mode.

2. Which measure of central tendency (arithmetic mean, median, mode) cannot be determined if the distribution has one open-end class?

D. Geometric mean.

E. $\dfrac{\Sigma X}{n}$

F. $L + \dfrac{\Delta_1}{\Delta_1 + \Delta_2}(i)$

3. Which graph represents a negatively skewed distribution?

4. Which formula is used for computing the arithmetic mean of ungrouped data?

G. $L + \dfrac{\dfrac{n}{2} - CF}{f}(i)$

H. $\dfrac{\Sigma fX}{n}$; or $\bar{X}_0 + \dfrac{i(\Sigma fd)}{n}$

5. Which average (arithmetic mean, median, mode) is the smallest measure of central tendency in a positively skewed distribution?

I.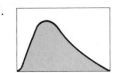

6. Which chart represents a symmetrical distribution?

7. Which is the formula for computing the arithmetic mean when the data have been tallied into a frequency distribution?

J.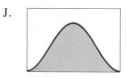

8. Which measures is used when determining the average annual percent increase in sales from one time period to another?

K.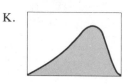

9. Referring to the following distribution, the midpoint of 84.5 grams is which measure of central tendency?

Weight (in grams)	f
60- 69	2
70- 79	5
80- 89	12
90- 99	3
100-109	1

10. Which measure of central tendency should not be used when the distribution is highly skewed?

L. $\left(\sqrt[n-1]{\dfrac{\text{Value at End}}{\text{Value at Beginning}}} \right) - 1$

Questions 11 and 12 refer to the following lengths of service for several employees who are retiring.

Employee	Length of service (years)
Mr. Archer	13
Miss Jones	22
Mr. Saam	27
Mr. Sorel	24
Mrs. Archer	19

11. What is the arithmetic mean length of service?
12. What is the median length of service?

Questions 13–16 refer to the following frequency table showing the annual sales of 50 small firms.

Sales ($000)	Number of firms
$100-$119	5
120- 139	7
140- 159	9
160- 179	16
180- 199	10
200- 219	3
Total	50

13. What is the median sales?
14. What is the arithmetic mean sales?

15. What is the estimated (crude) mode?

16. Is the distribution of sales symmetric, positively skewed, or negatively skewed? Explain.

17. Production of plywood sheets increased from 30 million in 1976 to 456 million in 1981. What is the approximate average annual percent increase in production from 1976 to 1981?

18. Which measure of central tendency (arithmetic mean, median, mode) cannot be computed if the distribution has open-end classes? Explain.

19. Which measure of central tendency (arithmetic mean, median, mode) is affected by extreme values?

20. The arithmetic mean of a moderately skewed distribution was computed to be 230 and the mode 200. What is the estimated median? Explain.

Bonus: The preceding problems total 100 percent. You need not do the following problem. However, if you try it and solve it correctly, add 10 points to your grade. If you get it wrong, deduct 10 points from your score.

Referring back to the distribution of sales for 50 small firms, what is the computed mode (to the nearest dollar)?

5

INTRODUCTION

Chapter 3 was concerned with organizing data into a frequency distribution. Several charts, including a histogram, helped to describe the shape and other important characteristics of the distribution graphically. Chapter 4 dealt with describing the central location of the data numerically. The arithmetic mean, median, and mode was used to do this. These descriptive measures pinpointed a typical value near the center of the distribution.

Equally important is the scatter, or dispersion, in data. Several descriptive measures are available to give an insight into the spread of a set of observations. These are alternatively called measures of **spread, scatter, dispersion, variation,** and **variability**. Seven of these measures of dispersion are considered in this chapter, namely, the **range,** the **average deviation,** the **variance,** the **standard deviation,** the **interquartile range,** the **quartile deviation,** and the **percentile range**.

Measures of dispersion
and skewness

WHY STUDY DISPERSION?

To answer this question, suppose that the arithmetic mean age of a group of union executives is 50 years. Likewise, the mean age of a group of management executives is also 50 years. Judging by the two means, one might conclude that the two distributions of ages are quite similar or in fact identical. An examination of the two sets of ages in Chart 5–1, however, reveals that this is not true. The youngest union executive is 45, the oldest 55. The ages of the management executives are more spread out from the mean, with the youngest being 40, the oldest 60.

CHART 5–1

Ages of union executives

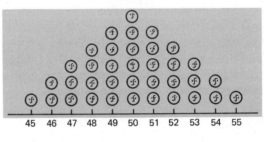

Ages

Ages of management executives

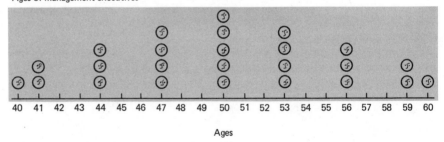

Ages

What is needed, therefore, is a measure, or measures, that will allow us to compare the spread in two or more sets of observations. One of these measures, the range, will be discussed first.

MEASURES OF DISPERSION —UNGROUPED DATA

The **range** of a set of ungrouped data is simply the difference between the two extreme values of a set of observations, that is, it is the *difference between the highest and lowest values*.

The range

$$\text{Range} = \text{Highest value} - \text{Lowest Value}$$

EXAMPLE

The capacities of several metal containers are: 38, 20, 37, 64, and 27 liters, respectively. What is the range for this set of ungrouped observations?

SOLUTION

The range is 44 liters, found by 64 − 20.

SELF-REVIEW 5-1

54.3, found by 297.9 − 243.6.

A reminder: cover the answers in the left-hand column.

The consumer price indexes for selected cities are: 285.1, 297.9, 256.7, 284.7, 243.6, and 277.2. What is the range?

Returning to the ages of the union and management executives in Chart 5-1, note that the range of the ages of the union executives is 10 years (55 − 45 = 10). The range of the ages of the management executives is 20 years (60 − 40 = 20). It can be concluded, therefore, that (1) there is less dispersion in the ages of the union executives than in the ages of the management executives (because the range of 10 years is less than the range of 20 years) and (2) the ages of the union executives are clustered more closely about the mean of 50 years than the ages of the management executives (because the range of 10 years is less than the range of 20 years). Thus, the mean age of the union executives (50 years) is more representative as an average than is the mean age of 50 years for the management group.

The average deviation

A serious defect of the range is that it does not take into consideration all the values. The **average deviation** does. It is the *arithmetic mean of the absolute values of the deviations from the arithmetic mean.* In terms of a formula, the average deviation, designated A.D., is computed by:

$$\text{A.D.} = \frac{\Sigma|X - \bar{X}|}{n}$$

where:

X is the value of each observation.
$\bar{X}$ is the arithmetic mean of the values.
n is the number of observations.
| | indicates the absolute value. In other words, the signs of the deviations from the mean are disregarded.

98

EXAMPLE

The weights of several crates ready for shipment to France are (in kilograms): 103, 97, 101, 106, and 103.

1. What is the average deviation?
2. How is it interpreted?

SOLUTION

The arithmetic mean weight is 102 kg., found by $(103 + 97 + 101 + 106 + 103)/5$.

1. To find the average deviation:
   a. The mean is subtracted from each value.
   b. The absolute deviations are summed.
   c. The sum of the absolute deviations is divided by the number of values.

Weights (in kg.) X	$X - \bar{X}$		Absolute deviations	
103	$\mid +1 \mid$	=	1	$\text{A.D.} = \dfrac{\Sigma\mid X - \bar{X}\mid}{n}$
97	$\mid -5 \mid$	=	5	
101	$\mid -1 \mid$	=	1	$= \dfrac{12}{5}$
106	$\mid +4 \mid$	=	4	
103	$\mid +1 \mid$	=	$\dfrac{1}{12}$	$= 2.4 \text{ kg}$

The average deviation is 2.4 kilograms.

2. Interpretation: The crates deviate, on the average, 2.4 kilograms from the arithmetic mean weight of 102 kilograms.

SELF-REVIEW 5–2

$\bar{X} = \dfrac{824}{8} = 103$

a. 5.25 kg., found by

X	$X - \bar{X}$		Absolute deviation
95	$\mid - 8 \mid$	=	8
103	$\mid 0 \mid$	=	0
105	$\mid + 2 \mid$	=	2
110	$\mid + 7 \mid$	=	7
104	$\mid + 1 \mid$	=	1
105	$\mid + 2 \mid$	=	2
112	$\mid + 9 \mid$	=	9
90	$\mid -13 \mid$	=	13
		Total	$\overline{42}$

The weights of a group of crates being shipped to Ireland are: (in kilograms) 95, 103, 105, 110, 104, 105, 112, and 90.

a. Compute the average deviation.
b. Interpret your findings.
c. Compare the dispersion in the weights of the shipments going to France and to Ireland.

$$\text{A.D.} = \frac{42}{8}$$

$$= 5.25 \text{ kg.}$$

b. The weights of the crates going to Ireland deviate 5.25 kilograms on the average from the mean of 103 kilograms.
c. There is more dispersion in the crates going to Ireland compared with those going to France (because 5.25 kilograms is greater than 2.4 kilograms).

The average deviation uses all the value in its computation. In that sense it is a more satisfactory measure of dispersion than the range, which only uses two—the highest and the lowest values. The average deviation is easy to interpret: it is the average amount the values deviate from the mean. However, it does have one disadvantage. Because the signs of the deviations are disregarded—that is, all the deviations from the mean are considered to be positive—the average deviation cannot be manipulated algebraically.

EXERCISES

(A reminder: Answers and method of solution for selected exercises are in Appendix A.)

1. The closing prices of IBM common stock for the past five days have been 61½, 62, 61¼, 60⅞, and 61½. What is the range?
2. Ten experts rated a newly developed chocolate chip cookie on a scale of 1 to 50. Their ratings were: 34, 35, 41, 28, 26, 29, 32, 36, 38, and 40.
   a. What is the range?
   b. What is the arithmetic mean rating?
   c. What is the average deviation? Interpret.
   d. A second group of experts rated the same chocolate chip cookie. The range was 8, the mean 33.9, and the average deviation 1.9. Compare the dispersion in these ratings with that of the first group of experts.
3. A sample of the personnel files of eight male employees revealed that, during a six-month period, they lost the following number of days due to illness: 2, 0, 6, 3, 10, 4, 1, and 2.
   a. What is the range?
   b. What is the arithmetic mean number of days lost?
   c. What is the average deviation? Interpret.
   d. A sample of the personnel files of female employees revealed that they lost 3.48 days on the average during the same six-month period due to illness. The range was computed to be 10 and the average deviation 2.381. Compare the two groups.

The variance

The **variance** and the **standard deviation** are also based on the deviations from the mean. However, in computing the variance one does not ignore the signs, as for the average deviation. The variance is computed by squaring the deviations from the arithmetic mean. First we will show how the variance of a population is determined. (Recall that a population is the totality of all observations being studied.) The **population variance** is found by:

$$\sigma^2 = \frac{\Sigma(X - \mu)^2}{N}$$

where:

σ^2 is the symbol for the population variance (σ is the lowercase Greek letter sigma).

X is the value of the observations in the population.

μ is the mean of the population.

N is the total number of observations in the population.

EXAMPLE

The ages of the inhabitants of Yazu City are 38, 26, 13, 41, and 22 years. What is the population variance?

SOLUTION

	Ages	
X	$X - \mu$	$(X - \mu)^2$
38	+10	100
26	− 2	4
13	−15	225
41	+13	169
22	− 6	36
140	0*	534

*Deviations from mean must equal zero.

$$\mu = \frac{\Sigma X}{N} = \frac{140}{5} = 28$$

$$\sigma^2 = \frac{\Sigma(X - \mu)^2}{N}$$

$$= \frac{534}{5}$$

$$= 106.8$$

SELF-REVIEW 5–3

X	X − μ	(X − μ)²
104	−6	36
115	+5	25
107	−3	9
112	+2	4
114	+4	16
108	−2	4
	0	94

$$\mu = \frac{\Sigma X}{N}$$

$$= \frac{660}{6}$$

$$= 110 \text{ kg.}$$

$$\sigma^2 = \frac{\Sigma(X - \mu)^2}{N}$$

$$= \frac{94}{6}$$

$$= 15.67$$

A population consists of all the weights of the defensive tackles on Sociable University's football team. They are: Johnson, 104 kilograms; Patrick, 115 kilograms; Juniors, 107 kilograms; Kendron, 112 kilograms; Nicko, 114 kilograms; and Cochran 108 kilograms. What is the population variance?

The above approach for determining the population variance was used mainly to show that the variance is based on the *squared deviations from the population mean*. The mean was a whole number, so that the computations for this small population of ages was relatively easy. Usually, however, the population is large, and the mean is not a whole number. In more realistic problems a shortcut formula is preferred. Note it is not based on deviations from the mean, but rather on the actual values of the observations. This formula saves a large number of subtractions.

$$\sigma^2 = \frac{\Sigma X^2}{N} - \left(\frac{\Sigma X}{N}\right)^2$$

Applying it to the previous problem:

$$\sigma^2 = \frac{(38)^2 + (26)^2 + (13)^2 + (41)^2 + (22)^2}{5} - \left(\frac{38 + 26 + 13 + 41 + 22}{5}\right)^2$$

$$= \frac{4,454}{5} - \left(\frac{140}{5}\right)^2$$

$$= 106.8 \text{ (which is the same answer as before)}$$

The variance can be used to compare the dispersion in two or more sets of observations. For example, the variance cf the ages of the people living in Yazu City was just computed to be 106.8. If the variance of the ages for the population of Kzonk Junction is 342.9, it can be said that (1) there is less dispersion in the distribution of the ages of the Yazu population than in the age distribution for Kzonk Junction (because 106.8 is less than 342.9), and (2) the ages of the people living in Yazu City are clustered more closely about the mean of 28 years than those in the Kzonk distribution. Thus, the mean age for the Yazu set of observations is a more representative or typical average.

The population standard deviation

The variance is difficult to interpret for a single set of observations. The variance of 106.8 for the Yazu City ages is not in terms of ages, but rather "ages squared." In the self-review the variance for the set of defensive tackles is 15.67 kilograms squared, which again is difficult to interpret.

By taking the square root of the population variance, we can transform it to the same unit of measurement as the original data. Taking the square root of the variance of 106.8 gives 10.3 years. Taking the square root of the variance of 15.67 for the weights of the defensive tackles at SU gives 3.96 kilograms. The square root of the population variance is called the **population standard deviation.**

> The population standard deviation of a set of observations is the square root of the mean of the squared deviations from the mean. It can also be defined as the positive square root of the population variance.

In terms of a formula:

$$\sigma = \sqrt{\frac{\Sigma(X - \mu)^2}{N}} \quad \text{or} \quad \sigma = \sqrt{\frac{\Sigma X^2}{N} - \left(\frac{\Sigma X}{N}\right)^2}$$

EXERCISES

4. Rainbow Trout, Inc., feeds fingerling trout in special ponds and markets them when they attain a certain weight. A group of 10 trout (considered the population) were isolated in a pond and fed a special food mixture called Grow Em Fast. At the end of the experimental period, the weights of the trout were (in grams): 124, 125, 125, 123, 120, 124, 127, 125, 126, and 121.
   a. What is the range?
   b. What is the arithmetic mean of the population?
   c. Compute the population variance.
   d. Compute the standard deviation of the population.
   e. Another special mixture, Fatso 1B, was used in another pond. The mean of the population was computed to be 126.9 grams, the standard deviation 1.20 grams. Which food results in a more uniform weight?

5. The annual incomes of the five vice presidents of Erlen Industries are: $41,000, $38,000, $32,000, $33,000, and $50,000.
   a. What is the range?
   b. What is the arithmetic mean income?
   c. What is the population variance? The standard deviation?
   d. The annual incomes of another firm similar to Erlen Industries were also

studied. $\mu = \$38,900$, $\sigma = \$6,612$. Compare the means and dispersions in the two firms.

The sample variance as an estimator of the population variance

The formula for the population mean was given in Chapter 4 as $\mu = \Sigma X/N$. We just changed symbols when referring to the sample mean, that is, $\bar{X} = \Sigma X/n$. Unfortunately, the conversion from the population variance to the sample variance is not quite that direct. It requires a slight change in the denominator. Instead of substituting n (number in the sample) for N (number in the population), the denominator is $n - 1$. Thus, the formula for the **sample variance** is:

$$s^2 = \frac{\Sigma(X - \bar{X})^2}{n - 1}$$

where:

s^2 is the symbol used to represent the sample variance.
X is the value of the observations in the sample.
$\bar{X}$ is the mean of the sample.
n is the total number of observations in the sample.

Converting the shortcut formula for the population variance σ^2 to the **sample variance** s^2 we have:

$$s^2 = \frac{\Sigma X^2 - \dfrac{(\Sigma X)^2}{n}}{n - 1}$$

Why is this seemingly insignificant change made in the denominator? It can be proven that, had the sample variance been computed using just n in the denominator, the result would *underestimate* the population variance.[1] That is, the sample variance would be a **biased** estimator of the population variance. This would be especially true when the sample size was small. Using $n - 1$ compensates for this underestimate. Thus the sample variance s^2 is considered an **unbiased** estimator of the population variance.[2]

---

[1] To state it another way, the formula for the sample variance should be

$$\frac{\Sigma(X - \mu)^2}{n}$$

However, $\bar{X}$ is used to estimate μ. Thus the sum in the numerator will be too small. Dividing by $n - 1$, instead of n, compensates for the underestimate in the numerator.

[2] If the sample variance of a sample has been computed using just n in the denominator, it can been converted to the unbiased estimator s^2 by:

$$s^2 = \frac{n}{n - 1}(\hat{s}^2)$$

where $\hat{s}^2$ is the sample variance computed using just n.

EXAMPLE

The hourly wages selected in a sample are: $2, $10, $6, $8, and $9. What is the sample variance?

SOLUTION

Using the squared deviations from the mean

The mean wage is $7, found by

$$\bar{X} = \frac{\Sigma X}{n} = \frac{\$35}{5} = \$7$$

Hourly wage X	$X - \bar{X}$	$(X - \bar{X})^2$
$ 2	−$5	25
10	3	9
6	− 1	1
8	1	1
9	2	4
$35	0	40

$$s^2 = \frac{\Sigma(X - \bar{X})^2}{n - 1}$$

$$= \frac{40}{5 - 1}$$

$$= 10$$

Using the shortcut formula:

Hourly wage X	X^2
$ 2	4
10	100
6	36
8	64
9	81
$35	285

$$s^2 = \frac{\Sigma X^2 - \dfrac{(\Sigma X)^2}{n}}{n - 1}$$

$$= \frac{285 - \dfrac{(35)^2}{5}}{5 - 1}$$

$$= \frac{40}{5 - 1}$$

$$= 10$$

SELF-REVIEW 5-4

2.33, found by:

$$\bar{X} = \frac{\Sigma X}{n} = \frac{28}{7} = 4$$

X	$X - \bar{X}$	$(X - \bar{X})^2$	X^2
4	0	0	16
2	−2	4	4
5	1	1	25
4	0	0	16
5	1	1	25
2	−2	4	4
6	2	4	36
28	0	14	126

The weights of the contents of several small bottles are (in grams) 4, 2, 5, 4, 5, 2, and 6. What is the sample variance?

$$s^2 = \frac{\Sigma(X - \bar{X})^2}{n - 1} \qquad s^2 = \frac{\Sigma X^2 - \dfrac{(\Sigma X)^2}{n}}{n - 1}$$

$$= \frac{14}{7 - 1} \qquad = \frac{126 - \dfrac{(28)^2}{7}}{7 - 1}$$

$$= 2.33 \qquad = \frac{126 - 112}{6}$$

$$= 2.33$$

The sample standard deviation as an estimator of the population standard deviation

As noted previously, the population standard deviation is the square root of the population variance. Likewise, the **sample standard deviation** (s) *is the square root of the sample variance.* The sample standard deviation (s) is found:

Using the squared deviations from the mean:

$$s = \sqrt{\frac{\Sigma(X - \bar{X})^2}{n - 1}}$$

Using the shortcut formula:

$$s = \sqrt{\frac{\Sigma X^2 - \dfrac{(\Sigma X)^2}{n}}{n - 1}}$$

EXAMPLE

The sample variance in the previous example involving hourly wages was computed to be 10. What is the sample standard deviation?

SOLUTION

The sample standard deviation is $3.16, found by $\sqrt{10}$. It can be determined by using either a hand calculator or Appendix C. Note again that the sample variance is in terms of dollars squared, but taking the square root of 10 gives us $3.16, which is in the same units (dollars) as the original data.

SELF-REVIEW 5–5

a. 1.53 grams, found by $\sqrt{2.33}$.
b. Yes, the original data were in grams. The standard deviation is 1.53 grams.

Refer to the previous self-review.

a. What is the sample standard deviation?
b. Is it in the same unit of measurement as the original problem?

6. The hourly outputs of a group of employees assembling plug-in units were selected at random. The sample outputs were: 8, 9, 8, 10, 9, 10, 12, and 10. What is the standard deviation of the sample?

7. The ages of a sample of tourists flying to Hong Kong were: 32, 21, 60, 47, 54, 17, 72, 55, 33, and 41. What is the standard deviation of the sample?

Before discussing the uses of the standard deviation, we will turn our attention to the computation of the range, average deviation, variance, and the standard deviation from data grouped into a frequency distribution.

MEASURES OF DISPERSION FOR DATA GROUPED INTO A FREQUENCY DISTRIBUTION

The range

Recall that the range is defined as the difference between the highest and lowest values. There are two methods of determining the range from data already grouped into a frequency distribution. To illustrate, the distribution of the daily commissions of 120 salespersons from Table 3–3 is reintroduced in Table 5–1.

Method 1. Find the difference between the upper *true* limit of the highest class and the lower true limit of the lowest class. Recall from Chapters 3 and 4 that, since the daily commissions were rounded to the nearest dollar, the first class really goes from $29.50 to $34.50 (the true limits of the class). The true limits of the next class are $34.50 and $39.50, and so on. The true limits of the highest class are $64.50 and $69.50. Computing the range using this method, Highest real limit − lowest true limit = $69.50 − $29.50 = $40.

Method 2. Find the difference between the *midpoint* of the highest class and the *midpoint* of the lowest class. The range using this method is $35, found by $67 − $32. In practice, both are used.

TABLE 5–1
Frequency distribution of the daily commissions of 120 salespersons

Daily commissions	Number
$30–$34	3
35– 39	7
40– 44	11
45– 49	22
50– 54	40
55– 59	24
60– 64	9
65– 69	4

SELF-REVIEW 5–6

Method 1: Highest true limit − lowest true limit = 54,500 − 24,500 = 30,000 miles.

Method 2: Midpoint of highest class − midpoint of lowest class = 52,000 − 27,000 = 25,000 miles.

The mileage some tires traveled before they went bald was rounded to the nearest 1,000 miles and tallied into the following frequency distribution.

Mileage	Number of tires
25,000–29,000	16
30,000–34,000	45
35,000–39,000	78
40,000–44,000	56
45,000–49,000	21
50,000–54,000	9

Using both methods, what is the range in mileage?

The average deviation

The formula for the average deviation as applied to data grouped in a frequency table is:

$$\text{A.D.} = \frac{\Sigma f |X - \bar{X}|}{n}$$

where:

X is the midpoint of each class.
$\bar{X}$ is the arithmetic mean.
f is the number of observations in each class.
n is the total number of observations.

Since the average deviation derived from grouped data is used only infrequently, its computation will not be shown. Instead, more emphasis will be placed on the standard deviation.

The variance and the standard deviation

Recall that for *ungrouped* data, one formula for the sample standard deviation is:

$$s = \sqrt{\frac{\Sigma X^2 - \frac{(\Sigma X)^2}{n}}{n - 1}}$$

If the data of interest are in *grouped* form (in a frequency distribution), the sample standard deviation can be approximated by substituting $\Sigma f X^2$ for ΣX^2 and $\Sigma f X$ for ΣX. The formula for the **sample standard deviation** then converts to:

$$s = \sqrt{\frac{\Sigma f X^2 - \frac{(\Sigma f X)^2}{n}}{n - 1}}$$

where:

X is the midpoint of a class.
f is the class frequency.
n is the total number of sample observations.

EXAMPLE

Refer to the distribution of daily commissions in Table 5-1. What is the standard deviation of these grouped commissions?

SOLUTION

Following the same practice used in Chapter 4 when computing the arithmetic mean of grouped data, X represents the midpoint of each class. For example, the midpoint of the \$30–\$34 class is \$32 (see Table 5–2 which follows). It is asssumed that all three commissions in that class fall at \$32, that all seven commissions in the \$35–\$39 class are concentrated at \$37, and so on. To find the standard deviation:

Step 1: Each class frequency is multiplied by its class midpoint. As an example, for the first class multiply f times X, written $fX = 3 \times \$32 = \$96$. For the second class, $fX = 7 \times \$37 = \$259$, and so on.

Step 2: Calculate fX^2. This could be written $fX \cdot X$. For the first class it would be $\$96 \times \$32 = 3{,}072$, for the second class, $\$259 \times \$37 = 9{,}583$, and so on.

Step 3: Sum the fX and fX^2 columns. They are \$6,125 and 319,345.

TABLE 5–2
Calculations needed for the sample standard deviation

Commissions	Number f	Midpoint X	fX	$fX \cdot X$ or fX^2
\$30–\$34	3	\$32	\$ 96	3,072
35– 39	7	37	259	9,583
40– 44	11	42	462	19,404
45– 49	22	47	1,034	48,598
50– 54	40	52	2,080	108,160
55– 59	24	57	1,368	77,976
60– 64	9	62	558	34,596
65– 69	4	67	268	17,956
	120		\$6,125	319,345

Substituting these sums in the formula and solving for the sample standard deviation:

$$s = \sqrt{\frac{\Sigma fX^2 - \dfrac{(\Sigma fX)^2}{n}}{n-1}}$$

$$= \sqrt{\frac{319{,}345 - \dfrac{(\$6{,}125)^2}{120}}{120 - 1}}$$

$$= \sqrt{\frac{319{,}345 - 312{,}630.2}{119}}$$

$$= \$7.51$$

The sample variance is found by $(\$7.51)^2$, or about 56.4.

─────────────── **SELF-REVIEW 5–7** ───────────────

a. A frequency distribution.

b. 3.2 years, found by:

Ages	*f*	Midpoint *X*	*fX*	*fX²*
2- 4	2	3	6	18
5- 7	5	6	30	180
8-10	10	9	90	810
11-13	4	12	48	576
14-16	2	15	30	450
	23		204	2,034

$$s = \sqrt{\frac{2{,}034 - \dfrac{(204)^2}{23}}{23 - 1}}$$

$$= \sqrt{\frac{2{,}034 - 1{,}809.3913}{22}}$$

$$= \sqrt{10.209486}$$

$$= 3.195228 \text{ years}$$

c. 8.9 years, found by 204/23.

d. 10.209486, found by $(3.195228)^2$.

The ages of a sample of the typewriters used by the typists in the typing pool were organized into the following table:

Ages (in years)	Number
2- 4	2
5- 7	5
8-10	10
11-13	4
14-16	2

a. What is the table called?

b. Estimate the sample standard deviation.

c. Estimate the mean age of the typewriters (to nearest 10th of a year).

d. What is the sample variance?

The calculations required for the standard deviation of the daily commissions were relatively simple. However, if the midpoints are large and there is a large number of class frequencies (and the class intervals are equal), the **coding** described in the preceding chapter for the arithmetic mean can be used. Class deviations (*d*) from the mean are merely substituted for the midpoints (*X*). Otherwise the procedure followed in the coded method is the same as in the more direct method, except that the square root of the number under the square root sign is multiplied by the class interval (*i*) to return it, in the case of the daily commissions, to dollars. (Note the similarity in the two formulas.)

The formula for the direct method is:

$$s = \sqrt{\frac{\Sigma fX^2 - \dfrac{(\Sigma fX)^2}{n}}{n - 1}}$$

The formula for the coded method is:

$$s = i\sqrt{\dfrac{\Sigma fd^2 - \dfrac{(\Sigma fd)^2}{n}}{n - 1}}$$

EXAMPLE

Estimate the standard deviation of the distribution of the daily commissions in Table 5–2 using the coded method.

SOLUTION

Step 1. Set the midpoint of any class equal to the origin of zero. The usual procedure is to let a class midpoint near the center of the distribution be zero. Note that in Table 5–3 we let the $50–$54 class midpoint be the origin, zero. Then code the classes prior to the origin -1, -2, -3, etc. and the classes following the origin $+1$, $+2$, $+3$, etc.

Step 2. Multiply these class deviations, designated d, by the corresponding class frequencies to get fd. Then multiply fd by d to get fd^2.

Step 3. Sum the appropriate columns and insert the totals in the formula.

TABLE 5–3
Calculations needed to compute the standard deviation using the coded method

Commissions	Number f	Class deviations d	fd	$fd \cdot d$ or fd^2
$30–$34	3	−4	−12	48
35– 39	7	−3	−21	63
40– 44	11	−2	−22	44
45– 49	22	−1	−22	22
50– 54	40	0	0	0
55– 59	24	1	24	24
60– 64	9	2	18	36
65– 69	4	3	12	36
	120		−23	273

Substituting these sums in the formula:

$$s = i\sqrt{\dfrac{\Sigma fd^2 - \dfrac{(\Sigma fd)^2}{n}}{n - 1}}$$

$$= 5 \sqrt{\frac{273 - \frac{(-23)^2}{120}}{120 - 1}}$$

$$= 5 \sqrt{\frac{273 - 4.4083333}{119}}$$

$$= 5 \sqrt{2.2570728}$$

$$= \$7.51 \text{ (same answer as before)}$$

―――――――――――――― **SELF-REVIEW 5–8** ――――――――――――――

3.195228 years, or 3.2 years (rounded), found by:

Ages	f	d	fd	fd²
2- 4	2	−2	−4	8
5- 7	5	−1	−5	5
8-10	10	0	0	0
11-13	4	1	4	4
14-16	2	2	4	8
	23		−1	25

$$s = 3 \sqrt{\frac{25 - \frac{(-1)^2}{23}}{23 - 1}}$$

$$= 3 \sqrt{\frac{25 - .0434782}{22}}$$

$$= 3(1.065076)$$
$$= 3.195228$$

which is the same answer as computed using the direct method.

Returning to the ages of the typewriters in Self-Review 5-7:

Ages (in years)	Number
2- 4	2
5- 7	5
8-10	10
11-13	4
14-16	2

Approximate the sample variance using the coded method.

EXERCISES

8. Each person who applies for an assembly job at Philagree Electronics is given a mechanical aptitude test. One part of the test involves assembling a plug-in unit based on numbered instructions. A sample of the length of time it took 42 persons to assemble the unit was organized into the following frequency distribution.

Length of time (in minutes)	Number
1- 3	4
4- 6	8
7- 9	14
10-12	9
13-15	5
16-18	2

a. What is the range? Use both methods.

b. What is the standard deviation. It is suggested that you use both the direct and coded methods as a check.

c. What is the variance?

9. A sample of the amounts paid for parking on Saturday at the Downtown Parking Garage was organized into the following frequency distribution.

Amount paid	Number
$0.50–$0.74	2
0.75– 0.99	7
1.00– 1.24	15
1.25– 1.49	28
1.50– 1.74	14
1.75– 1.99	9
2.00– 2.24	3
2.25– 2.49	2

a. Compute the range using both methods.

b. Compute the sample standard deviation. It is suggested that you use both methods as a check.

c. What is the sample variance?

INTERPRETATION AND USES OF THE STANDARD DEVIATION

The standard deviation is used as a common measure to compare the spread in two or more sets of observations. For example, the standard deviation of the daily commissions for a sample of salespersons was just computed to be $7.51. Suppose these salespersons are located in the South. If the standard deviation for a group from the West is $10.47, and the means are about the same, it indicates that the commissions of the southern salespersons are not dispersed as much as those of the western group (because $7.51 < $10.47). Further, the commissions of the southern group are clustered more closely about its mean compared with the western group. Thus, the mean for the southern group is more reliable or useful average compared with the average for the western group.

The standard deviation can be used to estimate the proportion of a distribution which lies within a specified number of standard deviations from the mean. In this regard, we will consider two theorems, or rules—one which applies to *any set of observations* and the other which is *only applicable to a mound-shaped distribution*.

Chebyshev's Theorem, developed by the Russian mathematician Chebyshev, applies to any set of observations. The theorem states:

The proportion of *any* set of observations that lies within k standard deviations from the mean is *at least*

$$1 - \frac{1}{k^2}$$

where:

k is any positive number.

EXAMPLE

The arithmetic mean of the daily commissions was computed to be $51.04 (Chapter 4), and the standard deviation was just computed to be $7.51. At least what percent of the commissions lie within two standard deviations of the mean?

SOLUTION

About 75 percent, found by

$$1 - \frac{1}{k^2} = 1 - \frac{1}{2^2} = 1 - \frac{1}{4} = \frac{3}{4} = 0.75$$

EXAMPLE

What percent of the commissions are either above $66.06 or below $36.02?

SOLUTION

Both $66.06 and $36.02 are two standard deviations from the arithmetic mean, found by

$$\frac{X - \bar{X}}{s} = \frac{\$66.06 - \$51.04}{\$7.51} = \frac{\$15.02}{\$7.51} = 2$$

and

$$\frac{\$36.02 - \$51.04}{\$7.51} = -2$$

Logically, if 75 percent of the commissions are between $36.02 and $66.06, no more than 25 percent of the commissions can be either above $66.06 or below $36.02.

The histogram representing the frequency distribution of the daily commissions is portrayed in Chart 5–2. Also shown is the area encompassing at least 75 percent of the values.

**CHART 5-2
Histogram
representing the
distribution of
commissions**

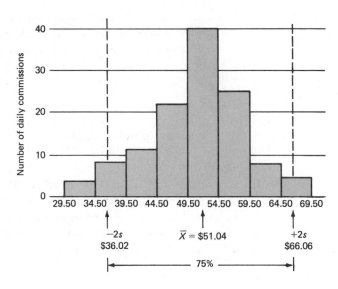

Daily commissions (in dollars)

—————————————————— SELF-REVIEW 5-9 ——————————————————

a. At least 88.9%, found by:

$$1 - \frac{1}{3^2} = 1 - \frac{1}{9} = \frac{8}{9} = 0.889$$

b. About 80.2 percent, found by:

$$1 - \frac{1}{(2.25)^2} = 1 - \frac{1}{5.0625} = 1 - 0.198$$

Both $34.14 and $67.94 are 2.25 standard deviations from the mean. ($34.14 − $51.04)/$7.51 = −2.25, and ($67.94 − $51.04)/$7.51 = + 2.25.

Refer to the previous example regarding the commissions of a sample of 120 salespersons.

a. At least what percent of the commissions lie within three standard deviations of the mean?

b. At least what percent of the commissions lie between $34.14 and $67.94?

The **Empirical Rule**, sometimes referred to as the **Normal Rule**, states that:

> For a symmetrical, bell-shaped frequency distribution, approximately 68 percent of the observations will lie within one standard deviation of the mean; about 95 percent of the observations will lie within two standard deviations of the mean; and practically all (99.7 percent) will lie within three standard deviations of the mean.

These relationships are portrayed graphically in Chart 5–3.

**CHART 5–3
Histogram of a
mound-shaped
distribution**

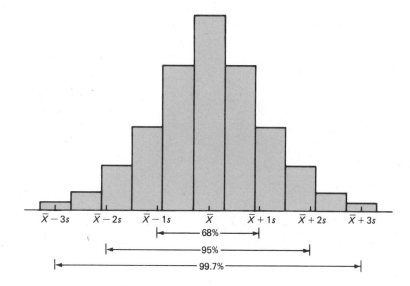

EXAMPLE

A sample of the monthly amounts spent for food by families of four receiving food stamps approximates a symmetrical, bell-shaped frequency distribution. The sample mean is $150, the standard deviation $20. Using the empirical rule:

a. About 68 percent of the monthly food expenditures are between what two amounts?
b. About 95 percent of the monthly food expenditures are between what two amounts?
c. Almost all of the monthly expenditures are between what two amounts?

SOLUTION

a. About 68 percent are between $130 and $170, found by $\bar{X} \pm 1s = \$150 \pm 1(\$20)$.
b. About 95 percent are between $110 and $190, found by $\bar{X} \pm 2s = \$150 \pm 2(\$20)$.
c. Almost all (99.7 percent) are between $90 and $210, found by $\bar{X} \pm 3s = \$150 \pm 3(\$20)$.

SELF-REVIEW 5-10

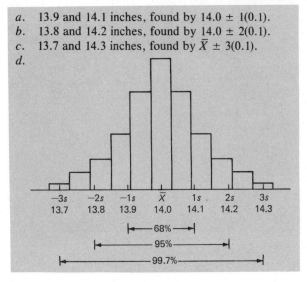

a. 13.9 and 14.1 inches, found by 14.0 ± 1(0.1).
b. 13.8 and 14.2 inches, found by 14.0 ± 2(0.1).
c. 13.7 and 14.3 inches, found by $\bar{X}$ ± 3(0.1).
d.

The distribution of a sample of the outside diameters of PVC gas pipes approximates a symmetrical, bell-shaped distribution. The arithmetic mean outside diameter of the sample is 14.0 inches and the standard deviation is 0.1 inches.

a. About 68 percent of the outside diameters lie between what two amounts?
b. About 95 percent lie between what two amounts?
c. Almost all (99.7 percent) lie between what two amounts?
d. Portray the above percents and amounts in the form of a mound-shaped histogram.

EXERCISES

10. Regarding Chebyshev's Theorem, at least what percent of any set of observations will be within 1.8 standard deviations of the mean?

11. The mean income of a group of sample observations is $500; the standard deviation is $40. According to Chebyshev's Theorem, at least what percent of the incomes will lie between $400 and $600?

12. Based on the Empirical Rule, what percent of the observations will lie
    a. Between $\bar{X} - 2s$ and $\bar{X} + 2s$?
    b. About $\bar{X} + 2s$? Below $\bar{X} - 2s$?

13. The figure below portays the mound-shaped appearance of a sample distribution of efficiency ratings.

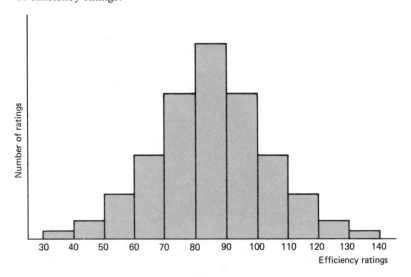

a. Estimate the mean efficiency rating.
b. Estimate the standard deviation to the nearest whole number. (Hint: Since the mean plus and minus three standard deviations encompass practically all the values, the range divided by six should give a good approximation of the standard deviation.
c. About 68 percent of the efficiency ratings fall between what two values?
d. About 95 percent of the efficiency ratings fall between what two values?

SOME OTHER MEASURES OF DISPERSION

Three other measures of dispersion will be considered briefly. They are: the **interquartile range,** the **quartile deviation,** and the **percentile range.**

The interquartile range

The **interquartile range** is the distance between the third quartile and the first quartile.

$$\text{Interquartile range} = \text{Third quartile} - \text{First quartile}$$
$$= Q_3 - Q_1$$

Recall that the median value Q_2 separates the top 50 percent of a set of observations from the bottom 50 percent. In a similar fashion, the **first quartile,** Q_1, is the value corresponding to the point below which 25 percent of the observations lie. The **third quarter,** Q_3, is the value corresponding to the point above which 25 percent of the observations lie. Therefore, the middle 50 percent of the observations are located between Q_3 and Q_1.

The formulas for Q_1 and Q_3 are:

$$Q_1 = L + \frac{\frac{n}{4} - CF}{f}\ (i) \qquad\qquad Q_3 = L + \frac{\frac{3n}{4} - CF}{f}\ (i)$$

where:

L is the true lower limit of the class containing the first quartile.

n is the total number of frequencies (not classes).

CF is the cumulative number of frequencies in all of the classes immediately preceding the class containing the first quartile.

f is the frequency in the class containing the first quartile.

i is the width of the class in which the first quartile lies.

where:

L is the true lower limit of the class containing the third quartile.

n is the total number of class frequencies (not classes).

CF is the cumulative number of frequencies in all of the classes immediately preceding the class containing the third quartile.

f is the frequency in the class containing the third quartile.

i is the width of the class in which the third quartile lies.

What is the first quartile for the distribution of daily commissions?

SOLUTION

TABLE 5–4
Calculations needed
for the first and third
quartiles

Stated limits	True limits	Class frequency	Cumulative frequency
$30–$34	$29.50–$34.50	3	3
35– 39	34.50– 39.50	7	10
40– 44	39.50– 44.50	11	21
45– 49	44.50– 49.50	22	43
50– 54	49.50– 54.50	40	83
55– 59	54.50– 59.50	24	107
60– 64	59.50– 64.50	9	116
65– 69	64.50– 69.50	4	120

You will no doubt notice that the procedure for determining the first and third quartiles is quite similar to that presented in Chapter 4 for the median (which is the second quartile Q_2). Interpolating for the first quartile:

Step 1.   Determine the class in which Q_1 lies. Note that there are 120 commissions. One fourth of 120 = 30. Counting down from the lowest commission class, observe in the *CF* column that there are 21 commissions below the *true* upper class limit of $44.50, and 43 commissions below the upper true limit of $49.50. Logically, the 30th commission falls in the $44.50–$49.50 class. So L, the lower true limit of the class containing Q_1, is $44.50.

Step 2.   Determine the cumulative number of frequencies *CF* in all of the classes immediately preceding the class containing the first quartile. Referring to Table 5–4, *CF* is 21.

Step 3.   Determine f, the frequency of the class containing the first quartile. There are 22 frequencies in the $44.50–$49.50 class.

Step 4.   Determine i, the class interval of the class containing Q_1. $49.50 − $44.50 = $5, the class interval i.

Substituting all these values in the formula for Q_1:

$$Q_1 = L + \frac{\frac{n}{4} - CF}{f} \quad (i)$$

$$= \$44.50 + \frac{\frac{120}{4} - 21}{22} \,(\$5)$$

$$= \$44.50 + \frac{9}{22}(\$5)$$

$$= \$46.55$$

The interpretation is that one fourth of the commissions are below $46.55.

─────────────── SELF-REVIEW 5–11 ───────────────

$Q_3 = \$55.96$, found by ¾ of $120 = 90$. Q_3 lies in the $54.50–$59.50 class. $L = \$54.50$, $CF = 83$, $f = 24$.
Solving:

$$\$54.50 + \frac{\frac{3(120)}{4} - 83}{24}(\$5) = \$55.96$$

One fourth of the commissions are above $55.96.

Refer to the daily commissions in Table 5–4. What is the third quartile? Interpret.

The interquartile range is $9.41, found by $Q_3 - Q_1 = \$55.96 - \$46.55$. Thus, the distance between the third and first quartiles is $9.41. Suppose the interquartile range of another distribution of daily commissions is $14.96. It can be said that (1) the set of commissions with the interquartile range of $9.41 is clustered more closely to its mean than is the set of commissions with an interquartile range of $14.96 (because $9.41 < $14.96) and (2) the arithmetic mean of the daily commissions with the interquartile range of $9.41 is a more representative or typical average than is the mean of the distribution with an interquartile range of $14.96.

The quartile deviation

The quartile deviation is half the distance between the third quartile, Q_3, and the first quartile, Q_1.

$$\boxed{Q.D. = \frac{Q_3 - Q_1}{2}}$$

For the daily commissions:

$$Q.D. = \frac{Q_3 - Q_1}{2}$$

$$= \frac{\$55.96 - \$46.55}{2}$$

$$= \$4.71$$

The percentile range

As noted, there are three quartiles (Q_1, Q_2, Q_3). They divide a distribution into four parts. Likewise, the 99 **percentiles** divide a distribution into 100 parts. The 10-to-90 **percentile range** is the distance between the 10th and

90th percentiles. The percentiles are computed and interpreted in a manner similar to the quartiles. The formulas for the 10th and 90th percentiles are:

10th percentile

$$L + \frac{\frac{10n}{100} - CF}{f} \ (i)$$

90th percentile

$$L + \frac{\frac{90n}{100} - CF}{f} \ (i)$$

EXAMPLE

What is the 10th percentile for the distribution of daily commissions in Table 5–4?

SOLUTION

$$L + \frac{\frac{10n}{100} - CF}{f} \ (i)$$

$$= \$39.50 + \frac{\frac{10(120)}{100} - 10}{11} \ (\$5)$$

$$= \$39.50 + \frac{2}{11} \ (\$5)$$

$$= \$40.41$$

SELF-REVIEW 5–12

$60.06, found by:

$$\$59.50 + \frac{\frac{90(120)}{100} - 107}{9} \ (\$5)$$

Refer back to Table 5–4. What is the 90th percentile?

The percentile range is $19.65, found by $60.06 − $40.41. The middle 80 percent of the commissions lie between $40.41 and $60.06 (approximately). Twenty percent lie either below $40.41 or above $60.06.

EXERCISES

14. The weekly incomes of part-time employees were tallied into the following distribution:

Weekly incomes	Number
$0–$49	8
50– 59	16
60– 69	24
70– 79	48
80– 89	22
90– 99	14
100–109	11
110–119	7

a. What is the first quartile?
b. What is the third quartile?
c. What is the interquartile range? Interpret.
d. What is the quartile deviation? Interpret.
e. Determine the 10 to 90 percentile range. Interpret.

15. The number of air miles logged by a sample of executives during the year were grouped into the following distribution:

Number of miles	Class frequency
10,000–19,000	16
20,000–29,000	31
30,000–39,000	86
40,000–49,000	103
50,000–59,000	120
60,000–69,000	99
70,000–79,000	71
80,000–89,000	30
90,000–99,000	10
100,000 and over	4

a. Estimate the interquartile range. Interpret.
b. Estimate the quartile deviation. Interpret.
c. What is the 20-to-80-percentile range? Interpret.

RELATIVE DISPERSION

Sometimes we may want to express the variation in a distribution relative to an average. Carl Pearson (1857–1936), who contributed significantly to the early development of the science of statistics, originated a relative measure called the **coefficient of variation (C.V.).** It is the *ratio of the standard deviation to the arithmetic mean expressed as a percent.*

$$C.V. = \frac{s}{\bar{X}}(100)$$

EXAMPLE

Suppose that the arithmetic mean quarterly sales for a distribution are $100,000 and the standard deviation of this distribution is $10,000. What is the coefficient of variation?

SOLUTION

$$C.V. = \frac{s}{\bar{X}}(100)$$

$$= \frac{\$10,000}{\$100,000}(100)$$

$$= 10 \text{ percent}$$

This indicates that the standard deviation is 10 percent of the mean.

It is often necessary to compare the variation of two or more distributions which are *in different units*. A measure of absolute variation, such as the standard deviation, cannot be applied because one distribution may be in dollars and the other in days. In such cases, the coefficient of variation can be used.

EXAMPLE

The arithmetic mean of the distribution of daily commissions was computed to be $51.04, and the standard deviation $7.51. The relative variation in that distribution is to be compared with the absenteeism of the salespersons. The mean number of days absent was found to be 12.1, and the standard deviation 1.6 days. Compare the relative variation in the two distributions.

SOLUTION

For the daily commissions:

$$C.V. = \frac{s}{\bar{X}}(100)$$

$$= \frac{\$7.51}{\$51.04}(100)$$

$$= 14.7 \text{ percent}$$

For the absenteeism:

$$C.V. = \frac{s}{\bar{X}}(100)$$

$$= \frac{1.6}{12.1}(100)$$

$$= 13.2 \text{ percent}$$

The relative variation in the two distributions is about the same.

The coefficient of variation can also be used to compare the relative dispersion in two or more distributions which are in the same units. As an example, we may want to compare the relative variation in the prices of two groups of homes being studied. One group of homes is low priced and the other is high priced.

EXAMPLE

The study of the low-priced homes revealed that the arithmetic mean price is $43,925. The standard deviation is $4,010. The statistics for the high-priced homes are: $\overline{X} = \$324,905$, and $s = \$30,140$. Compare the relative dispersion of the two groups.

SOLUTION

For the low-priced homes　　　　　　For the high-priced homes

$$\text{C.V.} = \frac{s}{\overline{X}}(100) \qquad\qquad \text{C.V.} = \frac{s}{\overline{X}}(100)$$

$$= \frac{\$4,010}{\$43,925}(100) \qquad\qquad = \frac{\$30,140}{\$324,905}(100)$$

$$= 9.1 \text{ percent} \qquad\qquad = 9.3 \text{ percent}$$

It is evident that the relative dispersion in the low-priced and high-priced groups is about the same.

SELF-REVIEW 5–13

C.V. for mechanical is 5 percent, found by 10/200. For finger dexterity C.V. is 20 percent, found by 6/30. Thus, relative dispersion in finger dexterity scores greater than relative dispersion in mechanical, because 20 percent > 5 percent.

A large group of inductees was given two experimental tests, a mechanical aptitude test and a finger dexterity test. The arithmetic mean score on the mechcanical aptitude test is 200, with a standard deviation 10. The mean and standard deviation for the finger dexterity test are: $\overline{X} = 30$, $s = 6$. Compare the relative dispersion in the two groups.

MEASURES OF SKEWNESS

Two descriptive characteristics of a distribution have been studied, namely, measures of central tendency and measures of dispersion. Another characteristic which can be described is its **skewness**. As noted in the previous chapter, a frequency distribution that is symmetrical has no skewness; that is, the skewness is zero. The introduction of extreme observations into the distribution tends to influence the mean more than the mode or median. Recall that if the observations are extremely large, the mean is greater than the median or mode and the distribution is said to be positively skewed. Conversely, if extremely low items are included in the distribution, the mean is weighted down and is smaller than the median or mode. The distribution is then described as being negatively skewed. Karl Pearson developed a **coefficient of skewness** (Sk) to measure the amount and direction of skewness. For a sample:

$$Sk = \frac{3(\bar{X} - \text{Median})}{s}$$

The daily commissions for the sample of 120 salespersons are not distributed symmetrically since the mean is $51.04 and the median is $51.63. The standard deviation was computed previously to be $7.51. The coefficient of skewness is −0.24, found by:

$$Sk = \frac{3(\bar{X} - \text{Median})}{s} = \frac{3(\$51.04 - \$51.63)}{\$7.51} = -0.24$$

The Pearsonian coefficient of skewness generally falls between −3 and +3, and in this case the −0.24 indicates that there is a slight negative skewness in the distribution of commissions, meaning that the longer tail of the distribution is on the negative side (to the left).

SELF-REVIEW 5–14

2.5, found by:

$$Sk = \frac{3(87 - 73)}{16.9} = 2.5$$

There is considerable positive skewness in the distribution of the typing speeds, meaning that the longer tail of the distribution is on the positive (right) side.

A sample of experienced typists revealed that their mean typing speed is 87 words per minute and the median is 73. The standard deviation is 16.9 words per minute. What is the coefficient of skewness? Interpret.

EXERCISES

16. The mean weight of a sample of slugs is 87 grams, the standard deviation 2 grams. The mean outside diameter of the same slugs is 2.54 centimeters, the standard deviation 0.25 centimeters. Is it true that because 2 grams > 0.25 centimeters there is more dispersion in the weights of the slugs than in their outside diameters? Explain.

17. The sample statistics with respect to a sample of new home prices are: $\bar{X} =$ $64,900, median = $62,700, mode = $58,600, and $s =$ $5,000.
    a. What is the coefficient of skewness? Interpret.
    b. If $\bar{X} =$ $63,000, median = $63,000, mode = $63,000, and $s =$ $5,000, what is coefficient of skewness? What does this indicate?

A COMPUTER APPLICATION

A number of computer packages are available which can be applied to problems involving descriptive statistics. These packages are used extensively in business, the social sciences, education, and other areas and require very little knowledge of computer programming. One of the more widely used is called the Statistical Package for the Social Sciences, abbreviated SPSS. The output with respect to the daily commissions of 120 salespersons is given below. First, a frequency distribution is given, then a histogram is drawn, and finally various averages and measures of dispersion are computed.

CATEGORY LABEL	CODE	ABSOLUTE FREQ	RELATIVE FREQ (PCT)	ADJUSTED FREQ (PCT)	CUM FREQ (PCT)
$30-34	32.	3	2.5	2.5	2.5
$35-39	37.	7	5.8	5.8	8.3
$40-44	42.	11	9.2	9.2	17.5
$45-49	47.	22	18.3	18.3	35.8
$50-54	52.	40	33.3	33.3	69.2
$55-59	57.	24	20.0	20.0	89.2
$60-64	62.	9	7.5	7.5	96.7
$65-69	67.	4	3.3	3.3	100.0
	TOTAL	120	100.0	100.0	

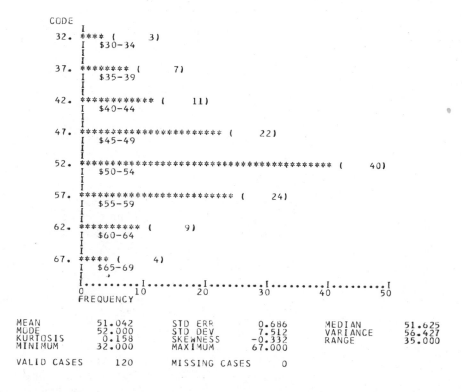

MEAN	51.042	STD ERR	0.686	MEDIAN	51.625	
MODE	52.000	STD DEV	7.512	VARIANCE	56.427	
KURTOSIS	0.158	SKEWNESS	-0.332	RANGE	35.000	
MINIMUM	32.000	MAXIMUM	67.000			

VALID CASES	120	MISSING CASES	0

CHAPTER SUMMARY

Chapters 4 and 5 dealt with measures a statistician uses to describe frequency distributions. The measures fall into three categories: measures of central tendency, measures of dispersion, and measures of skewness. Chapter 4 was concerned with four measures of central tendency, namely, the arithmetic mean, the median, the mode, and the geometric mean. One of the measures of dispersion discussed in this chapter is the range. It measures the spread from the lowest to the highest value. It is simple to compute, but if there is an extremely small or large value, the range may be a very unreliable measure of dispersion.

The percentile range and the interquartile range are not based on the two extreme values, and so they correct this weakness of the range. The 10-to-90 percentile range, for example, is the difference between the 10th and 90th percentiles and thus includes only the middle 80 percent of the observations. The interquartile range, which is the difference between the third and first quartiles (the 25th and 75th percentiles) measures the spread of the middle 50 percent of the observations.

Three measures of dispersion—the average deviation, the variance, and the standard deviation—are based on the deviation of each item from its mean. If the observations are clustered close to the mean, they will be small. If there is considerable dispersion from the mean, they will be large. The average deviation is the average of the deviations from the mean. The variance and standard deviation are based on the squared deviations from the mean.

If two or more distributions are in different units, or their means are far apart, a direct comparison of their standard deviations may be misleading. Instead, they should be converted to coefficients of variation (percents), and then the comparisons made.

The degree of skewness in a distribution can be measured by the coefficient of skewness. Generally it ranges from -3 (negative skewness) to $+3$ (positive skewness). A coefficient of skewness of zero indicates no skewness.

CHAPTER OUTLINE

Measures of dispersion and skewness

I. Measures of dispersion and skewness.
    A. *Purpose*. To arrive at one value which either describes the spread (variation) in the data, or the extent of skewness.
II. Measures of absolute dispersion.
    A. Range.
        1. *Definition*. The difference between the two extreme values of a set of numbers.
        2. *Computation*.
            a. *Ungrouped data*. The range is the difference between the highest and lowest values.
            b. *Grouped data*. The true upper limit of the largest class minus the true lower limit of the smallest class, or the midpoint of the largest class minus the midpoint of the smallest class.
        3. *Advantages*. Simple to compute.

        4. *Limitations*. An extremely high and/or low value makes it an unreliable measure of dispersion.

  B. Percentile range.

        1. *Definition*. The difference between two selected percentiles, such as the 10th and 90th percentiles.

        2. *Advantages*. Corrects the limitation of the range by measuring the spread in the middle 80 percent of the observations.

  C. Interquartile range.

        1. *Definition*. The difference between the third and first quartiles. Similar in computation and use to the percentile range.

  D. Quartile deviation.

        1. *Definition*. Half the distance between the first and third quartiles.

        2. *Computation*.

$$Q.D. = \frac{Q_3 - Q_1}{2}$$

where:

$$Q_3 = L + \frac{\frac{3n}{4} - CF}{f}\ (i) \qquad Q_1 = L + \frac{\frac{n}{4} - CF}{f}\ (i)$$

For the third quartile, Q_3:

    L is the lower limit of the class containing the third quartile.

    n is the total number of frequencies.

   CF is the cumulative number of frequencies in all the classes immediately preceding the class containing the third quartile.

    f is the frequency in the class containing the third quartile.

    i is the width of the class in which the third-quartile falls.

(For the first quartile, Q_1: substitute the word *first* for the word *third* in the above.)

        3. *Use*. To compare the dispersion between two or more distributions.

        4. *Advantages*. Relatively easy to compute. Not affected by extreme values. Can be determined if the distribution has unequal class intervals.

        5. *Limitations*. Does not include all observations in its computation; that is, it describes only the dispersion for the middle half of distribution.

  E. Mean deviation (also called average deviation).

        1. *Definition*. The arithmetic mean of the absolute differences of each value from the mean.

2. *Formula for ungrouped data.*

$$\text{A.D.} = \frac{\Sigma|X - \bar{X}|}{n}$$

3. *Use.* To compare the dispersion between two or more distributions.

F. Variance.
   1. *Definition.* The arithmetic mean of the squared deviations from the mean.
   2. *Formulas for a population.*

   Ungrouped data:

   $$\sigma^2 = \frac{\Sigma(X - \mu)^2}{N}$$

   Grouped data:

   $$\sigma^2 = \frac{\Sigma fX^2}{N} - \left(\frac{\Sigma fX}{N}\right)^2$$

   or

   $$\frac{\Sigma X^2}{N} - \left(\frac{\Sigma X}{N}\right)^2$$

   3. *Use.* To compare the dispersion between two or more distributions.
   4. *Limitations.* Difficult measure to interpret because, for example, it might be in terms of (dollars)^2, or (ages)^2.

G. Standard deviation.
   1. *Definition.* Square root of the variance—that is, the square root of the arithmetic mean of the squared deviations from the mean.
   2. *Formulas for a sample.*

   Ungrouped data:

   $$s = \sqrt{\frac{\Sigma(X - \bar{X})^2}{n - 1}}$$

   Grouped data:

   $$s = \sqrt{\frac{\Sigma fX^2 - \frac{(\Sigma fX)^2}{n}}{n - 1}}$$

   or

   $$\sqrt{\frac{\Sigma X^2 - \frac{(\Sigma X)^2}{n}}{n - 1}}$$

   or

   $$i\sqrt{\frac{\Sigma fd^2 - \frac{(\Sigma fd)^2}{n}}{n - 1}}$$

   3. *Use.* Widely used in sampling and other facets of statistical inference. Used to estimate the dispersion of two or more populations and the representativeness of their means. Using the standard deviation and the mean, the empirical rule states:

   $\mu \pm \sigma$ encompasses about 68 percent of the values.
   $\mu \pm 2\sigma$ encompasses about 95 percent of the values.
   $\mu \pm 3\sigma$ encompasses about 99.7 percent of the values.

III. Measures of relative dispersion.
    A. Coefficient of variation.
        1. *Definition.* The standard deviation divided by the mean.
        2. *Formula.*

$$\text{C.V.} = \frac{s}{\bar{X}}(100)$$

        3. *Uses.* When (1) there is a *wide difference* in the magnitude of the means, or (2) the distributions being compared are in *different units*. A direct comparison of the standard deviations might result in an erroneous conclusion.
IV. Measures of skewness.
    A. Coefficient of skewness.
        1. *Formula.*

$$Sk = \frac{3(\bar{X} - \text{Median})}{s}$$

        2. *Use.* To measure the degree of skewness in a distribution. An *Sk* of zero indicates that there is no skewness, i.e., the distribution is symmetrical; a negative value indicates that the distribution is negatively skewed; and a positive value of *Sk* reveals positive skewness. Illustrations:

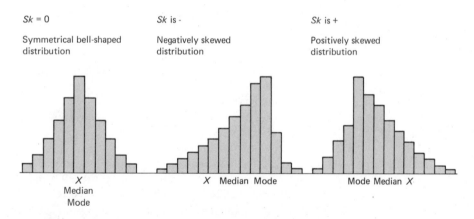

Sk = 0 — Symmetrical bell-shaped distribution

Sk is - — Negatively skewed distribution

Sk is + — Positively skewed distribution

CHAPTER EXERCISES

Record the letter of the correct answer in front of the number of the problem.

Questions 18 through 23 are based on the weights (in centigrams) of a *sample* of several transistors selected from the production line. They are:

12, 6, 7, 3, 10

18. The mean weight of the sample is: (a) 7.0, (b) 38.0, (c) 7.6, (d) 9.0, (e) none of these is correct.

19. The range of the sample is (a) 0.0, (b) 7.6, (c) 7.0, (d) 9.0, (e) none of these is correct.

20. The standard deviation of the sample is (a) 7.6, (b) 3.8, (c) 50 percent, (d) −14.44, (e) none of these is correct.

21. The coefficient of variation is (a) $38, (b) 3.8, (c) 14.44, (d) 50 percent, (e) 7.0, (f) none of these is correct.

22. The variance is (a) 14.44, (b) 3.80, (c) 50.00 percent, (d) 0.47, (e) none of these is correct.

23. The coefficient of skewness is (a) −14.44, (b) 47 percent, (c) 19.01, (d) 38, (e) none of these is correct.

Questions 24 through 30 are based on the following problem.

The quality control department constantly monitors three assembly lines producing built-in ovens for home use. The oven is designed to preheat to a temperature of 240° Celsius in four minutes and then shut off. However, the oven may not reach 240° C in the allotted time because of improper installation of the insulation and other reasons. Likewise, the temperature might go over 240° C during the four-minute preheat cycle.

A large number of ovens were sampled, and the following measures were computed on each line:

	Temperature (in degrees Celsius)		
Statistical measure	Line 1	Line 2	Line 3
Arithmetic mean	238.1	240.0	242.9
Median	240.0	240.0	240.0
Mode	241.5	240.0	239.1
Standard deviation	3.0	0.4	3.9
Mean deviation	1.9	0.2	2.2
Quartile deviation	1.0	0.1	1.7

24. The distribution of the oven readings from which line is a symmetrical, bell-shaped distribution? (a) line 1, (b) line 2, (c) line 3, (d) cannot determine based on the information given.

25. The coefficient of variation for the temperatures from line 3 is (a) 1.6 percent, (b) 60.6 percent, (c) 3.9° C, (d) 242.9 degrees C, (e) cannot be computed based on the information given.

26. According to the empirical rule, about 95 percent of the temperatures from line 2 were between (a) 238.8 and 241.2, (b) 239.9 and 240.1, (c) 239.2 and 240.8, (d) 239.6 and 240.4, (e) none of these is correct.

27. The distribution of the oven temperatures at the end of the four-minute preheat period for line 1 is (a) not skewed, (b) negatively skewed, (c) positively skewed, (d) none of these is correct.

28. About half the temperature readings for line 3 are above (a) 242.9, (b) 240.0, (c) 239.1, (d) 1.7, (e) none of these is correct.

29. About half the temperature readings for line 2 fall between (a) 239.2 and 240.8, (b) 239.8 and 240.2, (c) 239.9 and 240.1, (d) 0.1 and 0.4, (e) none of these is correct.

30. The variance for the line 1 temperature readings is (a) 1.0, (b) 3.0, (c) 3.61, (d) 9.0, (e) 241.5, (d) none of these is correct.

31. The range of the temperatures for line 2 is about (a) 3.0 degrees C, (b) 50

degrees C, (c) 0.4 degrees C, (d) 2.4 degrees C, (e) 1.0 degrees C, (f) none of these is correct.

32. A large hospital wanted to compare its annual patient turnover rate per bed with those published by the American Hospital Association, shown in Chapter 3. The turnover rates for a sample of 80 beds were organized into the following frequency distribution. (An annual turnover rate of 21.0 per bed indicates that, during a year, 21 different patients occupied the same hospital bed.)

Annual turnover rate per bed	Number	Annual turnover rate per bed	Number
17–19	4	32–34	7
20–22	9	35–37	5
23–25	13	38–40	5
26–28	20	41–43	2
29–31	15		

a. Compute the arithmetic mean turnover rate per bed.
b. Determine the standard deviation.
c. What is the coefficient of variation?
d. Is the distribution negatively or positively skewed? Cite evidence.

CHAPTER SELF-REVIEW EXAMINATION

Do all of the problems and then check your answers against those given in Appendix A.

Score each problem 10 points.

Question 1–5 are based on the following statistics: Samples of copper wire were submitted for testing by two companies. The sample pieces for each company were tested for tensile strength and the results organized into a frequency distribution. Then the mean, median, and other measures were computed. (Tensile strengths are in pounds per square inch.)

Statistic	Company Doma	Betz
Arithmetic mean	500	600
Median	500	500
Mode	500	300
Standard deviation	40	20
Mean deviation	32	16
Quartile deviation	25	14
Range	240	120
Number in sample	100	80

1. According to the empirical rule, the middle 95 percent of the wires from the Doma Company tested between approximately what two values?
2. The middle 50 percent of the wires of the Doma Company tested between what two values?
3. What is the coefficient of variation for the Doma distribution?
4. Which distribution has the larger dispersion? Explain.
5. What is the variance for the Doma distribution?

Questions 6 and 7 are based on the following weights: 7, 9, 11, 9, and 4 grams.

6. Compute the average deviation.

7. Compute the variance and the standard deviation.

Questions 8–10 are based on the following frequency distribution.

Days absent during year	Number f
2– 5	7
6– 9	11
10–13	20
14–17	30
18–21	14
22–25	10
26–29	8

8. Determine the range. Explain what it indicates.

9. Determine the 10-to-90-percentile range.

10. Is the distribution symmetrical, positively skewed, or negatively skewed? (It is not necessary to compute any measures, such as the coefficient of skewness.)

6

INTRODUCTION

A perusal of newspapers and business-oriented magazines reveals many references to **index numbers.** As examples, newspapers, television, radio, and other media give considerable attention every month to the release of the consumer price index (CPI). From *The Wall Street Journal*:

> On an unadjusted basis, the price index for all-urban consumers—which covers about 80% of the population—stood last month at 263.2% of the 1967 average, up 11.3% from a year earlier. This means that a market-basket item costing $1.00 in 1967 cost $2.632 last month.[1]

From the *Sarasota (Florida) Herald-Tribune*:

> Before seasonal adjustment, the Labor Department's comparative measure of wholesale prices, which it calls the producer price index (PPI), reached 265.3 over the 1967 base of 100. This means it cost $265.30 to buy the Labor Department's sampling of wholesale commodities that cost $100 14 years ago.[2]

In this chapter we will examine the descriptive measure called an index number. We will discuss what it is, how it is determined, and how it is used.

---

[1] *The Wall Street Journal,* March 25, 1981, pp. 1, 3.

[2] *Sarasota (Florida) Herald-Tribune*, April 4, 1981, p. 1.

Index numbers

SOME BASIC CONCEPTS

What is an index number? An **index number** is *a ratio that is usually on a base of 100 and is used to measure a change in magnitude over periods of time.*

EXAMPLE

The main use of an index number in business is to show the percent change from one time period to another. To illustrate this, the average hourly earnings in mining in 1978 were $7.67, and in January 1981, $9.53.[3] What is the index of hourly earnings in mining for February 1981 based on 1978?

SOLUTION

It is 124.3, found by:

$$\frac{\text{Hourly earnings in 1981}}{\text{Hourly earnings in 1978}} \times 100 = \frac{\$9.53}{\$7.67} \times 100 = 124.3$$

indicating that hourly earnings in mining in 1981 compared with 1978 were 124.3 percent, or they increased 24.3 percent during that period.

EXAMPLE

The Bureau of the Census reported that in 1980 there were 29.0 million white females under 19 years. The projected number in 1988 is 28.5 million. What is the index for 1988 based on 1980?

SOLUTION

The index is 98.3, found by

$$\frac{\text{1988 estimate}}{\text{1980 population}} \times 100 = \frac{28.5 \text{ million}}{29.0 \text{ million}} \times 100 = 98.3$$

indicating that if the 1988 estimate is correct, the number of white females under 19 will have decreased 1.7 percent during the eight-year period (the 1.7 percent is calculated by 100 percent − 98.3 percent).

---

[3] U.S. Department of Commerce, *Survey of Current Business,* February 1981, pp. 5–13.

EXAMPLE

As an illustration of the construction of an index to show one thing compared with another, the Department of Transportation, National Highway Safety Administration, reported that for 1980 the death rate from motor vehicle accidents in the United States was 22 per 100,000 population. For Italy it was 16 per 100,000 population. What is the death rate for Italy compared with the United States expressed as an index?

SOLUTION

The index for Italy is 72.7, found by:

$$\frac{\text{Death rate for Italy}}{\text{Death rate for U.S.}} \times 100 = \frac{16}{22} \times 100 = 72.7$$

indicating that the death rate in Italy is 72.7 percent of that in the United States, or the death rate in Italy is 27.3 percent less than in the United States.

SELF-REVIEW 6–1

1. 119.5, found by

$$\frac{\$10.35}{\$8.66} \times 100$$

Hourly earnings in 1981 were 119.5 percent of the 1978 earnings, or earnings increased 19.5 percent from 1978 to 1981.

2. 165.3, found by

$$\frac{\$2,037,000}{\$1,232,000} \times 100$$

Mahoney's income is 165.3 percent of Stamper's income, or Mahoney's income is 65.3 percent greater than Stamper's.

(A reminder: cover the answers in the left-hand column).

1. The average hourly earnings in contract construction in January 1981 were $10.35, and in 1978, $8.66. Express the hourly earnings in 1981 as an index using the hourly earnings in 1978 as the base (denominator). Interpret.

2. David J. Mahoney, chairman of the board of Norton Simon, has an annual income of $2,037,000, and Malcolm T. Stamper, chairman of the board at Boeing, has an income of $1,232,000. Express the income of David J. Mahoney as an index using the income of Malcolm T. Stamper as the base. Interpret.

Note from the previous discussion that:

1. The index of the hourly earnings in mining of 124.3 and the index of 72.7 for the motor vehicle death rate problem are actually percents. The percent sign is usually omitted.

2. Each index number has a **base**. The **base period** for the hourly earnings in mining is 1978. The death rate of 22 per 100,000 population for the

United States is the base for the death rate problem involving Italy and the United States. If there is a base period, such as 1978, it is usually designated as 1978 = 100. At this writing, most of the indexes compiled and published by the federal government have a base period of 1967 = 100. There are some notable exceptions, however. The index of the prices received and paid by farmers, for example, still has 1910–14 as the base period.

3. The **base number** of most indexes is 100. (The plural of *index* is *indexes* or *indices*.) Thus, when we computed the index of hourly earnings in mining, the quotient of 1.243, found by $9.53/$7.67, was multiplied by 100. There is no reason, however, why 10, 50, 1,000, or any other number cannot be used as the base number.

4. Most business and economic indexes are carried either to the nearest whole percent, such as 254 or 76, or to the nearest 10th of a percent, such as 77.5 or 178.6.

Compiling index numbers, such as the producer price indexes, (PPI), is not a recent innovation. An Italian, G. R. Carli, has been credited with originating the first index numbers in 1764. They were incorporated in a report he made regarding price fluctuations in Europe from 1500 to 1750. No systematic approach to collecting and reporting data in index form was evident in the United States until about 1900. The cost-of-living index (now called the consumer price index) was introduced in 1913, and the list of indexes has increased steadily since then.

Why convert data to indexes? An index is a convenient way of expressing a change in a heterogeneous group of items. The consumer price index (CPI), for example, encompasses about 400 items including golf balls, lawn mowers, hamburgers, funeral services, and stereo phonograph records, which are expressed in pounds, boxes, yards, and many other different units. Only by converting the prices of these many diverse goods and services to one index number every month can the federal government and others concerned with inflation keep informed of the overall movement of consumer prices.

Converting data to indexes also makes it easier to compare the trend in a series composed of exceptionally large numbers. For example, if the total retail sales in 1981 were $185,679,432,621.87, and in 1967 total retail sales were $185,500,000,000.00, the increase of $179,432,621.87 appears significant. Yet, if the 1981 sales were expressed as an index based on 1967 sales, the increase is less than one tenth of 1 percent!

$$\frac{\text{Total Retail Sales in 1981}}{\text{Total Retail Sales in 1967}} = \frac{\$185,679,432,621.87}{\$185,500,000,000.00} \times 100 = 100.09$$

Indexes can be classified as a **price index**, a **quantity index**, a **value index**, or a **special-purpose index**. A few examples of the four types of indexes published on a regular basis follow.

Price Indexes

Consumer price index. Actually there are two consumer price indexes, one for all-urban consumers and the other for urban wage earners and clerical workers. Also, there are separate indexes to show the change in the price of food, transportation, etc. (1967 = 100).

Producer price indexes. These measure the average changes in prices received in the primary markets of the United States by producers of commodities in all stages of processing (1967 = 100).

Prices received and paid by farmers. Published monthly along with a parity index in the *Survey of Current Business* (1910–14 = 100).

Quantity indexes

Federal Reserve Board indexes of quantity output. In addition, there are output indexes by market grouping and industry grouping. They also are given monthly in the *Survey of Current Business* (1967 = 100).

Index of employment in manufacturing. (1967 = 100).

Value indexes

Value of construction contracts awarded in 50 states. (1967 = 100).

McCann-Erickson Advertising Index. Subdivided into network TV, spot TV, magazine, and newspaper, this index is reported monthly in *Survey of Current Business* (1967 = 100).

Special-purpose indexes

There are several indexes which reflect the overall economic activity in the United States. The federal government puts out an index of leading economic indicators. It includes such diverse economic indicators as stock prices, new orders for plant and equipment, and building permits issued. Another such index, the Forbes Index, combines production, money turnover, employment, department stores sales, and several other business indicators.

CONSTRUCTION OF INDEX NUMBERS

Unweighted index numbers

Unweighted indexes are also called **simple indexes**. To illustrate the construction of a simple price index, the price of an A78–10 boat trailer tire for selected years (see Table 6–1) has been converted to an index number. The indexes in this first illustration are often called **relatives**. The base period is 1967; that is, 1967 = 100.

The base-period price is designated as p_0, and the price other than the base period is often referred to as the **given period**, and designated p_n. To calculate the simple price index (relative) P for any given period:

$$P = \frac{p_n}{p_0} (100)$$

TABLE 6–1
Price indexes for
trailer tire, 1966–82

Year	Price of tire	Index (1967 = 100)
1966	$18	$\frac{18}{20} \times 100 = 90.0$
1967	20	$\frac{20}{20} \times 100 = 100.0$
1968	22	$\frac{22}{20} \times 100 = 110.0$
1969	23	$\frac{23}{20} \times 100 = 115.0$
1982	38	$\frac{38}{20} \times 100 = 190.0$

For 1982, the price index for the trailer time is 190.0.

$$P = \frac{\$38}{\$20} (100) = 190.0$$

In interpreting, one could say that the price of the tire increased 90 percent from the base period of 1967 to 1982.

Had the years 1967–68 been selected as the base period, i.e., $1967 - 68 = 100$, the arithmetic mean of the two prices ($20 and $22) would be the representative value in the base year; and the prices $20, $22, and $23 would be averaged if 1967–69 were selected as the base. The mean price would be $21.67. The indexes constructed using the three different base periods are presented in Table 6–2. (Note that when 1967–69 = 100, logically the index numbers for 1967, 1968, and 1969 average 100.0.)

TABLE 6–2
Prices of the tire
converted to indexes
using three different
base periods

Year	Price of tire	Price index (1967 = 100)	Price index (1967–68 = 100)	Price index (1967–69 = 100)
1966	$18	90.0	$\frac{18}{21} \times 100 = 85.7$	$\frac{18}{21.67} \times 100 = 83.1$
1967	20	100.0	$\frac{20}{21} \times 100 = 95.2$	$\frac{20}{21.67} \times 100 = 92.3$
1968	22	110.0	$\frac{22}{21} \times 100 = 104.8$	$\frac{22}{21.67} \times 100 = 101.5$
1969	23	115.0	$\frac{23}{21} \times 100 = 109.5$	$\frac{23}{21.67} \times 100 = 106.2$
1982	38	190.0	$\frac{38}{21} \times 100 = 181.0$	$\frac{38}{21.67} \times 100 = 175.4$

If the data involved the *quantities* of the A78–10 tires manufactured (instead of the price), the index of the quantity manufactured for 1982 (1967 = 100) would be 190.0. $Q = (q_n/q_0)(100)$ or $(38/20)(100) = 190.0$. The 190.0 would indicate that the quantity manufactured in 1982 was 90 percent greater than in 1967.

—————————————————— SELF-REVIEW 6-2 ——————————————————

a. 250.2, found by:

$$\frac{\$5.63}{\$2.25} \times 100$$

Average hourly earnings in January 1981 were 250.2 percent compared with 1967. Or, average hourly earnings in January 1981 were 150.2 percent above those in 1967.

b. 241.6, found by ($2.25 + $2.41)/2 = $2.33. Then,

$$\frac{\$5.63}{\$2.33} \times 100 = 241.6$$

c. 47.1, found by:

$$\frac{\$1.06}{\$2.25} \times 100$$

Average hourly earnings in 1949 were 47.1 percent of those in 1967. Or, earnings in 1949 were 52.9 percent below those in 1967.

The average hourly earnings in wholesale and retail trade for selected periods are:

Year	Average hourly earnings
1949	$1.06
1967	2.25
1968	2.41
1981 (January)	5.63

Source: *Monthly Labor Review*, March 1981, Tables 14, 17.

a. Using 1967 as the base period, determine an index number for January 1981 which might aptly be called the index of average hourly earnings in wholesale and retail trade. Interpret.

b. Now, using the average of 1967 and 1968 (that is, 1967–68 = 100), determine the index for January 1981.

c. What is the index for 1949 using 1967 = 100? Interpret.

A more complex problem would be to determine an index of food prices. Assume for this illustration that the typical family eats only three food items: milk, bread, and avocados. Using the procedure for calculating simple indexes, we find that the unweighted index of food prices for 1982 in the following example would be 122.9 (1967 = 100). The index for 1982 was computed by dividing the total of the prices for 1982 by the 1967 total (Table 6–3).

TABLE 6–3
Computation of the food price using the simple unweighted method

Item	1967 price p_0	1982 price p_n
Milk (quart)	$0.64	$0.61
Bread (loaf)	0.65	0.59
Avocado (each)	0.50	1.00
Total	$1.79	$2.20

The index of price is:

$$P = \frac{\Sigma p_n}{\Sigma p_0}(100) = \frac{220\cancel{c}}{179\cancel{c}} = 122.9$$

The unweighted price index of 122.9, however, seems illogical because the two major food items *declined* in price from 1967 to 1982 and only the price of avocados increased. Avocados are eaten only infrequently by most consumers. It seems, therefore, that the prices of bread and milk should be given more weight than the price of avocados.

Also, the simple method of computing an index illustrated in the preceding problem does not meet the **units test**. This means that if the items were quoted in different units, the answer would be different from 122.9. For example, if the price of milk were quoted in gallons instead of quarts and avocados were quoted by the box instead of singly, the price index would not be 122.9. Because of these inadequacies, the simple aggregative method is seldom used in actual practice for this type of problem. Instead the weighted method described in the following section is used.

Weighted indexes

Price index. A **weighted price index** is computed by:

$$P = \frac{\Sigma p_n q_0}{\Sigma p_0 q_0} (100)$$

EXAMPLE

The prices of the three foods and the quantities consumed by a typical consumer in 1967 are:

Item	1967 price p_0	1967 amount consumed q_0	1982 price p_n
Milk (quart)	$0.64	100	$0.61
Bread (loaf)	0.65	1,000	0.59
Avocado (each)	0.50	1	1.00

What is the weighted index of price for 1982 using 1967 = 100?

SOLUTION

The total amount spent for food by the typical consumer in the base period, 1967, is determined first. The total amount spent on the three food items was $714.50 (see Table 6–4). In order to measure the effect of price, it is assumed that the amount of food consumed *did not change* between the base period and 1982. Thus, to find how much the typical consumer spent on food in 1982, the 1982 prices are multiplied by the corresponding quantities consumed in 1967. The total is $652.00. The weighted index of price for 1982 is 91.3, found by:

$$P = \frac{\Sigma p_n q_0}{\Sigma p_0 q_0} (100) = \frac{\$652.00}{\$714.50} (100) = 91.3$$

Interpretation. The average price of food declined about 9 percent from 1967 to 1982. The weighted method results in a more logical answer (91.3) than the unweighted index (122.9), which indicated an increase of about 23 percent in the price of food.

TABLE 6–4
Computation of a
weighted price index
(1967 = 100)

Item	1967 price p_0	1967 amount consumed q_0	p_0q_0	1982 price p_n	p_nq_0
Milk (quart)	$0.64	100	$ 64.00	$0.61	$ 61.00
Bread (loaf)	0.65	1,000	650.00	0.59	590.00
Avocado (each)	0.50	1	0.50	1.00	1.00
			$714.50		$652.00

Note that the weighted method, alternatively called the **weighted aggregative method**, uses the amounts consumed in the base period (q_0) as weights. It assumes that the eating habits of the typical consumer did not change from 1967 to 1982. Thus, *only price* fluctuated, causing the decrease in the index from 100 in the base period to 91.3 in 1982.

SELF-REVIEW 6–3

a. 214.5, found by:

p_0	q_0	p_0q_0	p_n	p_nq_0
$35	500	$17,500	$65	$32,500
40	1,200	48,000	90	108,000
		$65,500		$140,500

$$P = \frac{\$140,500}{\$65,500} \times 100 = 214.5$$

b. The price of clothing in 1981 was 214.5 percent of the price in 1976. Or, the price of clothing increased 114.5 percent from 1976 to 1981.

An index of clothing prices for 1981 based on 1976 is to be constructed. The prices for 1976 and 1981 and the quantity consumed in 1976 are shown below.

Item	1976 price	1981 price	1976 amount sold
Dress (each)	$35	$65	500
Shoes (pair)	40	90	1,200

a. Assuming that the number sold remained constant—that is, the same number were sold in 1981 as in 1976—what is the weighted index of price for 1981 using 1976 as the base?
b. Interpret.

EXERCISES

(A reminder: The answers and method of solution for selected exercises are given in Appendix A.)

1. The spendable average weekly earnings for a married worker with three dependents working in manufacturing for selected periods are:

Year	Spendable average weekly earnings
1960	$ 80.11
1967	100.93
1975	166.29
1976	181.32
1977	200.06
1980	246.96

Source: *Monthly Labor Review,* February 1981, Table 20.

a. Using 1967 as the base period, what is the index of spendable weekly earnings for 1980? Interpret.

b. Using 1967 = 100, what is the index for 1960? Interpret.

c. Using 1975–77 = 100, what is the index of spendable weekly earnings for 1980?

2. The hourly earnings in selected durable-goods manufacturing groups for December 1979 and December 1980 follow.

	Hourly earnings	
Manufacturing group	*December 1979*	*December 1980*
Lumber and wood products	$6.24	$6.77
Furniture and fixtures	5.26	5.71
Stone, clay, and glass	7.11	7.83
Instruments and related products	6.50	7.09

Source: *Monthly Labor Review,* February 1981, Table 17.

a. Convert the hourly earnings for December 1980 to indexes for each of the four groups, using December 1979 = 100.

b. Interpret your findings.

3. Fruit prices and the amounts of fruit consumed for 1973 and 1981 are:

Fruit	*Price 1973*	*Amount consumed 1973*	*Price 1981*
Bananas (pound)	$0.23	100	$0.35
Grapefruit (each)	0.29	50	0.27
Apples (pound)	0.35	85	0.35
Strawberries (basket)	1.02	8	1.69
Oranges (bag)	0.89	6	0.99

a. Assuming that the amounts of fruit consumed did not change between 1973 and 1981, determine the weighted index of price for 1981 using 1973 as the base period.

b. Interpret your findings.

Quantity index. The foregoing weighted method of computing a price index using the quantities consumed in the base period as constants was developed during the latter part of the 18th century by Etienne Laspeyres. The Laspeyres method of weighting is also used to compute a quantity index. The procedure is similar to the method of constructing a weighted price index, except that *base-year prices* are used as weights instead of base-year quantities. The formula for the **weighted index of quantity** is:

$$Q = \frac{\Sigma p_0 q_n}{\Sigma p_0 q_0} (100)$$

EXAMPLE

The prices of selected commodities for 1973 and the quantities mined in 1973 and 1981 follow.

Commodity	1973 price p_0	1973 quantity mined q_0	1981 quantity mined q_n
Oil (barrels)	$ 2	100	110
Coal (ton)	20	10	9
Sulfur (tank car)	15	90	80
Granite (block)	60	5	5

What is the index of the quantity mined in 1981 using 1973 as the base period?

SOLUTION

One might be tempted to add the quantities in 1981 and divide this total by the total of the 1973 quantities. Of course, it is impossible to add barrels, tank cars, and blocks. The quantities, therefore, have to be converted to a common denominator using 1973 prices.

It is assumed in computing the quantity index that 1973 prices still prevailed in 1981—that is, the price of each commodity is held constant. Thus, any change in the quantity index is *due only to the quantity mined*. In this problem the quantity of minerals mined declined 7.3 percent from 1973 to 1981. (See Table 6–5 for computations.)

$$Q = \frac{\Sigma p_0 q_n}{\Sigma p_0 q_0} (100) = \frac{\$1,900}{\$2,050} (100) = 92.7$$

TABLE 6–5
Computation of weighted index of the quantity of minerals mined for 1981 using the Laspeyres method (1973 = 100)

Commodity	1973 price p_0	1973 quantity mined q_0	$p_0 q_0$	1981 quantity mined q_n	$p_0 q_n$
Oil (barrels)	$ 2	100	$ 200	110	$ 220
Coal (ton)	20	10	200	9	180
Sulfur (tank car)	15	90	1,350	80	1,200
Granite (block)	60	5	300	5	300
			$2,050		$1,900

---

a. 235.4, found by:

$$Q = \frac{\$8240}{\$3500} \times 100$$

$p_0 q_0$	$p_0 q_n$
$ 200	$1,400
300	240
3,000	6,600
$3,500	$8,240

b. Quantity produced between 1975 and 1982 increased 135.4 percent.

The prices and the number produced for selected agricultural items are:

Item	Price 1975	Price 1982	Production 1975	Production 1982
Wheat (bushel)	$ 2.00	$ 4.00	100	700
Eggs (dozen) ...	0.30	0.20	1,000	800
Pork (cwt.)	60.00	70.00	50	110

a. Using the Laspeyres method, compute an index of the quantity of agricultural production for 1982 (1975 = 100).
b. Interpret the index.

Several years after Laspeyres introduced the concept of using base-period figures as weights, Paasche suggested a similar procedure—except that present-year weights were substituted for base-period weights. The Paasche formula for a weighted price index using present-year figures as weights is:

$$P = \frac{\Sigma p_n q_n}{\Sigma p_0 q_n} (100)$$

The weighted price index applying the Paasche formula is illustrated in Table 6-6. The data are the same as used previously:

$$P = \frac{\Sigma p_n q_n}{\Sigma p_0 q_n} (100) = \frac{\$655}{\$714} (100) = 91.7$$

TABLE 6-6
Computation of a weighted price index for 1982 using the Paasche formula (1967 = 100)

Commodity	1967 price p_0	1982 price p_n	1982 quantity consumed q_n	$p_0 q_n$	$p_n q_n$
Milk (quart)	64¢	61¢	200	$128	$122
Bread (loaf)	65¢	59¢	900	585	531
Avocado (each)	50	100	2	1	2
				$714	$655

The interpretation of the index of price using the Paasche method (91.7) is as follows: A market basket of food selected in 1982 would cost 8.3 percent less than the same food would have cost at 1967 prices, found by 100.0 − 91.7.

The Paasche method has the advantage of using current consumption figures as weights; that is, the consumption pattern is always up-to-date. However, the method poses a practical problem. The index must be revised every year using new present-year weights. If the Paasche method were used to compute the producer price indexes, for example, the consumption of approximately 2,800 wholesale items would have to be determined every year in order to weight the base-year and present-year prices. The Laspeyres method of using base-period weights, therefore, is the most commonly used (with some modification).

Value index. A **value index**, such as the index of department store sales, needs the base-year prices, the base-year quantities, the present-year prices, and the present-year quantities for its construction. Its formula is:

$$V = \frac{\Sigma p_n q_n}{\Sigma p_0 q_0} (100)$$

EXAMPLE

Suppose the price and quantity sold for various items of apparel for 1972 and 1981 are:

Item	1972 price p_0	1972 quantity sold (000) q_0	1981 price p_n	1981 quantity sold (000) q_n
Ties (each)	$ 1	1,000	$ 2	900
Suits (each)	30	100	40	120
Shoes (pair)	10	500	8	500

What is the index of value for 1981 using 1972 as the base period?

SOLUTION

Total sales in 1981 were $10,600,000 and the comparable figure for 1972 is $9,000,000. Thus, the index of value for 1981 using 1972 = 100 is 117.8. The value of apparel sales in 1981 was 117.8 percent of the 1972 sales. To put it another way, apparel sales increased 17.8 percent from 1972 to 1981.

$$V = \frac{\Sigma p_n q_n}{\Sigma p_0 q_0} (100) = \frac{\$10,600,000}{\$9,000,000} (100) = 117.8$$

The needed calculations are in Table 6–7.

**TABLE 6–7
Construction of a
value index for 1981
(1972 = 100)**

Item	1972 price p_0	1972 quantity sold (000) q_0	(000) $p_0 q_0$	1981 price p_n	1981 quantity sold (000) q_n	(000) $p_n q_n$
Ties (each)	$ 1	1,000	$1,000	$ 2	900	$ 1,800
Suits (each)	30	100	3,000	40	120	4,800
Shoes (pair)	10	500	5,000	8	500	4,000
			$9,000			$10,600

a. 127.1, found by:

$$V = \frac{\$77,000}{\$60,600} \times 100$$

p_0q_0	p_nq_n
$30,000	$36,000
600	1,000
30,000	40,000
$60,600	$77,000

b. Value of the sales up 27.1 percent from 1973 to 1980.

The number of items produced and the price per item for the Wejipum Manufacturing Company are:

Item produced	Price 1973	1980	Number produced 1973	1980
Shear pins (box) ...	$ 3	$4	10,000	9,000
Cutting compound (pound)	1	5	600	200
Tie rods (each)	10	8	3,000	5,000

a. Find the index of the value of production for 1980, using 1973 as the base period.

b. Interpret the index.

EXERCISES

4. The prices and production of grains for 1977 and 1982 are:

Grains	1977 price	1977 quantity produced (in millions of bushels)	1982 price	1982 quantity produced (in millions of bushels)
Oats	$1.52	200	$1.87	214
Wheat........	2.10	565	2.05	489
Corn	1.48	291	1.48	203
Barley........	3.05	87	3.29	106

a. Using 1977 as the base period and the Laspeyres method, determine the weighted index of the quantity of grains produced for 1982.

b. Using 1977 as the base period, find the index of the value of grains produced for 1982.

5. A company manufactures a variety of products. The prices and quantities produced for 1974 and 1981 are:

Product	1974 price	1981 price	1974 quantity produced	1981 quantity produced
Small motor (each)	$23.60	$28.80	1,760	4,259
Scrubbing compound (gallon)	2.96	3.08	86,450	62,949
Nails (pound)	0.40	0.48	9,460	22,370

a. Using 1974 as the base period and the Laspeyres method, determine the weighted index of the quantity produced for 1981.

b. Using 1974 as the base period, find the index of the value of goods produced for 1981.

Special-purpose index. Special-purpose indexes are usually a combination of a number of business and economic indicators, such as sales, employment, and stock prices.

The construction of a special-purpose index designed to measure general business activity is shown using the data in Table 6–8. Note that weights based on the judgments of the statistician are assigned to each series, and the series are in different units—dollars, freight car loadings, and so on.

TABLE 6–8
Data for the computation of the index of general business activity

Year	Department store sales ($ billions)	Index of employment (1967 = 100)	Freight carloadings (millions)	Unemployment (thousands)
Weight	40	30	10	20
1967	$20	100	50	500
1977	41	110	30	900
1982	44	125	18	700

To compute the index of general business activity for 1982 using 1967 = 100, for example, each 1982 figure is first expressed as a relative using the base period figure as the denominator. For illustration, retail sales for 1982 are converted to a relative by ($44/$20) × 100 = 220.

The relatives are then weighted by the appropriate weights. For the department store relative, 220 × 0.40 = 88.0.

$$\text{Department store sales:} \quad \left(\frac{\$44}{\$20}\right) 100 \times 0.40 = 88.0$$

$$\text{Employment:} \quad \left(\frac{125}{100}\right) 100 \times 0.30 = 37.5$$

$$\text{Freight carloadings:} \quad \left(\frac{18}{50}\right) 100 \times 0.10 = 3.6$$

$$\text{Unemployment:} \quad \left(\frac{700}{500}\right) 100 \times 0.20 = \underline{28.0}$$
$$157.1$$

The index of general business activity for 1982 is 157.1. Interpreting, business activity increased 57.1 percent from the base period (arbitrarily selected as 1967) to 1982.

SELF-REVIEW 6–6
---

a. 1976 = 100

1981 = 139, found by:

$$\begin{array}{l} \textit{Weight} \\ (50¢/20¢)(100) \times 0.10 = 25 \\ (80{,}000/100{,}000)(100) \times 0.30 = 24 \\ (120/80)(100) \times 0.60 = \underline{90} \\ 139 \end{array}$$

b. Business activity in 1981 was 139 percent of the activity in 1976. Or, business activity in 1981 was 39 percent higher than in 1976.

As chief statistician for the county, you want to compute and publish every year a special-purpose index which you plan to call the *Index of County Business Activity*. Three series seem to hold promise as the basis for the index; namely, the price of cotton, the number of new automobiles sold, and the rate of money turnover for the county published by a local bank. Arbitrarily you decide that money turnover should have a weight of 60 percent; number of new automobiles sold, 30 percent; and the price of cotton, 10 percent.

a. Construct the *Index of County Business Activity* for 1976 (the base) and for 1981.

Year	Price of cotton (per pound)	Number of automobiles sold	Rate of money turnover (an index)
1976	20¢	100,000	80
1981	50	80,000	120

b. Interpret the indexes.

CONSUMER PRICE INDEX

Frequent mention has been made of the consumer price index (CPI) in the preceding pages. It is a statistical measure of the average change in prices found in a fixed market basket of goods and services. In January 1978, the Bureau of Labor Statistics began publishing CPIs for two groups of the population. One index, a new CPI for all-urban consumers, covers about 80 percent of the total noninstitutional population. The other index is for urban wage earners and clerical workers and covers about 40 percent of the population.[1]

In brief, the CPI serves several major functions. It allows consumers to determine the degree to which their purchasing power is being eroded by price increases. In that respect, it is a yardstick for revising wages, pensions, and other income payments to keep pace with changes in prices. Equally important, it is an economic indicator of the rate of inflation in the United States.

The index includes about 400 items, and about 250 part-time and full-time agents collect price data monthly. Prices are collected from over 18,000 tenants, 24,000 retail establishments, and 18,000 housing units in 85 urban areas across the country. The prices of baby cribs, bread, beer, cigars, gasoline, haircuts, mortgage interest rates, physicians' fees, taxes, and operating-room charges are just a few of the items included in what is often termed a typical "market basket" of goods and services.

Originated in 1913 and published regularly since 1921, the standard reference period (called the base period) has been revised approximately every 10 years. The base periods prior to the present 1967 base were the average of 1957–59, 1947–49, 1935–39, and 1925–29.

The need for this rather frequent rebasing is somewhat obvious. Consumption patterns have changed drastically. The automobile has replaced the horse as a mode of transportation. In the 1910s and 1920s a relatively small proportion of the income of wage earners and clerical workers was spent on higher education. Now the typical family spends a sizable amount on the higher education of its children, and the CPI reflects any changes in costs of tuition and books.

---

[1] For an excellent article on the methodology used to construct the CPI see Janet L. Norwood, "The Anatomy of Price Change," *Monthly Labor Review,* March 1981, pp. 58.

In addition to changing the base period periodically, the Bureau of Labor Statistics conducts an extensive consumer expenditure survey from time to time to determine what items are to be included in the CPI and the relative weights to be put on stereo cassettes, bananas, gasoline, rent, and so on. The latest survey was made in 1972–73.[2]

The CPI is not just one index. Instead, it includes a large number of groups, subgroups, and selected items. And there are separate indexes for a number of large cities. A few of them are shown below for all-urban consumers for November 1980.

Items	November 1980
All items	256.2
Food and beverages	257.4
Apparel and upkeep	184.8
Transportation	259.0
Medical care	274.5
Entertainment	211.2
Rent, residential	198.3
Energy.........................	366.1
All items less energy	247.7

Source: *Monthly Labor Review,* February 1981, Table 23.

A perusal of the above listing shows that the price of all items combined increased 156.2 percent since 1967, energy increased the most (266.1 percent), and apparel and upkeep went up the least (84.8 percent).

SPECIAL USES OF THE CONSUMER PRICE INDEX

Real income

In addition to measuring the change in prices of goods and services, both consumer price indexes have a number of other applications. One use is to determine the **real income** of individuals. As an example, assume for the sake of simplicity that the consumer price index is presently 300 (1967 = 100). Also, assume that a typical consumer earned $7,000 in the base period of 1967 and that his current income is $21,000. Note that although his **money income** tripled from $7,000 to $21,000, the prices the typical consumer pays for food, gasoline, clothing, and other items also tripled. Thus, the typical consumer's standard of living remained the same from 1967 to the present time. In other words, despite the fact that income tripled from $7,000 to $21,000, the typical consumer's present standard of living is the same as it was in 1967. Price increases have exactly offset his increase in income, and so his present buying power (real income) is still $7,000. (See Table 6–9 for computations.)

In general:

$$\text{Real income} = \frac{\text{Money income}}{\text{CPI}} \times 100$$

[2] For a description of this survey, see U.S. Department of Labor, *Consumer Expenditure Survey: Diary Survey,* Bulletin 1959.

**TABLE 6–9
Computation of real income**

Year	Money income	Consumer price index (1967 = 100)	Real income	Computation of real income
1967	$ 7,000	100	$7,000	$\dfrac{\$7,000}{100}(100)$
Present year	$21,000	300	$7,000	$\dfrac{\$21,000}{300}(100)$

The concept of real income is sometimes called **deflated income**. The CPI is called the **deflator**. Also, a popular term for deflated income is **income expressed in constant dollars**. Thus, in Table 6–9, in order to determine whether the typical consumer raised his or her standard of living, money income was converted to constant dollars. It was found that purchasing power expressed in 1967 dollars (constant dollars) remained the same at $7,000.

SELF-REVIEW 6–7

a. $5,000, found by:

$$\frac{\$5000}{100.0} \times 100.$$

b. $4,000, found by:

$$\frac{\$11,200}{280.0} \times 100.$$

c. Although the employee's take-home pay increased $6,200 between 1967 and 1981, his or her real income decreased from $5,000 to $4,000. This means purchasing power was $1,000 less in 1981 than in 1967.

The take-home pay of an employee working in an urban area and the consumer price index for 1967 and 1981 are:

Year	Take-home pay	CPI (1967 = 100)
1967	$ 5,000	100.0
1981	11,200	280.0

a. What was the "real" take-home pay of the employee in 1967?
b. What was the "real" take-home pay of the employee in 1981?
c. Interpret your findings.

Deflated sales

A price index can also be used to "deflate" sales figures, or similar money series. The producers price index for finished goods has been used in Table 6–10 to deflate sales to account for changes in the price the company paid for its raw materials.

**TABLE 6–10
Conversion of money sales to real sales**

Year	Sales	Producers price index* (1967 = 100)	Computation of deflated sales		Sales in constant 1967 dollars
1967	$482,000	100.0	$\dfrac{\$482,000}{100.0} \times 100$	=	$482,000
1979	980,000	216.1	$\dfrac{\$980,000}{216.1} \times 100$	=	453,494
1980	991,000	244.7	$\dfrac{\$991,000}{244.7} \times 100$	=	404,986

* Source: *Monthly Labor Review*, February 1981, Table 26.

The conclusion is that although the actual dollar sales of the manufacturer increased by more than $500,000 from 1967 to 1980, sales deflated for the rise in prices the company paid for raw materials actually declined (from about $482,000 down to about $405,000). This is so because the prices the manufacturer paid at wholesale for raw materials increased at a more rapid rate than did the sales.

Purchasing power of the dollar

The consumer price index is also used to determine the **purchasing power of the dollar**.

$$\text{Purchasing power of dollar} = \frac{\$1}{\text{CPI}} \times 100$$

EXAMPLE

Suppose that the consumer price index this month is 200.0 (1967 = 100). What is the purchasing power of the dollar?

SOLUTION

It is 50 cents, found by:

$$\text{Purchasing power of dollar} = \frac{\$1}{200.0}(100) = \$0.50$$

Interpretation. The CPI of 200.0 indicates that prices doubled from 1967 to this month. Thus, the purchasing power of a dollar has been cut in half. That is, a 1967 dollar is worth only 50 cents this month. To put it another way, if you lost $1,000 in 1967 and just found it, the $1,000 could only buy half of what it could buy in 1967.

Table 6–11 shows the computations of the purchasing power of the dollar for a few actual periods. Note that the purchasing power of the dollar for January 1981 was 38.4 cents. Theoretically, if $1,000 could purchase 1,000 porterhouse steaks at $1 each in 1967, by 1981 the same $1,000 could buy only 384 steaks.

TABLE 6–11
Computation of the purchasing power of the dollar

Year	Consumer price index* (1967 = 100)	Computations $\frac{\$1}{\text{CPI}}(100)$		Purchasing power of the dollar (1967 = $1)
1967 .... 100.0		$\frac{\$1}{100.0}(100)$	=	$1.000
1969 .... 109.8		$\frac{\$1}{109.8}(100)$	=	0.911
1979 .... 217.7		$\frac{\$1}{217.7}(100)$	=	0.459
1981 (January) 260.5		$\frac{\$1}{260.5}(100)$	=	0.384

* Source: *Survey of Current Business,* March 1981, Tables 22, 23.

34.5¢, found by

$$\frac{\$1}{290.0}(100)$$

Due to price increases since 1967, a 1967 dollar is worth only 34.5 cents today.

Suppose the consumer price index for the latest month is 290.0. What is the purchasing power of the dollar? Interpret.

Cost-of-living increases

The consumer price index is also the basis for so-called cost-of-living increases in many management-union contracts. The specific clause in the contract is often referred to as the "escalator clause." These clauses vary somewhat, but the contract between American Airlines and the Transport Workers Union of America is rather typical. "Effective August 6, 1977, all employees shall receive one cent (1¢) per hour for each 0.3 rise in the Consumer Price Index All Cities (1967) published by the Bureau of Labor Statistics."[3]

In addition, about 31 million social security beneficiaries, 2.5 million retired military and federal civil service employees and survivors, and 600,000 postal workers have their incomes or pensions pegged to the consumer price index.[4]

Finally, the CPI is used to adjust alimony and child-support payments; attorneys' fees; workers' compensation payments; rentals on apartments, homes, and office buildings; welfare payments; and so on.[5]

SHIFTING THE BASE

If two or more series have the same year as the base period, they can be compared directly. As an example, suppose that the trend since 1967 in the price for food, housing, services, transportation (new cars), and all items combined is to be analyzed. Note in Table 6–12 that all of these price indexes are on the same base (1967). Thus, it can be said that during the 13-year period, the prices of all items combined increased about 148 percent; housing, 167 percent; and so on.

───────

[3] Robert H. Ferguson, *Cost-of-Living Adjustments in Union-Management Agreements,* Bulletin 65, New York State School of Industrial and Labor Relations, Cornell University, 1976, p. 52. This bulletin contains a large number of escalator clauses. An interesting article on the history of escalator clauses in the United States is "Adjusting Wages to Living Costs: A Historical Note," *Monthly Labor Review,* July 1974, pp. 21–26.

[4] U.S. Department of Labor, Bureau of Labor Statistics, "Revising the CPI: A Brief Review of Methods," Report 484, p. 4.

[5] For a discussion of the legal aspects, see an article by Leonard I. Reiser, "Legal Recognition of Changes in the Cost of Living," *Case & Comment,* March–April 1975, pp. 9–14.

TABLE 6–12
Consumer prices (U.S. Department of Labor indexes, 1967 = 100)

Year	All items	Food	Housing	Services	Transportation
1967	100.0	100.0	100.0	100.0	100.0
1970	116.3	114.9	118.9	121.6	112.7
1971	121.3	118.4	124.3	128.4	118.6
1972	124.7	122.2	128.5	132.7	119.9
1980	247.8	245.7	266.7	274.2	249.7

Source: *Survey of Current Business.*

A problem arises when two or more series being compared are not on the same base. This is the case for the two price series in Table 6–13. The prices received by farmers for their farm products are based on 1910–14, but the consumer price indexes for food are based on 1967.

TABLE 6–13
Prices received by farmers and the consumer index of food prices, 1967–1980

Year	Index of prices received by farmers (1910–14 = 100)	Index of food prices paid by consumers (1967 = 100)
1967	253	100.0
1970	280	114.9
1971	285	118.4
1972	317	122.2
1980	586	245.7

Source: *Survey of Current Business.*

Suppose that the two sets of prices since 1970 (the base period) are to be compared. In order to do this, the bases of both series are shifted to 1970 = 100 (see Table 6–14). Now it can be said that since 1970 the prices received by farmers for their products increased at a slightly less rapid rate (109 percent) than did the prices consumers paid for food (about 114 percent).

TABLE 6–14
Procedure for shifting the base

Year	Index of prices received			Index of food prices		
	1910–14 = 100	1970 = 100	Calculations	1967 = 100	1970 = 100	Calculations
1967	253	90	$\frac{253}{280}(100)$	100.0	87.0	$\frac{100}{114.9}(100)$
1970	280	100	$\frac{280}{280}(100)$	114.9	100.0	$\frac{114.9}{114.9}(100)$
1971	285	102	$\frac{285}{280}(100)$	118.4	103.0	$\frac{118.4}{114.9}(100)$
1972	317	113	$\frac{317}{280}(100)$	122.2	106.4	$\frac{112.2}{114.9}(100)$
1980	586	209.3	$\frac{586}{280}(100)$	245.7	213.8	$\frac{245.7}{114.9}(100)$

—————————————— SELF-REVIEW 6–9 ——————————————

a.

Year	Production (1968 = 100)	Raw material prices (1968 = 100)
1968	100	100
1972	80	97
1982	64	88

b. Production decreased more rapidly (36 percent) from 1968 to 1982 than did raw material prices (12 percent).

The trends in two series since 1968 are to be compared. Unfortunately, they are on different bases.

Year	Production index (1967 = 100)	Index of raw material prices (1957 − 59 = 100)
1968	110	200
1972	88	194
1982	70	176

a. Shift the base to 1968 to make the two series comparable.

b. Interpret the trend in the two series.

CHAPTER SUMMARY

This chapter deals with a descriptive measure called an index number. Its principal use in business is to describe the percent change in price, quantity, or value from one time period to another. A few, designated as special-purpose indexes, measure changes in overall business and economic activity. They combine into one index such diverse series as stock prices, industrial production, and money turnover.

The federal government, magazines devoted to business matters, such as *Forbes* and *Business Week*, universities, banks, private organizations, and the United Nations, collect data for thousands of indexes which appear regularly in such publications as the *Survey of Current Business,* the *Monthly Labor Review,* and the *Federal Reserve Bulletin.*

Indexes have a base period. At this writing it is 1967, written 1967 = 100. The base number for all practically all indexes is 100. Thus a price index of 265.3 for March indicates that prices increased 165.3 percent from the base period to March.

One of the most watched index is the consumer price index which is compiled and published monthly. As the name implies, it is a price index which reflects the percent change in the price of a market basket consisting of about 400 items including bread, doctors' fees, taxes, tires, and baby cribs. Social security old-age pensions, many apartment leases, and management-union contracts are tied to the change in the CPI. As prices rise so do pensions, rents, and wages.

Some indexes are classified as being simple (unweighted). Most, however, are weighted indexes. The CPI, for example, is a weighted price index with the price of each item in the market basket weighted by an amount established by a survey of consumers in 1972–73.

Price indexes can be used as deflators to deflate income, sales, the gross national product, and other series, for changes in price. This is accomplished by dividing the income, or sales, by an appropriate price index and multiplying the quotient by 100. Real or deflated income, for example, is determined by dividing an employee's money income by the CPI and multiplying the quotient by 100.

CHAPTER OUTLINE

Index numbers

I. Index numbers.
   A. Purpose. To show the change in price, quantity, or value from one time period to another.
   B. Characteristics.
      1. An index number such as 185.0 is a *percent*, but the percent sign is usually omitted.
      2. An index number has a base *period*. Currently the most commonly used is the year 1967, written 1967 = 100.
      3. The base *number* of most indexes is 100. Thus, a price index of 185.0 for last month, using 1967 = 100, means that prices increased 85 percent from 1967 to last month.
      4. Most indexes are carried to the nearest whole percent, such as 164 or 96, or to the nearest tenth of a percent, such as 185.6 and 83.2.
   C. Reasons for computing indexes.
      1. Indexes facilitate a comparison of unlike series such as the change in wholesale prices, employment, and exports since 1967.
      2. A convenient way to express the change in the total of a heterogeneous group of items. Example: Industrial production in the United States consists of the total production of automobiles, girdles, books, antifreeze, detergent, and so on.
      3. A percent change is sometimes easier to comprehend compared with actual numbers. Example: The Gross National Product increased from $785 billion in 1967 to $2,732 billion for the latest quarter.[6] The change of $1,947 billion is hard to grasp. Instead, the index for the latest quarter of 348.0 (1967 = 100) is easy to interpret—GNP rose 248 percent from 1967 to the latest quarter.
   D. Types of index numbers.
      1. *Price.* Its purpose is to measure the change in prices from a selected base period to another period, such as this year. Example: Consumer Price Index (1967 = 100).
      2. *Quantity.* Portrays change in quantity from base period to another period. Example: Index of Industrial Production (1967 = 100).
      3. *Value.* Likewise, shows change in value from say 1967 to the

---

[6] *Survey of Current Business,* March 1981, p. 7.

present month. Example: Federal Reserve Board Index of
Quantity Output (1967 = 100).
   4. *Special-purpose index*. It combines and weights a heteroge-
      neous group of series, such as employment, prices, produc-
      tion, and bank debits, usually to arrive at an overall index to
      show the change in business activity from the base period to
      the present. Example: Index of leading economic indicators.
II. Construction of index numbers.
   A. Unweighted index numbers.
      1. *Formula:* Price index $(p_n/p_0) \times 100$ where p_0 is the price in the
         base period and p_n is the price in a period other than the base
         period. Example: Price of a pen was $2 in 1974, price now is
         $2.20. Index is 110.0, found by ($2.20/$2.00)100 (1974 = 100).
         Quantity index $(q_n/q_0) \times 100$ where q_0 is the quantity during
         the base period and q_n the quantity during another period.
      2. *Use*. To show the change in a single price or a single commod-
         ity from one time period to another.
      3. *Limitations*. To determine the change in the quantity of a
         group of items, such as food items, it is impossible to add
         quarts of milk, pounds of coffee, and heads of lettuce.
   B. Weighted index numbers.
      1. *Formulas*.
         a. Value.

$$V = \frac{\Sigma p_n q_n}{\Sigma p_0 q_0} (100)$$

         b. Price:

         Laspeyres method   **Paasche method**

$$P = \frac{\Sigma p_n q_0}{\Sigma p_0 q_0} (100) \qquad\qquad P = \frac{\Sigma p_n q_n}{\Sigma p_0 q_n} (100)$$

         c. Quantity:

$$Q = \frac{\Sigma p_0 q_n}{\Sigma p_0 q_0} (100) \qquad\qquad Q = \frac{\Sigma p_n q_n}{\Sigma p_n q_0} (100)$$

      2. *Use*. Using the weighted aggregative method, (1) a price
         index reflects the change in the price paid *only* (because the
         quantity consumed is held constant), and (2) a quantity index
         reflects the change in the quantity consumed *only* (because
         price is held constant).
      3. *Laspeyres and Paasche methods*. The Laspeyres method
         uses base-period weights, the Paasche method uses present-
         year weights. Laspeyres method is most commonly used.
III. Consumer price index.
   A. Description. Starting in 1978 two consumer price indexes were

published—one designed for urban wage earners and clerical workers, which covers about 40 percent of the population, and another for all urban households, which covers about 80 percent of the population.

B. Function.

1. Allows consumers to determine the effect of price increases on their purchasing power.
2. A yardstick for revising wages, pensions, alimony payments, and so on.
3. An economic indicator of the rate of U.S. inflation.

C. Other uses of the consumer price indexes.

1. *Real income.* Computed by dividing income by consumer price index. Example: Ms. Smith's income increased from $8,000 in 1967 to $12,000 in 1982. Meanwhile, the CPI went from 100 to 200. She could buy $8,000 worth of goods in 1967, found by ($8,000/100) × 100. In 1982 her buying power (real income) was only $6,000, found by ($12,000/200) × 100. Her income has been eroded by sharp price increases.
2. *Purchasing power of the dollar,* found by ($1/*CPI*) (100). Example: Suppose the CPI this month is 295.6 (1967 = 100). The purchasing power of the dollar this month compared with 1967 is only 33.8 cents, found by ($1/295.6)(100).
3. *Escalator clauses.* Millions of employees in automobile, steel, and other industries have their wages adjusted upward when the CPI increases. The specifics are in the management-union contracts.

D. Shifting the base.

1. *Need.* When two or more series of index numbers to be compared do not have the same base period.
2. *Procedure.* Select a common base period for all series. Use the respective base numbers as the denominators and convert each series to the new base.

CHAPTER EXERCISES

6. The net sales of the Occidental Petroleum Corporation since 1971 are:

Year	Net sales ($ billion)
1971	$ 2.3
1972	2.4
1973	3.0
1974	5.5
1979	9.6
1980	12.5

Source: 1980 *Annual Report,* Occidental Petroleum Co., p. 82.

a. Using 1971 as the base period, express the 1979 and 1980 net sales as indexes.

b. Using 1971–73 as the base period, express the 1979 and 1980 net sales as indexes.

c. Refer to *b*. What does the index for 1980 indicate?

7. The percents of the civilian labor force unemployed for selected years are:

Year	Percent unemployed
1967	3.8
1968	3.6
1969	3.5
1975	5.6
1975	8.5
1979	5.8
1980	7.1

Source: *Monthly Labor Review,* March 1981, p. 83.

a. Using 1967 as the base period, express the 1979 and 1980 unemployment rates as indexes.

b. Interpret the 1980 index.

c. Using 1967–69 as the base period, express the 1979 and 1980 unemployment rates as indexes.

8. The median money incomes of year-round, full-time workers with income, by sex, for 1970, 1975, and 1979 are:

Year	Women median income	Men median income
1970	$ 5,440	$ 9,184
1975	7,719	13,144
1979	10,548	17,553

Source: U.S. Bureau of the Census, *Current Population Reports,* Series P–60, No. 125.

a. Convert the incomes for 1975 and 1979 to indexes using 1970 as the base period.

b. Compare the dollar incomes and the percent changes since 1970.

9. a. Using the Laspeyres formula, calculate a weighted index of price for 1982 (1967 = 100). Interpret.

b. Using the Laspeyres formula, determine a weighted index of quantity for 1982 (1967 = 100). Interpret.

c. Calculate an index of value for 1982 (1967 = 100). Interpret.

Item	1967 Price	1967 Amount produced	1982 Price	1982 Amount produced
Cabbage (pound)	6¢	2,000	5¢	1,500
Carrots (bunch)	10	200	12	200
Peas (quart)	20	400	18	500
Endive (bunch)	15	100	15	200

Problems 10–12 are based on the following indexes.

Year	Producers price index, all commodities (1967 = 100)	Consumer price index, all-urban consumers (1967 = 100)
1965	96.6	94.5
1966	99.8	97.2
1967	100.0	100.0
1968	102.5	104.2
1969	106.5	109.8
1970	110.4	116.3
1974	160.1	147.7
1979	235.6	217.4
1980	268.7	246.8
1981 (Feb.)	282.4	263.2

Source: *Survey of Current Business*, April 1981, pp. 5–7.

10. Using the consumer price index and 1967 as the base period, determine the purchasing power of the dollar for February 1981. Interpret.

11. Note that the producers price index, which represents the price of goods at wholesale, was 282.4 in February 1981. The consumer price index, representing the price of goods paid by the consumer, was 263.2 that month. Does this indicate that wholesale prices for that month were higher than retail prices? Explain.

12. Patricia Greene's annual income in 1967 was $8,240. In 1980 her annual income was $19,500. Evaluate her real income in 1980 compared with her real income in 1967. Explain.

13. Discuss the main features of the consumer price index (what it measures, base period, and so on).

14. Discuss the escalator clause (also called the cost-of-living clause) found in many management-union contracts.

15. A special-purpose index is to be designed to monitor the overall movements of the economy. Four key series were selected. Arbitrarily it was decided to weight retail sales 20 percent, total bank deposits 10 percent, industrial production 40 percent, and nonagricultural employment 30 percent.

Year	Retail sales (billions)	Bank deposits (billions)	Industrial production index (1967 = 100)	Total nonagricultural employment (thousands)
1974	$538	$30.6	129.3	78,413
1982*	985	41.3	135.0	82,100

*Estimated.

Source: *Survey of Current Business*, February 1977, pp. S-4, 12, 17; and *Monthly Labor Review*, February 1977, pp. 105 and 106 for 1974.

a. Compute a special-purpose index for 1982 (1974 = 100).
b. Interpret.

16. The changes in four economic series since 1971 are to be examined. Note in the following table that the CPI is on a 1967 base, employment is in millions of persons, and so on. A direct comparison, therefore, is not feasible.

a. Make whatever calculations are necessary to compare the trend in the four series since 1971.

b. Interpret.

Year	Consumer price index (1967 = 100)	Total labor force (millions)	Index of productivity in manufacturing (1967 = 100)	Gross national product (billions)
1950	72.1	64	64.9	$ 286.2
1967	100.0	81	100.0	789.6
1971	121.3	87	110.3	1,063.4
1975	161.2	95	114.9	1,516.3
1980	246.8	107	146.6	2,626.0

Source: *Monthly Labor Review*, April 1977, pp. 91, 103, 109; *National Income and Products Accounts of the United States; Survey of Current Business*, March 1981, p. S-1.

CHAPTER SELF-REVIEW EXAMINATION

Do all of the problems and then check your answers against those given in Appendix A. Score each problem 12½ points.

1.

Year	Price of aluminum scrap (per ton)
1967	$50.00
1970	40.20
1982	80.65

a. Using 1967 as the base, determine a price index for 1982.

b. Interpret.

Questions 2–5 are based on the following prices and quantities consumed for 1967 and 1981.

	1967		1981	
Item	Price (bushel)	Amount consumed (millions of bushels)	Price (bushel)	Amount consumed (millions of bushels)
Corn	$2	10	$4	12
Wheat	3	6	1	8
Oats	7	2	5	9

2. Using the Laspeyres formula and 1967 as the base, determine a weighted price index for 1981.

3. Using the Laspeyres formula and 1967 as the base, determine a weighted quantity index for 1981.

4. Compute a value index for 1981 using 1967 = 100.

5. *a.* Using the Paasche formula and 1967 as the base, determine a weighted price index for 1981.

   b. Why is this price index different from the one found in Problem 2? Which one is the more commonly used?

Questions 6 and 7 are based on the following.

Year	Consumer Price Index (1967 = 100)	Mr. Martin's monthly take-home pay
1967	100.0	$ 600
1971	121.3	700
1981 (Feb.)	263.2	1000

6. What is the purchasing power of the dollar for February 1981 based on 1967?

7. *a.* Determine Mr. Martin's "real" monthly income for each of the three years.
    b. Interpret.

8. Suppose that the producers price index (1967 = 100) and the sales of a firm for 1969 and 1982 are:

Year	Producers price index (1967 = 100)	Sales of the Nogood Company
1969	120.0	$2,400,000
1982	265.9	3,500,000

a. What are the "real" sales (also called "deflated" sales) for the two years?
b. Interpret.

7

INTRODUCTION

According to an article in *Forbes,* "Thirteen years hence, TI's [Texas Instruments'] bosses intend to make seven times today's profit on six times today's sales. Are they serious? You bet"[1] Predictions such as the one made by Texas Instruments with respect to some future event that will probably occur are referred to as **forecasts**, and the processes used to arrive at these predictions is called **forecasting**.

The forecast by Texas Instruments is considered to be a long-term forecast. Long-term forecasts are usually more than one year into the future; and 5-, 10-, 15-, and 20-year projections are common. Long-range predictions are considered essential in order to allow sufficient time for the procurement, manufacturing, sales, finance, and other departments of a company to develop plans for possible new plants, financing, development of new products, and new methods of assembling.

Forecasting the level of sales, both short term and long term, is almost dictated by the very nature of business organization in the United States. Competition for the consumer's dollar, stress on earning a profit for the stockholders, a desire to procure a larger and larger share of the market, and the ambitions of executives are some of the prime motivating forces in business. Thus, a statement of the goals of management, called *forecasts,* is considered necessary in order to have the raw materials, production facilities, and staff available to meet the projected demand.

The alternative, of course, is not to plan ahead. In a dynamic business environment, however, the lack of planning might be disastrous. An electronics firm which ignored the trend to solid-state circuitry a few years ago would no doubt have lost most of its share of the market by now.

Forecasts may be based only on the judgment of management. This is common in small firms. The management of a small firm is concerned mainly with day-to-day problems and seldom has the time to make an extensive study of the market, the effect of governmental actions on the firm, the sales of the competition, and other factors which must be considered in making a forecast; and many managers do not have the specialized knowledge necessary to make forecasts based on quantitative data. Many large firms, however, have planning departments (sometimes called statistical departments or control departments) which are constantly making and revising both long-range and short-range forecasts. Their activities involve all departments—

---

[1] *Forbes,* April 1, 1977, p. 29.

Time series analysis

accounting, finance, procurement, production, advertising, personnel, and sales.

This is not to imply, however, that judgment is not a factor in making forecasts. What is important is that statistical forecasting techniques are available, which, when supplemented with management's experience, will provide a better basis for decision making than would result from decisions based on judgment alone. Nor does the use of statistical techniques in forecasting guarantee that forecasts, and the decisions based on the forecasts, are infallible.

One of the many approaches to forecasting is called **time series analysis**. Time series are the records of past sales, production, or other variables over a period of time. Examples of time series are:

The number of persons 65 years and over from the decennial censuses of 1890, 1900, 1910. . . .

The annual birth rate in the United States since 1903.

The gross national product, by quarter, since 1971.

The monthly production of Schlitz beer since 1976.

The daily sales of J C Penney since 1972.

The daily slaughter of hogs, all markets, since 1967.

The chapter deals with the use of past data to forecast future events. First we look at the components of a time series, and then we develop some of the techniques used in analyzing past data.

COMPONENTS OF A TIME SERIES

Secular trend

As suggested in the preceding examples, one component of a time series is the **secular trend**. It is the smooth movement of a series over a long period of time. For illustration, the long-term trend in the gross national product since 1946 is portrayed in Chart 7–1. Note that there has been a rather smooth upward trend in the GNP since 1960.

CHART 7–1
The gross national product, United States, 1960–1980.

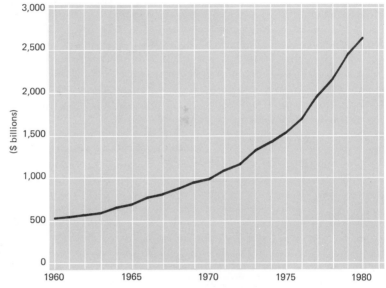

Source: *Survey of Current Business*, December 1980, p. 17, and March 1981, p. 7.

Seasonal variation

Another component of a time series is **seasonal variation**. Many sales, production, and other series fluctuate with the seasons. The unit of the time may be either quarterly, monthly, weekly, daily, or even hourly.

Practically all business and economic series have a recurring seasonal pattern. A few exceptions are found in certain electronic and aircraft firms under contract to the federal government to supply aerospace and military parts. Sales of men's and boys' wear stores, for example, have extremely high sales prior to Christmas and relatively low sales after Christmas and in the summer, as shown in Chart 7–2.

Measurement of the seasonal component is described in detail in the following chapter.

Cyclical variation

Cyclical variation is another component of a time series. A typical business cycle consists of a period of prosperity followed by periods of recession, depression, and recovery (see Chart 7–3).

A study of business-cycle history since 1919 reveals a number of recurring cycles. The depression phase of the cycle has varied in length from a few months to over 10 years. The typical cycle in the American economy appears to last about eight years. Many theories concerning the causes of

**CHART 7–2
Sales of men's and
boys' wear stores by
month, 1977–1981**

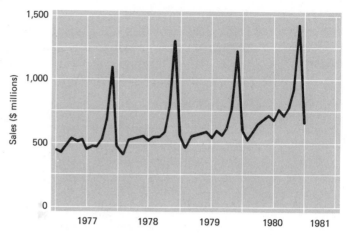

Source: *Survey of Current Business,* April 1981, p. S-10; and previous March issues.

**CHART 7–3
Typical business
cycle**

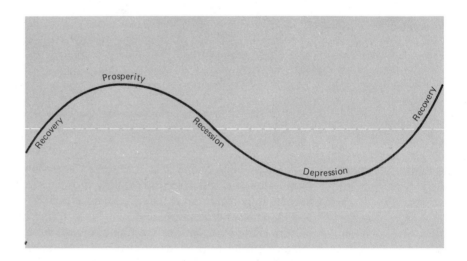

cyclical fluctuations have been suggested, but none has received widespread acceptance as the complete explanation of the causes of the fluctuations.

Irregular variation

Many analysts prefer to subdivide the irregular variation into **episodic** and **residual** variations. Episodic fluctuations are unpredictable, but they can be identified. The initial impact on the economy of a major strike or a war can be identified, but the strike or war could not have been predicted. After the episodic fluctuations have been removed, the remaining variation is called the residual variation. The residual fluctuations, often called chance fluctuations, are unpredictable, and they cannot be identified. Of course neither episodic or residual variation can be projected into the future.

LINEAR TREND

The long-term trend of many business series, such as sales, exports, and production, often approximates a straight line. If so, the equation to describe this growth is:

$$\overline{Y}_p = a + bX$$

where:

$\overline{Y}_p$ is the projected value of the Y variable for a selected X value.

a is the Y-intercept. It is the estimated value of Y when $X = 0$. Another way to put it is: a is the estimated value of Y where the straight line crosses the Y-axis when X is zero.

b is the slope of the line, or the average change in $\overline{Y}$ for each change of one (either increase or decrease) in X.

X is any value of X (time) that is selected.

To illustrate further meaning of $\overline{Y}_p, a, b,$ and X in a time series problem, a straight line has been drawn on Chart 7–4 to represent the typical trend of sales. Assume that this company started in business in 1974. This beginning year (1974) has been arbitrarily designated as the zero year. Note that sales increased $2 million on the average every year; that is, sales increased from $3 million in 1974, to $5 million in 1975, to $7 million in 1976, to $9 million in 1977, and so on. The slope, or b, therefore, is 2. Note too that the line intercepts the Y-axis (when $X = 0$) at $3 million. This point (3) where the line crosses the Y-axis is a.

CHART 7–4
A straight-line trend

The plots on the line are:

Year	X	$\overline{Y}_p$
1974	0	$3
1975	1	5
1976	2	7
1977	3	9
1978	4	11
1979	5	13
1980	6	15
1981	7	17
1982	8	19

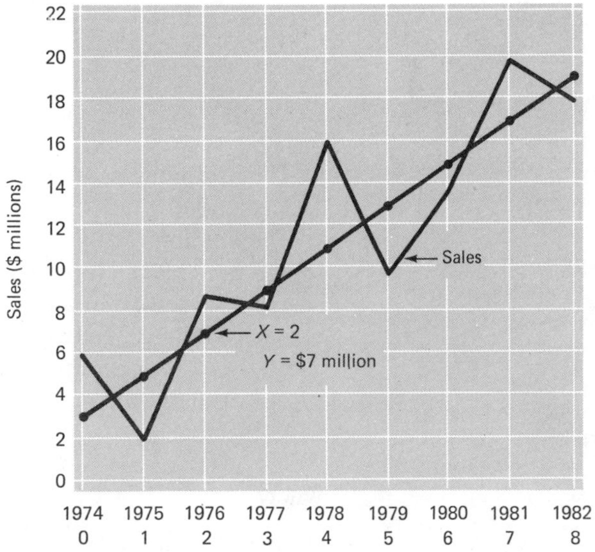

Two methods of determining the linear-trend equation are considered, namely, the **freehand method** and the **method of least squares**.

Freehand method

EXAMPLE

The **freehand method** can be used if an *approximate* linear-trend equation is deemed satisfactory. Using a ruler, the first step is to draw a straight line through the data. It should be drawn through the middle of all of the plots, as shown in Chart 7–5.

a. What is the linear trend equation for the data plotted in Chart 7–5?
b. Based on the equation, what are the predicted sales for 1992 and 1995?

**CHART 7–5
A linear freehand
trend line**

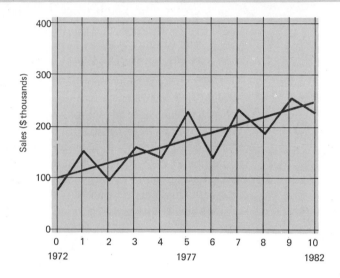

SOLUTION

The beginning year (1972) is designated the origin, or zero year. The year 1973 is coded 1; 1974 is coded 2; . . . ; and 1982 is coded 10.

The line intercepts the Y-axis in the zero year (1972) at $100,000. Therefore, a is 100,000. Note that the straight line representing the path of average sales increased from about $100,000 in 1972 to $250,000 in 1982. Sales increased $150,000, found by $250,000 − $100,000, in the 10-year period, or $15,000 per year on the average. Therefore, b is 15,000.

The straight-line equation is:

$$\overline{Y}_p = 100 + 15X \text{ (in \$ thousands)}$$

where:

Sales are in thousands of dollars.
The origin, or zero year, is 1972.
X increases by one unit for each year.

The trend equation can be used to forecast sales for 1992 (year 20), for example, and for 1995 ($X = 23$.)

For 1992 ($X = 20$):

$$\bar{Y}_p = a + bX$$
$$= 100,000 + 15,000(20)$$
$$= 400,000 \text{ dollars}$$

For 1995 ($X = 23$):

$$\bar{Y}_p = a + bX$$
$$= 100,000 + 15,000(23)$$
$$= 445,000 \text{ dollars}$$

— SELF-REVIEW 7-1 —

a. $\bar{Y}_p = a + bX$
     $= 300 - 10X$ (in thousands of units)

Production decreased from 300 to 100 in 20 years.
$b = (100 - 300)/20 = -200/20 = -10$.

b.   1987 is time period 25.
     $\bar{Y}_p = 300 - 10(25) = 50$ (in thousands).

(A reminder: cover the answers in the left-hand column.)

The production of gears since 1962 for the Rosalind Gear Company is portrayed in the following chart. A straight line has been drawn through the production data.

a.   What is the equation for the straight line drawn through the production data?

b.   Based on the trend equation, what is the forecast of production for 1987?

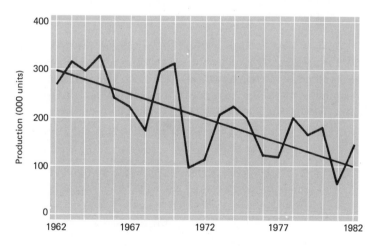

The freehand method for determining the straight-line equation has a serious drawback—namely, the position of the line depends on the judgment of the individual who drew the line. For example, three different individuals might arrive at three different equations for the same data (see Chart 7-6).

Individual A's equation would be approximately $\bar{Y}_p = 15 + 2.3X$.
Individual B's equation would be approximately $\bar{Y}_p = 20 + 1.6X$.
Individual C's equation would be approximately $\bar{Y}_p = 25 + 1.0X$.

**CHART 7–6
Three possible
straight lines**

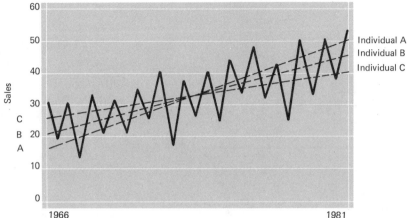

The three equations are not identical because the *Y*-intercepts and the slopes of the three lines are different.

Because of the subjective judgment involved, the freehand method should be used only when a quick approximation of the trend-line equation is needed.

**Least squares
method**

The **least squares method** of arriving at the straight line gives the "best-fitting" line. The equation for the line can be computed using either a **direct method** or a **coded method**. There are two differences in the methods—the placement of the zero period of time (the origin) and the formulas used.

Using the direct method, two equations are solved simultaneously to arrive at the least squares trend equation. They are:

$$\text{I:} \quad \Sigma Y = Na + b\Sigma X$$
$$\text{II:} \quad \Sigma XY = a\Sigma X + b\Sigma X^2$$

EXAMPLE

The sales of a grocery chain since 1978 are (in $ millions)

Year	Sales (000,000)
1978	$ 7
1979	10
1980	9
1981	11
1982	13

Using the direct method, what is the least squares trend equation?

SOLUTION

The first time period (1978) is called the origin, and X is given the value of 0. The second time period (1979) becomes 1; the year 1980 becomes 2; and so on. These are shown in Table 7–1 along with the needed calculations.

TABLE 7–1
Computations for the least squares method (direct method) of determining the trend equation

Year	Y Sales ($000,000)	X	XY	X²
1978	$ 7	0	0	0
1979	10	1	10	1
1980	9	2	18	4
1981	11	3	33	9
1982	13	4	52	16
Total	$50	10	113	30

N is the number of years of data. Substituting the appropriate values from Table 7–1, we get:

$$\text{I:} \quad \Sigma Y = Na + b\Sigma X$$
$$\text{II:} \quad \Sigma XY = a\Sigma X + b\Sigma X^2$$
$$50 = 5a + 10b$$
$$113 = 10a + 30b$$

Equation I was multiplied by 10, and equation II by 5 to eliminate a:

$$500 = 50a + 100b$$
$$565 = 50a + 150b$$

Subtracting equation II from equation I, we get:

$$\text{I:} \quad 500 = 50a + 100b$$
$$\text{II:} \quad -565 = -50a + -150b$$
$$\overline{\quad -65 = \qquad\qquad -50b}$$
$$b = 1.3$$

This b value can be substituted in the original equation I, or equation II, to solve for a.

$$\text{Equation I:} \quad 50 = 5a + 10b$$
$$50 = 5a + 10(1.3)$$
$$a = 7.4$$

The equation is:

$$\overline{Y}_p = 7.4 + 1.3X$$

where:

Sales are in millions of dollars.
The origin, or zero time period is midyear 1978, that is, July 1, 1978.
X increases by 1 unit for each year.

The average monthly amount of scrap produced by a machine shop during the years 1977–81 is:

Year	Average monthly amount of scrap (tons)
1977	 2
1978	 4
1979	 3
1980	 5
1981	 6

a. Using the direct method, determine the least squares trend equation.

b. What is the predicted average monthly amount of scrap for 1987?

a. $\overline{Y}_p = 2.2 + 0.9X$ (origin 1977).

$$20 = 5a + 10b$$
$$49 = 10a + 30b$$

Multiplying equation I by 2:

$$40 = 10a + 20b$$
$$49 = 10a + 30b$$
$$\overline{-9 = -10b}$$
$$b = 0.9$$

Then,

$$20 = 5a + 10(0.9)$$
$$11 = 5a$$
$$a = 2.2$$

b. 1987 is year 10. Then, $\overline{Y}_p = 2.2 + 0.9(10) = 11.2$ tons.

The direct method of determining the least squares trend equation by solving two equations simultaneously is time consuming if there are a large number of time periods, say 15 years, and the magnitude of the numbers is large. An alternative method, called the **coded method**, is recommended in such cases.

For an *odd* number of years, the origin (zero time period), using the coded method, is the center year. For an odd number of months, the origin would be the center month. The lowercase letter x, representing time, has been substituted in the coded method to distinguish it from the capital X which was used in the direct method.

The formulas for a and b using the coded method are:[2]

---

[2] The two equations solved simultaneously using the direct method have the first time period as the origin.

$$\text{I: } \Sigma Y = na + b\Sigma X$$
$$\text{II: } \Sigma XY = a\Sigma X + b\Sigma X^2$$

The origin using the coded method is the middle time period. Therefore, $\Sigma x = 0$. Thus, the first equation becomes:

$$\text{I: } \Sigma Y = na$$

and:

$$a = \frac{\Sigma Y}{n}$$

The second equation becomes:

$$\text{II: } \Sigma xY = b\Sigma x^2$$

and:

$$b = \frac{\Sigma xY}{\Sigma x^2}$$

$$a = \frac{\Sigma Y}{n} \qquad b = \frac{\Sigma x Y}{\Sigma x^2}$$

EXAMPLE

The sales of a grocery chain since 1978 are repeated below.

Year	Sales ($000,000)
1978	$ 7
1979	10
1980	9
1981	11
1982	13

What is the least squares trend-line equation using the coded method?

SOLUTION

Note that there are an odd number of years. The center year (1980) is the origin. The time period prior to the origin (1979) is coded -1, the year following the origin (1981) is coded $+1$, and so on.

The trend equation is $\bar{Y}_p = 10 + 1.3x$

where:

Sales are in millions of dollars.
The origin, or zero year, is midyear 1980, i.e., July 1, 1980.
x increases by 1 unit for each year.

The needed calculations are in Table 7–2.
Determining a and b:

$$a = \frac{\Sigma Y}{n} = \frac{50}{5} = 10$$

$$b = \frac{\Sigma x Y}{\Sigma x^2} = \frac{13}{10} = 1.3$$

$$\bar{Y}_p = 10 + 1.3x \text{ (in \$ millions)}$$

TABLE 7–2
Computations for the least squares method (coded method) of determining the trend equation

Year	Sales Y ($000,000)	x	xY	x²
1978	$ 7	−2	−14	4
1979	10	−1	−10	1
1980	9	0	0	0
1981	11	1	11	1
1982	13	2	26	4
	50		+13	10

Note that the equations derived using the direct method and the coded method have the same b value because the slope is identical. The a values are different only to the extent that each method has a different origin.

$$\text{Direct method:} \quad \bar{Y}_p = 7.4 + 1.3X \text{ (origin 1978)}$$
$$\text{Coded method:} \quad \bar{Y}_p = 10.0 + 1.3x \text{ (origin 1980)}$$

The equations would yield the same predictions for 1992. The year 1992 is year 14, using the direct method, and year 12, using the coded method.

$$\text{Direct method:} \quad \bar{Y}_p = 7.4 + 1.3(14) = \$25.6 \text{ million}$$
$$\text{Coded method:} \quad \bar{Y}_p = 10.0 + 1.3(12) = \$25.6 \text{ million}$$

SELF-REVIEW 7-3

a. $\bar{Y}_p = 4 + 0.9x$ (origin 1979)

Y	X	XY	X²
2	-2	-4	4
4	-1	-4	1
3	0	0	0
5	1	5	1
6	2	12	4
20		9	10

$$a = \frac{\Sigma Y}{n} = \frac{20}{5} = 4$$

$$b = \frac{\Sigma xY}{\Sigma x^2} = \frac{9}{10} = 0.9$$

b. $\bar{Y}_p = 4 + 0.9x = 4 + 0.9(8) = 11.2$ tons—same answer as in Self-Review 7-2.

The data on the average monthly amount of scrap produced by a machine shop is repeated from Self-Review 7-1.

Year	Average monthly scrap (tons)
1977	2
1978	4
1979	3
1980	5
1981	6

a. What is the equation for the straight line using the coded method?

b. What is your prediction for 1987? Does it agree with your predicted average monthly scrap computed in Self-Review 7-2?

If there is an *even* number of time periods, the origin falls between the middle two. The time periods *prior to* the center period are scaled -1, -3, -5, and so on. The time periods *following* the center period are scaled $+1$, $+3$, $+5$, and so on. Thus, since the distance between each year is 2 units, x is half that distance, or equal to 6 months.

A partially solved problem involving an even number of time periods is given in Self-Review 7-4.

=========================== **SELF-REVIEW 7–4** ===========================

a. The straight-line equation is:

$$\overline{Y}_p = 5 + 0.657x$$

where:

Exports (Y) are in millions of dollars.
The origin is January 1, 1980 (that is, halfway between July 1, 1979, and July 1, 1980).
x increases by 2 units for each year (or x increases by 1 unit for each six months).

$$a = \frac{\Sigma Y}{n} = \frac{30}{6} = 5 \qquad b = \frac{\Sigma xY}{\Sigma x^2} = \frac{46}{70} = 0.657$$

b. 1977: $x = -5$, $\overline{Y}_p = \$1.715$ million
    1981: $x = +3$, $\overline{Y}_p = \$6.971$ million
c. 1990 is coded 21. $\overline{Y}_p = \$18.797$ million.

Computations for the least squares method (coded method) of determining the trend equation

Year	x	Exports Y (000,000)	xY	x^2
1977	−5	$ 2	−10	25
1978	−3	4	−12	9
1979	−1	3	− 3	1
1980	+1	6	+ 6	1
1981	+3	5	+15	9
1982	+5	10	+50	25
		$30	$46	70

a. Determine the straight-line equation.
b. Find the plots on the straight line for 1977 and 1981.
c. What are the predicted exports for 1990?

EXERCISES

(A reminder: The answers and method of solution for selected exercises are in Appendix A.)

1. *a.* Using the freehand method, draw a straight line through the data and estimate the linear equation for the following sales series. Use 1962 as the origin.
   b. What was the average annual increase in sales?
   c. Based on the trend equation, what is the sales forecast for 1988?

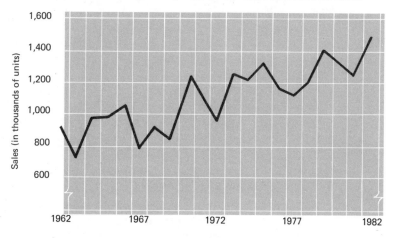

2. *a.* Using the freehand method, estimate the trend equation for the following production series. Use 1966 as the origin, or zero year.
   b. What was the average annual change in production?
   c. What is the predicted production in 1986 based on the trend equation?

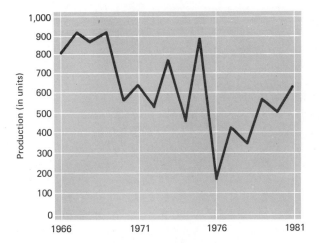

Questions 3 and 4 are based on the following birth and death rates per 1,000 population in the United States since 1930.

Year	Birth rate	Death rate
1930 .... 21.3		11.5
1935 .... 18.7		11.2
1940 .... 19.4		10.8
1945 .... 20.5		11.0
1950 .... 23.9		9.6
1955 .... 24.9		9.3
1960 .... 23.8		9.5
1965 .... 19.6		9.4
1970 .... 18.2		9.4
1975 .... 14.7		8.9
1980 .... 15.3		8.8

Source: U.S. Bureau of the Census, *Current Population Reports*, series P-25, nos. 601, 632, and 802.

3. *a.* Plot the birth rates in the form of a chart.

   b. Using either the direct method (solving two equations simultaneously) or the coded method, determine the least squares trend equation (to the nearest 10th).

   c. Compute the coordinates for three points and plot the straight line on the chart.

   d. Based on the straight-line equation, what is the estimated birth rate for 1990? Explain what it indicates.

4. *a.* Plot the death rates in the form of a chart.

   b. Using either the direct method (solving two equations simultaneously) or the coded method, determine the least squares trend equation (to the nearest 10th).

   c. Compute the coordinates for three points and plot the straight line on the chart.

   d. Based on the straight-line equation, what is the estimated death rate in 1990? Explain what it indicates.

NONLINEAR TRENDS

A straight-line trend is used when it is believed that the time series data are increasing (or decreasing) by *equal amounts*, on the average, from one time period to another.

Logarithmic straight-line trend

Data that increase (or decrease) by *increasing amounts* over a period of time appear *curvilinear* when plotted on paper having an arithmetic scale. To put it another way, data that increase (or decrease) by *equal percents, or proportions*, over a period of time appear curvilinear on arithmetic paper. (See Chart 7–7).

**CHART 7–7
Imports of a firm
plotted on paper
having an arithmetic
scale**

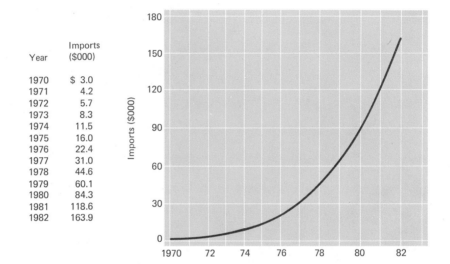

Year	Imports ($000)
1970	$ 3.0
1971	4.2
1972	5.7
1973	8.3
1974	11.5
1975	16.0
1976	22.4
1977	31.0
1978	44.6
1979	60.1
1980	84.3
1981	118.6
1982	163.9

The same data plotted on paper having a ratio (semilogarithmic) scale approximates a straight line. (See Chart 7–8).

The trend equation for a time series which does approximate a linear trend when plotted on ratio paper can be computed by using the logarithms of the data and the least squares method.

The general equation for the logarithmic trend equation using the coded method is:

$$\log \bar{Y}_p = \log a + \log b(x)$$

where:

$$\log a = \frac{\Sigma \log Y}{n}$$

$$\log b = \frac{\Sigma(x \log Y)}{\Sigma x^2}$$

**CHART 7–8
Imports of a firm
plotted on paper
having a ratio
(semilogarithmic)
scale**

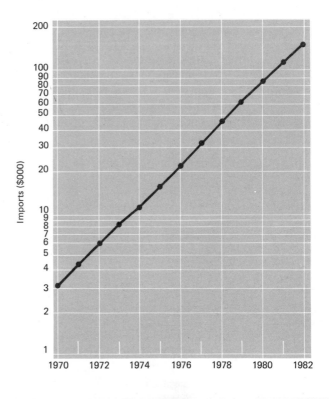

EXAMPLE

The imports of the firm plotted previously in Charts 7–7 and 7–8 are
repeated in Table 7–3.

**TABLE 7–3
Imports of a firm,
1970–1982**

Year	Imports ($000)
1970	$ 3.0
1971	4.2
1972	5.7
1973	8.3
1974	11.5
1975	16.0
1976	22.4
1977	31.0
1978	44.6
1979	60.1
1980	84.3
1981	118.6
1982	163.9

What is the logarithmic trend equation for the import data?

SOLUTION

The computations for the various sums are shown in Table 7-4. The logarithms are from Appendix B.

TABLE 7-4
Computations needed for the logarithmic straight-line equation

Year	Imports (000) Y	Log of Y	x	x(log Y)	x^2
1970	$ 3.0	0.4771	−6	−2.8626	36
1971	4.2	0.6232	−5	−3.1160	25
1972	5.7	0.7559	−4	−3.0236	16
1973	8.3	0.9191	−3	−2.7573	9
1974	11.5	1.0607	−2	−2.1214	4
1975	16.0	1.2041	−1	1.2041	1
1976	22.4	1.3502	0	0.0000	0
1977	31.0	1.4914	1	1.4914	1
1978	44.6	1.6493	2	3.2986	4
1979	60.1	1.7789	3	5.3367	9
1980	84.3	1.9258	4	7.7032	16
1981	118.6	2.0740	5	10.3700	25
1982	163.9	2.2145	6	13.2870	36
		17.5242		26.4019	182

$$\log a = \frac{\Sigma \log Y}{n} = \frac{17.5242}{13} = 1.3480$$

$$\log b = \frac{\Sigma(x \log Y)}{\Sigma x^2} = \frac{26.4019}{182} = 0.1451$$

The logarithmic equation is:

$$\log \overline{Y}_p = 1.3480 + 0.1451x$$

where:

Imports (Y) are in thousands of dollars.
The origin, or zero year, is 1976 (July 1, 1976).
x increases by 1 unit for each year.

Since the straight-line trend is logarithmic, the slope of the line, or b, represents a *percent change* in Y for each increase of one in X. Thus, the concept and computation of b are similar to the geometric mean, discussed in Chapter 4, which gives the percent change in Y (sales production, and so on) from one time period to another.

The logarithm of b is 0.1451 and its antilog is 1.40. Subtracting one from this number, it indicates that the imports of the firm increased about 40 percent on the average each year from 1970 to 1982.

SELF-REVIEW 7-5
---

a. Log $Y_p = 1.4292 + 0.409x$ (coded method) (origin is 1980) (x increases by 1 unit for each year) (sales in millions).

Year	Y	Log of Y	x	x log Y	x²
1978	$ 2.13	0.3284	-2	-0.6568	4
1979	18.10	1.2577	-1	-1.2577	1
1980	39.80	1.5999	0	0	0
1981	81.40	1.9106	1	1.9106	1
1982	112.00	2.0492	2	4.0984	4
		7.1458		+4.0945	10

$$a = \frac{\Sigma \log Y}{n} \qquad \frac{7.1458}{5} = 1.4292$$

$$b = \frac{\Sigma(x \log Y)}{\Sigma x^2} \qquad \frac{+4.0945}{10} = +0.4094$$

b. 157 percent. (The antilog of b [0.4094] is about 2.57. One [1] is subtracted from the antilog of b.)

Sales of Loviedovie Manufacturing Company since 1978 are:

Year	Sales ($000,000)
1978	$ 2.13
1979	18.10
1980	39.80
1981	81.40
1982	112.00

a. Using the coded method, find the logarithmic straight-line equation for the sales data.
b. Sales increased about what percent annually on the average?

The coordinates of a point on the line can be arrived at by substituting the appropriate value of x in the logarithmic trend line equation, $\log \bar{Y}_p = \log a + \log b(x)$.

EXAMPLE

Returning to the import problem, what are the coordinates of the point on the line for 1976?

SOLUTION

The year 1976 is the origin where $x = 0$. Substituting:

$$\log \bar{Y}_p = \log a + \log b(x)$$
$$= 1.3480 + 0.1451(0)$$
$$= 1.3480$$

The antilog of 1.3480 is about 22.3. Thus, the coordinates of one point on the line are $x = 0$, $Y = 22.3$. The coordinates of several other points are computed as follows:

Year	x	Log of $\bar{Y}_p$	Antilog	Coordinates x	Coordinates Y
1970	-6	0.4774	3.002	-6	3.0
1972	-4	0.7676	5.856	-4	5.9
1979	+3	1.7833	60.720	+3	60.7
1982	+6	2.2186	165.400	+6	165.4

The actual imports and the straight-line trend values have been plotted on Chart 7–9.

**CHART 7–9
Imports of a firm and the logarithmic trend line (semilog scale)**

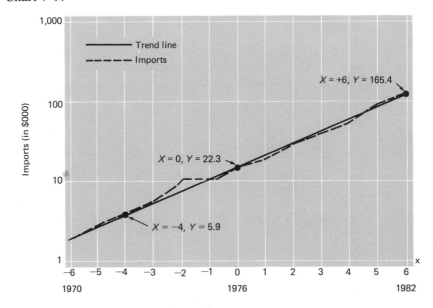

The logarithmic straight line permits forecasts. The forecast of imports for 1990 ($x = 14$) is found by:

$$\log \bar{Y}_p = 1.3480 + 0.1415(14)$$
$$= 3.3794$$

The antilog of 3.3794 is about 2,400. Thus, estimated sales for 1990 are $2,400 thousand, or $2,400,000.

EXERCISES

5. If plotted on arithmetic paper, the following sales series would appear curvilinear. This indicates that sales are increasing at a somewhat constant annual rate (percent).

Year	Sales ($ millions)
1972	$ 8.0
1973	10.4
1974	13.5
1975	17.6
1976	22.8
1977	29.3
1978	39.4
1979	50.5
1980	65.0
1981	84.1
1982	109.0

a. Plot the sales series on semilogarithmic paper.

b. Using the coded method, determine the logarithmic straight-line equation.

c. Determine the coordinates of the points on the straight line for 1973 and 1982.

d. What percent did sales increase on the average during the period 1972–82?

e. Based on the equation, what are the estimated sales for 1986?

6. It appears that the imports of carbon black have been increasing about 10 percent annually on the average.

Year	Imports of carbon black (thousands of tons)
1975	92
1976	101
1977	112
1978	124
1979	135
1980	149
1981	163
1982	180

a. Plot the imports on semilogarithmic paper.

b. Using the coded method, determine the logarithmic straight-line equation.

c. Determine the coordinates of the points on the straight line for 1975 and 1981.

d. Plot the points on your graph.

e. What percent did imports increase, on the average, during the period 1975–82?

f. Based on the equation, what are the estimated imports of carbon black for 1985?

Other trend equations

It should be noted that there are other trend equations which can be applied to time series that do not follow a linear trend. For example, a second-degree polynomial has the equation $\bar{Y}_p = a + bx + cx^2$. Three equations are solved simultaneously.

The second-degree polynomial and other such forecasting techniques will not be considered in this introductory text. Instead, it might be of interest that several computer programs have been designed to fit a number of equations to a set of data in order to find the one that best fits the series. For example, there are several kinds of **contributed programs**. *BASIC* has one entitled REGOR, contributed by Walt Nichols, Woods Hole Oceanographic Institute. It is designed to fit four different equations to the data of interest. The commercial bank prime rates from 1945 to 1976 are used to illustrate.

**Commercial bank
prime rates**

Year	Rate	Year	Rate
1945 .... 1.50%		1961 .... 4.50%	
1946 .... 1.50		1962 .... 4.50	
1947 .... 1.52		1963 .... 4.50	
1948 .... 1.85		1964 .... 4.50	
1949 .... 2.00		1965 .... 4.54	
1950 .... 2.07		1966 .... 5.62	
1951 .... 2.56		1967 .... 5.63	
1952 .... 3.00		1968 .... 6.28	
1953 .... 3.17		1969 .... 7.95	
1954 .... 3.05		1970 .... 7.91	
1955 .... 3.16		1971 .... 5.70	
1956 .... 3.77		1972 .... 5.25	
1957 .... 4.20		1973 .... 8.02	
1958 .... 3.83		1974 .... 10.80	
1959 .... 4.48		1975 .... 7.86	
1960 .... 4.82		1976 .... 6.83	

Source: *The Wall Street Journal,* March 4, 1977, p. 1.

Briefly, EQUATION 1 in the following computer output is the least squares equation found by solving two equations simultaneously and EQUATION 3 is the logarithmic trend equation examined previously. Note that of the four different equations tried, EQUATION 1 explains the largest percent of the variance (84.6393 percent) and is, therefore, considered the best-fitting equation. The semilogarithmic equation (EQUATION 3) is a close second, with 82.2177 percent explained. Another contributed program in the same series includes the second-degree polynomial and other polynomials.

```
EQUATION 1
VARIABLE 2 =    .928508           +         .22189       *LOG OF VAR 1
    84.6392       PERCENT OF THE VARIANCE IN VARIABLE 2 EXPLAINED

EQUATION 2
VARIABLE 2 =   -.993318           +        2.19054       *LOG OF VAR 1
    68.662        PERCENT OF THE VARIANCE IN VARIABLE 2 EXPLAINED

EQUATION 3
LOG(VAR 2)=     .509274           +         .538066E-1   *  VARIABLE 1
ALTERNATE FORM ---
VARIABLE 2 = 1.66408              * 1.05528                 ^VAR 1
    82.2177       PERCENT OF THE VARIANCE IN VARIABLE 2 EXPLAINED

EQUATION 4
LOG(VAR 2) =   -.899734E-1    *(VAR 1^       .58346        )
ALTERNATE FORM --
VARIABLE 2 = .913956           *(VAR 1 ^      .58346        )
    79.0842       PERCENT OF THE VARIANCE IN VARIABLE 2 EXPLAINED
NUMBER OF OBSERVATIONS<TO END TYPE 0>? 0
```

**THE MOVING
AVERAGE METHOD**

The **moving average method** not only is useful in smoothing out a time series, but it is the basic method used in measuring the seasonal fluctuation described in Chapter 8. In contrast to the least squares method, which resulted in expressing the trend in a mathematical equation ($\overline{Y}_p = a + bX$), the *moving average method merely smooths out the fluctuations in the data.* This is accomplished by "moving" the arithmetic mean values through the time series.

To apply the moving average method to a time series, the data should follow a fairly linear trend and have a definite rhythmic pattern of fluctuations which repeats (say, every three years). The data in the following example have three components—trend, cycle, and irregular, abbreviated T, C, and I. There is no seasonal variation because the data are recorded annually. What the moving average method does, in effect, is average out C and I. The residual is trend.

If the duration of the cycles is constant and if the amplitudes of the cycles are equal, the cyclical and irregular fluctuations can be removed entirely using the moving average method. The result is a straight line. For example, in the following time series, the cycle repeats itself every seven years; and the amplitude of each cycle is four. That is, there are exactly four units from the trough (lowest time period) to the peak. The seven-year moving average, therefore, averages out the cyclical and irregular fluctuations perfectly, and the residual is a straight-line trend. (Refer to Table 7–5 and to Chart 7–10.)

The first step in computing the seven-year moving average is to determine the seven-year moving totals. The total of the sales for the first seven years (1957–63 inclusive) is $22 million. This total is positioned opposite the middle

**TABLE 7–5
Exhibit of the
Computations for the
Seven-Year Moving
Average**

Year	Sales ($ millions)	Seven-year moving total	Seven-year moving average
1957	$1		
1958	2		
1959	3		
1960	4	$22	$3.143
1961	5	23	3.285
1962	4	24	3.429
1963	3	25	3.571
1964	2	26	3.714
1965	3	27	3.857
1966	4	28	4.000
1967	5	29	4.143
1968	6	30	4.286
1969	5	31	4.429
1970	4	32	4.571
1971	3	33	4.714
1972	4	34	4.857
1973	5	35	5.000
1974	6	36	5.143
1975	7	37	5.286
1976	6	38	5.429
1977	5	39	5.571
1978	4	40	5.714
1979	5	41	5.857
1980	6		
1981	7		
1982	8		

**CHART 7-10
Sales and seven-year
moving average**

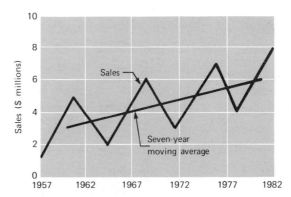

year (1960). Then the total sales for the next seven years (1958–64 inclusive) are computed. A convenient method is to subtract the sales for 1957 from the first seven-year total and then add the sales for 1964. This total ($23 million) is positioned opposite the middle year (1961). This procedure is repeated until all possible seven-year totals are determined. Note that there are no totals for the first three years and the last three years.

Sales, production, and other economic and business series usually do not have (1) periods of oscillation which are of equal length or (2) oscillations which have identical amplitudes. Thus, in actual practice, the application of the moving average method to data does not result precisely in a straight line. For example, the following production series repeats about every five years, but the amplitude of the data varies from one oscillation to another. The trend appears to be upward and somewhat linear. Two moving averages—a three-year moving average and a five-year moving average—have been computed in Table 7–6. The procedure is the same as employed in determining the seven-year moving average in the previous illustration.

**TABLE 7-6
Exhibit of a three-year
moving average and a
five-year moving
average**

Year	Production Y	Three-year moving total	Three-year moving average	Five-year moving total	Five-year moving average
1963	5				
1964	6	19	6.3		
1965	8	24	8.0	34	6.8
1966	10	23	7.7	32	6.4
1967	5	18	6.0	33	6.6
1968	3	15	5.0	35	7.0
1969	7	20	6.7	37	7.4
1970	10	29	9.7	43	8.6
1971	12	33	11.0	49	9.8
1972	11	32	10.7	55	11.0
1973	9	33	11.0	60	12.0
1974	13	37	12.3	66	13.2
1975	15	46	15.3	70	14.0
1976	18	48	16.0	72	14.4
1977	15	44	14.7	73	14.6
1978	11	40	13.3	75	15.0
1979	14	42	14.0	79	15.8
1980	17				
1981	22				

The three-year and the five-year moving averages from Table 7–6 have been plotted in Chart 7–11.

CHART 7–11
Exhibit of a three-year moving average and a five-year moving average

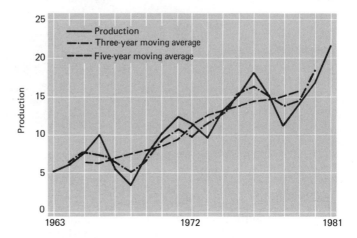

A four-year six-year, and other even-numbered-year moving averages present one minor problem regarding the centering of the moving totals and moving averages. Note in Table 7–7 that there is no center time period, and so the moving totals are positioned between two time periods. The total of the first four years ($42) is positioned between 1975 and 1976. The total of the next fours years is $43. The average of the first four years and the second four years ($10.50 and $10.75 respectively) are averaged and the resulting figure centered on 1976. This procedure is repeated until all possible four-year averages are computed.

TABLE 7–7
Exhibit of a four-year moving average

Year	Sales Y	Four-year moving total	Four-year moving average	Centered four-year moving average
1974	$ 8			
1975	11			
		$42(8 + 11 + 9 + 14)	$10.50($42 ÷ 4)	
1976	9			$10.625
		43(11 + 9 + 14 + 9)	10.75(43 ÷ 4)	
1977	14			10.625
		42	10.50	
1978	9			10.625
		43	10.75	
1979	10			10.000
		37	9.25	
1980	10			9.625
		40	10.00	
1981	8			
1982	12			

SELF-REVIEW 7-6

a.

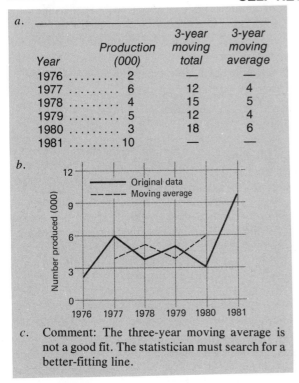

Year	Production (000)	3-year moving total	3-year moving average
1976	2	—	—
1977	6	12	4
1978	4	15	5
1979	5	12	4
1980	3	18	6
1981	10	—	—

b.

c. Comment: The three-year moving average is not a good fit. The statistician must search for a better-fitting line.

a. Compute a three-year moving average for the following production series.

b. Then plot both the original data and the moving average.

Year	Number produced (000)
1976	2
1977	6
1978	4
1979	5
1980	3
1981	10

c. Comment on the fit.

EXPONENTIAL SMOOTHING

The moving-average method discussed in the previous section has traditionally been used to smooth out unwanted fluctuations in a time series. A somewhat more sophisticated method aimed at accomplishing this is called **exponential smoothing**. In its simplest form to be discussed here it is especially useful for short-term forecasts of sales (demand), or a level of inventory needed, where there is no significant long-term trend in the data and no erratic fluctuations from one time period to another. The objective of exponential smoothing, therefore, is twofold—to average out irregular fluctuations and to use the smoothed values for forecasting future demand.

Although the moving-average method and the exponential smoothing technique are designed to smooth out unwanted fluctuations using past data, a fundamental difference exists between the two approaches. The three-year moving average, for example, uses only three time periods to arrive at an average value. And all three time periods are weighted equally. The exponential smoothing technique, however, uses all the past data in order to arrive at an average value. Also, as will be shown shortly, the method gives more weight to more-recent time periods than to earlier periods. The weight given to the actual values (sales, number of items in stock, etc.) decreases exponentially, which is why the method is called exponential smoothing.

Putting more weight on recent data and less on data in the more distant past is logical. For example, recent demand for a product such as alkaline batteries, which has increased rapidly due to the popularity of electronic games and toys, is much more closely related to demand in the near future than is the demand, say, one or two years ago.

The formula for a smoothed value for a time period designated S_t is:

$$S_t = \alpha A_t + (1 - \alpha) S_{t-1}$$

where:

S_t is the smoothed value for time period t.
A_t is the actual value for time period t.
α is a **smoothing constant**. It can assume any value between 0 and 1.

Using this general formula, we will now design specific formulas for the first, second, and third periods of a time series. The time series may encompass days, weeks, months, quarters, years, or other periods.

The smoothed value for the first time period in a series, designated S_1, is the same as the actual value for the first time period.

$$S_1 = A_1$$

The smoothed value for the second time period, S_2, is:

$$S_2 = \alpha A_2 + (1 - \alpha)S_1$$

Similarly, the smoothed value for the third period, S_3, is:

$$S_3 = \alpha A_3 + (1 - \alpha)S_2$$

EXAMPLE

The actual sales (demand) for SilverBand, a new alkaline battery, for the first eight months since its introduction are shown in Table 7–8.

TABLE 7–8
Sales of SilverBand

Month	Time period	Sales ($000)
March	1	$203
April	2	196
May	3	198
June	4	206
July	5	210
August	6	209
September	7	206
October	8	199

Using a smoothing constant α (the Greek letter alpha) of 0.2, what are the smoothed values for March, April, and May?

SOLUTION

March is time period 1. The actual sales A_1 for that month total $203 thousand, as shown in Table 7–8. So, the smoothed value for March $S_1 = A_1 = \$203,000$.

April is time period 2. The actual sales for that month, A_2, are $196,000. The smoothed sales from the previous month, S_1, are $203,000. Solving for the smoothed value for April:

$$\begin{aligned}
S_2 &= \alpha A_2 + (1 - \alpha)S_1 \\
&= 0.2(\$196) + (1 - 0.2)\,(\$203) \\
&= \$39.20 + \$162.40 \\
&= \$201,600
\end{aligned}$$

May is time period 3. The actual sales for that month, A_3, are $198,000. The smoothed sales from the previous month, S_2, are $201,600. Solving for the smoothed value for May:

$$\begin{aligned}
S_3 &= \alpha A_3 + (1 - \alpha)S_2 \\
&= 0.2(\$198) + (1 - 0.2)\,(\$201.6) \\
&= \$39.60 + \$161.28 \\
&= \$200,880.
\end{aligned}$$

SELF-REVIEW 7–7

a.

$$\begin{aligned}
S_4 &= \alpha A_4 + (1 - \alpha)S_3 \\
&= 0.2(\$206) + (1 - 0.2)(\$200.88) \\
\end{aligned}$$

b.

$$\begin{aligned}
&= \$41.20 + \$160.704 \\
&= \$201.900.
\end{aligned}$$

For June:

a. Design a formula to determine the smoothed sales.
b. Solve for the smoothed sales.

The actual sales and the smoothed sales for the eight-month period are in Table 7–9, and they are portrayed graphically in Chart 7–12. Note that the

TABLE 7–9
Actual sales and smoothed sales
($\alpha = 0.2$)

	Sales	
Month	Actual A_t	Smoothed S_t
March	$203	$203.00
April	196	201.60
May	198	200.88
June	206	201.90
July	210	203.52
August	209	204.62
September	206	204.90
October	199	203.72

CHART 7–12
Actual sales and smoothed sales ($\alpha = 0.2$)

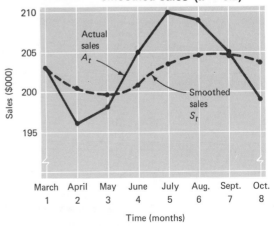

smoothed series using $\alpha = 0.2$ averages out the month-to-month fluctuations quite well. This is the intent of the exponential smoothing technique.

How would the smoothed data appear for other smoothing constants? Alphas of 0.1, 0.2, 0.6, and 0.8 were selected and the smoothed values computed using the same alkaline battery sales data. (See Table 7–10.)

TABLE 7–10
Actual values and smoothed values for alphas of 0.1, 0.2, 0.6, and 0.8

Month	Actual sales ($000)	Smoothed sales ($000)			
		0.1	0.2	0.6	0.8
March	$203	$203.00	$203.00	$203.00	$203.00
April	196	202.30	201.60	198.80	197.40
May	198	201.87	200.88	198.32	197.88
June	206	202.28	201.90	202.93	204.38
July	210	203.06	203.52	207.17	208.88
August	209	203.65	204.62	208.27	208.98
September	206	203.88	204.90	206.91	206.60
October	199	203.40	203.72	202.16	200.52

The smoothed curves for the alphas selected are in Chart 7–13. Note that the smoothing constants of 0.1 and 0.2 tend to smooth out the irregular fluctuations in the actual data more than do the constants of 0.6 and 0.8. Thus, if the alpha selected is too high, an excessive amount of weight is placed by the formula on the most recent actual values (sales in this illustration). As a result, the unwanted fluctuations are not satisfactorily averaged out. The smoothed curve for $\alpha = 0.8$, for example, rather closely follows the actual data. Conversely, selecting a smoothing constant that is too low (such as 0.1 in the sales illustration) puts very little weight on recent actual values. The smoothed values, therefore, might not reflect any changes in the actual sales data. Which smoothing constant is used depends in part on the type of application and to what use the smoothed data is put.

CHART 7–13
Actual sales and smoothed sales for selected smoothing constants

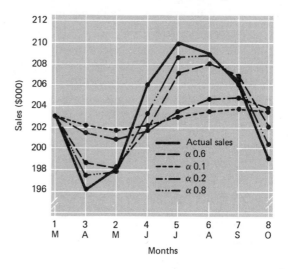

The computations for the smoothed values for a large number of periods can be done quickly by a computer. A program in the BASIC language was written to compute the smoothed value and to give the absolute differences between the actual value and the smoothed value. Also included in the program is the calculation of the mean absolute deviation (MAD). It is computed using the following formula:

$$MAD = \frac{\Sigma|A_t - S_t|}{n}$$

where:

S_t is the smoothed value in period t.
A_t is the actual value for period t.
| | indicates the absolute value; that is, the value without regard to sign.
n is the number of periods considered.

The MAD value is used as a basis to compare different values of α. In comparing two values for α, the smaller MAD value indicates a closer tracking of the actual data by the smoothed data.

EXAMPLE

The factory sales of trucks and busses in the United States since 1964 are to be smoothed using (1) a smoothing constant (α) of 0.3, and (2) a MAD value, computed using a BASIC computer program.

SOLUTION

The actual factory sales are in the left column of the following computer output, and the smoothed sales are in the center column for the 17-year period. The MAD value is at the end of the listing.

```
TYPE A 1 IF YOU WISH TO TRY ANOTHER ALPHA VALUE
? 1
INPUT THE VALUE OF ALPHA? .3


    PERIOD          ACTUAL          SMOOTHED          DIFFERENCE
                    VALUE           VALUE

       1            1540.00         1540.00              0.00
       2            1751.00         1603.30            147.70
       3            1731.00         1641.61             89.39
       4            1539.00         1610.83             71.83
       5            1896.00         1696.38            199.62
       6            1923.00         1764.37            158.64
       7            1692.00         1742.66             50.66
       8            2053.00         1835.76            217.24
       9            2446.00         2018.83            427.17
      10            2979.00         2306.88            672.12
      11            2727.00         2432.92            294.08
      12            2272.00         2384.64            112.64
      13            2979.00         2562.95            416.05
      14            3442.00         2826.66            615.34
      15            3706.00         3090.47            615.54
      16            3037.00         3074.43             37.43
      17            1667.00         2652.20            985.20

   THE MEAN ABSOLUTE DEVIATION (MAD) IS   300.625
```

The actual factory sales and the smoothed values for an alpha of 0.3 are portrayed in Chart 7–14.

**CHART 7–14
Actual sales and
smoothed sales of
trucks and busses
($\alpha = 0.3$)**

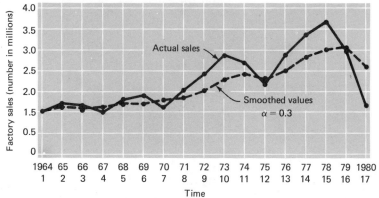

Source: *Survey of Current Business,* April 1981, p. 36, and previous issues.

The problem was rerun for selected alphas. As expected, the MAD value decreased as the value of alpha increased. (See Table 7–11).

**TABLE 7–11
MAD values for
selected alphas**

Alpha	MAD value
0.1	524
0.2	377
0.3	301
0.4	251
0.8	79
0.99	4

The listing for the BASIC program for this problem is at the end of the chapter.

**CHAPTER
SUMMARY**

It was pointed out that firms manufacturing items such as television sets, books, lamps, or ice cream cannot wait until consumers decide what they want. Instead, management tries to anticipate future demand and have the goods on hand ready to satisfy expected demand. Time series analysis is concerned with describing past trends, and, with predicting the future on the basis of past internal data.

A time series may include secular trends and seasonal, cyclical, and irregular variations. The emphasis in this chapter is on describing secular trends. If the past data approximate a straight line, the equation used is $\overline{Y}_p = a + bX$, where a is the Y-intercept and b the slope of the line.

If the data, when plotted on paper having an arithmetic scale, appear to be curvilinear, it is evident that the series is changing by equal percents. In those instances, the logarithmic trend equation in the form of $\log \bar{Y}_p = \log a + \log b(x)$ is used.

If there is interest in smoothing out unwanted fluctuations in a time series, a moving average or exponential smoothing may be employed. Exponential smoothing is particularly useful to smooth out irregular fluctuations and to use the smoothed values for forecasting future demand. It has the advantage of giving more weight to recent data, and the weights decrease exponentially as the time periods are moved forward.

CHAPTER OUTLINE

Time series analysis

I. Time series analysis.
    A. Definition. Loosely defined, time series are the records of sales, production, and so on over a period of time. The time period can be years, months, weeks, days, etc.
    B. Purpose. To make long-term or short-term forecasts.
    C. Components of a time series.
        1. *Trend.*
        2. *Seasonal.*
        3. *Cyclical.*
        4. *Irregular.*
    D. Linear trend. Long-term trend of sales and other business series often approximates a straight line. Equation for straight line is

$$\bar{Y}_p = a + bX$$

where:

    a   is the *Y*-intercept, that is, the estimated value of *Y* when $X = 0$.
    b   is the slope of line, that is, the average change in $\bar{Y}$ for each change of one in *X*.
    X   is any value of *X* (time) selected.

    E. Freehand method of determining straight-line equation.
        1. *Use.* Used for quick approximation. Draw a straight line through data. In the equation $\bar{Y}_p = a + bX$, the value of *a* is the point where the line crosses the *Y*-axis. Example:

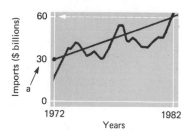

Note imports went from \$30 billion to \$60 billion in 10 years, or increased $3 billion on the average every year. $b = 3$. Equation is

$$\bar{Y}_p = 30 + 3X$$

    2. *Disadvantage.* Position of freehand line subject to human error. Resulting forecast, therefore, might contain sizable error.

F. Least squares method of determining straight-line equation.
    1. *Use.* When the best-fitting straight line is required.
    2. *Direct method* of computation involves solving two equations simultaneously.

$$\Sigma Y = na + b\Sigma X$$
$$\Sigma XY = a\Sigma X + b\Sigma X^2$$

where the origin, or zero, is the first year (or first time period)
    3. *Coded method.* The middle time period is the origin. To find a and b:

$$a = \frac{\Sigma Y}{n} \qquad b = \frac{\Sigma xY}{\Sigma x^2}$$

G. Nonlinear trends.
    1. *Logarithmic straight-line trend equation* should be used for forecasts when the time series is increasing, or decreasing, by increasing amounts; that is, the series is increasing by equal percents. For logarithmic line: $\log \bar{Y}_p = \log a + \log b(x)$.

$$\log a = \frac{\Sigma \log Y}{n} \qquad \log b = \frac{\Sigma(x \log Y)}{\Sigma x^2}$$

H. Moving average.
    1. *Purpose.* To smooth out unwanted fluctuations.
    2. *Procedure.* Replace actual sales, production, etc. with a three-year or five-year moving average.

I. Exponential smoothing.
    1. Purpose. To average out irregular fluctuations and to forecast future demand or sales.
    2. General formula for time period S_t is:

$$S_t = \alpha A_t + (1 - \alpha)S_{t-1}$$

where:

    S_t is the smoothed value for time period t.
    A_t is the actual value for time period t.
    α is a smoothing constant that can assume any value between 0 and 1.

**CHAPTER
EXERCISES**

7. *a.* Using the freehand method, estimate the linear equation for the following production series. Use 1960 as the origin.

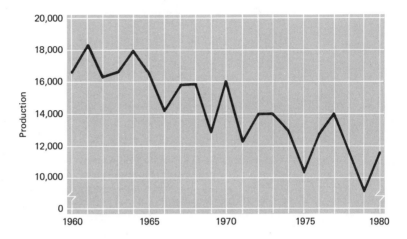

b. What was the average annual decrease in production?

c. Based on the trend equation, what is the forecast for 1985?

8. *a.* Using the freehand method, estimate the trend equation for the following personal income series. Use 1967 as the origin, or zero year.

b. What is the average annual increase in personal income?

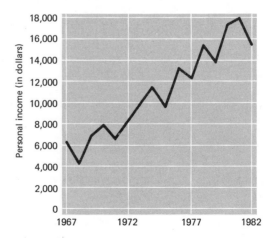

Questions 9–12 are based on the following historical information from the annual reports of the respective firms.

Year	Kaiser Aluminum total revenues ($ millions)	Boise Cascade production of newsprint (000 tons)	American Electric Power coal purchased (millions of tons)	Merrill Lynch earnings per share
1971	$ 922	—	—	—
1972	1,007	—	—	—
1973	1,314	—	—	—
1974	1,773	389	—	—
1975	1,597	332	26.0	—
1976	1,860	328	28.1	$3.01
1977	2,234	379	30.3	1.25
1978	2,542	329	30.5	2.00
1979	3,021	379	30.2	3.26
1980	3,351	418	28.3	5.51

9. Using the revenues of the Kaiser Aluminum & Chemical Corporation:
   a. Plot the revenues in the form of a line chart.
   b. Using the direct method (solving two equations simultaneously), or the coded method, determine the least squares trend equation (to nearest whole number).
   c. Compute the coordinates for three points and plot the straight line on the chart.
   d. Based on the straight-line equation, estimate the total revenues for 1985.

10. Using the production of newsprint of the Boise Cascade Corporation:
    a. Plot the production in the form of a line chart.
    b. Using either the direct method or the coded method, determine the least squares trend equation (to the nearest whole number).
    c. Compute the coordinates for three points and plot the straight line on the chart.
    d. Based on the straight-line equation, estimate production for 1984.

11. Using the amount of coal purchased by American Electric Power:
    a. Plot the data in the form of a line chart.
    b. Using either the direct method or the coded method, determine the least squares trend equation (to the nearest 10th).
    c. Compute the coordinates for three points and plot the straight line on the chart.
    d. Based on the straight-line equation, estimate the amount of coal to be purchased in 1985.

12. Using the earnings per share of Merrill Lynch and Company,
    a. Plot the earnings in the form of a line chart.
    b. Using either the direct method or the coded method, determine the least squares trend equation (to the nearest cent).
    c. Compute the coordinates for three points and plot the straight line on the chart.
    d. Based on the straight-line equation, estimate the earnings for 1984.

13. It appears that the sales of the firm shown in the following table are increasing about 20 percent each year on the average. In order to emphasize this steady growth:
    a. Plot the sales data on semilogarithmic paper.
    b. Compute the logarithmic straight-line equation.

c. For 1979, what are the coordinates of the point on the line?
d. What percent per annum are the sales increasing on the average?

Year	Sales (in $ thousands)
1977	$ 820
1978	990
1979	1,190
1980	1,430
1981	1,720
1982	2,060

14. The sales of a product since 1967 are:

Year	Sales (in millions)	Year	Sales (in millions)
1967	$ 8	1975	$14
1968	6	1976	12
1969	5	1977	12
1970	7	1978	13
1971	10	1979	16
1972	8	1980	19
1973	9	1981	14
1974	10	1982	9

The sales series seems to have recurring periods of high sales and low sales.
a. Plot the data on arithmetic paper.
b. Describe these rhythmic fluctuations by applying the moving average method to data. (It may take some experimentation to arrive at an appropriate average to smooth out the fluctuations. You might want to try a three-, four-, five-, six-, or seven-year moving average.)
c. Plot the average, or averages, on the chart.
d. Which average seems to best smooth out the fluctuations?

15. If a computer is available, use the BASIC program given at the end of this chapter designed for exponential smoothing and apply it to the following sales of passenger cars. (Only 900 and 901 need to be changed.)

Year	New factory sales of passenger cars from U.S. plants (000)	Year	New factory sales of passenger cars from U.S. plants (000)
1964	7,751	1973	9,658
1965	9,305	1974	7,331
1966	8,598	1975	6,713
1967	7,436	1976	8,498
1968	8,822	1977	9,201
1969	8,223	1978	9,165
1970	6,546	1979	8,419
1971	8,584	1980	6,400
1972	8,823		

Source: Survey of Current Business, April 1981, p. 36, and previous issues.

    a. Plot the data on arithmetic paper.

    b. Using an alpha of 0.3, determine the smoothed values for each of the years.

    c. Plot the smoothed values.

CHAPTER SELF-REVIEW EXAMINATION

Do all of the problems and then check your answers against those given in Appendix A.

Score each problem 25 points.

Questions 1–3 are based on the following problem:

A large manufacturing firm gathered data on the number of worker-days lost during the year. The results were:

Year	Worker-days lost (000)	Year	Worker-days lost (000)
1972	3	1977	10
1973	6	1978	9
1974	4	1979	11
1975	5	1980	10
1976	8	1981	14

1. *a.* Plot the worker-days lost.

    b. Draw a freehand straight line through the data.

    c. Using 1972 as the origin, estimate the trend equation.

2. Refer to the above series. Determine the least squares trend equation using either the direct method or the coded method.

3. Referring to Problem 2:

    a. Interpret the meaning of the *b* value in the least squares equation.

    b. Using the least squares equation, arrive at two points on the straight line.

    c. Using the least squares equation, make a forecast for 1987.

4. The imports of a commodity in millions of tons since 1976 are:

Year	Imports (in millions of tons)
1976	6.00
1977	8.44
1978	11.70
1979	15.50
1980	21.90
1981	30.80
1982	43.00

    a. Plot the data on arithmetic paper.

    b. Note that the data, when plotted, tend to approximate a curvilinear trend line. This suggests that a logarithmic trend equation would give the best-fitting line. Using the coded method, determine the equation for that line.

    c. Find the coordinates of the point on the line for 1982.

    d. Based on the equation, predict the value of imports for 1989.

    e. What was the average annual percent increase in imports during the years 1976 to 1982?

**BASIC PROGRAM
FOR EXPONENTIAL
SMOOTHING**

```
Ready

LISTNH
5 REM THIS PROGRAM CAN BE USED TO SMOOTH DATA EXPONENTALLY
10 REM DATA SHOULD BE ENTERED AT LINE 900
11 DIM S(100),M(100),D(110)
19 PRINT
20 PRINT "INPUT THE NUMBER OF DATA POINTS";
25 INPUT N
28 FOR I = 1 TO N
30 READ D(I)
32 NEXT I
50 PRINT "INPUT THE VALUE OF ALPHA";
60 INPUT A
65 IF A>1 GO TO 400
66 IF A<0 GO TO 400
130 S(1)=D(1)
135 M(1)=ABS(S(1)-D(1))
140 FOR I=2 TO N
150 S(I)=A*D(I)+(1-A)*S(I-1)
155 M(I)=ABS(S(I)-D(I))
170 NEXT I
175 A$="   ##        #####.##        #####.##        #####.##"
198 PRINT
199 PRINT
200 PRINT "PERIOD","ACTUAL","SMOOTHED","DIFFERENCE
201 PRINT ,"VALUE","VALUE"
202 PRINT
220 FOR I=1 TO N
230 PRINT USING A$,I,D(I),S(I),M(I)
232 X1=X1+M(I)
240 NEXT I
245 X=X1/N
249 PRINT
250 PRINT "THE MEAN ABSOLUTE DEVIATION (MAD) IS ";X
251 X,X1=00
298 PRINT
299 PRINT
300 PRINT "TYPE A 1 IF YOU WISH TO TRY ANOTHER ALPHA VALUE"
310 INPUT P
320 IF P=1 THEN 50
325 GO TO 999
400 PRINT "THE VALUE OF ALPHA MUST BE BETWEEN 0 AND 1"
900 DATA 1540,1751,1731,1539,1896,1923,1692,2053,2446
901 DATA 2979,2727,2272,2979,3442,3706,3037,1667
999 END
```

INTRODUCTION

Business series such as automobile sales, shipments of soft-drink bottles, and residential construction have periods during the year of above-average and below-average activity. Most department stores, for example, have a period of high sales just prior to Christmas, and relatively low sales at the beginning of the year and for a short period during the summer, as shown in Chart 8–1.

**CHART 8–1
Sales of department
stores, 1977–1981***

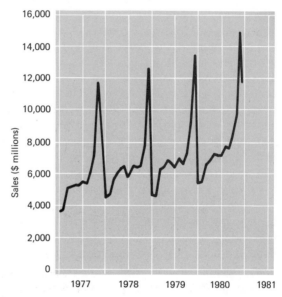

* Excludes mail-order sales.
Sources: *Survey of Current Business,* April 1981, p. S–10, and previous issues.

In the area of production, one of the reasons for analyzing seasonal fluctuations is to have a sufficient supply of raw materials on hand to meet the varying seasonal demand. The glass-container division of a large glass company, for example, manufactures nonreturnable beer bottles, returnable beer bottles, iodine bottles, aspirin bottles, bottles for rubber cement, and so on. The production scheduling department must know how many bottles to produce and when to produce each kind. A run of too many bottles of one kind may cause a serious storage problem. Production cannot be based entirely on orders on hand because many orders are telephoned in for immediate

Seasonal analysis

shipment. Since the demand for many of the bottles varies according to the season, a forecast a year or two in advance, by month, is essential to good scheduling.

Another reason for studying and measuring seasonal fluctuations is to eliminate them. For example, until recently many processors of jams and jellies hired local and migratory workers during the harvest season. Machines and people worked around the clock to process the fruits and berries. Several problems became evident. The continuous operation of the presses and other machines caused maintenance problems, and the time lost on breakdowns was often costly. Further, the inability of various machines to process the crop rapidly often extended the harvest season beyond the normal period. The last of the crop often had to be sold as B or C grade because of the loss of flavor. At the end of the canning season, machines had to be coated with a rust preventative and then cleaned again the next season. The costs of idle machines and maintaining a large inventory of jams and jellies had to be added to the selling price. In order to reduce the harvest period to a minimum and to allow time for systematic maintenance of machines, the management of some firms has smoothed out some of the seasonal fluctuation by introducing several innovations. Grape-processing plants in western New York, for example, now merely remove the stems, wash, and quick-freeze the incoming grapes in large, plastic-lined, steel barrels. The actual canning begins after all the harvest is frozen, and it extends throughout the remainder of the year. The presses and other canning equipment are also used to process frozen cranberries shipped in from New England, as well as other fruits and berries such as strawberries and currants.

Several savings are self-evident. A permanent work force can be retained throughout the year. The picking season for the grapes, currants, and other crops has been shortened considerably. Regular maintenance of machines is now possible. Machine breakdowns no longer create a problem of spoilage. Also, the production of specific jams and jellies can be oriented to actual demand. If a blend of current and apply jelly is selling well in grocery stores, more of the frozen currants and apples can be diverted to this blend and less to other blends that are not in such great demand. This was not possible heretofore because all the crops were canned during the harvest season.

An analysis of seasonal fluctuations over a period of years can also be of help in evaluating current trends. The typical sales of department stores in the United States, excluding mail-order sales, are expressed as indexes in Table 8–1. Each index represents the average sales for a period of seven years. The actual sales for some months were above the average (which is represented by an index of 100.0) and the sales for other months were below average. The index of 126.8 for December (Table 8–1) indicates that typically

TABLE 8–1
Typical seasonal indexes for U.S. department store sales, excluding mail-order sales

January	87.0	July	86.0
February	83.2	August	99.7
March	100.5	September	101.4
April	106.5	October	105.8
May	101.6	November	111.9
June	89.6	December	126.8

Source: Computed from data in the *Survey of Current Business.*

sales for December are 26.8 percent above the average for the year; and the index of 86.0 for July indicates that department store sales for July are typically 14 percent below the average for the year.

DESEASONALIZING DATA

A set of seasonal indexes can be used to adjust, say, a sales series for seasonal fluctuations. The resulting sales series is called **deseasonalized sales** or **seasonally adjusted sales**. The reason for deseasonalizing the sales series is to remove the seasonal fluctuations so that the trend and cycle can be studied. To illustrate the procedure, the sales of a women's apparel store for 1981 and for the first six months of 1982 are given in the first column of Table 8–2. Note that it is very difficult to determine whether the sales have been increasing or decreasing because of the month-to-month variation.

TABLE 8–2
Sales and deseasonalized sales for a women's apparel store

1981	Sales (000) TSCI	Typical index S	Deseasonalized sales (000) $\frac{TSCI}{S} = TCI$
January	$160	80.0	$200
February	183	92.0	199
March	195	99.1	197
April	198	101.2	196
May	201	103.8	194
June	191	99.0	193
July	187	97.0	193
August	174	91.2	191
September	193	101.6	190
October	196	103.8	189
November	197	104.7	188
December	234	126.6	185
1982			
January	146	80.0	182
February	167	92.0	181
March	179	99.1	181
April	182	101.2	180
May	187	103.8	180
June	177	99.0	179

To remove the effect of the seasonal variation, the sales for each month (which contain trend, cyclical, irregular, and seasonal variations) are divided by the seasonal index for that month, i.e., $TSCI/S = TCI$. The seasonal indexes act the same as the deflator discussed in Chapter 7. Logically, the deseasonalized data then only contain trend, cycle, and irregular components. The seasonal component has been divided out (removed).

For example, the actual sales for January 1981 were $160,000. The typical seasonal index for January is 80.0, indicating that usually sales for that month are 20 percent below the average for the year. By dividing the actual sales of $160,000 by the seasonal index of 80.0 (and multiplying the quotient by 100), the deseasonalized sales of $200,000 were determined.

By dividing out the effect of seasonal variation, the deseasonalized series might be used to suggest a turning point in the cycle. In this problem suppose that the long-term trend in sales has been upward (see Chart 8–2). Actual sales fluctuate with the season. Note that although deseasonalized sales were above the trend line in 1981 (indicating an above-average level of sales), they declined to a point in early 1982 where one might wonder whether the peak in cyclical sales has been reached and a downturn in the sales cycle is underway.

CHART 8–2
Sales, deseasonalized sales, and the least squares trend line for a women's apparel store

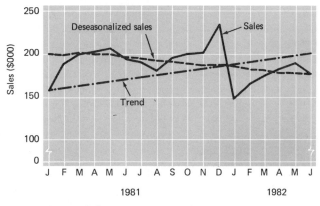

Source: Table 8–2.

METHODS OF DETERMINING THE SEASONAL INDEXES

To recapitulate, a typical seasonal consists of a set of indexes. If the data being analyzed are monthly data, the typical seasonal pattern consists of 12 indexes. Logically, there are four typical seasonal indexes for data that are reported quarterly.

Each index is a percent, with the average for the year equal to 100.0; that is, each monthly index indicates the level of sales, production, or other variable in relation to the annual average of 100.0. A typical index of 96.0 for January indicates that sales (or whatever the variable is) are usually 4 percent below the average for the year. An index of 107.2 for October means that the variable is typically 7.2 percent above the annual average.

A large number of methods have been developed to measure the typical seasonal fluctuation in a time series. The methods vary from a rather simple approach to sophisticated methods employing computers. Only two methods will be discussed: (1) a method using averages, and (2) the commonly used ratio-to-moving-average method.

A method using averages

Since a typical seasonal index represents the seasonal fluctuations for a number of years, one simple approach is to find the average sales for each month (i.e., all the January values are averaged, all the February values, and so on).

CHART 8–3
Monthly sales of the
Staat Company, 1979,
1980, and 1981

EXAMPLE

The actual sales for several years may be plotted first to make sure that there is a recurring seasonal pattern (Chart 8–3).

The chart indicates that definite seasonal fluctuations exist. There are periods of high sales in the spring and at the end of the year. There are low periods at the beginning of the year and during the summer.

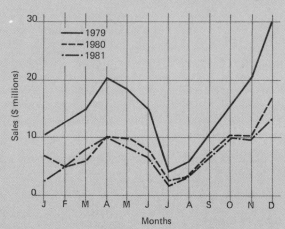

What are the typical seasonal indexes for the sales of the Staat Company?

SOLUTION

Referring to the monthly sales in Table 8–3, note that sales for January for the years 1977–81 were $2, $5, $4, $6, and $10 million. The total is $27 million, and the average sales are $5.4 million, found by $27/5. Continuing, total sales for all five Februarys were $34 million, and the average was $6.8 million. This process is continued for all months.

The next step is to determine the average monthly sales. It is $9.483 million, found by $113.8 million/12. Then the value of the sales for each month is divided by $9.483 million and the quotients are multiplied by 100. For January, ($5.4/$9.483)(100) = 57.0. For February, ($6.8/$9.483) (100) = 71.8, and so on. Logically, the sum of the 12 monthly indexes must equal 1,200.

This crude method of measuring the seasonal pattern has several advantages. The procedure is very simple, and time involved in calculating is minimal. However, this and other similar approaches have several disadvantages. Theoretically, each year should have equal weight in determining the value of each monthly index. This is not true in this problem. The trend was upward from 1977 to 1981, with the 1981 level of sales much higher than sales

TABLE 8-3
Sales of the Staat Company by month, 1977–1981 ($000,000)

Year	Jan.	Feb.	Mar.	Apr.	May	June	July	Aug.	Sept.	Oct.	Nov.	Dec.	Total
1977	$ 2	$ 4	$ 8	$10	$ 8	$ 6	$ 1	$ 4	$ 7	$10	$10	$14	$ 84
1978	5	6	7	10	9	6	2	5	8	10	11	15	94
1979	4	7	8	11	9	8	21	4	7	10	11	17	117
1980	6	5	7	10	9	7	1	4	9	11	11	17	97
1981	10	12	15	20	18	14	3	7	11	17	22	28	177
Total	$27	$34	$45	$61	$53	$41	$28	$24	$42	$58	$65	$91	$569
Average	5.4	6.8	9.0	12.2	10.6	8.2	5.6	4.8	8.4	11.6	13.0	18.2	113.8
Index	57.0	71.8	94.9	128.6	111.7	86.5	59.0	50.6	88.6	122.3	137.1	191.9	1,200.0

in previous years. As a result, sales for each month in 1981 are weighted disproportionately. Note too the sales for July 1979. This one irregular value (21) unduly affected the index for July.

Ratio-to-moving-average method

The simple average method is used primarily in problems where only a quick approximation of the seasonal pattern is needed. As noted above, the method has several theoretical disadvantages. The method most commonly used to compute the typical seasonal pattern is called the **ratio-to-moving-average method**. It eliminates the trend, cyclical, and irregular components from the original data (Y). This is accomplished in six steps. Briefly, SI is isolated from the data, using a 12-month moving average. By dividing the original data ($TCSI$) by TC, the SI component is reintroduced; that is, $TCSI/TC = SI$. The SIs are called **specific seasonals**. There is one specific seasonal for each month of the series. To eliminate the irregular component (I) from the specific seasonals (SI), an average of all the specific seasonals for January is computed using either the median or the modified mean. Then an average of all the specific seasonals for the month of February is determined, and so on. The 12 numbers that result are called the **typical seasonal index**.

Now to discuss in detail the procedure followed in arriving at the typical seasonal indexes using the ratio-to-moving-average method. As before, simple figures are used to illustrate the steps. A time series representing the sales of the Cann-Farber Department Stores are found in the first column of Table 8–4. As noted previously, the initial step is to remove the seasonal and irregular components from the time series using a 12-month moving average.

1. The sales for the 12 months of 1976 are totaled, and the toal is centered in the middle of the year. Since there is an even number of months, the total ($56) is positioned *between* June and July. The total of the next 12 months (February 1976 through January 1977) is calculated by subtracting the sales for January 1976 ($1) and adding the sales for January 1977 ($2). This total ($57) is positioned between July and August. The total is moved along by subtracting the sales for February 1976 ($2) from the new total ($57) and adding the sales for February 1977 ($3). The new total ($58) is positioned between August and September of 1976. The procedure is repeated until all possible 12-month moving totals are computed.

A technical note. A system should be devised to ensure accuracy. In Table 8–4, a sales figure was crossed out lightly with a (/) mark when it was subtracted. When a figure was added, it was checked (✔). Also, a frequent check of the 12-month moving total is recommended. For example, the $61 million˙ total positioned between June and July 1977 is the total of the six months preceding it and the six months following it. The figure between a June and July should equal the total sales for that particular year.

2. The next step is to compute a 12-month moving average. Each 12-month moving total can be divided by 12, or multiplied by the reciprocal of 12.

Note that the 12-month moving average, which was determined either by

TABLE 8–4
Sales of Cann-Farber
Department Stores
**($000,000)*

1976	Sales TSCI	(1) 12-month moving total	(2) 12-month moving average $\frac{Col\ (2)}{12}$	(3) Centered 12-month moving average TC	(4) Specific seasonal indexes $\frac{TCSI}{TC} \times 100 = SI$	(5)
January ......$ 1					
February 2					
March 4					
April 6					
May.......... 3					
June 3					
		$56	4.67			
July 2				4.71	42.5
		57	4.75			
August 2				4.79	41.8
		58	4.83			
September.... 5				4.79	104.4
		57	4.75			
October 7				4.71	148.6
		56	4.67			
November 9				4.71	191.1
		57	4.75			
December 12				4.75	252.6
1977		57	4.75			
January 2				4.79	41.8
		58	4.83			
February 3				4.83	62.1
		58	4.83			
March 3				4.87	61.6
		59	4.91			
April 5				4.96	100.8
		60	5.00			
May.......... 4				.	.
		59				
June 3			.	.	.
		61	.	.	.
July 3			.	.	.
		62				
August 2					
		61				
September.... 6		.			
			.			
October 8		.			
			.			
November 8					
December 14					
1978					
January 3					
February 2					

*Dots on this and other tables indicate that the calculations would be continued to the present year.

dividing each moving total by 12 or by using the reciprocal method, is still positioned between two months. The first average (4.67), for example, is between June and July 1976 (see Table 8–4).

3. In order to center the 12-month moving averages directly on the months, two moving averages are averaged. As an example:

1976	12-month moving average	Centered 12-month moving average
	4.67	
July ⟶		⟶ 4.71
	4.75	
August ⟶		⟶ 4.79
	4.83	
September ⟶		⟶ 4.79
	4.75	

To reemphasize, the calculations up to this point were necessary to eliminate seasonal and irregular fluctuations from the original sales. The centered 12-month moving average, therefore, contains only trend and cycle variations. The original data and the centered 12-month moving averages are shown graphically in Chart 8–4.

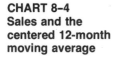

**CHART 8–4
Sales and the
centered 12-month
moving average**

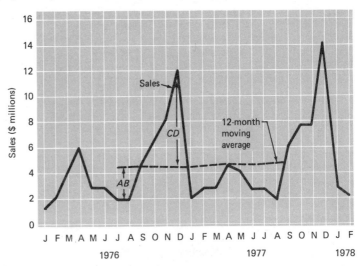

4. The next step is to convert the distances between the original data (*TCSI*) and the centered 12-month moving average (*TC*) to indexes.

The moving average contains only the trend and cyclical components, whereas the original sales have all four components (*TSCI*).[1] The distances between the two represent *SI*. Two points have been identified in Chart 8–4 (*AB* and *CD*) which illustrate the concept. The distance between the sales of $12 million in December 1976 and the centered-moving-average value of 4.75 (distance *CD*) can be expressed as an index. The index is 252.6, computed by

---

[1] Theoretically, some seasonal and irregular variations still exist in the moving average.

($12/4.75)(100). This specific seasonal of 252.6 indicates that sales for December 1976 were 152.6 percent above the average for the year, or that sales were 252.6 percent of the average. The distance *AB* for August 1976 indicates that sales were only 41.8 percent of the average annual sales ($2/4.79)(100) = 41.8; that is:

$$\frac{TCSI}{TC}(100) = SI$$

As examples of the necessary calculations:

1976:	Sales ($000,000)	Specific seasonals SI*
July	$\dfrac{\$2\text{ sales}}{4.71\text{ moving average}}$ = 0.425 × 100 =	42.5
August	$\dfrac{\$2\text{ sales}}{4.79\text{ moving average}}$ = 0.418 × 100 =	41.8
December	$\dfrac{\$12\text{ sales}}{4.75\text{ moving average}}$ = 2.526 × 100 =	252.6

* These specific seasonals are found in column (5) of Table 8–4.

The specific seasonal indexes (*SI*) for each year contain seasonal and irregular variations. The tier chart (Chart 8–5) portrays the extent of those fluctuations. This graphic technique can also be used to uncover any change in the seasonal pattern. Chart 8–5 indicates that there has been no major change since 1976.

**CHART 8–5
The specific
seasonals**

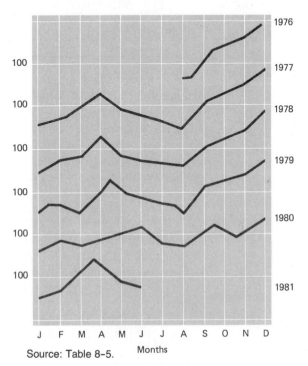

Source: Table 8–5.   Months

5. The irregular fluctuations must now be removed and one index for each month determined. (As noted previously, the resulting 12 monthly figures are called the typical seasonal index. This is often shortened to the **typical seasonal**, or just the **seasonal**.)

A convenient way to accomplish this is to assemble the specific seasonals in a table. (The specific seasonals from July 1976 through April 1977 in Table 8–5 are copied from Table 8–4. The remaining specific seasonals are hypothetical and are added merely to illustrate how the typical seasonal indexes are computed.) Note that the ratio-to-moving-average method produced no specific seasonals for the first six months of 1976 and the last six months of 1981.

TABLE 8–5
Specific seasonals and the computation of the typical seasonal index

Year	Jan	Feb	Mar	Apr	May	June	July	Aug	Sept	Oct	Nov	Dec	TOTAL
1976							42.5	41.8	104.4	148.6	191.1	252.6	
1977	41.8	62.1	61.6	100.8	99.3	91.6	69.6	45.2	105.8	135.9	158.4	210.2	
1978	51.9	65.2	72.8	103.1	98.2	90.2	44.8	50.1	102.6	150.9	161.7	211.6	
1979	54.1	65.9	55.7	106.9	92.7	98.6	62.8	49.7	103.9	140.6	157.9	212.2	
1980	70.7	72.9	54.6	99.9	100.3	92.7	44.2	39.6	103.6	82.8	162.3	200.1	
1981	50.0	67.1	69.8	190.6	97.1	92.5							
Total after omitting high/low	143.7	198.2	187.1	310.8	294.6	276.8	150.1	136.7	311.9	425.1	482.4	634.0	
Modified Mean	47.9	66.1	62.4	103.6	98.2	92.3	50.0	45.6	104.0	141.7	160.8	211.3	1,183.9
Typical Index	48.6	67.0	63.2	105.0	99.5	93.6	50.7	46.2	105.4	143.6	163.0	214.2	1,200.0

Either the modified mean or median can be used to eliminate the irregular fluctuations. The **modified mean** is used here. To determine it, the *highest* and *lowest* specific seasonals for each month have been omitted, and the arithmetic mean of the remaining indexes has been determined. In effect, this eliminates the irregular variations. For example, the April 1981 specific seasonal of 190.6 was unusually high compared with the other seasonals for that month, and the specific seasonal for October 1980 (82.8) was extremely low in comparison with the other figures for October. Both of these irregular figures were omitted in the calculation of the modified mean.

6. The total of the 12 modified means should theoretically be equal to 1,200 because the average of the 12 months is designated as 100. However, the total may not be equal to 1,200 due to rounding and the omission of some data (the highs and lows). A correction factor, therefore, can be applied to each modified mean to arrive at the typical seasonal. The correction factor is computed by:

$$\text{Correction factor} = \frac{1200.0}{\text{Total of modified means}}$$

If we were working with quarterly data, the correction factor would be 400/total.

EXAMPLE

Suppose the modified means totaled a ridiculous 600.0. The modified means would be multiplied by what correction factor?

SOLUTION

$$\text{Correction factor} = \frac{1200.0}{600.0}$$

$$= 2.0$$

Had the total of the modified means been 2,400, the correction factor would be 0.5, computed by (1,200/2,400). The correction factor for this illustration is the ratio of 1,200 to the actual total. It is 1.0136, computed by (1,200/1,183.9). This correction factor is multiplied by each modified mean. The corrected 12 figures are the typical seasonal indexes. (If the modified means total between 1,198.9 and 1,201.1, no correction factor is necessary.)

The typical seasonal indexes are given in Table 8–6 and portrayed graphically in Chart 8–6.

TABLE 8–6
Typical seasonal indexes for the sales of the Cann-Farber Department Stores

Month	Index	Month	Index
January	48.6	July	50.7
February	67.0	August	46.2
March	63.2	September	105.4
April	105.0	October	143.6
May	99.5	November	163.0
June	93.6	December	214.2

Source: Table 8–5.

CHART 8–6
Typical seasonal indexes for the sales of the Cann-Farber Department Stores

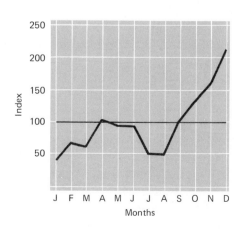

Since the calculations needed to determine the typical seasonal index are routine, they can be programmed for the computer. The monthly sales of drug and proprietary stores starting with 1963 are used for illustration. The actual sales are in the left margin, with $649 million being the sales for January 1963; for month 2 (February 1963) sales were $641 million, and so on.

YEAR	MON	DATA	12 MOV TOT	12 MOV AVE	CEN MOV AV	SEAS INDEX
1963	1	649				
	2	641				
	3	667				
	4	652				
	5	676				
	6	664				
			8170.00	680.83		
	7	660			681.74	96.80
			8192.00	682.66		
	8	680			683.29	99.51
			8207.00	683.91		
	9	647			684.45	94.52
			8220.00	685.00		
	10	667			685.54	97.29
			8233.00	686.08		
	11	666			687.62	96.85
			8270.00	689.16		
	12	901			690.87	130.41
			8311.00	692.58		
1964	1	671			694.54	96.61
			8358.00	696.50		
	2	656			697.66	94.02
			8386.00	698.83		
	3	680			701.08	96.99
			8440.00	703.33		
	4	665			705.70	94.23
			8497.00	708.08		
	5	713			709.04	100.55
			8520.00	710.00		
	6	705			712.70	98.91
			8585.00			
	7	707		41	717.37	98.55

SELF-REVIEW 8–1

(A reminder: cover the answers in the margin.)

a. The production of pencils, in millions, is shown below, starting with January 1978. Compute a typical seasonal index using the ratio-to-moving-average method. Production has been adjusted for the number of working days per month. Assume that all the data given are correct.

	Monthly pro- duction	12- month moving total	12- month moving average	Centered 12-month moving average	Specific sea- sonals
1978					
January	2				
February	3				
March	2				

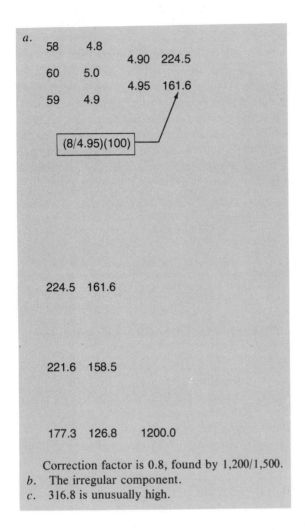

a.

58	4.8		
		4.90	224.5
60	5.0		
		4.95	161.6
59	4.9		

(8/4.95)(100) → 161.6

224.5	161.6	
221.6	158.5	
177.3	126.8	1200.0

Correction factor is 0.8, found by 1,200/1,500.

b. The irregular component.

c. 316.8 is unusually high.

April	4					
May	6					
June	8					
		?	?			
July	11			?	?	
		?	?			
August	8			?	?	
		?	?			
September	7					
October	4					
November	2					
December	1					
1979						
January	4					
February	2					
March	4					
April	3					

	Jan	*Feb*	*Mar*	*Apr*	*May*	*June*	*July*	*Aug*	*Sept*	*Oct*	*Nov*	*Dec*	
1978							?	?					
1979							218.7	154.8					
1980							208.4	155.5					
1981							316.8	187.0					
													Total
Modified Mean							?	?	*Sum of modified means is*				= 1,500.0
													Total
Seasonal Index							?	?	*Correct to*				= ?

b. The modified mean was used as an average to represent the months. Why? That is, what component of the time series (*TCSI*) did this average eliminate?

c. What seasonal relative for July is somewhat irregular?

CHAPTER SUMMARY

Seasonal variation is quite common in many industries, especially in retail and wholesale trade. Motels, resorts, and manufacturers of seasonal goods, such as bathing suits, also have seasonal ups and downs. An analysis of past seasonal fluctuations can be helpful in planning production and in buying such items as toys, dolls, Easter eggs, and other holiday-oriented goods. Knowing the seasonal pattern in the form of indexes also allows the retailer to deseasonalize sales. This is accomplished by dividing the actual sales for a month by the seasonal index for that month. The deseasonalized sales, therefore, only include trend, cycle, and irregular fluctuations. An examination of the deseasonalized data allows management to determine, for example, whether the trend in sales has been upward, downward, or remained the same, and to forecast the future.

Two methods of isolating the seasonal pattern were presented. A simple method using averages requires only that an average be determined for all the January values, all the February values, and so on. This method gives satisfactory results if the data do not express any marked upward or downward trend. A more commonly used method is referred to as the ratio-to-moving-average method. Briefly, an index for each month, called the specific seasonal, is computed first. Then, using the modified mean, one index is arrived at for each of the 12 months of the year. These 12 numbers are called the typical seasonal index and represent all the past data.

CHAPTER OUTLINE

Seasonal analysis

I. Seasonal analysis.
   A. Reasons for developing a typical seasonal pattern.
      1. *Identify typical seasonal fluctuations* for better production and sales planning.
      2. *Eliminate seasonal fluctuations,* if possible. Result might be more economical use of labor.
      3. *Assist in evaluating current trends* by seasonally adjusting the sales, production, or other time series.
      4. *Uncover possible shift* in seasonal pattern in recent years.
      5. *Detect possible change* in the business cycle.
   B. Average method of determining the seasonal indexes.
      1. *Advantages.* Quick approximation of the seasonal pattern. Minimal amount of calculations.
      2. *Disadvantages.* If trend in sales, or other series, is upward or downward, the latest years receive disproportionate weight. Also one irregular value unduly affects a monthly index.
   C. Ratio-to-moving-average method.
      1. *Advantages.* Most commonly used method of eliminating trend (T), cycle (C), and irregular (I) components from the original time series. Many computer programs use this method.
      2. *Disadvantages.* More time consuming than the average method.

CHAPTER EXERCISES

1. The production of the Gogetter Manufacturing Company for 1977 and part of 1978 follows.

Month	1977 production (000)	1978 production (000)
January	6	7
February	7	9
March	12	14
April	8	9
May	4	5
June	3	4
July	3	4
August	5	
September	14	
October	6	
November	7	
December	6	

a. Using the ratio-to-moving-average method, determine the specific seasonals for July, August, and September 1977.

b. Assume the specific seasonal indexes in the following table are correct. Insert in the table the specific seasonals you computed in Part a for July, August, and September 1977 and determine the 12 typical seasonal indexes.

Year	Jan.	Feb.	Mar.	Apr.	May	June	July	Aug.	Sept.	Oct.	Nov.	Dec.
1977							?	?	?	92.1	106.5	92.9
1978	88.9	102.9	178.9	118.2	60.1	43.1	44.0	74.0	200.9	90.0	101.9	90.9
1979	87.6	103.7	170.2	125.9	59.4	48.6	44.2	77.2	196.5	89.6	113.2	80.6
1980	79.8	105.6	165.8	124.7	62.1	41.7	48.2	72.1	203.6	80.2	103.0	94.2
1981	89.0	112.1	182.9	115.1	57.6	56.9						

c. Interpret the typical seasonal index.

2. The sales of Andre's Boutique for 1978 and part of 1979 are:

Month	1978 sales ($000)	1979 sales ($000)
January	$ 78	$65
February	72	60
March	80	72
April	110	97
May	92	86
June	86	72
July	81	65
August	85	61
September	90	75
October	98	
November	115	
December	130	

a. Using the ratio-to-moving-average method, determine the specific seasonals for July, August, September, and October 1978.

b. Assume the specific seasonals in the following table are correct. Insert in the table the specific seasonals you computed in Part a for July, August, September, and October 1978 and determine the 12 typical seasonal indexes.

Year	Jan.	Feb.	Mar.	Apr.	May	June	July	Aug.	Sept.	Oct.	Nov.	Dec.
1978							?	?	?	?	123.6	150.9
1979	83.9	77.6	86.1	118.7	99.7	92.0	87.0	91.4	97.3	105.4	124.9	140.1
1980	86.7	72.9	86.2	121.3	96.6	92.0	85.5	93.6	98.2	103.2	126.1	141.7
1981	85.6	65.8	89.2	125.6	99.6	94.4	88.9	90.2	100.2	102.7	121.6	139.6
1982	77.3	81.2	85.8	115.7	100.3	89.7						

    c. Interpret the typical seasonal index.

3. Following are the sales ($000,000) of men's and boys' clothing in the United States for the period 1977–81.

Year	Jan.	Feb.	Mar.	Apr.	May	June	July	Aug.	Sept.	Oct.	Nov.	Dec.
1977	470	419	475	542	508	526	469	495	484	543	675	1,088
1978	480	421	582	536	542	563	508	554	552	609	763	1,293
1979	561	462	564	582	586	615	553	612	570	625	753	1,242
1980	604	538	614	645	691	711	633	767	683	789	900	1,440
1981	636											

Source: *Survey of Current Business,* April 1981, p. S–10, and previous issues.

Using the ratio-to-moving-average method:
a. Determine the 12 typical seasonal indexes.
b. Interpret the typical seasonal pattern of sales.

4. Following are the sales ($000,000) of liquor stores in the United States for the period 1977–81.

Year	Jan.	Feb.	Mar.	Apr.	May	June	July	Aug.	Sept.	Oct.	Nov.	Dec.
1977	919	950	1,012	1,066	1,064	1,087	1,135	1,067	1,028	1,067	1,106	1,583
1978	939	922	1,038	1,010	1,086	1,138	1,181	1,161	1,147	1,123	1,196	1,675
1979	1,061	1,034	1,146	1,110	1,197	1,320	1,346	1,354	1,284	1,270	1,361	1,954
1980	1,294	1,258	1,301	1,297	1,425	1,378	1,429	1,452	1,305	1,377	1,439	1,969
1981	1,315											

Source: *Survey of Current Business,* April 1981, p. S–10, and previous issues.

Using the ratio-to-moving-average method:
a. Determine the 12 typical seasonal indexes.
b. Interpret the typical seasonal pattern of sales.

5. Following are the sales ($000,000) of department stores in the United States for the period 1977–81.

Year	Jan.	Feb.	Mar.	Apr.	May	June	July	Aug.	Sept.	Oct.	Nov.	Dec.
1977	3,840	3,873	5,044	5,470	5,457	5,487	5,492	5,837	5,797	6,179	7,290	11,817
1978	4,345	4,424	5,894	6,010	6,431	6,552	5,965	6,520	6,468	6,610	7,908	12,635
1979	4,747	4,700	6,304	6,511	6,946	6,810	6,396	7,180	6,886	7,686	9,076	13,513
1980	5,488	5,571	6,770	6,975	7,736	7,116	7,023	7,889	7,350	8,255	9,709	14,963
1981	5,958	5,766										

Source: *Survey of Current Business,* April 1981, p. S–10, and previous issues.

Using the ratio-to-moving-average method:
a. Determine the 12 seasonal indexes.
b. Interpret the seasonal pattern of sales.

6. The undergraduate enrollment in the College of Business Administration, the University of Toledo, by quarter, 1977–81, follows.

	Quarter			
Year	Winter	Spring	Summer	Fall
1977	2,033	1,871	714	2,318
1978	2,174	2,069	840	2,413
1979	2,370	2,254	927	2,704
1980	2,625	2,478	1,136	3,001
1981	2,803	2,668	—	—

Source: Institutional Research Office, The University of Toledo, Toledo, Ohio, *Resource Consumption Report,* 1981.

Using the ratio-to-moving-average method:
a. Determine the four quarterly indexes.
b. Interpret the quarterly pattern of enrollment.

CHAPTER SELF-REVIEW EXAMINATION

Do the problem first and then check your answer against that given in Appendix A. Score the problem 100 points.

1. Suppose that a drug and proprietary store had these sales (in $000).

Month	1978	1979	1980
January	$ 2	$ 1	$4
February	1	3	2
March	3	4	
April	5	6	
May	4	3	
June	3	4	
July	3	5	
August	4	8	
September	5	8	
October	6	9	
November	8	11	
December	12	14	

a. Using the ratio-to-moving-average method, compute the specific seasonals for months given in the foregoing table. *Note:* Carry the calculations to the nearest 100th, such as 5.68. The specific seasonals should be to the nearest 10th, such as 114.6.

Assume that specific seasonals for additional months were computed. They are shown in the following table.

Month	1979	1980	1981	1982
January		22.8	46.1	26.8
February		58.2	41.6	55.5
March		77.1	73.9	71.6
April		102.9	101.6	104.7
May		49.7	49.4	41.2
June		64.1	60.0	40.6
July		68.2	65.6	
August		120.6	118.6	
September	106.4	105.9	109.7	
October	126.2	124.7	113.6	
November	160.7	161.6	162.8	
December	240.6	249.9	250.0	

b. Insert the specific seasonals computed in Part *a* and determine the typical seasonal indexes for the drug and proprietary store.

c. Interpret the seasonal pattern.

9

INTRODUCTION

The emphasis in Chapters 2 through 8 was on **descriptive statistics**. In Chapter 2, various types of graphs, such as line charts, bar charts, and pie charts, were used to describe the past trends in sales, production, exports, and so on. Chapter 3 dealt with organizing data into a frequency distribution and portraying the data graphically. In Chapter 4 several averages, namely, the arithmetic mean, median, and mode were computed to describe typical value in a distribution. The dispersion of the data was described in Chapter 5 using the range, standard deviation, and other measures. Index numbers which describe the change in price, quantity, and value over periods of time were examined in Chapter 6. Chapters 7 and 8 dealt with describing the trend and seasonal pattern of sales, production, and other such series over a period of time.

The field of descriptive statistics, therefore, is concerned with *describing something which has already occurred.* We now turn to the second facet of statistics, namely, *the chance that something will occur*. This facet of statistics is called **inductive statistics** or **statistical inference**.

Seldom does the decision maker have complete information on which to make a decision. A cereal manufacturer, an automobile manufacturer, and thousands of other producers of consumer-oriented goods must decide, on the basis of incomplete information, whether to manufacture and market such items as a new cereal having a mint flavor, a pickle with an apple flavor, or a new magazine for devotees of Ping-Pong. A television network must decide whether to retain a soap opera for the forthcoming season. One way of minimizing the risk of making a wrong decision is to take a sample from the population. The market researcher does this in order to assess consumer preference for the pickle with the apple flavor. A test market might be selected and 2,000 persons asked to try the pickle and give their opinions. Statistical inference deals with inferences about a population based on a sample taken from that population. (The populations for the above illustrations are: all consumers who eat cereal, all pickle lovers, all devotees of Ping-Pong, and all television viewers who watch the soaps.)

Since there is considerable uncertainty in decision making, it is important that all the known risks involved be scientifically evaluated. Helpful in this evaluation is *probability theory*, which has often been referred to as the science of uncertainty. The use of probability theory allows the decision maker with only limited information to analyze the risks and minimize the gamble inherent, for example, in marketing a new product, or accepting an incoming shipment containing defective parts.

A survey of probability concepts

WHAT IS PROBABILITY?

No doubt you are familiar with terms such as *probability*, *chance*, *likelihood*, and *odds*. They are often used interchangeably. The weather forecaster announces that there is a 70 percent chance of rain for Super Bowl Sunday. The odds that the Boston Celtics will win their division are quoted as three to one. The probability that man will go to Saturn in the 1980s is rather remote. And the chance that you will pass the forthcoming examination without further study is 50-50. To answer the question in the heading,

> *A probability is a measure of one's belief that a particular outcome of an experiment will happen.*

The **experiment** referred to in the definition is an activity which is either observed or measured. Some examples of an experiment are:

1. Asking a panel of children their preference with respect to several new toys.
2. Counting the number of inmates in cell block M.
3. Measuring the outside diameter of piston rings to determine the number defective.
4. Weighing the contents of cereal boxes to determine how many are overweight.
5. Turning the ignition key of an automobile as it comes off the assembly line to determine whether the engine will start.

Note that experiments 2, 3, and 4 result in numbers. There might be, for example, 26 inmates in cell block M. The outcomes of experiments 1 and 5 are not numerical.

A particular result of an experiment is called an **outcome**. Any set of outcomes of an experiment is called an **event**. To illustrate:

Experiment: Observe whether the automobile starts when the ignition is turned to the ON position.
    Event: *a.* Yes, it starts.
             b. No, it does not start.

Experiment: Ask a child which toy he likes best: toy A, toy B, or toy C.
    Event: *a.* Likes toy A best.
             b. Likes toy B best.
             c. Likes toy C best.

Experiment: Roll a die.
    Event: *a.* Observe a 1.
             b. Observe a 2.
             c. Observe a 3.
             d. Observe a 4.
             e. Observe a 5.
             f. Observe a 6.

A probability is expressed as a decimal, such as 0.70, or 0.27, or 0.50. However, it may be given as a fraction, such as $7/10$, $27/100$, or $1/2$. It can assume a number from 0 to 1 inclusive. If a company has only five sales regions, and each region's name or number is written on a slip of paper and the slips put in a hat, the probability of selecting one of the five regions is 1.00. The probability of selecting a slip of paper from the hat which reads "Pittsburgh Steelers" is 0.00. Thus, the probability of 1.00 represents something that is certain to happen, the probability of 0.00 something that cannot happen.

─────────────────────── **SELF-REVIEW 9–1** ───────────────────────

1. *a.* Testing of the new computer game.
   b. Seventy-three players liked the game.
2. *a.* No. Probability cannot be greater than 1.00. The probability that the game, if put on the market, will be successful is $^{65}/_{80}$, or 0.8125.
   b. Cannot be less than 0.00. Perhaps a mistake in arithmetic.

(A reminder: cover the answers in the left column.)

1. A new computer game has been developed. Its market potential is to be tested by 80 veteran game players.
   a. What is the experiment?
   b. What is one possible event?
2. *a.* Suppose 65 players liked the game. Is 65 a probability?
   b. The probability that the new computer game will be a success is computed to be −1.00. Comment.

APPROACHES TO PROBABILITY

Three approaches to probability will be considered, namely, the **classical approach**, the **relative frequency approach**, and the **subjective approach**.

1. The **classical** approach to probability is predicated on the assumption that the simple outcomes of an experiment are *equally likely*. Using the classical viewpoint, the probability of an event's happening is computed by dividing the number of favorable outcomes by the total number of possible outcomes.

$$\text{Probability of an event} = \frac{\text{Number of favorable outcomes}}{\text{Total number of possible outcomes}}$$

EXAMPLE

The experiment is to observe the up face on a six-sided die. What is the probability that a two-spot will appear face up?

SOLUTION

The possible events are: a one-spot , a two-spot , a three-spot , a four-spot , a five-spot , and a six-spot . All six outcomes of the toss of the die are equally likely. Therefore,

$$\text{Probability of a two-spot} = \frac{1}{6} \begin{array}{l} \leftarrow \boxed{\text{Number of favorable outcomes}} \\ \leftarrow \boxed{\text{Total number of possible outcomes}} \end{array}$$

$$= 0.167$$

SELF-REVIEW 9–2

1. ¼ = 0.25.

2. *a.* $\dfrac{\text{13 spades in deck}}{\text{52 cards total}}$
   $= {}^{13}/_{52} = {}^{1}/_{4} = 0.25.$

   b. $\dfrac{\text{1 jack of hearts in deck}}{\text{52 cards total}}$
   $= {}^{1}/_{52} = 0.0192.$

   c. $\dfrac{\text{4 queens in deck}}{\text{52 cards total}}$
   $= {}^{4}/_{52} = 0.0769.$

3. Classical.

1. A company has warehouses in four regions—southern, midwestern, Rocky Mountain, and far western. One of the regions is to be selected at random to store a seldom-used item. What is the probability that the warehouse selected would be the one in the Rocky Mountain region?

2. One card from a standard 52-card deck of cards is to be selected at random. Express as a fraction and as a decimal—
   a. The probability the card will be a spade.
   b. The probability the card will be the jack of hearts.
   c. The probability the card will be a queen.

3. The above two examples illustrate what approach to probability?

The **classical** (objective) view of probability is by its definition limited to situations having equally likely outcomes, such as games of chance. What if the probabilities of the various outcomes are not equally likely? As an example, high-speed machines mass-producing goods generally turn out only a relatively few defective parts during a one-hour period. Logically, the probability of selecting a defective part at random and the probability of selecting a good part are not equally likely. The relative frequency approach is used in these situations.

2. The **relative frequency** (historical) interpretation of probability is based on past experience. We can then estimate the probability an event will occur again the long run by:

$$\text{Probability of an event's happening} = \frac{\text{Number of times event occurred in past}}{\text{Total number of observations}}$$

EXAMPLE

As an example of the relative frequency interpretation of probability, a study of 751 graduates of a midwestern university revealed that 383 were *not* employed in their major area of study in college. (For illustration, a person who majored in accounting is the marketing manager of a tomato-processing firm.) What is the probability that any graduate selected will be employed in an area other than his or her college major?

SOLUTION

$$\begin{array}{l} \text{Probability of} \\ \text{event happening} \end{array} = \dfrac{\begin{array}{c}\text{Number of times}\\ \text{event occurred in past}\end{array}}{\begin{array}{c}\text{Total number}\\ \text{of observations}\end{array}}$$

$$P(A) = \frac{383}{751}$$

$$= 0.51$$

To simplify, letters, or numbers, may be used. P stands for probability, and in this case $P(A)$ stands for probability that a graduate is not employed in his or her major area of college study.

Thus, we can say that the likelihood of outcome A, a graduate who is *not* employed in his or her major area of study in college, is 0.51.

SELF-REVIEW 9–3

a. $\dfrac{24}{883} = 0.027.$

b. $\dfrac{182}{883} = 0.206$

The National Center for Health Statistics reported that of every 883 deaths in recent years, 24 resulted from an automobile accident, 182 from cancer, and 333 from heart disease.

a. Using the relative frequency approach, approximate the probability that a particular death is due to an automobile accident. Express it as a fraction and as a decimal.

b. Using the relative frequency approach, estimate the probability that a particular death is caused by cancer. Express it as a fraction and as a decimal.

3. If there is little or no past experience on which to base a probability, the **subjective**, or **personal**, viewpoint can be used. Essentially this means evaluating whatever indirect information, opinions, and other subjective factors are available and then making an educated guess. Illustrations of subjective probability:

    a. Estimating the likelihood that Mount Saint Helens will continue to erupt for the next 10 years.

    b. Estimating the probability that a retail outlet specializing in badminton and Ping-Pong equipment will be a financial success in a medium-sized city.

    c. Estimating the probability that the prime rate will increase to 25 percent next year.

SELF-REVIEW 9–4
---

1. 0.02. No doubt your estimate is different.
2. 0.00001, indicating that the chance that this will happen is rather remote.

1. What probability would you assign to the likelihood that the Green Bay Packers will advance to the Super Bowl this year?
2. What probability do you assign to the possibility that the Dow-Jones Industrial Average will fall below 300 this month?

In brief summary, there are three viewpoints regarding probability—the classical (objective), the relative frequency (historical), and the subjective viewpoints. We noted that a probability statement always constitutes an estimate of an unknown value which will govern an event that has not yet occurred. Many statisticians, therefore, think that all probability statements are basically subjective—that is, statements of an individual's knowledge and feelings concerning the event of interest. There is, of course, a considerable difference in the degree of uncertainty that surrounds this estimate, based primarily on the knowledge possessed by the individual concerning the underlying process. He possesses a great deal of knowledge about the toss of a die. He can state that the probability that a one-spot will appear face up on the toss of a true die is one sixth. But he knows very little concerning the acceptance by the marketplace of a new and untested product. For example, even though the market research director tests a newly developed product in, say, 40 retail stores and states that there is a 70 percent chance that the product will have sales of over 1 million units, he still has very little knowledge of how consumers will react when it is marketed nationally. In both cases (the case of the person rolling a die and the marketing research testing a new product) the individual is assigning a value to an event of interest, and a difference exists only in the predictor's confidence in the precision of the estimate.

USES OF PROBABILITY

What use does probability have in decision making? This question can be answered by citing two problems which will be discussed in forthcoming chapters.

Problem 1. Based on past experience a publishing company determined that at least 20 percent of a certain group, such as musicians, must subscribe to a monthly magazine to make it a financial success. The company is considering a monthly magazine for bird-watchers. A special copy was designed and mailed to a sample of 1,000 bird-watchers. In response, 190 out of 1,000, or 19 percent, said they would subscribe to the magazine if it were published. Should we state that this proportion is less than 20 percent and make an immediate decision not to publish the magazine? Or could the difference between the needed percent (20) and the sample percent (19) be attributed to sampling, that is, chance? Probability will help us arrive at a decision for this type of problem, which will be discussed in Chapter 14.

Problem 2. A very large construction project requires thousands of concrete blocks. Specifications state that the blocks must stand up to pressures of 1,050 pounds per square inch (psi) on the average. Two firms manufacturing these blocks submitted samples for testing. The arithmetic mean strength of the Strong Block Company blocks was 1,070 psi, those from the Taylor Company, 1,062 psi. Strong Block thinks it should be awarded the contract because its blocks have a higher psi. Taylor disagrees, saying that the difference of only 8 psi could be due to sampling (chance). If Strong Block's claim is correct, it will be awarded the contract. If Taylor's statement is correct, the contract will be divided between the two companies. Probability will help the decision maker reach the decision.

SOME BASIC RULES OF PROBABILITY

Recall that three approaches to probability were discussed—the classical, the relative frequency, and the subjective viewpoints. Regardless of the viewpoint, the same laws of probability apply. Two basic ways of combining probabilities are considered in this section—namely, by addition and by multiplication.

Rules of addition

Special rule of addition. To apply this rule, the events must be **mutually exclusive**. Mutually exclusive means that when one event occurs, none of the other events can occur *at the same time*. As illustrations, if a two-spot comes face up on the roll of a die, none of the other faces (1, 3, 4, 5, or 6) can be face up at the same time. And a product coming off the assembly line cannot be defective and satisfactory at the same time.

If two events A and B are mutually exclusive, the **special rule of addition** states that the probability of one *or* the other event's occurring equals the sum of their probabilities. The rule shown symbolically is:

$$P(A \text{ or } B) = P(A) + P(B)$$

For three mutually exclusive events designated *A*, *B* and *C*, the rule is written:

$$P(A \text{ or } B \text{ or } C) = P(A) + P(B) + P(C)$$

EXAMPLE

An automatic machine inserts a mixture of beans, broccoli, and other vegetables in a plastic bag. Most of the bags contain the correct weight, but because of the slight variation in the size of the beans and other vegetables, a package might be slightly underweight or overweight. A check of many packages in the past revealed:

Weight	Event	Number of packages	Probability of occurrence	
Underweight	A	100	0.025	← $\frac{100}{4000}$
Satisfactory	B	3,600	0.900	
Overweight	C	300	0.075	
		4,000	1.000	

What is the probability that a particular package will be either underweight or overweight?

SOLUTION

The outcome "underweight" is the event *A*.
The outcome "overweight" is the event *C*.
Applying the special rule of addition:

$$P(A \text{ or } C) = P(A) + P(C)$$
$$= 0.025 + 0.075$$
$$= 0.10$$

Note that the events are mutually exclusive, meaning that a package of mixed vegetables cannot be underweight, satisfactory, and overweight at the same time. Also note that $P(A \text{ or } B \text{ or } C) = 1.000$.

SELF-REVIEW 9–5

a. 0.025, found by

$$\frac{50}{2000}$$

b. 0.034, found by

$$\frac{68}{2000}$$

A selected group of employees of Nordeen Enterprises is to be surveyed with respect to a new pension plan. In-depth interviews are to be conducted with each employee selected in the sample. The employees are classified as follows.

Classification	Event	Number of employees
Supervisors ....A		120
Maintenance ....B		50
Production C		1,460
Management.........D		302
Secretarial ....E		68

a. What is the probability that the first person selected is classified as a maintenance employee?
b. What is the probability that the first person selected is a secretary?
c. What is the probability that the first person selected is either in maintenance or a secretary?
d. What rule of probability did you use to determine the answer to c?
e. What is the probability that the first person chosen to be interviewed is either a supervisor or in maintenance or a production worker or a manager or a secretary?

Venn diagrams   English logician J. Venn (1834–88) developed a diagram to portray graphically the outcome of an experiment. The mutually exclusive concept and various other rules for combining probabilities can be seen using this device. To construct a Venn diagram, a space is first enclosed representing the total of all possible outcomes. This space is called the **sample space** and it is usually in the form of a rectangle. Some outcome (for example, that the bag of mixed vegetables was overweight) is called a **sample point**. The total of all sample points equal the **sample space**. The following Venn diagrams represent the mutually exclusive concept. Note that there is no overlapping of events, meaning that the events are mutually exclusive.

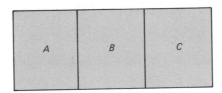 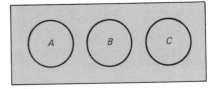

Complement rule. The probability that a bag of mixed vegetables selected at random is underweight, $P(A)$, plus the probability that it is not an underweight bag, written $P(\sim A)$, must logically equal 1. This is written:

$$P(A) + P(\sim A) = 1$$

The Venn diagram might appear as:

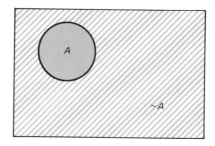

This can be revised to read:

$$P(A) = 1 - P(\sim A)$$

and is called the **complement rule**.

EXAMPLE

Recall that the probability that a bag of mixed vegetables is underweight is 0.025 and that the probability of an overweight bag is 0.075. How might this situation appear in the form of a Venn diagram?

SOLUTION

The Venn diagram portraying this situation might appear as:

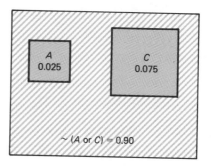

SELF-REVIEW 9–6

The Venn diagram might appear as:

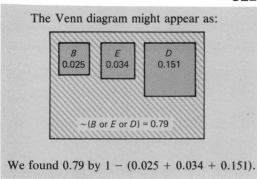

We found 0.79 by $1 - (0.025 + 0.034 + 0.151)$.

Refer back to Self-Review 9–5. Portray the following in the form of one Venn diagram. On the first selection, what is the probability of

a. Selecting a maintenance employee (designated event B).
b. Selecting a secretary (designated event E).
c. Selecting a person in management (designated event D).
d. Not selecting events B, D, and E.

General rule of addition. The outcomes of an experiment might not be mutually exclusive. To illustrate, one might ask, What is the probability that a card selected at random from a standard deck of cards will either be a king or a heart? There is some chance that the card chosen will be both a king and a heart—i.e., the king of hearts. To put it another way, there is an overlapping of outcomes, meaning that there is a chance that both A (a king) and B (a heart) can occur at the same time. The probability that this will happen is called the **joint probability** of A and B. It is referred to as a **compound event** and is usually written $P(A \text{ and } B)$.

It seems logical that the joint probability of a king and a heart should be subtracted once or it will be included twice in finding the probability that a card chosen from the deck will be either a king or a heart. What is needed, therefore, for these outcomes is a more general rule of addition. The **general rule of addition** for two events designated A and B is:

$$P(A \text{ or } B) = P(A) + P(B) - P(A \text{ and } B)$$

EXAMPLE

What is the probability that a card chosen at random from a standard deck of cards will either be a king or a heart?

SOLUTION

Card	Probability		Explanation
King ....$P(A)$	=	4/52	There are 4 kings in a deck of 52 cards,
Heart ....$P(B)$	=	13/52	13 hearts in a deck of 52 cards,
King of hearts ....$P(A \text{ and } B)$ =		1/52	1 king of hearts in a deck of 52 cards.

Solving:

$$P(A \text{ or } B) = P(A) + P(B) - P(A \text{ and } B)$$
$$= 4/52 + 13/52 - 1/52$$
$$= 16/52, \text{ or } 0.3077$$

A Venn diagram portrays these outcomes which are not mutually exclusive.

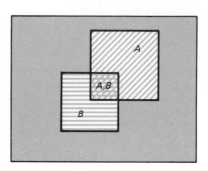

SELF-REVIEW 9–7

a. Need for corrective shoes is event *A*. Need for major dental work is event *B*.

$$P(A \text{ or } B) = P(A) + P(B) - P(A \text{ and } B)$$
$$= 0.08 + 0.15 - 0.03$$
$$= 0.20$$

b. One possibility is:

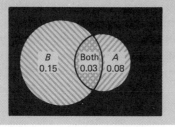

Routine physical examinations are conducted annually as part of a health service program for the employees. It was discovered that 8 percent of the employees needed corrective shoes, 15 percent needed major dental work, and 3 percent needed both corrective shoes and major dental work.

a. What is the probability that an employee selected at random will need either corrective shoes or major dental work?

b. Show this situation in the form of a Venn diagram.

EXERCISES

(A reminder: the answers and method of solution for selected exercises are in Appendix A.)

1. The marketing research department plans to survey teenagers regarding their reactions to a newly developed soft drink. They will be asked to compare it with their favorite soft drink.
   a. What is the experiment?
   b. What is one possible event?

2. The number of times an event occurred in the past is divided by the total number of occurrences. What is this approach to probability called?

3. The probability that the cause and the cure of cancer will be discovered before 1990 is 0.02. What viewpoint of probability does this statement illustrate?

4. Is it true that, if there is absolutely no chance a person will recover from 50 bullet wounds, the probability assigned to this event is -1.00?

5. On the throw of one die, what is the probability that a one-spot or a two-spot or a six-spot will appear face up?

Questions 6–10 are based on a study of the weekly offering in the envelopes at the First Baptist Church in Warren, Pennsylvania.

Offering in envelope	Number
$ 0–$ 0.99	6
1– 2.99	26
3– 4.99	16
5– 9.99	34
10– 14.99	17
15– 19.99	8
20– 24.99	9
25– 29.99	3
$30 or over	4

6. What is the probability of selecting an envelope at random and finding $30 or over in it?

7. Are the classes $0–$0.99, $1.00–$2.99, and so on considered mutually exclusive or non–mutually exclusive? Why?

8. If the probabilities associated with each class were totaled, what would the total be?

9. What is the probability of selecting an envelope at random and finding it contained either $30 or over, or under $1?

10. What is the probability of not finding at least $30 in an envelope selected at random?

11. *a.* What is the following picture called?

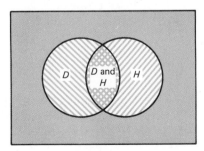

b. What is the name of the total area encompassed by the large rectangle?
c. Are the events D and H mutually exclusive? Explain.
d. What is the formula for arriving at the probability of D or H happening?

12. Design a formula and then determine the probability that a card selected at random from a standard deck of cards will be a queen or a spade or a diamond. Which rule of probability does this illustrate?

Rules of multiplication

Special rule of multiplication. If there are two independent events A and B, the probability that A and B will occur is found by multiplying the two probabilities. Thus, for two events A and B, the **special rule of multiplication** shown symbolically is:

$$P(A \text{ and } B) = P(A) \times P(B) \text{ or}$$
$$= P(A) \cdot P(B) \leftarrow$$

Raised dot means to *multiply*.

This rule for combining probabilities presumes that a second outcome does *not* depend on the first outcome. To illustrate what is meant by independence of outcomes, suppose two coins are tossed. The outcome of one coin (head or tail) is unaffected by the outcome of the other coin (head or tail). For three independent events A, B, and C, the special rule of multiplication used to determine the probability all three events will occur is:

$$P(A \text{ and } B \text{ and } C) = P(A) \cdot P(B) \cdot P(C)$$

EXAMPLE

Two coins are tossed. What is the probability that both will land tail up?

SOLUTION

The probability of a tail's showing face up on one of the coins, written $P(A)$, is one half, or 0.50. The probability that the other coin will land tail up, written $P(B)$, is one half, or 0.50. The probability that both will happen is one fourth, or 0.25, found by:

$$P(A \text{ and } B) = P(A) \cdot P(B)$$
$$= \tfrac{1}{2} \times \tfrac{1}{2}$$
$$= \tfrac{1}{4}, \text{ or } 0.25$$

This can be shown by listing all of the possible outcomes. Two tails is only one of the four possible outcomes.

(T) (T)

or (T) (H)

or (H) (T)

or (H) (H)

—————————————————— **SELF-REVIEW 9–8** ——————————————————

1. Assuming that "average life" means that the probability is one-half that a tire will not last 40,000 miles, and $P = \frac{1}{2}$ that a tire will last over 40,000 miles. Then, probability that all four will need adjustment is $\frac{1}{16}$, found by $\frac{1}{2} \times \frac{1}{2} \times \frac{1}{2} \times \frac{1}{2}$.

2. *a.*

$$0.0000156$$

found by

$$0.025 \times 0.025 \times 0.025$$

b. The chance of selecting three bags and finding all are underweight is rather remote.

1. A tire manufacturer advertises that "the average life of our new tire XB-70 is 40,000 miles. An immediate adjustment will be made on any tire which does not last 40,000 miles." You purchased four XB-70s. What is the probability that you will return all four tires for adjustment (meaning all four will wear out before traveling 40,000 miles)?

2. As cited in an earlier example, an automatic machine inserts mixed vegetables in a plastic bag. Past experience revealed that some packages were underweight and some overweight, but most of them had satisfactory weight.

Weight	Percent of total
Underweight	0.025
Satisfactory	.900
Overweight	.075

a. What is the probability of selecting three packages from the food-processing line today and finding that all three of them are underweight?

b. What does this probability mean?

General rule of multiplication. If two events are *not* independent they are referred to as being **dependent**. To illustrate dependency, suppose there are 10 rolls of film in a box and it is known that 3 are defective. A roll of film is selected from the box. Obviously, the probability of selecting a defective roll is $\frac{3}{10}$, and the probability of selecting a good roll is $\frac{7}{10}$. Then a second roll is selected from the box. The probability that it is defective *depends on* whether the first roll selected was defective or good. The probability that the second roll is defective is—

$\frac{2}{9}$, if the first roll selected was defective. (Only two defective rolls remained in the box containing nine rolls.)

$\frac{3}{9}$, if the first roll selected was good. (All three defective rolls are still in the box containing nine rolls.)

The $\frac{2}{9}$ (or $\frac{3}{9}$) is aptly called a **conditional probability** because its value is conditional on (dependent on) whether a defective or good roll of film is chosen in the first selection from the box.

The **general rule of multiplication** is used to find the **joint probability** that two events will occur, such as selecting defectives rolls from the box of 10 rolls. In general, the rule states that for two events, A and B, the joint probability that both events will happen is found by multiplying the probability that event *A* will happen by the conditional probability of event *B*'s occurring. Symbolically, the joint probability $P(A \text{ and } B)$ is found by:

$$P(A \text{ and } B) = P(A) \cdot P(B|A)$$

where $P(B|A)$ stands for the probability that *B* will occur *given that* A *has already occurred*. The vertical line means "given that."

EXAMPLE

To repeat the previous illustration: There are 10 rolls of film in a box and 3 are defective. Two rolls are to be selected, one after the other. What is the probability of selecting a defective roll followed by another defective roll?

SOLUTION

The first roll of film selected from the box is event *A*. $P(A) = {}^3/_{10}$ because 3 out of the 10 are defective. The second roll selected is event *B*. Assuming the second roll is defective, $P(B|A) = {}^2/_9$, because after the first selection was defective only two defective rolls of film remained in the box containing nine rolls. Determining the probability of two defectives:

$$P(A \text{ and } B) = P(A) \cdot P(B|A)$$

$$= \frac{3}{10} \times \frac{2}{9}$$

$$= \frac{6}{90}, \text{ or about } 0.07$$

The interpretation of the equation is that, if this experiment was conducted about 100 times, in the long run 7 times out of the 100 defectives rolls would be on both the first two selections.

Incidentally, it is assumed that this experiment was conducted **without replacement**—that is, the defective roll of film was not thrown back in the box before the next roll was selected. It should also be noted that the general rule of multiplication can be extended to more than two events. For three events, A, B, and C, the formula would be:

$$P(A \text{ and } B \text{ and } C) = P(A) \cdot P(B|A) \cdot P(C|A \text{ and } B)$$

For illustration, the probability that the first three rolls chosen from the box will all be defective is 0.00833, found by:

$$P(A \text{ and } B \text{ and } C) = P(A) \cdot P(B|A) \cdot P(C|A \text{ and } B)$$

$$= \frac{3}{10} \times \frac{2}{9} \times \frac{1}{8}$$

$$= \frac{6}{720}$$

$$= 0.00833$$

or, $0.300 \times 0.222 \times 0.125 = 0.00833$.

SELF-REVIEW 9–9

a. 0.002, found by:

$$\frac{4}{12} \times \frac{3}{11} \times \frac{2}{10} \times \frac{1}{9} = \frac{24}{11,880} = 0.002$$

b. 0.14, found by:

$$\frac{8}{12} \times \frac{7}{11} \times \frac{6}{10} \times \frac{5}{9} = \frac{1680}{11,880}$$

c. No, because there are other possibilities such as three women and one man.

1. A board of directors consists of eight men and four women. A four-member search committee is to be chosen at random to recommend a new company president.

    a. What is the probability that all four members of the search committee will be women?

    b. What is the probability that all four members will be men?

    c. Does the sum of the probabilities for *a* and *b* equal 1.00? Explain.

Another application of the general rule of multiplication follows. A survey of executives dealt with their loyalty to the company. One of the questions asked was, "If you were given an offer by another company equal to or slightly better than your present position, would you remain with the company or take the other position?" The responses of the 200 executives in the survey were cross-classified with their length of service with the company (see Table 9–1). The type of table that resulted is usually referred to as a **contingency table**.

TABLE 9–1
Loyalty of executives and length of service with company

Loyalty	Length of service				
	Less than 1 year	1–5 years	6–10 years	Over 10 years	Total
Would remain	10	30	5	75	120
Would not remain	25	15	10	30	80
					200

EXAMPLE

What is the probability of randomly selecting an executive who is loyal to the company (would remain) and who has over 10 years of service?

SOLUTION

Notice that two events occur at the same time—the executive would remain with the company, and he or she has over 10 years service.

1. Event A is an executive who would remain with the company despite an equal or slightly better offer from another company. To find the probability that event A will happen, refer back to Table 9–1. Note that there are 120 executives out of the 200 in the survey who would remain with the company. So $P(A) = 120/200$, or 0.60.
2. Event B is an executive who has over 10 years of service with the company. Thus $P(B|A)$ is the probability that an executive with over 10 years of service would remain with the company despite an equal or slightly better offer from another company. Note in the contingency table, Table 9–1, that 75 out of the 120 executives who would remain have over 10 years of service. So $P(B|A) = 75/120$.

Solving for the probability that an executive randomly selected will be one who would remain with the company and who has over 10 years service with the company, and using the general rule of multiplication:

$$P(A \text{ and } B) = P(A) \cdot P(B|A)$$

$$= \frac{120}{200} \times \frac{75}{120}$$

$$= \frac{9,000}{24,000}$$

$$= 0.375$$

SELF-REVIEW 9–10

$$P(A \text{ and } B) = P(A) \cdot P(B|A)$$

$$= \frac{80}{200} \times \frac{25}{80}$$

$$= 0.125$$

Refer to Table 9–1. Using the general rule of multiplication, what is the probability of selecting at random an executive who would not remain with the company and has less than one year of service?

TREE DIAGRAMS   A tree diagram is very useful for portraying conditional and joint probabilities. The contingency table (Table 9–1) is reintroduced to show the construction of a tree diagram.

	Length of service				
Loyalty	Less than 1 year	1–5 years	6–10 years	Over 10 years	Total
Would remain	10	30	5	75	120
Would not remain	25	15	10	30	80
					200

1. The construction of a tree diagram is begun by drawing a heavy dot on the left to represent the trunk of the tree (see Chart 9-1).

CHART 9-1
Tree diagram showing loyalty and length of service

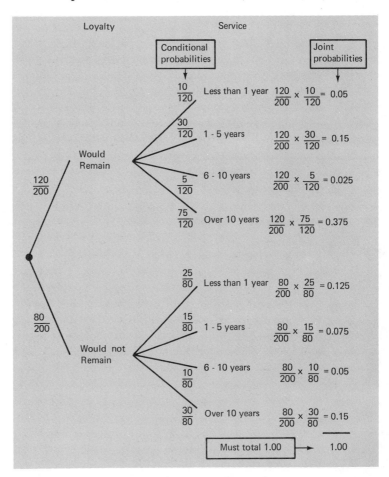

2. For this problem, two main branches go out from the trunk, the upper one representing "would remain" and the lower one "would not remain." Their probabilities are written on the branches, namely, 120/200 and 80/200. These are $P(A)$ and $P(\sim A)$.
3. Four branches "grow" out of each of the two main branches. These branches represent the length of service—less than 1 year, 1–5 years, 6–10 years, and 10 years and over. The conditional probabilities 10/120, 30/120, 5/120, and so on are written on the appropriate branches. These are $P(B_1|A)$, $P(B_2|A$, and so on.
4. Finally, joint probabilities, that A and B will occur together, are shown on the right side. These are $P(A \text{ and } B)$. For example, the joint probability of randomly selecting an executive who would remain with the company and who has less than one year of service is:

$$P(A \text{ and } B) = \frac{120}{200} \times \frac{10}{120}$$

$$= \frac{1,200}{24,000}$$

$$= 0.05$$

Note that because the joint probabilities represent all possible selections (would remain, 6–10 years service; not remain, over 10 years service; etc.) they must sum to 1.00.

SELF-REVIEW 9–11

1. Go out from the tree trunk on the lower branch, "would not remain." The probability of that event is 80/200. Continuing on the same path, find the branch labeled "6–10 years." That conditional probability is 10/80. To get the joint probability,

$$P(A \text{ and } B) = \frac{80}{200} \times \frac{10}{80}$$

$$= \frac{800}{16,000}$$

$$= 0.05$$

2. *a.* Contingency table.
   b.

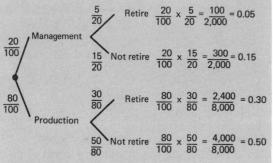

   c. Yes, all possibilities are included.

1. Refer to the tree diagram in Chart 9–1. Explain the path you would follow to find the joint probability of selecting an executive at random who has 6–10 years' service and who would not remain with the company having received an equal or slightly better offer from another company.

2. A random sample of the employees of a company was chosen in order to determine their plans after age 65. Those selected in the sample were divided into either management or production. The results were:

Employee	Plans after age 65		
	Retire	Not retire	Total
Management.......	5	15	20
Production	30	50	80
			100

a. What is the table called?

b. Draw a tree diagram and determine the joint probabilities.

c. Do the joint probabilities total 1.00? Why?

EXERCISES

13. A coin is tossed four times.
    a. What is the probability that all four tosses will result in a head face up?
    b. Using the letters A, B, C, and D, write the formula for the probability of this outcome.
    c. Suppose four heads did appear face up on the toss of the coin. What is the probability that a head will appear face up on the next toss of the coin?

14. Three young children approach a gum-ball machine, each with a nickle to spend. The machine has just been filled with 50 black, 150 white, 100 red, and 100 yellow balls, which have been thoroughly mixed.

   a. Sue and Jim approached the machine first. They both said they wanted red gum-balls. What is the likelihood they will get their wish?

   b. Sue and Jim did get red gum-balls. Sammie approached the machine next and said he did not want a red gum-ball. What is the chance he will get his wish?

   c. What is the probability that Sammie will not get his wish?

15. Three defective electric toothbrushes were accidently shipped to a drugstore by the manufacturer along with 17 nondefective ones.

   a. What is the probability that the first two electric toothbrushes sold will be returned to the drugstore because they were defective?

   b. What is the probability that the first two electric toothbrushes sold will not be defective?

16. Each salesperson in a large department store chain is rated either below average, average, or above average with respect to his or her sales ability. Each salesperson is also rated with respect to his or her potential for advancement—either fair, good, or excellent. These traits for the 500 salespersons were cross-classified into the following table.

Sales ability	Potential for advancement		
	Fair	Good	Excellent
Below average	16	12	22
Average	45	60	45
Above average	93	72	135

   a. What is this kind of table called?

   b. Using one of the rules for combining probabilities, what is the probability that a salesperson selected at random will have above-average sales ability and excellent potential for advancement?

   c. Construct a tree diagram showing all the probabilities, conditional probabilities, and joint probabilities.

17. In a management trainee program 80 percent of the trainess are female, 20 percent male. Ninety percent of the females attended college, 78 percent of the males attended college.

   a. A management trainee is selected at random. What is the probability that the person selected is a female who did not attend college?

   b. Construct a tree diagram showing all the probabilities, conditional probabilities, and joint probabilities.

   c. Do the joint probabilities total 1.00? Why?

PRINCIPLES OF COUNTING

The total number of possible outcomes in an experiment may be difficult to determine. The following principles of **multiplication**, **permutations**, and **combinations** merely facilitate counting. For example, suppose there are three different parts which must be assembled into a plug-in unit for a television chassis. If it makes no difference in which order the three parts are assembled, how many different ways must the production supervisor try before the most efficient sequence of assembly is found?

The multiplication principle

The multiplication principle states: *if there are* m *ways of doing one thing and* n *ways of doing another thing there are* m × n *ways of doing both.* The multiplication formula is:

> Total number of arrangements = $m \times n$

This can be extended to more than two events. For three events, *m, n,* and *o*:

> Total number of arrangements = $m \times n \times o$

EXAMPLE

A building of villas has developed three exterior home plans which he has named the Mediterranean, the Timeless, and the Classic. Two floor plans are offered, the Norfolk and the Sarasota. How many different arrangements of exterior and interior plans can the builder offer?

SOLUTION

Of course the builder could determine the total number of arrangements by picturing all possible options and then counting them. There are six.

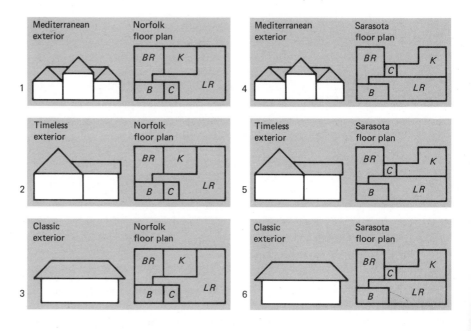

Using the multiplication formula as a check (m is the number of exterior styles, n the number of interior floor plans):

$$\text{Total possible arrangements} = m \times n$$
$$= 3 \times 2$$
$$= 6$$

It was not difficult to picture and count all the possible exterior and interior arrangements in this example. Suppose, however, that the builder developed eight exterior styles and six interior floor plans. It would be tedious to picture and count all the possible alternatives. Instead, the multiplication formula is used. In this case $m \times n = 8 \times 6 = 48$ possible arrangements.

───────────────── **SELF-REVIEW 9–12** ─────────────────

1. There are 20, found by 5×4.

2. There are 72, found by $3 \times 2 \times 4 \times 3$.

1. A lamp manufacturer has developed five lamp bases and four lamp shades which could be used together. How many different arrangements of base and shade can be offered?

2. An electronics firm manufactures three models of stereo receivers, two cassette decks, four speakers, and three turntables. When the four types of components are sold together, they form a "system." How many different systems can the electronic firm offer?

Permutations

In the previous illustrations there were two or more groups. In the problem regarding villas, there were two groups: an exterior design was selected, and an interior floor plan was chosen. The multiplication formula is applied to find out how many different arrangements are possible.

Another type of counting problem is concerned with only *one* group. As illustrations of this type of problem:

1. A group of three electronic parts is to be assembled into a plug-in unit for a television set. The parts can be assembled in any order. The question involving counting is: How many different ways can the three parts be assembled?

2. A machine operator must make four checks before starting to machine a part. He must tighten a clamp, and so on. It does not matter in which order the checks are made. How many different ways can the operator make the checks?

In both illustrations, the order of selection is important. One order might be: transistor first, the LEDs second, and the synthesizer third. This arrangement is called a **permutation**. *A permutation is an arrangement of a set of objects in which there is a first, a second, and a third order through* n.

Notice that the order of arrangement is important in permutations. The arrangements *a, b, c,* and *b, a, c* are *different* permutations.

The **permutation formula** employed to count the total number of arrangements is:

$$_nP_r = \frac{n!}{(n-r)!}$$

where:

- *P* is the number of permutations, or ways, the objects can be arranged.
- *n* is the total number of objects. In the previous illustration, there are three electronic parts. So, *n* = 3.
- *r* is the number of objects to be used at one time. In the electronics problem all the objects (electronic parts) are to be assembled. So *r* = 3. If only two out of the three electronic parts were to be inserted in the plug-in unit, *r* would be 2.

Before solving the above two problems it should be noted that permutations and combinations use a notation called *n* **factorial**. It is written *n*! and means the product of $n(n-1)(n-2)(n-3) \ldots [n-(n-1)]$. For instance, 5! would be found by $5(5-1)(5-2)(5-3)[5-(5-1)]$. Thus, $5 \cdot 4 \cdot 3 \cdot 2 \cdot 1 = 120$.

As shown below, $5 \cdot 4 \cdot 3 \cdot 2 \cdot 1$ are numbers and can be canceled when the same numbers are included in the numerator and denominator.

$$\frac{6! \, 3!}{4!} = \frac{6 \cdot 5 \cdot \cancel{4} \cdot \cancel{3} \cdot \cancel{2} \cdot \cancel{1}(3 \cdot 2 \cdot 1)}{\cancel{4} \cdot \cancel{3} \cdot \cancel{2} \cdot \cancel{1}} = 180$$

By definition, zero factorial, written 0!, is set equal to one. That is, 0! = 1.

EXAMPLE

Referring back to the group of three electronic parts which are to be assembled in any order, how many different ways can they be assembled?

SOLUTION

n = 3 because there are three electronic parts to be assembled.

r = 3 because all three are to be inserted in the plug-in unit.

Solving:

$$_nP_r = \frac{n!}{(n-r)!} = \frac{3!}{(3-3)!} = \frac{3!}{0!} = \frac{3!}{1} = 6$$

SELF-REVIEW 9-13

1. 720, found by $6 \times 5 \times 4 \times 3 \times 2 \times 1$.
2. 10, found by:

$$\frac{6 \cdot 5 \cdot \cancel{4 \cdot 3 \cdot 2 \cdot 1}(2 \cdot 1)}{4 \cdot 3 \cdot 2 \cdot 1(3 \cdot 2 \cdot 1)}$$

3. 24, found by:

$$\frac{4!}{(4-4)!} = \frac{4!}{0!}$$

$$= \frac{4!}{1}$$

$$= \frac{4 \cdot 3 \cdot 2 \cdot 1}{1}$$

4. 5,040, found by

$$\frac{10!}{(10-4)!} = \frac{10!}{6!}$$

$$= \frac{10 \cdot 9 \cdot 8 \cdot 7 \cdot \cancel{6 \cdot 5 \cdot 4 \cdot 3 \cdot 2 \cdot 1}}{\cancel{6 \cdot 5 \cdot 4 \cdot 3 \cdot 2 \cdot 1}}$$

1. What does 6! equal?
2. What does $\dfrac{6! \, 2!}{4! \, 3!}$ equal?
3. Referring back to the second illustration: A machine operator must make four checks before starting to machine a part. It does not matter in which order the checks are made. How many different ways can the operator make the checks?
4. The ten numbers 0 through 9 are to be used in code groups of four to identify an item of clothing. Code 1083 might identify a blue blouse, size medium. The code group 2031 might identify a pair of pants, size 18, and so on. Repetitions of numbers are not permitted. That is, the same number cannot be used twice (or more) in a total sequence. As examples, 2,256, 2,562, or 5,559 would not be permitted. How many different code groups can be designed?

Another way of looking at the question of permutations is considering how many spaces have to be filled and what are the various possibilities for each space. In the problem involving three electronic parts, there are three locations in the plug-in unit for the three parts. There are three possibilities for the first space, two for the second (one has been used up), and one for the third, as follows:

$$(3)(2)(1) = 6 \text{ permutations}$$

The six ways the three electronic parts lettered A, B, C can be arranged are:

$$\begin{array}{ccc} ABC & BAC & CAB \\ ACB & BCA & CBA \end{array}$$

To cite another example, suppose that there are eight machines but only three spaces on the floor of the machine shop for the machines. How many different ways (permutations) can the eight machines be arranged in the three spaces? The commonsense approach would be as follows. There are eight possibilities for the first space, seven for the second space (one has been used up), and six for the third space. Then:

$$(8)(7)(6) = 336 \text{ permutations}$$

As before, this may also be expressed mathematically by saying the number of permutations, P, of n items is dependent on the number of spaces, r, available.

$$_nP_r = \frac{n!}{(n-r)!} = \frac{8!}{(8-3)!} = \frac{8!}{5!} = \frac{(8)(7)(6)\cancel{5!}}{\cancel{5!}} = 336$$

SELF-REVIEW 9–14

a. 60, found by (5)(4)(3).
b. 60, found by:

$$\frac{5!}{(5-3)!} = \frac{5 \cdot 4 \cdot 3 \cdot \cancel{2} \cdot \cancel{1}}{\cancel{2} \cdot \cancel{1}}$$

A musician wants to write a score based on only five notes (A-flat, B-natural, C-sharp, D-flat, and E-sharp). However, only three notes out of the five will be used in succession, such as C-sharp, A-flat, and E-sharp. Repetitions, such as A-flat, A-flat, and E-sharp, will not be permitted.

a. Using the commonsense approach just discussed, how many permutations of the five notes taken three at a time are possible?
b. Using the permutation formula, how many permutations are possible?

The previous discussion of permutations did not allow for any repetition. For example, the three electronic parts to be placed in the plug-in unit for the television set were all different. Repetitions, such as two transistors and one synthesizer, were not allowed (or the television set probably would not operate correctly).

If repetitions are permitted, the permutation formula is:

$$\boxed{_nP_r = n^r}$$

To illustrate the point, assume that two letters, *A* and *B*, are to be taken two at a time. The number of permutations *without* repetitions is two (*AB* and *BA*). Or, it could be found by—

$$P = \frac{n!}{(n-r)!} = \frac{2!}{(2-2)!} = 2$$

With repetitions, such as *AA*, there are four permutations possible, found by $P = n^r = 2^2$. The four permutations are *AA*, *AB*, *BA*, and *BB*.

SELF-REVIEW 9–15

125, found by $_nP_r = n^r = 5^3$

In Self-Review 9–14, the musician decided to use five notes taken three at a time. Repetitions—such as A-flat, A-flat, and E-sharp—were not permitted. There are 60 possible arrangements (permutations) of three notes. If repetitions are permitted, how many permutations are possible?

In brief review of permutations, if a set of objects designated by *a*, *b*, *c*, *d*, and e can also be arranged $a, c, d, e,$ and $b,$ and if they can be arranged $c, a,$ $e, b,$ and d and so on, then there are 120 *permutations* of these five objects taken five at a time, found by:

$$_nP_r = \frac{n!}{(n-r)!} = \frac{5!}{(5-5)!}$$

where:

> n is the total number of objects.
> r is the number of objects considered for each permutation.

If only two of the five objects were considered—such as $a, b; d, a;$ or $c,$ e—then there is a total of 20 permutations possible, found by:

$$_nP_r = \frac{n!}{(n-r)!} = \frac{5!}{(5-2)!}$$

Note then that in permutations, *the order in which the objects are listed differs from one arrangement to the next* (that is, a, b differs from b, a; from e, a; and so on). And each arrangement is counted.

If repetitions are permitted, such as a, a, a, b, b or $a, a, b, b, d,$ the number of permutations can be determined by $_nP_r = n^r$. For the five objects $(n = 5)$ taken five at a time $(r = 5),$ there are 3,125 possible arrangements found by $_nP_r = n^r = 5^5$.

Combinations

In determining the number of permutations of n different things taken r at a time, the order of things was of concern. For example, in painting three color dots on a resistor, the order could be red, orange, and blue (meaning, say, a 500-ohm resistor). Or the order could be orange, blue and red (meaning a 1,000-ohm resistor), and so on. There are six permutations of the three colors, found by:

$$_nP_r = \frac{n!}{(n-r)!} = \frac{3 \cdot 2 \cdot 1}{(3-3)!} = 6$$

Suppose, however, it has been decided that any **combination** of red, orange, and blue will be used on a resistor to identify it as a 750-ohm resistor. *The order is not important.* In effect, the many different ways of ordering the three colors are being disregarded; that is, the combination of red, blue, and orange on a resistor is considered the same as orange, blue, and red. Both would identify a 750-ohm resistor. This means that the combination of red, orange, and blue can be used only once for identification purposes. The **combination formula** is:

$$_nC_r = \frac{n!}{r!(n-r)!}$$

EXAMPLE

The paint department has been given the assignment of designing color codes for 42 different parts. Three colors are to be used on each part, but a combination of three colors used for one part cannot be rearranged and used to identify a different part. This means that if green, yellow, and violet were used to identify a cam shaft, yellow, violet, and green (or any other combination of these three colors) could not be used to identify, say, a pinion gear. Would seven colors taken three at a time be adequate to color-code the 42 parts?

SOLUTION

There are 35 combinations, found by:

$$_7C_3 = \frac{n!}{r!(n-r)!} = \frac{7!}{3!(7-3)!} = \frac{7!}{3!4!} = 35$$

The seven colors taken three at a time (i.e., three colors to a part) would not be adequate to color-code the 42 different parts because they would provide only 35 combinations. Eight colors taken three at a time would give 56 different combinations. This would be more than adequate to color-code the 42 different parts.

─── SELF-REVIEW 9–16 ───

1. 56 is correct, found by:

$$_8C_3 = \frac{n!}{r!(n-r)!} = \frac{8!}{3!(8-3)!}$$

$$= \frac{8!}{3!5!}$$

$$= \frac{8 \cdot 7 \cdot 6 \cdot 5!}{3 \cdot 2 \cdot 1 \cdot 5!}$$

$$= 56$$

2. Yes. There are 45 combinations, found by:

$$_{10}C_2 = \frac{n!}{r!(n-r)!}$$

$$= \frac{10!}{2!(10-2)!}$$

$$= \frac{10!}{2!8!}$$

$$= \frac{10 \cdot 9 \cdot 8!}{2 \cdot 1 \cdot 8!}$$

$$= 45$$

1. Verify the 56 combinations cited in the previous paragraph.
2. As an alternate plan for color-coding the 42 different parts, it has been suggested that only two colors be placed on a part. Would 10 colors be adequate to color-code the 42 different parts? (Again, a combination of two colors could only be used once—that is, if pink and blue were coded for one part, blue and pink could not be used to identify a different part.)

To reemphasize the difference between a permutation and a combination, note again that for a **permutation** the order *a, b, c, d,* and *e* is one order; *a, c, d, e,* and *b* form another order; and so on. With five letters, a total of 120 such permutations are possible. Thus, a permutation is an arrangement where order is important.

If the order of selection is not important, the total number of orders is called a **combination**. If, for example, Able, Baker, Chauncy, Delbecque, and Eberlin were chosen as a committee to handle the forthcoming negotiations with the union, there is only one possible combination of these five executives. Logically, a committee consisting of Chauncy, Baker, Eberlin, Delbecque, and Able is the same as the first one listed.

EXERCISES

18. Six basic colors are to be used in decorating a new condominium. They are to be applied to a unit in groups of four colors. One unit might have gold as the principal color, blue as the complimentary color, and red as the accent color with touches of white. Another unit might have blue as the principal color, white as the complimentary color, and gold as the accent color with touches of red.

    a. If repetitions are not permitted (such as gold, gold, gold, and white), how many different units can be decorated?

    b. If repetitions are permitted, how many different units can be decorated? (Of course, this would probably not be very good decorating!)

19. A rug manufacturer has decided to use seven compatible colors in her rugs. However, in weaving a rug only five spindles can be used. In her advertising the rug manufacturer wants to indicate the number of different color groupings she has for sale. How many color groupings using the seven colors taken five at a time are there? (This assumes that five different colors will go into each rug— i.e., there are no repetitions of color.)

20. Consideration is being given to forming a Super Ten football conference. The top ten football teams in the country based on past records would be members of the Super Ten Conference. Each team would play every other team in the conference during the season. The team winning the most games would be declared the national champion. How many games would the conference commissioner have to schedule each year? (Remember, Oklahoma versus Michigan is the same as Michigan versus Oklahoma.)

CHAPTER SUMMARY

A probability is expressed as a number and indicates the chance that a specific event will happen. The highest probability, 1.00, means that the event is certain to occur, and 0.00 means it will not occur. A 0.90 probability of rain reveals that the chance the event (rain) will happen is quite high. A probability of 0.02, on the other hand, indicates that the likelihood the event will happen is almost nil.

Three viewpoints of probability, namely, the classical (objective), the relative frequency (historical), and the subjective were discussed. The classical viewpoint is based on the assumption that the outcomes of an experiment are equally likely. On the toss of a coin, for example, the probabilities of a head or a tail showing face up are equally likely (one half, or 0.50).

The relative frequency viewpoint of probability is based on past experience. If, for example a field goal kicker made 12 out of 36 field goals this year from the 40-yard line, the probability of a successful kick from that distance is $^{12}/_{36} = ^{1}/_{3} = 0.33$.

The subjective, or personal, viewpoint of probability is based on whatever information is available—subjective judgment, hunches, and so on.

Rules for combining probabilities—namely, the rules of addition and multiplication—were presented. The special rule of addition can be applied when the events are mutually exclusive. This means that when one event occurs none of the other events can happen at the same time. The rule for adding two probabilities is: $P(A \text{ or } B) = P(A) + P(B)$.

The general rule of addition is used when the events are not mutually exclusive—that is, there is an overlapping of outcomes. Symbolically, for two events: $P(A \text{ or } B) = P(A) + P(B) - P(A \text{ and } B)$.

The special rule of multiplication assumes that the second outcome does not depend on the first outcome. For example, the outcome of the roll of one die does not depend on the roll of the second die. For two events: $P(A \text{ and } B) = P(A) \cdot P(B)$.

The general rule of multiplication is applied to find the probability that two events will occur. For example, if there are 100 numbers in a box and 20 are winning numbers, the probability that you will select two winning numbers on the first two draws from the box is 0.038, found by

$$P(A) \text{ and } B) = P(A) \cdot P(B|A)$$

$$= \frac{20}{100} \times \frac{19}{99}$$

The multiplication, permutation, and combination formulas facilitate counting the total number of arrangements. The multiplication formula for two events is $m \times n$ where m is the number of ways of doing one thing and n the number of ways of doing a second thing. If there is only one group, the permutation formula is applied.

$$_nP_r = \frac{n!}{(n - r)!}$$

is the formula for the number of arrangements of n things taken r at a time. Order is important. a, b, c is one permutation of three letters, b, c, a another, c, b, a another way, and so on. If repetitions are permitted, the formula becomes $_nP_r = n^r$.

If the order of the objects is not important, the combination formula

$$_nC_r = \frac{n!}{r!(n - r)!}$$

CHAPTER OUTLINE

A survey of probability concepts

I. Probability.
   A. *Definition.* A probability is a numerical value that measures the degree of certainty with which a particular event of interest will occur.
   B. *Rules of probability.*
      1. *Special rule of addition.* If there are two mutually exclusive events designated A and B, $P(A$ or $B) = P(A) + P(B)$. To apply the rule, two conditions must be met: (*a*) one of two outcomes must happen (example: on one flip of a coin, a head A or a tail B must show face up), (*b*) events must be mutually exclusive, meaning in tossing one coin, a head and a tail cannot show face up at the same time. If there are three events the formula would be written $P(A$ or B or $C) = P(A) + P(B) + P(C)$.
      2. *Complement rule.* $P(A) = 1 - P(\sim A)$. The probability of event A's happening can be found by subtracting the probability that it will *not* happen from one. In the coin-tossing problem, the probability of a head is $P(A) = 1 - P$(head will not show face up). Solving: $P(A) = 1 - 0.50 = 0.50$.
      3. *General rule of addition.* If the events are not mutually exclusive: $P(A$ or $B) = P(A) + P(B) - P(A$ and $B)$, where $P(A$ and $B)$ is called the **joint probability** and is usually referred to as a **compound event.** There is a chance that both event A and event B will happen.
      4. *Special rule of multiplication.* $P(A$ and $B) = P(A) \cdot P(B)$. This rule requires independence, meaning that the outcome of one event in no way affects the outcome of another event. Illustration: The probability of three heads on three tosses of a coin would be found by $P(A$ and B and $C) = 0.5 \times 0.5 \times 0.5$.
      5. *General rule of multiplication.* Applied when probabilities are *not* independent, meaning that the outcome of one event is conditional on the outcome of another event. For two events the rule is written $P(A$ and $B) = P(A) \cdot P(B|A)$.
II. Permutations and combinations.
   A. *Purpose.* To facilitate counting.
   B. *Permutations.* The order in which objects are arranged is important, and each order is counted. If repetitions are not permitted,

$$_nP_r = \frac{n!}{(n-r)!}$$

where:

   P is the number of permutations or ways the objects can be arranged.
   n is the total number of objects.
   r is the number of objects to be used at one time.

Example: If there are three letters, a, b, and c, and arrangements of two letters are to be made, there are six permutations, found by

$$_3P_2 = \frac{3 \cdot 2 \cdot 1}{1!}$$

To check: a, b; a, c; b, a; b, c; c, a; c, b. If repetitions are permitted, such as a, a, then the number of permutations is found by $_nP_r = n^r$. In the previous problem $_3P_2 = 3^2 = 9$. To check: a, a; a, b; a, c; b, a; b, b; b, c; c, a; c, b; c, c.

C. *Combinations.* If it is immaterial how the r objects are arranged, then—

$$_nC_r = \frac{n!}{r!(n-r)!}$$

Example: From three persons, Mr. A, Ms. B, and Ms. C., a committee of two is to be formed. The order in which the names are listed is immaterial. A committee of A and B is the same as a committee of B and A. There are three possible combinations, found by

$$_3C_2 = \frac{3 \cdot 2 \cdot 1}{2 \cdot 1(1)}.$$

Check: A and B, A and C, B and C.

CHAPTER EXERCISES

21. Forty percent of the families in precinct A are white, and 60 percent are nonwhite. Seven families are to be chosen by random sampling and interviewed in depth.
    a. What is the probability that all seven families chosen will be white?
    b. What is the probability that all seven families chosen will be nonwhite?

22. The odds on Stumblebum in the fifth race are 50 to 1. What is the likelihood (probability) that she will win?

23. The first card selected from a standard 52-card deck was a king.
    a. If it was returned to the deck, what is the probability that a king will be drawn on the second selection?
    b. If the king was not replaced, what is the probability that a king would be drawn on the second selection?
    c. What is the probability that a king would be selected on the first draw from the deck and another king on the second draw (assuming that the first king was not replaced)?

    Questions 24–26 are based on the following:
    A manufacturer of traffic-light systems found that under accelerated life tests, 95 percent of a newly developed system lasted three years before failing to change the signals properly.

24. If a city purchased five of these systems, what is the probability that all five systems would operate properly for at least three years?

25. Which rule of probability does this illustrate?

26. Using letters to represent the five systems, design an equation to show how you arrived at the answer to Problem 24.

27. There are five vacant parking places left in a parking lot. Four cars arrive at the parking lot at the same time. In how many different ways can these four cars be arranged in the five spaces?

28. A new game consists of three phases. The first phase is called ACCOM-PLISHMENTS. It consists of 20 cards. On the back of six cards there are accomplishments, such as "you solved a major crime" or "you discovered a cure for cancer." The backs of the remaining cards are blank. One of the participants starts the game by drawing a card. If he draws an accomplishment, he is eligible to draw another card. What is the probability that he will draw two accomplishments?

29. Refer to Problem 28. Phase 2 of the game, called MONEY, contain 15 cards, and 5 of them have statements on the back such as "you win $1 million" or "you broke the bank at Monte Carlo." The backs of the remaining cards are blank. Phase 3 of the game is called HONORS and consists of 30 cards, 8 of which have honors on the back, such as "you have been elected to Congress." One of the rules of the game states that if the first participant draws an accomplishment, he is eligible to draw a card from Phase 2 (MONEY). If he does win some money, he is then eligible to draw a card from Phase 3 (HONORS.) If he receives an honor, he wins the game. What is the probability that the first participant will win the game by accomplishing something, winning money, and receiving an honor?

CHAPTER SELF-REVIEW EXAMINATION

Do all of the problems and then check your answers against those given in Appendix A.

Score each problem 10 points.

Questions 1–4 are based on the following picture.

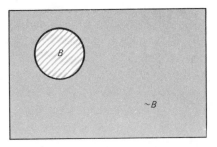

1. What is the picture called?

2. What is the total area called?

3. What rule of probability is being illustrated?

4. B represents the event of choosing a family that receives welfare payments. What does $P(B) + P(\sim B)$ equal?

5. Out of every 100 employees in a manufacturing plant, 57 are production workers

(designated as A), 40 are supervisors (designated as B), 2 are secretaries (designated as C), and 1 is with either middle or top management (designated as D). If an employee is selected at random, what does $P(A$ or B or $C)$ equal?

6. A punchboard has 50 squares numbered 1, 2, 3, . . . 50. It was announced that there are three winning numbers on the board.
   a. Using letters, design a formula to indicate how to calculate the probability that a winning number will be chosen on both the first and second selections from the punchboard.
   b. Compute the probability.

7. A test contains four multiple-choice questions. Each question has five answers, labeled a, b, c, d, e. Only one answer is correct. What is the probability of scoring 100 percent on the test, assuming that the person taking the test knows nothing about the subject and just guessed the answers?

8. A round-robin chess tournament involving the 20 members of the chess club must be scheduled. (In a round-robin tournament, each member plays every other member.) How many matches must be scheduled? (Of course, if Mr. Smith plays Mr. Jones, it is the same as Mr. Jones playing Mr. Smith.)

9. A new job consists of assembling four different parts. All four have different color codes, and they can be assembled in any order. The production department wants to determine the most efficient way to assemble the four parts. The supervisors are going to conduct some experiments to solve the problem. First, they plan to assemble the parts in this order—green, black, yellow, and blue— and record the time. Then the assembly will be accomplished in a different order. In how many different ways can the four parts be assembled?

10. A study by the Wyoming Tourist Bureau revealed that 60 percent of the state's tourists visit Yellowstone National Park, 40 percent visit Jackson Hole, and 30 percent visit both. What is the probability that a particular tourist will visit at least one of the attractions?

10

INTRODUCTION

Chapters 2 through 8 are devoted to **descriptive statistics**. In Chapter 2 we described the trend in sales and other business series using line graphs and other graphs. The daily commissions of 120 salespersons were described in Chapters 3 to 5, using such descriptive tools as a frequency distribution, averages, and measures of dispersion. Chapter 6 dealt with describing price, quantity, and value changes using an index. Chapters 7 and 8 were concerned with describing long-term and short-term trends using equations and smoothing techniques. These chapters focused on describing *something that had already happened*. A sales series, for example, is simply a listing of the amount of money received for products which have already been sold.

The emphasis changes starting with Chapter 9. We began describing *something that will probably happen*. This facet of statistics is called **statistical inference**. The objective is to make inferences about a population based on a small number, called a sample, selected from the population. Probability is a very valuable aid in making inferences about a population. Recall that a probability is a measure on the scale of 0 to 1 of a person's belief that a specific outcome of an experiment will occur.

We will go a step further in this chapter by generating a **probability distribution**. Two particular families of probability distributions will be discussed, namely, the **binomial probability distribution** and the **Poisson probability distribution**. They are referred to as being **discrete probability distributions**. Another very important probability distribution will be introduced in Chapter 11, the **normal probability distribution**. It is a **continuous probability distribution**. The difference between a discrete and a continuous distribution will be discussed shortly.

Discrete probability distributions

WHAT IS A PROBABILITY DISTRIBUTION?

> A probability distribution is a listing of the outcomes of an experiment and the probability associated with each outcome. The listing is usually exhaustive, and the outcomes are not overlapping—that is, they are mutually exclusive.

A probability distribution can be presented in the form of a table, a graph, or a formula. A probability distribution is quite similar to a frequency distribution. Like a frequency distribution, its purpose is to summarize all the possible outcomes and indicate the "shape of the future." A simple example is used to illustrate.

EXAMPLE

Suppose we are interested in the number of heads showing face up on three tosses of a coin. This is the experiment. The possible outcomes are zero heads, one head, two heads, and three heads. What is the probability distribution for the number of heads?

SOLUTION

The toss of the coin three times might result in:

First toss	Second toss	Third toss	First toss	Second toss	Third toss
T	T	T	H	T	T
T	T	H	H	T	H
T	H	T	H	H	T
T	H	H	H	H	H

Note that the outcome "zero heads" occurred only once, "1 head" occurred three times, "two heads" occurred three times, and the outcome "three heads" occurred only once. That is, zero heads happened one out of eight times. Thus the probability of zero heads is one eighth. The probability of one head is three eighths, and so on. The distribution of probabilities is shown in Table 10–1.

TABLE 10–1
Probability distribution for the outcome of zero, one, two, and three heads showing face up on three tosses of a coin

Number of heads	Probability of outcome
0	$\frac{1}{8}$ = 0.125
1	$\frac{3}{8}$ = 0.375
2	$\frac{3}{8}$ = 0.375
3	$\frac{1}{8}$ = 0.125
Total	$\frac{8}{8}$ = 1.000 ← Total must equal 1

The same information can be portrayed graphically, using a bar graph:

CHART 10–1
Graphical presentation of the number of heads and the associated probability resulting from three tosses of a coin

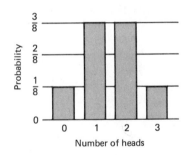

SELF-REVIEW 10–1

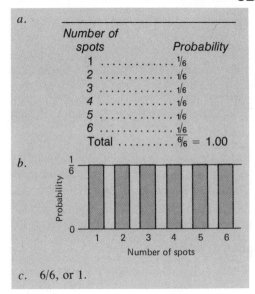

a.

Number of spots	Probability
1	$\frac{1}{6}$
2	$\frac{1}{6}$
3	$\frac{1}{6}$
4	$\frac{1}{6}$
5	$\frac{1}{6}$
6	$\frac{1}{6}$
Total	$\frac{6}{6} = 1.00$

b.

c. 6/6, or 1.

(A reminder: cover the answers in the left column.)

The possible outcomes of an experiment involving the roll of a six-sided die are: a one-spot, a two-spot, a three-spot, a four-spot, a five-spot, and a six-spot.

a. Develop a probability distribution for these outcomes.
b. Portray the probability distribution graphically.
c. What is the total of the probabilities?

Before we continue, notice that the individual probabilities in both the example and the self-review were between zero and one inclusive, and the total of the probabilities equaled one.

DISCRETE PROBABILITY DISTRIBUTIONS

The two previous probability distributions are called **discrete probability distributions** because the numerical outcomes can only have specified values. In the coin-tossing experiment, the numerical outcomes can only be zero, one, two, and three heads. There cannot be 2¼ heads or −6 heads. In the die-rolling experiment, the numerical outcomes can only be one, two, three, four, five, and six spots. We cannot have a one-half-spot or a nine-spot coming face up on a six-sided die. These values, which we designated earlier as X, are called **discrete random variables** because they are random outcomes of the experiment. A four-spot, for example, is a discrete random variable because it comes face up on the toss of a die by chance. Other examples of discrete random variables are:

The number of defectives in a sample of eight light bulbs, the discrete random variable, can be only zero, one, two, three, four, five, six, seven, and eight. There cannot be, for example 6⅞ defective light bulbs.

The number of executives in a sample of 100 who changed jobs last year can only assume values of 0, 1, 2, 3 . . . 100.

A definition will sum up the discussion.

> A discrete random variable is one which can have only certain clearly separate values resulting from a count of some item of interest.

Two discrete probability distributions will be discussed in this chapter.

CONTINUOUS PROBABILITY DISTRIBUTIONS

As the name implies, a **continuous probability distribution** is based on a **continuous random variable**. If we can *measure* something like the width of a room, the height of a person, or the outside diameter of a bushing, the variable is called a continuous random variable. It can assume one of an infinitely large number of values, within certain limitations. As examples:

The distance between Atlanta and Los Angeles could be 2,254 miles, 2,254.1 miles, 2,254.16 miles, 2,254.162 miles, and so on, depending on the accuracy of our measuring device.

Tire pressure could be 28 pounds, 28.6 pounds, 28.2 pounds, 28.626 pounds, and so on depending on the accuracy of the gauge.

The normal probability distribution developed in Chapter 11 is a continuous probability distribution.

BINOMIAL PROBABILITY DISTRIBUTIONS

The **binomial probability distribution** is a discrete probability distribution. Its prefix *bi* indicates that it is concerned with experiments where each outcome can take only two forms. For example, the answer to a true-false question is either true or false. The outcomes are *mutually exclusive* meaning in this case that the answer to a true-false question cannot be correct and wrong *at the same time*. A common way to designate the two outcomes is "success" and "failure." If, for example, you guessed the correct answer to a true-false question, the outcome would be classified as a success. If not, it is a failure. Other illustrations of experiments which might have only two outcomes:

Experiment: Selecting a mechanical toy from the production line.
Outcomes: Toy works correctly (a success).
Toy does not work correctly (a failure).

Experiment: Asking a five-year old child whether he likes a newly developed cereal.

Outcomes: He likes it (a success).

He does not like it (a failure).

A second characteristic of a binomial distribution is that the data collected are the *result of counts*. This is one reason that the binomial distribution is classified as a discrete distribution.

A third characteristic of a binomial distribution is that the probability of a success remains the same from one trial to another. Examples:

The probability that you will guess the first question of a true-false test correctly (a success) is one half. This is the first "trial." The probability that you will guess right on the second question (referred to as the second trial) is also one half, the probability of success on the third trial is one half, and so on.

If past experience revealed that the drawbridge over the Gulf Intracoastal Waterway was raised one out of every four times you approached it, then the probability is one fourth that it will be raised (a success) the next time you approach it, one fourth the following time, etc.

A fourth characteristic of a binomial probability distribution is that one trial is *independent* of any other trial. In effect this is the same as saying that there is no rhythmic pattern with respect to the outcomes. As an example, the answers to a true-false test are not arranged *T, T, T, F, F, F, T, T, T,* etc.

In summary, a binomial distribution has these characteristics;

1. An outcome of an experiment is classified into one of two mutually exclusive categories—namely, a success or a failure.
2. The data collected are the result of counts.
3. The probability of a success stays the same for each trial. So does the probability of a failure.
4. The trials are independent, meaning that the outcome of one trial does not affect the outcome of any other trial.

SELF-REVIEW 10-2

1. For each multiple-choice question, a student either guesses the answer correctly (a success) or does not (a failure).
2. The distribution of successes is discrete, resulting from a count of the number of successes.
3. The probability that a student will guess each question correctly is one-fifth, or 0.20.
4. The trials are independent, meaning that a success, or failure, on any question does not affect the outcome of any other question.

The professor teaching Horticulture 101 made an assignment involving the memorization of the Latin names of flowers. Unfortunately, none of the students studied the chapter. A "pop quiz" the next day consisted of 20 multiple-choice questions, each having five answers. Each student guessed the answer to each question. Why would the probability distribution resulting from this experiment be considered a binomial probability distribution?

How is a binomial distribution constructed?

To construct a binomial probability distribution, we must know (1) the number of trials, and (2) the probability of success on each trial. For example, if a market research questionnaire has 20 multiple-choice questions, the number of trials is 20. If each question on the questionnaire has five choices and only one choice is correct, the probability of success on each trial is one fifth, or 0.20. Thus, the probability is 0.20 that a person with no knowledge of the subject matter will guess the answer to a question correctly.

The binomial probability distribution can be described using the formula:

$$P(r) = \frac{n!}{r!(n-r)!}(p)^r(q)^{n-r}$$

where:

n is the number of trials.
r is the number of observed successes.
p is the probability of success on each trial.
q is the probability of a failure, found by $1 - p$.

EXAMPLE

As we all know, the answer to a true-false question is either correct or incorrect. Assume that (1) an examination consists of four true-false questions, and (2) a student has now knowledge of the subject matter. The chance (probability) that the student will guess the correct answer to the first question is one-half, or 0.50. Likewise, the probability of guessing each of the remaining questions correctly is also 0.50. What is the probability of—

1. Getting exactly none out of four correct?
2. Getting exactly one out of four correct?

SOLUTION

1. The probability of guessing exactly none out of the four correctly is 0.0625, found by solving the following equation. (Recall from Chapter 9 that 0! is equal to 1.)

$$P(r) = \frac{n!}{r!(n-r)!}(p)^r(q)^{n-r}$$

Substituting:

$$P(0) = \frac{4!}{0!(4-0)!}(0.50)^0(1-0.50)^{4-0}$$

$$= \frac{4 \cdot 3 \cdot 2 \cdot 1}{(1)(4 \cdot 3 \cdot 2 \cdot 1)}(1)(0.50)^4$$

$$= (1)(1)(0.50)^4$$

$$= 0.0625$$

2. The probability of getting exactly one out of four correct is 0.2500, found by:

$$P(1) = \frac{4!}{1!(4-1)!}(0.50)^1(1-0.50)^{4-1}$$

$$= \frac{4 \cdot 3 \cdot 2 \cdot 1}{1(3 \cdot 2 \cdot 1)}(0.50)^1(0.50)^3$$

$$= (4)(0.50)(0.125)$$

$$= 0.2500$$

SELF-REVIEW 10–3

0.3750 found by:

$$P(2) = \frac{4!}{2!(4-2)!}(0.50)^2(0.50)^{4-2}$$

$$= (6)(0.50)^2(0.50)^2$$

$$= (6)(0.25)(0.25)$$

What is the probability of getting exactly two of the four questions correct?

The probabilities of getting exactly zero, one, two, three, and four questions correct out of a total of four questions are shown in Table 10–2.

TABLE 10–2
Binomial probability distribution for $n = 4$, $p = 0.50$

Number of correct guesses	Probability Fraction	Decimal
0	$\frac{1}{16}$	0.0625
1	$\frac{4}{16}$	0.2500
2	$\frac{6}{16}$	0.3750
3	$\frac{4}{16}$	0.2500
4	$\frac{1}{16}$	0.0625
Total	$\frac{16}{16}$	1.0000

The data in Table 10–2 have been plotted in a bar chart to show the symmetrical nature of the binomial probability distribution when $p = 0.50$ (Chart 10–2).

CHART 10–2
Binomial distribution
for $n = 4, p = 0.50$

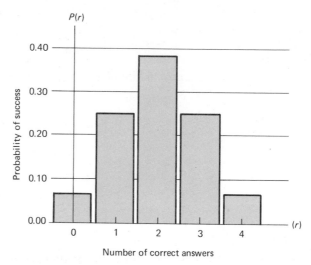

Number of correct answers

Binomial probability tables

A binomial probability distribution is a theoretical distribution which, as has been shown, can be generated mathematically. However, except for problems involving a small n (say an n of 3 or 4), the calculations for the probabilities of 0, 1, 2, . . . successes can be rather tedious.

As an aid, a table has been developed (in Appendix I) which gives the probabilities of 0, 1, 2, . . . successes for a selected n and p. To illustrate its use, consider the following example.

EXAMPLE

Judging from past experience, 5 percent of the worm gears produced by an automatic, high-speed machine are defective. What is the probability that out of six gears selected at random, exactly zero gears will be defective? Exactly one? Exactly two? Exactly three? Exactly four? Exactly five? Exactly six out of the six? (Note: $n = 6, p = .05$.)

SOLUTION

Refer to Appendix I. To find the probability of exactly zero defectives, go down the left margin to an n of 6 and an r of 0. Now move horizontally to the column headed by a p of 0.05 to find the probability. It is 0.7351.

The probability of exactly one defective in a sample of six worm gears is found similarly. It is 0.2321. The complete binomial probability distribution is: ($n = 6, p = 0.05$).

Number of defective gears r	Probability of occurrence P(r)
0	0.7351
1	0.2321
2	0.0305
3	0.0021
4	0.0001
5	0.0000*
6	0.0000*

* Appendix Table I gives the probabilities to only four decimal places.

Of course, there is some chance of getting exactly five defective gears out of six random selections. It is 0.00000178, found by inserting the appropriate values in the binomial formula.

$$P(5) = \frac{6!}{5!(6-5)!} (0.05)^5(0.95)^1$$

$$= (6)(0.05)^5(0.95)$$
$$= 0.00000178.$$

For six out of six it is 0.000000016, indicating that the probability is very small that five or six defective gears will be selected in a sample of six.

SELF-REVIEW 10-4

$n = 7, p = 0.25.$

	r	Probability
a.	0	. . . . 0.1335
b.	1	. . . . 0.3115
c.	2	. . . . 0.3115
	3	. . . . 0.1730
	4	. . . . 0.0577
	5	. . . . 0.0115
	6	. . . . 0.0013
	7	. . . . 0.0001

d. 1.0000, but in this case there is a slight discrepancy due to rounding.

Recall from a previous illustration that one out of every four times you approached the drawbridge over the Gulf Intracoastal Waterway it was raised and you had to wait. Using the binomial probability table:

a. What is the probability that on your next seven approaches to the drawbridge it will not be raised?
b. What is the probability that it will be raised exactly once out of the seven approaches?
c. What is the probability that it will be raised exactly twice? Exactly four times? Exactly five times ?Exactly six times? All seven times?
d. What should the probabilities in a, b, and c total?

Referring back to the binomial probability distribution for the defective worm gears, what is the probability that two *or more* out of the six selected at random will be defective? The probability is found by $P(2) + P(3) + P(4) + P(5) + P(6) = 0.0305 + 0.0021 + 0.0001 + 0.0000 + 0.0000 = 0.0327.$

SELF-REVIEW 10-5

a. 0.0706, found by 0.0577 + 0.0115 + 0.0013 + 0.0001.
b. 0.4450, found by 0.1335 + 0.3115.

Refer back to Self-Review 10-4.

a. On the next seven approaches to the drawbridge, what is the probability that you will discover the bridge raised four or more times?

b. What is the probability that you will discover the drawbridge raised one or less times out of the seven?

Appendix Table I is somewhat limited in that it only gives probabilities for an n of 1 to 20 and p values of 0.05, 0.10, 0.15 . . . 0.50. There are two methods for arriving at a binomial distribution for an n over 20, and/or a p not found in the table, say 0.07: (1) The normal approximation to the binomial may be used. This will be presented in Chapter 11. (2) A computer can generate the probabilities for a specified number of successes given an n and a p.

Two final points should be made about binomial distributions:

1. If n remains constant but p becomes larger and larger, the shape of the binomial probability distribution becomes more symmetrical. To illustrate, Table 10-3 gives the probabilities for an n of 10 and the probabilities of success of 0.05, 0.10, 0.20, and 0.50. They are plotted in Chart 10-3. Note that for the probability of success of 0.05, the distribution is highly skewed, but for a p of 0.50, it is symmetrical.

TABLE 10-3
Probability of 0, 1, 2, . . . successes for a p of 0.05, 0.10, 0.20, and 0.50 and an n of 10

| p | *Number of successes (r)* | | | | | | | | | | |
	0	1	2	3	4	5	6	7	8	9	10
0.05 $p(r)$	0.5987	0.3151	0.0746	0.0105	0.0010	0.0001	0.0000	0.0000	0.0000	0.0000	0.0000
0.10 $p(r)$	0.3487	0.3874	0.1937	0.0574	0.0112	0.0015	0.0001	0.0000	0.0000	0.0000	0.0000
0.20 $p(r)$	0.1074	0.2684	0.3020	0.2013	0.0881	0.0264	0.0055	0.0008	0.0001	0.0000	0.0000
0.50 $p(r)$	0.0010	0.0098	0.4039	0.1172	0.2051	0.2461	0.2051	0.1172	0.0439	0.0098	0.0010

Source: Appendix I.

2. If p, the probability of success, remains the same, but n becomes larger and larger, the shape of the binomial distribution becomes more symmetrical. Chart 10-4 shows a situation where p remains constant at 0.10, but n increases from left to right from 7 to 40.

CHART 10-3
Bar chart representing the binomial probability distribution for a _p_ of 0.05, 0.10, 0.20, and 0.50, and an _n_ of 10

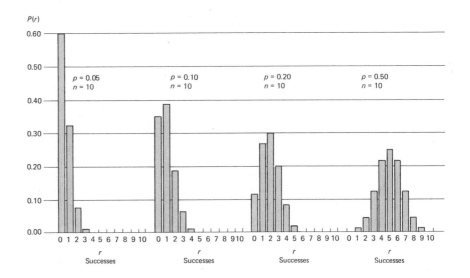

CHART 10-4
Bar chart representing the binomial probability distribution for a _p_ of 0.10 and an _n_ of 7, 12, 20, and 40.

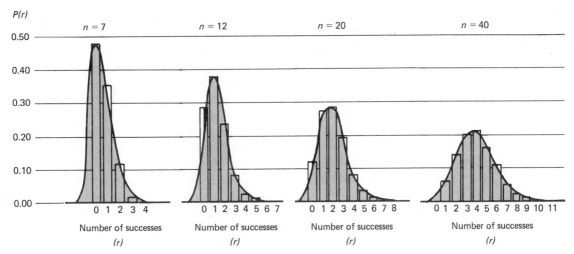

THE IMPORTANCE OF PROBABILITY DISTRIBUTIONS IN DECISION MAKING

Now that we have developed a probability distribution, what use is it in making business decisions? The answer to this question applies to all probability distributions which will be discussed in the next section and in the forthcoming chapters. To give some idea of their importance, two illustrations are presented.

1. Suppose that past experience revealed that 5 percent of the automobile doors coming off the production line are defective. A defective door is defined by quality control as a door with one or more defects, such as an exposed sharp burr, faulty paint, a dent, etc. Ten doors are to be selected at random by quality control. The binomial distribution for the number of defects in 10 trials with $p = 0.05$ is shown in Table 10–4.

TABLE 10–4
Binomial probability distribution for an n of 10 and a p of 0.05

Number of defects	Probability of occurrence
0	0.5987
1	0.3151
2	0.0746
3	0.0105
4	0.0010
5	0.0001
6	0.0000
7	0.0000
8	0.0000
9	0.0000
10	0.0000

Notice that the most probable number of defective doors in the sample of 10 is either 0 or 1. Three or more defective doors are quite improbable. If 6 doors were defective out of the 10, quality control would no doubt investigate the causes of the defects and have corrective action taken. So, knowledge of the distribution tells us, in advance of the experiment, what we can expect to occur and what are unusual results.

2. Surveys are conducted continuously by various research groups regarding voting preference, consumer protection policies, product preference, and so on. A set of multiple-choice questions is often used. The respondent checks what he or she considers the correct answer. The researcher is always concerned that uninformed respondents may merely guess the answers to avoid embarassment. The researcher, therefore, generates a probability distribution and matches it with the actual responses in order to help identify the guesses. For example, for a six-query questionnaire in which each question has five choices but only one answer, the binomial probability distribution for the number of correct answers given *by chance* is shown in Table 10–5.

TABLE 10–5
Binomial probability distribution for an n of 6 and a p of 0.20

Number of correct answers	Probability of occurrence
0	0.2621
1	0.3932
2	0.2458
3	0.0819
4	0.0154
5	0.0015
6	0.0001

The combined probabilities of 4, 5, and 6 are 17 out of 1,000. If 992 of the 1,000 respondents who completed the questionnaire had either 4, 5, or 6 correct answers, we would no doubt conclude that they knew the answers and were not simply guessing. That is, it is highly improbable that 992 out of 1,000 could answer 4, 5, or 6 questions correctly by chance—that is, "dumb luck."

EXERCISES

(A reminder: the answers and method of solution for selected exercises are given in Appendix A.)

1. Records of the Alcorn Glass Company revealed that during a hot summer day an employee who works on the furnaces has a 0.10 probability of being absent. Five such employees were selected at random for a special in-depth study on absenteeism.
   a. What is the probability the research will reveal that none of the employees are absent on a particular hot summer day?
   b. Develop a probability distribution for this experiment.
   c. Portray the distribution in the form of a graph.
   d. Is the distribution of absences discrete or continuous? Why?

2. Past studies revealed that 15 percent of the cameras sold in the United States are manufactured in Europe. If 20 cameras are selected at random, what is the probability of finding that at least one of them was manufactured in Europe?

   Questions 3–5 are based on the following problem.

   The marketing department is to conduct an experiment to find out if consumers can identify the taste of Cola-Cola. Five small glasses, labeled A, B, C, D, and E, are placed before a consumer. One of the five glasses contains Cola-Cola. The remaining four contain other soft drinks such as Tab, Pepsi, and so on. The consumer is told that only one contains Cola-Cola. He sips each and indicates which one he thinks is Cola-Cola. The experiment is repeated until the consumer has done a total of four such experiments; that is:

3. Suppose that the consumer really could not identify Cola-Cola. What is the probability that he will guess either exactly three or exactly four correctly?

4. Suppose that 10,000 elderly consumers took the same test. If none of them had ever tasted Cola-Cola (and thus could not identify it), theoretically about how many out of the 10,000 would guess all four correctly?

5. Suppose that 10,000 young consumers took the same taste test. Results:

Number of correct identifications	Number of consumers
Exactly 0 out of 4 3,992	
Exactly 1 out of 4 4,019	
Exactly 2 out of 4 1,603	
Exactly 3 out of 4 219	
Exactly 4 out of 4 167	

Based on a comparison of this distribution and the binomial probability distribution, what general conclusions can be made?

POISSON PROBABILITY DISTRIBUTION

The binomial probability distributions for probabilities of success (p) less than 0.05 could be computed, but the calculations would be quite time consuming (especially for a large n of say 100 or more). Intuitively, the distribution of probabilities would become more and more skewed as the probability of success became smaller. The limiting form of the binomial distribution where the probability of success is very small and n is large is called the **Poisson probability distribution**. The distribution is named after Simeon Poisson, who described it in 1837. It is often referred to as the **law of improbable events**, meaning that the probability p of a particular event's happening is quite small. The Poisson distribution is a discrete probability distribution because *it is formed by counting something*.

This distribution has many applications. It is used as a model to describe such phenomena as the distribution of errors in punch cards, the number of scratches and other imperfections in newly painted panels, the number of defective parts in outgoing shipments, the number of customers waiting to be served at a restaurant or waiting to get into an attraction at Disney World, and the number of accidents on route I-75 during a three-month period.

The Poisson distribution can be described mathematically using the formula:

$$P(x) = \frac{\mu^x e^{-\mu}}{x!}$$

where:

μ (mu) is the arithmetic mean number of occurrences (successes) in a particular interval of time.

e is the constant 2.71828 (base of the Naperian logarithmic system).

x is the number of occurrences (successes).

$P(x)$ is the probability to be computed for a specified value of x.

The mean number of successes μ can be determined in binomial situations by np, where n is the total number of trials and p the probability of success.

$$\mu = np$$

If, for example, the probability that a check cashed by a bank will bounce is 0.0003, and 10,000 checks are cashed, the mean number of bad checks is 3.0, found by $\mu = np = 10,000\ (0.0003) = 3.0$.

Recall that for binomial distribution there is a determinable number of successes. For example, for a four-question multiple-choice test there can only be zero, one, two, three, and four successes (number correct). The random variable x for a Poisson distribution, however, can assume an *infinite number of values*, that is, 0, 1, 2, 3, 4, 5. . . . But the probabilities *become very small after the first few occurrences (successes)*.

To illustrate the computation of a Poisson probability, assume that in the keypunching of 80-column keypunch cards, experienced operators rarely make an error. Many cards, of course, have no mistakes, some have one, a very few have two mistakes, rarely will one card have three mistakes, and so on. A random sample of 1,000 cards revealed 300 errors. Thus, the arithmetic mean number of mistakes per card is 0.3, found by 300/1,000. This is a sample mean $\bar{X}$ which is used to estimate the population mean μ for a model (Poisson) of the process.

The probability of no (0) mistakes appearing in a keypunch card is computed by:

$$P(x) = \frac{\mu^x e^{-\mu}}{x!}$$

Substituting:

$$P(0) = \frac{0.3^0 (2.71828)^{-0.3}}{0!} = 0.7408$$

However, the computations of the probabilities for a Poisson distribution using the formula are time consuming. As an aid, a table of Poisson probabilities are given in Appendix J for various values of μ.

EXAMPLE

Recall from the previous illustration that the mean number of mistakes per punch card was estimated to be 0.3. That is, $\mu = 0.3$. What is the probability that exactly no mistakes will appear in a card selected at random? What is the probability that exactly one mistake will be found?

270

SOLUTION

Refer to Appendix J. Locate the column headed by $\mu = 0.3$. Reading down that column, the probability of zero successes (no errors in the card) is 0.7408182. The probability of exactly one error is 0.2222455. The Poisson distribution for zero, one, two, three, four, five, and six successes (errors) is given in Table 10–6 and graphed in Chart 10–5.

TABLE 10–6
Poisson probability distribution for $\mu = 0.3$

Number of occurrences	Probability the occurrence will happen
0	0.7408182
1	0.2222455
2	0.0333368
3	0.0033337
4	0.0002500
5	0.0000150
6*	0.0000008

* As noted previously, there is an infinite number of values for x. In this distribution, the probability of an occurrence after 2 or 3 successes is extremely small.

CHART 10–5
Poisson probability distribution for $\mu = 0.3$

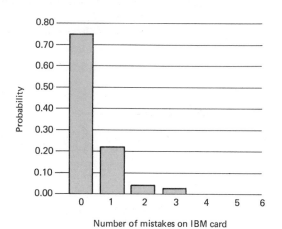

Number of mistakes on IBM card

SELF-REVIEW 10–6

$\mu = 0.7$, found by 3500/5000

a. 0.496585. Refer to Appendix J and a μ of 0.7 and an x of 0.

A hybrid-seed grower is experiencing trouble with corn borers. A random check of 5,000 ears revealed that many of the ears contained no borers,

b.

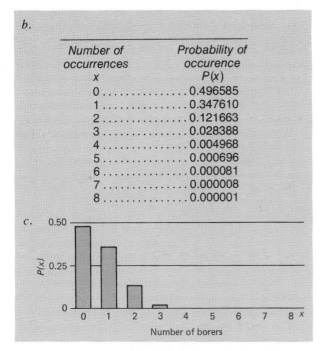

Number of occurrences x	Probability of occurence P(x)
0	0.496585
1	0.347610
2	0.121663
3	0.028388
4	0.004968
5	0.000696
6	0.000081
7	0.000008
8	0.000001

but some ears had one borer, a few had two borers, etc. The distribution of the number of borers per ear approximated the Poisson distribution. The grower counted 3,500 borers in the 5,000 ears.

a. What is the probability that an ear of corn selected at random will contain no borers?

b. Develop a Poisson probability distribution for this experiment.

c. Graph the distribution in the form of a bar graph.

The Poisson probability distribution is always positively skewed. Notice that the Poisson distributions for the punchcard experiment, where $\mu = 0.3$, and the corn borer experiment, where $\mu = 0.7$, is highly skewed. As the mean μ becomes larger, the Poisson distribution becomes almost symmetrical. As illustrations, the distributions for a μ of 0.7, 2.0 and 6.0 are shown in Chart 10–6.

CHART 10–6
Poisson probability distribution for a μ of 0.7, 2.0, and 6.0

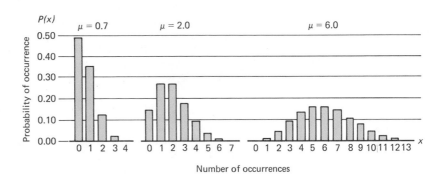

In brief summary, the Poisson distribution is actually a group of discrete distributions. To apply it, n must be large, such as the 1,000 sheared pieces. Conversely, the probability p of a defect, error, and the like must be small. All that is needed to construct a Poisson probability distribution is the average number of defects, errors, and so on, designated as μ. Mu is computed by np.

6. A new chassis was put into production. It involved soldering, inserting transistors, and so on. Each chassis was inspected at the end of the assembly line and the number of defects per unit recorded. For the first 100 chassis produced, there were 40 defects. Of course, some of the chassis had no defects, a few had one defect, and so on. The distribution of defects followed a Poisson distribution. Based on the first 100 produced, about how many out of every 1,000 chassis assembled will have one or more defects?

7. The production department has installed a new spray machine to paint automobile doors. As is common with most spray guns, unsightly blemishes often appear because of improper mixture or other problems. A worker counted the number of blemishes on each door. Most doors had no blemishes, a few had one, a very few had two, and so on. The average number was 0.5 per door. The distribution of blemishes followed the Poisson distribution.
   a. Out of 10,000 doors painted, about how many would have no blemishes?
   b. Out of 10,000 doors painted, how many would have two or more blemishes?

8. A mail-order house advertised "same day" service. Unfortunately, the movement of orders did not go as planned. There was a large number of complaints. A complete change in the handling of incoming and outgoing orders was then made. An internal goal was set to have less than five unfilled orders on hand (per picker) at the end of 95 out of every 100 working days. Frequent checks of the unfilled orders at the end of the day revealed that the distribution of the unfilled orders approximated a Poisson distribution; that is, most of the days there were no unfilled orders, some of the days there was one order, and so on. The average number of unfilled orders per picker was 2.0.
   a. Has the mail-order house lived up to it internal goal? Cite evidence.
   b. Draw a histogram representing the Poisson probability distribution of unfilled orders at the end of the day.

9. A machine shop has 100 drill presses and other machines in constant use. The probability that a machine will become inoperative during a given day is 0.002. During some days no machines are inoperative, but during some days one, two, three, or more are broken down.
   a. What is the probability that for a particular day no machines will be inoperative?
   b. What is the probability that fewer than two machines will be inoperative during a particular day?

10. Refer back to Exercise 9. A machine operator claims that he noticed on many occasions three or more machines broken down during the day. Does his claim seem logical? Why or why not?

CHAPTER SUMMARY

Two families of discrete probability distributions were presented in this chapter: the binomial distribution and the Poisson distribution. The binomial probability distribution describes the result of an experiment which takes only two forms. For example, a tape cassette deck coming off the assembly line either operates correctly, or it does not operate correctly. If it operates correctly, the outcome is designated a **success**. Otherwise it is a **failure**.

To apply the binomial distribution it is assumed that the probability of a success remains the same for each trial, the total number of trials is known, and the trials are independent, meaning the outcome of one trial does not affect the outcome of another trial.

A binomial probability distribution can be expressed using the formula:

$$P(r) = \frac{n!}{r!(n - r)!} (p)^r (q)^{n-r}$$

Instead of using the formula to compute the probability of various numbers of successes, a table (Appendix I) is readily available.

A Poisson distribution is concerned with experiments where the number of trials is very large and the probability of success is very small. To find the probability of various numbers of successes, one can use the formula—

$$P(x) = \frac{\mu^x e^{-\mu}}{x!}$$

Again, it is more convenient to read these probabilities from a table (Appendix J). To generate a Poisson distribution, only mu (μ) is required. It is found by np where n is the number of trials and p is the probability of success.

CHAPTER OUTLINE	I. Probability distribution.

CHAPTER OUTLINE

Probability distributions

I. Probability distribution.
    A. *Definition.* A probability distribution is a mutually exclusive listing of the outcomes of an experiment which can occur by chance and the corresponding probabilities of occurrence.
    B. *Purpose.* To develop a probability distribution that provides a foundation upon which to make generalizations about a population, or two or more populations, based on sample evidence.
II. Binomial probability distribution.
    A. *Characteristics.*
        1. Only two outcomes possible for each trial. Example: Pass the test, don't pass the test.
        2. Data result from counts. Therefore a binomial probability distribution is a discrete distribution; n and p are needed for its construction.
        3. Probabilities of a success and a failure stay the same for all trials.
        4. No pattern to outcomes of the trials; that is, trials are independent.
    B. *Formula.*

$$P(r) = \frac{n!}{r!(n - r)!} (p)^r (q)^{n-r}$$

where:

p is the probability of success.
q is $1 - p$, or the probability of a failure.
n is the total number of trials.
r is the number of successes out of n trials.

C.   *Application.* If it is known that 10 percent of a lot is defective, one might ask what the probability is of selecting four pieces at random and finding two of them defective. To solve:

$$P(2) = \frac{4!}{2!(4 - 2)!} (0.10)^2(0.90)^{4-2} = 0.0486$$

Using this approach, or referring to Appendix I, we find that the binomial probability distribution for an n of 4 and a p of 0.10 would be:

Number of defectives r	Probability $P(r)$
0	0.6561
1	0.2916
2	0.0486
3	0.0036
4	0.0001

III.   Poisson probability distribution.
A.   *Characteristics.* In addition to the four characteristics of a binomial probability distribution, two other characteristics are: (1) probability of success is very small, and (2) n is very large. It is also a discrete distribution.
B.   *Formula.*

$$P(x) = \frac{\mu^x e^{-\mu}}{x!}$$

C.   *Application.* Suppose that the average number of mistakes per form on the income tax Form 1040 was found to be 0.2. What is the probability of selecting a form at random and finding no errors ($\mu = 0.2, x = 0$)?

$$P(x) = \frac{\mu^x e^{-\mu}}{x!} = \frac{(0.2)^0(2.71828)^{-0.2}}{0!} = 0.8187308$$

Over 81 percent of the forms will have no errors. The probability of finding various numbers of errors can be found in Appendix J. Only μ is needed for its construction.

CHAPTER EXERCISES

11.   A machine is producing 15 percent defective, which is abnormally high for this machine. The quality control engineer has been checking the output by almost

continuous sampling since the abnormal condition began. What is the probability that in a sample of 10 pieces—

a. Exactly five will be defective?

b. Five or more will be defective?

12. A mechanical aptitude test includes five problems to determine whether the person taking the test can distinguish between the size of objects. For example, he is shown a square hole □ and given four blocks of slightly different sizes.

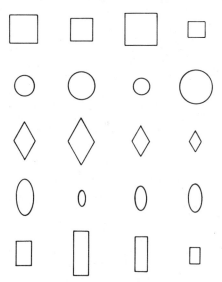

He can choose only one block. Thus, his choice is either right or wrong. This is repeated with round blocks, diamond-shaped blocks, and so on.

Assuming that a person cannot distinguish between sizes:

a. What is the probability that the person will guess all five identifications correctly?

b. What is the probability that the person will get none out of the five correct?

c. What is the probability of getting one or more identifications correct?

13. The first-grade classes in the Perrysburg school district are filled, and several new classes must be added. A survey revealed that half of the seven year olds who will enroll are boys and the other half are girls. The class size is limited to 18 children.

a. What is the probability that exactly nine boys and nine girls will be in the class?

b. What is the probability that there will be 11 or more boys in the newly created class? Is this the same as the probability of having less than 7 girls in the class of 18?

c. What is the probability that exactly 7 girls and 11 boys will enroll in the new class?

d. The doors were opened the first day of classes. What is the probability that the first seven-year-old child who walks into the room is a girl?

14. Thirty percent of the population in a southwestern community are Spanish-speaking Americans. A Spanish-speaking person is accused of killing a non-Spanish-speaking American. Of the first 12 potential jurors, only 2 were Spanish-speaking Americans, and 10 were not. The defendant's lawyer challenged the jury selection, claiming bias against his client. The government lawyer disagreed, saying that the probability of this particular jury composition is common. What do you think?

15. Suppose that 1.5 percent of the plastic spacers produced by a high-speed mold ejection machine are defective. The distribution of defectives follows a Poisson distribution. For a random sample of 200 spacers, find the probability that:

a. None of the spacers are defective.

b. Three or more of the spacers are defective.

16. A study of the lines at the checkout registers of a supermarket revealed that during a certain period at the rush hour there were four customers on the average waiting. What is the probability that during that period:

a. No customers were waiting?

b. Four customers were waiting?

c. Four or less were waiting?

d. Four or more were waiting?

CHAPTER SELF-REVIEW EXAMINATION

Do all of the problems and then check your answers against those given in Appendix A.

Score each problem 10 points.

Indicate whether a statement is true or false. If false, give the correct answer.

1. A probability distribution is a listing of the outcomes of an experiment and the probabilities associated with each outcome.

2. To construct a binomial probability distribution, the number of trials and the probability of success must be known.

3. The Poisson distribution is a continuous probability distribution.

4. A binomial distribution can be described using the formula:

$$P(r) = \frac{n!}{r!(n-r)!}(p)^r(q)^{n-r}$$

5. If we can measure something, such as the weight of a carton of eggnog, the variable is referred to as being a discrete random variable.

6. Both the binomial distribution and the Poisson distribution deal with experiments that have only two possible outcomes, a success or a failure.

7. If 20 percent of a group are nearsighted, and if a large number of random samples of 20 persons are selected, it is reasonable to expect that slightly over half of the samples will contain either none or exactly one nearsighted person.

8. If 0.1 percent of the light bulbs produced by a machine (written 0.001) are defective, the probability is about 0.90 that no defective light bulbs will be discovered in a sample of 100.

9. If the number of trials remains constant, the shape of a binomial distribution tends to become more symmetrical as p increases.

10. If you did not read this chapter and guessed the answer to each of these 10 true-false questions, the odds that you guessed all 10 correct are 1 in 1,000.

INTRODUCTION

Chapter 10 dealt with two *discrete* probability distributions, the binomial distribution and the Poisson distribution. Recall that these distributions are based on discrete random variables which can only be nonnegative integers and can only assume a specified number of values. For example, the number of correct responses to a survey containing 10 questions can only be 0, 1, 2, 3 . . . 10. There cannot be a negative number of responses, such as −7 responses, nor can there be 7¼ or 15 correct responses.

We will continue our study of probability distributions in this chapter by examining a very important **continuous** probability distribution, namely, the **normal probability distribution.** As noted in the preceding chapter, a continuous random variable is one *which can assume an infinite number of possible values.* It may result from measuring something such as the weight of an individual. The weight might be 112.0 kilograms, 112.1 kilograms, 112.12 kilograms, and so on, depending on the accuracy of the scale. Other continuous random variables which can assume an infinite number of values are: the life expectancy of alkaline batteries, the volume of a shipping container, and the amount of impurities in a steel ingot.

The probability distributions of the life of products such as batteries, tires, and light bulbs tend to follow a "normal" pattern. So do the weights of boxes of Sugar Dab cereal, the lengths of rolls of wallpaper, and other variables which are measured on a continuous scale. This "normal" pattern of continuous variables is referred to as a **normal distribution.** When this distribution is portrayed graphically, the curve is called a **normal curve.** The normal curve for the life of an alkaline battery, type D, might appear as shown in Chart 11–1.

CHART 11–1
The normal curve representing the life of alkaline batteries, type D

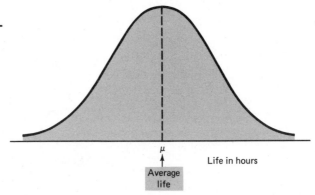

μ

Average life

Life in hours

The main features of a normal distribution are presented first. Then the **standard normal distribution** and its uses are examined.

The normal probability distribution

**SOME FEATURES
OF THE NORMAL
DISTRIBUTION**

Notice these characteristics of the normal curve (which represents a normal distribution) by referring to Chart 11–1, above, and Chart 11–2, below.

**CHART 11–2
The normal curve**

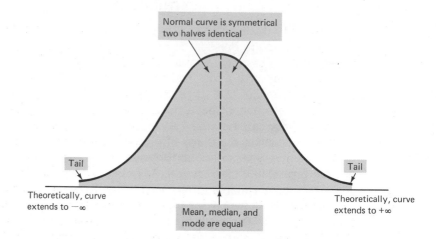

Normal curve is symmetrical two halves identical

Tail

Tail

Theoretically, curve extends to −∞

Mean, median, and mode are equal

Theoretically, curve extends to +∞

1. The curve is **bell shaped.** The arithmetic mean, median, and mode of a normal distribution are equal. Half the values are above this center point, half below. it.

2. It is **symmetrical.** That is, if the normal curve is cut in half along the vertical line representing the three averages, the two halves will be identical.

3. The normal curve is **asymptotic,** meaning that it gets closer and closer to the X-axis, but the tails never actually touch it. (See Chart 11–2.) In real-world problems, such as the life of alkaline batteries, it is inconceivable that a battery would last, say, 100 years. It should be stressed, however, that the variable is considered to extend indefinitely in both directions.

4. A particular normal distribution is unique and described by its mean μ and its standard deviation σ. Chart 11–3 portrays three normal distributions.

**CHART 11–3
Normal distributions
with equal means but
different standard de-
viations**

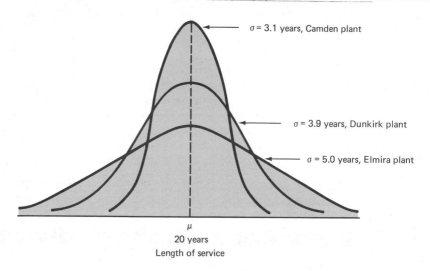

$\sigma = 3.1$ years, Camden plant

$\sigma = 3.9$ years, Dunkirk plant

$\sigma = 5.0$ years, Elmira plant

μ
20 years
Length of service

5. There is not just one normal distribtuion, but a "family" of them. For example, there is a normal distribution for the lengths of service for employees in our Camden plant, another normal distribution for the lengths of service of the employees in our Dunkirk plant, and so on. Chart 11-3 shows the normal curves for a family of distributions having the same mean (20 years of service), but with different standard deviations.

Chart 11-4 portrays the weights of the boxes of three different cereals. The distributions are normal, with equal standard deviations but different means.

**CHART 11-4
Three normal
distributions with
equal standard
deviations but
different means**

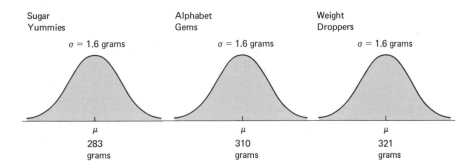

Finally, Chart 11-5 shows the curves for three normal distributions having different means and standard deviations. They show the distribution of tensile strengths measured in pounds per square inch (psi) for three types of cables.

**CHART 11-5
Three normal
distributions with
different means and
different standard
deviations**

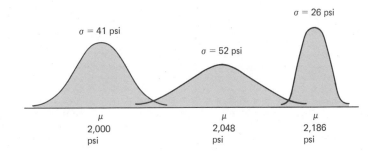

**THE STANDARD
NORMAL
DISTRIBUTION**

What is the standard normal distribution? How do we compute specific probabilities? What are some of its applications? To suggest a few research-type problems which can be solved using the standard normal distribution:

1. Mashed potatoes are packaged in boxes with a listed weight of 757 grams. Some boxes, of course, weigh less than 757 grams, others more. A large number of weight checks revealed that the weights are distrib-uted normally around the mean of 757 grams with a standard deviation of 1.5 grams. If a box is selected at random by the quality control inspec-tor, what is the probability that it will weigh less than 754 grams? More than 761 grams?

2. A tire manufacturer wants to set a mileage guarantee on its new XB 70 radial tire. The guarantee is to read "The XB 70 is guaranteed to travel —— miles before it becomes bald and fails to pass state inspection." To set the mileage on the guarantee, a life test was made. The mean of the normally distributed mileage is 47,900 miles, the standard deviation, 1,050 miles. The manufacturer does not want to set the guaranteed mileage too low, or consumers will think the tire does not wear well. Nor does the manufacturer want to set it too high, or a large number of tires will have to be replaced. What guaranteed mileage should the manufacturer set, if only about 5 percent of the tires will have to be replaced?

These questions and others of this nature involving the normal distribution can be answered by transforming the normal distribution into a **standard normal distribution.** This is accomplished by converting the units of measurement, such as tire lives, weights, or incomes, into **standard units,** or **z scores.** A z score is computed by:

$$z = \frac{X - \mu}{\sigma}$$

where:

X   is any particular observation.
μ is the mean of the distribution.
σ is the standard deviation of the distribution.

EXAMPLE

The mean μ of a normally distributed group of weekly incomes is $1,000; the standard deviation σ is $100. What is the z score for an income X of $1,100? For $900?

SOLUTION

For X = $1,100

$$z = \frac{X - \mu}{\sigma}$$

$$= \frac{\$1,100 - \$1,000}{\$100}$$

$$= 1.00$$

For X = $900

$$z = \frac{X - \mu}{\sigma}$$

$$= \frac{\$900 - \$1,000}{\$100}$$

$$= -1.00$$

The z of 1.00 indicates that a weekly income of $1,100 is one standard deviation above the mean, and a z of −1.00 shows that $900 is one standard deviation below the mean. Notice that both incomes ($1,100 and $900) are the same distance ($100) from the mean.

a. 2.25, found by:

$$z = \frac{\$1,225 - \$1,000}{\$100} = \frac{\$225}{\$100} = 2.25$$

b. −2.25, found by:

$$z = \frac{\$775 - \$1,000}{\$100} = \frac{-\$225}{\$100} = -2.25$$

A reminder: cover the answers in the left-hand column.)

Using the same information as in the previous example ($\mu = \$1,000$, $\sigma = \$100$), convert:

a. The weekly income of $1,225 to a standard unit (*z* score).

b. The weekly income of $775 to a *z* score.

Transforming measurements to standard units changes the scale. For example, $\mu + 1\sigma$ is converted to a *z* score of $+1.00$. Likewise, $\mu - 2\sigma$ is transformed to a *z* score of -2.00. This conversion is shown below. Note that the center of the *z* distribution is zero, indicating no deviation from the mean μ.

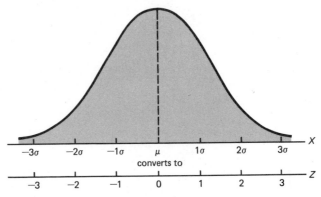

APPLICATIONS OF THE STANDARD NORMAL DISTRIBUTION

The first application of the standard normal distribution involves determining *what percent of the observations lie between two observations*. To illustrate, the weekly income example ($\mu = \$1,000$, $\sigma = \$100$) is used. What percent of the weekly wages is between $1,000 and $1,100? To put it another way, what is the area under the normal curve between $1,000 and $1,100? We have already converted $1,100 to a *z*-score of 1.00. To repeat:

$$z = \frac{X - \mu}{\sigma}$$

$$= \frac{\$1,100 - \$1,000}{\$100}$$

$$= \frac{\$100}{\$100}$$

$$= 1.00$$

The probability associated with a *z* of 1.00 has been computed and is in

Appendix G. To locate the probability, go down the left column marked (1) to 1.00, the computed z-score. Then move horizontally to the right and read the area under the curve in the column marked (2). It is 0.34134. Shown in a diagram:

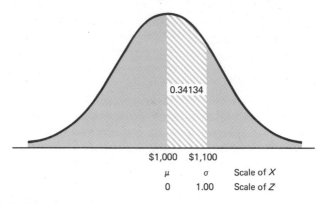

EXAMPLE

Refer to the previous problem ($\mu = \$1,000$ $\sigma = \$100$).

a. What is the probability that any weekly income selected at random is between $790 and $1,000?
b. What is the probability that the income is less than $790?

SOLUTION

Computing the z score for $790:

$$z = \frac{X - \mu}{\sigma}$$

$$= \frac{\$790 - \$1,000}{\$100}$$

$$= \frac{-\$210}{\$100}$$

$$= -2.10$$

a. The area under the normal curve between μ and X given for a z score of -2.10 is 0.48214 (from Appendix G). Since the normal curve is symmetrical, the minus sign in front of 2.10 indicates that the area is to the left of the mean.
b. The mean μ divides the normal curve into two identical halves. The area under the half to the left of the mean is 0.50000, and to the right of the mean is also 0.50000. Since the area under the curve between $790 and $1,000 is 0.48214, the area below $790 can be found by subtracting

0.48214 from 0.50000. Thus, $0.50000 - 0.48214 = 0.01786$. Shown in a diagram:

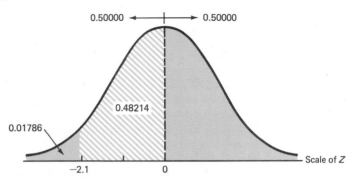

SELF-REVIEW 11-2

a. Computing the z score:

$$z = \frac{482 - 400}{50} = +1.64$$

Referring to Appendix G, the area is 0.44950.

b. 0.05050, found by $0.50000 - 0.44950$.

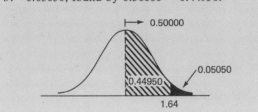

The employees of Cartwright Manufacturing are awarded efficiency ratings. The distribution of the ratings approximates a normal distribution. The mean is 400, the standard deviation 50.

a. What is the area under the normal curve between 400 and 482?

b. What is the area under the normal curve over 482?

c. Show the facets of this problem in a diagram.

EXERCISES   A reminder: The answers and method of solution to selected exercises are given in Appendix A.

1. The lengths of service of a large group of employees are approximately normally distributed, with a mean of 20 years and a standard deviation of 5 years.
    a. What is the probability of selecting any employee at random and finding the employee has less than 28 years, 9 months of service?
    b. What is the probability that the employee has over 28 years, 9 months of service?

2. The distribution of the lengths of time needed to assemble a subassembly is normal with a mean of 16.0 minutes and a standard deviation of 1.5 minutes.
    a. What is the probability that a subassembly picked at random took between 16.0 minutes and 19.0 minutes to assemble?
    b. What is the probability that it took over 19.0 minutes to assemble?
    c. What is the probability that it took less than 19.0 minutes to assemble?

3. Based on the responses of many users in regard to major maintenance of their

20-inch, heavy-duty Skie chain saw, the manufacturer concluded that the saw will operate 500 hours on the average before any major maintenance is required. The distribution of hours is normally distributed, with a standard deviation of 40 hours.

a. What is the probability that a chain saw will operate over 590 hours before requiring major maintenance?

b. What is the probability that any chain saw selected at random will require major maintenance before operating 420 hours?

EXAMPLE

As a final problem involving areas under the normal curve, suppose that for a group, normally distributed monthly incomes $\mu = \$1,000$ and $\sigma = \$50$. What is the area under the normal curve between $920 and $1,100? Shown in a diagram:

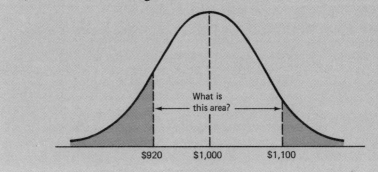

SOLUTION

The problem is divided into two parts:

For the area between $920 and the mean of $1,000

$$z = \frac{\$920 - \$1,000}{\$50}$$

$$= \frac{-\$80}{\$50}$$

$$= -1.60$$

The area under the curve for a z of -1.60 is 0.44520 (from Appendix G).

For the area between the mean of $1,000 and $1,100

$$z = \frac{\$1,100 - \$1,000}{\$50}$$

$$= \frac{\$100}{\$50}$$

$$= 2.00$$

The area under the curve for a z of 2.00 is 0.47725.

Adding the two areas: $0.44520 + 0.47725 = 0.92245$ (answer).

Thus, the probability of selecting a monthly income between $920 and $1,100 is 0.92245. Or, 92.245 percent of the persons have a monthly income between $920 and $1,100.

SELF-REVIEW 11-3
---

z for area between $960 and $1000 is -0.80, found by:

$$\frac{\$960 - \$1,000}{\$50}.$$

Area from Appendix G is 0.28814.
z for area between $1,000 and $1,120 is 2.40, found by:

$$\frac{\$1,120 - \$1,000}{\$50}.$$

Area is 0.49180.
Adding: $0.28814 + 0.49180 = 0.77994$ (answer).
In terms of a percent, it is 77.994 percent.

Using the same monthly income data—$\mu = \$1,000$, $\sigma = \$50$—what is the area under the normal curve between the monthly incomes of $960 and $1,120? (This is the same as asking what percent of the persons have monthly incomes between $960 and $1,120.)

EXERCISES

4. The annual commissions per salesperson employed by a manufacturer of light machinery averaged $40,000, with a standard deviation of $5,000. What percent of the salespersons earn between $32,000 and $42,000?

5. The weights of cans of fruit are normally distributed with a mean of 1,000 grams and a standard deviation of 50 grams. What percent of the cans weigh either 860 grams or less or between 1,055 and 1,100 grams?

In the previous examples we found the percent of the observations located between two observations. Or, the problem computed the percent of the observations above or below a particular observation X.

A second application of the standard normal distribution involves *finding the value of the observation* X, *when the percent above or below the observation is given.*

EXAMPLE

Suppose a tire manufacturer wants to set a mileage guarantee on its new XB 70 tire. Life tests revealed that the mean mileage is 47,900 and the standard deviation of the normally distributed distribution of mileages is 2,050 miles. The manufacturer wants to set the guaranteed mileage so that no more than 5 percent of the tires will have to be replaced. What guaranteed mileage should the manufacturer announce?

SOLUTION

The facets of this problem are shown in a diagram on the next page. X represents the guaranteed mileage.

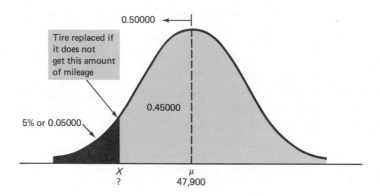

Inserting these values in the formula for z:

$$z = \frac{X - \mu}{\sigma} = \frac{X - 47{,}900}{2{,}050}$$

There are two unknowns, z and X. To find z, note that the area under the normal curve to the left of X is 0.05000. Logically, the area between μ and X is 0.45000, found by $0.50000 - 0.05000$. Refer to Appendix G. Go down the column labeled "area under the curve between μ and X" and locate the area closest to 0.45000. It is 0.44950. Then move left and read the z score. It is 1.64. (The 1.64 is really -1.64 because it is to the left of the mean.) Knowing there are $-1.64\,z$'s between μ and X, we can now solve for X, the guaranteed mileage.

$$z = \frac{X - 47{,}900}{2{,}050}$$

$$-1.64 = \frac{X - 47{,}900}{2{,}050}$$

Solving for X:

$$-1.64(2050) = X - 47{,}900$$

$$X = 44{,}538$$

SELF-REVIEW 11-4

a. 85.24 (instructor would no doubt make it 85 or 86). The closest area to 0.40000 is 0.39973. z is 1.28. Then:

$$1.28 = \frac{X - 75}{8}$$

$$10.24 = X - 75$$

$$X = 85.24$$

An analysis of the grades on the first test in Math 127 revealed that they approximate a normal curve with a mean of 75 and a standard deviation of 8. The instructor wants to award the grade of A to the upper 10 percent of the test grades.

a. What is the dividing point between an A and a B grade?

b. Show the facets of this problem graphically.

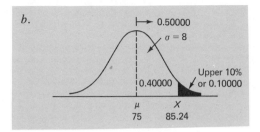

b.

In Chapter 5 it was pointed out that for a normal distribution:

About 68.27 percent of the observations lie within one standard deviation of the mean.

About 95.45 percent of the observations lie within two standard deviations of the mean.

About 99.73 percent of the observations lie within three standard deviations of the mean.

Shown diagramatically:

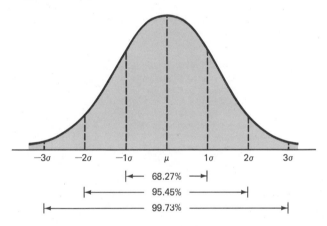

This same concept can be stated in terms of **areas under the normal curve.** The area under the normal curve within one standard deviation of the mean is about 0.6827, the area within two standard deviations of the mean is about 0.9545, and the area within three standard deviations of the mean is about 0.9973. The total area under the normal curve is 1.0000.

EXAMPLE

An accelerated life test on a large number of type D alkaline batteries revealed that the mean life for a particular use before they failed was 19.0 hours. The distribution of the lives approximated a normal distribution. The standard deviation of the distribution was 1.2 hours.

a. About 68.27 percent of the batteries failed between what two values?

b. About 95.45 percent of the batteries failed between what two values?

c. About 99.73 percent of the batteries failed between what two values?

SOLUTION

a. About 68.27 percent failed between 17.8 hours and 20.2 hours, found by $19.0 \pm 1(1.2)$.

b. About 95.45 percent failed between 16.6 hours and 21.4 hours, found by $19.0 \pm 2(1.2)$.

c. About 99.73 percent failed between 15.4 hours and 22.6 hours, found by $19.0 \pm 3(1.2)$.

Shown in a diagram:

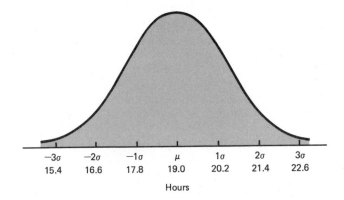

Hours

SELF-REVIEW 11-5

a. $36,400 and $38,000, found by $37,200 ± 1($800).

b. $35,600 and $38,800, found by $37,200 ± 2($800).

c. $34,800 and $39,600, found by $37,200 ± 3($800).

d. $37,200. Mean, median and mode are equal for a normal distribution.

e. Yes, a normal distribution is symmetrical.

The distribution of the annual incomes of a group of middle-management employees approximated a normal distribution with a mean of $37,200 and a standard deviation of $800.

a. About 68.27 percent of the incomes lie between what two incomes?

b. About 95.45 percent of the incomes lie between what two incomes?

c. About 99.73 percent of the incomes lie between what two incomes?

d. What are the median and the modal incomes?

e. Is the distribution of incomes symmetrical?

EXERCISES

6. The mean score of a college entrance test is 500, the standard deviation is 75. The scores are normally distributed.
   a. What percent of the students scored below 320?
   b. Twenty percent of the students had a test score above what score?
   c. Ten percent of the students had a test score below what score?

7. A study of a company's practice regarding the payment of invoices revealed that on the average an invoice was paid 20 days after it was received. The standard deviation equaled five days.
   a. What percent of the invoices were paid within 15 days of receipt?
   b. What is the probability of selecting any invoice and finding it was paid between 18 and 26 days after it was received?
   c. Five percent of the invoices were paid at least how many days after receipt?

OTHER USES OF THE STANDARD NORMAL DISTRIBUTION

The standard normal distribution can also be used to *compare two or more observations which are on different scales, or in different units.*

EXAMPLE

Suppose a study of the inmates of a correctional institution is concerned with the social adjustment of the inmates in prison and their prospect for rehabilitation upon being released. Each inmate was given a test regarding social adjustment. The scores are normally distributed, with a mean of 100 and a standard deviation of 20. Prison psychologists rated each of the inmates with respect to the prospect for rehabilitation. These ratings were also normally distributed, with a mean of 500 and a standard deviation of 100.

Inmate number 16412 scored 146 on the social adjustment test, and her rating with respect to rehabilitation is 335. How does inmate number 16412 compare with the group with respect to social responsibility and the prospect for rehabilitation?

SOLUTION

Converting her social responsibility test score of 146 to a z-score

$$z = \frac{X - \mu}{\sigma}$$

$$= \frac{146 - 100}{20}$$

$$= \frac{46}{20}$$

$$= 2.30$$

Converting her rehabilitation rating of 335 to a z-score

$$z = \frac{X - \mu}{\sigma}$$

$$= \frac{335 - 500}{100}$$

$$= \frac{-165}{100}$$

$$= -1.65$$

The standardized test score and the standardized rating are shown on the following diagram.

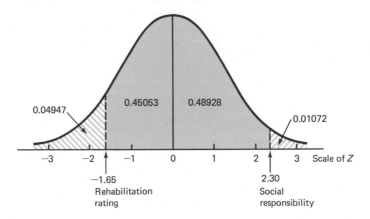

Interpretation. With respect to social responsibility, inmate number 16412 is in the highest 1 percent of the group. However, compared with the other inmates, she is among the lowest 5 percent in regard to the prospect for rehabilitation.

The following self-review illustrates the use of the standard normal distribution when comparing data in different units—ratios and percent changes in this case.

SELF-REVIEW 11-6

The price-earnings (PE) ratios and the changes in price over a three-year period for a group of selected stocks were studied. For the PE ratios, $\mu = 10.0$, $\sigma = 2.0$. For the price changes, $\mu = 50$ percent, $\sigma = 10$ percent. Both distributions are normally distributed.

Radnor Industries had a PE of 11.2, and a 75 percent increase in the three-year period.

a. Convert Radnor's PE and percent change to z scores.
b. Show the two z-scores on a standardized normal curve.
c. Compare Radnor's PE ratio and percent change with the other selected stocks.

a. $z = 0.60$ for PE ratio, found by:

$$\frac{11.2 - 10.0}{2.0}$$

$z = 2.50$ for percent change, found by:

$$\frac{75 - 50}{10}$$

b.

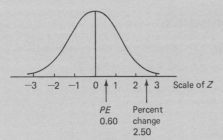

c. Compared with the other selected stocks, Radnor's PE is slightly above average; the percent increase well above average.

EXERCISES

8. The net sales and the number of employees for firms with similar characteristics were organized into frequency distributions. Both were normally distributed. For the net sales, $\mu = \$180$ million, $\sigma = \$25$ million. For the number of employees, $\mu = 1,500$, $\sigma = 120$. Clarion Corporation had sales of $170 million and 1,850 employees.

   a. Convert Clarion's sales and number of employees to z-scores.
   b. Locate the two z-scores on a standard normal distribution.
   c. Compare Clarion's sales and number of employees with those of the other firms.

9. A mechanical aptitude test designed for entering college students has a mean of 1,000 and a standard deviation of 150. An IQ test designed for college students has a mean of 110 and a standard deviation of 10. Shawn Bucci scored 1,310 on the mechanical aptitude test and 122 on the IQ test. Evaluate his test scores relative to those of others who took the tests.

THE NORMAL APPROXIMATION TO THE BINOMIAL

The binomial table in Appendix I is for a sample of up to 20. The **normal approximation to the binomial** is useful when the number in the sample is greater than 20. *The normal probability distribution is generally deemed a good approximation for the binomial probability distribution when* np *and* n(1 − p) *are both greater than five.*

EXAMPLE

Suppose that the management of the Santoni pizza restaurant chain revealed that 70 percent of their customers returned for another meal. In a week in which 80 new (first-time) customers dined at Santoni's, what is the probability that 60 *or more* will return for another meal?

Of course, we could use the binomial formula

$$P(r) = \frac{n!}{r!(n-r)!}(p)^r(q)^{n-r}$$

to calculate this probability. This would mean, however, computing the probabilities of 60, 61, 62 . . . 80 and adding them to arrive at the probability of 60 or more. This could be a time-consuming job! No doubt you will agree that using the normal approximation to the binomial is a much more efficient method of computing the probability of 60 or more.

SOLUTION

First, we must make sure we have a binomial problem. Recall from Chapter 10 that the binomial distribution can be applied if the following four criteria are met:

1. There are only two mutually exclusive outcomes, a "success" and a "failure." If a customer returns for another meal, it is a "success." Otherwise it is a "failure."
2. A binomial distribution results from counting the number of successes. The number of customers—namely, 0, 1, 2, 3 . . . 80—are the number of successes.
3. Each trial is independent, meaning in this problem that the decision of a customer to either return or not return for another meal does not affect the decision of any other customer.
4. The probability p must remain the same from trial to trial. In this problem it is 0.70, and it remains the same from trial to trial.

Further, the normal distribution can be used to approximate the binomial in this problem distribution because both np and $n(1 - p)$ are over five.

$$np = 80(0.70) = 56$$

$$n(1 - p) = 80(1 - 0.70) = 24$$

Now to determine the probability that 60 or more out of the 80 first-time customers who dined at Santoni's during the week will return.

First, compute the mean μ and the variance σ^2 of the binomial distribution:

$$\mu = np$$
$$\sigma^2 = np(1 - p)$$

Solving for μ and σ^2:

$$\mu = 80(0.70) = 56$$

$$\sigma^2 = np(1 - p) = 80(0.70)(1 - 0.70) = 16.8$$

Second, determine the z-score for 60, the number who will return to Santoni's for another meal.[1] $X = 60$, $\mu = 56$, and $\sigma = \sqrt{\sigma^2} = \sqrt{16.8} = 4.1$. Solving for z:

$$z = \frac{X - \mu}{\sigma} = \frac{60 - 56}{4.1} = \frac{4}{4.1} = 0.98$$

Third, locate the area under the normal curve between μ and X given a z of 0.98. It is 0.33646 from Appendix G. This is the area under the curve between the mean of 56 and 60. The area beyond 60 is 0.16354, found by $0.50000 - 0.33646$.

---

[1] This number should be 59.5 instead of 60. If 59.5 were used, it would be a **continuity correction**. A continuity correction is made because a discrete distribution (the binomial distribution) is being approximated by a continuous distribution (the normal distribution). In this case, however, because the sample size (number of trials) is large, the correction will have a negligible effect.

What does 0.16354 indicate? It indicates that the probability is 0.16354 that 60 or more of the 80 first-time customers will return to Santoni's for another meal. To put it another way, if records were kept on weeks during which Santoni's had 80 first-time customers, it would be noticed that for 16.354 percent of those weeks, 60 or more customers out of the 80 would return for another meal.

The facets of this problem are shown graphically:

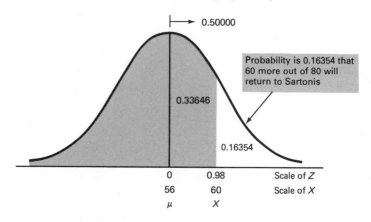

------ **SELF-REVIEW 11-7** ------

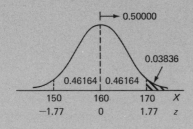

a. 0.03836, found by $\mu = np = 200(0.80) = 160$, and $\sigma^2 = np(1-p) = 200(0.80)(1-0.80) = 32$. Then,

$$\sigma = \sqrt{32} = 5.6568542$$

$$z = \frac{170 - 160}{5.6568542} = 1.77$$

Area from Appendix G is 0.46164. Subtracting from 0.50000 gives 0.03836.

b. 0.96164, found by 0.46164 + 0.50000.

A study by an insurance underwriter revealed that none of the stolen goods were recovered by the homeowners in 80 percent of the reported thefts.

a. During a period in which 200 thefts occurred, what is the probability that no stolen goods were recovered in 170 or more of the robberies?

b. During a period in which 200 thefts occurred, what is the probability that no stolen goods were recovered in 150 or more robberies?

EXERCISES

10. A study conducted by a nationally-known health club revealed that 30 percent of its new members were significantly overweight. A membership drive in a metropolitan area resulted in 500 new members.

    a. It has been suggested that the normal approximation to the binomial be used to determine the probability that out of the 500 new members, 175 will be significantly overweight. Does this problem qualify as a binomial problem? Explain.

    b. What is the probability that 175 or more of the new members are overweight?

    c. What is the probability that 140 or more new members will be significantly overweight?

    d. Show the areas and other facets of *b* and *c* in the form of a diagram.

11. Research on new juvenile delinquents who were put on probation by the judge revealed that 38 percent of them committed another crime.

    a. What is the probability that out of the last 100 new juvenile delinquents put on probation, 30 or more will commit another crime?

    b. Portray the areas under the curve and other facets of this problem in the form of a diagram.

CHAPTER SUMMARY

    This chapter has dealt with a widely used continuous probability distribution, namely, the **normal probability distribution.** The normal curve which portrays the normal distribution graphically is:

1. Bell shaped and symmetrical, and not extremely peaked or flat.
2. Fifty percent of the area under the curve is to the right of the mean, and 50 percent is to the left of the mean.
3. The normal curve is asymptotic. It gets closer and closer to the X-axis but never actually touches it.
4. About 68.27 percent of the observations lie within one standard deviation of the mean; about 95.45 percent within two standard deviations of the mean; and about 99.73 percent within three standard deviations of the mean.
5. Further, there is not just one normal curve, but rather there is a family of them—one for each mean and standard deviation. The mean and the standard deviation of a normal distribution are used to transform it into a **standard normal distribution.** To accomplish this the observations of interest are converted to z-scores by:

$$z = \frac{X - \mu}{\sigma}$$

    The standard normal distribution is very useful in determining the percent of the observations between two values (see Figure 11–6A). Conversely, given the percent above or below an observation, the value of that observation can be determined (see Figure 11–6B). If two or more observations are in different units, or on different scales, they can be transformed to z-scores in order to make a comparison (see Figure 11–6C).

    The normal probability distribution is also a useful tool to approximate the binomial distribution. It is considered a good approximation when np and

FIGURE 11-6

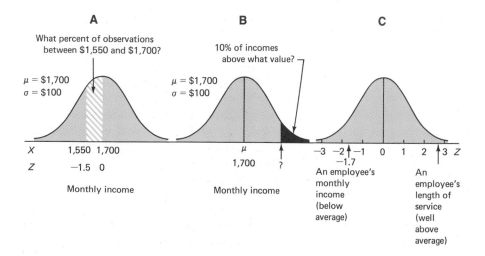

$n(1 - p)$ are both greater than five. The steps in approximating the binomial area:

1. Compute the mean and the variance.

$$\mu = np$$
$$\sigma^2 = np(1 - p)$$

2. Determine the z-score for X, the observation of interest, by:

$$z = \frac{X - \mu}{\sigma}$$

3. Using Appendix G, locate the area under the normal curve between μ and X, given the z-score computed in Step 2.
4. Subtract that area from 0.50000, if necessary, to arrive at the probability of X or more.

CHAPTER OUTLINE

**The normal
probability
distribution**

I. Normal probability distribution.
   A. Features.
     1. A continuous distribution based on a continuous random variable.
     2. Bell shaped. Mean, median, and mode located at center and are equal.
     3. Symmetrical in shape.
     4. Normal curve is asymptotic, meaning tails become closer and closer to X-axis but never touch it.
     5. The mean μ and standard deviation σ are needed to construct a normal distribution.

6. There is a family of normal curves, a different one for each mean and standard deviation.
   B. Some relationships between mean and standard deviation.
      1. About 68.27 percent of observations lie within one standard deviation of the mean.
      2. About 95.45 percent of the observations lie within two standard deviations of the mean.
      3. About 99.73 percent of the observations lie within three standard deviations of the mean.
II. Standard normal distribution.
   A. Applications.
      1. Determining what percent of the observations lie between two observations.
      2. Determining the value of the observation X when the area above or below X is known.
      3. Comparing two or more observations which are on different scales, or in different units.
III. The normal approximation to the binomial.
   A. Advantage.
      1. Eliminates the need to compute a large number of probabilities and find their sum.
   B. Use.
      1. When np and $n(1 - p)$ are both greater than five.
   C. Steps needed to compute probability of X or more.
      1. Compute mean by $\mu = np$. Compute variance by $\sigma^2 = np(1 - p)$.
      2. Determine z-score by

$$z = \frac{X - \mu}{\sigma}$$

      3. Locate area under normal curve between μ and X for computed z-score (refer to Appendix G for area).
      4. Subtract area in Step 3 from 0.50000 to find probability of X or more.

CHAPTER EXERCISES

12. Past experience with respect to the number of passengers on a large ship offering one-week cruises to the Caribbean revealed that the mean number of passengers is 1,820 and the standard deviation of the normal distribution is 120.
   a. What percent of the cruises will have between 1,820 and 1,970 passengers?
   b. What percent of the cruises will have 1,970 passengers or more?
   c. What percent of the Caribbean cruises will have 1,600 or fewer passengers?

13. Management is considering adopting a bonus system to increase production. One suggestion is to pay a bonus on the highest 5 percent of production based on past experience. Past records indicated that, on the average, 4,000 units of a small assembly are produced during a week. The distribution of the weekly

production is approximately normally distributed with a standard deviation of 60 units. If the bonus is paid on the upper 5 percent of production, the bonus would be paid on how many units or more?

Question 14–16 are based on the following.

Past experience of a large manufacturing firm with administering a test to recent college graduates who had applied for a job revealed that the mean test score was 500 and the standard deviation was 50. The distribution of the test scores was normal.

14. Based on this experience, management is considering placing a person whose score is in the upper 6 percent of the distribution directly into a responsible position. What is the lowest score a college graduate must earn to qualify for a responsible position?

15. Also based on past performance, the personnel director plans to give no consideration to anyone who scores 400 or less on the test. About what percent of the applicants will receive no consideration?

16. Because of the limited number of vacancies this year, applicants with scores between 400 and 485 will be put on a HOLD status.
    a. What *percent* of the applicants will be put on this HOLD status?
    b. If a total of 1,000 applied for a job with the company, *how many* would be put in the HOLD classification?

17. The tensile strengths of a large number of wires were determined and then organized into a frequency distribution. The distribution approximated a normal distribution with a mean of 300 pounds and a standard deviation of 20 pounds.
    a. What percent of the wires tested between 296 pounds and 310 pounds?
    b. What percent tested over 332 pounds?
    c. Eighty percent of the wires tested over what amount?

18. Fast Service Truck Lines uses the Ford Super 1310 exclusively and wants to make a study of maintenance costs and so on. Rather than study all 3,500 trucks, a sample was selected. It revealed that during the past year the arithmetic mean distance traveled per truck was 60,000 kilometers. The distances were normally distributed, and the standard deviation of the sample was 2,000 kilometers. Based on the sample data:
    a. What percent of the Ford Super 1310s logged 65,200 kilometers or more?
    b. Recall that the truck line owns 3,500 Ford Super 1310s. Based on the sample findings, how many of them traveled 55,000 kilometers or less?
    c. How many of the Fords traveled 62,000 kilometers or less during the year?

19. For many years a large company has been using a standardized test as a guide in hiring new secretaries. The test scores are normally distributed with a mean of 800 and a standard deviation of 100. There has been an unusually large number of applicants in recent months, and it has been suggested that only the applicants who score in the upper 10 percent be considered further. An applicant would have to have a test score of at least what to be considered further?

20. The annual incomes of a large group of supervisors are normally distributed, with a mean of $18,000 and a standard deviation of $1,200. The length of service of the same supervisors is also normally distributed, with a mean of 20 years and a standard deviation of 5 years. John McMaster earns $20,400 annually and has 10 years of service.
    a. Compare his income with those of the other supervisors.
    b. Compare this length of service with that of the other supervisors.

21. The county traffic division reported that 40 percent of the high-speed chases involving automobiles result in a minor or major accident. During a month in which 50 high-speed chases occur, what is the probability that 25 or more will result in a minor or major accident?

22. Cruise ships report that 80 percent of their rooms are occupied during September. For a cruise ship having 800 rooms, what is the probability that 665 or more are occupied in September?

CHAPTER SELF-REVIEW EXAMINATION

Do all the problems and then check your answers against those given in Appendix A.

Score each problem 25 points.

1. You missed two weeks of class due to illness. The day you returned, a 100-question, multiple-choice examination was distributed. Each question had four possible answers. The professor stated that at least 40 correct answers would be needed to earn a "satisfactory" grade. You decided to take the test and guess the answers to each question.
   a. This problem qualifies for the use of the normal approximation to the binomial. Explain.
   b. Calculate the probability of guessing 40 or more correctly.
   c. Depict the various facets of this problem graphically.

2. Large ceramic vases are made by hand. Due to fluctuations in the composition of the clay and the skill of the person making the vase, there is some variation in the weights. The mean weight was computed to be 1,200 grams, the standard deviation 20 grams. The distribution of weights approximated a normal distribution. What percent of the vases will weigh 1,250 grams or more?

3. You are enrolled in History 321 and Science 382. The mean class grade on the first history test was 75, with a standard deviation of 8. The mean grade on the science test was 60, with a standard deviation of 5. The grades on both tests roughly follow the shape of a normal distribution. You scored 74 on the history test and 74 on the science test.
   a. Evaluate your score on the history test relative to the other students in the class.
   b. Evaluate your score on the science test relative to the other students in the class.
   c. Show your position on the tests using the standard normal curve.

4. The seasonal output of a new experimental strain of pepper plants was carefully weighed. The mean weight per plant is 15.0 pounds, and the standard deviation of the normally distributed weights is 1.75 pounds. Of the 200 plants in the experiment, how many produced peppers weighing between 13 and 16 pounds?

INTRODUCTION

What do these four cases have in common?

Case 1: The quality control department has the job of assuring the quality of production. To check the tensile strength of drawn steel wire, five small pieces are selected every three hours, and the tensile strength of each piece is determined by stretching it until it breaks.

Case 2: The marketing department of a large soap manufacturer has the responsibility of finding out consumer opinion with respect to new products. To determine the sales potential of a new soap named Ahhh, 452 women were asked to try it for one week. At the end of one week each woman completed a questionnaire regarding Ahhh.

Case 3: A polling firm was hired to gather the opinions of registered voters regarding policies of the federal government. Two thousand registered voters were selected at random, and their opinions regarding our immigration policy, measures being taken to curb inflation, and so on were recorded.

Case 4: In order to study the migratory pattern of seals, 50 seals were tagged by marine biologists, and their movements were charted for a period of three years.

The cases have these common characteristics: (1) It would be very expensive, if not impossible, to contact all the registered voters in the United States, all the seals, and all the women. Further, checking all the drawn wire produced in a three-hour period for tensile strength would destroy it, and none would be available for sale! (2) Only a relatively small group were involved in each study. Only five pieces of wire were tested, only 50 seals were tagged, etc.

The cases illustrate one way of finding such facts as the quality of a product or the opinions of consumers about a product—namely, to take a **sample** from the **population** of interest. *A sample is merely a part of the population.* The populations in these cases are all the seals in the ocean, all the registered voters in the United States, all the adult women, and all the wire drawn in a three-hour period. Notice that the population might be persons, objects, or other phenomenan of interest.

These four cases can also be used to illustrate how sample data are used to make statements about the entire population. Reasoning from statistical information obtained from a small group (the sample) to general conclusions about the entire group (the population) is called **statistical inference**. If, for example, the quality control inspector finds that all five pieces of wire tested for tensile strength exceed specifications, he would conclude that production during the three-hour period has been satisfactory. If 403 out of the 452

An introduction to sampling

women in the sample *disliked* Ahhh, no doubt the soap manufacturer would not manufacture and market Ahhh.

Making decisions based on incomplete information is not new. For centuries wine tasters, for example, have made predictions about the vintage based on a few sips. Many shoppers purchase a pizza at the grocery store after sampling a small wedge. (The inference is that if the small sample tastes good, the whole pizza will taste equally good.) In industry, a random sample of 50 ball bearings might result in an inference (generalization) that 5 percent of all ball bearing produced are defective. Similarly, an inventory of a few items in a department store might result in a prediction that if the present security measures remain unchanged, 8 percent of the stock will be stolen during the month. In medicine, a sample of blood might result in an inference that the patient is anemic.

The following section expands on the reasons why, in many problems, taking a sample is the only logical way of finding out something about a population. Then, some of the basic methods of selecting a sample are discussed.

REASONS FOR SAMPLING

As noted previously, it is often not feasible to study the entire population. Some of the major reasons why sampling is necessary are:

1. *The destructive nature of certain tests.* If the wine tasters drank all of the wine in order to evaluate the vintage, they would destroy the entire crop, and none would be available for sale. In the area of industrial production, steel plates, wires, and other similar products often must have a certain minimum tensile strength. To assure that the product meets the minimum standard, a relatively small sample is selected. Each piece is stretched until it breaks, and the breaking point (usually measured in pounds per square inch) is recorded. Obviously, if all the wire or all the plates were tested for tensile strength, none would be available for sale or use. And for this same reason, only a sample of photographic film is selected to determine the quality of all the film produced. Only a few seeds are tested for germination prior to the planting season.

2. *The physical impossibility of checking all items in the population.* The populations of fish, birds, snakes, mosquitoes, and the like are large and are constantly moving, being born, and dying. Instead of even attempting to count all the ducks in Canada or all the fish in Lake Erie, estimates are made using various techniques such as counting all the ducks on a pond picked at random, creel checks, or setting nets at predetermined places in the lake.

3. *The cost of studying all the items in a population is often prohibitive.* Public opinion polls and consumer testing organizations usually contact less than 2,000 families out of approximately 50 million families in the United States. One consumer panel–type organization charges about $10,000 to mail out and tabulate the responses in order to test a product such as cereal, cat food, or perfume. The same product test using all 50 million families would cost $250 million!

4. *The adequacy of sample results.* Even if funds were available, it is doubtful whether the additional accuracy of a 100 percent sample—i.e., studying all the population—is essential in most problems. For example, the federal government uses a sample of grocery stores scattered throughout the United States to determine the monthly index of food prices. The prices of bread, beans, milk, and other major food items are included in the index. The monthly index would probably not differ by one tenth of 1 percent from the published figure if minor items not now included, such as avocadoes, pomegranates, and watercress, were priced every month and added to the computation of the index. Moreover, it is unlikely that the inclusion of all grocery stores in the United States would significantly affect the index, since the prices of milk, bread, and other major foods usually do not vary by more than one cent from one chain store to another.

5. *To contact the whole population would often be time consuming.* A candidate for a national office may wish to determine his chances for election. A sample poll using the regular staff and field interviews of a professional polling firm would take only one or two days. By using the same staff

and interviewers and working seven days a week, it would take nearly 200 years to contact all the voting population!

Even if a large staff of interviewers could be assembled, the cost of contacting all of the voters would probably not be worth the expense. If the candidate were extremely popular, the sample poll might indicate that he would most certainly receive between 79 percent and 81 percent of the popular vote. The additional expense to find out that he might receive exactly 80 percent of the popular vote does not seem to be justified.

METHODS OF SELECTING A SAMPLE

There is no one "best" method of drawing a sample from the population of interest. A sample method used to select a sample from invoices in a file drawer might not be an appropriate method to use when choosing a national sample of voters. Basically, there are two methods of selecting a sample— **probability methods** and **nonprobability methods.** If all the items in the population of interest have a chance of being included in the sample, samples drawn are considered *probability* samples. If the selection of the items in the sample is based on the judgment of the selector rather than on randomness, the methods are called *nonprobability* methods. Following is a brief description of some of the methods used in selecting a sample.

Probability sampling

Simple random sampling. Suppose that the population consists of 845 students enrolled at Sociable University, and a sample of 52 students is to be selected from that population. One way of assuring that every student in the population has a chance of being chosen is to first write the name of each student on a small slip of paper and deposit all of the slips in a box. After they have been thoroughly mixed, the first selection is made. This process is repeated until the sample of size 52 is chosen. This type of sampling is often referred to as **simple random sampling.**

A more convenient method would be to use the identification number of each student and a *table of random numbers*. As the name implies, the table is developed by simply selecting numbers at random and forming them into a table. Thus, no matter where the researcher starts choosing numbers from the table, he or she is assured that they have been completely randomized (that is, thoroughly mixed).

Several tables of random numbers are available in published form, and random number programs have been written for most computers. The partial table which follows and the table of random numbers in Appendix D were emitted by a computer.

A partial table of random numbers

219	716	200	418	732	864	001	821
642	123	998	565	445	686	902	656
051	212	107	981	422	192	327	537
199	659	297	849	771	900	113	455

Arbitrarily starting in the upper right corner of the table, student no. 821 would be the first one chosen at random. Reading down that column, students represented by nos. 656, 537, 455, and so on would be part of the sample.

A study conducted by Marion Bryson and Robert Mason[1] further illustrates the use of a table of random numbers.

Located in 18 warehouses on a U.S. Army ordnance depot were 186,810 different ordnance items such as tires, nuts, bolts, tank treads, and tire irons. In each warehouse there were bays, and in each bay there were bins. For example, in warehouse No. 17 motor vehicle parts were stored. Bay 260, bin 2, contained Jeep cranks. Bay 260, bin 3, had Jeep radiator caps.

The problem involved selecting a bin at random from a warehouse and counting all the items found in the bin. This physical count was compared with the count which machine records indicated should be on hand. Thus, the problem was essentially a physical inventory problem involving sampling methods. The objective of the research project was to determine how accurate the machine records were.

To assure that each bin had an equal chance of being selected, a table of random numbers was used to choose the warehouse, bay, and bin. Since a random table is already randomized, the selection process may start any place in the table. To select a warehouse, it was necessary to read down the first two columns of figures in the preceding exhibit of random numbers until an actual warehouse number was found; that is (reading down), 21, 64, 05, 19, 71, 12, etc. There was no warehouse number 21 or number 64; so the first warehouse to be studied was number 5. Next, a bay in warehouse number 5 was selected. The bays were numbered 001, 002 . . . 999. Bay number 455 was selected by reading up in the extreme right column. (A start could be made at any place in the table.) To select a bin, or bins, to be sampled, the same random procedure was used. If bin 6 had been picked, the checker went to warehouse number 5, bay 455, and counted the number of items in bin 6.

Why was such a time-consuming method used for randomly selecting a few bins to sample? The alternative would have been to allow the checkers to count the items in any bins they wished. No doubt the checkers would have avoided counting the items in the bins containing heavy or greasy parts. The omission of these items from a study might have **biased** the results, that is, not given a true picture of the accuracy of the machine records.

Systematic sampling. A simple random sample may be awkward to select in certain cases. Assume that the population consists of 3,200 invoices in a file drawer. If each invoice were selected using a simple random sample, then each invoice would have to be numbered from 0001 up to 3,200. If the sample size was 800, a total of 800 numbers would have to be selected from a table of random numbers. The invoice to match each of the random numbers

---

[1] Office of Ordnance Research, *Physical Inventory Accounting Program,* Technical Report Number 1.

would have to be located in the file. This simple random sampling method would be very time consuming.

Instead, a **systematic sampling** procedure may be used if the population is organized in an orderly way. For example, invoices may be filed according to date received, the names of the alumni of a university may be filed either in alphabetical order or in alphabetical order by year of graduation, the telephone directory is in alphabetical order. If the population contains 3,200 names and 800 names are to be sampled, it may be more convenient, as well as more economical, to select every fourth name. The name of the first person should be selected using a random device such as a table of random numbers. If the number 2 were selected, then the 2d, 6th, 10th, 14th, 18th . . . names would constitute the sample.

A systematic sample should not be used if there is a predetermined pattern to the population. For example, in the physical inventory study mentioned previously, some of the warehouses in the ordnance depot had bays six bins high. On the bottom bins were fast-moving ordnance items such as grease, touch-up spray paint, and hardware. These items were stored on the floor-level bins to speed the work of the pickers who had to fill the requisitions. In the top row of bins were slow-moving items such as tire rims, half-track treads, and firing pins. The middle rows were stocked with moderately fast-moving items such as tires, headlights, and cotter pins. If a systematic sample were used to check the inventory, then it is quite possible that a biased sample would be selected. Suppose that the sampling procedure called for a selection of every third bin and No. 1 bin was selected first. Then bins No. 1, 4, 7, 10, 13, 16, 19, and 22 would be selected systematically.

The systematic procedure automatically selected four bins filled with moderately fast-moving items and a total of four bins filled with either fast-moving or slow-moving items. This 50–50 division of the sample does not coincide with the actual population characteristics. The population consists of 16 bins of moderately fast-moving items, four bins of fast-moving items, and four bins of slow-moving items. The sample results would undoubtedly be biased toward the slow- and fast-moving items.

Stratified random sampling.   To correct the inadequacy of a simple random sample when used in certain problems, a **stratified random sample** may be selected. The first step is to stratify the population into subpopulations (also called subgroups, or strata). Then each subpopulation is sampled, independent of the other subpopulations.

After the population has been divided into strata, either a **proportional** or a **nonproportional** sample can be selected. As the name implies, a proportional sampling procedure requires that the number of items in each stratum be in the same proportion as found in the population. For instance, the problem might be to study the advertising expenditures of the 352 largest companies in the United States. Suppose that the objective of the study is to determine whether firms with high returns on equity (a measure of profitability) spent more or less of each sales dollar on advertising than firms with a low return or a deficit. Assume that the 352 firms were divided into five strata. If, say, 50 firms are to be selected for intensive study, then one firm with a level of profitability of 30 percent and over would be studied, five firms in the 20 percent up to 30 percent stratum would be selected at random, and so on.

Stratum	Profitability (return on equity)	Number of firms	Percent of total	Number sampled
1	30 percent and over	8	2	1*
2	20 up to 30 percent	35	10	5*
3	10 up to 20 percent	189	54	27
4	0 up to 10 percent	115	33	16
5	Deficit	5	1	1
		352	100	50

*2 percent of 50 = 1; 10 percent of 50 = 5; etc.

Any sample statistics computed for each stratum would have to be weighted by the number of firms in the stratum to arrive at one figure to represent the population. For example, if the firms in the first stratum spent nine cents of their sales dollar on advertising, that amount (nine cents) would be weighted by one; and if the firms in stratum two spent six cents, the six cents would be weighted by five, and so forth. The arithmetic mean amount spent on advertising by the 352 largest firms would be 3.6 cents, found by $1.80/50.

Profitability	Number in sample	Amount of sales dollar spent on advertising (cents)	Weighted values
30 percent and over	1	9	9
20 up to 30 percent	5	6	30
10 up to 20 percent	27	4	108
0 up to 10 percent	16	2	32
Deficit	1	1	1
	50		180

In a **nonproportional stratified sample,** the number of items studied in each stratum would be disproportionate to their number in the population. If a research project involves sampling grocery stores to determine stocking practices, advertising expenditures, number of employees, and the like, the stores could be stratified according to the volume of sales. Stratification might result in the following figures:

Annual sales	Number of stores	Number in sample
$2 million and over	10	1
$1 million up to $2 million	50	5
Under $1 million	940	94
	1,000	100

If a proportional stratified procedure were followed, only 1 large grocery store would be sampled to 94 small stores. However, the 10 large stores probably sell more than the remaining 990 stores combined. It would be more desirable, therefore, to sample all 10 large stores and fewer small stores.

Another consideration in determining the sampling procedure might be cost. If there is a fixed budget (and there usually is), it may be more advantageous to sample more large grocery stores and fewer small ones. The large stores are concentrated in shopping areas and in cities, while many of the small stores are in rural areas. The cost of traveling from one rural store to another might not be worth the expense. Thus, nonproportional sampling has the additional advantage of getting the most out of the interview dollar. This is often called the principle of *optimum allocation*.

In summary, a stratified random sample is a refinement of probability sampling. The method of stratification still assures each item in the population a chance of being chosen in the sample. Proportional stratification merely prevents a disproportionate number of one group from being represented in the sample.

There are other probability methods designed to assure that every item in the population has a chance of being selected and the resulting measures will be unbiased, but they will not be considered in this introductory text.

Nonprobability sampling

There is a significant amount of nonprobability sampling done in the United States. The users and supporters claim that nonrandom sampling is less expensive, not so time consuming, more convenient, and gives results as valid as the results obtained from probability sampling. Nonprobability sampling lacks one or more of the conditions of probability sampling. One of the usual conditions lacking is that all of the items in the population being studied do not have a chance of being selected.

Chunk sampling, also called **convenience sampling** and **incidental sampling,** is one type of nonprobability sampling. A research firm periodically takes a busload of persons from Toledo to Detroit to view mock-up models of new automobiles and to rate parts of an automobile, such as grille designs and interior styling. The persons are usually a group of office workers from a glass-manufacturing plant, production supervisors from a local assembly plant, and so on. (The firm offers a steak dinner, tickets to a stage play, and a bus prize as inducement.) The responses of many such groups are analyzed and decision made on grille design, overall design, interior colors, and so forth.

Test marketing of a new product in one locality is also considered convenience sampling. Thus, the marketing research team can concentrate its efforts in one small area. Consumer-testing organizations or companies originating new products often use small groups of neighbors for product testing. For example, a nationally known company wanted to test a newly developed Danish roll. A homemaker who had conducted other surveys for the company was asked to invite 10 women to her home for a "party." The women were told in advance they were to test a new product. Mrs. H. invited mostly friends and neighbors.

The new Danish pastry was compared with two other nationally known Danish pastries. Brand names of the three were not known to the 10 women, nor was the name of the company sponsoring the party divulged. The party was informal, and the psychologist from the home office of the sponsor used a tape recorder to record the likes, dislikes, and suggestions. These sessions usually last about one hour. The psychologist indicated that the company considered these convenient groups a desirable way of sampling because they produce more usable information per interview dollar than any other method.

Theoretically, sampling using **panels** is nonprobability sampling. Persons who volunteer to test products and give opinions are organized into panels. One panel usually consists of from 1,000 to 2,000 persons. The firm usually has a number of different panels. One may consist of only teenagers, another only homemakers, another only professional persons, another only farmers, and another only families with small children. The characteristics of the panelists such as age and sex are usually keypunched on cards or stored in a computer so that a panel can be formed for almost any project. For example, if a processor of cat food wanted a newly developed cat food tested, a panel could be quickly organized. Participation is voluntary. Most firms do not pay the respondents, but some firms send them gifts from time to time. Many polling firms using panels guarantee the sponsor over 70 percent response.

The advantages of a panel-type sample compared with a probability sample are lower cost, a higher percent response, and less time consumed because the participants are readily available. Some advocates of the panel method also claim results equally valid as from probability sampling. However, since all the persons in the United States do not have a chance of being selected (such as those who cannot read or write), this method cannot be considered probability sampling.

The main disadvantage of nonprobability sample is that the reliability (accuracy) of the sample results cannot be accurately measured. Therefore, the subsequent discussion involving the reliability of sample results concerns only probability sampling.

EXERCISES

A reminder: the answers and method of solution for selected exercises are given in Appendix A.

1. Briefly explain:
   a. The fundamental reason for sampling.
   b. Some of the reasons why a sample is used instead of contacting, enumerating, or testing the entire population.

2. Identify each of the following types of sampling.
   a. Auditors may select every 20th file starting with, say, the 5th file in the top drawer. Then file numbers 25, 45, 65, 85, . . . are audited.
   b. Manufacturers were subdivided into groups by volume of sales. Those with over $100 million in sales were classified as class A large; those from $50 to $100 million as class A medium size; and those between $25 and $50 million . . . and so on. Samples were then selected from each of these groups. What is this type of sampling called?

3. Ten passengers are to be selected at random from the New York–to–Los Angeles flight and interviewed in depth regarding airport facilities, service, food, and so on. Each passenger boarding the aircraft was given a number. The numbers started with 001 and ended with 250.
   a. Select 10 numbers at random using the table of random numbers in Appendix D.
   b. The sample of 10 could have been chosen using a systematic sample. Choose the first number using Appendix D, and then list the numbers to be interviewed.
   c. Evaluate the two methods by giving the advantages and possible disadvantages.

4. Briefly explain each of the following nonprobability types of sampling.
   a. Panel sampling.
   b. Convenience sampling.

SAMPLING ERROR

The previous section stressed the importance of selecting a sample so that every member of the sample has a known chance of being selected. Logically, we cannot expect a sample characteristic to be exactly identical to that characteristic in the population. That is, it is unlikely that a sample mean would be identical to the population mean. The differences between the sample statistic and the corresponding population value are referred to as **sampling errors.** They are simply *chance* variations.

As an example, suppose it were known that the mean grade for all students on an examination was 75 (the population mean). And suppose the mean of the first random sample of 10 grades was 73. The sample mean deviates −2 from the population mean. If another sample of 10 grades resulted in a mean of 76, that sample mean deviates +1 from the population mean. These deviations (−2 and +1) between what we get and what we expect are the sampling errors.

Continuing with this example, the means of 15 samples were computed to be (rounded to the nearest whole number): 73, 76, 79, 75, 74, 73, 77, 77, 76, 76, 77, 76, 73, 79, and 76. The sample means were organized into a distribution (Table 12–1) and portrayed graphically in the form of a histogram (Chart

Sample means	Number
73–74	4
75–76	6
77–78	3
79–80	2

TABLE 12–1
Distribution of sample means

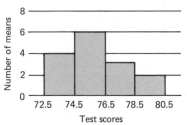

CHART 12–1
Histogram portraying the distribution of sample means

12–1). This distribution is aptly called the **sampling distribution** of the sample mean. Based on the table and histogram, notice that, even though only 15 samples were selected, the sampling distribution of the means is starting to be somewhat bell shaped and symmetrical about the population mean of 75. If a large number of samples were selected, and if the means were not rounded to the nearest whole number, the sample means would, when plotted, appear as a smooth, bell-shaped, symmetrical curve about the mean of 75. This concept will be examined further in the following section.

SAMPLING DISTRIBUTION OF THE MEAN

The discussion in the previous section emphasized that it is unlikely the mean of a sample will be identical to the mean of the population. Further, it was pointed out that if all possible samples of a given size are selected from a population, the distribution of their sample means, called the **sampling distribution of the mean**, will tend to approximate a normal curve.

EXAMPLE

These concepts will now be demonstrated by taking all possible samples of size four from a population consisting of the hourly incomes of the seven employees of Tartus Industries. The hourly earnings for the population are listed in Table 12–2.

TABLE 12–2
Hourly earnings of the seven employees of Tartus Industries

Employee	Hourly earnings
Joe	$7
Sam	9
Sue	8
Bob	8
Jan	7
Art	8
Ted	9

a. What is the population mean?
b. What is the sampling distribution of the mean?
c. What is the mean of the sampling distribution?
d. What observations can be made with respect to the population and the sampling distribution?

SOLUTION

a. The population mean is $8, found by:

$$\frac{\$7 + \$9 + \$8 + \$8 + \$7 + \$8 + \$9}{7}$$

b. In order to arrive at the sampling distribution of the means, all possible samples of size four without replacement were selected from the population, and their means were computed (see Table 12–3).[2]

TABLE 12–3
Sample means for all possible samples of size four

Names	Hourly earnings	Sum		Sample mean
Joe, Sam, Sue, Bob	$7, $9, $8, $8	$32/4	=	$8.00
Joe, Sam, Sue, Jan	7, 9, 8, 7	31/4	=	7.75
Joe, Sam, Sue, Art	7, 9, 8, 8	32/4	=	8.00
Joe, Sam, Sue, Ted	7, 9, 8, 9	33/4	=	8.25
Joe, Sam, Bob, Jan	7, 9, 8, 7	31/4	=	7.75
Joe, Sam, Bob, Art	7, 9, 8, 8	32/4	=	8.00
Joe, Sam, Bob, Ted	7, 9, 8, 9	33/4	=	8.25
Joe, Sam, Jan, Art	7, 9, 7, 8	31/4	=	7.75
Joe, Sam, Jan, Ted	7, 9, 7, 9	32/4	=	8.00
Joe, Sam, Art, Ted	7, 9, 8, 9	33/4	=	8.25
Joe, Sue, Bob, Jan	7, 8, 8, 7	30/4	=	7.50
Joe, Sue, Bob, Art	7, 8, 8, 8	31/4	=	7.75
Joe, Sue, Bob, Ted	7, 8, 8, 9	32/4	=	8.00
Joe, Sue, Jan, Art	7, 8, 7, 8	30/4	=	7.50
Joe, Sue, Jan, Ted	7, 8, 7, 9	31/4	=	7.75
Joe, Sue, Art, Ted	7, 8, 8, 9	32/4	=	8.00
Joe, Bob, Jan, Art	7, 8, 7, 8	30/4	=	7.50
Joe, Bob, Jan, Ted	7, 8, 7, 9	31/4	=	7.75
Joe, Bob, Art, Ted	7, 8, 8, 9	32/4	=	8.00
Joe, Jan, Art, Ted	7, 7, 8, 9	31/4	=	7.75
Sam, Sue, Bob, Jan	9, 8, 8, 7	32/4	=	8.00
Sam, Sue, Bob, Art	9, 8, 8, 8	33/4	=	8.25
Sam, Sue, Bob, Ted	9, 8, 8, 9	34/4	=	8.50
Sam, Sue, Jan, Art	9, 8, 7, 8	32/4	=	8.00
Sam, Sue, Jan, Ted	9, 8, 7, 9	33/4	=	8.25
Sam, Sue, Art, Ted	9, 8, 8, 9	34/4	=	8.50
Sam, Bob, Jan, Art	9, 8, 7, 8	32/4	=	8.00
Sam, Bob, Jan, Ted	9, 8, 7, 9	33/4	=	8.25
Sam, Bob, Art, Ted	9, 8, 8, 9	34/4	=	8.50
Sam, Jan, Art, Ted	9, 7, 8, 9	33/4	=	8.25
Sam, Bob, Jan, Art	8, 8, 7, 8	31/4	=	7.75
Sue, Bob, Jan, Ted	8, 8, 7, 9	32/4	=	8.00
Sue, Bob, Art, Ted	8, 8, 8, 9	33/4	=	8.25
Sue, Jan, Art, Ted	8, 7, 8, 9	32/4	=	8.00
Bob, Jan, Art, Ted	8, 7, 8, 9	32/4	=	8.00

The sample means from all the distinct possible equal-size samples of four

---

[2] Note that there are 35 possible samples (combinations), found by applying the formula for combinations from Chapter 9, namely—

$$_nC_r = \frac{n!}{r!(n-r)!} = \frac{7!}{4!(7-4)!}$$

that can be drawn from the population are in Table 12–4. This probability distribution is the **sampling distribution of the means.**

TABLE 12–4
Sampling distribution of the mean for $n = 4$

Sample mean	Number of means	Probability
$7.50	3	3/35 = 0.0857
7.75	8	8/35 = 0.2286
8.00	13	13/35 = 0.3714
8.25	8	8/35 = 0.2286
8.50	3	3/35 = 0.0857
	35	35/35 1.0000

c. The mean of the sampling distribution is $8.00, found by adding all of the sample means and dividing the total of $280 by 35.

d. These observations can be made:

(1) The mean of the sample means (eight dollars) is equal to the population mean (also eight dollars). This is always true if all distinct possible samples of a given size are selected from the population of interest.

(2) Notice from Chart 12–2 that the dispersion in the distribution of sample means is *less than* the dispersion in the population. The sample means vary from $7.50 to $8.50, the population values from $7.00 to $9.00.

(3) The histogram representing the distribution of the sample means is tending to approximate a normal curve (see Chart 12–2).

CHART 12–2
Histogram representing the sample means and the population values

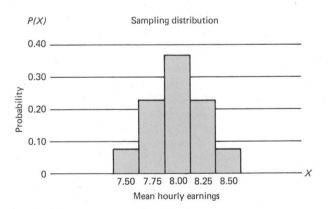

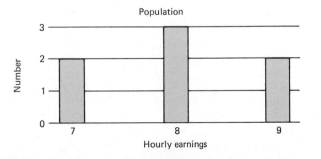

314

a. 10, found by:

$$\frac{5!}{2!(5-2)!}$$

	Service	Sample mean
b. Snow, Tolson	20, 22	21
Snow, Kraft	20, 26	23
Snow, Irwin	20, 24	22
Snow, Jones	20, 28	24
Tolson, Kraft	22, 26	24
Tolson, Irwin	22, 24	23
Tolson, Jones	22, 28	25
Kraft, Irwin	26, 24	25
Kraft, Jones	26, 28	27
Irwin, Jones	24, 28	26

c. Means	Number	Probability
21	1	0.10
22	1	0.10
23	2	0.20
24	2	0.20
25	2	0.20
26	1	0.10
27	1	0.10
	10	1.00

d. Identical: population mean $\mu = 24$ and mean of sample means also 24.

e. Dispersion of means less (range from 21 to 27). Population values go from 20 to 28.

f. Nonnormal.

g. yes.

A reminder: cover the answers in the left column.)

The lengths of service of all the executives employed by Standard Chemicals are:

Name	Years
Mr. Snow	20
Ms. Tolson	22
Mr. Kraft	26
Ms. Irwin	24
Mr. Jones	28

a. Using the combination formula, how many samples of size two are possible?

b. Select all possible samples of size two from the population and compute their means.

c. Organize the means into a sampling distribution.

d. Compare the population mean and the mean of the sample means.

e. Compare the dispersion in the population with that of the distribution of sample means.

f. Is the distribution of population values normally distributed or nonnormal?

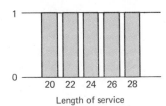

g. Is the distribution of sample means starting to show some tendency toward being bell shaped?

The population and the sample size in both the example and the self-review were intentionally kept small to simplify the calculations. Both these illustrations, however, highlighted two important concepts:

1. If the population is normally distributed, the sampling distribution of the mean will also be normally distributed. Roughly speaking, the case involving the hourly earnings of the employees of Tartus Industries illustrated this concept. Shown graphically:

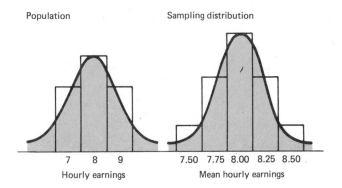

2. If the population is not normally distributed, the sampling distribution still tends to approximate the normal distribution. The lengths of service of the executives of Standard Chemicals illustrated this concept.

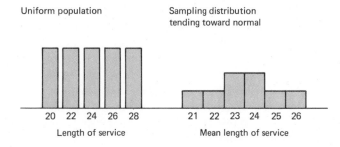

Of what importance are these two concepts? They are the basis for one of the most important theorems in statistics, namely, the **Central Limit Theorem.**

THE CENTRAL LIMIT THEOREM

The Central Limit Theorem states:

> If the sample size n is sufficiently large, the sampling distribution of the mean will be approximately normal.

There is no common agreement as to what constitutes a "sufficiently large" sample size. Some statisticians say 30, others go as low as 12. The example concerned with the hourly earnings of all the employees at Tartus Industries worked quite well with a sample of four. However, unless the population is approximately normal, such small sample sizes generally do not result in a sampling distribution which is normally distributed. As the sample size becomes larger and larger, the distribution of the sample mean becomes closer and closer to the bell-shaped normal distribution. As an arbitrary figure, many researchers consider that a sample size of 30 or more qualifies as a large sample.

Some applications of the central limit theorem

The Central Limit Theorem provides the theoretical framework for most **statistical estimation** and **tests of hypotheses.** Problems of estimation will be examined in this chapter. Several chapters are devoted to testing hypotheses, starting with Chapter 13.

Statistical estimation can be divided into **point estimation** and **interval estimation.**

> A point estimate is one number (called a point) which is used to estimate a population parameter.

For illustration, we may want to estimate a **population parameter**, such as the population mean μ. One problem might involve estimating the hourly earnings of all coal miners in the United States. Another problem might involve estimating the knee-bend strength of all steel plates welded during a three-hour period. As pointed out earlier, it is usually impractical to include all the miners in a study to determine the arithmetic mean hourly earnings. Instead, a statistical estimator based on a sample is used. The **point estimator** of the population mean μ is the sample mean $\overline{X}$, found by:

$$\overline{X} = \frac{\Sigma X}{n}$$

Likewise an **interval estimator** is used to estimate the interval within which the population mean probably lies. The idea of a point estimate and an interval estimate is shown diagrammatically for the mean weight of the contents of boxes of cereal.

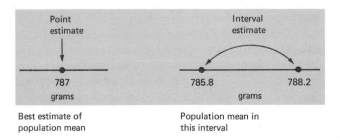

The interval within which the population parameter probably lies is called a **confidence interval.** In the illustration we are stating that the mean weight of all boxes of cereal is probably in the interval between 785.8 grams and 788.2 grams. The end points (785.8 and 788.2 grams) are called the **confidence limits.** The measure of confidence one has in the interval estimate is referred to as the **degree of confidence.**

An interval estimate is based on the Central Limit Theorem which, as has been pointed out, states that if the sample size is large enough the distribution of sample means approximates a normal probability distribution.

Sampling distribution of means

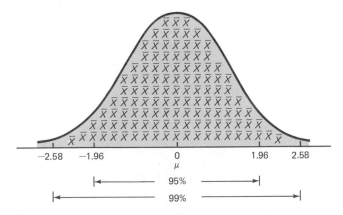

About 95 percent of the sample means fall within 1.96 **standard errors** of the population mean μ, and about 99 percent of the sample means fall within 2.58 standard errors of the population mean.

The standard error of the mean is computed by:

$$\sigma_{\bar{x}} = \frac{\sigma}{\sqrt{n}}$$

where:

$\sigma_{\bar{x}}$ is the symbol for the standard error of the mean.
σ is the standard deviation of the population.
n is the size of the sample.

If the 0.95 degree of confidence is selected, the confidence interval is determined by:

$$\bar{X} \pm z\,\frac{\sigma}{\sqrt{n}} = \bar{X} \pm 1.96\,\frac{\sigma}{\sqrt{n}}$$

For the 0.99 degree of confidence, the confidence interval is determined by:

$$\bar{X} \pm z\,\frac{\sigma}{\sqrt{n}} = \bar{X} \pm 2.58\,\frac{\sigma}{\sqrt{n}}$$

The above formulas for the standard error and the confidence intervals assume that the population standard deviation σ is known or can be approximated accurately. If it is not known and $n = 30$ or more (considered a large sample), the standard deviation of the sample, designated by s, is used to approximate the population standard deviation σ. The formula for the standard error then becomes:

$$\sigma_{\bar{x}} = \frac{s}{\sqrt{n}}$$

and the formulas for setting the 0.95 and 0.99 confidence intervals are:

$$\bar{X} \pm 1.96 \frac{s}{\sqrt{n}} \qquad \text{and} \qquad \bar{X} \pm 2.58 \frac{s}{\sqrt{n}}$$

EXAMPLE

An experiment involves selecting a random sample of 256 middle managers at random for study. One item of interest is their mean annual income. The sample mean is computed to be $35,420 and the sample standard deviation $2,050.

a. What is the estimated mean income of all middle managers (the population)? That is, what is the point estimate?
b. What is the 0.95 confidence interval (rounded to the nearest $10)?
c. What are the 0.95 confidence limits?
d. What degree of confidence is being used?
e. Interpret the findings.

SOLUTION

a. $35,420, the sample mean.
b. The population mean is in the interval between $35,170 and $35,670, found by:

$$\bar{X} \pm 1.96 \frac{s}{\sqrt{n}} = \$35,420 \pm 1.96 \frac{\$2,050}{\sqrt{256}}$$

$$= \$35,420 \pm 1.96 \left(\frac{\$2,050}{16}\right)$$

$$= \$35,168.875 \text{ and } \$35,671.125$$

c. $35,170 and $35,670 are the confidence limits.
d. 0.95 is the degree of confidence.
e. Interpretation: The probability is 0.95 that the mean annual income of 'all middle managers is in the interval between $35,170 and $35,670.

Theoretically for this problem, if we had time to select 100 samples of size 256 from the population of middle managers and compute the sample means, and confidence intervals, the population mean annual income would be found in about 95 out of the 100 confidence intervals. About 5 out of the 100 confidence intervals would *not* contain the population mean annual income μ. Shown schematically for a few samples we selected:

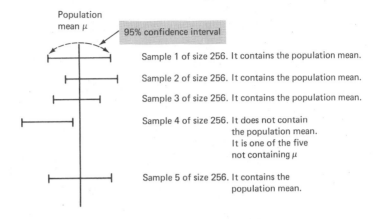

a. 402.7 grams. The point estimate
b. Population mean in interval between 399.1 and 406.3 grams found by

$$\bar{X} \pm 2.58 \frac{s}{\sqrt{n}} = 402.7 \pm 2.58 \frac{8.8}{\sqrt{40}}$$

$$= 402.7 \pm 2.58 \frac{8.8}{6.32455}$$

c. 399.1 and 406.3 grams
d. 0.99
e. The probability is 0.99 that the population mean weight of the trout in the pond is in the interval between 399.1 and 406.3 grams.

The wildlife department has been feeding a special food to rainbow trout fingerlings in a pond. A sample of the weights of 40 trout revealed that the mean weight is 402.7 grams, the standard deviation 8.8 grams.

a. What is the estimated mean weight of the population? What is that estimate called?
b. What is the 0.99 confidence interval (to the nearest tenth of a gram)?
c. What are the 0.99 confidence limits?
d. What degree of confidence is being used?
e. Interpret your findings.

EXERCISES

5. Suppose that a research firm conducted a survey to determine the average (mean) amount of money steady smokers spend on cigarettes during a month. A sample of 500 steady smokers revealed that $\bar{X} = \$30$ and $s = \$5$.
   a. What is the point estimate? Explain what it indicates.
   b. Using the 0.95 confidence coefficient, determine the confidence interval for μ.

6. Refer to problem 5. Suppose that 1,000 smokers (instead of 500) had been surveyed, and the sample mean and the sample standard deviation remained the same ($30 and $5, respectively).
   a. What is the 95 percent confidence interval estimate of μ?
   b. Explain why this confidence interval is narrower than the one determined in Problem 5.

SIZE OF THE SAMPLE

There are several misconceptions about the number to sample. One fallacy is that a sample consisting of 5 percent (or a similar constant percent) is adequate for all problems (A sample of 3 out of a population of 60 might be too small, and a sample of size 50,000 from a population of 1 million too large.) Another is that a larger sample of consumers or voters must be selected from a heavily populated state, such as California, than from a small state, such as New Hampshire. There are three factors that determine the size of the sample—*none of which have any direct relationship to the size of the population*. They are:

1. *The degree of confidence selected*. This is usually 0.95 or 0.99, but it may be any level. The researcher specifies the degree of confidence.
2. *The maximum allowable error*. The researcher must decide on this too. It is the maximum error the researcher will tolerate at a specified level of confidence.
3. *The variation of the population*. It is measured by the standard deviation. (Of course, a population with little variation requires smaller samples.)

The role each of these factors plays in determining the sample size is now examined.

Degree of confidence

Recall again that the purpose of taking a sample is to estimate a population parameter. Suppose that the parameter to be estimated is the arithmetic mean and the degree of confidence selected is 0.90. And, based on a sample, it was estimated that the population mean is in the interval between $89,050 and $91,050. Logically, if the degree of confidence were increased to 0.95 or 0.99, the sample size would have to be increased (assuming the interval remained the same). Carrying this to the extreme, if the researcher wanted to be 100 percent sure that the true mean was in the interval between $89,050 and $91,050, he or she would have to survey the entire population—that is, take a 100 percent sample. Thus, one of the factors related to the sample size is the **degree of confidence**—the higher the degree of confidence, the larger the sample required to give a certain precision.

Maximum error allowed

To illustrate, suppose that a developer is considering building a shopping mall near several subdivisions. One important statistic needed is the mean income in the area. A leisurely drive through the subdivisions indicated that the family incomes range from a probable low of $9,000 to a high of about $29,000. On the assumption that these are reasonable estimates, does it seem likely that the developer would be satisfied with this statement resulting from a sample of area residents? "I am 95 percent confident that the population mean is between $13,000 and $25,000." Probably not! Confidence limits that wide indicate little or nothing about the population mean. Instead, the developer stated that "Using the 0.95 probability, the total error in predicting the population mean should not exceed $200"; that is, $1.96\sigma_{\bar{x}} = \$200$. So, the standard error of the mean $\sigma_{\bar{x}}$ is $102.04, found by:

$$\sigma_{\bar{x}} = \frac{\$200}{1.96}$$

$$= \$102.04$$

Shown schematically:

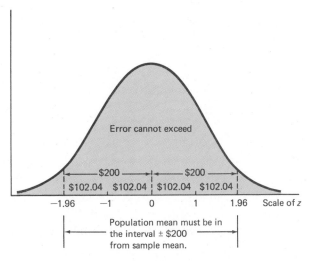

The size of the sample is computed by solving for n in the formula:

$$\boxed{\sigma_{\bar{x}} = \frac{s}{\sqrt{n}}}$$

where:

$\sigma_{\bar{x}}$ is the standard error of the mean.

s is the standard deviation of the pilot survey.

n is the sample size.

Thus far:

$$\sigma_{\bar{x}} = \frac{s}{\sqrt{n}}$$

$$\frac{\text{Total allowable error}}{z \text{ standard deviates}} = \frac{\text{Sample standard deviation}}{\sqrt{\text{Sample size}}}$$

$$\sigma_{\bar{x}} = \frac{s}{\sqrt{n}}$$

$$\frac{\$200}{1.96} = \frac{s}{\sqrt{n}}$$

$$\$102.04 = \frac{s}{\sqrt{n}}$$

Estimating the variation in the population

There are still two unknowns, s and n. To solve for the number to be sampled, the standard deviation of the population must be estimated. This can be done either by taking a small pilot survey (say 50) and using the standard deviation of the pilot sample as an estimate of the population standard deviation, or by estimating the standard deviation based on a knowledge of the population. Suppose that a pilot survey was conducted and the sample standard deviation computed to be $3,000. The number to be sampled can now be estimated.

$$\sigma_{\bar{x}} = \frac{s}{\sqrt{n}}$$

$$\frac{\$200}{1.96} = \frac{\$3,000}{\sqrt{n}}$$

$$\$102.04\sqrt{n} = \$3,000$$

$$\sqrt{n} = \frac{\$3,000}{\$102.04}$$

$$n = 864$$

A more convenient computational formula for determining n is:

$$\boxed{n = \left(\frac{z \cdot s}{E}\right)^2}$$

where:

E is the allowable error.
z is the z-score associated with the degree of confidence selected.
s is the sample standard deviation of the pilot survey.

For this problem:

$$n = \left(\frac{z \times s}{E}\right)^2$$

$$= \left(\frac{1.96 \times \$3,000}{\$200}\right)^2$$

$$= \left(\frac{\$5,880}{\$200}\right)^2$$

$$= 864$$

which is the same answer as above.

The sample of size 864 may or may not give the developer what he wants—an estimate of the true mean within plus and minus $200. The sample of 864 may be the correct sample size, or it may prove to be too small or too large. If it proves that too many families were interviewed, the cost of surveying all 864 was not warranted. If the sample of size 864 is too small, more families must be contacted if the error is to be reduced to within $200 (as originally specified by the developer).

It is highly unlikely that the standard deviation of the sample of 864 families will be exactly $3,000 (the same as the pilot survey of about 50 families). If the standard deviation of the sample resulted in a sample standard deviation of $2,500, the correct sample size should have been 600. This is found by solving for n in the following: $\$200/1.96 = \$2,500/\sqrt{n}$. Obviously, the sample of 864 was too large.

***

SELF-REVIEW 12–3

***

207, found by:

$$\sigma_{\bar{x}} = \frac{s}{\sqrt{n}}$$

$$\frac{0.05}{2.58} = \frac{0.279}{\sqrt{n}}$$

$$0.0193798 = \frac{0.279}{\sqrt{n}}$$

$$0.0193798\sqrt{n} = 0.279$$

$$\sqrt{n} = \frac{0.279}{0.0193798}$$

$$n = (14.396433)^2$$

$$= 207$$

Or, $n = \left(\dfrac{z \times s}{E}\right)^2 = \left(\dfrac{2.58 \times 0.279}{0.05}\right)^2 = 207$

Will you assist the college registrar in determining how many transcripts to study? The registrar wants to estimate the arithmetic mean final grade point average of all graduating seniors during the past 10 years. GPAs range between 2.0 and 4.0. The mean grade point average is to be estimated within 0.05, and the 0.99 degree of confidence is to be used. Thus, the registrar wants to report something like this (hypothetical): "I am 99 percent sure that the mean grade point average of graduating seniors is in the interval between 2.45 and 2.50." The standard deviation of a small pilot survey is 0.279. How many transcripts should be sampled?

EXERCISES

7. A survey is being planned to determine the average amount of time preschool children watch television. A pilot survey indicated that the mean time per week is 12 hours, with a standard deviation of 3 hours. It is desired to estimate the mean viewing time within one quarter hour. The 0.95 degree of confidence is to be used. How many preschool children should be surveyed?

8. A processor of carrots cuts the green top off each carrot, washes the carrots, and inserts six to a package. Twenty packages are inserted in a box for shipment. As a check on the weight of the boxes, a few were checked. The mean weight was 20.4 pounds, the standard deviation 0.5 pounds. How many boxes must the processor sample to be 95 percent confident that the sample mean does not differ from the population mean by more than 0.2 pounds?

CONFIDENCE INTERVAL FOR A POPULATION PROPORTION

The theory and procedure for determing a point estimator and an interval estimator for a **population proportion** are quite similar to those described in the previous section. Therefore, the following discussion regarding **point estimates** and **interval estimates** will be rather brief.

A point estimate for the population proportion is found by X/n, where X is the number of successes and n the size of the sample.

SOLUTION

The *point estimate* is 0.80, found by 1,600/2,000. This proportion can be converted to a percent by multiplying it by 100; that is, $0.80 \times 100 = 80$ percent. Note that this proportion is based on a count of the number of persons who favor the Democratic candidate (1,600 successes) relative to the total number surveyed (2,000).

The *confidence interval* for the population proportion is estimated by:

$$p \pm z \ \sqrt{\frac{p(1-p)}{n}}$$

where:

p is the sample proportion.
z is the z-score for the degree of confidence selected.
n is the sample size.

SOLUTION

$$p \pm z \ \sqrt{\frac{p(1-p)}{n}} = 0.80 \pm 1.96 \ \sqrt{\frac{0.80(1-0.80)}{2,000}}$$

$$= 0.80 \pm 1.96 \ \sqrt{0.00008}$$
$$= 0.78247 \text{ and } 0.81753$$

As is the usual practice in this type of problem, the percents are rounded to one decimal place. Thus, the probability is 0.95 that between 78.2 percent and 81.8 percent of the voting population favor the Democratic candidate.

Interpreting. We are 95 percent sure that the population proportion is in the interval between 78.2 percent and 81.8 percent. To put it another way, if the election were held today we are 95 percent sure that the Democratic candidate for governor would receive between 78.2 percent and 81.8 percent of the vote.

SELF-REVIEW 12-4
---

a. The population proportion lies between 0.268 and 0.332, found by 420/1,400 = 0.30. Then:

$$0.30 \pm 2.58 \sqrt{\frac{0.30(1 - 0.30)}{1,400}}$$

$$= 0.30 \pm 2.58 \sqrt{0.00015}$$
$$= 0.30 \pm 2.58 (0.0122474)$$
$$= 0.30 \pm 0.0315982$$
$$= 0.268 \text{ and } 0.332$$

b. 0.268 and 0.332.

c. We are 99 percent sure the population proportion is in the interval between 26.8 percent and 33.2 percent.

A market survey was conducted to estimate the proportion of homemakers who could recognize the brand name of a cleanser based on the shape and color of the container. Out of the 1,400 homemakers, 420 were able to identify the brand name. The 0.99 confidence coefficient was used.

a. Based on the 0.99 degree of confidence, the population proportion lies within what interval?

b. What are the confidence limits?

c. Interpret your findings.

SIZE OF THE SAMPLE FOR PROPORTIONS

Again, the same procedure as for interval data is applicable for determining the sample size when proportions are involved. Specifically: (1) The sponsor of the survey must specify how precise the estimate of the population proportion must be. (2) The degree of confidence, such as the 0.90, 0.95, or 0.99, must be given. (3) The proportion p must be either approximated from past experience (such as past elections) or approximated from a small pilot survey of, say, 50 or 100.

The formula for determining the sample size in the case of a proportion is:

$$n = p(1 - p) \left[\frac{z}{E} \right]^2$$

where:

p is the estimated proportion based on past experience, or a pilot survey.

z is the z-score associated with the degree of confidence selected.

E is the maximum allowable error the researcher will tolerate.

EXAMPLE

A congressman wants to determine his popularity in a certain part of the state. He indicated that the proportion of voters who will vote for him must be estimated with ±2 percent. Further, the 0.95 degree of confidence is to be used. In past elections he received 40 percent of the popular vote in that area of the state. He doubts whether it has changed much. How many registered voters should be sampled?

326

SOLUTION

Sample size should be 2,305, found by:

$$n = p(1 - p)\left[\frac{z}{E}\right]^2$$

$$= 0.40(1 - 0.40)\left[\frac{1.96}{0.02}\right]^2$$

$$= 0.24[98]^2$$

$$= 2,304.96$$

Again, the sample size of 2,305 might be too large, too small, or exactly correct, depending on the accuracy of $p = 0.40$.

Note: If there is no logical estimate of p, the sample size can be estimated by letting $p = 0.50$. (The size of the sample will never be larger than the one obtained for n when $p = 0.50$.)

SELF-REVIEW 12–5

a. True. $p = 922/2,305 = 0.40$. Substituting:

$$0.40(1 - 0.40)\left[\frac{1.96}{0.02}\right]^2 = 2,304.96$$

$$= 2,305$$

b. True. $p = 461/2,305 = 0.20$. Substituting:

$$0.20(1 - 0.20)\left[\frac{1.96}{0.02}\right]^2 = 0.16[98]^2$$

$$= 1,537$$

The sample of 2,305 was too large. Only 1,537 voters needed to be surveyed.

The following statements refer to the previous problem regarding the popularity of the congressman. For each statement, indicate whether it is true or false and give supporting evidence.

Suppose 2,305 registered voters were surveyed.

a. If 922 out of the 2,305 registered voters surveyed said they planned to vote for the congressman, the sample of size 2,305 was exactly correct.

b. If 461 of the 2,305 registered voters surveyed said they planned to vote for the congressman, the sample size of 2,305 was too large.

EXERCISES

9. Out of 1,000 persons surveyed regarding the foreign policy of the United States with respect to Cuba, 750 persons said they approved of it. Using the 0.95 degree of confidence, set the interval within which the population proportion falls.

10. Past surveys revealed that 30 percent of the tourists going to a gambling resort during a weekend spent over $1,000. Management wants to update that percent.
    a. Using the 0.90 degree of confidence, management wants to estimate the percent of the tourists spending over $1,000 within 1 percent. What sample size should be employed?
    b. Management said that the sample size suggested in Part *a* is much too large. Suggest something which could be done to reduce the sample size. Based on your suggestion, recalculate the sample size.

CHAPTER SUMMARY

Sampling is used extensively in business, public opinion polling, education, and other areas. The quality control department might select only 50 transistors at random in order to estimate the percent defective. The advertising department might ask 126 persons to rate five proposed advertising programs. The federal government uses sampling to determine the percent unemployment in the population, to find the average hourly earnings in contract construction, and to construct the monthly consumer price index.

A study of the entire population is usually not feasible for these reasons: (1) Many tests, such as tensile strength tests, destroy the product. (2) It may not be possible to count or measure every member of the population. This would apply to rainbow trout, sea gulls, light bulbs, and ears of corn. (3) The cost may be prohibitive. It would be very expensive to contact all television viewers, all college students, or all senior citizens. (4) Contacting the entire population may be too time consuming.

It was pointed out that the researcher must be careful to assure that the members of the sample are representative of the entire population. To accomplish this, many sampling plans are available. Some of the simple ones are random sampling, systematic sampling, and stratified random sampling.

Even though the members of the sample are carefully selected, it is unlikely that, say, the mean of a sample will be exactly equal to the population mean. The deviations between "what we get" (sample statistics) and "what we expect" (population parameters) are referred to as sampling errors.

To examine the concept of sampling variation further, all possible samples of a constant size were selected from a population and the mean of each sample computed. The distribution of those means is aptly called the sampling distribution of the mean. It was observed that the distribution of sample means tended to approximate a normal distribution. This fact is the basis for the Central Limit Theorem. It states that regardless of the shape of the population, the sampling distribution of the mean will be approximately normal, if the sample size is sufficiently large. Many statisticians consider 30 or more as qualifying as a large sample.

A point estimate is simply one number which is used to estimate a population parameter, such as the population mean μ. An interval estimate gives the interval within which the population parameter probably falls. The Central Limit Theorem provides the foundation for interval estimates. As an example, it might be said that "we are 95 percent confident that the mean age of the population of all executives is in the interval between 50.3 years and 51.3 years."

Three factors must be known before the size of a recommended sample can be determined. (1) The degree of confidence placed on the results. The 0.90, the 0.95, and the 0.99 are three used extensively. (2) The maximum allowable error the researcher will tolerate. (3) An estimate of the variation within the population. The standard deviation is used to represent this variation. It can be estimated by conducting a pilot study, or it may be based on past experience.

**CHAPTER
OUTLINE**

**An introduction to
sampling**

I. Statistical inference.
  A. *Definition.* Statistical inference is the process by which estimates, predictions, or decisions about the value of a population parameter are made based on limited sample information.
II. Sampling.
  A. *Reasons for sampling.*
    1. Destructive nature of certain tests.
    2. Physical impossibility of surveying all items in the population.
    3. Prohibitive cost of checking all items in population.
    4. Adequacy of sample results.
    5. Contacting entire population is too time consuming.
  B. *Methods of selecting a sample.*
    1. *Simple random sampling.* Examples: To assure that all items in the population have a chance of being chosen, a table of random numbers could be used.
    2. *Systematic sampling.* Select every nth item, such as items numbered 4, 14, 24, 34, and so on. Every item in the population has a chance of being selected.
    3. *Stratified random sampling.* Subdivide the population into subgroups and select either a proportional or a nonproportional sample. Every item has a chance of being selected.
    4. *Nonprobability sampling.* Convenience and panel sampling are two types of nonprobability sampling used extensively by market research groups. Every item in the population does not have a chance of being selected. Research groups claim that results are equally representative of the population.
III. Point estimates and interval estimates.
  A. *Point estimate.* One of the concerns of statistical inference is to make a statement about a population parameter (such as a population mean or a population proportion) based on a sample statistic. This one value is called a point estimate.
  B. *Interval estimate.* Because of sampling variation, an estimate of a population parameter cannot be precise. However, based on sample information, the interval in which the population value will fall can be identified. This estimate is called an interval estimate.
IV. Confidence interval for the mean. If population standard deviation is not known and a large sample is used, the confidence interval is constructed by:

$$\overline{X} \pm z \left(\frac{s}{\sqrt{n}} \right)$$

where:

$\overline{X}$ is the sample mean.
s is the sample standard deviation.
n is the size of the sample.
z is the number of standard deviates associated with the confidence level selected.

V. Confidence interval for proportions.

$$p \pm z \sqrt{\frac{p(1-p)}{n}},$$

where:

p is the sample proportion.
n is the sample size.

VI. Size of sample.
  A.   For interval level data:

$$n = \left(\frac{z \cdot s}{E}\right)^2$$

where:

E is the allowable error.
z is the z-score associated with the degree of confidence selected.
s is the sample standard deviation based on a pilot study.

  B.   For a proportion, the corresponding sample size is computed by:

$$n = p(1-p)\left[\frac{z}{E}\right]^2$$

where:

p is the estimated proportion based on past experience or a pilot study.
z is the z-score associated with the degree of confidence selected.
E is the maximum allowable error the researcher will tolerate.

**CHAPTER
EXERCISES**

11. The commercial banks in Region III are to be surveyed. Some of them are very large, with assets over $500 million; others are medium-sized, with assets between $100 million and $500 million; and the remaining banks have assets under $100 million. Explain how you would select a sample of these banks.

12. A small company is concerned about the inside diameter of the plastic PVC pipe it produces. A machine extrudes the pipe, and then it is cut into 10-foot lengths. About 720 pipes are produced per machine during a two-hour period. How would you go about taking a sample from the two-hour production period?

13. The ages of the six executives of the Ace Manufacturing Company are:

Name	Age
Mr. Jones	54
Ms. Smith	50
Mr. Kirk	52
Ms. Small	48
Mr. Hugh	50
Mr. Sioto	52

   a.   How many possible samples of size two are possible?
   b.   Select all possible samples if size two from the population of executives and compute the means.
   c.   Organize the means into a sampling distribution.
   d.   What is the mean of the population? Of the sample means?
   e.   What is the shape of the population?
   f.   What is the shape of the sampling distribution?

14. A random sample of 85 foremen, supervisors, and similar personnel revealed that on the average a person spent 6.5 years on the job before being promoted. The standard deviation of the sample was 1.7 years. Using the 0.95 degree of confidence, construct the confidence interval within which the population mean lies.

15. Out of 900 consumers surveyed, 414 said they were very enthusiastic about a new home decor scheme. Construct the 0.99 confidence interval for the population proportion.

16. The mean number of travel days per year for the outside salespersons employed by hardware distributors is to be estimated. The 0.90 degree of confidence is to be used. The mean of a small pilot study was 150 days, with a standard deviation of 14 days. If the population mean is to be estimated within two days, how many outside salespersons should be sampled?

17. The proportion of junior executives leaving large manufacturing companies within three years is to be estimated within 3 percent. The 0.95 degree of confidence is to be used. A study conducted several years ago revealed that the percent of junior executives leaving within three years was 21. To update this study, the files of how many junior executives should be studied?

CHAPTER SELF-REVIEW EXAMINATION

Do all the problems, and then check your answers against those given in Appendix A.

Score each problem 25 points.

1. It was discovered that some of the small steel shafts stored in warehouse E rusted and will have to be cleaned before they can be sold. In order to approximate the percent that need cleaning, a sample of 200 was selected at random. It was found that 80 out of the 200 needed cleaning.

   Using a confidence coefficient of 0.90, set confidence limits between which the population proportion should fall.

2. A probability sample of size 200 was selected to estimate the average (mean) amount of time adults over 65 years old, retired, and living in Florida listened to the radio during the day. The sample mean was calculated to be 110 minutes, and the standard deviation of the sample was 30 minutes.

   What are the 95 percent confidence limits for the population mean listening time?

3. There are 2,000 eligible voters in a precinct. Despite protests from knowledge-able persons that a sample size of 500 was too large in relation to the total, the 500 selected at random were asked to indicate whether they planned to vote for the

Democratic incumbent or the Republican challenger. Of the 500 surveyed, 350 said they were going to vote for the Democratic incumbent.

Using the 98 percent confidence coefficient, set the confidence limits for the proportion who plan to vote for the Democratic incumbent.

4. A sample survey is to be conducted to determine the mean family income in an area. The question is, How many families should be sampled? In order to get more information about the area, a small pilot survey was conducted, and the standard deviation of the sample was computed to be $500. The sponsor of the survey wants you to use the 0.95 confidence coefficient. Further, *if* you find the mean family income to be, say, $9,500, you could make a statement such as "I am 95 percent sure that the true mean family income is in the interval between $9,400 and $9,600." Or, *if* you find the sample mean to be, say, $8,800, you would state with 95 percent confidence that the population mean is in the interval between $8,700 and $8,900.

Based on the pilot information and the demands of the sponsor, how many families should be interveiwed?

13

INTRODUCTION

Chapter 12 dealt with one aspect of statistical inference—namely, estimating, or predicting an unknown population parameter, such as the population mean or the population proportion. We noted that a single sample is selected, and based on the sample statistic (the sample mean or the sample proportion) a point estimate and an interval estimate of the population parameter are made. As an example, if a sample of 2,000 union members revealed that 1,600 favored the position the executive board took regarding import tariffs, the point estimate of the population proportion in favor of the board's position is 1,600/2,000 = 0.80, or 80 percent. However, it was stressed that sample statistics vary from sample to sample according to their sampling distribution. Because of this variability, we estimate a confidence interval in which the population mean or proportion lies with a known probability. In the labor union example we might estimate with a high degree of confidence (say 95 percent) that the population proportion lies in the interval between 78 and 82 percent.

This chapter begins our study of another aspect of statistical inference, namely, hypothesis testing. Some of the types of questions we could be concerned with are:

1. Is the mean impact strength of the plate glass being produced on production line B 70 pounds per square inch?
2. Are more than 10 percent of the 50-millimeter shells in storage defective?
3. Is there a difference in the proportion of consumers who purchased Smell Sweet soap before our television advertising campaign and after the campaign?
4. Is there a difference in the mean usable life of Always Ready and Hotshot type C batteries?

What is a **hypothesis**? It is a statement which you tentatively accept as true in order to study its logical consequences. For example, you generally hypothesize that your instructor is proficient in arithmetic until he or she says something like 2 + 4 = 12, which contradicts the hypothesis that he or she is proficient in arithmetic. Testing a hypothesis will help us check the reasonableness of the statement in Question 1 that the arithmetic mean impact strength of the glass is 70 psi. In Question 4, the statement (hypothesis) to be tested is "There is no difference between the usable life of Always Ready and Hotshot batteries. *Hypothesis testing is a formal procedure which is used in order to make a decision with respect to the reasonableness of a statement.* After applying the hypothesis-testing procedure we might, for example, agree with the hypothesis that there is no difference between the usable life of Always Ready and Hotshot batteries.

Tests of hypotheses: Large samples

THE PROCEDURE IN HYPOTHESIS TESTING

The hypothesis-testing procedure as used by statisticians does not provide proof that something is true in the manner in which a mathematician "proves" a statement. But it does provide a kind of "proof beyond a reasonable doubt" in the manner of an attorney. Hence there are specific rules of evidence, or procedure, which are followed. They are:

1. The **null hypothesis** and the **alternate hypothesis** are stated.
2. The **level of significance** is stated.
3. The appropriate **test statistic** is selected.
4. A **decision rule** is formulated.
5. Based on sample information, a decision to **accept or reject the null hypothesis** is made.

Each of these steps will now be discussed in more detail.

The null and alternate hypotheses

Step 1. The first step is to state the hypothesis to be tested. It is called the **null hypothesis**, designated H_0. The capital letter H stands for hypothesis, and the subscript zero implies "no difference." There is usually a *not* or a *no* in the null hypothesis. The null hypothesis for Question 1 of the introduction would be, "The impact strength of the glass is *not* different from 70 psi." This is the same as saying the mean μ impact strength of the glass is equal to 70 psi. The null hypothesis H_0 would then be written H_0: $\mu = 70$. For Question 3, it would be, "There is *no* difference in the proportion of consumers who purchased Smell Sweet before and after the television advertising campaign." This is the same as saying that the two proportions are equal, written H_0: $p_1 = p_2$. Generally speaking, *the null hypothesis is set up for the purpose of either accepting or rejecting it.*

The **alternate hypothesis** describes what you will believe if you reject the null hypothesis. Hence the name alternate hypothesis. It is often called the research hypothesis and designated H_1. If the null hypothesis is rejected, the alternate hypothesis will be accepted.

If the alternate hypothesis does not state the direction of the difference, the test is considered to be a **two-tailed test**, often referred to as a **two-sided test**. For the two illustration: ($\neq$ indicates "not equal"):

$$H_0: \mu = 70 \qquad H_0: p_1 = p_2 \quad \leftarrow \quad \boxed{p_1 \text{ equals } p_2}$$

$$\text{Read}$$

$$H_1: \mu \neq 70 \qquad H_1: p_1 \neq p_2 \quad \leftarrow \quad \boxed{p_1 \text{ does not equal } p_2}$$

If the alternate hypothesis states a direction, the test is referred to as a **one-tailed test**. Suppose there is interest in whether the mean impact strength of the glass is *greater* than 70 psi, the alternate hypothesis would then be written H_1: $\mu > 70$. However, if there is interest in determining whether the mean impact strength is *less* than 70 psi, the alternate hypothesis is written H_1: $\mu < 70$.

The level of significance

Step 2. The researcher must decide on the **level of risk** he or she will tolerate. If a true hypothesis is accepted, or a false hypothesis is rejected, it is obvious that a correct decision has been made. The fact that tests of hypotheses are based on samples, however, suggests two potential types of errors. (1) The null hypothesis is rejected when it should have been accepted, and (2) the null hypothesis is accepted when it should have been rejected. The first potential error (rejecting the null hypothesis when it is actually true) is called a **Type I error**. If expressed in terms of a probability, such as 0.10, 0.05, or 0.01, it is called the **level of significance** and designated by α (the Greek letter alpha). It is also called the **alpha risk** or the **level of risk**. The latter may be a more appropriate term because it is the risk one takes of rejecting the null hypothesis when it is really true. It should be noted that the level of significance is decided upon *before* going on to Steps 3, 4, and 5. It is needed to set up a decision rule (Step 4).

It would seem that instead of using the 0.05 level of significance (again meaning that there is a 5 percent chance of rejecting a null hypothesis when it is true), the 0.001 level, or even the 0.00001 level, should be chosen. Thus, only rarely would a Type I error be committed. But as the probability of making a Type I error decreases, the risk of accepting the null hypothesis when it is actually false increases. This is called a **Type II error**. It is also referred to as the **beta error** and designated by the Greek letter β.

The following table summarizes the decisions which the researcher could make and the possible consequences. For example, if the researcher rejects a null hypothesis which is actually true, a Type I decision error has been committed.

Null hypothesis	Researcher	
	Accepts H_0	Rejects H_0
H_0 is true	Correct decision	Type I error
H_0 is false	Type II error	Correct decision

Attempting to strike an ideal balance between the two types of errors is difficult. Some judgment of the relative costs of making either type of error will lead to a reasonable level of significance. Generally speaking, pollsters use the 0.10 level, and quality control engineers the 0.01 level. The 0.05 level of risk is applied to many research problems in marketing, medicine, sociology, and so on.

The test statistic

Step 3. An appropriate **test statistic**, depending on the parameter being tested, is decided upon. The value of the test statistic is used to test the null hypothesis. It may be the z-statistic discussed in Chapter 14, or the t-statistic which will be applied in Chapter 15, or the chi-square statistic introduced in Chapter 17. A number of factors must be considered in selecting an appropriate test. To mention just a few:

1. Does the problem involve a single sample, two samples, or many (k) samples? The Wilcoxon test (Chapter 17), for example, is a test for two samples, but to apply the Friedman test (Chapter 18), more than two samples are needed.
2. Are the samples related or independent? A sample of persons who smoke and a sample of persons who do not smoke are considered unrelated (independent) samples. Some tests require independence, whereas others must have related samples.

Identifying the test statistic allows us to develop the **sampling distribution of the test statistic**. Table 13–1 is an example of a sampling distribution. It is a distribution of all possible mean hourly wages selected from a population of 10 using a sample size of 2, with replacement. The population consists of hourly wages of $4, $5, $5, $6, $6, $6, $6, $7, $7, and $8.

**Table 13–1
Sampling distributions of the means, $N = 10, n = 2$, with replacement**

Mean hourly wage	Number of means	Probability
$4.00	1	0.01
4.50	4	0.04
5.00	12	0.12
5.50	20	0.20
6.00	26	0.26
6.50	20	0.20
7.00	12	0.12
7.50	4	0.04
8.00	1	0.01
	100	1.00

Generally speaking, the distribution is somewhat typical of most sampling distributions: (1) It is a probability distribution; (2) all possible outcomes for a given population and a given sample size are included; and (3) the distribution is symmetrical. (Some, however, are skewed or have other shapes.) Again, it should be noted that there is not just one sampling distribution. There are many different sampling distributions such as chi square, F, binomial, z, and so on. Each of these will be examined when the statistical test is introduced.

The decision rule

Step 4. Identification of the sampling distribution is important because it allows a **decision rule**, which has a known probability of committing a Type I error, to be formulated. A decision rule is simply a statement of the conditions under which the null hypothesis is accepted or rejected. To accomplish this, the sampling distribution is divided into two regions, aptly called the **region of acceptance** and the **region of rejection**. The region or area of rejection defines the location of all those values that are so large or so small that the probability of their occurrence under a true null hypothesis is rather remote. Chart 13–1 shows the region of rejection for a test of significance which will be made later in the chapter. The test is called the z-test. The sampling distribution of the statistic z is normally distributed. The 0.05 level of significance has been selected. How far away from the hypothesized value of the mean μ should we locate the dividing point between the regions of acceptance and rejection? It is sufficient at this point to indicate that if the value of z computed from sample observations is equal to or greater than 1.645, the null hypothesis is rejected. If, for example, the computed z was 4.132, it is highly unlikely that such a large value (compared with 1.645) could occur *if H_0 is true*. Thus, since 4.132 falls in the region beyond 1.645, the hypothesis is rejected. The z of 1.645 is called the **critical value**, and it is the dividing point between the area of acceptance and the area of rejection.

CHART 13–1
Sampling distribution for the statistic z, regions of acceptance and rejection for a one-tailed test, 0.05 level of significance

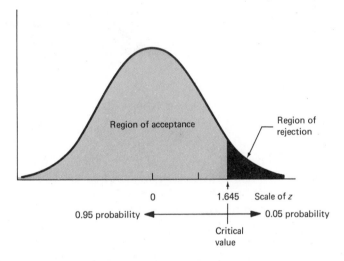

Chart 13–1 indicates that a *one-tailed* test is being applied. The entire 5 percent representing the area of rejection is found in one tail of the curve. Recall that *a test is one-tailed when the alternate hypothesis states a direction* such as:

H_0: There is *no* difference between the mean income of males and the mean income of females.

H_1: The mean income of males is *greater than* the mean income of females.

If, however, no direction is specified under the alternative hypothesis, a *two-tailed* test is applied. Changing the previous alternate hypothesis to illustrate:

H_0: There is *no* difference between the mean income of males and the mean income of females.

H_1: There *is* a difference in the mean income of males and females.

If the null hypothesis is rejected and H_1 accepted, the mean income of males could be greater than that of females or vice versa. To accommodate these two possibilities, the 5 percent representing the area of rejection is divided equally into the two tails of the sampling distribution (2½ percent each). Chart 13-2 shows the two areas and the critical values.

CHART 13-2
Region of acceptance and rejection, 0.05 level of significance for a two-tailed test

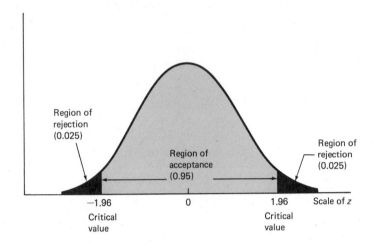

Making a decision

Step 5. The fifth and final step in hypothesis testing is making a *decision* (to accept or reject the null hypothesis). Referring to the previous two-tailed test, if the value of z was computed to be, say, either -3.45 or $+3.45$, the null hypothesis is rejected at the 0.05 level (refer back to Chart 13-2). A computed z-value of, say, -1.03, or $+0.89$, would cause the null hypothesis to be accepted. H_0 would be accepted because it would be reasoned that such a small difference between the mean sample income of males and the mean sample income of females (as represented by the computed z of say $+0.89$) *could be attributed to chance, i.e., sampling variation.* As noted, a computed z of, say, -3.45 would cause the null hypothesis to be rejected. The reasoning behind this decision is that it is highly improbable that a computed z-value this large could be due to sampling variation. Of course there is always the somewhat remote possibility that the null hypothesis was rejected when it should have been accepted (a Type I error). And, in accepting the null hypothesis based on a computed z of 0.89, there is also a definable chance that a false hypothesis has been accepted (Type II error).

Several tests are now conducted using this five-step hypothesis-testing procedure. These tests will be continued in subsequent chapters.

TESTING A HYPOTHESIS FOR THE POPULATION MEAN

This first test involves determining whether a reported population mean is consistent with sample data.

EXAMPLE

It is known that the distribution of efficiency ratings for production employees at Roller Bearings, Inc., is normally distributed with a population mean μ of 200 and a population standard deviation σ of 16. The research department is challenging this mean, stating it is different from 200. Using the 0.01 level of significance, test the hypothesis that the population mean is not different from 200.

SOLUTION

Step 1. The null hypothesis H_0 is, "The population mean is not different from 200." To put it another way, the mean is 200. The alternate hypothesis is: "The mean is different from 200." The two hypotheses are written as:

$$H_0: \mu = 200$$

$$H_1: \mu \neq 200$$

This is a *two-tailed test* because the alternate hypothesis does not state the direction of the difference. That is, it does not state whether the mean is greater than or less than 200.

Step 2. As noted, the 0.01 level of significance is to be used. This is α, the Type I error, and it is the probability of rejecting a true hypothesis.

Step 3. The appropriate test statistic is z. This is the z-score introduced in Chapter 11. Transforming the data to standard units (z-scores) permits their use in a great number of different problems. The formula is:

$$z = \frac{\overline{X} - \mu}{\dfrac{\sigma}{\sqrt{n}}}$$

where:

$\overline{X}$ is the sample mean.

μ is the population mean.

$\dfrac{\sigma}{\sqrt{n}}$ is the standard error of the mean discussed earlier in Chapter 12. σ is the population standard deviation and n the sample size.

Step 4. The decision rule is formulated by finding the critical value of z from Appendix G. Since this is a two-tailed test, half of 0.01, or 0.005, is in each tail. The acceptance area, which is located between the two tails, is therefore 0.99. Appendix G is based on just half of the area under the curve of 0.50000. Half is 0.49500. Go down the column marked "Area under the Curve between μ and X" until 0.49500 is located. The value nearest to 0.49500 is 0.49506. Then read the *critical value* in the margin opposite 0.49500. It is 2.58. It is shown in the form of a diagram in Chart 13–3.

**CHART 13–3
Areas of acceptance
and rejection for an
alpha of 0.01**

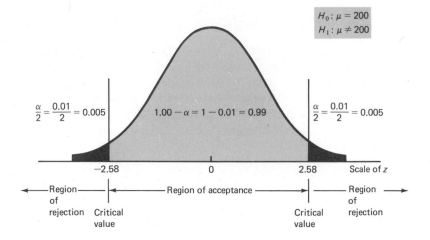

$H_0: \mu = 200$
$H_1: \mu \neq 200$

$\frac{\alpha}{2} = \frac{0.01}{2} = 0.005$ $1.00 - \alpha = 1 - 0.01 = 0.99$ $\frac{\alpha}{2} = \frac{0.01}{2} = 0.005$

-2.58 0 2.58 Scale of z

Region of rejection   Critical value   Region of acceptance   Critical value   Region of rejection

The decision rule is, therefore: Reject the null hypothesis and accept the alternate H_1 (which states that the population mean μ is not 200), if the computed value of z does not fall in the region between -2.58 and $+2.58$. Otherwise, we fail to reject the null hypothesis.

Step 5. Take a sample from the population (efficiency ratings), compute z, and based on the decision rule arrive at a decision to reject or fail to reject H_0.

The efficiency ratings of 100 production employees were analyzed. The mean of the sample $\overline{X}$ was computed to be 203.5. Computing z:

$$z = \frac{\overline{X} - \mu}{\dfrac{\sigma}{\sqrt{n}}}$$

$$= \frac{203.5 - 200}{\dfrac{16}{\sqrt{100}}}$$

$$= \frac{3.5}{1.6}$$

$$= 2.19$$

Since 2.19 falls in the region of acceptance, the null hypothesis, which states that the population mean is not different from 200, is not rejected at the 0.01 level. The difference between 203.5 and 200 can be attributed to chance variation.

SELF-REVIEW 13–1

a. $H_0: \mu = 6.0.$ $H_1: \mu \neq 6.0.$
b. 0.05.

A reminder: cover the answers in the left column.

c.
$$z = \frac{\overline{X} - \mu}{\frac{\sigma}{\sqrt{n}}}$$

d. Accept the null hypothesis if computed z falls between -1.96 and $+1.96$. Otherwise reject.

e. Yes. Computed $z = -2.56$, found by:

$$\frac{5.84 - 6.0}{\frac{0.5}{\sqrt{64}}} = \frac{-0.16}{0.0625}$$

Reject H_0 at the 0.05 level. Accept H_1.

The mean turnover rate of a brand of allopurinol is 6.0. (This indicates that the stock of the medicine turns over on the average six times a year.) The standard deviation is 0.5. It is suspected that the average turnover is not 6.0. The 0.05 level of significance is to be used to test this hypothesis.

a. State H_0 and H_1
b. What is the Type I error?
c. Give the formula for the test statistic.
d. State the decision rule.
e. A sample of 64 bottles of allopurinol was selected at random. The mean turnover rate was computed to be 5.84. Shall we reject the null hypothesis at the 0.05 level?

As noted previously, if the alternate hypothesis states a direction (either "greater than" or "less than"), the test is *one-tailed*. The hypothesis-testing procedure is generally the same as for a two-tailed test, except that the critical value is different. Let us change the alternate hypothesis in the previous problem involving the efficiency rating of the production workers at Roller Bearing, Inc., from:

$$H_1: \mu \neq 200 \quad \text{(a two-tailed test)}$$

to:

$$H_1: \mu > 200 \quad \text{(a one-tailed test)}$$

The region of rejection for this one-tailed test is in the right tail (the inequality sign, $>$, points to the rejection region). The critical values for the previous two-tailed test were -2.58 and $+2.58$. For this one-tailed test the critical value is $+2.33$, found by (1) subtracting 0.01 from 0.50000, and (2) finding the critical value associated with 0.49000 in Appendix G. The decision rules for the two-tailed test and the one-tailed test are shown graphically in Chart 13–4.

CHART 13–4
Regions of acceptance and rejections, two-tailed and one-tailed tests, $\alpha = 0.01$

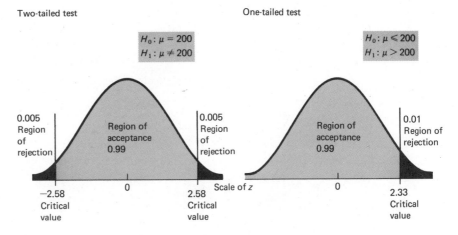

Notice the way the null hypothesis for the one-tailed test is given on the graph. It is H_0: $\mu \leq 200$, read "the population mean is equal to or less than 200." This is effectively the same as $\mu = 200$, but we will continue to write the null hypothesis in such cases the conventional way, either as $\mu \leq$ or $\mu \geq$ depending on the problem.

SELF-REVIEW 13-2

a. H_0: $\mu \geq 6.0$.

b. H_1: $\mu < 6.0$.

c. Note that the inequality $<$ in the alternate hypothesis points in the direction of the region of rejection.

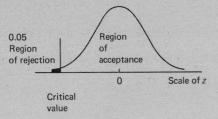

0.05
Region
of rejection

Region
of
acceptance

0   Scale of z

Critical
value

To determine the critical value: $0.50000 - 0.05 = 0.45000$. z from Appendix G is about 1.645.

Refer back to Self-Review 13–1.

a. If this hypothesis-testing problem were changed to a one-tailed test, how would the null hypothesis be stated if it read "the population mean is equal to or greater than 6.0."

b. How would the alternate hypothesis be written? (Watch the direction of the inequality.)

c. Show the decision rule graphically. Show the regions of acceptance and rejection, and the critical value.

Note in the preceding problems that we knew σ, the population standard deviation. In most cases, however, it is unlikely that the population standard deviation is known. Thus, σ must be based on prior studies, or estimated using the sample standard deviation s. To safely substitute s for σ, the sample size must be 30 or more (considered a large sample). A procedure for samples of less than 30 will be presented in Chapter 15. The population standard deviation in the following example is not known; so the sample standard deviation will be used to estimate σ.

EXAMPLE

A large department chain issues its own credit card. The research director wants to find out whether the mean monthly unpaid balance for the population is equal to or less than $400. The level of significance is set at 0.05. A random check of 172 unpaid balances revealed the sample mean to be $407, and the standard deviation of the sample $38. Should the research director conclude that the population mean is greater than $400, or is it reasonable to assume that the difference of $7 is due to chance?

SOLUTION

As before, the null and alternate hypotheses are stated as:

$$H_0: \mu \leq \$400$$

$$H_1: \mu > \$400$$

Because the alternate hypothesis states a direction, a one-tailed test is applied. In a sense, the researcher hopes the null hypothesis will be rejected. The critical value of z is 1.645. The computed value of z is 2.42, found by:

$$z = \frac{\overline{X} - \mu}{\frac{s}{\sqrt{n}}}$$

$$= \frac{\$407 - \$400}{\frac{\$38}{\sqrt{172}}}$$

$$= \frac{\$7}{\frac{\$38}{13.114877}}$$

$$= \frac{\$7}{2.897428}$$

$$= 2.42$$

A value this large will occur less than 5 percent of the time. So, the research director would reject the null hypothesis that the mean unpaid balance is $400 in favor of H_1, which states that the mean is greater than $400.

EXERCISES

(A reminder: The answers and method of solution for selected exercises are in Appendix A.)

1. The mean gross annual incomes of certified tack welders are normally distributed with a mean of $20,000 and a standard deviation of $2,000. The shipbuilding association wishes to find out whether their tack welders earn more or less than $20,000 annually. The alternate hypothesis is that the mean is *not* $20,000. The 0.10 level of significance is to be used.
    a. State the null and alternate hypothesis using symbols.
    b. What is the alpha risk?
    c. State the decision rule.
    d. A sample of 120 welders employed in shipbuilding was selected. The sample mean was computed to be $20,500. Should H_0 be rejected?

2. The new director of the local office of the state unemployment service thought the average wait in line of 28 minutes to file a claim was much too long. Therefore, she instituted a number of changes to speed up the filing process. Three weeks later a sample of size 127 was selected. As each of the 127 unemployed

persons entered the office to file a claim, he or she was given a number with the time of arrival stamped on it. When the claim was filed, the time was again recorded. The sample average wait was computed to be 26.9 minutes, and the standard deviation of the sample 8 minutes. Shall we reject the null hypothesis that $\mu \geq 28$ (or, as noted $\mu = 28$) in favor of the alternate hypothesis $\mu < 28$ at the 0.02 level of significance?

HYPOTHESIS TESTING: TWO MEANS

The following illustration involving a test of significance between two sample means typifies a practical industrial problem.

Concrete blocks are to be used in the foundations of several buildings. The specifications state that the minimum arithmetic mean compressive strength of a sample of blocks must be 1,000 pounds per square inch (psi). If two companies submit samples of blocks which have mean compressive strengths over the minimum (1,000 psi), then the specifications state that one of two actions will be taken: (1) If a statistical test applied to the sampling results indicates that both samples could have come from the same, or identical, populations, the contract for the blocks will be divided equally. (2) If the sample statistics indicate that there are two populations involved, the company submitting the blocks having the higher compression strength will be awarded the contract.

Suppose that two suppliers plan to submit samples of concrete blocks for testing—the Stanblock Company and the Hicompressive Company. Prior to testing the blocks for compressive strength, a null and alternate hypothesis will be stated, a level of significance selected, an appropriate statistical test decided upon, and a decision rule formulated.

Step 1. The null hypothesis. There is *no* difference between the mean compressive strength of the concrete blocks manufactured by the Stanblock Company and the mean compressive strength of the concrete blocks manufactured by the Hicompressive Company. Thus, they constitute a single, identically overlapping population of concrete blocks. The alternative hypothesis H_1 is that there *is* a significant difference between the two mean compressive strengths; that is,

$$\text{Null } H_0\text{: } \mu_1 = \mu_2$$

$$\text{Alternative } H_1\text{: } \mu_1 \neq \mu_2$$

Since the alternative hypothesis does not specify direction (such as that the mean compressive strength of the blocks from the Stanblock Company is greater than the mean of the Hicompressive blocks), a two-tailed test will be used. The null hypothesis could have been written $\mu_1 - \mu_2 = 0$ (which indicates that the difference between the two means is zero), and the alternative hypothesis $\mu_1 - \mu_2 \neq 0$.

Step 2. Level of significance. The 0.01 level of significance has been chosen. This is the same as saying that the probability of a Type I error is 0.01.

Step 3. The statistical test. At least 30 blocks (n_1) will be selected at random from the blocks of the Stanblock Company and at least 30 will be selected from Hicompressive (n_2). As noted previously, when n_1 and n_2 are 30 or more, the samples are considered large and the z-test can be applied as the test of significance. The selection process also meets one other assumption underlying the z-test, namely, independence. This means that the selection of one concrete block in no way affects the selection of another block. And, the z-test assumes that the data are interval scaled. Of course, either of the two populations could be called number one. However, once you have labelled a particular population number one, you must continue to call it that.

The theory underlying the sampling distribution of z (called the *critical ratio*) will be examined briefly. It states in part that—

> If a large number of independent random samples are selected from the two populations, the distribution of the differences between the two means divided by the standard error of the difference between the two means (the critical ratio) will approximate a normal distribution.

$$z = \frac{\overline{X}_1 - \overline{X}_2}{\sqrt{\left(\frac{s_1}{\sqrt{n_1}}\right)^2 + \left(\frac{s_2}{\sqrt{n_2}}\right)^2}} \quad \text{or} \quad \frac{\overline{X}_1 - \overline{X}_2}{\sqrt{\frac{s_1^2}{n_1} + \frac{s_2^2}{n_2}}}$$

← Difference between two sample means

← Standard error of the difference between the two means

To illustrate this theory, assume that many samples of size 100 were taken of blocks from the Stanblock Company and many samples of 100 blocks were taken from the Hicompressive Company. And for the sake of simplicity, assume that the standard deviation for each sample was computed to be 20 psi. Then to compute z:

Sample	$\overline{X}_1$	$\overline{X}_2$	$\overline{X}_1 - \overline{X}_2$	$\dfrac{\overline{X}_1 - \overline{X}_2}{\sqrt{\left(\frac{s_1}{\sqrt{n_1}}\right)^2 + \left(\frac{s_2}{\sqrt{n_2}}\right)^2}}$	z
1	1,020	1,020	0	$\frac{0}{2.8} =$	0
2	1,022	1,020	+2	$\frac{+2}{2.8} =$	+0.7
3	1,030	1,021	+9	$\frac{+9}{2.8} =$	+3.2
4	1,018	1,021	−3	$\frac{-3}{2.8} =$	−1.1

Thus, in theory, if the two population means are equal and if the z-values of 0, +0.7, +3.2, −1.1, and so on were plotted, the distribution of these z-values would approximate a normal distribution.

Reference to the areas under the normal curve (Appendix G) reveals that about 68 percent of the z-values would fall within 0 ± 1.0; about 95 percent of the z-values within 0 ± 1.96; and about 99 percent within 0 ± 2.58 (see Chart 13–5).

CHART 13–5
Distribution of z when
$\mu_1 - \mu_2 = 0$

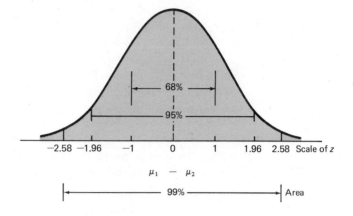

Step 4. The decision rule. It was shown in the preceding section that about 99 percent of the computed z-values will be between -2.58 and $+2.58$ under the assumption that there is no difference between the means of the two populations. Recall again that the 0.01 level of significance was selected. A two-tailed test will be used (because the alternative hypothesis H_1 does not state that the mean compressive strength of the blocks of one company is greater than the mean compressive strength of the other firm's blocks). So, if the computed z-value does fall within the region between ±2.58, the null hypothesis is *accepted*. It would be concluded that the difference between the two sample means was due to chance.

If the computed z-value is 2.58 or greater, the null hypothesis is *rejected*. The null hypothesis would be rejected on the basis that is highly unlikely that a computed z-value could be 2.58 or greater *by chance*. This decision rule is portrayed in Chart 13–6.

CHART 13–6
Two-tailed test, areas of acceptance and rejection, with a level of risk of 0.01

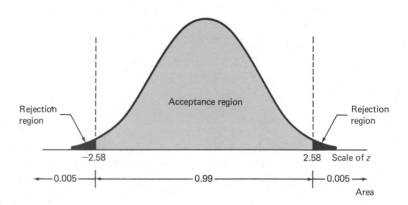

Step 5. The sample results and the decision. A total of 81 blocks was selected at random from the Stanblock Company production, and the compressive strength of each determined. The standard deviation of the sample and the mean compressive strength were computed. Sixty-four blocks from the Hicompressive Company were selected, and the same procedure was followed. The sample statistics are:

Stanblock Company	Hicompressive Company
$\overline{X}_1 = 1{,}070$ psi	$\overline{X}_2 = 1{,}020$ psi
$n_1 = 81$	$n_2 = 64$
$s_1 = 63$ psi	$s_2 = 57$ psi

The test statistic (z) is $+5.0$, found by:

$$z = \frac{\overline{X}_1 - \overline{X}_2}{\sqrt{\left(\frac{s_1}{\sqrt{n_1}}\right)^2 + \left(\frac{s_2}{\sqrt{n_2}}\right)^2}}$$

$$= \frac{1{,}070 - 1{,}020}{\sqrt{\left(\frac{63}{\sqrt{81}}\right)^2 + \left(\frac{57}{\sqrt{64}}\right)^2}}$$

$$\cong \frac{50}{\sqrt{100}} = 5.0$$

The computed z value of 5.0 falls in the area of rejection. The null hypothesis H_0 is *rejected* at the 0.01 level, and the alternative hypothesis H_1 is accepted. This indicates that $\mu_1 \neq \mu_2$, or putting it another way, $\mu_1 - \mu_2$ is not 0. Thus, it can be said that it is highly unlikely that the population mean compressive strength of the blocks of the Stanblock Company is equal to the population mean of the blocks of the Hicompressive Company and that the difference in the sample means (1,070 and 1,020) represents a real difference.

A logical decision would be to buy the blocks from the Stanblock Company.

In using a two-tailed test and the 0.01 level of significance, note in the previous chart (Chart 13–6) that there are two rejection areas, one above $+2.58$ and the other below -2.58. Thus, the null hypothesis that $\mu_1 = \mu_2$ would also be rejected at the 0.01 level of significance if the test statistic (z) were computed to be -5.0 instead of $+5.0$. That is, in the problem regarding the concrete blocks, the null hypothesis would also be rejected if the mean compressive strengths were reversed and the Stanblock Company blocks had a mean of 1,020 and Hicompressive blocks 1,070 $(1{,}020 - 1{,}070)/10 = -5.0$. And regardless of whether z is $+5.0$ or -5.0, the alternative hypothesis $\mu_1 \neq \mu_2$ would be accepted.

SELF-REVIEW 13–3

Yes, Fatear is effective. Computed z is 6.15, found by:

$$z = \frac{16.0 - 15.2}{\sqrt{\left(\frac{1}{\sqrt{400}}\right)^2 + \left(\frac{1.2}{\sqrt{100}}\right)^2}}$$

$$= \frac{0.8}{\sqrt{(0.05)^2 + (0.12)^2}}$$

$$= \frac{0.8}{\sqrt{0.0169}}$$

$$= \frac{0.8}{0.13}$$

$$= 6.15$$

Since $6.15 > 1.645$ (critical value), the null hypothesis that $\mu_1 \leq \mu_2$ is rejected and the alternate, that $\mu_1 > \mu_2$, is accepted.

Fatear is a chemical specifically designed to add weight to corn during the growing season. Alternate acres were treated with Fatear during the growing season. In order to determine whether Fatear was effective, 400 ears of corn receiving the Fatear treatment were selected at random. Each was weighed, and the mean weight was computed to be 16 ounces, with a standard deviation of 1 ounce. Likewise, 100 ears of untreated corn were weighed. The mean was 15.2 ounces, and the standard deviation was 1.2 ounces.

Using a one-tailed test and the 0.05 level, can we say that Fatear was effective in adding weight to the corn?

EXERCISES

3. A small motor for use in power tools is assembled on both the first and second shifts and requires critical attention and painstaking care to provide the motor with optimum operating conditions. Due to increasing complaints concerning motor performances, a review is made of the quality control records for the motor rpms inspected on both shifts during the previous week. The records indicate that 64 units from the first shift had an average rpm value of 2,175 with a standard deviation of 12, and that 36 units from the second shift had an average value of 2,050 with a standard deviation of 20. As the company wishes to spend its analysis efforts in the most productive way possible, it is interested in determining whether there is enough of a difference between the first and second shift values to concentrate efforts in this area. The company is willing to take a 10 percent risk of not recognizing when there is a significant difference.

    a. State the null and alternative hypotheses.
    b. Test the shift difference at $\alpha = 0.10$.
    c. What decision should be made? Any recommendations?

4. A study was being conducted of the annual incomes of probation officers in metropolitan areas of less than 100,000 population and in metropolitan areas having more than 500,000 population. Some sample statistics:

Sample statistic	Population less than 100,000	Population more than 500,000
Sample size	45	60
Sample mean	$21,290	$21,330
Sample variance	$ 1,060	$ 1,900

Test the hypothesis that the annual incomes of probation officers in areas having more than 500,000 population are significantly greater than those paid in areas of less than 100,000. Use the 5 percent level of risk. It is suggested that a systematic approach be followed by stating the null and alternative hypotheses, the statistical test to be used, and so on.

TYPE II ERRORS, OPERATING CHARACTERISTIC CURVES, AND POWER CURVES

Type II errors

Recall that Type I error, interchangeably called the alpha risk of a statistical test, is the risk of rejecting the hypothesis when it is really true. This risk is the same as the level of significance selected. As noted, the most commonly used are the 0.05, 0.01, and the 0.10. It is the probability of rejecting the hypothesis when in fact it is true.

Type II error, designated by β, is the probability of accepting the hypothesis as true when it is really not true.

To illustrate the computation of the probability of committing a Type II error, suppose that a manufacturer purchases steel bars to make cotter pins. Past experience revealed that the true mean of all incoming shipments is, in fact, 10,000 psi and the standard deviation (σ) 400 psi.

In order to make a decision about incoming shipments of steel bars, the manufacturer set up this rule for the quality control inspector to follow: Take a sample of 100 pieces of steel bars and if the mean $\overline{X}$ strength falls between 9,922 psi and 10,078 psi, accept the lot. Otherwise the lot is to be rejected. Chart 13–7A shows the acceptance region and the regions of rejection. The mean of this distribution is designated μ_0. The tails of the curve represent the probability of making a Type I error, that is, rejecting the incoming lot of

CHART 13–7

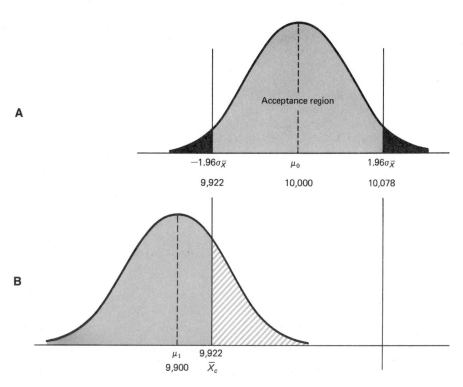

steel bars when in fact it is a good lot with a mean of 10,000 psi. How is the probability of a Type II error computed? (Recall it is the probability of accepting an incoming lot as a "good lot" when in fact the mean is not 10,000 psi.)

EXAMPLE

Suppose that the unknown mean of an incoming lot, designed μ_1, is really 9,900 psi. What is the probability that the quality control inspector will fail to reject the shipment (a Type II error)?

SOLUTION

The probability of committing a Type II error, as represented by the striped area in Chart 13–7B, can be computed by determining the area under the normal curve which lies above 9.922 pounds. The calculation of the areas under the normal curve was discussed in Chapter 11. Reviewing briefly, it is necessary first to determine the probability of the sample mean falling between 9,900 and 9,922. Then this probability is subtracted from 0.5000 (which represents all the area beyond the mean of 9,900) to arrive at the probability of making a Type II error.

Recall that the number of standard units (z-scores) between the mean of the incoming lot (9,900), designated μ_1, and $\overline{X}_c$, representing the critical value for 9,922, is computed by:

$$z = \frac{\overline{X}_c - \mu_1}{\dfrac{\sigma}{\sqrt{n}}} \quad \text{or} \quad z = \frac{\overline{X}_c - \mu_1}{\sigma_{\bar{x}}}$$

z is 0.55. Assuming n and σ are the same as before, the answer is found by:

$$z = \frac{\overline{X}_c - \mu_1}{\dfrac{\sigma}{\sqrt{n}}}$$

$$= \frac{9,922 - 9,900}{\dfrac{400}{\sqrt{100}}}$$

$$= \frac{22}{40}$$

$$= 0.55$$

The area under the curve between 9,900 and 9,922 (a z of 0.55) is 0.2088 (from Appendix G).

The area under the curve beyond 9,922 pounds is $0.5000 - 0.2088$ or 0.2912; this is the probability of making a Type II error—that is, accepting an incoming lot of steel bars when its mean is actually not 10,000 psi.

───────── **SELF-REVIEW 13-4** ─────────

0.1469, found by: (1) determining the area under the curve between 10,078 and 10,120 (Figure 13-C).

$$z = \frac{\bar{X}_c - \mu_1}{\dfrac{\sigma}{\sqrt{n}}}$$

$$= \frac{10,078 - 10,120}{\dfrac{400}{\sqrt{100}}}$$

$$= -1.05$$

The area under the curve for a z of -1.05 is 0.3531 (Appendix G), and $0.5000 - 0.3531 = 0.1469$, which is the area between 10,078 and 10,120.

Suppose that the mean of an incoming lot of steel bars is 10,120 psi. What is the probability that the quality control inspector will accept the bars as having a mean of 10,000 psi?

(It sounds inconsistent that steel bars will be rejected if the tensile strength is higher than specified, but it may be that the cotter pin has a dual function in an outboard motor—not to shear off if the motor hits a small object, but to shear off if it hits a rock. Therefore, the steel cannot be too strong.) The striped area in Chart 13-7C below represents the probability of falsely accepting the hypothesis that the mean tensile strength of the incoming lot of steel is 10,000 psi. What is the probability?

CHART 13-7

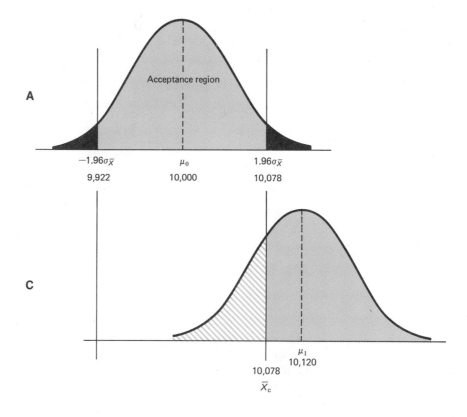

Using the methods illustrated by Charts 13–7B and 13–7C, the probability of accepting a hypothesis as true when it is actually false can be determined for any particular value of mu. The probabilities computed in the preceding three examples and other Type II probabilities are shown in the center column of Table 13–2 for various selected values of mu.

TABLE 13–2
Probabilities of a Type II
error and power functions for $\mu_0 =$ 10,000 pounds and selected alternative means, 0.05 level of significance

Selected alternative means (pounds)	Probability of Type II error (β)	Probability of not making a Type II error ($1 - \beta$)
9,820	0.0054	0.9946
9,880	0.1469	0.8531
9,900	0.2912	0.7088
9,940	0.6734	0.3266
9,980	0.9194	0.0806
10,000	—*	—
10,020	0.9194	0.0806
10,060	0.6734	0.3266
10,100	0.2912	0.7088
10,120	0.1469	0.8531
10,180	0.0054	0.9946

*It is not possible to make a Type II error when $\mu = \mu_0$.

Operating characteristic curves

The beta probabilities in Table 13–2 are used to plot an **operating characteristic curve** (see Chart 13–8).

CHART 13–8
Operating characteristic curve

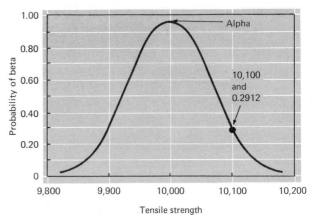

Source: Table 12–6.

The operating characteristic (OC) curve is merely a convenient way of showing graphically the probability of accepting a false hypothesis when it should have been rejected. The OC curves vary according to the sample size, the standard error of the mean, and the level of significance selected.

Power curves

Referring back to Table 13–2, the third column is simply the probability of *not* committing a Type II error—that is, $1 - \beta$. These probabilities are the basis for the **power curve** shown in Chart 13–9.

CHART 13–9
Power curve

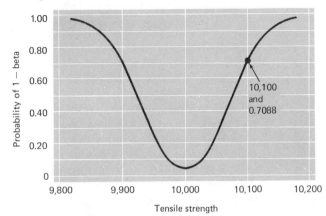

Source: Table 12–6.

The power curve is merely a graphic presentation of the probabilities of not committing a Type II error. The set of $1 - \beta$ probabilities in column 3 of Table 13–2 is called the **power function** of the test. The higher the probabilities, the greater the discriminatory power of the test. To explain, suppose the mean tensile strength of an incoming shipment of steel bars is 9,880 pounds per square inch. If a large number of samples of 100 bars were tested for tensile strength, about 85.31 percent of the samples would yield the correct decision to reject the incoming shipment.

If management wishes to be more discriminatory, one possibility is to increase the size of the sample. Suppose that the sample size was increased from 100 to 200 and the probability of $1 - \beta$ was computed to be 0.9200. It can be said that the sample of size 200 has more power to discover that the mean of the incoming shipment is not 10,000 psi (because 0.9200 > 0.8531).

CHAPTER SUMMARY

This chapter began our study of hypothesis testing. A systematic five-step approach is followed, namely, (1) two hypotheses are stated (a null hypothesis and an alternate hypothesis), (2) a level of significance is selected, (3) a test statistic is decided on, (4) a decision rule is formulated, and (5) based on the sample results, the null hypothesis is either accepted or rejected.

Both types of problems considered in this chapter require that the sample, or samples, selected be large (defined as being 30 or more). The tests can also be used any time the population under study is normally distributed with a known standard deviation. The first test of hypothesis involved determining whether a hypothesized population mean μ is reasonable. Suppose the null hypothesis H_0 stated that $\mu = \$25,000$ and the alternate hypothesis H_1 is $\mu \neq \$25,000$ (read the population mean is not $\$25,000$). Since the alternate hypothesis did not state a direction, the test is two-tailed. Had the alternate hypothesis been either $\mu < \$25{,}000$ or $\mu > \$25{,}000$, the test would be one-tailed.

The appropriate test statistic for this type of problem is z. The formula when the population standard deviation σ is known is:

$$z = \frac{\overline{X} - \mu}{\dfrac{\sigma}{\sqrt{n}}}$$

When σ is not known, the sample standard deviation s is substituted for σ.

The decision rule consists of two areas—a region of acceptance and a region, or regions, of rejection. The value separating the two regions is called the critical value.

The second type of hypothesis-testing problem concerned two means. Again, the test can be either two-tailed or one-tailed. If two-tailed, the null hypothesis states that $\mu_1 = \mu_2$ and the alternate hypothesis, $\mu_1 \neq \mu_2$. The null hypothesis for a one-tailed test could be written $\mu_1 = \mu_2$, but the usual way the null and alternate hypotheses are given is:

$$\boxed{\begin{array}{l} H_0\colon \mu_1 \leq \mu_2 \\[1ex] H_1\colon \mu_1 > \mu_2 \end{array}} \quad \text{or} \quad \boxed{\begin{array}{l} H_0\colon \mu_1 \geq \mu_2 \\[1ex] H_1\colon \mu_1 < \mu_2 \end{array}}$$

The procedure used to test whether the mean of one population is equal to the mean of a second population is similar to that followed for one mean, except for the computation of the test statistic z. It is:

$$z = \frac{\overline{X}_1 - \overline{X}_2}{\sqrt{\left(\dfrac{s_1}{\sqrt{n_1}}\right)^2 + \left(\dfrac{s_2}{\sqrt{n_2}}\right)^2}}$$

Two decision errors are possible, namely, Type I and Type II. Type I is the same as the level of significance which is selected before starting the test. It is the probability of rejecting the null hypothesis when it is actually true. A Type II error is the reverse—that is, the probability of accepting the null hypothesis when it is actually false.

An operating characteristic curve shows the probability of making a Type II error for various unknown population means, and a power curve depicts the probabilities of not making a Type II error.

CHAPTER OUTLINE

Tests of Hypotheses: Large sample

I. A. *Objective.* To check the validity of quantitative statements. Examples of quantitative statements involving interval level measurement: (1) There is no difference between the length of time needed to assemble a plug-in unit for a color television set using method A and method B. (2) There is no difference in the average income of males and the average income of females.

II. Procedures in hypothesis testing.
    A. *State the null hypothesis H_0 and the alternative hypothesis H_1.*
        1. Null hypothesis H_0. Example: There is no difference in the average income of males and the average income of females.
        2. Alternative hypothesis H_1. *Two-tailed* if no direction given. Example: There is a difference in the average incomes of males and females. *One-tailed* test if direction given. Example: The average income of males is greater than that of females.
    B. *Select the level of significance.* The 0.10, the 0.05, and the 0.01 are three of the levels most commonly used. It is the probability of rejecting a true hypothesis.
    C. *Decide on the statistical test to be used.* Depending on the problem, the Wilcoxon test, the chi-square test, or the z-test are a few which might be applied. The z-test is used for the problems in this chapter.
    D. *State the decision rule.* Based on the sampling distribution, an *area of acceptance* and an *area of rejection* can be identified. Example: The following drawings show the areas of acceptance and rejection for a two-tailed and a one-tailed test for which the z-test will be applied. If a two-tailed test is applied, the decision rule states that if the computed value of z falls between ± 1.96, the null hypothesis is accepted. Otherwise it is rejected.

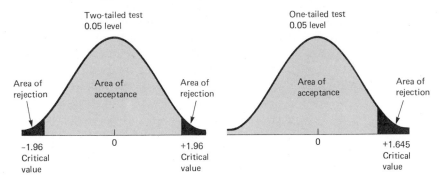

    E. *Take a sample, make a decision.* If the computed test statistic falls in the area of acceptance, accept H_0. Otherwise reject H_0 and accept H_1.
III. Testing a hypothesis about the population mean.
    A. *Examples.* The 1980 census revealed that the mean age of the state's population is 41.3 years. Has the mean age changed since then? The label of a commercial detergent gives the net weight as 640 grams. The jets filling the bottles seem to be malfunctioning. Has there been a change in the net weight?
    B. *Formula,* if the standard deviation of the population σ is known:

$$z = \frac{\bar{X} - \mu}{\frac{\sigma}{\sqrt{n}}}$$

If σ is unknown, substitute the sample standard deviation s when s can reasonably be expected to approximate σ.

IV. Hypothesis testing: two means, large samples.
  A. *Objective.* Using the usual hypothesis-testing procedures, determine if there is a difference between two population means using large samples (30 or more). Example: To test the lasting quality of paint for center highway markers, 45 strips of paint A and 60 strips of paint B were used. The number of days each strip lasted was recorded. Paint A lasted 261 days on the average, paint B, 268. Is there a difference in the lasting quality, or is it reasonable to assume that the difference of seven days is due to sampling variation?
  B. *Formula.*

$$z = \frac{\bar{X}_1 - \bar{X}_2}{\sqrt{\frac{s_1^2}{n_1} + \frac{s_2^2}{n_2}}}$$

V. Type I and Type II errors, operating characteristic curves, and power curves.
  A. *Type I error,* designated by α, is the same as the level of significance selected. A Type I error of 0.05 is the probability that a true null hypothesis will be rejected.
  B. *Type II error,* designated by β, is the probability of accepting the null hypothesis as true when it is really not true. The beta probabilities for selected alternative means when plotted are called an *operating characteristic curve.*
  C. *Power curve.* The probability of not committing a Type II error for selected alternative means when plotted is called a *power curve.* The higher the probabilities, the greater the discriminatory power of the test.

CHAPTER EXERCISES

5. A food processor is concerned that the 16-ounce can of sliced pineapple is being overfilled. The quality control department took a random sample of 50 cans and found that the arithmetic mean weight was 16.05 ounces, with a sample standard deviation of 0.03 ounces. At the 5 percent level of significance, can the hypothesis that the mean weight is equal to 16 ounces be rejected?

6. The Board of Education of a suburban school district wants to consider a new academic program funded by the Department of Health, Education and Welfare. In order to be eligible for the federal grant, the arithmetic mean income per household must not be more than $15,000. The board hired a research firm to gather the required data. In its report the firm indicated that the arithmetic mean income in the district is $17,000. They further reported that 75 households were

surveyed and the standard deviation of the sample was $3,000. Can the board argue that the difference between the mean income resulting from the sample survey and the mean specified by HEW is due to chance (sampling)? Cite evidence. Use the 0.05 level.

7. Frequent checks, during the past several years, of U.S. citizens returning from a vacation abroad (of 21 days or less) indicated that they spend on the average $1,010 on such items as souvenirs, meals, and travel. A recent survey of size 400 by a nationally known research organization resulted in a sample mean of $1,250 and a sample standard deviation of $205. Test the hypothesis that $\mu = $1,010$; that is, can the difference in the two means be attributed to sampling, or has there been a recent shift upward in the mean amount spent? Test at the 0.01 level. It is suggested that a systematic approach be followed by stating the null and alternative hypotheses, the statistical test to be used, and so on.

8. The U.S. Public Health Service publishes the *Annual Data Tabulations, Continuous Air Monitoring Projects,* which indicates that a large midwestern city has an annual mean level of sulfur dioxide of 0.12 (concentration in parts per million). Suppose that in order to reduce this excessively high concentration, many steel mills and others installed pollution equipment. In 900 random checks made throughout the past year, it was found that the sample mean was 0.09 and the sample standard deviation, 0.03. Assess the efforts of these industries. Use the 0.05 level.

9. After extensive tests, Tropico was adopted as the official paint for tropical rainy regions. Continuous tests are made in the laboratory by spraying water on test panels painted with Tropico. Records indicate that on the average the paint will withstand 200,000 tons of water before it loses its color. The standard deviation of the many panels tested was computed to be 12,000 tons of water. The Painto Manufacturing Company claims that its tropical paint (Painto II) is as good as the official paint, if not better. Painto II was tested by painting 144 test strips and giving them the usual water test. The arithmetic mean amount of water sprayed on the panels before they lost color was 190,000 tons. Although Painto II did not quite withstand the average of 200,000 tons, the manufacturers of Painto II claim that this difference was probably due to sampling. Using the 0.05 level, accept or reject their claim.

10. A study was being conducted of the annual incomes of probation officers in metropolitan areas of less than 100,000 population and in metropolitan areas having more than 500,000 population. Some sample statistics:

Sample statistic	Population less than 100,000	Population more than 500,000
Sample size	45	60
Sample mean	$1,290	$1,330
Sample variance	$1,060	$1,900

Test the hypothesis that the annual incomes of probation officers in areas having more than 500,000 population are significantly greater than those paid in areas of less than 100,000. Use the 5 percent level of risk. It is suggested that a systematic approach be followed by stating the null and alternative hypotheses, the statistical test to be used, and so on.

CHAPTER SELF-REVIEW EXAMINATION

Do all of the problems and then check your answers against those given in appendix A.

Score each probelm 50 points.

1. Experience with a steel-belted radial tire indicates that, on the average (mean), a tire travels 40,000 miles before it needs to be replaced. In an effort to increase the mileage still further, the tread design was redesigned and other changes were made. One hundred tires were road tested, and it was found that the average mileage was 43,000 and the standard deviation of the sample, 2,000 miles. Using the 0.10 level of significance, ascertain whether or not there has been a significant increase in the mean mileage.

    a. State the null hypothesis and the alternative hypothesis.
    b. Is the test being used a one-tailed or a two-tailed test? Explain.
    c. What is the critical value?
    d. Arrive at a decision. Explain the rationale underlying your decision.

2. A random sample of large manufacturing firms of size 100 indicated that the mean age of the president of the firm at the time he first became president was 47 years. Similarly, a random sample of 80 medium-sized manufacturing firms revealed an average age of 45 years. The standard deviations of the two samples were: large manufacturing firms, 15 years, and medium-sized firms, 5 years.

    H_0: There is no significant difference in the mean ages.
    H_1: There is a significant difference in the mean ages.

    a. Is a one-tailed or a two-tailed test being used? Explain.
    b. In testing the null hypothesis at the 0.05 level, what is the critical value?
    c. Arrive at a decision. Explain.
    d. Could it be reasonably assumed that the difference of two years is due to sampling variation?

INTRODUCTION

Chapter 13 began our study of tests of hypotheses. The data with which we were concerned were interval scaled. Testing a hypothesis involves setting up some systematic procedures to follow in order to ultimately make a decision about a hypothesis. We either accept it or reject it. The previous chapter dealt with two types of questions: (1) Is it reasonable to conclude, based on some sample data, that the mean of the population is not a certain value, say $32,000?, and (2) Is the difference between two sample means so large that one can conclude that the samples were selected from two different populations?

This chapter deals with tests of hypotheses about **proportions**. A proportion is *a fraction or a ratio which indicates what part of a population has a particular trait of interest*. A proportion is usually expressed as a percent or a probability.

The questions explored in this chapter are similar to those in the previous chapter. As examples: Are 50 percent of the union members in favor of the proposed changes in the constitution? Is there a difference in the proportion of male executives and female executives willing to move to gain a promotion?

The five-step hypothesis-testing procedures developed in Chapter 13 will be followed to arrive at a decision, namely:

1. Statements regarding the null hypothesis and alternative hypothesis are made.
2. The level of significance is given.
3. A statistical test is chosen.
4. A decision rule is stated.
5. A sample or samples are chosen and the null hypothesis is either rejected or not rejected.

Tests of hypotheses about proportions

A TEST ABOUT A POPULATION PROPORTION

The first test involves comparing a single-sample proportion with a hypothesized population proportion. It is assumed that a random sample is taken from a population for which the binomial assumptions hold, namely, (1) the data collected are the result of counts; (2) an outcome of an experiment is classified into one of two mutually exclusive categories—a "success" or a "failure"; (3) the probability of a success stays the same for each trial; and (4) the trials are independent, meaning that the outcome of one trial does not affect the outcome of any other trial.

Before proceding with a test of a hypothesis involving one proportion, it should be stressed that this particular test can be used when *both* np *and* n(1 − p) *are greater than five.* n is the sample size, and p is the population proportion. The test is introduced here because it is a special extension of the test presented in the previous chapter and also is widely used. This test is a good example of the case where the normal probability distribution is used to approximate a binomial probability distribution with a great deal of accuracy. Notice n and p are the parameters of the binomial.

To illustrate a typical test, suppose prior elections in a state indicated that it is necessary for a candidate for governor to receive at least 80 percent of the vote in the northern section of the state to be elected. The incumbent governor is interested in assessing his chances of returning to office. He has a sample survey conducted. Two thousand potential voters in the northern part of the state are surveyed. The following test can be used, therefore, because np and n(1 − p) both exceed five. np = 2,000(0.80) = 1,600, and n(1 − p) = 2,000(1 − 0.80) = 400.

Step 1: The null hypothesis H_0 is that the population proportion p is 0.80 or more. The alternate hypothesis H_1 is that the proportion is less than 0.80. From a practical standpoint, the incumbent governor is concerned only when the sample proportion is less than 0.80. If it were equal to or greater than 0.80, he would have no problem that is, the data would indicate he will probably be elected. These hypotheses are written symbolically as:

Null hypothesis H_0: $p \geq 0.80$

Alternate hypothesis H_1: $p < 0.80$

H_1 states a direction. Thus, the test is one-tailed, with the inequality pointing to the tail of the curve containing the region of rejection.

Step 2. The level of significance is 0.05. This is the likelihood of committing a Type I error—that is, it is the probability that a true hypothesis is rejected.

Step 3. The z-test is an appropriate statistical test, found by:

$$z = \frac{\dfrac{X}{n} - p}{\sigma_p}$$

where:

n is the number in the sample.

X is the observed number of "successes" in the sample. In this problem is the number of voters who will vote for the incumbent governor.)

σ_p is the standard error of the population proportion. It is computed by $\sqrt{p(1-p)/n}$, so the formula for z becomes:

$$z = \frac{\dfrac{X}{n} - p}{\sqrt{\dfrac{p(1-p)}{n}}}$$

Notice that $X/n = \bar{X}$, the sample mean, and p is the hypothesized population proportion (parameter).

Step 4. The **critical value** or values of z, form the dividing point or points between the region of acceptance and the region of rejection. Since the alternate hypothesis stated a direction, this is a one-tailed test. The inequality pointed to the left, so only the left half of the curve is used (see Chart 14–1). Alpha was given as 0.05 in Step 2. This probability is in the left tail and determines the region of rejection. The area between zero and the critical value is 0.4500, found by 0.5000 − 0.0500. Referring to Appendix G and searching the column "Area under the Curve" in the column marked (2) for 0.45000, we find the critical value of z to be about −1.645. The decision rule, therefore, is: Reject the null hypothesis and accept the alternate hypothesis if the computed value of z falls to the left of −1.645; otherwise we fail to reject H_0.

**CHART 14–1
Acceptance and
rejection regions for
the 0.05 level of
significance,
one-tailed test**

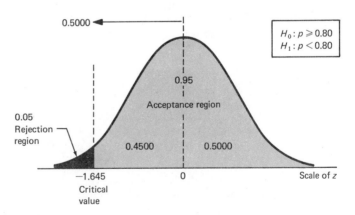

Step 5. The sample survey of 2,000 potential voters in the northern part of the state revealed that 1,500 planned to vote for the incumbent governor. Is the proportion of 0.775 (found by 1,550/2,000) "close enough" to the required proportion of 0.80 to say that he will be reelected?

In this problem:

$X = 1,550$, the number who plan to vote for the governor.

$n = 2,000$, the number of voters surveyed.

$p = 0.80$, the hypothesized population proportion.

z is a normally distributed test statistic when the hypothesis is true and the other assumptions are true.

Computing z:

$$z = \frac{\dfrac{X}{n} - p}{\sqrt{\dfrac{p(1 - p)}{n}}}$$

$$= \frac{\dfrac{1,550}{2,000} - 0.80}{\sqrt{\dfrac{0.80(1 - 0.80)}{2,000}}}$$

$$= \frac{0.775 - 0.80}{\sqrt{0.00008}} = \frac{-0.025}{0.0089442} = -2.80$$

The computed value of z (-2.80) is in the rejection region, and the null hypothesis is rejected at the 0.05 level. The difference of 2.5 percentage points between the sample percent (77.5 percent) and the hypothesized population percent in the northern part of the state necessary to carry the state (80 percent) is statistically significant. It is probably not due to sampling variation. To put it another way, the evidence at this point does not support the claim that the incumbent governor will return to the governor's mansion for another four years.

EXAMPLE

Test at the 0.01 level the statement that 55 percent of those families who plan to purchase a vacation residence in Florida want a condominium. The null hypothesis is $p = 0.55$, and the alternate $p \neq 0.55$. A random sample of 400 families who said they planned to buy a vacation residence reveals that 228 families want a condominium. What decision should be made regarding the null hypothesis?

SOLUTION

The z-test can be used because both np and $n(1 - p)$ exceed 5, $np = 220$, and $n(1 - p) = 180$.

Since no direction was given in the alternate hypothesis, the test is two-tailed. The decision rule is shown graphically in Chart 14-2.

CHART 14–2
Areas of acceptance and rejection, 0.01 level of significance for a two-tailed test

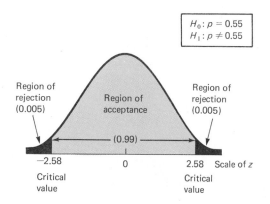

In this problem:

$X = 228$, the number in the sample who want a condominium.
$n = 400$, the number in the sample.
$p = 0.55$, the claimed percent in the population who want a condominium.

Computing z:

$$z = \frac{\dfrac{X}{n} - p}{\sqrt{\dfrac{p(1-p)}{n}}}$$

$$= \frac{\dfrac{228}{400} - 0.55}{\sqrt{\dfrac{0.55(1-0.55)}{400}}}$$

$$= \frac{0.02}{0.0248736}$$

$$= 0.80$$

The null hypothesis that the true proportion is 0.55 is not rejected at the 0.01 level. Although there is a difference between the hypothesized proportion (0.55) and the sample proportion (0.57), it can be attributed to sampling error. We conclude that, of the families who plan to buy a vacation residence in Florida, 55 percent plan to buy a condominium.

SELF-REVIEW 14–1

a. Yes, because both np and $n(1-p)$ exceed five. $np = 200(0.40) = 80$, and $n(1-p) = 200(0.60) = 120$.

b. $H_0: p \geq 0.40$
$H_1: p < 0.40$

(A reminder: cover the answers in the left column.)

This claim is to be investigated at the 0.02 level: "At least 40 percent of those persons who retired from an industrial job before the age of 60 would

c.

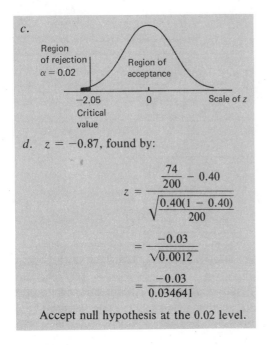

Region of rejection
$\alpha = 0.02$

Region of acceptance

−2.05   0   Scale of z
Critical value

d. $z = -0.87$, found by:

$$z = \frac{\dfrac{74}{200} - 0.40}{\sqrt{\dfrac{0.40(1 - 0.40)}{200}}}$$

$$= \frac{-0.03}{\sqrt{0.0012}}$$

$$= \frac{-0.03}{0.034641}$$

Accept null hypothesis at the 0.02 level.

return to work if a suitable job was available." Seventy-four persons out of the 200 sampled said they would return to work.

a.   Can the z-test be used?
b.   State the null and alternate hypotheses.
c.   Show the decision rule graphically.
d.   Compute z and arrive at a decision.

EXERCISES

(A reminder: The answer and method of solution for selected exercises are given in Appendix A.)

1.   Past experience at a university indicates that 50 percent of the students change their major area of study after their first year in the program.[1] Suppose a random sample of 100 students revealed that 48 of them had changed their major area of study during their first year of the program. Has there been a significant decrease in the proportion of students who change their major after the first year in the program? Test at the 0.05 level of significance.

2.   Past experience of a travel agency indicated that 44 percent of those persons who wanted the agency to plan a vacation for them wanted to go to Europe. During the most recent busy season, a sampling of 1,000 plans was selected at random from the files, and it was found that 480 persons wanted to go to Europe on vacation. Has there been a significant shift upward in the percent of persons who want to go to Europe? Test at the 0.005 level. Use the usual hypothesis-testing steps.

A TEST FOR THE DIFFERENCE BETWEEN TWO POPULATION PROPORTIONS

Several typical cases involving two population proportions are cited.

Case 1:   A mock model of a proposed new automobile was shown to two groups of 150 each. One group consisted of persons between 18 and 25 years of age, and the other group consisted of persons over 50 years old. About 80 percent of the younger group rated the styling satisfactory, but only 50

---

[1] Unpublished study, Office of Institutional Research, University of Toledo.

percent of the older group gave it a similar rating. In evaluating the market potential of this proposed automobile, is it reasonable to expect that it would appeal primarily to younger persons? Or is it possible that this difference of 30 percentage points could be due to sampling and, in fact, might not the two age groups in the population like the proposed automobile equally well?

Case 2:   Two new high-speed machines designed by different companies are being considered for purchase. One factor in the final choice is the percent defective which each machine produces. A sample of the output of one of the machines revealed that 6 percent were defective. A sample of the output of the other machine indicated that 10 percent of the total were defective. Is the machine with the 6 percent scrap significantly better than the one with the 10 percent scrap, or is there a chance that the two machines are producing an equal percent defective?

Case 3:   Hybrid corn seed was divided into two piles before planting. The seeds in one pile were soaked with a chemical claimed to significantly reduce corn borers. The other pile was not treated. The seed corn was planted in alternate rows and clearly identified. Samples from each row were selected at random during the harvest season, and it was discovered that 20 percent of the treated corn had corn borers and 80 percent of the untreated sample had borers. Was the treatment effective?

Case 4:   A perfume manufacturer has developed a new perfume called Stay-Away. A number of comparison tests indicate that the perfume has a good market potential. The marketing and advertising departments, however, want to plan their strategy so as to reach and impress the largest possible segment of the buying public. One of the questions is whether the perfume is preferred by a larger proportion of younger women or a larger proportion of older women. There are two populations, therefore, a population consisting of young women and one consisting of older women. A standard smell test is used. Women selected at random are asked to sniff several perfumes in succession, including the one they most frequently use and, of course, Stay-Away. The names of the perfumes are known only to the person administering the test. Each woman selects the one perfume she likes best.

Note that the proposed automobile styling was either satisfactory or unsatisfactory, the output of the machine was either defective or not defective, the corn borer treatment was either effective or ineffective, and the women either preferred Stay-Away over all others or she did not. So, each case describes a proportion. And, all of the cases are concerned with two samples.

The procedures followed in making a decision involving the difference between two proportions will now be examined. The perfume problem has been selected.

Step 1.   A statement of the hypothesis H_0 and the alternative hypothesis H_1.   Again, the hypothesis is stated as a null hypothesis. In this problem it is "There is no difference between the proportion of young women who prefer Stay-Away and the proportion of older women who prefer Stay-Away." If the proportion of young women in the population is designated as p_1 and the proportion of older women as p_2, then the null hypothesis is $p_1 = p_2$. The alternate hypothesis is that the two proportions are not equal, or $p_1 \neq p_2$.

(Note again that the lowercase letter p represents the population proportions.)

Step 2.   *The level of significance.*   It was decided to use the 0.05 level.

Step 3.   *The statistical test.*   If the size of the random sample of young women n_1 and the size of the sample of older women n_2 *both* meet the requirement that np and $n(1 - p)$ are greater than five, the z-test which follows may be used. The test statistic z, as before, follows the standard normal distribution and is computed by:

$$z = \frac{\dfrac{X_1}{n_1} - \dfrac{X_2}{n_2}}{\sqrt{\dfrac{\bar{p}(1 - \bar{p})}{n_1} + \dfrac{\bar{p}(1 - \bar{p})}{n_2}}}$$

where:

X_1 is the number of young women in sample one who prefer Stay-Away.
X_2 is the number of older women in sample two who prefer Stay-Away.
n_1 is the number of young women selected in the sample.
n_2 is the number of older women selected in the sample.
$\bar{p}$ is the *weighted* mean of the two sample proportions computed by:

$$\bar{p} = \frac{\text{Total number of successes}}{\text{Total number of samples}} = \frac{X_1 + X_2}{n_1 + n_2}$$

$\bar{p}$ is generally referred to as the *pooled estimate of the proportion*. This is the best estimate of the proportion of women in the population who prefer Stay-Away and does not consider whether they are old or young. Hence it is called a "pooled", or common, estimate.

Step 4.   *The decision rule.*   Recall that the null hypothesis H_0 states that $p_1 = p_2$, and the alternative hypothesis H_1 is $p_1 \neq p_2$. Since H_1 does not state any direction (such as $p_1 < p_2$) the test is *two-tailed*. Thus, the critical value for the 0.05 level is ± 1.96. As before, if the computed z-value falls in the region between ± 1.96, the null hypothesis is not rejected. If that does occur, it is assumed that any difference between the two sample proportions is due to chance variation (see Chart 14–3).

**CHART 14–3
Two-tailed test, areas
of acceptance and
rejection, 0.05 level of
significance.**

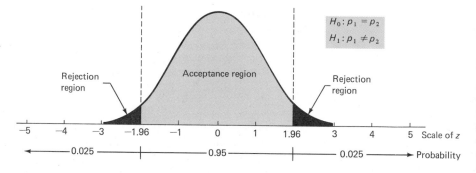

Step 5. The decision. A total of 100 young women were selected at random, and each was given the standard smell test. Twenty out of the 100 young women chose Stay-Away as the perfume they liked best. A total of 200 older women were selected at random and each was given the same standard smell test. Out of the 200 older women, 100 preferred Stay-Away.

Young women

X_1 is the number preferring Stay-Away = 20
n_1 is the number in sample = 100

$$p_1 = \frac{X_1}{n_1} = \frac{20}{100} = 0.20$$

Older women

X_2 is the number preferring Stay-Away = 100
n_2 is the number in sample = 200

$$p_2 = \frac{X_2}{n_2} = \frac{100}{200} = 0.50$$

The pooled weighted mean $\bar{p}$ is:

$$\bar{p} = \frac{X_1 + X_2}{n_1 + n_2} = \frac{20 + 100}{100 + 200} = \frac{120}{300} = 0.40$$

Note that the weighted mean of 0.40 is closer to 0.50 than to 0.20. (More older women were sampled than younger women.)

Computed z:

$$z = \frac{\dfrac{X_1}{n_1} - \dfrac{X_2}{n_2}}{\sqrt{\dfrac{\bar{p}(1 - \bar{p})}{n_1} + \dfrac{\bar{p}(1 - \bar{p})}{n_2}}}$$

$$= \frac{0.20 - 0.50}{\sqrt{\dfrac{0.40(1 - 0.40)}{100} + \dfrac{0.40(1 - 0.40)}{200}}}$$

$$= \frac{-0.30}{\sqrt{\dfrac{0.24}{100} + \dfrac{0.24}{200}}}$$

$$= \frac{-0.30}{\sqrt{0.0024 + 0.0012}}$$

$$= \frac{-0.30}{\sqrt{0.0036}}$$

$$= \frac{-0.30}{0.06}$$

$$= -5.0$$

The computed z of -5.0 falls in the area of rejection beyond -1.96. The null hypothesis is rejected at the 0.005 level of significance. To put it another way, the hypothesis that the proportion of young women in the population who prefer Stay-Away is equal to the proportion of older women in the population who prefer Stay-Away is rejected at the 0.05 level. It is highly unlikely that such a large difference between the two sample proportions (0.30) could be due to sampling errors.

The probability of committing a Type I error is 0.05, which is the same as the level of significance selected before the project started. This indicates there is a 5 percent risk of rejecting the true hypothesis that $p_1 = p_2$.

EXAMPLE

The following illustration requires a one-tailed test.

Guymon, Inc., is testing two high-speed shearing machines. One is manufactured by Royal Industries, the other by Cordell. Royal claims that its machine produces a lower percent of defective pieces. To investigate this claim, 200 sheared pieces of copper were selected at random from the output of the Royal machine. A count revealed that 14 were defective. A similar experiment with the Cordell machine revealed that 10 out of the 100 selected at random were defective. At the 0.05 level, does the statistical evidence support Royal's claim?

SOLUTION

The z-statistic can be used because np and $n(1 - p)$ for both samples are more than five.

For Royal

$$np = 200 \left(\frac{14}{200} \right) = 200(0.07) = 14$$

$$n(1 - p) = 200 \, (1 - 0.07) = 186$$

For Cordell

$$np = 100 \left(\frac{10}{100} \right) = 100(0.10) = 10$$

$$n(1 - p) = 100(1 - 0.10) = 90$$

The null hypothesis is: For the Royal machine, the percent defective p_1 is not less than the Cordell percent defective p_2. This would be written $H_0: p_1 \geq p_2$. The alternate hypothesis is that p_1 is less than p_2, written $p_1 < p_2$. Thus, since the alternate hypothesis states a direction, the test is one-tailed. The inequality points to the direction of the region of rejection.

Using the same procedure as before, the decision rule would be: Reject the null hypothesis if the computed value of z falls in the area of the curve to the left of -1.645 and accept the alternate hypothesis. Otherwise, do not reject the null hypothesis.

The pooled estimated of the proportion $\bar{p}$ is 0.08, found by:

$$\bar{p} = \frac{\text{Total number of ''successes''}}{\text{Total number sampled}} = \frac{X_1 + X_2}{n_1 + n_2} = \frac{14 + 10}{200 + 100} = 0.08$$

where:

X_1 is the number of defective pieces produced by the Royal machine in the sample (14).

n_1 is the number of pieces produced by the Royal machine in the sample (200).

X_2 is the total number of defective pieces produced by the Cordell machine in the sample (10).

n_2 is the total number of pieces produced by the Cordell machine in the sample (100).

If, in fact, there is no difference between the machines, this pooled estimate $\bar{p}$ of 8 percent is the best estimate of the proportion defective.

Computing z:

$$z = \frac{p_1 - p_2}{\sqrt{\dfrac{\bar{p}(1 - \bar{p})}{n_1} + \dfrac{\bar{p}(1 - \bar{p})}{n_2}}}$$

$$= \frac{0.07 - 0.10}{\sqrt{\dfrac{0.08(1 - 0.08)}{200} + \dfrac{0.08(1 - 0.08)}{100}}}$$

$$= \frac{-0.03}{\sqrt{0.000736 + 0.000368}}$$

$$= \frac{-0.03}{0.0332264}$$

$$= -0.90$$

Since -0.90 is to the right of -1.645, that is, in the region of acceptance, the null hypothesis is not rejected at the 0.05 level of significance. The difference between the two sample proportions of 0.03 can be attributed to chance. Based on these sample data, Royal cannot claim that its shearing machine produces fewer defectives.

SELF-REVIEW 14–2
---

a. Yes because both np and $n(1 - p)$ exceed five. For adults: $np = 150(87/150) = 87.$ $n(1 - p) = 150(1 - 0.58) = 63.$ For children: $np = 200 (123/200) = 123.$ $n(1 - p) = 200(1 - 0.615) = 77.$

b. $H_0: p_1 = p_2.$

c. 0.10.

d. Two-tailed.

e. $-1.645.$

Out of 150 adults who tried Smack Smack, a new candy, 87 rated it excellent. Out of 200 children sampled, 123 rated it excellent. Using the 0.10 level of significance and the alternate hypothesis $p_1 \neq p_2$:

a. Does this data meet the requirement for the use of z-test?

b. What is the null hypothesis?

c. What is the Type I error?

d. Is this a one-tailed or a two-tailed test?

e. What is the critical value?

f. Accepted. Computed $z = -0.66$.

$$\bar{p} = \frac{87 + 123}{150 + 200} = \frac{210}{350} = 0.60$$

then:

$$z = \frac{0.58 - 0.615}{\sqrt{\dfrac{0.60(0.40)}{150} + \dfrac{0.60(0.40)}{200}}}$$

$$= \frac{-0.035}{\sqrt{0.0028}} = \frac{-0.35}{0.052915} = -0.66$$

f. Should the null hypothesis be accepted or rejected?

EXERCISES

3. The manufacturer of the NEW Go-Away, a tablet used to prevent headaches, is convinced that it is more effective than the old Go-Away, which it will replace. To evaluate the manufacturer's conviction, 200 persons were asked to take the NEW Go-Away. During the trial period, 180 of them did not have a headache. A different group of 300 took the old Go-Away, and 261 had no headaches during the trial period. The manufacturer's conviction that the NEW Go-Away is more effective is to be tested at the 0.05 level.

   a. Do the sample data meet the requirement for the use of the z-test?

   b. What is the proportion of successes with the NEW Go-Away? With the old Go-Away?

   c. What are the null and alternate hypotheses?

   d. What is the critical value?

   e. What is the computed z-value? Your decision?

4. Suppose that a random sample of 1,000 American-born citizens revealed that 198 favored resumption of diplomatic relations with Cuba. Similarly, 117 out of a sample of 500 foreign-born citizens favored it. Test at the 0.05 level that there is no difference in the proportion of American-born citizens and the proportion of foreign-born citizens who favor resumption of diplomatic relations with Cuba. H_1 states that there is a difference, that is, the two proportions are not equal.

CHAPTER SUMMARY

This chapter is a continuation of hypothesis testing started in Chapter 13. The tests required that the data be of the "yes-or-no" type—that is, data that can only be classified into categories such as defective or not defective; will vote for the incumbent governor, will not vote for the incumbent governor,—and that the random samples be selected according to a binomial model meaning that there is a constant probability of "success," the trials are independent, and so forth.

One problem involved testing a statement about a population proportion. Examples are: The percent defective is 7 percent. Ten percent of the newlywed couples plan to purchase a mobile home within three years. Twenty percent of the recent college graduates went into business for themselves.

In order to employ this particular test statistic, it is essential to make sure that np and $n(1 - p)$ exceed five. If they do, the usual five-step hypothesis-testing procedure is followed. (If they do not, a test based on the exact binomial probability distribution can be used.)

The first step is to state the null and alternate hypotheses. In the previous examples H_0 would be $p = 0.07, p = 0.10$, or $p = 0.20$. The way the alternate hypothesis H_1 is stated tells us whether a one-tailed or a two-tailed test is to be used. If it states a direction (either $<$ or $>$), a one-tailed test is employed.

After formulating a decision rule, z is computed and compared with the critical value. If the computed value of z falls outside the region of acceptance, the null hypothesis is rejected. Otherwise, it is not rejected.

The second test involved two population proportions. Example: Is the proportion of cures using vaccine A greater than the proportion of cures using vaccine B? We conducted this type of test by taking samples from each population and computing z. Based on the magnitude of the computed z-value, the null hypothesis is either rejected or not rejected.

CHAPTER OUTLINE

Tests of hypotheses about a proportion or two proportions

I. Procedure.
  A. For one proportion, in order to safely use this particular test make sure that np and $n(1 - p)$ are greater than five. For two proportions, np and $n(1 - p)$ for both samples must exceed five.
  B. Follow the usual five-step hypothesis-testing procedure.
    1. State the null and alternate hypothesis.
    2. Decide on the level of significance.
    3. Choose an appropriate statistical test.
    4. Formulate a decision rule.
    5. Take a sample, or samples, and based on the computed z-value arrive at a decision to reject or fail to reject the null hypothesis.

II. A test about a population proportion.
  A. Null hypothesis H_0:, for example, might be $p = 0.42$. Alternate hypothesis H_1 could be either $p \neq 0.42$, or $p < 0.42$, or $p > 0.42$. Summarizing the three possibilities:

$H_0: p = 0.42$	$H_0: p \geq 0.42$	$H_0: p \leq 0.42$
$H_1: p \neq 0.42$	$H_1: p < 0.42$	$H_1: p > 0.42$

  B. Computed z found by:

$$z = \frac{\frac{X}{n} - p}{\sqrt{\frac{p(1 - p)}{n}}}$$

  where:

  X is the observed number in the sample possessing the trait.
  n is the size of the sample.
  p Is the hypothesized population proportion.

III. A test for the statistically significant difference between two population proportions.

   A. Null hypothesis H_0: $p_1 = p_2$.
      Alternate hypothesis H_1 either $p_1 \neq p_2$, or $p_1 < p_2$, or $p_1 > p_2$

   B. Computed z found by:

$$z = \frac{\dfrac{X_1}{n_1} - \dfrac{X_2}{n_2}}{\sqrt{\dfrac{\bar{p}(1-\bar{p})}{n_1} + \dfrac{\bar{p}(1-\bar{p})}{n_2}}}$$

where:

X_1 is the number possessing the trait in the first sample.
X_2 is the number possessing the trait in the second sample.
n_1 is the total number in the first sample.
n_2 is the total number in the second sample.
$\bar{p}$ is the pooled estimate of the population proportion, found by

$$\frac{X_1 + X_2}{n_1 + n_2}$$

CHAPTER EXERCISES

5. A prefabricator of garages has found from past experience that in metropolitan areas having 50,000 or more persons, at least 20 percent of the homes must be without garages to make it profitable for him to establish a branch office in the area. He is considering establishing a branch in Anniston, Alabama. A random sample of 1,000 homes revealed that 180 did not have garages. Using the 0.05 level of significance, determine whether or not it would be profitable for him to establish a branch there. Follow a formal approach; that is, cite the null hypothesis, and so on.

6. A new breakfast cereal is being test marketed in selected cities on the east and west coasts. Consumer panels are being used for the evaluation in each of the selected cities, and after four weeks of product use, the consumer reactions have been obtained as follows:

	East coast	West coast
Total responses	632	428
Preferred cereal or considered cereal equivalent to others	468	327

   a. Past test marketing experience has indicated that at least 76 percent consumer panel acceptance must be demonstrated before a product has a chance to be successful. Do the results indicate the 76 percent criterion has been reached with an alpha risk of 0.01?

   b. There is also interest in determining whether there are regional differences in consumer acceptance of the product. To answer this question, conduct a test of hypotheses on the results of the two samples at an alpha level of 0.01. State your recommendations.

7. A manufacturer of stereophonic equipment introduces the new models of receivers, tape cassettes, and other audio components in the fall. Retail dealers are surveyed immediately after the Christmas selling season regarding their stock on hand of each piece of equipment. It has been discovered that unless 40 percent of the new equipment ordered by the retailers in the fall had been sold by Christmas, immediate production cutbacks are needed.

   The manufacturer has found contacting all of the dealers after Christmas by mail rather frustrating because many of them never respond. This year the manufacturer selected 80 dealers at random and telephoned them regarding the new Model TX 3040 receiver. It was discovered that 38 percent of those receivers had been sold. Since 38 percent is less than 40 percent, does this mean that immediate production cutbacks are needed—or can this difference of 2 percentage points be attributed to sampling? Test at the 0.05 level.

CHAPTER SELF-REVIEW EXAMINATION

Do all the problems. Then check your answers against those in Appendix A. Score each problem 50 points.

1. A high-speed automatic machine mass produces a small washer. Past experience reveals that 70 percent of each day's production is perfect. Most of the remaining washers have a rough burr which must be filed off before they can be inserted in the assembly. In an attempt to increase the percent of production which is perfect, the machine was modified somewhat. A sample of 100 washers was then checked, and it was found that 72 percent were perfect. The boss thinks that there has been no change. The plant manager, however, believes that the production of the modified machine has definitely improved. That is, the percent of perfect washers is greater than 70 percent. Is the plant manager correct? Test at the 0.02 level.

2. A committee studying employer-employee relations proposed that a rating system be adopted. Each employee would rate his or her immediate supervisor and in turn the supervisor would rate each employee. In order to find out if there is a difference between the reactions of the office personnel and the plant personnel regarding the proposal, 120 office personnel and 160 plant personnel were selected at random. Seventy-eight of the office personnel and 90 of the plant personnel were in favor of the proposal. Is there sufficient evidence to support the belief that the proportion of office personnel in favor of the proposal is greater than that of the plant personnel at α 0.05?

INTRODUCTION

Chapter 13 deals with tests of hypotheses based on the test statistic z which arises when one has a normal distribution with a known standard deviation. That chapter shows that, if the population of interest is approximately normal and the population standard deviation σ is known, the test statistic z is:

$$z = \frac{\overline{X} - \mu}{\dfrac{\sigma}{\sqrt{n}}}$$

If the population standard deviation σ is not known but the sample size is reasonably large (30 or more), the standard deviation of the sample s is used to estimate it. The formula then used is:

$$z = \frac{\overline{X} - \mu}{\dfrac{s}{\sqrt{n}}}$$

When the sample size is small—that is, less than 30—the standard deviation of the sample may not be a good estimator of σ and the z-statistic is generally not used. Fortunately, there is a test statistic available for small-sample problems. It is called **Student's t**.

Student's t test: Small samples

THE t DISTRIBUTION

The characteristics of Student's t distribution will be examined before considering its application in testing a hypothesis. It was developed by William S. Gosset, a brewmaster for the Guinness Brewery in Ireland, who published it in 1908 using the pen name "Student." Gosset was concerned with the behavior of

$$\frac{\overline{X} - \mu}{\dfrac{s}{\sqrt{n}}}$$

when s had to be used as an estimator of σ. He was especially worried about the discrepancy between s and σ when s was calculated from a very small sample.

The following characteristics of the t distribution are based on the assumption that the population of interest is normal, or nearly normal.

1. It is (like the z distribution) a continuous distribution.
2. It is (like the z distribution) bell shaped and symmetrical.
3. There is not one t distribution, but rather a "family" of t distributions. All have the same mean of zero, but their standard deviations differ according to the sample size n.
4. The t distribution is more spread out and flatter at the center than is the standard normal distribution (see Chart 15–1). However, as the sample size increases, the curve representing the t distribution approaches the standard normal distribution.

**CHART 15–1
The standard normal distribution and the Student t distribution**

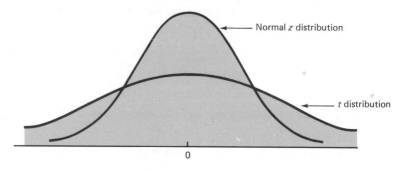

As noted above, the Student t distribution has a greater spread than the z distribution. As a result, the critical values of t for a given level of significance are larger in magnitude than the corresponding z critical values. Chart 15–2 shows the regions of acceptance and rejection for a one-tailed test using the 0.05 level of significance. The critical value for the z-test is 1.645, but for t it is 2.132 (determining the critical value of 2.132 will be discussed shortly).

Of what importance is the fact that the critical value for a given level of significance is greater for small samples than for large samples? It indicates that for small samples (which employ the t distribution) (1) the confidence interval will be wider than for large samples, (2) the region of acceptance will be wider than for large samples, and (3) a larger computed t-value will be needed to reject the null hypothesis than for large samples using z. In other

CHART 15–2
Regions of acceptance for the z and t distributions, 0.05 level, one-tailed test

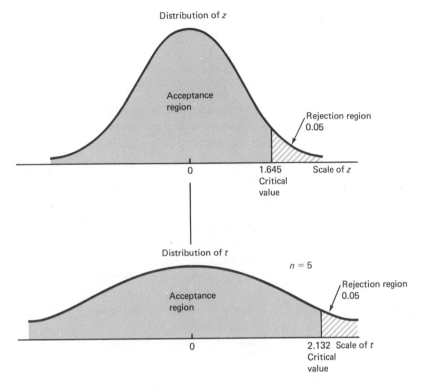

Distribution of *z*

Acceptance region

Rejection region 0.05

0   1.645   Scale of *z*
Critical value

Distribution of *t*

n = 5

Acceptance region

Rejection region 0.05

0   2.132 Scale of *t*
Critical value

words, because there is more variability in sample means computed from smaller samples, we have less confidence in the resulting estimates and are less apt to reject hypotheses.

A TEST FOR THE POPULATION MEAN

If the population from which the sample is selected is near normal, and the population standard deviation σ is unknown, the test statistic *t* is computed by:

$$t = \frac{\overline{X} - \mu}{\frac{s}{\sqrt{n}}}$$

with $n - 1$ degrees of freedom,[1]

---

[1] In brief summary, because sample statistics are being used, it is necessary to determine the number of variables which are free to vary. To illustrate, if the sum of four numbers totals 20, various combinations of three numbers can be written down, such as 7, 4, and 1, but the fourth number which can be written down is restricted in this case to 8 because the sum must total 20. Because of this restriction, it is said that "one degree of freedom is lost."

For example, assume that the mean of four numbers is known to be 5. The four numbers are 7, 4, 1, and 8. The deviations of these numbers from the mean must total 0. The deviations of +2, −1, −4, and +3 do total 0. If the deviations of +2, −1, and −4 are known, then the value of +3 is fixed (restricted) in order to satisfy the condition that the sum of the deviations must equal 0. Thus, one degree of freedom is lost in a sampling problem involving the standard deviation of the sample because one number (the arithmetic mean) is known.

where:

$\overline{X}$ is the mean of the small sample.
μ is the hypothesized population mean.
s is the standard deviation of the sample.
n is the sample size.

Notice that this is the same formula used in Chapter 13 for large samples. However, Student's t distribution is used to locate the critical value.

EXAMPLE

As an example of the use of the Student t, suppose that experience investigating accident claims revealed that it costs $60 on the average to handle the paperwork, pay the investigator, and make a decision. This cost compared with that of other insurance firms was deemed exorbitant, and cost-cutting measures were instituted. In order to evaluate the impact of these new measures, a sample of 26 recent claims was selected at random and cost studies were made. It was found that the sample mean $\overline{X}$ and the standard deviation s of the sample were $57 and $10, respectively. At the 0.01 level is there a reduction in the average cost—or can the difference of three dollars be attributed to sampling?

SOLUTION

First, state the null and the alternate hypotheses. The null hypothesis H_0 is that the population mean is $60. The alternate H_1 is that the population mean is less than $60. This is written:

$$H_0: \mu \geq \$60$$
$$H_1: \mu < \$60$$

The test is *one-tailed* because there is interest only in whether there has been a *reduction* in cost. The inequality in the alternate hypothesis points to the region of rejection in the left tail of the distribution.

A decision rule is formulated by referring to Appendix E. Go down the far left-hand column labeled df (degrees of freedom) until $n - 1$, or $26 - 1 = 25$ degrees of freedom is located. The critical value for 25 df, a one-tailed test, and the 0.01 level is 2.485. Shown schematically in Chart 15-3, the decision rule for this one-tailed test is to reject the null hypothesis if the computed value of t is -2.485 or it falls in any part of the left tail (the reject area). Otherwise, do not reject the null hypothesis that the mean is $60.

In the formula for the test statistic,

$$t = \frac{\overline{X} - \mu}{\frac{s}{\sqrt{n}}}$$

CHART 15–3
Regions of
acceptance and
rejection, *t*
distribution, 0.01 level
of significance

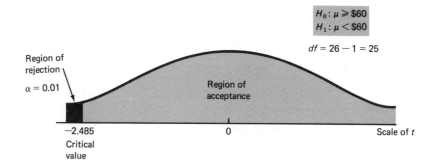

$$H_0: \mu \geqslant \$60$$
$$H_1: \mu < \$60$$

$$df = 26 - 1 = 25$$

Region of
rejection

$\alpha = 0.01$

Region of
acceptance

−2.485
Critical
value

0

Scale of *t*

$\overline{X} = \$57$, the sample mean.
$\mu = \$60$, the hypothesized population mean.
$s = \$10$, the sample standard deviation.
$n = 26$, the number of items in the sample.

Computed *t* is −1.530, found by:

$$t = \frac{\overline{X} - \mu}{\frac{s}{\sqrt{n}}} = \frac{\$57 - \$60}{\frac{\$10}{\sqrt{26}}} = \frac{\$-3}{\$1.9611613} = -1.530$$

The evidence is not sufficient to reject the null hypothesis. The decrease of $3 in the average cost can be explained by sampling variation. The cost-cutting measures apparently were not effective.

SELF-REVIEW 15–1
---

a. $H_0: \mu \leq 305$.
$H_1: \mu > 305$.

b.

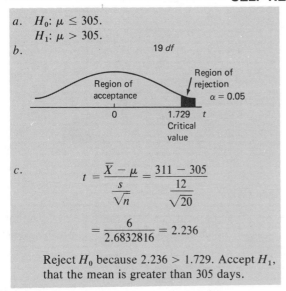

19 *df*

Region of
acceptance

Region of
rejection

$\alpha = 0.05$

0

1.729 *t*
Critical
value

c.
$$t = \frac{\overline{X} - \mu}{\frac{s}{\sqrt{n}}} = \frac{311 - 305}{\frac{12}{\sqrt{20}}}$$

$$= \frac{6}{2.6832816} = 2.236$$

Reject H_0 because 2.236 > 1.729. Accept H_1, that the mean is greater than 305 days.

(*A reminder: cover the answers in the left column.*)

From past records it is known that the average life of a battery used in a digital clock is 305 days. The lives of the batteries are normally distributed. The battery was recently modified to last longer. A sample of 20 of the modified batteries was tested, and it was discovered that the mean life was 311 days, the sample standard deviation, 12 days. At the 0.05 level of significance, did the modification increase the mean life of the battery?

a. State the null and alternate hypotheses.
b. Show the decision rule graphically.
c. Compute *t* and reach a decision.

In the previous examples the mean and standard deviation of the sample were given. The following example requires that they be computed from the sample observations.

EXAMPLE

The mean length of a small counterbalance bar is 43 millimeters. There is concern that the adjustments of the machine producing the bars have changed. The null hypothesis to be tested at the 0.02 level is that there has been no change in the mean length ($\mu = 43$). The alternate hypothesis is there has been a change ($\mu \neq 43$).

Twelve bars ($n = 12$) were selected at random and their lengths recorded. The lengths are (in millimeters) 42, 39, 42, 45, 43, 40, 39, 41, 40, 42, 43, and 42. Has there been a statistically significant change in the mean length of the bars?

SOLUTION

The null and alternate hypotheses are:

$$H_0: \mu = 43$$
$$H_1: \mu \neq 43$$

The alternate hypothesis does not state a direction. So, the test is two-tailed. There are 11 degrees of freedom, found by $n - 1 = 12 - 1 = 11$. Then, referring to Appendix E, a two-tailed test, and the 0.02 level, the critical value is 2.718. The critical values for the 0.02 level are shown in Chart 15–4. The decision rule, therefore, is to reject the null hypothesis if the computed t is not between ± 2.718. Otherwise, fail to reject H_0, that the mean length of the bars is 43 millimeters.

**CHART 15–4
Regions of acceptance and rejection, two-tailed test, Student t distribution, $\alpha = 0.02$**

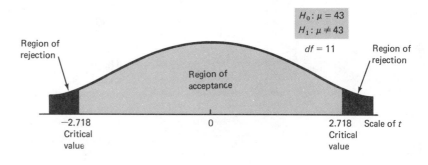

The standard deviation of a sample can be determined using either squared deviations from the mean, or an equivalent shortcut formula. The formulas from Chapter 5 are:

Using squared deviations

$$s = \sqrt{\frac{\Sigma(X - \overline{X})^2}{n - 1}}$$

Using the shortcut formula

$$s = \sqrt{\frac{\Sigma X^2 - \frac{(\Sigma X)^2}{n}}{n - 1}}$$

Unless the sample mean is a whole number, the shortcut formula is usually applied because it saves the effort of many subtractions.

The necessary calculations for these methods are in Table 15–1. The mean $\overline{X}$ is 41.5 millimeters, and the standard deviation s is 1.78 millimeters.

TABLE 15–1
Calculations needed for the sample standard deviation

X (in mm)	$X - \overline{X}$	$(X - \overline{X})^2$	X^2
42	0.5	0.25	1,764
39	-2.5	6.25	1,521
42	0.5	0.25	1,764
45	3.5	12.25	2,025
43	1.5	2.25	1,849
40	-1.5	2.25	1,600
39	-2.5	6.25	1,521
41	-0.5	0.25	1,681
40	-1.5	2.25	1,600
42	0.5	0.25	1,764
43	1.5	2.25	1,849
42	0.5	0.25	1,764
498	0	35.0	20,702

$\overline{X} = \frac{498}{12} = 41.5$ mm

Squared deviation method:

$$s = \sqrt{\frac{\Sigma(X - \overline{X})^2}{n - 1}} = \sqrt{\frac{35}{12 - 1}} = 1.7837651$$

Shortcut formula:

$$s = \sqrt{\frac{\Sigma X^2 - \frac{(\Sigma X)^2}{n}}{n - 1}} = \sqrt{\frac{20,702 - \frac{(498)^2}{12}}{12 - 1}}$$

$$= \sqrt{\frac{20,702 - 20,667}{12 - 1}} = \sqrt{\frac{35}{12 - 1}} = 1.7837651$$

Now you are ready to compute the actual t test statistic.

$$t = \frac{\overline{X} - \mu}{\frac{s}{\sqrt{n}}} = \frac{41.5 - 43.0}{\frac{1.7837651}{\sqrt{12}}} = \frac{-1.5}{0.5149286} = -2.913$$

The null hypothesis that the population mean is 43 millimeters is rejected at the 0.02 level (because the computed t of 2.913 falls in the area of the tail beyond the critical value of 2.718). The alternate hypothesis that the mean is not 43 millimeters is accepted. Apparently the machine is out of adjustment.

————————————————— **SELF-REVIEW 15–2** —————————————————

a. $H_0: \mu = 9.0$
$H_1: \mu < 9.0$

b. 7 df, found by $n - 1 = 8 - 1 = 7$.

A machine is set to fill a small bottle with 9.0 grams of medicine. It is claimed that the mean weight is less than 9.0 grams. The hypothesis is to

c. Accept the null hypothesis if the computed value of t falls between -2.998. Otherwise, reject H_0 and accept H_1.

d. $t = -2.494$, found by:

X	$X - \overline{X}$	$(X - \overline{X})^2$	X^2
9.2	0.4	0.16	84.64
8.7	−0.1	0.01	75.69
8.9	0.1	0.01	75.21
8.6	−0.2	0.04	73.96
8.8	0.0	0.00	77.44
8.5	−0.3	0.09	72.25
8.7	−0.1	0.01	75.69
9.0	0.2	0.04	81.00
70.4	0.0	0.36	619.88

$$\overline{X} = \frac{70.4}{8} = 8.8$$

$$s = \sqrt{\frac{0.36}{8 - 1}} = 0.2267785$$

or

$$s = \sqrt{\frac{619.88 - \frac{(70.4)^2}{8}}{8 - 1}} = 0.2267785$$

Then:

$$t = \frac{8.8 - 9.0}{\frac{0.2267785}{\sqrt{8}}} = -2.494$$

Since -2.494 does not fall below -2.998, the null hypothesis that $\mu = 9.0$ is accepted at the 0.01 level.

be tested at the 0.01 level. A sample revealed these weights (in grams): 9.2, 8.7, 8.9, 8.6, 8.8, 8.5, 8.7, and 9.0.

a. State the null and alternate hypotheses.
b. How many degrees of freedom are there?
c. Give the decision rule.
d. Compute t and arrive at a decision.

A COMPUTER OUTPUT

The Statistical Package for the Social Sciences, developed at the University of Chicago and presented in Chapter 5, is an efficient way of doing routine calculations. Another package, called MINITAB, was developed at The Pennsylvania State University. First, the null hypothesis is entered in the form TTEST MU = 43.

```
MTB >TTEST MU=43, USING C1
   WEIGHT     N =  12      MEAN =      41.500     ST.DEV. =      1.78

   TEST OF MU =    43.0000 VS. MU N.E.    43.0000
   T = -2.913
   THE TEST IS SIGNIFICANT AT   0.0141

MTB >PRINT C1
COLUMN   WEIGHT
COUNT       12
          42.        39.        42.        45.        43.
          40.        39.        41.        40.        42.
          43.        42.
```

Note: Student's t is the same as computed previously (-2.913).

EXERCISES

(A reminder: The answers and method of solution for selected exercises are given in Appendix A.)

1. The records of the owner of a fleet of trucks revealed that the average life of a set of spark plugs is 22,100 miles. The distribution of the life of the plugs is near normally distributed. A spark plug manufacturer claimed that its plugs had an average life in excess of 22,100 miles. The fleet owner purchased a large number of sets, and a sample of the life of 18 sets revealed that the sample average life is 23,400 miles, the sample standard deviation 1,500 miles. Is there enough evidence to accept the manufacturer's claim at the 0.05 level?

2. Based on past experience with raising Pure Rock chickens, their average weight at age five months is 1.35 pounds. The weights are normally distributed. In an effort to increase their weight during that period, a special additive was mixed with the chicken feed. The weights of a sample of five-month-old chickens were (in pounds): 1.41, 1.37, 1.33, 1.35, 1.30, 1.39, 1.36, 1.38, 1.40, and 1.39. At the 0.01 level, has the special additive increased the weight of the chickens?
   a. State the null and alternate hypotheses.
   b. What is the decision rule?
   c. What decision did you reach regarding the effectiveness of the new additive?

3. The liquid chlorine added to swimming pools to combat algae has a relatively short shelf life before it loses its effectiveness. (The effectiveness is measured on a scale of 1 to 10, with readings below 7 meaning it is ineffective.) Past records indicate that the average shelf life of a five-gallon jug of chlorine is 2,160 hours (90 days). As an experiment, Holdlonger was added to the chlorine to find out if it would increase the shelf life. A sample of nine jugs of chlorine gave these shelf lifes (in days): 2,159, 2,170, 2,180, 2,179, 2,160, 2,167, 2,171, 2,181, and 2,185. At the 0.025 level, has Holdlonger increased the shelf life of the chlorine?

A TEST FOR THE DIFFERENCE BETWEEN TWO POPULATION MEANS

EXAMPLE

Two different procedures have been proposed to assemble a small subassembly. The question is: Which procedure is more efficient—the procedure developed by Manley (designated as procedure number 1) or the procedure developed by Fox (designated as procedure number 2)? To objectively evaluate the two proposed methods, it was decided to conduct time and motion studies on a few subassemblies. The objective of the studies is to determine a mean assembly time per unit for each of the two procedures. If there is a difference between the two means, a statistical test will be applied to the data to determine whether or not the difference is significant.

The null hypothesis states that there is no difference in the mean assembly time for the Manley procedure and the mean assembly time for the Fox procedure.

$$\text{Null } H_0: \mu_1 = \mu_2$$
$$\text{Alternate } H_1: \mu_1 \neq \mu_2$$

This use of Student's *t* assumes that (1) the observations in the Manley sample are *independent* of those observations in the Fox sample, and of each other, (2) the two populations are approximately normal, and (3) the two populations have equal variances.

The basic formula for t is:

$$t = \frac{\overline{X}_1 - \overline{X}_2}{\sqrt{\dfrac{s_p^2}{n_1} + \dfrac{s_p^2}{n_2}}}$$

with $n_1 + n_2 - 2$ degrees of freedom

where:

$$s_p^2 = \frac{\Sigma(X_1 - \overline{X}_1)^2 + \Sigma(X_2 - \overline{X}_2)^2}{n_1 + n_2 - 2}$$

It is the pooled estimate of the population variance, and it is the weighted average of the two sample variances.

Note that the formula for t is quite similar to the one used for z in Chapter 13 to test the difference between two population means when large samples are employed. However, this particular test statistic presumes that the two population standard deviations are equal.

You may find the following a more convenient computational formula for t:

$$t = \frac{\overline{X}_1 - \overline{X}_2}{\sqrt{\dfrac{\dfrac{\Sigma(X_1 - \overline{X}_1)^2 + \Sigma(X_2 - \overline{X}_2)^2}{n_1 + n_2 - 2}(n_1 + n_2)}{n_1 n_2}}}$$

The 0.10 level of significance is to be used in testing for the difference between the two means in this example.

SOLUTION

The alternate hypothesis H_1 does not specify that one procedure is superior to the other procedure. Thus, a two-tailed test is used. The decision rule depends on the combined sample size and, of course, the level of significance selected. As noted, the degrees of freedom are computed by $n_1 + n_2 - 2$. Five Manley subassemblies and six Fox subassemblies are to be selected, There are, therefore, 9 degrees of freedom, found by $5 + 6 - 2$. The critical values of t from Appendix E for 9 df, a two-tailed test, and the 0.10 level are ± 1.833. The decision rule is shown graphically in Chart 15–5.

The five sample observations from the Manley procedure (procedure

CHART 15–5
Region of acceptance
and rejection,
two-tailed test
(9 degrees of
freedom,
α = 0.10)

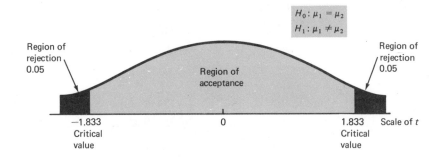

$H_0: \mu_1 = \mu_2$
$H_1: \mu_1 \neq \mu_2$

Region of
rejection
0.05

Region of
acceptance

Region of
rejection
0.05

−1.833   0   1.833   Scale of t
Critical   Critical
value   value

number 1) are (in minutes): two, four, nine, three, and two. So, the mean assembly time is four minutes, found by 20/5.

The six sample observations from the Fox procedure (procedure number 2) are (in minutes): three, seven, five, eight, four, and three. Hence the mean assembly time is five minutes, found by 30/6.

The deviations from each mean and the squared deviations for both samples are in Table 15–2.

TABLE 15–2
Calculations for
student t

Sample number	Procedure no. 1			Procedure no. 2		
	Minutes to assemble X_1	$X_1 - \overline{X}_1$	$(X_1 - \overline{X}_1)^2$	Minutes to assemble X_2	$X_2 - \overline{X}_2$	$(X_2 - \overline{X}_2)^2$
1	2	−2	4	3	−2	4
2	4	0	0	7	2	4
3	9	5	25	5	0	0
4	3	−1	1	8	3	9
5	2	−2	4	4	−1	1
6				3	−2	4
			$\overline{34}$			$\overline{22}$

In the formula for the test statistic t:

X_1 represents the length of time required to assemble the subassembly using procedure 1.

X_2 represents the length of time required to assemble the subassembly using procedure 2.

$\overline{X}_1$ is the arithmetic mean length of time required to assemble the subassembly using procedure 1.

$\overline{X}_2$ is the arithmetic mean length of time required to assemble the subassembly using procedure 2.

n_1 is the number in the sample using procedure 1.

n_2 is the number in the sample using procedure 2.

Inserting the numbers from Table 15–2 we get:

$$t = \frac{\overline{X}_1 - \overline{X}_2}{\sqrt{\dfrac{\Sigma(X_1 - \overline{X}_1)^2 + \Sigma(X_2 - \overline{X}_2)^2}{n_1 + n_2 - 2}\dfrac{(n_1 + n_2)}{n_1 n_2}}}$$

$$= \frac{4 - 5}{\sqrt{\dfrac{(34 + 22)}{5 + 6 - 2}\dfrac{(5 + 6)}{5 \times 6}}}$$

$$= -0.662 \text{ minutes}$$

The computed value of $t(-0.662)$ falls within the acceptance region, which was stated previously as being between ± 1.833. The null hypothesis is not rejected at the 0.10 level of significance. There is no difference between the two means; that is, $\mu_1 = \mu_2$ (using the 0.10 level of significance). The difference of one minute between the mean of four minutes (procedure number 1) and the mean of five minutes (procedure number 2) is probably due to sampling.

SELF-REVIEW 15-3

$\overline{X}_1 = 42/6 = 7$ H_0: $\mu_1 \geq \mu_2$

$\overline{X}_2 = 80/8 = 10$ H_1: $\mu_1 < \mu_2$

The critical value of t is -1.782 from Appendix E. $n_1 + n_2 - 2 = 6 + 8 - 2 = 12$ df.

$$t = \frac{7 - 10}{\sqrt{\dfrac{10 + 36}{6 + 8 - 2}\dfrac{(6 + 8)}{6 \times 8}}}$$

$$= \frac{-3}{\sqrt{\dfrac{\dfrac{46}{12}(14)}{48}}}$$

$$= \frac{-3}{1.0573814} = -2.837$$

Since -2.837 falls in the left tail beyond -1.782, the null hypothesis is rejected at the 0.05 level. Orno's mean weight is greater than Edne's mean weight.

The net weights of a sample of bottles filled by a machine manufactured by Edne, and the net weights of a sample filled by a similar machine manufactured by Orno, Inc., are (in grams):

Edne: 5, 8, 7, 6, 9, and 7
Orno: 8, 10, 7, 11, 9, 12, 14, and 9

Test the claim at the 0.05 level that the mean weight of the bottles filled by the Orno machine is greater than the mean weight of the bottles filled by the Edne machine.

The previous formula for t using deviations from the means is somewhat awkward to use if the means are decimal numbers, that is, not whole numbers. A convenient equivalent *shortcut formula* follows:

$$t = \frac{\overline{X}_1 - \overline{X}_2}{\sqrt{\frac{(n_1 - 1)s_1^2 + (n_2 - 1)s_2^2}{n_1 + n_2 - 2}\left(\frac{1}{n_1} + \frac{1}{n_2}\right)}}$$

with $n_1 + n_2 - 2$ degrees of freedom.

The shortcut formula will now be used to check the value of the computed t (-0.662) arrived at previously using squared deviations from the mean.

Note that the standard deviations s of the two samples are needed. The formula for the standard deviation was developed in Chapter 5 and used earlier in this chapter. The calculations for the standard deviations are in Table 15–3.

TABLE 15–3
Calculations needed for the sample standard deviations

Procedure 1		Procedure 2			
X	X²	X	X²		
2	4	3	9		
4	16	7	49	$s_1 = \sqrt{\dfrac{\Sigma X_1^2 - \dfrac{(\Sigma X_1)^2}{n_1}}{n_1 - 1}} = \sqrt{\dfrac{114 - \dfrac{(20)^2}{5}}{5 - 1}} = 2.9154759$	
9	81	5	25		
3	9	8	64		
2	4	4	16	$s_2 = \sqrt{\dfrac{\Sigma X_2^2 - \dfrac{(\Sigma X_2)^2}{n_2}}{n_2 - 1}} = \sqrt{\dfrac{172 - \dfrac{(30)^2}{6}}{6 - 1}} = 2.0976176$	
20	114	3	9		
		30	172		

Inserting the two standard deviations and other sample statistics in the shortcut formula for Student's t:

$$t = \frac{\overline{X}_1 - \overline{X}_2}{\sqrt{\frac{(n_1 - 1)s_1^2 + (n_2 - 1)s_2^2}{n_1 + n_2 - 2}\left(\frac{1}{n_1} + \frac{1}{n_2}\right)}}$$

$$= \frac{4 - 5}{\sqrt{\frac{(5 - 1)(2.9154759)^2 + (6 - 1)(2.0976176)^2}{5 + 6 - 2}\left(\frac{1}{5} + \frac{1}{6}\right)}}$$

$$= \frac{-1}{\sqrt{\frac{56}{9}(0.366667)}}$$

$$= \frac{-1}{1.5104572}$$

$$= -0.662, \text{ same as computed before}$$

EXERCISES

4. A sample of the scores on an examination given to both males and females are:

Males: 72, 69, 98, 66, 85, 76, 79, 80, and 77
Females: 81, 67, 90, 78, 81, 80, and 76

Test the hypothesis at the 0.01 level that the mean grade of the females is higher than for the males.

5. The scores of two groups of prison inmates on a rehabilitation test are:

	First offenders	Repeat offenders
Mean score	300	305
Sample variance	20	18
Sample size	16	13

Test at the 0.05 level that there is no difference between the mean scores of the two groups. The alternate hypothesis is there is a difference.

6. Refer to Self-Review 15–3. Use the shortcut formula to test the claim that the mean weight of the bottles filled by the Orno machine is greater than the mean weight of the bottles filled by the Edne machine.

CHAPTER SUMMARY

Testing hypotheses involving small samples using Student's t is covered in this chapter. By *small*, we mean the sample size is less than 30. To use the test statistic t in small-sample problems, the population, or populations, must be normally distributed or nearly normal. The t distribution is similar to the standard normal distribution z in that it is continuous, bell shaped, and symmetrical. Further, the curve for the t distribution is spread out more than the curve for the normal distribution and is flatter at the apex of the curve.

Two types of hypothesis-testing problems were examined. Both required interval levels of measurement. One was concerned with a single population mean, the other with two population means. In the first case, we assume that the population is normally distributed with some unknown standard deviation. In the second case, we assume that both populations are normally distributed and that they have equal (but unknown) standard deviations.

The usual five-step hypothesis-testing procedure is used. (1) The null and alternate hypotheses are stated, (2) a level of risk is selected, (3) the test statistic is identified, (4) a decision rule is formulated, and (5) a sample, or samples, are chosen and, based on a comparison of the computed t and the critical value of t, the null hypothesis is either rejected or not rejected.

CHAPTER OUTLINE

Student's *t* test: Small samples

I. *Objective*: To check the validity of quantitative statements. Examples of quantitative statements involving interval level measurements are: (A) The mean outside diameter of the bushing being machined is 31.19 centimeters; (B) There is no difference in the mean income of the executives in Carty Industries and the mean income of the executives employed by Dobel, Inc.

II. Student's t distribution.

    A. *Use*.

        1. When the sample size is less than 30, and

        2. The population, or populations are normally or near normally distributed.

B. *Characteristics*.
   1. It is a continuous distribution.
   2. It is bell shaped and symmetrical.
   3. There is a family of *t* distributions. All have the same mean, zero, but different standard deviations, depending on the sample size.
   4. It is spread out more than the standard normal distribution and is flatter at the apex of the curve.

III. A test of hypothesis about a population mean.

$$t = \frac{\bar{X} - \mu}{\frac{s}{\sqrt{n}}}$$

With $n - 1$ degrees of freedom

where:

$\bar{X}$ is the sample mean.
μ is the hypothesized population mean.
s is the sample standard deviation.
n is the number in the sample.

IV. A test for the difference between two population means.
   A. *Assumptions*.
      1. The observations in one sample are independent of those in the other sample and independent of each other.
      2. The two populations are normal.
      3. The two populations have equal variances.
   B. *Formulas*.
      1. The basic formula is:

$$t = \frac{\bar{X}_1 - \bar{X}_2}{\sqrt{\frac{s_p^2}{n_1} + \frac{s_p^2}{n_2}}}$$

with $n_1 + n_2 - 2$ degrees of freedom

where the pooled estimate of the population variance is:

$$s_p^2 = \frac{\Sigma(X_1 - \bar{X}_1)^2 + \Sigma(X_2 - \bar{X}_2)^2}{n_1 + n_2 - 2}$$

      2. An equivalent formula based on the squared deviations from the two means is:

$$t = \frac{\bar{X}_1 - \bar{X}_2}{\sqrt{\frac{\Sigma(X_1 - \bar{X}_1)^2 + \Sigma(X_2 - \bar{X}_2)^2}{n_1 + n_2 - 2} \cdot \frac{(n_1 + n_2)}{n_1 n_2}}}$$

Another equivalent formula for the test statistic *t* is:

$$t = \frac{\bar{X}_1 - \bar{X}_2}{\sqrt{\frac{(n_1 - 1)s_1^2 + (n_2 - 1)s_2^2}{n_1 + n_2 - 2}\left(\frac{1}{n_1} + \frac{1}{n_2}\right)}}$$

V. Hypothesis-testing steps.
    A. State H_0 and H_1.
    B. Decide on a level of risk.
    C. Chose the test statistic (t in this case).
    D. Formulate a decision rule.
    E. Select a sample, or samples and, based on a comparison of the critical t value (from Appendix E) and the computed t value, accept or reject the null hypothesis.

CHAPTER EXERCISES

7. The manufacturer of the Coochisaski motorcycle advertises that the cycle will average 87 miles per gallon on long trips. The mileages on eight long trips were 88, 82, 81, 87, 80, 78, 79, and 89. Test at the 0.05 level that the mean mileage is less than advertised.

8. The football coach said that, based on past records, the mean weight of the defensive linemen is 235 pounds. A sample of 10 defensive linemen this year revealed that the mean weight is 240 pounds and the standard deviation of the sample, 11 pounds. At the 0.01 level, is this sufficient evidence that the mean weight has increased?

9. Two equal groups of seedlings were selected for an experiment. All the seedlings were of equal height. One group of seedlings was fed with a 10-10-40 fertilizer, the other with a 20-20-20 fertilizer. The mean heights of the two groups of seedlings after a period of time and other pertinent information follow. (Remember, the variance is the square of the standard deviation.)

Group fed with	Sample mean height (in inches)	Sample standard deviation (in inches)	Sample size
10-10-40	12.92	0.25	15
20-20-20	12.63	0.20	13

At the 0.025 level, determine whether the group of seedlings fed with 10-10-40 fertilizer has a greater mean height than the group fed with 20-20-20 fertilizer.

10. Samples of efficiency ratings of employees in plant number 1 and plant number 2 are:

Efficiency ratings

Plant no. 1	Plant no. 2
160	163
158	161
162	160
161	162
160	163
160	162
161	164
159	163
159	165
160	162
	159
	160

At the 0.02 level, test H_0: $\mu_1 = \mu_2$ using the alternate hypothesis H_1: $\mu_1 \neq \mu_2$.

CHAPTER SELF-REVIEW EXAMINATION

Do all the problems and then check your answers against those given in Appendix A. Score each problem 10 points. Note whether the answer to each question is true or false. If false, give the correct answer.

1. T F To apply Student's t to a problem involving two means, it is assumed that the two populations are normal, or nearly normal.

2. T F A test was made about a population mean. A sample of 22 pieces of steel was selected at random. There are 22 degrees of freedom.

3. T F As the sample size increases, the t distribution tends to approximate the normal distribution.

4. T F There is only one t distribution, and it has a mean of zero.

5. T F Generally speaking, Student's t is used when the sample size is less than 30.

6. T F In testing the difference between two means, the use of Student's t requires that the two sets of sample observations be independent.

7. T F The t-test also assumes that the variances of the two populations are equal, or approximately equal.

Questions 8–10 are based on the following:

Given H_0: $\mu_1 = \mu_2$ and H_1: $\mu_1 \neq \mu_2$

Sample sizes are 12 and 11.
The 0.05 level of risk is to be used.

8. T F The test is two-tailed.

9. T F The critical value of t is ± 2.069.

10. T F If t was computed to be -0.999, the null hypothesis would be accepted.

16

INTRODUCTION

The previous three chapters dealt with tests of hypotheses designed to determine whether or not there is a difference between *two* populations. This was accomplished by selecting a sample from each population. The same procedure could be used in a problem involving more than two means, but it has several drawbacks. It would be very time consuming to compute all possible *z* values (large samples) or *t* values (small samples), if there were, say, 30 samples of size 10. First, a random sample would be selected from one of the populations and the mean and standard deviation computed. Likewise, a sample would be chosen from a second population and the mean and standard deviation determined. Then the *z* or *t* test would be applied and a decision made regarding the difference between μ_1 and μ_2. The procedure would be repeated for μ_1 and μ_3, μ_1 and μ_4, . . . , μ_{29} and μ_{30}. A total of 435 critical ratios would be required to include all possible differences among the 30 means! Suppose that 8 out of the 435 critical ratios indicated that the difference between the two means was significant. One might wonder: Does this indicate that there is an overall difference among the means?

To resolve the dilemma and to avoid having to compute a large number of critical ratios, a method has been developed called the **analysis of variance**, ANOVA for short. This method is not only less time consuming, but *it allows for a simultaneous comparison of all the populations to determine if they have identical means.* The analysis of variance procedure also has the advantage of allowing the sample data to be pooled for added stability. For example, in the previous illustration involving 30 samples of 10 observations each, if the Student *t* test were used, only 20 observations could be studied at one time. For the analysis of variance approach, all 30 samples of size 10 are pooled to give a total of 300 observations.

Analysis of variance: One-way and two-way classifications

ANOVA: THE GENERAL IDEA

Although the stated purpose of ANOVA is to determine whether more than two populations have the same mean, *it is actually accomplished by comparing the sample variances*. (Recall from Chapter 5 that the variance is the square of the standard deviation.) In order to do this, a probability distribution called the **F distribution** is used.

Basically, the analysis of variance technique uses sample information to determine whether or not three or more **treatments** produce different results. Following are several examples of what is means by a treatment.

1. Hydroponics, Inc., is a research firm which grows tomatoes and other plants in water. The question is how often to treat newly developed tomatoes with soluble plant food. For maximum growth, should they receive a full treatment of food at the beginning of the growing season and none thereafter? Or, should the plants be given one-half dose at the beginning and the other half in the middle of the four-month growing season? Or, should one quarter of the soluble solution be fed to the plants every month?

As an experiment, one tank was given the full treatment, another tank received half the two treatments, and a third tank got monthly doses. Samples of the ripe tomatoes from each of the three tanks were weighed, and the weights were recorded. A few results are shown in tabular form.

Sample number	Weight (grams)		
	Full treatment	Half treatment	Quarter treatment
1	12.3	15.6	13.8
2	25.8	11.4	15.2
etc.			

The question is: Do the treatments differ?

2. For a manufacturer, the different "treatments" may be four different grades of gasoline. Suppose, for example, that an automobile manufacturer designed a radically new lightweight engine and wants to recommend the grade of gasoline to use. The four grades, called the treatments, are below regular, regular, premium, and super premium. The test car made three trial runs on the test track using each of the four grades. The results:

Trial run number	Kilometers per liter			
	Below regular	Regular	Premium	Super premium
1	39.31	36.69	38.99	40.04
2	39.87	40.00	40.02	39.89
3	39.87	41.01	39.99	39.93

Again, the question to be answered by applying ANOVA is: Are the treatments (grades of gasoline) producing the same results (the same number of kilometers per liter)?

3. Finally, the "treatments" might be four different ways of doing a job. Suppose, for illustration, that five employees have submitted different methods of assembling a subassembly. Sample data for each of the four treatments are:

Sample number	Minutes required for assembly			
	Lind's method	Szabo's method	Carl's method	Manley's method
1	16.6	22.4	31.4	18.4
2	17.0	21.5	33.4	19.6
etc.				

Applying the analysis of variance technique to the sample observations, we might conclude that there is no difference in the time required, meaning that the differences in the sample data are due to chance.

ONE-WAY ANALYSIS OF VARIANCE

The ANOVA procedure can best be illustrated using an example. Suppose that the manager of the west end branch of Appliance Stores, Inc., resigned, and three salespersons at the branch are being considered for the position. All three have about the same length of service, education, and so on. In order to make a decision, it was suggested that each of their monthly sales records be examined. The sample results of each of their monthly sales are shown in Table 16–1. The "treatments" in this problem are the salespersons.

TABLE 16–1 Monthly sales of appliances for three salespersons

Sample number	Monthly sales (in $000)		
	Ms. Mapes	Mr. Sonnar	Mr. Mafee
1	$15	$15	$19
2	10	10	12
3	9	12	16
4	5	11	16
5	16	12	17
Mean	$11	$12	$16

The ANOVA procedure calls for the same hypothesis-testing procedure as outlined in Chapter 13 and used in Chapters 14 and 15.

Step 1. The null hypothesis. H_0 states that there is no statistical difference among the mean sales of the three salespersons; that is, $\mu_1 = \mu_2 = \mu_3$. H_1 states that at least one mean is different. As before, if H_0 is rejected, H_1 will be accepted.

Step 2. The level of significance. The 0.05 level was selected.

Step 3. The statistical test. The appropriate test to be applied is the **F test**. Underlying the use of this test are several assumptions. (1) The data must be at least interval level. (2) The actual selection of the sales must be chosen using a probability-type procedure. (3) the distributions of the monthly sales for each of the populations are normally distributed. (4) The variances of the three populations are equal, i.e., $\sigma_1^2 = \sigma_2^2 = \sigma_3^2$.

F is the ratio of two variances.

$$F = \frac{\text{Estimated population variance based on variation among the sample means}}{\text{Estimated population variance based on variation within samples}}$$

The numerator has $k - 1$ degrees of freedom. The denominator has $N - k$ degrees of freedom, where k is the number of treatments and N is the number of observations. It has these major properties:

1. The test statistic F is either zero of positive. It cannot be negative.
2. The F distribution's curve is positively skewed. The values go from zero to infinity. (Refer to the following schematic diagram.)
3. An F distribution is a continuous probability distribution, and there are many of them; that is, there is on F distribution and curve for the combination of 29 degrees of freedom in the numerator and 28 degrees of freedom in the denominator. And, there is a different F distribution and curve for the degree-of-freedom pair of 19 degrees of freedom in the numerator and 6 degrees of freedom in the denominator. Three of these are shown schematically:

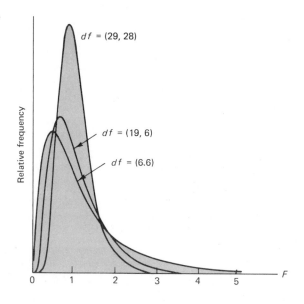

Step 4. The decision rule. As noted previously, the F distribution and curve are positively skewed and dependent on (1) the number of treatments k, and (2) the total number of observations N. For this problem involving a new store manager, there are three treatments (salespersons) so there are $k - 1 = 3 - 1 = 2$ degrees of freedom in the numerator. And, there are 15 observations (3 samples of 5 each). Therefore, there are $N - k = 15 - 3 = 12$ degrees of freedom in the denominator.

The critical value, that is, the dividing point between the region of acceptance and the region of rejection, is found by referring to Appendix O. (*Note:* There is one page for the 0.05 level and another for the 0.01 level.) The degrees of freedom for the numerator are listed at the top of the columns. The degrees of freedom for the denominator are in the left margin. Referring to the previous paragraph, we see that there are 2 degrees of freedom in the numerator and 12 degrees of freedom in the denominator. To locate the critical value, refer to Appendix O and the 0.05 level that was selected in Step 3. Move horizontally to 2 degrees of freedom in the numerator. Then go down that column until the number opposite 12 degrees of freedom in the margin is reached. That number is 3.89 and is the critical value for the 0.05 level.

In using the predetermined 0.05 level, the decision rule is to accept the null hypothesis H_0 if the computed F-value is less than 3.89; reject H_0 and accept H_1 if the computed F-value is 3.89 or greater. The decision rule is shown diagrammatically in Chart 16-1.

CHART 16-1
Distribution of F for a k of 3 and an N of 15, $\alpha = 0.05$

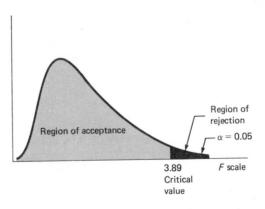

Step 5. Compute F and arrive at a decision. The first step is to set up an ANOVA table. It is merely a convenient form to record the sum of squares and other computations. The general format for a one-way analysis of variance problem is shown in Table 16-2.

TABLE 16–2
General format for one-way analysis of variance

Source of variation	(1) Sum of squares	(2) Degrees of freedom	(3) Mean square (1)/(2)
Treatments (between columns) .... SST		$k - 1$	$\dfrac{SST}{k - 1}$
Error (between rows) .... SSE		$N - k$	$\dfrac{SSE}{N - k}$
Total .... SS total			

$$F = \frac{\dfrac{SST}{k - 1}}{\dfrac{SSE}{N - k}}$$

SST is the abbreviation for sum of squares treatment and is found by:

$$SST = \sum \frac{T_c^2}{n_c} - \frac{(\Sigma X)^2}{N}$$

where:

$\dfrac{T_c^2}{n_c}$ directs one to square each column total and then divide each total by the number of observations in the column. Subscript c refers to a column.

n_c is the number of observations for each respective treatment (column). There are five sales figures for Ms. Mapes, five for Mr. Sonnar, and five for Mr. Mafee.

ΣX is the sum of all the observations (sales). It is $195 (see Table 16–3).

k is the number of treatments (salespersons). There are three.

N is the *total* number of observations. There are 15.

To compute *SST:*

TABLE 16–3
Calculations needed for the F ratio using the shortcut method

Sample number	Ms. Mapes Sales ($000) X_1	Ms. Mapes Sales squared X_1^2	Mr. Sonnar Sales ($000) X_2	Mr. Sonnar Sales squared X_2^2	Mr. Mafee Sales ($000) X_3	Mr. Mafee Sales squares X_3^2	
1	$15	225	$15	225	$19	361	
2	10	100	10	100	12	144	
3	9	81	12	144	16	256	
4	5	25	11	121	16	256	
5	16	256	12	144	17	289	Total
Column Totals: T_c	$55		$60		$80		$195
Sample size: n_c	5		5		5		15
Sum of squares: X^2		687		734		1,306	2,727

$$SST = \sum \frac{T_c^2}{n_c} - \frac{(\Sigma X)^2}{N}$$

$$= \frac{(\$55)^2}{5} + \frac{(\$60)^2}{5} + \frac{(\$80)^2}{5} - \frac{(\$195)^2}{15}$$

$$= 2,065 - 2,535$$

$$= 70$$

Now to compute SSE, which is the abbreviation for sum of squares error:

$$SSE = \Sigma(X^2) - \sum \frac{T_c^2}{n_c}$$

where $\Sigma(X^2)$ directs one to square each monthly sales figure and then sum the squares.

$$SSE = (\$15)^2 + (\$10)^2 + \$9^2 + \cdots + (\$17)^2 - \left[\frac{(\$55)^2}{5} + \frac{(\$60)^2}{5} + \frac{(\$80)^2}{5}\right]$$

$$= 2,727 - 2,605$$

$$= 122$$

Total variation (SS total) is the sum of the between-columns and the between-rows variation; that is, SS total $= SST + SSE = 70 + 122 = 192$. As a check:

$$SS \text{ total} = \Sigma(X^2) - \frac{(\Sigma X)^2}{N}$$

$$= 2,727 - \frac{(\$195)^2}{15}$$

$$= 2,727 - 2,535$$

$$= 192$$

The three sums of squares and the calculations needed for F are in Table 16–4.

TABLE 16–4
ANOVA table for the store managers problem

Source of variation	(1) Sums of squares	(2) Degrees of freedom	(3) Mean square (1)/(2)
Treatments (between columns)	$SST = 70$	$k - 1 = 3 - 1 = 2$	$\frac{SST}{k-1} = \frac{70}{2} = 35$
Error (between rows)	$SSE = 122$	$N - k = 15 - 3 = 12$	$\frac{SSE}{N-k} = \frac{122}{12} = 10.17$
SS total	192		

Computing F:

$$F = \frac{\dfrac{SST}{k-1}}{\dfrac{SSE}{N-k}} = \frac{35}{10.17} = 3.44$$

Referring back to the decision rule, we stated that, if the computed value of F was less than the critical value of 3.89, the null hypothesis would be accepted. If the F value was 3.89 or greater, H_0 would be rejected and H_1 accepted. Since $3.44 < 3.89$, the null hypothesis is not rejected at the 0.05 level. To put it another way, the differences in the mean monthly sales ($11,000, $12,000, and $16,000) can be attributed to chance (sampling). From a practical standpoint, the levels of sales of the three salespersons being considered for the store manager are the same. No decision with respect to the position can be made on the basis of monthly sales.

SELF-REVIEW 16–1

$$F_{3,16} = \frac{1.667}{1.625} = 1.026.$$

Do not reject H_0 because 1.026 is less than the critical value of 3.24. The ANOVA table is:

Treatments	Sum of squares	Degrees of freedom	Mean square
Between columns ... $SST = 5$		3	$\dfrac{SST}{k-1} = \dfrac{5}{3}$ $= 1.667$
Between rows ...... $SSE = 26$		16	$\dfrac{SSE}{N-k} = \dfrac{26}{20-4}$ $= 1.625$

(A reminder: Cover the answers in the left-hand column.)

In an effort to determine the most effective way to teach safety principles to a group of employees, four different methods were tried. Some employees were given programmed instruction booklets and worked through the course at their own pace. Other employees attended lectures. A third group watched a television presentation, and a fourth was divided into small discussion groups. At the end of the sessions, a test was given to the four groups. A high of 10 was possible. A sample of five tests was selected from each group. The results were:

Sample number	Test grades Programmed instruction	Lecture	TV	Group discussion
1	6	8	7	8
2	7	5	9	5
3	6	8	6	6
4	5	6	8	6
5	6	8	5	5

Test at the 0.05 level that there is no difference among the four means.

Another example of the one-way analysis of variance procedure follows.

EXAMPLE

A colleague had students in a large marketing class rate his perform-ance as either 1 (excellent), 2 (good), 3 (fair), or 4 (poor). A graduate assistant collected the ratings and assured the students that the profes-sor would not receive them until after the course grades had been filed in the office of the registrar. The rating (the treatment) a student gave the professor was matched with his final course grade. Logically, one might expect that in general the group of students who thought the professor was excellent would have a final average course grade sig-nificantly higher than those who rated him good, fair, or poor. And, it would seem that those who rated him poor would have the lowest course grades on the average. Samples from each rating group were selected. The results are:

Rating group 1 (excellent)	Rating group 2 (good)		Rating group 3 (fair)	Rating group 4 (poor)
85	80	78	73	81
77	70	75	71	85
74	78	73	70	76
77	72	80	79	81
70	74	82	73	79
74	77	73	76	70
	79	74	76	79
	78	76	68	
	82	91	80	
		78	78	

The question is whether or not there is a statistical difference among the mean scores of the four groups.

SOLUTION

As before, the *null hypothesis* states that there is no difference among the four arithmetic means. The 0.01 *level of significance* was selected.

The *decision rule:* The null hypothesis, which states that there is no difference among the means, will be accepted if the computed value of F is less than the critical value. Otherwise, the null hypothesis will be rejected and H_1 accepted.

Recall that the degrees of freedom in the numerator of the F ratio are found by $k - 1$, where k is the number of treatments (groups of faculty ratings in this problem). There are four treatments, so $4 - 1 = 3$ df. The degrees of freedom the denominator is 38, found by $N - k$, where N is the total number of students sampled. There were 42 students, so $42 - 4 = 38$ df.

Refer to Appendix O and the page for the 0.01 level of significance. Move horizontally at the top of the table to 3 degrees of freedom in the numerator. Then move down that column to the critical value opposite 40 degrees of freedom for the denominator (40 is the closest to 38). The critical value is approximately 4.31. The decision rule is shown diagrammatically in Chart 16–2. Accept the null hypothesis at the 0.01 level if the computed value of F if less than 4.31, but reject it if the computed value is 4.31 or greater.

CHART 16–2
Areas of acceptance and rejection, 0.01 level of significance

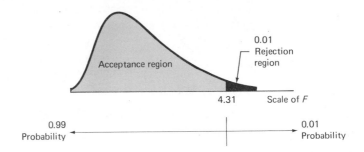

The calculations needed for the F ratio are shown in Table 16–5.

TABLE 16–5
Calculations needed for the F ratio using the shortcut method

Group 1 (excellent)		Group 2 (good)		Group 3 (fair)		Group 4 (poor)		
X_1	X_1^2	X_2	X_2^2	X_3	X_3^2	X_4	X_4^2	
85	7,225	80	6,400	73	5,329	81	6,561	
77	5,929	70	4,900	71	5,041	85	7,225	
74	5,476	78	6,084	70	4,900	76	5,776	
77	5,929	72	5,184	79	6,241	81	6,561	
70	4,900	74	5,476	73	5,329	79	6,241	
74	5,476	77	5,929	76	5,776	70	4,900	
		79	6,241	76	5,776	79	6,241	
		78	6,084	68	4,624			
		82	6,724	80	6,400			
		78	6,084	78	6,084			
		75	5,625					
		73	5,329					
		80	6,400					
		82	6,724					
		73	5,329					
		74	5,476					
		76	5,776					
		91	8,281					
		78	6,084					*Total*
Column totals: T_c 457		1,470		744		551		3,222
Sample size: n_c 6		19		10		7		42
Sum of squares: X^2 ...	34,935		114,130		43,505		55,500	248,070

Computing SST, SSE, and SS total, we get:

$$SST = \sum \frac{T_c^2}{n_c} - \frac{(\Sigma X)^2}{N}$$

$$= \frac{(457)^2}{6} + \frac{(1,470)^2}{19} + \frac{(744)^2}{10} + \frac{(551)^2}{7} - \frac{(3,222)^2}{42}$$

$$= 91.45$$

$$SSE = \Sigma(X^2) - \sum \frac{T_c^2}{n_c}$$

$$= (85)^2 + (77)^2 + (74)^2 + \cdots + (79)^2$$

$$- \left[\frac{(457)^2}{6} + \frac{(1,470)^2}{19} + \frac{(744)^2}{10} + \frac{(551)^2}{7} \right]$$

$$= 805.18$$

$$SS \text{ total} = SST + SSE = 91.45 + 805.18 = 896.63$$

As a check:

$$SS \text{ total} = \Sigma(X^2) - \frac{(\Sigma X)^2}{N}$$

$$= 248,070 - \frac{(3,222)^2}{42}$$

$$= 896.63$$

These values are inserted in the ANOVA table. (See Table 16–6.) Inserting the mean squares into the formula for F, we get:

$$F = \frac{30.48}{21.19} = 1.438$$

The decision: Since the computed F value of 1.438 is less than the critical value of 4.31 (from Appendix O), the null hypothesis that there is no difference among the means is *accepted* at the 0.01 level. Essentially this indicates that it is highly unlikely that the observed differences among the means are

TABLE 16–6
ANOVA table for the faculty evaluation problem

Source of variation	(1) Sum of squares	(2) Degrees of freedom	(3) Mean square (1)/(2)
Treatment (between columns)	$SST = 91.45$	$k - 1 = 4 - 1 = 3$	$\frac{SST}{k-1} = \frac{91.45}{4-1} = 30.48$
Error (between rows)	$SSE = 805.18$	$N - k = 42 - 4 = 38$	$\frac{SSE}{N-k} = \frac{805.18}{42-4} = 21.19$

attributable to chance. From a practical standpoint, it suggests that the grades students earn in a course are not related to the opinions they have of the overall competency and classroom performance of the instructor.

The calculations involved become quite tedious if there are a large number of observations. To show the application of the computer to an analysis of variance problem, an SPSS package mentioned in Chapter 5 was used. The same student opinions and grades resulted in the following output. Note that the computed F value is the same as that reached by hand.

```
                  SUM          MEAN       STD DEV       SUM OF SQ              N
Excellent      457.000       76.167        5.037        126.840       (    6)
Good          1470.000       77.368        4.705        398.500       (   19)
Fair           744.000       74.400        4.033        146.406       (   10)
Poor           551.000       78.714        4.716        133.434       (    7)
              -------------------------------------------------------------
Total         3222.000       76.714        4.676        805.180       (   42)
```

```
* * * * * * * * * * * * * A N O V A    T A B L E * * * * * * * * * * * * * *
*                                                                          *
*               SUM OF SQUARES     DEGREES OF FREEDOM     MEAN SQUARE       *
*                                                                          *
*  BETWEEN GROUPS      91.4453         (    3)             30.4818          *
*                                                                          *
*  WITHIN GROUPS      805.1797         (   38)             21.1889          *
*                                                                          *
*    TOTAL            896.6250         (   41)                              *
* * * * * * * * * * * * * * * * * * * * * * * * * * * * * * * * * * * * * * *
*                                                                          *
*   F =    1.4386         ETA SQRD =     0.1020                             *
* * * * * * * * * * * * * * * * * * * * * * * * * * * * * * * * * * * * * * *
```

TWO-WAY ANALYSIS OF VARIANCE

One-way analysis of variance deals with one treatment. One hypothesis is tested, namely, that all the means are equal. For illustration, recall from a case in the introduction to the chapter that Hydroponics, Inc., is a research firm which grows plants in water. As suggested in the case, one problem might involve the best way to treat the tomato plants with soluble plant food for maximum weight of fruit. The results would be summarized in a one-way table.

	Weights of tomatoes (grams)		
Sample number	Full solution beginning of season	Half solution every two months	Quarter solution once a month
1	9	12	16
2	10	11	17
etc.			

In the one-way ANOVA there is interest only in whether the mean weights of the tomatoes are equal; that is, H_0: $\mu_1 = \mu_2 = \mu_3$.

Two-way analysis of variance is concerned with making inferences about the underlying populations for two treatments.

EXAMPLE

Suppose that Hydroponics, Inc., wanted to determine what effect, if any, the plant food treatment and water temperature had on the weight of small cherry tomatoes used in salads. As an experiment, a group of plants was grown in tanks of cold water (4° Celsius) with some tanks being administered a full treatment of soluble plant food at the beginning of the growing season, others given a half solution every two months, and other tanks one-quarter solution every month.

Likewise, some plants were grown in cool water (10° Celsius) and given the same feeding treatments, and others were grown in warm and in hot water and given like food treatments. The sample results are shown in Table 16–7.

TABLE 16–7
Sample results of food and temperature treatments for tomato experiment

	Weights of tomatoes (grams)		
Temperature	Full solution beginning of season	Half solution every two months	Quarter solution once a month
Cold (4°C)	20	19	21
Cool (10°C)	16	15	14
Warm (16°C)	9	10	11
Hot (22°C)	8	7	6

There are two hypotheses to be tested. Thus, two F ratios must be computed.

1. H_0: The mean weights of the cherry tomatoes for the three food treatments are identical; that is, $\mu_1 = \mu_2 = \mu_3$.

   H_1: The mean weights resulting from the food treatment are not all equal.

2. H_0: The mean weights of the cherry tomatoes for the four water temperature treatments are identical; that is, $\mu_1 = \mu_2 = \mu_3 = \mu_4$.

   H_1: The mean weights resulting from the water temperature treatment are not all equal.

SOLUTION

The calculations needed for the two-way ANOVA are identical with the one-way analysis except for the addition of row sums, designated as B_r in Table 16–8.

TABLE 16–8
Calculations needed for two-way ANOVA

Temperature	Full solution Weight	Full solution Weight squared	Half solution Weight	Half solution Weight squared	Quarter solution Weight	Quarter solution Weight squared	Row sums B_r	
Cold	20	400	19	361	21	441	60	
Cool	16	256	15	225	14	196	45	
Warm	9	81	10	100	11	121	30	
Hot	8	64	7	49	6	36	21	Totals
Column totals: T_c	53		51		52			156
Sample size: n_c	4		4		4			12
Sum of squares: X^2		801		735		794		2,330

Analogous to the ANOVA table for a one-way analysis, the two-way general format is:

Source	(1) Sum of squares	(2) Degrees of freedom	(3) Mean square (1)/(2)
Treatment columns (food)	SST	$k - 1$	$\dfrac{SST}{k - 1}$
Treatment rows (temperature)	SSB	$n - 1$	$\dfrac{SSB}{n - 1}$
Error	SSE	$(k - 1)(n - 1)$	$\dfrac{SSE}{(k - 1)(n - 1)}$
Total	SS total		

As before, to compute STT:

$$SST = \sum \frac{T_c^2}{n_c} - \frac{(\Sigma X)^2}{N}$$

Inserting the appropriate values from Table 16–8 we get:

$$SST = \frac{(53)^2}{4} + \frac{(51)^2}{4} + \frac{(52)^2}{4} - \frac{(156)^2}{12}$$

$$= 2{,}028.50 - 2{,}028.00$$
$$= 0.50$$

$$SS \text{ total} = \Sigma(X^2) - \frac{(\Sigma X)^2}{N}$$

$$= 2{,}330 - \frac{(156)^2}{12}$$

$$= 2{,}330 - 2{,}028$$
$$= 302$$

SSB is found by:

$$SSB = \frac{\Sigma(B_r^2)}{k} - \frac{(\Sigma X)^2}{N}$$

$$= \frac{(60)^2 + (45)^2 + (30)^2 + (21)^2}{3} - \frac{(156)^2}{12}$$

$$= 2{,}322 - 2{,}028$$

$$= 294$$

Since SS total $= SST + SSB + SSE$, the sum of squares of SSE can be found by $SSE = SS$ total $- SST - SSB$. Solving: $SSE = 302 - 0.50 - 294 = 7.50$.

Table 16–9 shows the results of inserting these values in the two-way ANOVA table.

TABLE 16–9
ANOVA table for the food and temperature treatments

Sources of variation	(1) Sum of squares	(2) Degrees of freedom	(3) Mean square (1)/(2)
Treatment (food)	0.50	$3 - 1 = 2$	$\frac{0.50}{2} = 0.25$
Treatment (temperature)	294.00	$4 - 1 = 3$	$\frac{294}{3} = 98.00$
Error	7.50	$(2)(3) = 6$	$\frac{7.50}{6} = 1.25$
Total	302.00		

Computing F for the food treatment, we get:

$$F_{2,6} = \frac{0.25}{1.25} = 0.20$$

There are $k - 1$ degrees of freedom in the numerator and $(k - 1)(n - 1)$ df in the denominator. Referring to Appendix O for $F_{2,6}$, we see that the 0.05 level is 5.14. (The subscripts 2 and 6 indicate that there are 2 degrees of freedom in the numerator and 6 in the denominator.) As before, the decision is to accept the null hypothesis that the means are equal (because 0.20 is less than the critical value of 5.14). From a practical standpoint, it indicates that it does not matter whether the soluble food is applied full strength at the beginning of the season, or half strength every two months, or quarter strength every month.

Computing F for the temperature treatment, we get:

$$F_{3,6} = \frac{98.0}{1.25} = 78.4$$

For the numerator there are $n - 1$ degrees of freedom, and $(k - 1)(n - 1)$ in the denominator. The critical value is 4.76 for $F_{3,6}$. H_0 is rejected at the 0.05 level because $78.4 > 4.76$. As expected, the different temperatures of the water in which the tomatoes were grown did not produce equal results (weights).

A PRODUCTION PROBLEM

An actual problem in a mass-production plant located in Toledo, Ohio, might be of interest. Management noticed what seemed to be unequal production by four groups of swing-shift workers, designated shifts A, B, C, and D. The problem was somewhat complicated by the fact that the four shifts rotated. Some weeks shift A worked days, some weeks afternoons, and other weeks midnight to 7 A.M. Thus, there were two treatments—the four groups of shift workers and the three times of day worked. The two null hypotheses were (1) the average production amounts for the four shifts are equal, and (2) the average productions with respect to the times of day worked are equal. The ANOVA table for this two-way problem resulting from sample information follows.

```
* * * * * * * * * A N A L Y S I S   O F   V A R I A N C E * * * * * * * * * * *
        VAR004    HOURLY PRODUCTION
     BY VAR001    TIME OF DAY
        VAR003    SHIFT
* * * * * * * * * * * * * * * * * * * * * * * * * * * * * * * * * * * * * * * *

                                 SUM OF                    MEAN            SIGNIF
SOURCE OF VARIATION              SQUARES     DF           SQUARE      F     OF F
MAIN EFFECTS                    133347.875    5         26669.574   4.389   0.002
    VAR001                        8551.266    2          4275.633   0.704   0.999
    VAR003                      117726.375    3         39242.125   6.458   0.001

EXPLAINED                       133347.875    5         26669.574   4.389   0.002

RESIDUAL                        473934.000   78          6076.074

TOTAL                           607281.875   83          7316.648

    84 CASES WERE PROCESSED.
     0 CASES (  0.0 PCT) WERE MISSING.
```

The ANOVA table is only slightly different from the ones shown previously. The F-value for the shift treatment (VAR003 in the printout) is 6.458, found by 39,242.125/6,076.074. At the 0.05 level, the critical value of $F_{3,5}$ from Appendix O is 5.41. Since $6.458 \geq 5.41$, the null hypothesis of no difference with respect to the equal production of the four shifts is rejected; that is, the average productions of the four shifts are not all equal.

SELF-REVIEW 16-2

The second null hypothesis is accepted. There is no difference between the average production with respect to the time of day worked. $F_{2,5}$ is 0.704, found by 4,275.633/6,076.074. It is less than the critical value of 5.79 (Appendix O, 2 degrees of freedom in the numerator, 5 in the denominator).

Referring back to the computer output, make a decision regarding the second null hypothesis, that is, the time-of-day treatment. Give your reasoning.

The general conclusions at this point in the study are: (1) there is a difference in the average production among the four shifts, and (2) the fact that the shifts rotate from week to week has no bearing on the production differences. The logical next step is to determine the cause of the difference in production between the shifts.

CHAPTER SUMMARY	This chapter dealt with a technique called analysis of variance (ANOVA), which allows us to simultaneously test whether the means of more than two populations are equal. The five-step hypothesis-testing procedure used in Chapters 13, 14, and 15 is followed—that is, H_0 and H_1 are stated, the level of significance is decided on, the appropriate test statistic is selected (F in this case), a decision rule is formulated, and finally based on sample data a decision is reached to reject or not to reject the null hypothesis.

One-way analysis of variance is concerned with one "treatment." As an example, a research project might be to determine whether the mean heart beat is the same using five different medications.

Two-way analysis of variance is concerned with two treatments. For illustration, we may be interested not only in the effect of five different medications on the heart beat, but also the degree of exercise (practically none, some, strenuous exercise). Thus, two hypotheses are tested.

CHAPTER OUTLINE
 	
Analysis of variance: One-way and two-way classifications
	I. One-way analysis of variance.
	  A. *Purpose.* To determine if more than two populations have identical means.
	  B. *Example.* To determine the effect on gasoline mileage of four different additive treatments to regular gasoline.
	  C. *Procedure.*
	    1. As usual, state H_0 and H_1:

H_0: $\mu_1 = \mu_2 = \mu_3 = \mu_4$.
H_1: The means are not all equal.

    2. Select a level of significance—usually 0.05 or 0.01.
    3. Formulate a decision rule based on the F test. Formula:

$$F = \frac{\text{Estimated population variance based on variation among the sample means}}{\text{Estimated population variance based on variation within samples}}$$

    4. Method for computing F.
      a. Design an ANOVA table.

Source of variation	Sum of squares	Degrees of freedom	Mean square
Treatments (between columns) .... SST		$k - 1$	$\dfrac{SST}{k - 1}$
Error (between rows) .... SSE		$N - k$	$\dfrac{SSE}{N - k}$

b. Compute *F*:

$$F = \frac{\dfrac{SST}{k-1}}{\dfrac{SSE}{N-k}}$$

where:

$$SST = \sum \frac{T_c^2}{n_c} - \frac{(\Sigma X)^2}{N} \qquad SSE = \Sigma(X^2) - \sum \frac{T_c^2}{n_c}$$

N is the total number of observations and n_c is the number of observations for each respective treatment.

c. If the computed value of F is less than the critical value of F (from Appendix O), accept the null hypothesis. Otherwise reject it and accept H_1.

II. Two-way analysis of variance.
   A. *Purpose.* To make inferences about the underlying populations for two treatments.
   B. *Example.*

	Gasoline additive (mpg)			
Type of automobile	SPTT	GoGo	ZZZT	Flash
Subcompact	35.6	18.9	56.7	34.9
Compact	30.7	14.9	50.9	29.6
Standard	25.2	9.0	44.5	25.0
Medium	21.5	8.8	42.8	23.7
Luxury	12.6	5.4	34.1	19.5

   C. *Null and alternative hypotheses.*

   1. H_0: The mean miles per gallon for the four additives are identical.
      H_1: The mean miles per gallon for the four additives are not all equal.

   2. H_0: The mean miles per gallon for the five types of automobiles are identical.
      H_1: The mean miles per gallon for the five types of automobiles are not all equal.

   D. *Further procedure.*
   1. Set up ANOVA table.
   2. Compute two *F*-values.
   3. Accept or reject each of the two null hypotheses.

CHAPTER EXERCISES

1. One reads that a business school graduate with an undergraduate degree earns more than a high school graduate with no additional education, and one with a masters degree or a doctorate earns even more. To test this, a random sample of

25 top executives from companies with assets over $1 million was selected. Their incomes classified by highest level of education follow.

Incomes ($000)		
High school or less	Undergraduate degree	Masters degree or more
45	49	51
47	57	73
53	105	82
62	73	59
39	81	94
43	84	89
54	89	89
	92	95
	62	73

Test at the 0.05 level of significance that there is no difference in the arithmetic mean salaries of the three groups.

2. A research firm has been awarded a grant to study the management of large U.S. firms. One of the facets of the study concerns the salaries of chief executives officers who have held the position for five years or less. Specifically, a sample survey of chief executives is to be conducted to determine if there are differences between the regions where the home office is located and the years in the position. Using the 0.01 level, test these two hypotheses. A small pilot survey revealed these incomes:

Years in position	Annual salary ($000)		
	Eastern	Midwestern	Far western
1	$ 90	$ 75	$ 80
2	110	90	100
3	105	110	115
4	120	105	130
5	140	120	150

3. A mass producer of plastic toys is considering a change in the plastic used. In the process of making a toy, the raw plastic is fed into an injection molding machine where it is heated and the toy formed. When it cools to a certain point, the toy is automatically ejected. In this operation, one of the concerns is the length of time it takes the plastic to cool before it is ejected. Every second lost affects the profit picture of the company. Several brands of plastics have been selected for trial. One of the experiments involves the length of time it takes to cool each of the plastics in the four different injection molding machines. The sample results were:

Brand name of plastic	Cooling time (minutes)			
	Swiss	International	Comstock	Reich B
Crydon	3.0	4.9	4.5	4.0
Jaymer	2.7	3.1	2.9	3.3
Ansilcon	4.3	4.0	3.2	4.1
101 D	6.0	4.2	3.9	3.9

Using the 0.05 level of significance and the usual hypothesis-testing procedure, determine if there is (a) any difference among the four machines with respect to the arithmetic mean time required to cool and eject the toy, and (b) any difference in the mean times with respect to the brands of plastics.

4. It can be shown that when only two treatments are involved, ANOVA and the Student t test (Chapter 15) result in identical computed values. As an example, suppose that 14 randomly selected students were divided into two groups, one consisting of 6 students and the other of 8. One group was taught using a combination of lecture and programmed instruction, and the other using a combination of lecture and television. At the end of the course, each group was given a 50-item test. The following is a list of the number of correct for each of the two groups.

Lecture and programmed instruction	Lecture and television
19	32
17	28
23	31
22	26
17	23
16	24
	27
	25

a. Using analysis of variance techniques, test H_0 that the two mean test scores are equal; $\alpha = 0.05$.

b. Now using the t test from Chapter 15, compute t.

c. Interpret the results.

5. A sample survey of the annual income of a beginning probation officer, by size of city in which the income was earned, was conducted.[1] The annual incomes of those selected in the sample, by size of the city, are (in $000):

Less than 100,000	100,000 to 250,000	250,000 to 500,000	Greater than 500,000
$14.2	$11.7	$16.0	$13.2
16.9	15.8	17.2	19.0
12.3	21.3	11.6	25.5
15.6	13.3	14.9	11.8
11.5	11.4	15.9	17.1
24.7	13.0	11.6	16.9
12.2	15.9	13.2	—
10.2	11.7	12.9	—
13.3	10.8	25.3	—
13.1	16.2	—	—
—	15.6	—	—
—	13.7	—	—
—	21.4	—	—

---

[1] University of Toledo, Office of Institutional Research, "Probation Department Wage Comparison Study for the City of Toledo Municipal Court Probation Department."

The question to be explored is whether or not there is a significant difference in the four city sizes with respect to the mean annual income of a beginning probation officer.

a. State the null hypothesis and alternative hypothesis.
b. Using the 0.05 level, state the decision rule.
c. What is the computed F-value?
d. What conclusion can be drawn?

6. Suppose that the ages of *all* sophomore students at five small colleges are:

Student number	Hard Luck	Sociable U.	All American	Football U.	Study Hard
1	24	19	21	23	22
2	21	20	23	19	20
3	18	21	20	16	19
4	20	16	17	18	17
5	23	22	22	21	21
6	19	20	19	20	18
7	21	23	24	22	20
8	15	18	18	15	18
9	22	21	21	21	21
10	17	15	15	21	19
11	19	20	20	20	17
12	20	22	25	19	20
13	18	19	16	19	16
14	22	21	22	21	21
15	16	17	17	20	22
16	19	22	21	19	19
17	23	19	24	23	23
18	21	24	19	24	20
19	16	21	21	24	22
20	24	17	25	18	21
21	26	26	20	22	23
22	17	20	23	21	26
23	20	18	22	19	19
24	19	15	21	17	21
25	20	23	18	18	18
26	21	20	20	22	16
27	19	25	16	17	19
28	23	19	19	21	21
29	20	21	17	17	19
30	19	18	21	23	20
31	22	20	19	20	22
32	18	19	20	25	18
33	18	19	18	17	20
34	21	22	17	21	18
35	19	16	22	18	21
36	22	17	22	22	19
37	23	20	21	16	19
38	17	24	18	19	24
39	20	18	19	23	20
40	17	21	20	20	23
41	20	20	23	18	25
42	25	19	20	20	17
43	21	23	19	20	26

Student number	Hard Luck	Sociable U.	All American	Football U.	Study Hard
44 21		14	18	22	15
45 18		18	20	20	17
46 22		23	19	21	21
47 20		20	19	19	24
48 21		25	14	20	23
49 19		17	20	14	14
50 20		22	26	20	22
51 15		20	17	19	
52 20		15	21	20	
53 19		21	20	20	
54 22		21		18	
55 25				20	
56 14					
57 18					
58 17					
59 24					
60 20					

a. Choose at random eight students from each college and record their ages. Use the table of random numbers (Appendix D) or some other random system to select the ages.

b. Test the hypothesis that there is no significant difference with respect to the mean age of the sophomore students enrolled in the five colleges. Use the 0.01 level of significance.

7. Referring back to the five populations, choose 8 ages at random from Hard Luck College, 10 from Sociable University, 5 from All American College, 8 from Football University, and 6 from Study Hard College. At the 0.05 level, determine if there is a significant difference among the age distributions of the five populations.

8. If a computer is available, use it to do Problem 7 at the same level of significance.

9. Following are the number of emergency admissions by day of the week for a sample of weeks at St. Vincent Hospital and Medical Center in Toledo, Ohio. Test the hypothesis at the 0.05 level that the average numbers of emergency admissions by day of the week are equal. State H_0, H_1, and the decision rule. Show essential computations and summarize your findings.

Sun	Mon	Tues	Wed	Thurs	Fri	Sat
15	32	29	19	20	30	13
18	30	26	19	19	32	19
19	29	34	27	31	28	14
16	22	27	15	17	29	14
19	21	38	23	21	20	15
24	23	39	23	25	34	19
16	28	29	26	20	34	19
19	24	33	22	22	22	17
18	39	24	30	18	34	21
16	20	41	32	30	29	22
12	31	25	22	17	23	20
18	32	20	26	23	15	14
23	20	22	32	30	18	20
17	37	19	22	23	22	30

Sun	Mon	Tues	Wed	Thurs	Fri	Sat
24	35	22	23	24	20	18
18	21	36	28	27	25	23
18	33	33	20	26	27	19
18	33	19	22	27	22	24
15	21	25	21	29	28	17
15	23	24	24	25	28	24
23	24	33	27	31	41	16
16	28	28	20	28	22	25

Source: From a study of hospital practices conducted by Dr. William Marchal.

CHAPTER SELF-REVIEW EXAMINATION

Do the problem and then check your answers against the ones given in Appendix A.

Score the problem 100 points.

1. The company has four precision grinders. There is interest in determining (a) whether there is any overall difference in the performance of the four machines, and (b) whether there is any difference in the steel being supplied for the machines by three steel firms. Specifically, the first null hypothesis states that the tolerances maintained by the four machines are identical.

   a. State the alternative hypothesis.

   The second null hypothesis to be tested is that the tolerances resulting from the steel supplied by the three firms are identical. The alternative hypothesis is that the tolerances are not all equal.

   A sample of pieces ground by the Deitz machine using steel from U.S. Steel were selected, and it was found that the tolerance maintained was eight ten-thousandths of an inch. (This is the number 8 found in the upper left corner of the following table.) All the sample results are:

Source of steel	Tolerance (ten-thousandths of an inch)			
	Deitz	Arvis	Milcron	Hunt
U.S. Steel 8	8	6	10	7
Inland 7	7	9	8	8
Bethlehem 9	9	7	8	9

   b. Test the two hypotheses at the 0.05 level of significance.

   c. Write a brief summary of your findings.

17

Chapters 13, 15, and 16 dealt with data which are interval scaled (weights, ages, tensile strengths, and so on). Certain assumptions about the population, or populations, were made when applying the test. For example, to use Student's *t* to test a hypothesis about two population means, as shown in Chapter 15, one must assume that the populations from which the samples are selected are normal or approximately normal and that their variances are equal.

Can tests of hypotheses be made if the data are not interval scaled but are nominal or ordinal, and/or if they are not approximately normal with equal variances? Tests called **nonparametric tests** have been developed to deal with such situations. Another term used to identify these tests is **distribution-free tests**, implying that they are free of assumptions regarding the distribution of the parent population. These distribution-free tests are relatively easy to apply, and the computations are generally easy to perform. However, the power of a nonparametric test is generally less than that of a similar parametric test. So there is a price to pay for their easy application.

This chapter will concentrate on one-sample and two-sample tests, including the **chi-square test**, the **Mann-Whitney *U* test**, the **Kolmogorov-Smirnov test**, and the **Wilcoxon matched-pair signed rank test**. Chapter 18 will deal with nonparametric tests based on more than two samples.

Nonparametric tests of hypotheses: One-sample and two-sample tests

CHI-SQUARE: ONE-SAMPLE TEST OF SIGNIFICANCE

The **chi-square test** of significance is one of the most commonly used nonparametric tests. One use is the **chi-square test of goodness of fit**. Developed by Karl Pearson in the early 1900s, it is applied to data from a single sample and requires only nominal-level information. Recall that nominal-level measurement is the "lowest" level and involves such categories as male and female, or such job classifications as welder, milling-machine operator, secretary, and so on.

As the full name implies, the purpose of the chi-square test is to determine how well an observed set of data fits an expected set. An illustration can best describe the hypothesis-testing procedure. Suppose that there is some doubt that one of the slot machines in Nero's Palace in Las Vegas is true; that is, there is suspicion that the mechanism behind one of the windows in the slot machine has been altered.

It has been suggested that, as an experiment, the handle of this "one-armed bandit," as it is affectionately called, be pulled down, say, 120 times and the results recorded. Before doing so, however, let us state the null hypothesis, give the level of significance, etc.

The null hypothesis H_0 is that the mechanism behind the window has not been tampered with. To put it another way, when the slot machine is eventually operated 120 times, there will be no difference between the set of observed frequencies and the set of expected frequencies; that is, any differences can be attributed to sampling. The alternate hypothesis H_1 is that there is a difference between the two sets of frequencies—that is, the machine has been altered. If H_0 is rejected and H_1 accepted, it would mean that the mechanism has been altered to allow one fruit, or fruits, to appear in the window more frequently than other fruits.

The level of significance selected for the test is the 0.05 level. The sampling distribution of the test statistic chi-square, designated as χ^2, is:

$$\chi^2 = \sum \frac{(f_0 - f_e)^2}{f_e}$$

with $k - 1$ degrees of freedom.

There are six fruits that appear in the left window of the slot machine under suspicion, namely, banana, cherry, orange, peach, lemon, and pear. So, when the slot machine is ultimately operated 120 times, the counts will be tallied into these six categories, symbolized by k. There are $k - 1$ degrees of freedom, or $6 - 1 = 5$ df. The decision rule is formulated by referring to Appendix H, 5 df, and the 0.05 level. The critical value is 11.07. This is the dividing point between the regions of acceptance and rejection. Thus, the decision rule states that if the computed value of chi-square is less than 11.07, the null hypothesis H_0 will not be rejected. If it is equal to 11.07 or greater, the null hypothesis will be rejected and the alternate hypothesis H_1 accepted. Chart 17–1 shows these two areas.

CHART 17–1
Chi-square probability distribution for five degrees of freedom showing the regions of acceptance and rejection, 0.05 level of significance

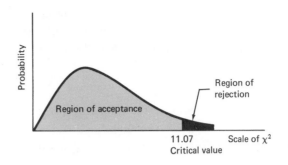

The sample results found by operating the slot machine 120 times are given in Table 17–1. The six categories are often called *cells*.

TABLE 17–1
Results of operating the slot machine 120 times

Fruit in left window (cells)	Number of times fruit appeared f_0
Banana	13
Cherry	33
Orange	14
Peach	7
Lemon	36
Pear	17
Total	120

The set of observed frequencies (f_0) is then matched with a set of expected frequencies (f_e). If the slot machine is true (not altered), out of 120 operations of the slot machine a banana would be expected to appear in the window 20 times, a cherry would appear 20 times, . . . and a pear would appear 20 times. The observed frequencies and the expected (theoretical) frequencies are shown in Table 17–2.

TABLE 17–2
Observed and expected frequencies for 120 operations of the slot machine

Fruit	Observed frequencies f_0	Expected frequencies f_e
Banana	13	20
Cherry	33	20
Orange	14	20
Peach	7	20
Lemon	36	20
Pear	17	20
Total	120	120

An examination of Table 17–2 indicates that a peach seldom appears in the left window and a lemon appears much more frequently than expected. Should the slot machine be declared altered? Perhaps, however, the differences between the observed and expected frequencies can reasonably be attributed to chance. Computing chi-square and comparing it with the critical value will resolve the dilemma.

Recall that the test statistic χ^2 is computed by:

$$\chi^2 = \sum \frac{(f_0 - f_e)^2}{f_e}$$

Referring to the following computations, we see that the steps required to determine chi-square are:

Column 1. The difference between each paired f_0 and f_e is calculated. (*Note:* The sum of the differences must logically equal zero.)

Column 2. The differences are squared.

Column 3. Each squared difference is divided by the appropriate frequency expected, f_e. These quotients are then summed. The sum (34.40) is the computed value of chi-square.

Fruit	f_0	f_e	(1) $f_0 - f_e$	(2) $(f_0 - f_e)^2$	(3) $\frac{(f_0 - f_e)^2}{f_e}$
Banana	13	20	-7	49	49/20 = 2.45
Cherry	33	20	13	169	169/20 = 8.45
Orange	14	20	-6	36	36/20 = 1.80
Peach	7	20	-13	169	169/20 = 8.45
Lemon	36	20	16	256	256/20 = 12.80
Pear	17	20	-3	9	9/20 = 0.45
			must be $\rightarrow$ 0		$\chi^2 \rightarrow$ 34.40

The computed statistic χ^2 of 34.40 falls in the rejection are beyond the critical value of 11.07. The decision, therefore, is to reject the null hypothesis H_0 at the 0.05 level that the slot machine has not been tampered with. The alternate hypothesis H_1, that the mechanism behind the left window of the slot machine has been tampered with, is accepted. In essence, rejecting H_0 means that it is highly unlikely that such large discrepancies between the frequencies observed and the frequencies expected would appear if the slot machine were true (unaltered). To repeat, the conclusion is that the mechanism has been tampered with.

SELF-REVIEW 12–1

a. Observed frequencies.
b. Six (six days of the week).
c. 10. Total observed frequencies ÷ 6 = 60/6 = 10.
d. 5; $n - 1 = 6 - 1$ or 5.
e. 15.09 (from the chi-square table in Appendix H).

(*A reminder: Cover the answers in the left-hand column.*)

The personnel manager is concerned about absenteeism. She decides to sample the records to determine if absenteeism is distributed evenly throughout the six-day workweek. The null hypothesis to be tested is: Absenteeism is distrib-

f. Computed:

$$\chi^2 = \sum \frac{(f_0 - f_e)^2}{f_e} = \frac{(12 - 10)^2}{10} + \frac{(9 - 10)^2}{10}$$

$$+ \frac{(11 - 10)^2}{10} + \frac{(10 - 10)^2}{10} + \frac{(9 - 10)^2}{10}$$

$$+ \frac{(9 - 10)^2}{10} = 0.8$$

g. Accepted.

h. Absenteeism is distributed evenly throughout the week. The observed differences are due to sampling variation.

i. 99 percent. (The null hypothesis was tested at the 1 percent level.)

uted evenly throughout the week. The 0.01 level is to be used. The sample results are:

	Number absent
Monday	12
Tuesday	9
Wednesday	11
Thursday	10
Friday	9
Saturday.......................	9

a. What kind of frequencies are the numbers 12, 9, 11, 10, 9, and 9 called?

b. How many cells are there?

c. What is the *expected* number of frequencies for each day?

d. How many degrees of freedom are there?

e. What is the chi-square critical table value at the 1 percent level?

f. Using the chi-square test of significance, compute χ^2.

g. Is the null hypothesis accepted or rejected?

h. Specifically, what does this indicate to the personnel manager?

i. How confident are you in this statement?

The expected frequencies (f_e) in the slot machine experiment were all equal; that is, out of 120 trials theoretically it is expected that a picture of a banana will appear 20 times in the left window of the slot machine, a cherry will appear 20 times, and so on. Chi-square can be used if the expected frequencies are not equal.

EXAMPLE

Suppose that the annual sales for the top seven cereals are as shown in Table 17–3. Based on the sales figures it is logical to assume that in the future Crinchies will account for 40 percent of the total sales, found

TABLE 17–3
Annual sales of the top seven cereals

Cereal	Annual sales ($000,000)	Percent of total
Crinchies	$20	40
Hooties	10	20
Pebbles	7	14
Sugar Dabs	5	10
Oat Crisps	4	8
Corn Kernels	3	6
Wheats	1	2
Total	50	100

by \$20/\$50. Hooties will account for 20 percent of the total, found by \$10/\$50, and so on. These percents are shown in the right-hand column of the table.

Several of the firms packaging these cereals conducted intensive advertising campaigns in an effort to increase their market shares. A sample survey conducted at supermarkets and independent grocery stores a month after the campaign revealed that total weekly sales of all cereals were \$400,000. As shown in Table 17–4, sales of Crinchies during the week were \$165,000; Hooties, \$78,000; and so on.

TABLE 17–4
Weekly sales for the top seven cereals after the advertising campaign

Cereal	Weekly sales
Crinchies	\$165,000
Hooties	79,000
Pebbles	50,000
Sugar Dabs	44,000
Oat Crisps	32,000
Corn Kernels	20,000
Wheats	10,000
Total	\$400,000

Has there been a significant change in the market share of the various cereals as the result of the intensive market campaign?

SOLUTION

The null hypothesis H_0 is: *there has been no change in the market share of the various cereals*. The alternate hypothesis H_1 states that *there has been a change in the market share*.

If there has been *no change* in the market share of each cereal as a result of the intensive market campaign, one would expect Crinchies to account for 40 percent of the total of \$400,000, or \$160,000. And Hooties would account for 20 percent of the weekly sales of \$400,000, or \$80,000. Weekly sales of Pebbles would be \$56,000, found by 14 percent of \$400,000, and so on. These expected sales (f_e) are shown in the fourth column of Table 17–5. Using the observed frequencies (f_0) resulting from the survey and these expected frequencies (f_e), we compute the chi-square to be 2.38 (see Table 17–5).

Referring to Appendix H, we see that the critical value of chi-square at the 5 percent level is 12.59. (There are 6 degrees of freedom, found by $k - 1$, or 7 cells − 1.) Since the computed statistic chi-square of 2.38 is less than 12.59, it falls in the region of acceptance.

You fail to reject the null hypothesis that there was no change in the sales pattern at the 5 percent level. That is, the advertising campaign sponsored by some firms to gain in sales at the expense of other firms was apparently not effective.

Limitations of chi-square

If there is an unusually small number of expected frequencies in a cell, chi-square (if applied) might result in an erroneous conclusion, because f_e

TABLE 17–5
Calculations needed for chi-square

Cereal	Annual sales		Weekly sales (000)				
	Sales (000,000)	Percent of total	f_0	f_e	$f_0 - f_e$	$(f_0 - f_e)^2$	$\dfrac{(f_0 - f_e)^2}{f_e}$
Crinchies	$20	40	$165	$160	$5	25	$\dfrac{25}{160} = 0.16$
Hooties	10	20	79	80	−1	1	$\dfrac{1}{80} = 0.01$
Pebbles	7	14	50	56	−6	36	$\dfrac{36}{56} = 0.64$
Sugar Dabs	5	10	44	40	4	16	$\dfrac{16}{40} = 0.40$
Oat Crisps	4	8	32	32	0	0	$\dfrac{0}{32} = 0.00$
Corn Kernels	3	6	20	24	−4	16	$\dfrac{16}{24} = 0.67$
Wheats	1	2	10	8	2	4	$\dfrac{4}{8} = 0.50$
Totals	$50	100	$400	$400	0	χ^2	2.38

appears in the denominator, and dividing by a very small number makes the quotient quite large! Two generally accepted rules regarding small cell frequencies are: (1) If there are only two cells, the **expected** frequencies in each cell should be five or more. The computation of chi-square would be permissible in the following problem.

Individual	f_0	f_e
Literate	643	642
Illiterate	4	5

(2) For more than two cells, χ^2 should not be applied if more than 20 percent of the f_e cells have frequencies less than five. According to this rule, it would be permissible to compute χ^2 for the management data in the left-hand section of the table shown below. Only one out of six expected cells, or 17 percent, contains a frequency less than five.

Level of management	Number		Level of management	Number	
	f_0	f_e		f_0	f_e
Foreman	18	16	Foreman	30	32
Supervisor	39	37	Supervisor	110	113
Manager	8	13	Manager	86	87
Middle management	6	4	Middle management	23	24
Assistant vice president	82	78	Assistant vice president	5	2
Vice president	10	15	Vice president	5	4
	163	163	Senior vice president	4	1

Chi-square should not be used for the management data in the right-hand section of the table because three out of the seven expected frequencies, or 43 percent, are less than five. Using this example to develop the reasoning behind the rule, note that most of the paired observed and expected frequencies are almost equal. The largest difference is just three. One might conclude, therefore, that there is no significant difference between the observed set and the expected set of frequencies. Yet, actually computing chi-square and evaluating it against the appropriate critical value will refute that conclusion. Instead, it would be concluded that there is a difference between the frequencies observed in the sample and the expected frequencies. This conclusion, however, does not seem logical. Verify this by solving the Self Review which follows.

SELF-REVIEW 17–2

χ^2 was computed to be 14.01, found by:

f_0	f_e	$f_0 - f_e$	$(f_0 - f_e)^2$	$\dfrac{(f_0 - f_e)^2}{f_e}$
30	32	−2	4	$\dfrac{4}{32} = 0.13$
110	113	−3	9	$\dfrac{9}{113} = 0.08$
86	87	−1	1	$\dfrac{1}{87} = 0.01$
23	24	−1	1	$\dfrac{1}{24} = 0.04$
5	2	3	9	$\dfrac{9}{2} = 4.50$
5	4	1	1	$\dfrac{1}{4} = 0.25$
4	1	3	9	$\dfrac{9}{1} = 9.00$
		0		14.01

The critical value of χ^2 for $k - 1 = 7 - 1 = 6\ df$, and the 0.05 level is 12.59. The computed χ^2 (14.01) is greater than this critical value, and the null hypothesis is rejected. There is a difference between the set of observed frequencies and the set of expected frequencies.

Using the management data shown on the right side of the preceding table, test the null hypothesis at the 0.05 level that there is no significant difference between the observed set and the expected set of frequencies.

The dilemma can be resolved if the data are such that some of the categories can be combined. This seems to be the case in the management problem. The three vice presidential levels were combined into one category in order to satisfy the 20 percent rule.

Level of management	Number in sample f_0	Expected number f_e
Foreman	30	32
Supervisor	110	113
Manager	86	87
Middle management	23	24
Vice president	14	7

The computed value of chi-square for the revised sets of frequencies is 7.26. This is less than the critical value of 9.49 for the 0.05 level. The null hypothesis is, therefore, not rejected at the 0.05 level of significance. This indicates that there is no difference between the sample results and the expected results. The small differences between the observed and expected observations can be attributed to sampling. This, of course, is a more logical conclusion.

SELF-REVIEW 17–3
---

a. $\chi^2 = 7.26$, found by:

f_0	f_e	$f_0 - f_e$	$(f_0 - f_e)^2$	$\dfrac{(f_0 - f_e)^2}{f_e}$
30	32	−2	4	0.13
110	113	−3	9	0.08
86	87	−1	1	0.01
23	24	−1	1	0.04
14	7	7	49	7.00
		0		7.26

b. The critical value of χ^2 for $k - 1 = 5 - 4\,df$, and the 0.05 level is 9.49. The computed value of 7.26 is less than 9.49, so the null hypothesis of no difference between the sample results and the expected results is accepted at the 0.05 level of significance.

c. Yes.

Refer to the previous discussion.

a. Verify that computed chi-square is in fact 7.26.
b. With the same level of significance (0.05), what is the decision rule? (Caution: The data have been reorganized.)
c. Do you agree that the null hypothesis should not be rejected at the 0.05 level?

EXERCISES

A reminder: The answers and method of solution for selected exercises are given in Appendix A.

1. A group of department store buyers viewed a new line of dresses and gave their opinions of them. The results were:

Opinion	Number of buyers
Outstanding	47
Excellent	45
Very good	40
Good	39
Fair	35
Undesirable	34

Source: Unpublished study, Office of Institutional Research, University of Toledo.

Because the largest number (47) indicated the new line is outstanding, the head designer thinks that this is a mandate to go into mass production of the dresses. The head sweeper (who somehow became involved in this) believes that there is not a clear mandate and claims that the opinions are evenly distributed among the six categories. He further says that the slight differences among the various counts are probably due to chance. Test the null hypothesis that there is no significant difference among the opinions of the buyers. Test at the 0.01 level of risk. Follow a formal approach, that is, state the null hypothesis, the alternative hypothesis, and so on.

2. The safety director of a large industrial plant took samples at random from the file of minor accidents and classified them according to the time the accident took place.

Time	Number of accidents
8– 9 A.M.	6
9–10 A.M.	6
10–11 A.M.	20
11–12 A.M.	8
1– 2 P.M.	7
2– 3 P.M.	8
3– 4 P.M.	19
4– 5 P.M.	6

Using the chi-square test and the 0.01 level of significance, determine whether the distribution of the number of accidents could be caused by chance. Write a brief explanation of your conclusion.

3. Column (1) gives the number of students enrolled, by college, at a midwestern university during the fall quarter.

College	(1) Number enrolled	(2) Number responding
Arts and sciences	4,700	90
Business administration	2,450	45
Education	3,250	60
Engineering	1,300	30
Law	850	15
Pharmacy	1,250	15
University college	3,400	45

The editor of the student newspaper selected names at random from each college and mailed the students chosen mail questionnaires dealing with campus activities, fees, the sports program, and so on. The numbers responding, by college, are in column (2). Using the 0.05 level, determine whether the sample response is representative of the student population.

4. A national study was conducted with respect to the major leisure indoor activity of males. The percent of the total for each activity is shown in the center column. The results of a similar study of a sample of males over 60 living in the Rocky Mountain area are given in the right column.

Major indoor activity	National results (percent of total)	Rocky Mountain study (number)
Photography	22	337
Stamp and coin collecting	19	293
Needlework, crocheting, and sewing	6	82
Greenhouse and indoor gardening	9	128
Metalworking and woodworking	12	182
Gourmet cooking	4	54
Painting and sculpture	7	99
Chess, checkers, and all others	21	325

Test at the 0.05 level that there is no difference between the national results and those of males over 60 in the Rocky Mountain area.

MANN-WHITNEY U TEST

The **Mann-Whitney test** of significance is an especially appropriate test when two *independent* and randomly selected sets of sample observations are at least *ordinal* level; that is, the data must be such that they can be ranked from low to high (or high to low).

The express purpose of the Mann-Whitney test is to *determine whether or not the two independent samples come from the same population.*

In addition to applying it to problems involving ordinal-level data, many researchers prefer to use the Mann-Whitney test instead of the Student t test (1) in cases where there is some doubt whether the level of measurement is truly interval scaled, and (2) is the data are interval level but the assumptions for the t test cannot be met.

*If the larger of the two samples has 20 or fewer observations, a **small sample** approach is followed.* Otherwise, the samples are considered large.

Small samples

Suppose there is interest in determining whether there is a difference in the mechanical aptitude of male and female assembly-line workers. To resolve the issue, nine males and five females were selected at random and each was given a mechanical aptitude test.

The usual five steps are followed in arriving at a decision regarding the observed differences in mechanical aptitude of the two groups.

Step 1. The null hypothesis H_0. There is no difference between the sexes with respect to mechanical aptitude. As usual, if the alternative hypothesis H_1 states that there is a difference, a two-tailed test would be used. If H_1, however, states that the men (or women) have *more* mechanical aptitude, a one-tailed test would be applied. A two-tailed test will be used in this illustration.

Step 2. The level of significance. It was decided that $\alpha = 0.05$.

Step 3. The statistical test. The Mann-Whitney U test is the appropriate test because the data (mechanical aptitude test scores) are to be converted to ordinal ranks for the purpose of the test. Also, it should be noted that the samples are independent—a prerequisite for the use of the Mann-Whitney U test.

Step 4. The decision rule. The critical values for the statistic U are given in Appendix L. It can be used for both one-tailed and two-tailed tests. Referring to Appendix L, note that the top table is used for a two-tailed test and the 0.05 level. Recall that nine men and five women were given the mechanical aptitude test, so $n_1 = 9$ and $n_2 = 5$. Now move horizontally across the top of the table until the number 9 is located. Then go down that column until the number opposite 5 is reached. It is 7, the critical value. The null hypothesis will be *rejected* if the computed value, designated as U, is 7 *or less*. Otherwise, it will not be rejected. (Note that this is just the opposite of the decision-making procedure followed for most other tests of significance.) The decision rule shown schematically:

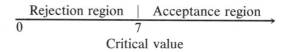

Critical value

Step 5. The decision. The nine men and five women were administered a mechanical aptitude test, and the raw test scores ranged from a high of 1,600 to a low of 600. The test scores for the males and females follow. Referring to the scores, the highest score (1,600) was earned by a man and ranked 1. The second-highest score was 1,500, also earned by a man, and it was ranked 2. The next-highest score of 1,400 was earned by a woman, and it was ranked 3. A woman was fourth ranked, a man fifth, a woman sixth, and so on. It does appear that the ranks are about evenly distributed between the two sexes. (*Note:* the scores could have been ranked from low to high, instead of from high to low.)

Men		Women	
Raw scores	*Rank*	*Raw scores*	*Rank*
1,500	2	1,400	3
1,600	1	1,200	6
670	13	780	12
800*	10.5	1,350	4
1,100	8	890	9
800*	10.5		34
1,320	5		
1,150	7		
600	14		
	71		

*Note that there are two scores of 800. Theoretically, these would be ranked 10 and 11. The tie was resolved by giving each score the arithmetic mean rank of 10.5. Had there been a tie for ranks 6, 7, and 8, each would have been awarded the arithmetic mean rank of 7. If there are a large number of ties, a correction factor is usually applied. It is somewhat involved and will not be discussed in this introductory text. (See: Siegel, S. *Nonparametric Statistics,* [New York: McGraw-Hill, 1956], pp. 123–25).

Two statistics are computed, U and U', found by:

$$U = n_1 n_2 + \frac{n_1(n_1 + 1)}{2} - \Sigma R_1 \qquad U' = n_1 n_2 + \frac{n_2(n_2 + 1)}{2} - \Sigma R_2$$

where:

n_1 is the size of one sample. There are nine men, so $n_1 = 9$.

n_2 is the size of the other sample. There are five women, so $n_2 = 5$.

ΣR_1 is the sum of the ranks for the sample designated as 1. The sum of the ranks for the men is 71.

ΣR_2 is the sum of the ranks for the sample designated as 2. The sum of the ranks for the women is 34.

Substituting the appropriate values, we get:

$$U = n_1 n_2 + \frac{n_1(n_1 + 1)}{2} - \Sigma R_1 \qquad U' = n_1 n_2 + \frac{n_2(n_2 + 1)}{2} - \Sigma R_2$$

$$= (5)(9) + \frac{9(9 + 1)}{2} - 71 \qquad = (5)(9) + \frac{5(5 + 1)}{2} - 34$$

$$= 19 \qquad\qquad\qquad\qquad = 26$$

As a check:

$$U' = n_1 n_2 - U$$
$$= (5)(9) - 19$$
$$= 26 \text{ (same as computed previously)}$$

The smaller computed U value, 19 in this problem, is used in arriving at the decision to either reject or accept the null hypothesis—namely, that there is no difference in the distribution of high and low ranks within the two samples. The computed U value of 19 is greater than the critical value of 7, and the decision rule directs that the null hypothesis not be rejected at the 0.05 level. There is no difference between the mechanical aptitude of the male and female assembly-line workers.

If, on the other hand, the mechanical aptitude test scores had resulted in the sets of scores shown in Table 17–6, a cursory examination of the rankings (which have been ordered from high to low) would lead one to conclude that these are two separate populations—one male and the other female. All the low ranks are associated with the scores of the men and all the women are ranked high. Either the computed U or U' will be decidedly less than the critical value, causing, as expected, H_0 to be rejected.

TABLE 17–6
Raw scores and ranks of males and females on the mechanical aptitude test

Males		Females	
Raw scores	Rank	Raw scores	Rank
1,200	8	1,600	1
1,190	9	1,580	2
1,175	10	1,450	3
1,160	11	1,310	4
1,097	12	1,275	5
940	13	1,250	6
800	14	1,230	7
790	15		
670	16		
650	17		
620	18		

SELF-REVIEW 17–4
---

a. H_0: There is no difference between the two sets of scores.
H_1: There is a difference.

b. 10.

Region of rejection	Region of acceptance
0	10

c.

Group 1		Group 2	
Score	Rank	Score	Rank
121	3	128	6
180	11.5	197	14
122	4	180	11.5
160	9	126	5
141	7	167	10
97	1	99	2
212	15	147	8
186	13		56.5
	63.5		

A company-sponsored course on principles of management was taken jointly be a group of middle managers and a group of supervisors. Random samples of the scores earned are:

Group 1: Middle managers. 121, 180, 122, 160, 141, 97, 212, and 186.

Group 2: Supervisors. 128, 197, 180, 126, 167, 99, and 147.

It is known that the population of scores is not normally distributed. The Student t test therefore, cannot be applied. Using the Mann-Whitney U test, a two-tailed test, and the 0.05 level:

a. State H_0 and H_1.
b. What is the critical value? Show the regions of acceptance and rejection (be careful).
c. Rank the scores from low to high (watch for ties), compute U and U' and make a decision.

$$U = (8)(7) + \frac{8(8 + 1)}{2} - 63.5$$

$$= 28.5$$

$$U' = (8)(7) + \frac{7(7 + 1)}{2} - 56.5$$

$$= 27.5$$

The smaller of the two values (27.5) falls in the region of acceptance. Accept H_0.

EXERCISES

5. Two groups of professional musicians—rock musicians and country-western musicians—are being studied. One facet of the study involves the ages of the two groups. It cannot be assumed that the two populations of ages are normal. Thus the Mann-Whitney U test is to be applied to the sample of ages. The ages of rock musicians selected at random for study are: 28, 16, 42, 29, 31, 22, 50, 42, 23, and 25. The ages of the country-western musicians: 26, 42, 65, 38, 29, 32, 59, 42, 27, 41, 46, and 18.

   Test at the 0.10 level that the country-western musicians are older than the rock musicians (be sure to use the lower table in Appendix L for the critical value).

6. One group was taught an assembly procedure using the usual sequence of steps. Another group was taught using an experimental technique. The times (in seconds) required to assembly the unit for two samples are:

   Group using
     usual steps: 41, 36, 42, 39, 29, 36, 48.

   Group using
     experimental
     technique: 21, 27, 36, 20, 19, 21, 39, 24, 22.

   Test, using the Mann-Whitney U test and the 0.05 level of risk, the statement that the experimental group required less time to assembly the unit. As usual, state the null and alternate hypothesis and the decision rule, compute U and U', and arrive at a decision.

Large samples

As the sizes of the two independent samples increase, the sampling distribution of the statistic U tends to become normally distributed. Thus, if one of the samples exceeds 20 observations, a form of the z-test is applied. The formula for z is:

$$z = \frac{\Sigma R_1 - \Sigma R_2 - (n_1 - n_2)\left[\dfrac{n_1 + n_2 + 1}{2}\right]}{\sqrt{n_1 n_2 \left[\dfrac{n_1 + n_2 + 1}{3}\right]}}$$

EXAMPLE

Continuing with the same type of problem, suppose that 15 men and 25 women were given a mechanical aptitude test. The mechanical aptitude test scores were ranked as follows.

Male ranks			Female ranks				
26	6	38	7	33	39	16	19
10	14	24	20	1	2	37	29
30	17	40	27	9	5	23	31
3	22	25	28	13	36	15	18
32	34	12	3	21	8	11	35

Is there a significant difference in the mechanical aptitude of the men and women?

SOLUTION

H_0 states that there is no difference in the mechanical aptitude of the men and women. A two-tailed test and the 0.05 level are to be used. The critical value of z is 1.96 from Appendix G. The areas of acceptance and rejection would appear as:

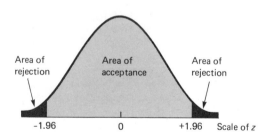

| Area of rejection | Area of acceptance | Area of rejection |

| -1.96 | 0 | +1.96 | Scale of z |

The number in each sample and the sum of the ranks are given below the following table.

Male ranks			Female ranks				
26	6	38	7	33	39	16	19
10	14	24	20	1	2	37	29
30	17	40	27	9	5	23	31
3	22	25	28	13	36	15	18
32	34	12	4	21	8	11	35
$n_1 = 15$	$\Sigma R_1 = 333$		$n_2 = 25$	$\Sigma R_2 = 487$			

Substituting the appropriate values in the formula for z, we get

$$z = \frac{\Sigma R_1 - \Sigma R_2 - (n_1 - n_2)\left[\dfrac{n_1 + n_2 + 1}{2}\right]}{\sqrt{n_1 n_2 \left[\dfrac{n_1 + n_2 + 1}{3}\right]}}$$

$$= \frac{333 - 487 - (15 - 25)\left[\dfrac{15 + 25 + 1}{2}\right]}{\sqrt{(15)(25)\left[\dfrac{15 + 25 + 1}{3}\right]}}$$

$$= 0.71$$

The computed value of z falls between 0 and ± 1.96, so the null hypothesis of no difference is not rejected at the 0.05 level.

KOLMOGOROV-SMIRNOV TWO-SAMPLE TEST

The **Kolmogorov-Smirnov two-sample test** is also a most useful test to determine whether two samples come from identical populations. It is assumed that the measurement is at least ordinal and that the two samples selected from their respective populations are independent.

To cite a simple example, suppose that samples were taken from two groups of workers, designated as Group A and Group B, and management rated their performances on the job. A rating of 3 meant that the worker was marginal and a rating of 22 indicated that the worker was outstanding (see Table 17–7).

TABLE 17-7
Performance ratings of two sample groups of workers

Performance rating		Number in
1 up to 5 (marginal) 0		5
5 up to 9 (fair) 1		3
9 up to 13 (good) 2		4
13 up to 17 (very good) 0		1
17 up to 21 (excellent) 5		2
21 up to 25 (outstanding) 7		0

A superficial examination of the ratings might lead one to conclude that there is a dramatic difference in the performance of the two groups. However, as with all sample information, there is the question of whether the observed sample differences can be attributed to chance. So the question to be explored is: Is it reasonable to assume that the two populations from which the samples were selected are different with respect to performance on the job?

The Kolmogorov-Smirnov test uses a cumulative principle. The class frequencies for both groups were cumulated (Table 17–8) and a less-than-cumulative frequency polygon was drawn.

The Kolmogorov-Smirnov (K-S) test statistic measures the maximum distance between the two cumulative distributions. That is, it is concerned with the "shapes" of the distributions and not just their means or variances. Based on the cumulative frequencies and the accompanying cumulative frequency polygon, it does seem that the wide divergences between the two sets of cumulative frequencies could not reasonably be attributed to chance. The function of the Kolmogorov-Smirnov test is to determine, at a specified level of significance, whether or not the samples came from the same (or identical) populations of workers.

TABLE 17-8
Scores and cumulative scores of Group A and Group B

Scores	Number in Group A	Number in Group B	Cumulative number for Group A	Cumulative number for Group B
1 up to 5	0	5	0	5
5 up to 9	1	3	1	8
9 up to 13	2	4	3	12
13 up to 17	0	1	3	13
17 up to 21	5	2	8	15
21 up to 25	7	0	15	15

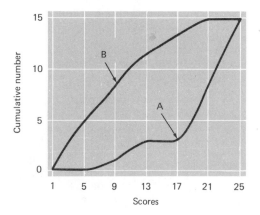

The actual test statistic depends on the size of the samples. If the numbers in each sample are equal or are 40 or less, a small-sample procedure is followed. If the samples are of unequal size or more than 40, then a large-sample approach is used. Only the large-sample approach will be presented.

EXAMPLE

Suppose that there is interest in exploring the differences among large and small banks in a region. One facet of the study concerns personnel in various levels of bank management and their knowledge of mergers, government regulations, balance sheet items, and so on. A random sample of 50 managerial personnel from large banks and 60 from small banks was selected at random. A test was administered to each manager. The results are shown in Table 17–9.

TABLE 17–9
Test results for managerial personnel in large and small banks

| | Type of bank | |
| | Large | Small |
Scores	f	f
20–29	1	30
30–39	3	15
40–49	4	8
50–59	6	5
60–69	12	2
70–79	24	0
Total	50	60

A *one-tailed test* will be considered first. The null hypothesis states that there is no difference between the two groups of managers with respect to knowledge of business matters. The alternate hypothesis is one-tailed, indicating that one group (managers from large banks) is more knowledgeable than the group of managers from small banks. The 0.05 level has been selected.

For large samples and one-tailed tests the sampling distribution follows closely chi-square with two degrees of freedom. The formula for the computed statistic χ^2 is:

$$\chi^2 = 4D^2 \left[\frac{n_1 n_2}{n_1 + n_2} \right] \text{ with 2 } df$$

where D is the largest absolute difference between the cumulative fractions, and n_1 and n_2 are the two sample sizes.

Is there a difference between the two groups of managers with respect to knowledge of business matters?

SOLUTION

Referring to Appendix H, the critical value for 2 df and the 0.05 level is 5.99. The decision rule, therefore, states that the null hypothesis will be accepted if the computed value of chi-square is less than 5.99. Otherwise, the null hypothesis will be rejected and the alternate hypothesis accepted.

As a first step, each class frequency from Table 17–9 for the large banks is expressed as a fraction of the total number (50). Likewise, each class frequency for the small banks is expressed as a fraction of the total (60). (See Table 17–10).

TABLE 17–10
Frequencies for large
and small banks
expressed as
fractions

Type of bank	Scores					
	20 up to 30	30 up to 40	40 up to 50	50 up to 60	60 up to 70	70 up to 80
Large	$\frac{1}{50}$	$\frac{3}{50}$	$\frac{4}{50}$	$\frac{6}{50}$	$\frac{12}{50}$	$\frac{24}{50}$
Small	$\frac{30}{60}$	$\frac{15}{60}$	$\frac{8}{60}$	$\frac{5}{60}$	$\frac{2}{60}$	$\frac{0}{60}$

Then (1) the fractions are cumulated (see Table 17–11), (2) the cumulative fractions are expressed as decimals, and (3) the largest absolute difference between the two sets of decimals is designated as D. It is 0.723.

TABLE 17–11
Computations for the
largest absolute
difference D

Type of bank	Scores					
	20 up to 30	30 up to 40	40 up to 50	50 up to 60	60 up to 70	70 up to 80
Large	$\frac{1}{50}$	$\frac{4}{50}$	$\frac{8}{50}$	$\frac{14}{50}$	$\frac{26}{50}$	$\frac{50}{50}$
Small	$\frac{30}{60}$	$\frac{45}{60}$	$\frac{53}{60}$	$\frac{58}{60}$	$\frac{60}{60}$	$\frac{60}{60}$
	Cumulative fractions expressed as decimals					
Large	0.020	0.080	0.160	0.280	0.520	1.000
Small	0.500	0.750	0.883	0.967	1.000	1.000
Absolute difference	0.480	0.670	0.723	0.687	0.480	0.000

$$\uparrow$$
$$\boxed{D}$$

Inserting the largest absolute difference D of 0.723 in the formula, we get:

$$\chi^2 = 4D^2\left[\frac{n_1 n_2}{n_1 + n_2}\right]$$

$$= 4(0.723)^2\left[\frac{(50)(60)}{50 + 60}\right]$$

$$= 57.0$$

We see that the critical value is 5.99. As expected, the computed value of χ^2 (57.0) falls in the area of rejection. The alternate hypothesis, which states that one group of managers (from large banks) has more knowledge of business matters, is accepted.

EXERCISES

7. A large retailer with several hundred stores throughout the country has instituted a wide-range study of its management-level associates. One of the questions to be explored is whether or not persons with master's degrees remain with the

company longer than those with bachelor's degrees. From the company's records the sample results were:

	Employees with	
Years employed	Bachelor's degree only	Master's degree
Less than 1	15	1
1 up to 3	17	9
3 up to 6	15	10
6 up to 10	10	15
10 or more	3	15

Is there sufficient evidence at the 0.05 level to conclude that the management-level associates with master's degrees tend to remain with the company longer than those with a bachelor's degree only?

8. Two groups rated a proposed advertising campaign.

Rating	Management (number)	Salespersons (number)
Superior	8	6
Good	20	15
Fair	30	20
Poor	12	9

Using a two-tailed test and the 0.05 alpha risk level, test whether there is a significant difference in the opinions of the two groups.

Now to the problem of a large sample and a *two-tailed test*. In order to apply the Kolmogorov-Smirnov test, D is determined in the usual way. Then the computed value of D is compared with the critical value from Appendix P. To illustrate, the problem from Table 17–11 will be used. The two sample sizes were 50 and 60. Suppose that $\alpha = 0.05$. Again from Table 17–11, the largest absolute difference D is 0.723. To find the critical value for this two-tailed test, refer to Appendix P and the 0.05 level. Note from Appendix P that it is determined by the following formula:

$$1.36 \sqrt{\frac{n_1 + n_2}{n_1 n_2}}$$

Inserting the appropriate values (sample sizes of 50 and 60, respectively), we find the critical value to be approximately 0.26.

$$1.36 \sqrt{\frac{n_1 + n_2}{n_1 n_2}} = 1.36 \sqrt{\frac{50 + 60}{(50)(60)}} = 0.26$$

The areas of acceptance and rejection for two samples of 50 and 60 are shown schematically:

438

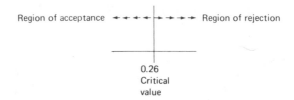

Region of acceptance ← ← ← |← → → → Region of rejection

0.26
Critical
value

Thus, for any two samples of sizes 50 and 60, the computed value of D (the largest absolute difference between the cumulative fractions) must be 0.26 or larger to reject the null hypothesis H_0 and accept H_1. The alternate hypothesis H_1 is two-tailed (merely stating that there *is* a difference).

Again, the null hypothesis is rejected (because 0.723 falls in the region of the rejection beyond [to the right of] 0.26). H_1 is accepted, indicating that there is a statistically significant difference between the managers from large banks and from small banks with respect to knowledge of business matters.

SELF-REVIEW 17-5

Sex	0	1-3	3-10	10-20	20†
			Fractions		
Male	$\frac{12}{100}$	$\frac{30}{100}$	$\frac{18}{100}$	$\frac{30}{100}$	$\frac{100}{100}$
Female	$\frac{24}{200}$	$\frac{50}{200}$	$\frac{40}{200}$	$\frac{60}{200}$	$\frac{26}{200}$
			Cumulative fractions		
Male	$\frac{12}{100}$	$\frac{42}{100}$	$\frac{60}{100}$	$\frac{90}{100}$	$\frac{100}{100}$
Female	$\frac{24}{200}$	$\frac{74}{200}$	$\frac{114}{200}$	$\frac{174}{200}$	$\frac{200}{200}$
			Cumulative fractions as decimals		
Male	0.12	0.42	0.60	0.90	1.00
Female	0.12	0.37	0.57	0.87	1.00
	0.00	0.05	0.03	0.03	0.00
		↑			
		$\boxed{D}$			

$$\text{Critical value} = 1.63 \sqrt{\frac{100 + 200}{(100)(200)}}$$

$$= 0.1996$$

0.05 is in the region of acceptance—that is, less than 0.1996. Accept the null hypothesis that there is no difference.

The numbers of days absent from work during a specified period for samples of male and female production workers are given below.

Days absent	Males	Females
0	12	24
1 up to 3	30	50
3 up to 10	18	40
10 up to 20	30	60
20 and over	10	26

Using the 0.01 level of significance and the Kolmogorov-Smirnov test, test the null hypothesis that there is no difference in the number of days absent from work for males and females. The alternate hypothesis that there is a difference.

THE WILCOXON MATCHED-PAIR SIGNED RANK TEST

A nonparametric test of significance developed by Frank Wilcoxon requires that the data be *ordinal* scaled and that the two samples be *related*. The test is usually referred to as the **Wilcoxon matched-pair signed rank test of differences.**

To illustrate its use, suppose that a radically new, experimental typewriter has been developed by the engineering section of a firm. A vice president is somewhat skeptical, however, that even after a period of transition the number of words per minute which a typist can achieve will differ significantly from those typed using the current models. Plans are to randomly select a group of typists and check their performance on the current model. Then each will be provided with the newly developed typewriter, and after a few weeks their performance will be again recorded. Thus, for each typist there will be a matched pair of data. For this type of experiment, it is said that each person is *acting as his own control*.

The difference between the two performances will be calculated and the differences ranked. The null hypothesis H_0 is that there is no difference between the typing speed using the current model and the new, experimental model.

The alternate hypothesis states that there *is* a difference. Since no direction is specified (such as, the speed attained on the new typewriter is greater than on the old model), the test of significance is *two-tailed*.

The null hypothesis is to be tested at the 0.01 level. In order to test the hypothesis, 29 typists selected at random were first given a typing test on the current models. Then each typist was assigned to one of the experimental typewriters. After a period of training, the typists were given another test. Table 17–12 shows the results and the differences.

The steps necessary to ultimately accept or reject the null hypothesis are:

1. The difference between the number of words per minute typed on the current model and the number typed on the experimental model is computed for each of the 29 typists. The differences are shown in Column (4) of Table 17–12 on the top of the following page.
2. Only the positive and negative changes are considered further; that is, if the difference between the words per minute typed on the current model and the words per minute typed on the newly developed typewriter is zero, those data will be ignored (because there is only interest in ranking actual differences). Seven out of the 29 typists showed no change in typing speed. Therefore, $N = 22$, found by $29 - 7$.
3. The 22 *absolute* differences are ordered. The 22 ordered differences are shown in column (1) of Table 17–13.
4. Each of the 22 absolute differences is ranked, starting with 1 and ending with 22 as shown in column (2) of Table 17–13.
5. Note that there are four differences of one (column 1) which have been ranked 1, 2, 3, and 4 (column 2). To resolve this tie, the average of these 4 ranks is then computed: $(1 + 2 + 3 + 4)/4 = 10/4 = 2.5$ (column 3).

TABLE 17–12
Number of words per minute typed on the current model typewriter and the number of words per minute typed on a newly developed typewriter (29 typists)

(1) Typist number	(2) Speed on current typewriter	(3) Speed on experimental typewriter	(4) Difference (3) − (2)
001	43	49	6
002	91	92	1
003	33	32	−1
004	54	54	—
005	45	65	20
006	55	90	35
007	65	64	−1
008	90	85	−5
009	53	56	3
010	70	70	—
011	76	74	−2
012	87	87	—
013	32	64	32
014	99	104	5
015	87	87	—
016	80	77	−3
017	88	88	—
018	23	32	9
019	75	90	15
020	54	51	−3
021	43	49	6
022	23	90	67
023	56	78	22
024	56	57	1
025	70	70	—
026	76	78	2
027	45	60	15
028	76	80	4
029	54	54	—

Further, the average of the rank for the differences of 2 is 5.5, found by $(5 + 6)/2$. The average of the ranks for the differences of 3 is 8, and so on. (See Table 17–13.)

6. Each assigned rank in column (3) is given the sign of the original difference. For example, two out of the four differences of one (1) are negative. Therefore, two out of the four assigned ranks of 2.5 are given a negative sign. The rank of 10 is positive because the difference of 4 opposite it is positive.

7. All the negative ranks in column (3) are summed (−38), and all the positive ranks are summed (+215). The *smaller* of the two sums (disregarding signs) is 38. The value of 38 is called the computed T. It was not really necessary to sum the positive ranks, since it could be seen that the sum of the negative ranks would be smaller than the sum of the positive ranks. However, a check on the accuracy of the computations can be made by summing the negative assigned ranks and the positive assigned ranks. This sum (disregarding signs) must equal the sum of the ranks in

TABLE 17–13
Computations for the computed *T* value for the Wilcoxon test

(1) Absolute differences ordered from smallest to largest	Rank	(2)	(3) Assigned ranks correctly signed
1	1		−2.5
1	2		−2.5
1	3		2.5
1	4		2.5
2	5		−5.5
2	6		5.5
3	7		−8
3	8		−8
3	9		8
4	10		10
5	11		−11.5
5	12		11.5
6	13		13.5
6	14		13.5
9	15		15
15	16		16.5
15	17		16.5
20	18		18
22	19		19
32	20		20
35	21		21
67	22		22

column (2). In this case $38 + 215 = 253$, which is the same as the sum of column (2).

Recall that the sum of the negative ranks is 38 and the sum of the positive ranks is 215. If any improvement in proficiency were exactly offset by a loss in proficiency, the two sums would have been about 126.5, found by $(38 + 215)/2$.

The Wilcoxon critical value in Appendix F for $N = 22$ at the 0.01 level of significance and a two-tailed test is 48. This indicates that a computed T value of greater than 48 to (and including) 126.5 could result by chance; that is, a computed T value greater than 48 but ≤ 126.5 would indicate that the sum of the positive and negative ranks do *not* depart significantly from zero.

The decision rule is shown schematically:

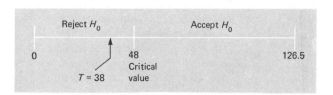

Since the computed T-value of 38 is less than the critical T-value of 48, the null hypothesis—which states that there is no difference in the typing speed using the current model and the experimental model—is *rejected* at the 0.01 level. H_1 is accepted. Such a large imbalance (-38 and $+215$) prevents us from accepting the null hypothesis.

SELF-REVIEW 17-6

a. $N = 10$.

b.

Before	After	Differ-ence	Ordered	Ranks	Signed ranks
17	18	+1	1	1	−1.5
21	23	+2	1	2	+1.5
25	22	−3	2	3	+3
15	25	+10	3	4	−5
10	28	+18	3	5	+5
16	16	—	3	6	+5
10	22	+12	6	7	+7
20	19	−1	10	8	+8
17	20	+3	12	9	+9
24	30	+6	18	10	+10
23	26	+3			

Sum of negative signed ranks is -6.5, the positive 48.5. From Appendix F, one-tailed test, $N = 10$, the critical value is 10. Since 6.5 is less than 10, reject the null hypothesis and accept the alternate. New procedures did increase production.

A record of production for each machine operator was kept over a period of time. Certain changes in the production procedure were suggested, and a group of 11 operators was picked as an experimental test group to determine whether new procedures were worthwhile. Their productions before and after the new procedures were established were as follows:

Operator	Production before	Production after
S.M.	17	18
D. J.	21	23
M. D.	25	22
B. B.	15	25
M. F.	10	28
A. A.	16	16
U. Z.	10	22
Y. U.	20	19
U. T.	17	20
Y. H.	24	30
Y. Y.	23	26

a. How many usable pairs are there? That is, what is N?

b. Using the Wilcoxon signed rank test, determine whether the new procedures actually increased production. Use the 0.05 level and a one-tailed test.

EXERCISES

9. A new assembly-line procedure has been suggested by Mr. Mump. In order to test whether the new procedure is superior to the old procedure, a sample group of 15 men was selected at random. First, their production under the old system was determined. Then the new Mump procedure was introduced. After an appropriate break-in period, their production was measured again. The results were:

Employee	Production Old system	Mump method
A 60		64
B 40		52
C 59		58
D 30		37
E 70		71
F 78		83
G 43		46
H 40		52
I 87		84
J 80		80
K 56		57
L 21		21
M 99		108
N 50		56
O 56		62

Test using the 0.05 level that production under the new Mump method is greater than under the old method.

a. State the null and alternate hypotheses.
b. State the decision rule.
c. Arrive at a decision regarding the null hypothesis.

CHAPTER SUMMARY

Tests of hypotheses about a population mean, two means, or more than two means in previous chapters made certain assumptions. One assumption is that the populations from which the samples are selected are normally distributed. Nonparametric tests, such as chi-square, the Mann-Whitney U test, the Kolmogorov-Smirnov test, and the Wilcoxon test are distribution-free, implying that they are free of assumptions. They are appropriate generally when the populations are not normally distributed.

The chi-square test is commonly used to find out if there is a difference between two sets of data, one called the observed frequencies and the other the expected frequencies. The data may be at any level of measurement. The usual five-step hypothesis-testing steps are used, namely, the null and alternate hypotheses are stated, a level of significance is chosen, the appropriate test statistic is selected, a decision rule is set up, and, based on the sample results, a decision is made. Chi-square should not be used, however, if more than 20 percent of the expected frequency cells have frequencies less than five.

The Mann-Whitney U test requires that the data be at least ordinal scaled (because to proceed with the test the observations must be ranked). If the larger of the two independent samples has 20 or fewer observations, a small-sample approach is followed. Two values are computed, U and U'. The smaller of the two values is compared with the critical value to arrive at a decision. If one of the samples is greater than 20, a large-sample approach is followed, with z, the standard normal distribution, being the test statistic.

The Kolmogorov-Smirnov two-sample test also requires that the measurement level be ordinal and the samples be independent. It is very useful for testing for a difference between two distributions when the observations have been organized into classes such as:

Job performance	Group A	Group B
Excellent	17	13
Very good	122	103
Good	81	97
Fair	19	67
Unsatisfactory	3	45

The two-tailed test uses a special table (Appendix P) for the critical value. A one-tailed test uses χ^2 as the test statistic with 2 degrees of freedom.

The Wilcoxon matched-pair signed rank test requires that the two samples be at least at the ordinal level of measurement, and related. As an example, employees perform tasks using the usual procedure, and the number of units each employee produces during a specified period is recorded. Then the same group is trained to do the task another way. The number of units each employee produces under this new method is also recorded. The matched pairs might appear as:

	Production	
Employee	Old method	New method
M. Szur	80	85
S. Jones	79	78
A. Ward	77	77

CHAPTER OUTLINE

Nonparametric tests of hypotheses: One-sample and two-sample tests

I. A. *Objective.* To check the validity of statements involving nominal- and ordinal-level measurement for one and two samples.

II. Chi-square one-sample test. Often referred to as the chi-square goodness of fit test. Can be applied if data are nominal. Also can be used for ordinal and interval levels of measurement.

A. *Assumptions.* Categories are mutually exclusive (a person cannot be male and female at same time). Also, sample observations are independent, meaning that the second random selection is in no way affected by the first selection, and so on.

B. *Formula.*

$$\chi^2 = \sum \frac{(f_0 - f_e)^2}{f_e}$$

C. *Illustration of use.* Question: Are the industrial accidents in the factory evenly distributed throughout the work week? As is common to all test of significance, the first step is to set up null and alternate hypotheses. Then a level of significance is selected, and so on. A review of 120 accident cases revealed:

	Mon	Tues	Wed	Thurs	Fri	Total
Observed number	24	24	25	26	21	120
Expected number	24	24	24	24	24	120

The expected number is based on the assumption that the null hypothesis is true; that is, there is no difference in the number of accidents with respect to the day of the week. By applying the χ^2 test, a decision can be made about whether the differences between the observed and expected frequencies are or are not due to sampling.

D. *Limitations.* If there are only two cells, the frequency in each cell should be five or more. And, for more than two cells, not more than one fifth of the cells containing the *expected* frequencies should have counts of less than five. Test cannot be applied if any of the expected frequencies are zero.

III. Mann-Whitney U test.

A. *Assumptions.* At least ordinal level of measurement. Two independent and randomly selected samples.

B. *Small samples.* Designated as small if larger of two samples has 20 or fewer observations.

1. *Procedure.* Rank all the data from low to high, or vice versa. Then compute U and U'.

$$U = n_1 n_2 + \frac{n_1(n_1 + 1)}{2} - \Sigma R_1$$

$$U' = n_1 n_2 + \frac{n_2(n_2 + 1)}{2} - \Sigma R_2$$

where:

n_1 and n_2 are the two sample sizes.
ΣR_1 is the sum of the ranks for one sample.
ΣR_2 is the sum of the ranks for the other sample.

The *smaller* computed U value is used in reaching a decision about whether to accept or reject the null hypothesis. Appendix L gives critical values.

C. *Large samples.* Designated as large, if larger of two samples has 21 or more observations.

1. *Procedure.* Again, rank all the data from low to high, or vice versa. Then compute z.

$$z = \frac{\Sigma R_1 - \Sigma R_2 - (n_1 - n_2)\left[\frac{n_1 + n_2 + 1}{2}\right]}{\sqrt{n_1 n_2 \left[\frac{n_1 + n_2 + 1}{3}\right]}}$$

Accept or reject H_0 based on the critical value of z in Appendix G.

IV. Kolmogorov-Smirnov two-sample test of significance.
   A. *Objective*. To accept or reject a null hypothesis of no difference with respect to two populations. Measurement must be at least ordinal level; the two samples must be independent.
   B. *Formulas*. For large samples (over 40):
      One-tailed test:

$$\chi^2 = 4D^2 \left[\frac{n_1 n_2}{n_1 + n_2} \right] \text{ with 2 } df$$

   Two-tailed test: Consult Appendix P. For the 0.05 level, it is

$$1.36 \sqrt{\frac{n_1 + n_2}{n_1 n_2}}$$

   C. *Procedure*.
      1. For each frequency distribution, express each class frequency as a fraction of the total number of frequencies.
      2. For each frequency distribution, cumulate the cumulative fractions.
      3. Express the cumulative fractions as decimals.
      4. Find the absolute difference between each of the two sets of decimals.
      5. Locate the largest absolute difference. It is designated as D.
   D. *Simple example:*

Hourly wages	Group A f	Group B f	Fractions A	Fractions B	Cumulative fractions A	Cumulative fractions B	Decimals A	Decimals B	Absolute difference
$2 up to $4	20	50	$\frac{20}{100}$	$\frac{50}{200}$	$\frac{20}{100}$	$\frac{50}{200}$	0.20	0.25	0.05
4 up to 6	50	100	$\frac{50}{100}$	$\frac{100}{200}$	$\frac{70}{100}$	$\frac{150}{200}$	0.70	0.75	0.05
6 up to 8	30	50	$\frac{30}{100}$	$\frac{50}{200}$	$\frac{100}{100}$	$\frac{200}{200}$	1.00	1.00	0
Totals	100	200							

   The largest absolute difference $D = 0.05$.
   E. *Rationale.* if the largest absolute difference D is so large that is cannot be attributed to chance, the null hypothesis is rejected.
V. Wilcoxon matched-pair signed rank test.
   A. *Assumptions*. Data must be at least *ordinal* scaled and the two samples *related*. One way to accomplish this is to have *each person act as his or her own control*, meaning that the same person (or item) is in both sample 1 and sample 2.
   B. *Uses*. Before and after situations. Example: Person assembles

plug-in unit using old method, then same person assembles it using new method. Is there any difference in the two methods?
C. *Procedure.*
1. Rank absolute differences between old method and new method.
2. Recognize ties and give ranks appropriate signs.
3. Sum negative ranks and positive ranks.
4. Disregarding signs, the smaller of the two sums is the computed T value.
5. Refer to Appendix F for critical value and accept or reject H_0.
D. *Simple example.*

Worker	Method Old	New	Difference	Absolute differences rank	Rank	Signed rank
Joe	16	20	−4	1	1	1
Sam	8	9	+1	4	2	−2.5
~~Sue~~	~~18~~	~~18~~	~~0~~	4	3	+2.5
Pete	36	44	+8	8	4	4
June	21	17	+4			

Note: Sum positives = 7.5, sum negative = −2.5.
Smaller absolute sum is $T.T = -2.5$
T of −2.5 is compared with critical value from Appendix F, and H_0 is either accepted or rejected.

CHAPTER EXERCISES

10. A sample of unpaid balances on Southwestern Charge accounts as of September 1 was organized into the following frequency distribution.

Size of unpaid balance	Number of accounts
Less than $20	13
$20 but under $40	10
$40 but under $60	15
$60 but under $80	14
$80 but under $100	9
$100 but under $150	12
$150 and over	11

The hypothesis that the unpaid balances are evenly distributed among the seven categories is to be tested at the 0.01 level of risk.
a. State the null and alternate hypotheses.
b. Show the decision rule graphically.
c. Arrive at a decision.

11. One statement in a questionnaire sent to both white and nonwhite persons dealt with housing integration. The null hypothesis states that there is no difference in the reactions of the whites and nonwhites to the statement. The alternate hypothesis states there is a difference in their reactions. A sample of the responses follows.

Reactions to statement	Whites (number)	Nonwhites (number)
Strongly agree	44	3
Agree	26	4
No opinion (neutral)	10	10
Disagree	12	11
Strongly disagree	8	52

a. What test should be applied?

b. State the decision rule.

c. Arrive at a decision.

12. A group of buyers of women's apparel were asked to view a rather innovative group of sportswear. Each male and female buyer was asked to rate the group on a scale of 1 to 100, with 1 representing absolutely no sales appeal and 100 substantial sales appeal. The ratings of the sample responses of 10 males and 12 females are:

Females		Males	
80	79	74	96
62	71	77	85
90	82	62	64
71	83	86	84
62	60	65	84
73	87	72	

Test whether there is a difference between the ratings of the female and male buyers. Use a two-tailed test and the 0.05 level.

13. The 950 faculty members of a large university decided that, although democratic, the meetings of the entire faculty to pass on matters of policy were too unmanageable. The faculty voted, therefore, to turn the decision making over to 80 faculty selected at random. The names of all 950 faculty were placed in a box, and 80 names were selected. The composition of the policy group, by rank, is:

Rank	Number in entire faculty	Number in policy group
Professor	124	11
Associate professor	247	18
Assistant professor	384	32
Instructor	195	19

A member of the faculty claims that the policy group selected at random is not representative of the faculty ranks. Explore this claim using an appropriate statistical test. You make a decision regarding the level of significance, etc.

14. It has been suggested that the daily production of a subassembly would be increased if better portable lighting was installed and background music and free coffee and doughnuts were provided during the day. Management agreed to try the scheme for a limited time. The number of subassemblies produced per week for a small test group of employees follows.

Employee	Past production record	Production after installing lighting, music, etc.
JD	23	33
SB	26	26
MD	24	30
RCF	17	25
MF	20	19
UHH	24	22
IB	30	29
WWJ	21	25
OP	25	22
CD	21	23
PA	16	17
RRT	20	15
AT	17	9
QQ	23	30

Using the Wilcoxon signed rank test, determine whether the suggested changes are worthwhile—that is, whether they increased production.

a. State the null hypothesis.

b. You decide on the alternate hypothesis.

c. You decide on the level of significance.

d. State the decision rule.

e. Compute T and arrive at a decision.

15. The employee-relations manager has been given the project of reviewing job satisfaction. As an experiment, she designed a simple questionnaire and selected a random sample from the Dorsett plant and another sample of employees from the Trenton plant. For one of the questions, the employee merely checked one of four possible alternatives. The results were:

Job satisfaction	Number of employees	
	Dorsett	Trenton
Extremely happy	10	15
Somewhat happy	20	30
Somewhat unhappy	10	20
Extremely unhappy	10	35

a. Using the 0.05 level and the appropriate test or hypotheses, test the null hypothesis and there is no difference in job satsifaction in the Dorsett and Trenton plants. Choose the alternate hypothesis.

b. State the decision rule.

c. Show the essential calculations.

d. Arrive at a decision and interpret your findings.

16. A large manufacturing company has a number of management training programs that are either voluntary or required. At the end of each program the participants are given a rating, part of which is based on objective tests and the other part on the subjective judgment of the persons conducting the course. The

ratings can be used by management for promotion and for pay raises. A group has charged that nonwhites are being discriminated against in the ratings. To explore the charges, a sample of the ratings given white employees and non-white employees during the past six months revealed the following ratings:

Nonwhite	White	Nonwhite	White
9	86	96	70
52	62	71	76
47	51	69	90
91	58	39	79
87	46	87	67
17	93	68	31
78	95	87	
87	21	70	
50	46	90	

Explore the charges by:

a. Stating the null hypothesis and deciding on an alternate hypothesis.
b. Selecting a level of significance.
c. Stating the decision rule.
d. Showing the computations.
e. Accepting or rejecting the null hypothesis and stating the findings.

CHAPTER SELF-REVIEW EXAMINATION

Do all the problems, and then check your answers against those in Appendix A. Score each problem 50 points.

1. Suppose past experience revealed that 1 out of every 10 automobiles sold of a certain make included practically all of the accessories (such as air conditioning, radio, tinted glass). Three out of 10 purchasers added a moderate amount; 5 out of 10, a few accessories; and 1 out of 10, none. A random sample of the purchases made during the first month of the current selling season revealed that 7 new owners added practically all of the accessories; 34 purchased a moderate amount; 48, a few accessories; and 11, none. Test at the 0.01 level of risk that there has been no change in the purchasing habits with respect to the purchase of accessories.

2. A study of the behavior of the residents of a prison revealed that for a random sample of first offenders, 12 had exemplary behavior, 13 had very good behavior, 20 had good behavior, 9 had fair behavior, and 6 had unsatisfactory behavior. A similar study of the residents who were second offenders revealed that 14 had exemplary behavior; 20, very good; 30, good; 12, fair; and 4, unsatisfactory behavior in prison. Test at the 0.01 level that there is no difference in the be-havior patterns of the two groups. H_1 states that there is a difference.

INTRODUCTION

Chapter 17 dealt with four **nonparametric tests of hypotheses**, commonly referred to as **distribution-free tests.** Recall that distribution-free tests do not require that any assumptions be made about the population (such as normality). The four tests we examined are designed to test a hypothesis involving one sample or two samples.

Three very useful nonparametric tests of significance are presented in this chapter to illustrate the testing procedure when *more than two samples are involved.* These are usually designated as *k* samples. The purpose of these tests is to find out whether the sample results differ from each other. To put it another way, *these tests have been designed to determine whether the k samples have been selected from identical populations (or from the same population).*

The first two tests—the *Cochran Q test* and the *Friedman two-way analysis of variance*—deal with random samples that are *related* in some way. The third test is another use of the chi-squared statistic discussed in the previous chapter.

Nonparametric tests of hypotheses: More than two samples

THE COCHRAN Q TEST

Designed by W. G. Cochran in the 1950s, the *Q test* requires only *nominal-level information* and is based on three or more *related* sets of observations.

EXAMPLE

Suppose management wants to evaluate the effectiveness of four different methods of presenting in-plant training topics to supervisory employees. The four different methods are television, lecture, programmed instruction, and a combination of methods. Before inaugurating the training program companywide, a randomly selected pilot group of 20 supervisors was chosen to test the effectiveness of the four proposed methods.

A topic, such as the supervision of new employees, was presented to the pilot group using one of the four methods. At the end of the presentation each supervisor was asked to rate the method as either "effective" or "not effective." The response of each supervisor was coded into either a 1 for "effective" or a 0 for "not effective." Note in Table 18–1 that a few of the supervisors rated all of the methods effective, but other supervisors considered some or none of them effective.

Further, note that a total of 4 out of the 20 supervisors indicated that television is an effective medium, 5 considered the lecture method to be effective, and so on.

TABLE 18–1
Responses of supervisors to four methods of presentation

Supervisor number	(1) Television only	(2) Lecture only	(3) Programmed instruction	(4) Combination of methods	L	L^2
1	0	0	1	1	2	4
2	1	0	0	1	2	4
3	0	1	0	0	1	1
4	0	0	0	0	0	0
5	0	0	0	1	1	1
6	0	0	1	1	2	4
7	0	1	0	0	1	1
8	0	0	0	0	0	0
9	1	0	0	1	2	4
10	1	1	1	1	4	16
11	0	0	1	1	2	4
12	0	0	0	0	0	0
13	0	0	0	0	0	0
14	1	1	0	1	3	9
15	0	0	0	1	1	1
16	0	0	1	1	2	4
17	0	1	0	1	2	4
18	0	0	0	1	1	1
19	0	0	1	0	1	1
20	0	0	1	1	2	4
Total	4	5	7	13	29	63
	ΣS_1	ΣS_2	ΣS_3	ΣS_4	ΣL	ΣL^2

The question to be resolved by the Cochran Q test is whether there is a difference in effectiveness among the four methods of presentation. (The two columns on the right will be explained shortly.)

SOLUTION

The null hypothesis H_0 is that there is no difference with regard to effective–not effective reactions to the methods of presentation. H_1, the alternate hypothesis, states that there is a difference among the k samples with respect to effective–not effective reactions. This test will always be two-tailed because there is no way to specify a direction in k dimensions.

The appropriate statistical test is the Cochran Q test because the data are nominal level, there are two related samples (meaning in this problem that each supervisor is acting as his own control), and the responses of the supervisors can be dichotomized into "effective" and "noneffective."

The 0.05 level of significance was selected. This means that there is a 5 percent chance of committing a Type I error—that is, rejecting the null hypothesis when it should have been accepted.

The general formula for Q is:

$$Q = \frac{(k-1)[k\Sigma S_1^2 - (\Sigma S_j)^2]}{k(\Sigma L) - \Sigma L^2}$$

Applied to this problem, Q would be:

$$Q = \frac{(k-1)[k(\Sigma S_1^2 + \Sigma S_2^2 + \Sigma S_3^2 + \Sigma S_4^2) - (\Sigma L)^2]}{k(\Sigma L) - \Sigma L^2}$$

where:

k is the number of samples. In this problem it is the number of different teaching methods. There are four.

ΣS_1 is the sum of the favorable (effective) responses to the television presentation. ΣS_2 is the sum of the favorable responses to the lecture method, and so on.

L is the total number of favorable (effective) responses for *each* supervisor. For example, the first supervisor sampled thought that two methods of instruction were effective. The total of all of the effective responses is ΣL, or 29. (Refer back to Table 18–1.)

ΣL^2 directs one to square the total number of favorable (effective) responses for each supervisor and then to sum them. The sum of L^2 is 63. (Refer back to Table 18–1.)

When the null hypothesis is true, the sampling distribution of Q approximates χ^2 with $k-1$ degrees of freedom. In this problem there are four samples, and $k-1=3$ df. Chart 18–1 shows the decision rule schematically—do not reject the null hypothesis if the computed value of Q

**CHART 18–1
Regions of
acceptance and
rejection for
Cochran's Q, $\alpha = 0.05$**

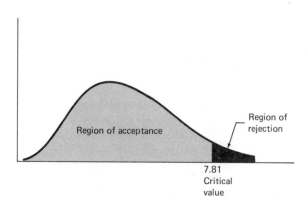

Region of acceptance

Region of rejection

7.81
Critical
value

is less than the critical value of 7.81, but reject H_0 if Q is 7.81 or greater. (The critical value is found in Appendix H, an α of 0.05 and 3 *df*.)

Solving for Q, we get

$$Q = \frac{(k-1)[k(\Sigma S_1^2 + \Sigma S_2^2 + \Sigma S_3^2 + \Sigma S_4^2) - (\Sigma L)^2]}{k(\Sigma L) - \Sigma L^2}$$

$$= \frac{(4-1)[4\{4^2 + 5^2 + 7^2 + (13)^2\} - (29)^2]}{4(29) - 63}$$

$$= 11.04$$

The computed value of Q falls in the area beyond 7.81, so the null hypothesis is rejected at the 0.05 level. The alternative hypothesis H_1, which states that there is a difference in the number of favorable responses with respect to the four teaching methods, is accepted.

It should be noted that the Cochran Q test is designed only to test whether or not there is an *overall difference* among the four teaching methods. In rejecting H_0 and accepting H_1 it does not indicate which teaching method is the most effective. It merely states that there is a difference among the k samples and the difference is not due to chance. If one wished to test whether the proportion of supervisors favoring the combination of methods is greater than, say, the proportion who thought the lecture methods was effective, the test for the difference between two population proportions covered in Chapter 14 would be applied.

SELF-REVIEW 18–1

a. The null hypothesis states that there is no overall difference in the responses of the tasters with respect to the three newly developed cakes.

b. Nominal level.

c. There are $k - 1$ or $3 - 1 = 2$ degrees of freedom. The critical value of chi-square at the 0.10 level of 9.21 (Appendix H). If the computed

(A reminder: Cover the answers in the left-hand column.)

The national known baker of that famous cupcake Yummy has developed three new cakes. They all look like Yummy, but they differ in taste. In order to collect some preliminary information, the baker asked a randomly selected group of 10 persons who eat Yummys regularly to test them. First,

value of Q is less than 9.21, the null hypothesis of no overall difference will be accepted. Otherwise, it will be rejected.

d. Cochran's Q was computed to be 16.2, found by (0 = no, 1 = yes):

Tester	No. 1	No. 2	No. 3	L	L²
1........	0	1	0	1	1
2........	0	1	1	2	4
3........	0	1	0	1	1
4........	0	1	0	1	1
5........	1	1	1	3	9
6........	0	1	0	1	1
7........	0	1	0	1	1
8........	0	1	0	1	1
9........	0	1	0	1	1
10........	0	1	0	1	1
S_j	1	10	2	13	21

Then:

$$Q = \frac{(3-1)[3(1^2 + (10)^2 + 2^2) - (13)^2]}{3(13) - 21}$$

$$= \frac{292}{18} = 16.2$$

The computed value of Q falls in the area beyond 9.21, and the null hypothesis is rejected at the 0.10 level. H_1, which states there is an overall difference, is accepted.

e. No. It only indicates that there is an overall difference in the responses with respect to the three cupcakes. If only one cupcake is to be marketed, the next logical step would be to design an experiment and determine the proportion who liked the original Yummy the best and the proportion who liked no. 2 the best.

each person tasted one of the new cakes designated only as no. 1. Each person then indicated whether he or she liked it better than Yummy. The same procedure was followed for cakes no. 2 and no. 3. The responses were as shown in the following table. (Yes indicates that the person liked it better than Yummy; no indicates that he did not like it better than Yummy.)

	Cake		
Tester	No. 1	No. 2	No. 3
1	No	Yes	No
2	No	Yes	Yes
3	No	Yes	No
4	No	Yes	No
5	Yes	Yes	Yes
6	No	Yes	No
7	No	Yes	No
8	No	Yes	No
9	No	Yes	No
10	No	Yes	No

The baker wants to determine if there is an overall difference with respect to the reactions of the test group toward the three newly developed cakes.

a. State the null hypothesis.
b. What level of measurement is implied in the problem?
c. Using the 0.10 level of significance and a two-tailed test, state the decision rule.
d. Arrive at a decision with respect to the three cakes.
e. Does this indicate that cake no. 2 is better than Yummy? Explain.

EXERCISES   A reminder: the answers and method of solution for selected exercises are given in Appendix A.

1. A unique product has been developed, and five different selling approaches have been suggested. They range from a very low profile (no pressure on the consumer to buy) to a very high-pressure sales approach. A test group has been selected to evaluate the approaches. After a selling demonstration is completed, each person rates it either positive or negative, with positive meaning that the approach is not objectionable. A negative reaction to the selling demonstration indicates that the consumer would probably not purchase the item. The results are shown in the following table. Note, for example, that Ms. Martin had no objections to the very low profile or the low profile approach. She did, however, object to the moderate, high-, and very high-pressure selling.

a. Test at the 0.05 level of risk whether or not there is an overall difference in their reactions. Use a systematic procedure by stating the null hypothesis, the alternate hypothesis, the decision rule, and so on.

b. What does your finding indicate to the developer of the new and unique product?

Name of person	Very low profile	Low profile	Moderate pressure	High pressure	Very high pressure
Ms. Martin	+	+	−	−	−
Ms. Urfer	+	−	−	−	−
Ms. Jones	−	−	−	−	−
Ms. Arnold	+	+	+	+	−
Ms. Cohan	+	+	+	+	+
Ms. Baker	−	−	+	+	−
Ms. Deward	−	−	−	−	+
Ms. James	−	−	+	+	+
Ms. Overlander	−	−	−	−	+
Ms. Solberg	+	−	−	−	−
Ms. Stephens	+	+	+	+	−
Ms. Kingsley	+	+	+	+	+

2. Travel Along, a manufacturer of campers and recreation trailers, had developed three new floor plans for its line of campers. In order to get the reactions of persons owning a Travel Along camper, the plans and other information were mailed to a random sample of the owners. If the respondent liked the plan, he or she merely wrote in "Yes." Those who did not like the suggested model wrote in "No." The results are shown below.

Owner no.	Floor plan		
	A	B	C
1	Yes	No	No
2	Yes	Yes	No
3	No	No	No
4	Yes	No	No
5	Yes	No	No
6	Yes	No	Yes
7	No	Yes	No
8	No	No	No
9	Yes	No	No
10	Yes	No	No
11	Yes	No	No
12	Yes	No	No
13	Yes	Yes	Yes
14	Yes	No	No
15	Yes	No	No

The problem involves determining whether or not there is an overall difference in reactions to the three newly developed models. Test at the 0.05 level.

a. State the null hypothesis and the alternate hypothesis.

b. What is the appropriate statistical test?

c. State the decision rule.

d. Show the necessary computations.

e. Interpret the findings.

THE FRIEDMAN TWO-WAY ANALYSIS OF VARIANCE

Cochran's Q test determines whether three or more samples are significantly different with respect to some characteristic. Its application assumes that the observations are nominal level and that the k samples are related (usually by having each subject act as his or her own control).

A test of significance designed by M. Friedman in the late 1930s is applicable when the observations are *ordinal level,* and there are k *related* samples. Because it is based on a higher level of measurement, Friedman's test will be generally more powerful than Cochran's test.

EXAMPLE

Suppose that a newly developed training program is divided into four units. Each unit is presented using a different technique. The first group to enter the program consisted of 14 employees selected at random. At the conclusion of each unit the 14 employees were given an examination and awarded a performance score (see Table 18–2).

TABLE 18–2 Performance scores for each training technique

Name of employee (N = 14)	Technique I	Technique II	Technique III	Technique IV
Mr. J. Jones	20	6	9	15
Ms. J. U. Urfer	5	12	19	10
Mr. J. Jones, Jr.	11	21	8	16
Ms. N. O. Smith	21	18	30	15
Ms. S. G. East	8	12	20	16
Mr. R. D. Stevens	9	7	10	12
Ms. S. M. Over	21	20	16	10
Mr. A. N. Papish	18	27	9	12
Mr. M. Y. Ort	30	16	22	21
Mr. A. Z. Arthur	22	27	19	18
Mr. L. K. Kimmel	10	8	4	12
Ms. O. N. Breezie	6	12	7	14
Mr. J. J. Brim	10	11	21	20
Mr. N. Goode	14	11	23	27

Before continuing, note the similarity between the problem and the previous problem to which the Cochran Q test was applied. The objective in both problems is the same—to determine if there is a difference in the overall effectiveness of four techniques or methods. In the previous section, however, the response of the supervisors could only be dichotomized into "effective" or "not effective"; that is, the data were nominal level of measurement. The Friedman test can be applied in this problem because the performance scores are *ordinal scaled,* meaning that the scores of an employee can be ranked from low to high, or vice versa.

Is there a difference in the overall effectiveness of the four techniques?

SOLUTION

The null and alternative hypotheses are:

H_0: There is no difference in the overall effectiveness of the four techniques.

H_1: There is a difference with respect to the overall effectiveness of the four techniques.

It was decided to test the null hypothesis at the 0.05 level.

The Friedman two-way analysis of variance is the appropriate statistical test because (1) there are k samples, (2) the samples are related (each employee acts as his or her own control by taking all four training units), and (3) the performance scores are ordinal level of measurement.

The statistic that Friedman designated as χ_r^2 approximates the chi-square distribution with $k - 1$ degrees of freedom. The decision rule can, therefore, be formulated by referring to the table of critical values of chi-square (Appendix H). The critical value of chi-square is 7.81. As before, k stands for the number of samples. There are four samples (techniques), $k - 1 = 3\ df$, and $\alpha = 0.05$. As usual, the null hypothesis will not be rejected if the computed value of χ_r^2 is less than the critical value of 7.81. Otherwise, it will be rejected.

In order to apply the Friedman test, the performance scores of each employee are ranked from low to high (or vice versa). It is immaterial which system is adopted, but the same procedure must be maintained throughout. As an example, referring back to Table 18–2, Mr. J. Jones scored 20, 6, 9, and 15, respectively, for the four samples (training units). The lowest number (6) is ranked 1, the score of 9 is ranked 2, 15 is ranked 3, and the highest score (20) is ranked 4. See Table 18–3 for these ranks.

TABLE 18–3
Performance scores ranked from low to high

Name of employee (N = 14)	Technique I	Technique II	Technique III	Technique IV
Mr. J. Jones	4	1	2	3
Ms. J. U. Urder	1	3	4	2
Mr. J. Jones, Jr.	2	4	1	3
Ms. N. O. Smith	3	2	4	1
Ms. S. G. East	1	2	4	3
Mr. R. D. Stevens	2	1	3	4
Ms. S. M. Over	4	3	2	1
Mr. A. N. Papish	3	4	1	2
Mr. M. Y. Ort	4	1	3	2
Mr. A. Z. Arthur	3	4	2	1
Mr. L. K. Kimmel	3	2	1	4
Ms. O. N. Breezie	1	3	2	4
Mr. J. J. Brim	1	2	4	3
Mr. N. Goode	2	1	3	4
Total	34	33	36	37
	T_1	T_2	T_3	T_4

The general formula for Friedman's χ_r^2 is:

$$\chi_r^2 = \frac{12}{Nk(k+1)} [T_1^2 + T_2^2 + \cdots + T_k^2] - [3N(k+1)]$$

Applied to this problem it is:

$$\chi_r^2 = \frac{12}{Nk(k+1)} [T_1^2 + T_2^2 + T_3^2 + T_4^2] - [3N(k+1)]$$

where:

N is the total number in the sample. There are 14.

k is the number of related samples (columns). There are four.

T_1 is the sum of the ranks for one of the samples (Technique I), T_2 is the sum of the ranks for the second sample (Technique II), and so on.

Substituting the appropriate values, we get

$$\chi_r^2 = \frac{12}{(14)(4)(4+1)} [(34)^2 + (33)^2 + (36)^2 + (37)^2] - [3(14)(4+1)]$$

$$= \frac{12}{280} [4{,}910] - 210$$

$$= 0.43$$

The computed value of χ_r^2 (0.43) is less than the critical value of chi-square (7.81). The null hypothesis H_0, therefore, is not rejected at the 0.05 level. There is no difference in the overall effectiveness of the four techniques.

SELF-REVIEW 18-2

a. H_0: There is no difference with respect to the overall agreement on the hood ornaments.

    H_1: There is a difference.

b. There are $k - 1 = 6 - 1 = 5$ degrees of freedom. The critical value is 15.09. Accept if computed chi-square is less than 15.09. Otherwise reject null hypothesis.

c.

			Hood ornament			
Expert	A	B	C	D	E	F
MM	4	3	5	1	6	2
GB	5	6	2	3	1	4
VR	2	1	3	6	5	4
UU	6	3	4	2	5	1
IN	1	2	5	4	6	3
	18	15	19	16	23	14

Hood ornament ranked from high to low

Six hood ornaments are being considered for a new prestige automobile. Each ornament was rated on a scale of 1 to 100 (with 100 being the most desirable) by a sample of design experts. Ties were not allowed. The 0.01 level is to be used. The results are:

Design	Hood ornament					
expert	A	B	C	D	E	F
MM	50	62	10	97	3	81
GB	61	8	86	71	91	64
VR	80	89	70	20	50	62
UU	40	70	60	80	50	90
IN	95	80	40	70	15	75

a. State the null and alternate hypotheses.

b. Give the decision rule.

c. Compute χ_r^2.

d. Arrive at a decision.

$\chi_r^2 = 3.06$, found by

$$\chi_r^2 = \frac{12}{5(6)(6 + 1)} [(18)^2 + (15)^2 + (19)^2 + (16)^2$$

$$+ (23)^2 + (14)^2] - 3(5)(6 + 1)$$

$$= [0.0571428(1891)] - 105 = 3.06$$

d. Since 3.06 is less than 15.09, do not reject the null hypothesis.

EXERCISES

3. The Lifeguard Association wants to publish instructions on how to tow a drowning person a considerable distance. A sample of experienced lifeguards was asked to try three methods and rate them 1, 2, 3, with 1 being the most desirable. The ratings are:

		Method	
Lifeguard	A	B	C
Feffers	1	2	3
Simon	2	1	3
Peters	1	2	3
Soski	1	3	2
Aterman	2	3	1
T. Byers	2	1	3
J. Byers	1	2	3
Conners	1	2	3

Is there a difference in the lifeguards' ratings (rankings) of the desirability of three methods? What does this indicate? Use the 0.05 level of risk.

4. A new unit can be assembled a number of different ways. Four engineering control personnel studied the process, and each recommended a different assembly method. A small group of assembly personnel tried the four methods. They each gave the methods an efficiency rating on a scale of 50 to 200. At the 0.05 level, is there a difference with respect to their ratings?

	Methods			
Employee	McGinty's method	Sobecki's method	Lope's method	Jackson's method
Carty	160	132	120	100
Gonzo	139	99	62	141
Suzo	97	109	112	103
Smith	113	121	118	111
Archer	114	130	160	118
Catlin	116	127	109	103
Utz	103	109	106	112

THE CHI-SQUARE TEST FOR _k_ SAMPLES

The **chi-square test**, developed by Karl Pearson in the early 1900s, was applied to a one-sample case in the previous chapter. It can also be used if there are _k independent_ samples.

EXAMPLE

Suppose that there is interest in testing if there is any relationship between the scholastic achievement (final grade point average in college) of business administration graduates and their level of income. The null hypothesis is: There is no relationship between the scholastic achievement of business administration graduates and their level of income. H_1 states that there is a relationship. For this test, the 0.05 level of significance was selected.

It was decided to classify the scholastic achievement of the business administration graduates into three groups: above average, average, and below average, represented by final grade point scores of 3.0–4.0, 2.5–2.9999, and 2.0–2.4999, respectively (2.0 is needed for graduation and 4.0 indicates that an alumnus had all A grades when in college). Therefore, there are three independent samples.

The incomes of the 751 respondents were classified into four levels: low, lower middle, upper middle, and high. The responses of the 751 graduates were tallied into a two-way table called a **contingency table** (Table 18–4). (This kind of table is often referred to as a 3 × 4 contingency table because there are 3 rows and 4 columns.)

**TABLE 18–4
Scholastic achievement and income level**

Scholastic achievement	Income level				
	Low	Lower middle	Upper middle	High	Total
Above average	22	31	31	8	92
Average	67	80	73	17	237
Below average	124	161	122	15	422

Source: Robert D. Mason, *Alumni Study* (Toledo, Ohio: University of Toledo, College of Business Administration).

Is there a relationship between scholastic achievement and level of income?

SOLUTION

Note in Table 18–5 that 92 out of the total of 751 graduates (12 percent) had an above-average grade point average (3.0 to 4.0). *If* there is *no* relationship whatsoever between scholastic achievement and income, it can be expected, therefore, that 12 percent of the 213 graduates who had low incomes would also have had an above-average college scholastic record. Thus the expected frequency (f_e) for that cell would be 26, found by 12 percent × 213. Further, if there is no relationship between scholastic achievement and income, it can be expected that 12 percent of the 272 graduates who were in the lower-middle income range would also have an above-average grade point. The expected frequency (f_e) for that cell is 33, found by 12 percent × 272. (See Table 18–5).

The computation of the expected frequency for one other cell will be shown. Note that 237 business administration graduates out of the 751 total,

TABLE 18–5
Scholastic achievement and income level

Scholastic achievement	Income level								Total	Percent of total
	Low		Lower middle		Upper middle		High			
	f_0	f_e	f_0	f_e	f_0	f_e	f_0	f_e		
Above average........	22	(26)	31	(33)	31	(27)	8	(5)	92	12
Average.............	67	(68)	80	(87)	73	(72)	17	(13)	237	32
Below average	124	(119)	161	(152)	122	(127)	15	(22)	422	56
Total............	213	(213)	272	(272)	226	(226)	40	(40)	751	100

or 32 percent, had average grades in college. If there is no relationship between scholastic achievement and income, logically 32 percent of those persons in the low-income bracket would have average grades. The expected frequency for that cell is 68, found by 32 percent $\times$ 213. This procedure is continued until the expected frequencies for all cells are determined. The observed frequencies (f_0) and the expected frequencies (f_e) for each cell are given in Table 18–5.

Due to rounding, the total of the expected frequencies for a column may not be exactly equal to the total of the observed frequencies for that column. If this does happen, the totals can be made equal by adjusting one or more of the expected frequencies in that column.

The statistic chi-square is:

$$\chi^2 = \sum \frac{(f_0 - f_e)^2}{f_e}$$

The decision rule is formulated by referring to the chi-square table of critical values (Appendix H). A convenient way to determine the degrees of freedom for a contingency table is to multiply the rows $-$ 1 times the columns $-$ 1. In Table 18–5 there are three rows and four columns of data. Therefore, $(3 - 1)(4 - 1) = 6$ degrees of freedom. The critical value for 6 df and an α of 0.05 is 12.59. H_0, the null hypothesis, will be accepted if the computed value of χ^2 is less than 12.59. Otherwise it will be rejected, and H_1, the alternative hypothesis, will be accepted.

Chi-square was computed to be 8.11 (see the following calculations). This computed value (8.11) is less than the critical value (12.59) and thus falls in the area of acceptance. The null hypothesis that there is no relationship between scholastic achievement in college and income level is accepted at the 5 percent level.

The information in this problem is ordinal scaled (because both income and scholastic achievement were ranked from low to high). It should be noted, however, that the chi-square test can be applied to nominal-, interval-, and ratio-level information.

Grade point average	Income	f_0	f_e	$f_0 - f_e$	$(f_0 - f_e)^2$	$\dfrac{(f_0 - f_e)^2}{f_e}$
Above average	Low	22	26	−4	16	16/26 = 0.62
Above average	Lower middle	31	33	−2	4	4/33 = 0.12
Above average	Upper middle	31	27	4	16	16/27 = 0.59
Above average	High	8	5	3	9	9/5 = 1.80
Average	Low	67	68	−1	1	1/68 = 0.01
Average	Lower middle	80	87	−7	49	49/87 = 0.56
Average	Upper middle	73	72	1	1	1/72 = 0.01
Average	High	17	13	4	16	16/13 = 1.23
Below average	Low	124	119	5	25	25/119 = 0.21
Below average	Lower middle	161	152	9	81	81/152 = 0.53
Below average	Upper middle	122	127	−5	25	25/127 = 0.20
Below average	High	15	22	−7	49	49/22 = 2.23
		751	751	0		8.11 ↑ $\boxed{\chi^2}$

The limitations for the use of the chi-square test discussed in the previous chapter bear repeating. It is recommended that if more than 20 percent of the cells have *expected* frequencies of less than 5, the test should not be used. And, as previously suggested, it may be possible to combine several categories to meet this requirement.

SELF-REVIEW 18–3

A sociologist was researching this question: Is there any relationship between the level of education and social activities of an individual? She decided on three levels of education: attended or completed college; attended or completed high school; and attended or completed grade school or less. Each individual kept a record of his or her social activities, such as bowling with a group, dancing, and church functions. The sociologist divided them into above-average frequency, average frequency, and below average.

Education	Social activity		
	Above average	Average	Below average
College	20	10	10
High school	30	50	80
Grade school	10	60	130

a. What is the above table called?

a. Contingency table.

b. There is no relationship between level of education and the frequency of social activity.

c. Computed $\chi^2 = 58.83$. Because it is greater than the critical value of 9.49, reject the null hypothesis. Computing χ^2:

f_0	f_e	f_0	f_e	f_0	f_e	Total	%
20	6	10	12	10	10	22	40	10
30	24	50	48	80	88	160	40
10	30	60	60	130	110	200	50
60	60	120	120	220	220	400	100

$$\chi^2 = \frac{(20 - 6)^2}{6} + \frac{(10 - 12)^2}{12} + \cdots \frac{(130 - 110)^2}{110}$$

$$= 32.67 + 0.33 + \cdots 3.64$$

$$= 58.83$$

d. There is a relationship between level of education and the frequency of social activity.

b. State the null hypothesis. It is to be tested at the 0.05 level.

c. Should the null hypothesis be accepted or rejected? Cite figures to substantiate your decision.

d. What specifically does this indicate in this problem?

EXERCISES

5. A survey of industrial salespersons who are either self-employed or work for small, medium-sized, or large firms revealed the following with respect to incomes:

Of those who earned under $20,000 a year, 9 are self-employed, and 12 are employed by small firms, 40 by medium-size firms, and 89 by large firms.

Of those who earned $20,000–$39,999, 11 are self-employed, and 10 are employed by small firms, 45 by medium-sized firms, and 104 by large firms.

Of those who earned $40,000 or over, 10 are self-employed, and 13 are employed by small firms, 50 by medium-sized firms, and 107 by large firms.

Examine the hypothesis that there is no relationship between the income level of the industrial salespersons and their employment status (self-employed or employed by small, medium-sized, or large firms). Test at the 0.05 level.

6. The survey mentioned in Exercise 5 included questions on the age of the respondent and the degree of pressure the industrial salesperson feels in connection with the job. Ages and the amount of job pressure were cross-clarified into the following table.

Age (years)	Degree of pressure (number of salespersons)		
	Low	Medium	High
Under 25	20	18	22
25–39	50	46	44
40–59	58	63	59
60 and over	34	43	43

Examine whether there is any relationship between age and the degree of job pressure. Use the 0.01 level.

CHAPTER SUMMARY

Three distribution-free tests of hypotheses were examined in this chapter—the Cochran Q test, the Friedman test, and the chi-square test. As implied, none of the tests required that any assumptions be made about the distribution of the parent population(s).

The Cochran Q test is applied to *nominal* scaled data. There must be three or more related samples. For example, a group of interior designers might be asked if they liked or disliked several color combinations. Their responses might be:

	Color		
Designer	Combination A	Combination B	Combination C
Pierre . . . . Like		Dislike	Like
Ollini . . . . Like		Like	Like
Susie . . . . Dislike		Like	Dislike

The Cochran Q test is used to evaluate the like-dislike responses to determine if there is an overall difference in the opinions of the designers.

The Friedman Two-Way Analysis of Variance is somewhat similar to Cochran's test, except that the data have to be at least ordinal level of measurement. The responses of each person are ranked 1, 2, 3 . . . from low to high (or vice versa). Using the previous example, suppose the interior designers were asked to rate the three color combinations on a scale of 1 to 50, instead of just like or dislike. The ratings might appear as:

	Color		
Designer	Combination A	Combination B	Combination C
Pierre 20		30	5
Ollini 32		19	7
Susie 20		40	3

The ratings would be ranked from low to high for the Friedman test.

	Color		
Designer	Combination A	Combination B	Combination C
Pierre 2		3	1
Ollini 3		2	1
Susie 2		3	1

The chi-square goodness of fit test was discussed in Chapter 17. It is concerned with only one sample. A set of observed frequencies is paired with a set of expected frequencies. Chi-square is applied to determine if there is a difference between what was observed and what was expected. This chapter extends the test to two or more independent samples. The objective of the experiment is to determine if there is a relationship between two variables, such as one's age and one's opinion regarding a new product. The data are cross-classified into a table called a contingency table. For this experiment the contingency table might appear as:

	Opinion regarding new product				
Age	Superior	Very good	Good	Fair	Unsatisfactory
20–39	19	27	25	52	81
30–39	10	17	15	29	41
40–49	51	40	31	21	27
50 and over	142	81	16	9	8

An expected frequency is calculated for each observed frequency in the table, and the chi-square test is applied. (Just from scanning the table, it does appear that there is a relationship between age and opinion regarding the new product. In general, the younger group view it as being fair or unsatisfactory, and the older groups think it superior or very good.)

I. Nonparametric tests of hypotheses: more than two samples.
  A. *Objective.* To check the validity of statements involving nominal and/or ordinal level of measurement for three or more samples. These tests have been designed to determine whether or not the k samples have been selected from identical populations (or from the same population).

II. Cochran Q test.
  A. *Assumptions. Nominal* level of measurement required. Samples are *related*, meaning that the person acts as his or her own control; that is, the person's responses are included in sample 1, sample 2. . . .
  B. *Use.* Example: Twenty persons are asked to give an opinion (either like or dislike) with respect to five mock-up models of a proposed medium-priced automobile. General format:

		Model				
Person		A	B	C	D	E
Ms. Bee	Like	Dislike	Like	Like	Like
Mr. See	Dislike	Dislike	Dislike	Dislike	Like

The null hypothesis is that there is no overall difference among the five samples with respect to like-dislike reactions to the mock-up models.

  C. *Formula.* After converting the word "like" to 1 and "dislike" to 0:

$$Q = \frac{(k - 1)[k(\Sigma S_1^2 + \Sigma S_2^2 + \Sigma S_3^2 + \Sigma S_4^2 + \Sigma S_5^2) - (\Sigma L)^2]}{k(\Sigma L) - \Sigma L^2}$$

where:

k is the number of samples.

ΣS_1 is the sum of the favorable (like) responses to model A, ΣS_2 is the sum of the favorable responses to model B, and so on.

L is the total number of favorable (like) responses to each person.

ΣL^2 directs one to square the total number of favorable responses for each person and then to sum them.

  D. *Decision procedure.* The sampling distribution of Q approximates chi-square with $k - 1$ degrees of freedom. Refer to Appendix H for the critical value for the level of significance selected.

III. Friedman two-way analysis of variance.
   A. *Assumptions*. Requires *ordinal* level data and *related* samples.
   B. *Use*. Instead of given like or dislike opinion on five mock-up models, the 20 respondents could rank them 1, 2, 3. . . .

Person	Rank of model				
	A	B	C	D	E
Ms. Bee	2	3	1	4	5
Mr. See	5	4	1	3	2

The null and alternative hypotheses are:

H_0: There is no difference in the overall ranking of the five models.

H_1: There is a difference with respect to the overall ranking of the five models.

   C. *Formula:*

$$\chi_r^2 = \frac{12}{Nk(k + 1)} [T_1^2 + T_2^2 + \cdots + T_k^2] - [3N(k + 1)]$$

where:

N is the total number of respondents in the sample.
k is the number of related samples (columns).
T_1 is the sum of the ranks for one of the samples (model A), T_2 is the sum of the ranks for the second sample, and so on.

   D. *Decision procedure*. The sample distribution of χ_r^2 approximates chi-square with $k - 1$ degrees of freedom. Refer to Appendix H for the critical value for the level of significance selected.

IV. Chi-square test for k samples.
   A. *Assumptions*. At least nominal level of measurement; k independent samples.
   B. *Use*. Example: There is no relationship between sex and income. Data are cast in a *contingency table*.

Sex	Income		
	Low	Average	High
Male	21	27	23
Female	62	55	68

Frequencies observed in the various categories are compared with frequencies expected.

   C. *Formula*.

$$\chi^2 = \Sigma \frac{(f_0 - f_e)^2}{f_e}$$

D. *Decision procedure.* Using the usual hypothesis-testing procedure, compute χ^2. Refer to Appendix H for the critical value for the level of significance selected.

7. It has been suggested that the name of Boomy Beans be changed and the can and label modernized. The choice has narrowed to four names. A sample of 20 "experts" who specialize in evaluating the impact of names, labels, and so on were asked to give their reactions to the four names. In order to prevent possible bias, the four names were given in a different order to each subject. Instructions were to rate the names from outstanding to unsatisfactory; they were directed not to give a name the exact same rating as another name. The words (from highest to lowest) they might give to describe their reaction to the proposed new name included: *outstanding, superior, excellent, very good, good, fair, poor, very poor,* and *unsatisfactory.* The results were:

Expert no.	Boston Back Bay Beans	Boomy's Brick Oven Beans	Boston's Favorite	Sweet & Lovely Boomy Beans
1	Very good	Poor	Excellent	Unsatisfactory
2	Good	Very poor	Very good	Poor
3	Outstanding	Good	Superior	Unsatisfactory
4	Superior	Fair	Excellent	Very poor
5	Excellent	Unsatisfactory	Outstanding	Very poor
6	Fair	Poor	Good	Unsatisfactory
7	Excellent	Very poor	Superior	Poor
8	Very good	Poor	Good	Unsatisfactory
9	Very good	Poor	Excellent	Unsatisfactory
10	Very good	Good	Superior	Fair
11	Superior	Good	Outstanding	Fair
12	Good	Poor	Very good	Very poor
13	Excellent	Fair	Superior	Poor
14	Excellent	Fair	Outstanding	Unsatisfactory
15	Good	Fair	Outstanding	Unsatisfactory
16	Good	Poor	Superior	Unsatisfactory
17	Superior	Good	Outstanding	Poor
18	Excellent	Very good	Outstanding	Fair
19	Excellent	Fair	Superior	Poor
20	Very good	Poor	Excellent	Unsatisfactory

Determine whether there is a difference in the responses to the four names. Use the usual five steps; that is, state the null hypothesis, and so on. Test at the 0.05 level.

8. A randomly selected group of fashion models were asked to try several newly developed waterproof makeups especially designed for use in photographic and television studios. They were requested to rate each cream, giving it a number from 1 to 50 with a low rating representing the most desirable makeup and a high number the least desirable. The results were:

Name of model	Rating for makeup				
	A	B	C	D	E
Sue	41	10	6	48	1
Sami	9	40	50	37	16
Jean	48	40	20	10	25
Pei	40	6	10	48	45
Gladys	30	40	5	10	50
Fifi	2	20	45	40	10

Test at the 0.05 level:

H_0: There is no difference in the overall appeal of the four makeup creams.

H_1: There is a difference.

a. State the decision rule.

b. Compute the appropriate statistic.

c. Arrive at a decision.

9. Male students selected at random from high schools in a large metropolitan area were asked about their plans after graduation. Their responses were:

Class	Work or military service	Attend college	Undecided
Freshman	50	50	300
Sophomore	75	125	100
Junior	45	105	50
Senior	20	70	10

a. Is there any difference in the plans of the students by class? Test at the 0.05 level of significance.

Suppose that the plans of the students in the large metropolitan area are to be compared with national figures. The U.S. figures (in percents) are:

Class	Work or military service	Attend college	Undecided
Freshman	10	10	80
Sophomore	27	40	33
Junior	21	50	29
Senior	19	72	9

b. Is there any difference in the plans of students in the metropolitan area and those of all students in the United States? Test at the 0.05 level.

CHAPTER SELF-REVIEW EXAMINATION

Do both problems and then check your answers against those in Appendix A. Score each problem 50 points.

1. A panel of 10 "experts" rated five designs for a sporty automobile on a scale from 0 (very unsatisfactory) to 100 (outstanding). The rating results were:

Expert no.	Design				
	A	B	C	D	E
1	40	90	10	46	18
2	60	8	98	12	3
3	2	80	90	98	99
4	82	60	5	50	55
5	42	99	3	2	60
6	86	3	99	40	45
7	8	50	9	10	82
8	14	3	29	19	10
9	9	10	5	7	1
10	12	8	7	6	50

Test at the 0.05 level that there is no difference in the overall ratings.

2. Two hundred men selected at random from various levels of management were interviewed regarding their concern about environmental issues. The response of each person was tallied into one of three categories—no concern, some concern, or great concern. The results were:

Level of management	No concern	Some concern	Great concern
Top management	15	13	12
Middle management	20	19	21
Supervisor	7	7	6
Foreman	28	21	31

Using the 0.01 level, determine if there is any difference in the responses with respect to the level of management.

19

INTRODUCTION

The objective of this chapter is to present a practical application of both descriptive statistics and statistical inference. To assess whether current production is satisfactory or unsatisfactory, charts, referred to as **control charts**, are drawn, and other descriptive measures, such as the arithmetic mean and range, are computed. Control charts are usually based on very small samples. For example, one chart to be discussed shortly is based on a sample of only five pieces selected from three hours of production. Based on tests conducted on these five pieces, an inference is made about *all* the pieces produced during a three-hour period. If the sample results are within acceptable limits, all of the pieces are stamped as being satisfactory and are moved to the assembly line. From this standpoint, statistical quality control can be considered as a practical application of statistical inference.

Statistical quality control is relatively new. Prior to the early 1900s, American industry was largely characterized by small shops making relatively simple products such as buggies, furniture, plows, and stoves. In these shops, the individual worker was generally a craftsman who was completely responsible for the "quality" of his work and could fulfill these responsibilities through his personal selection of material, skillful manufacture, and selective fitting and adjustment to assure that the finished product would work.

With the spread of the Industrial Revolution in the early 1900s, factories sprang up. People with only limited training were formed into long assembly lines. Products became increasingly more complex. The individual worker no longer had complete control over the quality of the product. A semiprofessional staff was developed (the inspection department), which became responsible for the quality. This responsibility was fulfilled by a 100 percent evaluation of all characteristics deemed important, with corrective action on discrepancies being handled by notifying the production department supervisors. During this period, quality was obtained by "inspecting it into the product."

During the 1930s, the concepts of *statistical quality control* were developed, primarily through the work of Dr. Walter A. Shewhart of the Bell Telephone Laboratories. Dr. Shewhart introduced the concepts of "controlling" the quality rather than inspecting it into the part. For the purpose of controlling the quality, the **Shewhart control chart technique** was developed for in-process manufacturing operations. In addition, he introduced the concept of *statistical sampling inspection* to determine whether manufactured lots were good or bad, replacing the old method of inspecting every part.

Statistical quality control

Statistical quality control, with its emphasis on in-process control of the quality, came into its own during World War II. The need for mass-produced, intricate bomb sights, accurate radar, and other electronic equipment at lowest cost accelerated the use of control charts and statistical sampling. These statistical techniques were retained, refined, and added to both during and after the war. Most manufacturers now utilize control charts and/or sampling plans for evaluating production quality. Numerous corporations have employed statisticians and quality control engineers to implement the statistical quality control program.

This chapter will be concerned with only one statistical technique used in quality control, namely, control charts.

THE CONTROL
CHART VIEWPOINT

Variation is a basic law of nature. The amount of rainfall in any of a number of years will vary, the heights of college freshmen will vary, and the parts produced by a manufacturing process will vary.

On the production line, a most important concept is that *there is no such thing as two identical parts*. The difference from one part to the next is minute (perhaps one millionth of an inch), but *they are different*. One automobile engine block is different from the next one, and any one valve is different from the next one produced. Even the tensile strength of a roll of steel wire varies throughout the length of the wire. This variation is recognized in the tolerances and limits specified on blueprints. A valve stem may be specified as being acceptable if it is between 1.32003 and 1.3300 inches in diameter. The roll of steel wire may be acceptable if it tests between 14,000 and 14,500 pounds per square inch tensile strength.

To illustrate the pattern of variation inherent in quantitative data, the weights of a sample of 23 incoming freshmen football players were recorded (Table 19–1).

TABLE 19–1
Variations in the
weights of football
players

Weight (in pounds)		Number of players
140 up to 160	/	1
160 up to 180	//	2
180 up to 200	⊬⊬	5
200 up to 220	⊬⊬ //	7
220 up to 240	⊬⊬	5
240 up to 260	//	2
260 up to 280	/	1

Note that the weights tend to cluster about an arithmetic mean weight of 210 pounds. Some weigh more; some less. Practically all of them weigh between 150 and 270 pounds. If all freshmen players were weighed, however, it is quite possible that a relatively few might weight less than 140 or more than 280 pounds.

Machined parts follow somewhat this inherent pattern. A gang drill drilling holes in bushings is set for 2.9870 inches diamater. A sample of bushings from this machine revealed the results shown in Chart 19–1.

CHART 19–1
Variations in the
inside diameters of
bushings

Inside diameter		Number of bushings
2.9873	O	1
2.9872	O O	2
2.9871	O O O O	4
2.9870	O O O O O O	6
2.9869	O O O O	4
2.9868	O O	2
2.9867	O	1

The inside diameters of the bushings can be considered normally distributed. The normal distribution has the form of a familiar bell-shaped curve, and its characteristics are generally described by measures of central tendency discussed in Chapter 4 and measures of dispersion and areas under the curve from Chapter 5.

The average most commonly used in quality control charts is the arithmetic mean. The most commonly used measures of dispersion are the range (R) and the standard deviation (σ).

These relationships are shown graphically in Chart 19–2.

CHART 19–2
Areas under the normal curve within Mu ± σ, Mu ± 2σ, and Mu ± 3σ

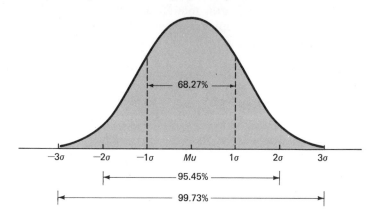

In order to understand why control charts are a basic tool in quality control, the following two questions must be answered:

1. What causes the basic pattern of variation in a manufacturing process?
2. What is the purpose of control charts?

Causes of variation

There are two general types of causes of variations in a manufacturing process: *chance* and *assignable*. **Chance causes** are usually large in number and random in nature, and they cannot be entirely eliminated. Internal machine friction, slight variations in materials or process conditions (temperature of a mold used to make glass containers), atmospheric conditions (temperature, humidity, dust content of the air), and vibrations transmitted to a machine from a passing forklift are a few chance causes.

Assignable causes of variation are usually few in number and nonrandom in nature, and they can readily be reduced or eliminated. If the hole being drilled in a piece of steel is much too large due to a dull drill, the drill may be sharpened or a new drill inserted. If an operator is continually setting up the machine incorrectly, he can be relieved. If the roll of steel to be used in the process does not have the correct tensile strength, it can be rejected.

Why be concerned with the causes of variation?

1. Variation can (and will) change the dispersion and/or the central tendency of the product characteristic distribution.
2. Assignable causes can generally be corrected easily, while chance causes cannot usually be corrected or stabilized economically.

To illustrate the effect of variation on distribution parameters, the frequency distribution of the inside diameter of the bushings noted previously (Chart 19–1) has been smoothed out to approximate a normal distribution curve and plotted in Chart 19–3A. Assuming that the upper and lower blueprint specifications are the same as the inherent pattern of variation, 99.73 percent of the bushings would be acceptable. This indicates that 997 bushings out of 1,000 would theoretically fall between the specified tolerances.

Chart 19–3B shows graphically the effect of an upward shift in the arithmetic mean inside diameter; that is, the mean inside diameter of the bushings has become much larger. This may be due to excessive vibration of the drill as it bites through the steel. Chart 19–3C shows the effect of a downward shift in the arithmetic mean diameter. The mean inside diameter has become much smaller. This may be due to excessive drill wear. In both cases, a large proportion of the output would be unacceptable.

In summary, if specifications have been established on the basis of the

CHART 19–3
The usual pattern of variation and the effects of upward and downward shifts in the arithmetic mean inside diameter

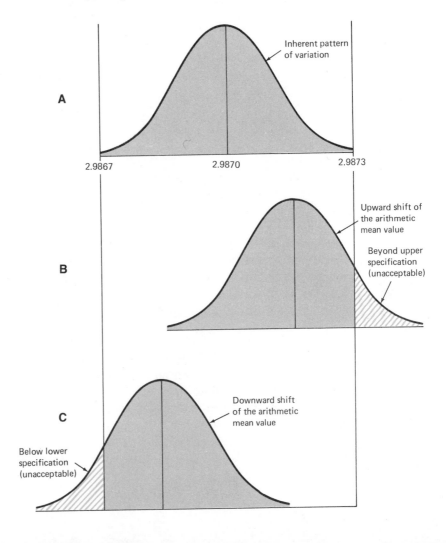

A

2.9867   2.9870   2.9873

Inherent pattern of variation

B

Upward shift of the arithmetic mean value

Beyond upper specification (unacceptable)

C

Downward shift of the arithmetic mean value

Below lower specification (unacceptable)

inherent pattern, then a shift in the arithmetic mean value results in defective parts. Chart 19–3A represents the pattern of *chance* variation. The areas above and below the upper and lower specifications in 19–3B and C represent *assignable* causes of variation.

Similarly, assuming that the upper and lower specifications of the bushings are the inherent pattern of variation, then any change in the range *R* in the distribution of bushings will cause a proportion of the bushings to be beyond the upper or lower specifications, even though the arithmetic mean inside diameter stayed the same at 2.9870. A change in the range indicates that some very small and/or very large bushings are being produced. The unusually small inside diameters may be caused by a dull drill. The large inside diameters may be caused by one of the gang drills which has expanded due to excessive heat. Chart 19–4D is the usual normal pattern of production, and 19–4E illustrates the effect of an increased range.

CHART 19–4
The usual pattern of variation and the effect of an increase in the range of the inside diameters

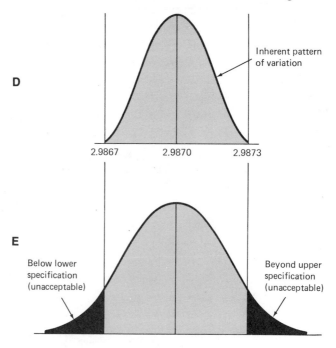

In summary, if specifications have been established on the basis of the inherent pattern, then an increase in the range results in defective parts. Chart 19–4D shows the pattern of chance variation. The areas above and below the upper and lower specifications in 19–4E represent assignable causes of variation.

Purpose and types of quality control charts

What is the purpose of a statistical quality control chart? Fundamentally, the purpose is to identify *when* assignable causes of variation or changes in process level have entered the production system. It is important to know *when* these changes have occurred so that the cuase may be identified and corrected.

Statistical quality control charts may be compared to a football scoreboard. By looking at the scoreboard, the fans, coaches, and players can tell which team is ahead. The scoreboard can do nothing to win or lose the game, for it is just lights and steel. It is merely a signal to the losing coach to try to do something about the situation. A new front four might turn the tide. Quality control charts are similar in function. These charts indicate to the workers, foremen, quality control engineers, or management whether the production of a part or parts is **in control** or **out of control**. If production is out of control, the quality control chart cannot correct the situation. It is just a piece of paper with figures and dots on it. Instead, the person responsible will adjust the machine manufacturing the part or do whatever is necessary to return production to the ''in control'' status. ''In control'' means satisfactory production; ''out of control'' indicates unsatisfactory production. Unsatisfactory production might mean that the part being produced is too heavy, too light, too large, too small, or has other manifestations of poor, unacceptable production.

Control charts have been developed for both *variables* and *attributes*. As has been pointed out previously, parts vary in length, inside diameter, outside diameter, tensile strength, and so on. One group of statistical quality control charts is for these variables. Two charts will be studied; namely, *bar X charts* (alternately called *mean charts*) and *range charts*.

CHARTS FOR VARIABLES

Statistical quality control charts utilize the same theoretical concepts with respect to sampling as those developed in the foregoing chapters. To illustrate, suppose that a small sample of, say, five pieces is selected from the population and the arithmetic mean is computed. Many additional samples of five pieces are selected and the means computed. The means of these samples could be designated $\bar{X}_1, \bar{X}_2, \bar{X}_3$, and so on. The mean of these sample means is denoted by $\bar{\bar{X}}$.

$$\bar{\bar{X}} = \frac{\Sigma \text{ of the means of the subgroups (samples)}}{\Sigma \text{ number of sample means}}$$

$$= \frac{\Sigma \bar{X}}{n}$$

The standard error of the distribution of sample (subgroup) means is $\sigma_{\bar{x}}$.

$$\sigma_{\bar{x}} = \frac{\sigma}{\sqrt{n}}$$

If all the sample means were plotted in a frequency distribution, the curve would approximate the bell-shaped curve in Chart 19–5. The relationship of the distribution of sample means superimposed on the distribution of the actual measurements might appear as shown in the chart.

**CHART 19–5
Distribution of sample
means and population
values**

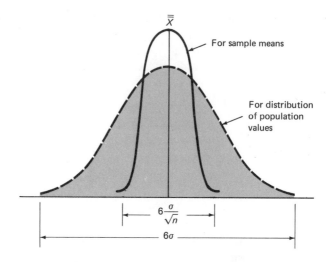

It is apparent that the arithmetic mean for the population is the same as that for the distribution of averages. Also, the total dispersion of the population is greater than that of the distribution of averages by the factor $\sqrt{n}$. It also should be noted that if the distribution of subgroup averages ($\bar{X}$'s) is normal, inferences concerning the distribution of averages ($\bar{X}$'s) can be made. They are:

68.27 percent of the subgroup averages ($\bar{X}$'s) will be within plus or minus *one* standard error of the mean ($\sigma_{\bar{x}}$) of the population mean ($\bar{\bar{X}}$).

95.45 percent of the subgroup averages ($\bar{X}$'s) will be within plus or minus *two* standard errors of the mean ($\sigma_{\bar{x}}$) of the population mean ($\bar{\bar{X}}$).

99.73 percent of the subgroup averages ($\bar{X}$'s) will be within plus or minus *three* standard errors of the mean ($\sigma_{\bar{x}}$) of the population mean ($\bar{\bar{X}}$).

These relationships allow limits to be set up around the subgroup averages to show how much variation can be expected for subgroup samples of a given size. These expected limits are called the *upper control limits*, usually abbreviated *UCL,* and the *lower control limits* (*LCL*).

**Bar X chart (mean
chart)**

EXAMPLE

Suppose that a new bottle-making machine has just been installed. The machine is set to produce 41-ounce bottles, but as pointed out previously, variation is expected. This expected variation is due to a number of factors, namely, the temperature of the glass, temperature of the molds, and the composition of the glass mixture. The quality control design calls for taking a sample of five bottles every hour, weighing them, and computing the arithmetic mean weight.

How is a mean chart constructed?

The upper control limit (*UCL*) and the lower control limit (*LCL*) of the mean chart are computed by:

$$UCL \text{ and } LCL = \bar{X} \pm A_2\bar{R}$$

where:

A_2 is a factor which greatly facilitates the computation of the upper and lower control limits. The factors for various sample sizes can be found in Appendix K. *Note:* The *n* in the table refers to the *number in the sample* (five in this problem.)

$\bar{\bar{X}}$ is the mean of the sample means computed by $\Sigma\bar{X}/N$ where N is the number of samples selected. In this problem a sample will be taken every hour for four hours. So, $N = 4$.

$\bar{R}$ is the mean of the ranges of the samples. $\bar{R}$ is computed by $\Sigma R/N$.

The quality control inspector recorded the weight of each of the five bottles he selected. The data for the samples taken at 8, 9, 10, and 11 o'clock are given in Table 19–2.

TABLE 19–2
Weights of five bottles selected at random, 8–11 o'clock (in ounces)

Time		Bottle				Arithmetic means $\bar{X}$	Range R
	1	2	3	4	5		
8 A.M.	41	43	42	41	43	42	2
9 A.M.	39	40	40	39	42	40	3
10 A.M.	41	44	43	46	41	43	5
11 A.M.	38	39	40	39	39	39	2
Total						164	12

SOLUTION

The centerline ($\bar{\bar{X}}$) for Chart 19–6 is 41, found by 164/4. The mean of the ranges ($\bar{R}$) is 3, found by 12/4.

To compute the upper control limit (*UCL*) of the bar X chart:

$$\bar{\bar{X}} + A_2\bar{R} = 41 + 0.577(3)$$
$$= 42.731$$

To compute the lower control limit (*LCL*) of the bar X chart:

$$\bar{\bar{X}} - A_2\bar{R} = 41 - 0.577(3)$$
$$= 39.269$$

The $\bar{\bar{X}}$, the *UCL* and *LCL*, and the means of the samples are portrayed in Chart 19–6.

There is considerable variation in the process averages, probably due to the newness of the bottling machine and the lack of experience of the opera-

480

CHART 19–6
A bar X chart

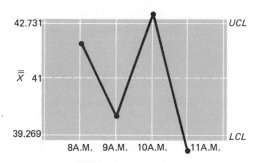

tor. Dr. Shewhart suggested that such a control chart not be set up until after 25 samples have been taken. Theoretically, this allows production to become somewhat stabilized.

Interpretation.   Based on just the first four hours of experience with this new bottling machine: (1) If a sample of five bottles is picked at random and weighed, the arithmetic mean weight will fall between 39.269 and 42.731 ounces about 99.73 percent of the time. (2) If many samples of five bottles are taken and the arithmetic means computed, the average of 41 ounces will appear more than any other average. The 41-ounce figure is the grand average of the subgroup means. The *UCL* and the *LCL* represent $\overline{\overline{X}} \pm 3\sigma_{\bar{x}}$.

SELF-REVIEW 19–1

Sample piece						
1	*2*	*3*	*4*	*Total*	*Average*	*Range*
1	4	5	2	12	3	4
2	3	2	1	8	2	2
1	7	3	5	16	4	6
					$\overline{9}$	$\overline{12}$

$$\begin{aligned}
UCL \text{ and } LCL &= X \pm 3\sigma_{\bar{x}} \\
&= \overline{\overline{X}} \pm A_2\overline{R} \\
&= 3 \pm 0.729(4) \\
&= 5.916 \ UCL \\
& 0.084 \ LCL
\end{aligned}$$

Bar X

(A reminder: Cover the answers in the left-hand column.)

Every half-hour the quality control inspector checks four pieces and records the outside diameters of each of the four pieces, as shown below:

	Sample piece			
Time	*1*	*2*	*3*	*4*
9:00 A.M.	1	4	5	2
9:30 A.M.	2	3	2	1
10:00 A.M.	1	7	3	5

Set up a bar X chart and plot the essential data.

Range chart

A **range** chart shows variation in the ranges of the samples. If the dots representing the ranges fall within the upper and lower limits, it is assumed that production is in control. According to chance, 997 times out of 1,000 the range of the samples will fall between the two limits. If a range should fall above or below the limits, it is assumed that some *assignable* cause affected the production, resulting in some individual pieces being too large, too small, too heavy, or too light, depending on what is being measured. The *UCL* and the *LCL* represent $\bar{R} \pm 3\sigma_R$.

The upper control limit of the range chart is computed by:

$$\boxed{UCL = D_4\bar{R}}$$

The lower control limit is found by:

$$\boxed{LCL = D_3\bar{R}}$$

where:

D_3 and D_4 are factors which greatly facilitate the computation of the upper and lower control limits of the range chart. These factors can also be found in Appendix K.

EXAMPLE

The weights of the five bottles selected at random every hour from 8 A.M. to 11 A.M., from Table 19–2, is repeated below.

		Weights (in ounces)			
Time	1	2	3	4	5
8 A.M.	41	43	42	41	43
9 A.M.	39	40	40	39	42
10 A.M.	41	44	43	46	41
11 A.M.	38	39	40	39	39

How is a range chart for these weights constructed?

SOLUTION

The first step is to find the average range $\bar{R}$. The range of the 8 A.M. sample is 2, found by $43 - 41$. The range of the 9 A.M. sample is 3, found by $42 - 39$. The ranges for the 10 A.M. samples are 5 and 2 respectively. The average range $\bar{R}$ is 3, found by $(2 + 3 + 5 + 2)/4 = 12/4 = 3$.

Referring to Appendix K for D_3 and D_4 and a sample size of 5, we get $D_4 = 2.115$ and $D_3 = 0$. Determining the upper and lower control limits for the range chart:

$$UCL = D_4\bar{R}$$
$$= 2.115(3)$$
$$= 6.345$$

$$LCL = D_3\bar{R}$$
$$= (0)(3)$$
$$= 0$$

Construction of the range chart and plotting of the 8 A.M.–11 A.M. ranges is shown in Chart 19–7.

CHART 19–7
A range chart

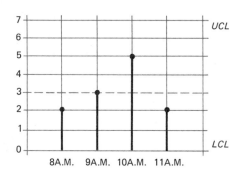

SELF-REVIEW 19–2

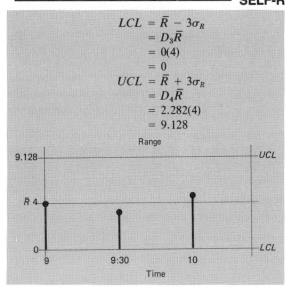

$$LCL = \bar{R} - 3\sigma_R$$
$$= D_3\bar{R}$$
$$= 0(4)$$
$$= 0$$
$$UCL = \bar{R} + 3\sigma_R$$
$$= D_4\bar{R}$$
$$= 2.282(4)$$
$$= 9.128$$

Using the data from Self-review 19–1 (repeated below), construct a range chart, and plot the essential data.

Time	Sample piece			
	1	*2*	*3*	*4*
9:00 A.M.	1	4	5	2
9:30 A.M.	2	3	2	1
10:00 A.M.	1	7	3	5

Chart 19–8 is an actual illustration of a mean chart and a range chart (only the name of the grinder has been changed). To plot the chart, a quality control inspector checks five pieces for inside diameter every three hours. The Sun Grinder in this operation is set to grind an inside diameter of 3.87525

CHART 19–8

MACH. NO.	13-271-64	UNIT OF MEASURE	.001	CHECK 5 PCS. EVERY 3 hrs.
DEPT. NO.	103	OPERATION	GRIND INSIDE DIAMETERS ON SUN GRINDERS	
PART NO.	1842B5	WEEK OF	8-17	CHART NO. 52

1	+1.0	+1.0	+2.0	-1.0	+2.0	(+5.0)	+2.0	+1.0	+1.0	-2.0	+1.0	-3.0	-3.0	+2.0	+4.0	+1.0	-1.0	0.0
2	-1.0	+1.0	+2.0	+3.0	-1.0	-1.0	-1.0	+2.0	+1.0	+1.0	-1.0	-3.0	-3.0	+1.0	-2.0	-1.0	+2.0	+1.0
3	+1.0	+1.0	-1.0	-1.0	-1.0	-1.0	0.0	+1.0	0.0	-1.0	-2.0	+3.0	-2.0	-2.0	-1.0	0.0	0.0	+1.0
4	+1.0	-2.0	-1.0	0.0	+1.0	+2.0	-3.0	-1.0	-1.0	-2.0	-2.0	-1.0	+1.0	+1.0	+3.0	+1.0	-2.0	+2.0
5	-2.0	+1.0	+1.0	+2.0	0.0	-2.0	0.0	-1.0	0.0	0.0	-1.0	+2.0	-1.0	-1.0	+3.0	+1.0	-1.0	+1.0
SUM	0.0	+2.0	+3.0	+3.0	+1.0	+3.0	-2.0	+2.0	+1.0	-4.0	-5.0	-2.0	-8.0	+1.0	+7.0	+2.0	-2.0	+5.0
AVER.	0.0	+0.4	+0.6	+0.6	+0.2	+0.6	-0.4	+0.4	+0.2	-0.8	-1.0	-0.4	-1.6	+0.2	+1.4	+0.4	-0.4	+1.0
RANGE	3.0	3.0	3.0	4.0	3.0	7.0	6.0	3.0	2.0	3.0	3.0	6.0	4.0	4.0	6.0	3.0	4.0	2.0
TIME	8:50	12:00	2:50	9:00	11:50	3:00	9:05	11:55	3:00	8:55	11:50	3:05	9:10	12:05	3:00	8:55	12:05	3:10

inches. The gauge the inspector uses is calibrated to the nearest ten-thousandth of an inch. He inserts the gauge in part number 1842B5 and records the reading on the chart, such as −1.0. He sums the five sample readings and computes the arithmetic mean and the range. The gauge reading of −1.0 indicates that the part was one ten-thousandth of an inch below the mean. A +2.0 reading would indicate that the part was two ten-thousandths above the mean.

Following are three illustrations of possible in-control and out-of-control production processes.

The bar X chart and the range chart together indicate that the process is in control.

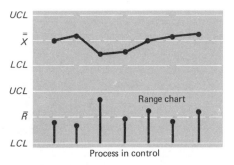

Process in control

The sample means are in control, but the ranges of the last two samples are out of control. This indicates that there is considerable variation from piece to piece. Some pieces are extremely large; others are extremely small.

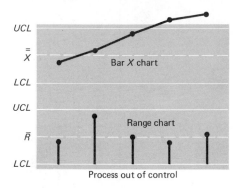

The arithmetic mean weight was in control for the first three samples, but the mean weights of the last two samples were out of control. The bar X chart and the range chart together indicate that all of the parts continued to become heavier and heavier.

EXERCISES

A reminder: The answers and method of solution for selected exercises are given in Appendix A.

1. A new industrial oven has just been installed. In order to develop experience regarding the temperature of the oven, the inspector reads the temperature in the oven at four different places every half-hour. The first reading, taken at 8 A.M., was 2,040 degrees Fahrenheit. (Only the last two digits are given in the following table to facilitate computations.)

Time	1	2	3	4
8:00 A.M.	40	50	55	39
8:30 A.M.	44	42	38	38
9:00 A.M.	41	45	47	43
9:30 A.M.	39	39	41	41
10:00 A.M.	37	42	46	41
10:30 A.M.	39	40	39	40

Reading

a. Based on this initial experience, set up a mean chart (also called a bar X chart). Insert the upper and lower control limits and the grand mean. Then plot the 8:00–10:30 experience.

b. Interpret the chart.

2. a. Design a range chart and plot it immediately below the bar X chart. Insert the upper and lower control limits and mean range.

b. Interpret the chart.

CHARTS FOR ATTRIBUTES

A weld has a crack in it or it doesn't; a relay works or it doesn't; a radiator leaks or it doesn't; the lock on a car door works or it doesn't; a tire fits on the rim or it doesn't. These are examples of *attributes*. If a part leaks, doesn't fit, won't lock, or doesn't work, it is said to be *defective*. Go and no-go gauges are one type of inspection tool for attributes; X ray is another. The **percent defective chart** shows the percent of production which is defective. A $\bar{c}$ **chart** shows the *number of defects per unit*.

Percent defective chart

Percent defective charts are also known as *P charts* or $\bar{p}$ *charts*; the latter is pronounced "*p* bar charts." The percent defective chart shows graphically the percent of the production that is not acceptable.

EXAMPLE

A new shearing machine is set to cut off a piece of steel from a long bar. For various reasons, the machine at times cuts off a piece that is too long or too short. These unacceptable pieces are automatically dropped in a box, and the operator of the shearing machine must count these defectives after every 100 pieces are sheared off. The record after the first day of operation is:

Number sheared off	Number defective	Percent defective
100	5	0.05
100	6	0.06
100	7	0.07
100	4	0.04
100	8	0.08
Total		0.30

How is a percent defective chart constructed?

SOLUTION

The arithmetic mean percent defective ($\bar{p}$) is 0.06, found by:

$$\bar{p} = \frac{\Sigma \text{ of the Percent Defective}}{\text{Number of Samples}}$$

$$= \frac{0.30}{5}$$

$$= 0.06$$

The upper control limit (*UCL*) and the lower control limit (*LCL*) are computed by the mean percent defective plus and minus three times the standard error of the percents.

$$UCL \text{ and } LCL = \bar{p} \pm 3 \sqrt{\frac{\bar{p}(1 - \bar{p})}{n}}$$

Determining the upper and lower control limits:

$$UCL \text{ and } LCL = \bar{p} \pm 3 \sqrt{\frac{\bar{p}(1 - \bar{p})}{n}}$$

$$= 0.06 \pm 3 \sqrt{\frac{(0.06)(0.94)}{100}}$$

$$= 0.06 \pm 3 \sqrt{\frac{0.0564}{100}}$$

$$= 0.06 \pm 3 \sqrt{0.000564}$$

$$= 0.132 \text{ and } -0.012$$

The upper control limit is 0.132, and the lower control limit is 0, since there cannot be less than 0 percent defective.

Note on Chart 19–9 that the average percent defective $\bar{p}$ of 0.06 and the *UCL* and *LCL* are shown. To complete the chart, the percent defective for each sample is plotted, namely, 0.05, 0.06, 0.07, 0.04, and 0.08, respectively.

CHART 19–9
A percent defective
chart

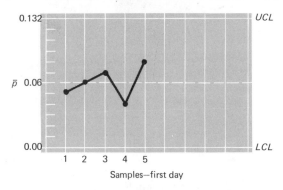

Samples—first day

Several observations can be made after the first day of operation: (1) The arithmetic mean percent defective is 6 percent. (2) About 99.7 percent of the time (which represents the mean percent defective plus and minus three times the standard error of the percents), there will be between 0 percent and 13.2 percent defective pieces. (3) Only in 3 out of 1,000 samples of size 100(1,000 − 997) will the percent defective either exceed 13.2 percent defective or theoretically be below 0 percent defective.

Management might or might not be satisfied with an average of 6 percent scrap or scrap as high as 13.2 percent. The chart cannot make a decision;

that is management's responsibility. The $\bar{p}$ chart merely sets limits based on actual experience.

An actual $\bar{p}$ chart from an automobile manufacturing plant is shown in Chart 19–10. (The name of the part has been changed slightly but the data have not been altered.)

CHART 19–10

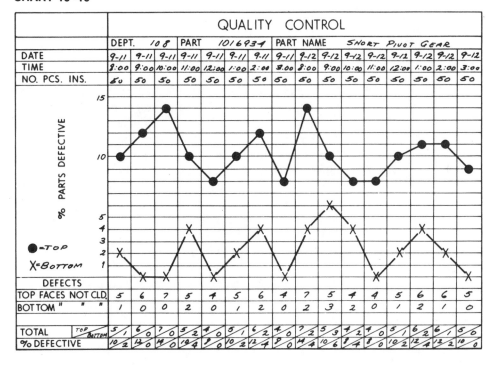

SELF-REVIEW 19–3

Day	Number checked	Number defective	Percent defective
1	200	4	0.02
2	200	3	0.015
3	200	5	0.025
4	200	4	0.02
			0.080

$$\bar{p} = \frac{0.08}{4} = 0.02$$

$$\begin{array}{l} UCL \\ \text{and} \\ LCL \end{array} = 0.02 \pm 3 \sqrt{\frac{0.02(0.98)}{200}}$$

$$= 0.047, \text{ and } 0$$

Samples of 200 parts were taken every day. The numbers of defectives were counted.

Day	Number checked	Number defective
1	200	4
2	200	3
3 .:..........	200	5
4	200	4

Set up a percent defective chart and plot the data.

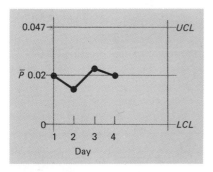

c̄ chart

The *c̄* **chart** is alternatively called a *C* **bar chart**. It portrays the *number of defects per unit*. A glass bottle might be considered defective if there are "stones" or imperfections 1/32 inch in size or more. If eight stones are found in a bottle picked at random from the assembly line, then the number of defects per unit is eight. In an automotive assembly plant, the number of defects per car door are counted. The defects might be two open seams, three slivers of steel which might scratch the new owner, one wavy section, and three small areas not completely painted. Thus, on this one car door there would be nine defects.

The purpose of a *c̄* chart, therefore, is to show graphically *how many defects appear in a unit of production*. *c̄* charts on subassemblies and final assembly show management weak areas in the construction process. Remedial action can be taken, including shift of personnel or closer supervision of certain subassemblies.

EXAMPLE

A high-fidelity tuner is subjected to a final inspection. It is plugged in and tested by tuning in to a local radio station. The tuners that work are packed and shipped. The others must be repaired before being released for sale. Possible defects might be in the soldering, or omission of parts. The quality control inspector checks these defective tuners and counts the number of defects per tuner. Checks on 10 new-model tuners revealed the following number of defects per tuner: 8, 5, 6, 4, 3, 8, 8, 10, 9, and 9.

How is a *C* bar chart constructed?

The formula for the upper and lower control limits of a *C* bar chart is:

$$UCL \text{ and } LCL = \bar{c} \pm 3\sqrt{\bar{c}}$$

SOLUTION

The total number of defects in the 10 new-model tuners is 70, found by $8 + 5 + 6 + 4 + 3 + 8 + 8 + 10 + 9 + 9$.

The arithmetic mean number of defects per tuner ($\bar{c}$) is:

$$\bar{c} = \frac{\Sigma \text{ of the number of defects}}{\text{Total number of tuners}}$$

$$= \frac{70}{10}$$

$$= 7$$

The upper control limit (UCL) and the lower control limit (LCL):

$$= \bar{c} \pm 3 \sqrt{\bar{c}}$$
$$= 7 \pm 3 \sqrt{7}$$
$$= 7 \pm 3(2.6)$$
$$UCL = 14.8$$
$$LCL = 0 \text{ (since the number of defects cannot be less than 0)}$$

The numbers of defects per tuner are plotted in Chart 19–11.

CHART 19–11
A $\bar{c}$ chart

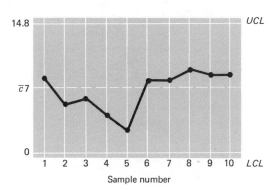

Interpretation. The average number of defects per unit is seven. In the long run, about 997 out of 1,000 tuners would have between 0 and 15 defects. The UCL and LCL represent $\bar{c} \pm 3\sigma_c$.

The $\bar{c}$ chart would no doubt be revised after more samples were taken. It is reasoned that during the production of the first units of a new model, the machine operators and foremen are somewhat unfamiliar with the process. Days or weeks are usually necessary before the process is stabilized.

Chart 19–12, an actual $\bar{c}$ chart from an automobile manufacturing plant, might be of interest. (The name of the part has been changed, but the data have not been altered.)

490

CHART 19-12

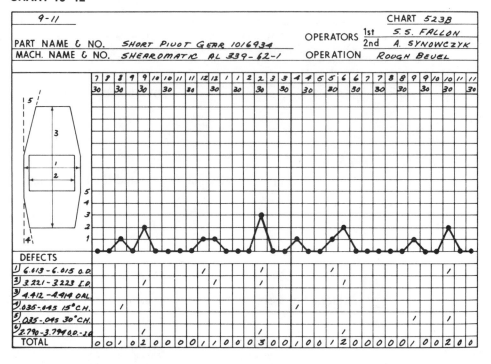

SELF-REVIEW 19-4

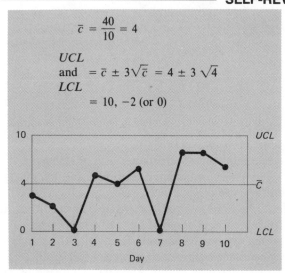

$$\bar{c} = \frac{40}{10} = 4$$

$$\begin{matrix} UCL \\ \text{and} \\ LCL \end{matrix} = \bar{c} \pm 3\sqrt{\bar{c}} = 4 \pm 3\sqrt{4}$$

$$= 10, -2 \text{ (or 0)}$$

A subassembly is thoroughly inspected, and the number of defects are recorded. A new group of assemblers began work Monday morning. The number of defects per subassembly for the first 10 they produced were: 3, 2, 0, 5, 4, 6, 0, 7, 7, and 6.

Set up a control chart for the average number of defects per subassembly and plot the essential data.

EXERCISES   3. A new high-speed machine appears to be producing a large percent of defective bolts. A frequent check of its output on Tuesday resulted in the following:

Sample number	Sample size	Number of defects	Sample number	Sample size	Number of defects
1 50		4	11 50		2
2 50		0	12 50		3
3 50		3	13 50		6
4 50		5	14 50		4
5 50		6	15 50		5
6 50		4	16 50		7
7 50		1	17 50		6
8 50		6	18 50		5
9 50		7	19 50		10
10 50		8	20 50		2

a. Design a percent defective chart. Insert the upper and lower control limits and $\bar{p}$ on the chart. Plot Tuesday's experience.

b. Interpret the chart.

4. The manufacturer of a newly designed metal storage cabinet ships the cabinet disassembled, and the purchaser assembles it. An increasing number of complaints have been received regarding missing parts, sharp edges, hinges that did not align properly, imperfections in the enamel, and so on. In order to eliminate these complaints as far as possible, starting with Monday's production each cabinet was fully assembled at the factory and the defects corrected before disassembling it for shipment. A record of the number of defects per cabinet for the first 12 cabinets checked was:

Cabinet designation	Number of defects	Cabinet designation	Number of defects
OA1 7		OA7 9	
OA2 6		OA8 3	
OA3 8		OA9 4	
OA4 10		OA10 6	
OA5 8		OA11 5	
OA6 4		OA12 2	

a. Design a chart to show the number of defects per unit. Show the upper and lower control limits and other essential data. Plot the experience for the first 12 cabinets inspected.

b. Interpret the chart.

CHAPTER SUMMARY

One facet of quality control is examined in this chapter—namely, control charts. The purpose of these charts is to keep management informed about the quality of incoming shipments or in-plant production.

We noted that two types of variation are present in a manufacturing process—chance and assignable variation. Chance variations are due to slight variations in the raw materials, slight vibrations of the machines, changes in temperature and humidity, and so on. These slight variations in the outside diameter, the weight, or the length of units of production are difficult to reduce or eliminate. Assignable causes, however, can be reduced or eliminated. If a bottle of cola is being overfilled, the machine can be adjusted. If an industrial band saw is damaging veneer, the teeth can be sharpened.

Four commonly used charts were presented—a mean chart, a range chart, a percent defective chart, and a chart designed to portray the average number of defects per unit, called a $\bar{c}$ chart. All have a centerline representing the average. There is a region of acceptance (referred to as the "in-control" region), and there is a region of rejection (referred to as the "out-of-control" region). These two regions are separated by the upper control limit, UCL, and the lower control limit LCL. If the sample taken from current production falls in the "in-control" region it is assumed that the production is satisfactory. If the sample results fall either above the upper control limit or below the lower control limit, production is considered "out of control," and remedial action is taken to correct the process.

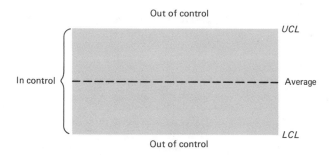

CHAPTER OUTLINE

Statistical quality control

I. Statistical quality control.
   A. *Objective.* To explore the application of quality control charts to manufacturing processes.
II. Control chart viewpoint.
   A. *Causes of variation in production.*
      1. *Chance causes.* Rare in number, random in nature, cannot be entirely eliminated.
      2. *Assignable causes.* Few in number, nonrandom, can be reduced or eliminated. Examples: If a shearing machine is cutting off a piece of steel that is too short. Solution: Reset the machine.
   B. *Purpose of quality control charts.* To determine and portray graphically just when an assignable cause enters the production system so that it can be identified and corrected. This is accomplished by selecting a very small random sample from current production periodically.
   C. *Types of charts.*
      1. *Mean charts.* Also called bar X charts. Designed to control variables, such as weights, lengths, and tensile strengths. Upper control limit and lower control limit found by $\bar{\bar{X}} \pm A_2\bar{R}$, where $\bar{\bar{X}}$ is the mean of the sample means, A_2 is a factor from

Appendix K, and $\bar{R}$ is the mean of the sample ranges. The chart on the left indicates that production is "in control." The one on the right is an "out-of-control" situation, with the outside diameter much too large and unacceptable at the last two checks.

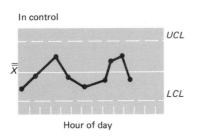

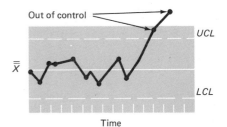

2. *Range chart*. Another chart for variables. Shows whether overall range of measurement is in or out of control. *UCL* and *LCL* found by $D_4\bar{R}$ and $D_3\bar{R}$, respectively. The factors D_4 and D_3 are given in Appendix K. $\bar{R}$ is the mean of the sample ranges.

3. *Percent defective chart*. A chart for an attribute. Example of an attribute is: Ball bearing is either good or defective. *UCL* and *LCL* found by:

$$\bar{p} \pm 3 \sqrt{\frac{\bar{p}(1 - \bar{p})}{n}}$$

where $\bar{p}$ is the mean percent defective based on samples taken from the production line.

4. *$\bar{c}$ charts*. Another attribute chart designed to control the *number of defects per unit*. Found by:

$$\bar{c} \pm 3\sqrt{\bar{c}}$$

where $\bar{c}$ is the mean number of defects per unit.

CHAPTER EXERCISES

5. An $\bar{X}$ and a range chart are to be designed. Every hour a quality control technician measures the thickness of the part and records the measurements. She also computes the mean thickness of the four parts and determines the range. After 30 hours had elapsed, the sum of the 30 means was computed to be 1,356 inches, and the sum of the ranges, 375 inches. Assume that the process is in control.
   a. Determine the central line, the upper control limit, and the lower control limit for the bar $\bar{X}$ chart.
   b. Determine the central line, the upper control limit, and the lower control limit for the range chart.

6. A glass manufacturer installed a new furnace and automatic equipment to make clear glass bowls. One of the problems associated with glassmaking is the ap-

494

pearance of unwanted stones. (Stones are small bubbles in the glass which are considered imperfections if over a specified diameter.)

In order to monitor the number of stones per bowl, a quality control inspector selected 15 bowls at random and counted the number of stones in each bowl over 1.5 millimeters in diameter. The number of stones per bowl were 14, 15, 10, 10, 14, 13, 12, 10, 11, 12, 9, 12, 12, 8, and 21, respectively.

a. Construct a chart specifically designed to monitor the number of defects (imperfections in this case) per unit. Show essential figures on the chart.

b. Plot the number of imperfections for the 15 bowls selected at random.

c. Interpret your chart.

7. An automatic machine produces 5.0 millimeter bolts at a high rate of speed. A quality control program has been started to control the number of defectives. The quality control inspector selects 50 bolts at random and determines how many are defective. The number defective for the first 10 samples follows.

Sample number	Size of sample	Number of defects
1	50	3
2	50	5
3	50	0
4	50	4
5	50	1
6	50	2
7	50	6
8	50	5
9	50	7
10	50	7

a. Design a percent defective chart. Insert $\bar{p}$, LCL, and other essential data on the chart.

b. Plot the number of defects for the first 10 samples on the chart.

c. Interpret the chart.

8. The following questions are based on Chart 19–13A, B, and C.

CHART 19–13

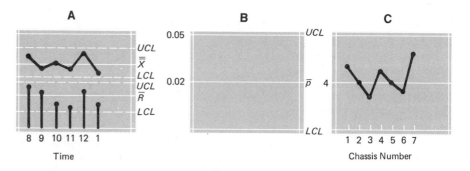

a. Chart 19–13A combines which two charts?

b. Referring back to A, is the process in control or out of control?

c. What will Chart 19–13B be called when its construction is completed?

d. For B, what is the lower control limit?

> *e.* Referring to Chart 19–13C, based on past experience how many defects are there per chassis on the average?
>
> *f.* What is C called?
>
> *g.* What are the upper and lower control limits of C?

9. A new machine has just been installed to cut and rough-shape large slugs. The slugs are then transferred to a precision grinder. One critical measurement is the outside diameter. The quality control inspector was instructed to select five slugs at random every half hour from the output of the new machine, measure the outside diameters, and record the results. The measurements (in millimeters) for the period from 8:00 A.M. to 10:30 A.M. follow.

	Sample piece number Outside diameter (in millimeters)				
Time	1	2	3	4	5
8:00 A.M.	87.1	87.3	87.9	87.0	87.0
8:30 A.M.	86.9	88.5	87.6	87.5	87.4
9:00 A.M.	87.5	88.4	86.9	87.6	88.2
9:30 A.M.	86.0	88.0	87.2	87.6	87.1
10:00 A.M.	87.1	87.1	87.1	87.1	87.1
10:30 A.M.	88.0	86.2	87.4	87.3	87.8

> *a.* Design a mean chart. Insert the control limits and other essential figures on the chart.
>
> *b.* Plot the means on the chart.
>
> *c.* Immediately below the mean chart, draw a range chart. Plot the ranges on the chart.
>
> *d.* Interpret the two charts.

CHAPTER SELF-REVIEW EXAMINATION

Do all of the problems and then check your answers against those given in Appendix A.

Score each problem 25 points.

For Problems 1 and 2, assume that the quality control inspector checks five pieces of the output of a shearing machine every hour. He measures and records each piece to the nearest hundredth of an inch. The record for the first four hours is:

Time	1	2	3	4	5
8 A.M.	6.04	6.01	6.05	6.02	6.06
9 A.M.	6.01	6.02	6.03	6.02	6.02
10 A.M.	6.01	6.05	6.07	6.03	6.04
11 A.M.	6.02	6.04	6.04	6.03	6.02

1. *a.* Design a bar X chart and plot the essential data for the four hours.
   b. Interpret the chart.

2. *a.* Design a range chart and plot the essential data for the four hours.
   b. Interpret the chart.

3. The quality control inspector then goes to another operation, where he checks 200 pieces. The piece is either good or defective. The record for nine hours is:

Time	Number of pieces checked	Number of defects
8 A.M.	200	0
9 A.M.	200	3
10 A.M.	200	4
11 A.M.	200	0
12 P.M.	200	5
1 P.M.	200	2
2 P.M.	200	0
3 P.M.	200	1
4 P.M.	200	3

a. Design a percent defective chart and plot the essential data.

b. Interpret the chart.

4. A new assembly operation has just been started. A small group of assemblyline employees inserts parts, solders, and so on to produce a radio chassis. The completed chassis is checked, and all defects must be repaired. The number of defects per chassis for the first 10 produced are:

Chassis number	Number of defects
1	0
2	1
3	0
4	2
5	3
6	0
7	1
8	1
9	2
10	4

a. Design a $\bar{c}$ chart and plot the essential data.

b. Interpret the chart.

INTRODUCTION

Many research projects involve the relationship between two variables. For example, an agronomist may be interested in the relationship between the amount of fertilizer applied to an acre of land and the number of bushels of corn harvested. The director of quality control may be interested in the relationship between the outside diameter of steel wires and their tensile strength. The admissions office may be interested in the relationship between the score earned by students on a newly developed entrance test and their grade point average at the end of their freshman year. If there is a strong relationship between the two variables, the admission counselors might try to dissuade some applicants with very low scores on the test from enrolling at the university.

Two techniques dealing with the relationship between two variables will be examined in this chapter—namely, **regression analysis** and **correlation analysis.**

Simple regression and correlation analysis

REGRESSION ANALYSIS

As noted, the major purpose of a study of two variables is to predict with reasonable accuracy one of the variables based on the other variable. For illustration, suppose that the personnel manager wishes to find out if the score on a test he designed can be used to predict the weekly sales of a salesperson. If so, the test score of an applicant could be used to predict weekly sales (should he or she be hired).

As a first step, the personnel manager selected five experienced salespersons at random and administered the test to each one. (Of course, in actual practice, in order to determine the validity of the test a much larger group would be selected. The size of the group was intentionally kept at a minimum in order to simplify the calculations.) The test score of each salesperson was then paired with weekly sales (see Table 20–1).

TABLE 20–1
Test scores and weekly sales of five salespersons

Salesperson	Test score	Weekly sales
Mr. J. A. Amber	4	$ 5,000
Mr. B. N. Archer	7	12,000
Ms. G. D. Smith	3	4,000
Mr. A. B. Malcolm	6	8,000
Ms. A. Goodwin	10	11,000

The variable being predicted is referred to as the *dependent* variable and frequently designated Y. The variable being used to make the prediction is called the *independent* variable and designated X.

Scatter diagram

The paired data can be portrayed graphically in a **scatter diagram** (Chart 20–1). To plot the data, the *dependent* variable (weekly sales in the problem) is *always* scaled on the Y-axis. The *independent* variable (test scores) is scaled on the X-axis. For example, the plot for the set of data for Mr. Amber is 4 on the X-axis and $5,000 on the Y-axis.

CHART 20–1
A scatter diagram

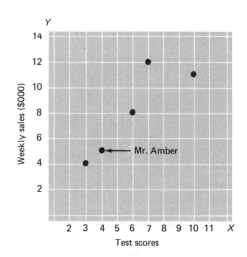

The scatter diagram shows: (1) As test scores increase so do sales. (2) A straight line seems to best describe the average path of the points. (3) Any prediction of sales based on test scores cannot be 100 percent accurate but can be fairly precise.

The regression equation

A linear equation, therefore, will be used as the **regression equation.**[1] It is alternately called an **estimating equation** or **predicting equation.** The scatter diagram in the previous chart is reproduced in Chart 20–2 and a ''freehand'' line using a ruler is drawn through the dots to illustrate that a linear straight line would probably fit the data best. However, the freehand line using a ruler or straight edge has one disadvantage: Its position is based on the judgment of the person drawing the line. The freehand lines on Chart 20–3 might represent the judgments of four persons. All the lines except line *A* seem to be reasonable. Each would, however, give a different prediction of sales.

CHART 20–2
Test scores and weekly sales of five salespersons

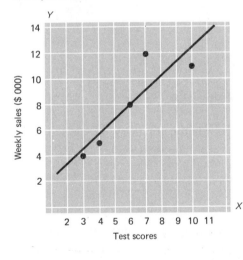

CHART 20–3
Many freehand lines superimposed on the scatter diagram

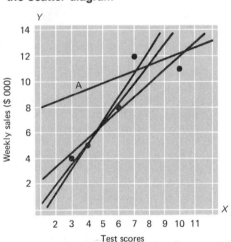

Least squares method of determining the regression equation

Judgment is eliminated by determining the regression line using a mathematical method called the **least squares method.** This method gives what is commonly referred to as the ''best-fitting'' straight line. The method minimizes the sum of the squares of the vertical deviations about the line. To illustrate this concept, the same data are plotted in the three charts which

---

[1] The word *regression* was introduced by Sir Francis Galton in 1877 in his study of heredity. He found that the heights of descendants of tall parents tended to regress (meaning to go back) toward the average height of the population. The mathematical line which he developed was called the line of regression. The term *line of regression* is commonly used even though *predictive equation* or *estimating equation* seems to be more appropriate.

follow. The regression line in Chart 20–4 was determined using the least squares methods. It is the best-fitting line because *the sum of the squares of the vertical deviations about it is at a minimum.* The first plot ($X = 3$, $Y = 8$) deviates 2 from the line, found by $10 - 8$. The deviation squared is 4. The deviation squared for the plot $X = 4$, $Y = 18$ is 16. The deviation squared for the plot $X = 5$, $Y = 16$ is 4. The sum of the squared deviations is 24, found by $4 + 16 + 4$.

Assume that the straight lines in Chart 20–5 and Chart 20–6 were drawn using the freehand method. The sum of the vertical deviations squared in Chart 20–5 is 44, and for Chart 20–6 it is 132. Both sums are greater than the one found using the least squares method.

CHART 20–4
A least squares line superimposed on a scatter diagram

CHART 20–5
A freehand line superimposed on a scatter diagram

CHART 20–6
A freehand line superimposed on a scatter diagram

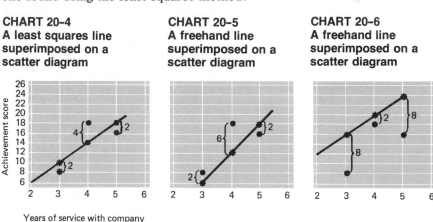

Years of service with company

Now to describe the relationship between test scores and weekly sales by determining the **regression equation.** It may be expressed in the form of:

$$\overline{Y}_p = a + bX$$

Recall from Chapter 7 on time series analysis that:

$\overline{Y}_p$ is the average predicted value of the Y variable for a selected X value.

a is the Y-intercept. It is the estimated value of Y when $X = 0$. Another way to put it is: a is the estimated value of Y where the regression line crosses the Y-axis when X is zero.

b is the slope of the line, or the average change in $\overline{Y}_p$ for each change of one (either increase or decrease) in X.

X is any value of X that is selected.

It should be noted that the linear regression equation for the sample of salespersons $\overline{Y}_p = a + bX$, is just an estimate of the relationship between the two variables in the population. Thus, the values of a and b in the regression equation are usually referred to as the *estimated regression coefficients,* or shortened to just the *regression coefficients.*

The equation for the regression line can be determined two ways. The first involves solving two equations simultaneously. The two equations are:

$$\boxed{\begin{aligned} &\text{Equation I:} \quad \Sigma Y = na + b\Sigma X \\ &\text{Equation II:} \quad \Sigma XY = a\Sigma X + b\Sigma X^2 \end{aligned}}$$

EXAMPLE

Returning to the test scores and weekly sales of the five salespersons, the sums and other essential figures, needed to solve the two equations simultaneously are given in Table 20–2.

**TABLE 20–2
Calculations
necessary for the
solution of the least
squares equation**

Salesperson	Test score X	Weekly sales ($000) Y	X²	XY	Y²
Mr. Amber	4	$ 5	16	20	25
Mr. Archer	7	12	49	84	144
Ms. Smith	3	4	9	12	16
Mr. Malcolm	6	8	36	48	64
Ms. Goodwin	10	11	100	110	121
Total	30	$40	210	274	370

What is the regression equation?

SOLUTION

The equations are:

$$\Sigma Y = na + b\Sigma X$$
$$\Sigma XY = a\Sigma X + b\Sigma X^2$$

Equation I: $\quad 40 = 5a + 30b$

Equation II: $\quad 274 = 30a + 210b$

To solve:

Multiply equation I by 6:	$240 = 30a + 180b$
Multiply equation II by 1:	$274 = 30a + 210b$
Then subtracting equation II from equation I:	$240 = 30a + 180b$
	$-274 = -30a + -210b$
	$-34 = -30b$
	$b = 1.133$

Insert the value of b in either equation I or II and solve for a.

$$40 = 5a + 30b$$
$$40 = 5a + 30(1.333)$$
$$40 = 5a + 33.99$$
$$6.01 = 5a$$
$$a = 1.202$$

The regression equation using the least squares method is:

$$\overline{Y}_p = 1.202 + 1.133X \text{ (in \$000)}$$

502

a. Yield is a dependent variable. The amount of fertilizer is the independent variable.

b.

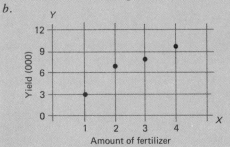

c.

X	Y	XY	X²	Y²
2	7	14	4	49
1	3	3	1	9
3	8	24	9	64
4	10	40	16	100
10	28	81	30	222

$$28 = 4a + 10b$$
$$81 = 10a + 30b$$

Multiply by 2.5: $70 = 10a + 25b$
Multiply by 1: $81 = 10a + 30b$
$$-11 = -5b$$
$$b = 2.2$$

Substituting:

$$28 = 4a + 10(2.2)$$
$$a = 1.5$$

Equation is:

$$\overline{Y}_p = a + bX$$

$$\overline{Y}_p = 1.5 + 2.2X \text{ (in hundreds of bushels)}$$

(A reminder: Cover the answers in the left-hand column.)

An agronomist experimented with different amounts of liquid fertilizer on a sample of equal-sized plots. The amount of fertilizer and the yield are:

Plot	Amount of fertilizer (tons)	Yield (hundreds of bushels)
A	2	7
B	1	3
C	3	8
D	4	10

a. The agronomist is interested in predicting yield. What is the dependent variable? The independent variable?
b. Draw a scatter diagram.
c. Determine the regression equation.

The relatively small size of the paired numbers in the previous problem made the computation of the least squares equation relatively easy. However, if there is a large number of paired observations, and if the numbers are large, solving the two equations simultaneously is rather tedious.

The second way of arriving at the least squares equation does not require that the two equations be solved simultaneously. Instead, a and b can be found directly, using the following equivalent shortcut formulas:

$$b = \frac{n(\Sigma XY) - (\Sigma X)(\Sigma Y)}{n(\Sigma X^2) - (\Sigma X)^2}$$

$$a = \frac{\Sigma Y}{n} - b\frac{\Sigma X}{n} \text{ or } \overline{Y} - b\overline{X}$$

EXAMPLE

What is the regression equation for the test score—weekly sales problem using the shortcut formulas?

SOLUTION

The sums from Table 20–2 are used to illustrate the computations of a and b in the regression equation. Note that the results are identical to the values of a and b found previously by solving the two equations simultaneously.

$$b = \frac{n(\Sigma XY) - (\Sigma X)(\Sigma Y)}{n(\Sigma X^2) - (\Sigma X)^2} \qquad a = \bar{Y} - b\bar{X}$$

$$= \frac{5(274) - (30)(40)}{5(210) - (30)^2} \qquad\qquad = \frac{40}{5} - 1.133 \left(\frac{30}{5}\right)$$

$$= \frac{1{,}370 - 1{,}200}{1{,}050 - 900} \qquad\qquad = 8 - 6.798$$

$$\qquad\qquad\qquad\qquad = 1.202$$

$$= \frac{170}{150}$$

$$= 1.133$$

$$\bar{Y}_p = 1.202 + 1.133X \text{ (in \$000)}$$

─────────────── **SELF-REVIEW 20-2** ───────────────

a.

$$b = \frac{4(81) - (10)(28)}{4(30) - (10)^2}$$

$$= \frac{324 - 280}{120 - 100} = 2.2$$

$$a = \frac{28}{4} - 2.2\left(\frac{10}{4}\right)$$

$$= 7 - 5.5 = 1.5$$

The equation is:

$$\bar{Y}_p = 1.5 + 2.2X \text{ (in hundreds of bushels).}$$

b. Yes.

The amount of fertilizer applied and the yield from Self-Review 20–1 are repeated below.

Plot	Amount of fertilizer (tons)	Yield (hundreds of bushels)
A	2	7
B	1	3
C	3	8
D	4	10

a. Determine the least squares equation using the shortcut formulas.
b. Does it agree with the one computed in Self-Review 20–1?

Determining the points on the straight line

EXAMPLE

Again referring back to the problem involving the weekly sales and test scores, how is the regression line superimposed on the scatter diagram?

SOLUTION

The least squares regression equation $\overline{Y}_p = 1.202 + 1.133X$ is used to determine various $\overline{Y}_p$ values for selected X values. For example, when the salespersons test score (X) is 3, predicted weekly sales $(\overline{Y}_p)$ are \$4,061, found by $\overline{Y}_p = 1.202 + 1.133(3)$, in \$000. The other points on the straight line can be determined by substituting the appropriate values of X into the equations. They are:

X when test score is	$\overline{Y}_p$ predicted weekly sales will be (\$000)	Solution
3	\$ 4.601	$\overline{Y}_p = 1.202 + 1.133(3)$
4	5.734	$= 1.202 + 1.133(4)$
6	8.000	$= 1.202 + 1.133(6)$
7	9.133	$= 1.202 + 1.133(7)$
10	12.532	$= 1.202 + 1.133(10)$

The plot for $X = 3$, $\overline{Y}_p = 4.601$ is located by moving to 3 on the X-axis and then going vertically to 4.601. The next plot is $X = 4$, $\overline{Y}_p = 5.734$. All the points are connected to give the straight line (see Chart 20–7). Note that the line goes through the middle of all the dots.

**CHART 20–7
The regression line plotted on the scatter diagram**

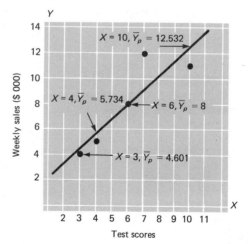

Errors in predicting   Notice in the preceding scatter diagram that all of the points do not fall on the regression line. Had they fallen on the line, and if the number of observations had been sufficiently large, there would be no error in predicting weekly sales. To put it another way, if all the points had fallen on the regression line, sales could be predicted with 100 percent accuracy. Thus, there would be no error in predicting the Y variable based on an X variable. This is true in the following hypothetical case (Chart 20–8). Theoretically, if

CHART 20–8
Perfect prediction

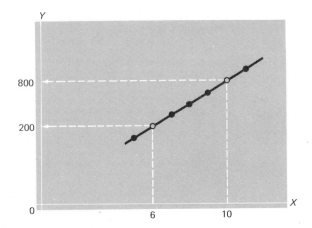

$X = 6$, then an exact Y of 200 could be predicted with 100 percent confidence. Or, if $X = 10$, then $Y = 800$. There is no error in this estimate.

Perfect prediction in problems involving economics and business is practically nonexistent. For example, the revenue for the year from gasoline sales (Y) based on automobile registrations (X) as of a certain date would no doubt be approximated fairly closely, but the prediction would not be exact to the nearest dollar, nor probably even to the nearest thousand dollars. Even predictions of tensile strengths of steel wires based on the outside diameters of the wires are not always exact (due to slight differences in the composition of the steel).

What is needed, then, is a measure that would indicate how precise the prediction of Y is based on X or, conversely, how inaccurate the prediction might be. This measure is called the **standard error of estimate.** The standard error of estimate, symbolized by $s_{y \cdot x}$, is the same concept as the standard deviation discussed in Chapter 5. The standard deviation measures the dispersion about an average, such as the mean. The standard error of estimate measures the dispersion about an average line, called the regression line.

The standard error of estimate is found by the equation shown below. (Note that the equation is quite similar to the one for the standard deviation of a sample.)

$$s_{y \cdot x} = \sqrt{\frac{\Sigma(Y - \overline{Y}_p)^2}{n - 2}}$$

EXAMPLE

The symbol for the standard error of estimate ($s_{y \cdot x}$) represents the standard deviation of the Y's based on the X's. Returning to the problem involving test scores and weekly sales, the first step is to determine each value of $\bar{Y}_p$ (the point on the straight line) for each X value. These $\bar{Y}_p$ points were computed previously in order to plot the straight line on the scatter diagram (Chart 20–7). The next step is to subtract each $\bar{Y}_p$ value from its corresponding Y value. These differences are squared and then summed (see Table 20–3).

**TABLE 20–3
Computations for the
standard error of
estimate**

Salesperson	Test score X	Sales ($000) Actual Y	Sales ($000) Predicted $\bar{Y}_p$	Deviations $Y - \bar{Y}_p$	Deviations squared $(Y - \bar{Y}_p)^2$
Mr. Amber	4	$ 5	$ 5.734	$-0.734	0.5388
Mr. Archer	7	12	9.133	+2.867	8.2200
Ms. Smith	3	4	4.601	−0.601	0.3612
Mr. Malcolm	6	8	8.000	0.000	0.0000
Ms. Goodwin	10	11	12.532	−1.532	2.3470
Total	30	$40	$40.000	$ 0.000	11.4670

What is the standard error of estimate?

SOLUTION

$$s_{y \cdot x} = \sqrt{\frac{\Sigma(Y - \bar{Y}_p)^2}{n - 2}}$$

$$= \sqrt{\frac{11.467}{5 - 2}}$$

$$= \sqrt{3.82}$$

$$= 1.954 \ (\text{in } \$000)$$

The figure 1.954 is really $1,954 (because the sales are in thousands of dollars).

The deviations $(Y - \bar{Y}_p)$ are vertical deviations from the regression line. To illustrate, the five deviations from Table 20–3 are shown in Chart 20–9. Note in Table 20–3 that the sum of the deviations is equal to zero, indicating that the positive deviations above the regression line on the scatter diagram are offset by the negative deviations below the line.

The formula for the standard error of estimate cited previously was given primarily to show the similarity in concept and computation between the standard deviation and the standard error of estimate. If a large number of observations are being studied and the numbers are large, computing each $\bar{Y}_p$ point on the regression line and then squaring the differences—that is, $(Y - \bar{Y}_p)^2$—is rather tedious. The following formula is algebraically identical to the preceding formula and facilitates computation.

$$s_{y \cdot x} = \sqrt{\frac{\Sigma Y^2 - a(\Sigma Y) - b(\Sigma XY)}{n - 2}}$$

CHART 20–9
Chart depicting the vertical deviations between each scatter point and the line of regression

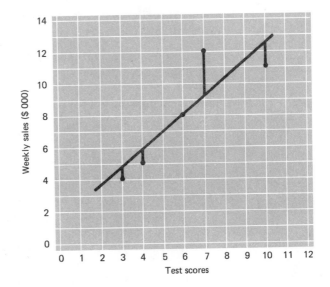

The squares, sums, and other numbers for the test score-weekly sales problem were calculated in Table 20–2.

$$s_{y \cdot x} = \sqrt{\frac{370 - 1.202(40) - 1.133(274)}{5 - 2}}$$

$$= \sqrt{\frac{370 - 48.08 - 310.44}{3}}$$

$$= 1.954 \text{ (in \$000)}$$

(This is the same standard error of estimate as computed previously.)

SELF-REVIEW 20–3

0.9487 (in hundreds of bushels) found by:

$$s_{y \cdot x} = \sqrt{\frac{\Sigma Y^2 - a(\Sigma Y) - b(\Sigma XY)}{n - 2}}$$

$$= \sqrt{\frac{222 - 1.5(28) - 2.2(81)}{4 - 2}}$$

$$= \sqrt{\frac{1.8}{2}} = \sqrt{0.9} = 0.9487 \text{ or } 94.87 \text{ bushels}$$

Refer back to Self-Review 20–1. Determine the standard error of estimate for this agricultural research project.

Theoretically, it is expected that the Y's will be distributed normally around the point on the line for any given X. In this sense, the standard error of estimate is similar to the standard deviation. Recall from Chapter 11 that if the distribution of values is somewhat normally distributed:

$\bar{X} \pm s$ encompassed approximately the middle 68 percent of the values.
$\bar{X} \pm 1.96s$ encompassed approximately the middle 95 percent of the values.
$\bar{X} \pm 3s$ encompassed approximately the middle 99.7 percent of the values.

If the distribution is highly skewed, these relationships would not be valid.

The same relationships exist between the average predicted value ($\bar{Y}_p$) and the standard error of estimate ($s_{y \cdot x}$). Again, if the scatter about the regression line is somewhat normally distributed, and the sample is large, then:

$\bar{Y}_p \pm s_{y \cdot x}$ encompasses the middle 68 percent of the dots.
$\bar{Y}_p \pm 1.96s_{y \cdot x}$ encompasses the middle 95 percent of the dots.
$\bar{Y}_p \pm 3s_{y \cdot x}$ encompasses the middle 99.7 percent of the dots.

Confidence limits for predictions

The standard error of estimate is a valid measure to use in setting **confidence limits** when the sample size is large and the scatter about the regression line is somewhat normally distributed. Neither of these assumptions is valid in this problem involving the weekly sales. The sample size of five, for example, is very small. Therefore, a correction factor for a small sample must be introduced.

Confidence limits will be set for:

1. The *mean* value of Y for a given value of X.
2. An *individual* value of Y for a given value of X.

To set confidence limits for the *mean* value of Y for a given value of X, the formula is:

$$\bar{Y}_p \pm t(s_{y \cdot x}) \sqrt{\frac{1}{n} + \frac{(X - \bar{X})^2}{\Sigma(X - \bar{X})^2}}$$

where in this problem:

$\bar{Y}_p$ is the predicted value for any selected X value. In the illustration above, $\bar{Y}_p$ is \$8,000 for an X value of 6.
X is any selected value of X.
$\bar{X}$ is the mean of the X's (six in this case).
n is the number of observations. There are five.
$s_{y \cdot x}$ is the standard error of estimate (computed previously to be 1,954).
t is the value of t from Appendix E for $n - 2 = 5 - 2 = 3$ *degrees of freedom* (3 *df*).

The formula compensates not only for the error of the predicting equation measured by $s_{y \cdot x}$, but also for the sampling error.

It is sufficient to note here again that the concept of t was developed by William Gosset in the early 1900s. He noticed that $\bar{X} \pm z(s)$ was not precisely correct for small samples. He observed, for example, for samples of size 120, that 95 percent of the items fell within $\bar{X} \pm 1.98s$ instead of $\bar{X} \pm 1.96s$. This is not too critical, but note what happens as the sample size becomes smaller.

df	t
120	.... 1.980
60	.... 2.000
21	.... 2.080
10	.... 2.228
3	.... 3.182

This is logical. The smaller the sample, the larger the possible error. The increase in the t value compensates for this possibility. Student's t (Gosset wrote under the pen name of Student) for a confidence level of 95 percent and $n - 2$ degrees of freedom is 3.182. What he found for the standard deviation (s) is directly applicable for the standard error of estimate ($s_{y \cdot x}$).

The confidence limits for the $\bar{Y}_p$ value of 8.0 are 5.219 and 10.781 (see Table 20-4 for some of the essential computations).

TABLE 20-4
Calculations necessary for constructing confidence limits

X	Y	$X - \bar{X}$	$(X - \bar{X})^2$
4	$ 5	−2	4
7	12	+1	1
3	4	−3	9
6	8	0	0
10	11	+4	16
		0	30

Now, substituting the values for n, t, and so on in the formula, we find:

$$\bar{Y}_p \pm t(s_{y \cdot x}) \sqrt{\frac{1}{n} + \frac{(X - \bar{X})^2}{\Sigma(X - \bar{X})^2}}$$

$$= 8.0 \pm 3.182(1.954) \sqrt{\frac{1}{5} + \frac{(6 - 6)^2}{30}}$$

$$= 8.0 \pm 3.182(1.954)\sqrt{0.20}$$

$$= 5.219 \text{ and } 10.781, \text{ or } \$5,219 \text{ and } \$10,781$$

Interpretation. For a group of applicants whose test scores are exactly 6, the personnel manager would be 95 percent confident that their average weekly sales would be in the interval between $5,219 and $10,781.

As another example of the construction of confidence limits for the mean value of Y for a given value of X, suppose a group of applicants had test scores of exactly 7. The essential numbers to compute the 0.95 confidence limits for $X = 7$ would be entered as follows (when $X = 7$, $\bar{Y}_p = 9.133$ from Table 20-3):

$$9.133 \pm 3.182(1.954) \sqrt{\frac{1}{5} + \frac{(7 - 6)^2}{30}}$$

SELF-REVIEW 20-4

$\bar{Y}_p$ for an X of 3 is 8.1, found by $\bar{Y}_p = 1.5 + 2.2(3) = 8.1$. $\bar{X} = 2.5$. Then:

X	$X - \bar{X}$	$(X - \bar{X})^2$
2	−0.5	0.25
1	−1.5	2.25
3	0.5	0.25
4	1.5	2.25
		5.00

t from Appendix E for $4 - 2 = 2df$ and 0.10 level is 2.290.

$$\bar{Y}_p \pm t(s_{y \cdot x}) \sqrt{\frac{1}{n} + \frac{(X - \bar{X})^2}{\Sigma(X - \bar{X})^2}}$$

$$= 8.1 \pm 2.290(0.9487) \sqrt{\frac{1}{4} + \frac{(3 - 2.5)^2}{5.00}}$$

$$= 8.1 \pm 2.290(0.9487)(0.5477)$$

$$= 6.91 \text{ and } 9.29 \text{ (in hundreds of bushels)}$$

The sample data for Self-Reviews 20–1, 20–2, and 20–3 are repeated.

Plot	Amount of fertilizer (tons) X	Yield (hundreds of bushels) Y
A	2	7
B	1	3
C	3	8
D	4	10

You computed the regression equation to be $\bar{Y}_p = 1.5 + 2.2X$ (in hundreds of bushels). The standard error was computed to be 0.9487 (in hundreds of bushels).

a. Realizing that this is a small sample, set the 0.90 confidence limits for a group of plots that received exactly three tons of fertilizer each.

b. Interpret your findings.

Now to set confidence limits for an *individual* value of Y for a given value of X. If confidence limits are to be set about an *individual* Y the formula is modified slightly. One (1) is added to the number under the radical:

$$\bar{Y}_p \pm t(s_{y \cdot x}) \sqrt{1 + \frac{1}{n} + \frac{(X - \bar{X})^2}{\Sigma(X - \bar{X})^2}}$$

The weekly sales of Mr. Archer are used for illustration. He scored 7 on the test (Table 20–1). The 95 percent confidence limits would be found by:

$$\$9.133 \pm 3.182(1.954) \sqrt{1 + \frac{1}{5} + \frac{(7 - 6)^2}{30}}$$

Review of regression analysis

The problem used to illustrate the concepts of regression analysis involved predicting the weekly sales of salespersons. In an attempt to estimate sales, a test was devised. A cursory examination of the paired test scores and sales indicated that weekly sales (Y) seemed to be dependent to some degree on test scores (X). It was noted that the relationship between the two variables was linear, i.e., a change in X produced a constant incremental change in Y. The linear *regression equation* was computed to be $\bar{Y}_p = 1.202 + 1.133X$ (in thousands of dollars). This equation, determined by the least squares method, gave the best-fitting straight line. A freehand line could have been superimposed on the data, but the resulting equation would not be as accurate as the one determined mathematically by the least squares method. The regression equation measures the average relationship between the two variables; and based on the regression equation, average weekly sales (Y) can be predicted for a test score (X).

A prediction is a valuable statistic, but equally important is a measurement of the preciseness of the prediction. This measure is called the *standard error of estimate*.

Caution. The fact that the X variable and Y variable move together does not necessarily indicate that an increase in the X variable *causes* the Y variable to increase (or decrease as the case may be). For example, it can be shown that the consumption of Georgia peanuts and the consumption of aspirin have moved together. However, this does not indicate that an increase in the consumption of peanuts caused the consumption of aspirin to increase. (Nor does it indicate that there is any relationship between the two variables.) Likewise, the incomes of professors and the number of inmates in mental institutions have increased proportionately. Further, as the population of donkeys decreased there was a proportional increase in the number of Ph.D.s. The foregoing illustrations show that the independent variable (X) used to predict the Y variable must be selected with discretion.

EXERCISES

(A reminder: The answer and method of solution for selected exercises are given in Appendix A.)

1. A research project to determine if there is a relationship between years on the job and the efficiency rating of employees was undertaken. The objective of the study is to predict the efficiency rating of an employee based on years on the job. The sample results are:

Employee	Years on job	Efficiency rating
Jones	1	6
Orlando	20	5
Ireland	6	3
Smith	8	5
Kordel	2	2
Harper	1	2
Lopez	15	4
Sobecki	8	3

   a. What is the dependent variable?
   b. Draw a scatter diagram.
   c. Based on the scatter diagram, does there appear to be any relationship between years on the job and efficiency?
   d. Compute the regression equation.
   e. Compute any three points for the straight line, and plot the line on the scatter diagram.
   f. Determine the standard error of estimate.
   g. Determine the 0.95 confidence limits for a group of employees who have exactly two years of service.

2. The production department wants to explore the relationship between the

number of employees who assemble a subassembly and the number produced. As an experiment two employees were assigned to assemble the subassembly. They produced 15 during a one-hour period. Then, four employees assembled it. They produced 25 during a one-hour period. The complete set of paired observations is as follows.

Number of assemblers	One-hour production (units)
2	15
4	25
1	10
5	40
3	30

The dependent variable is production, that is, it is assumed that the level of production depends upon the number of employees.

a. Draw a scatter diagram.
b. Based on the scatter diagram, does there appear to be any relationship between the number of assemblers and production? Explain.
c. Compute the regression equation.
d. Determine any three points for the straight line, and plot the line on the scatter diagram.
e. Determine the standard error of estimate.
f. Determine the 0.90 confidence limits for a group of exactly three assemblers.

CORRELATION ANALYSIS

In the previous section, a predictive line was fitted to paired data consisting of sales (Y) and test scores (X). The objective was to predict weekly sales based on a test score. The error of the predictions was measured by the standard error of estimate $(s_{y \cdot x})$. If the standard error of estimate is zero, there is no error in the prediction. The zero indicates that all of the dots fall on the predictive line, as shown in Chart 20–10A. However, as the scatter increases about the line, the error becomes larger (Chart 20–10B) and larger (Chart 20–10C) until $s_{y \cdot x} = s_y$. To put it another way, predicting Y based on X becomes less and less accurate as the scatter about the line increases.

The lack of scatter in Chart 20–10A indicates that *all* of the sales (Y) were accurately explained by the test scores. In Chart 20–10B a large proportion of the variation in sales is explained by the test scores. However, some of

CHART 20–10

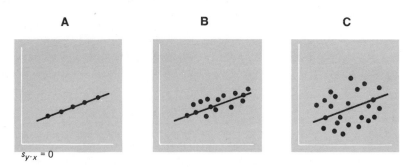

A　　　　　B　　　　　C

$s_{y \cdot x} = 0$

the variation in sales is *not* explained by the test scores. Thus, there is *explained* variation and *unexplained* variation. As will be examined in more detail in the following discussion, "variation" in a statistical sense refers to the sum of square deviations.

The standard error of estimate which measures the *unexplained* variation is rather difficult to interpret. Is the $s_{y \cdot x}$ of $1,954 in the foregoing problem large or small? Similarly, how is standard error of estimate of 842 tons, 107 inches, or 1,800 board-feet interpreted? A standard error of zero can be interpreted by saying that all (100 percent) of the variation in Y is explained by X. The abstract measure, such as the 100 percent, can be readily interpreted. Thus, if 842 tons could be converted to a percent, say 92 percent (hypothetical), then statements could be made such as "92 percent of the variation in Y is explained by X." If the problem involved predicting the tensile strength (Y) of a steel cable based on the outside diameter, then it could be said that outside diameter (X) is an excellent predictor of tensile strength because 92 percent of the variation in tensile strength is explained by the outside diameter. And, only 8 percent of the variation in tensile strength is unexplained by outside diameter. (Factors not measured by outside diameter might include slight differences in the physical properties of the steel from piece to piece.)

Coefficients of determination, nondetermination, and correlation

The proportion of the variation *explained* (92 percent in the foregoing illustration) is called the **coefficient of determination** (r^2). The unexplained variation (8 percent in the illustration) is called the **coefficient of nondetermination**, found by $1 - r^2$.

The value of the coefficient of determination may vary from zero to one. A coefficient of determination of zero indicates that none of the variation in Y is explained by the X variable; a coefficient of one indicates that 100 percent of the variation in Y is explained by X. An r^2 of 0.12 indicates that very little of the variation is explained by X, and a 0.93 coefficient suggests that a large proportion of the Y variable is determined by the X variable. In the latter case, 93 percent is explained by X; 7 percent is not explained by X. Thus, if the coefficient of nondetermination is known to be 0.07, the coefficient of determination is $1 - 0.07 = 0.93$. This is one way of computing the coefficient of determination, that is, $1 -$ coefficient of nondetermination.

The square root of the coefficient of determination is called the **correlation coefficient** and is designated by r. Originated by Karl Pearson, it is often referred to as the *Pearson product-moment correlation coefficient*, or *Pearson's r*. It measures the degree of linear relationship between the two variables of interest.

A convenient formula for computing the correlation coefficient is shown below. (Note that the numerator in the formula is the same as that used in determining the regression coefficient b.)

$$r = \frac{n(\Sigma XY) - (\Sigma X)(\Sigma Y)}{\sqrt{[n(\Sigma X^2) - (\Sigma X)^2][n(\Sigma Y^2) - (\Sigma Y)^2]}}$$

EXAMPLE

The data for the problem involving weekly sales and test scores and the calculations needed for the correlation coefficient are repeated from Table 20–2.

Salesperson	Test score X	Weekly sales (000) Y	X²	XY	Y²
Mr. Amber	4	$ 5	16	20	25
Mr. Archer	7	12	49	84	144
Ms. Smith	3	4	9	12	16
Mr. Malcolm	6	8	36	48	64
Ms. Goodwin	10	11	100	110	121
Total	30	$40	210	274	370

What is the coefficient of correlation, the coefficient of determination, and the coefficient of nondetermination?

SOLUTION

The coefficient of correlation is 0.87788, found by:

$$r = \frac{n(\Sigma XY) - (\Sigma X)(\Sigma Y)}{\sqrt{[n(\Sigma X^2) - (\Sigma X)^2][n(\Sigma Y^2) - (\Sigma Y)^2]}}$$

$$= \frac{5(274) - (30)(40)}{\sqrt{[5(210) - (30)^2][5(370) - (40)^2]}}$$

$$= \frac{170}{\sqrt{[150][250]}}$$

$$= \frac{170}{193.64916}$$

$$= 0.87788$$

The usual practice is to round r to the nearest hundredth; in this problem it would be 0.88. Squaring the r of 0.88 gives an r^2 of 0.77 which, as noted previously, is the *coefficient of determination*. The *coefficient of nondetermination* is 0.23, found by $1 - r^2$.

Recall that the coefficient of determination is defined as the *proportion of the variation in the Y variable which is explained by the X variable*. In this problem, about 77 percent of the variation in weekly sales is explained by the test scores. Logically, the coefficient of nondetermination of 0.23 is the *proportion of the sales which is not accounted for by the test scores*.

The coefficient of correlation r measures the *degree of linear relationship between the X and Y variables.* Its meaning is not as explicit as that of the coefficient of determination. Moreover, the Pearson product-moment coefficient tends to overstate the degree of relationship between the X and Y variables. For example, if the coefficient of determination $(r^2) = 0.75$ and the coefficient of nondetermination $(1 - r^2) = 0.25$, it indicates that only about three fourths of the variation in Y is attributable to X and one fourth of the variation is not explained. Pearson's $r = \sqrt{0.75} = 0.87$ indicates a rather high correlation between the two variables. Thus, the more conservative coefficient of determination seems to be a more desirable measure to use to explain the relationship between X and Y.

SELF-REVIEW 20–5

a. $r = 0.96$, found by:

$$r = \frac{4(81) - (10)(28)}{\sqrt{[4(30) - (10)^2][4(222) - (28)^2]}}$$

$$= \frac{44}{\sqrt{2080}} = \frac{44}{45.60717} = 0.9648$$

b. $r^2 = (0.96)^2 = 0.92$. About 92 percent of the variation in yield is explained by the amount of fertilizer applied to the plot.

c. $1 - r^2 = 1 - 0.92 = 0.08$. About 8 percent of the variation in yield is not explained by the amount of fertilizer applied to the plot.

The agriculture problem involving the amount of fertilizer X applied on a plot, and yield Y, is repeated from Self-Review 20–1. The sums and sum of squares needed for the three coefficients are also given.

Plot	X	Y	XY	X²	Y²
A	2	7	14	4	49
B	1	3	3	1	9
C	3	8	24	9	64
D	4	10	40	16	100
	10	28	81	30	222

a. Determine the coefficient of correlation.
b. What is the coefficient of determination? Interpret.
c. What is the coefficient of nondetermination? Interpret.

A **correlation coefficient** can assume any value between -1.00 and $+1.00$ inclusive. A coefficient of -1.00 indicates a perfect negative linear relationship between the two variables and $+1.00$ perfect positive relationship. An r of zero indicates no correlation. (See Charts 20–11D, E, and F.)

CHART 20–11

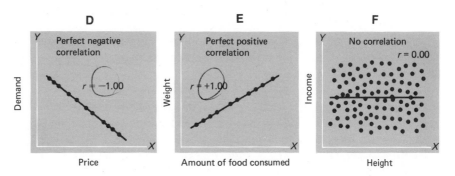

The strength of the relationship is summarized below. Note that the closer Pearson's r is to 1.00 (in either direction), the greater the strength of the relationship. Notice that the strength of the correlation does not depend on the direction. A -0.91 and a $+0.91$ are equal in strength (both very strong). Likewise, the strength of -0.14 and $+0.14$ are the same (both quite weak).

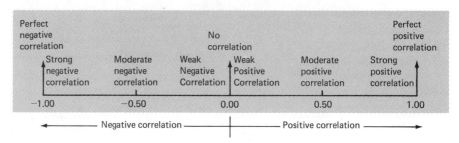

3. Refer back to Exercise 1 involving the relationship between years on the job and the efficiency ratings of the employees.
   a. Compute the coefficient of correlation.
   b. Compute the coefficient of determination.
   c. Compute the coefficient of nondetermination.
   d. Interpret the three measures.

4. Refer back to Exercise 2 involving the number of assemblers and hourly production.
   a. Compute the coefficient of correlation.
   b. Compute the coefficient of determination.
   c. Compute the coefficient of nondetermination.
   d. Interpret the three measures.

Testing the significance of the correlation coefficient

If the number of paired observations is less than 50, the t-test is usually used to test the significance of r. If the number is 50 or greater, the z-test is applied. The question is: *Is there zero correlation in the population from which the sample was selected?* To put it another way, did the computed r come from a population of paired observations with zero correlation?

Small samples. The test scores and weekly sales illustration is a small-sample case. The null hypothesis and the alternate hypothesis are:

H_0: The correlation coefficient r in the population is not different from zero, i.e., it is zero.

H_1: r in the population is different from zero. Thus, the way H_1 is stated, the test becomes a two-tailed test.

The formula for t is:

$$t = \frac{r\sqrt{n-2}}{\sqrt{1-r^2}}$$ with $n-2$ degrees of freedom

Using the 0.05 level of significance, the decision rule states that if the computed t falls in the area between ± 3.182, the null hypothesis will be accepted. To locate the critical value of 3.182, refer to Appendix E and $n - 2$, or $5 - 2 = 3$ df. Shown schematically:

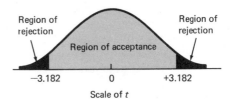

Region of rejection

Region of acceptance

Region of rejection

−3.182   0   +3.182

Scale of t

Applying the formula to the test scores and weekly sales problem, we get:

$$t = \frac{r\sqrt{n - 2}}{\sqrt{1 - r^2}} = \frac{0.87788 \sqrt{5 - 2}}{\sqrt{1 - (0.87788)^2}}$$

$$= \frac{1.5221262}{0.4788807} = 3.179$$

The computed value of t falls in the area of acceptance, so H_0 is at the 0.05 level, meaning that the correlation in the population could be zero.

Large samples. As noted, the z-test is used for samples of 50 or more. The formula is:

$$z = \frac{r}{\dfrac{1}{\sqrt{n - 1}}}$$

As an illustration, suppose that the sample consisted of 401 sets of paired observations and r was computed to be 0.30. If the 0.05 level of significance and a two-tailed test were applied, the decision rule would be to accept the null hypothesis if the computed z-value fell between ± 1.96 (from Appendix G). Shown diagrammatically:

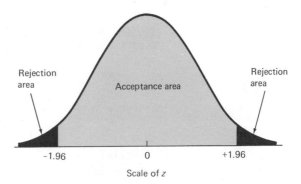

Rejection area

Acceptance area

Rejection area

−1.96   0   +1.96

Scale of z

In this problem, H_0 would be rejected at the 0.05 level because the computed value of 6.0 falls in the area of rejection. The calculations for z:

$$z = \frac{r}{\dfrac{1}{\sqrt{n-1}}} = \frac{0.30}{\dfrac{1}{\sqrt{401-1}}} = \frac{0.30}{\dfrac{1}{20}} = \frac{0.30}{0.05} = 6.0$$

Although the correlation (0.30) between the two sets of variables is rather weak, based on the test of significance it is highly unlikely that the relationship in the population is zero.

AN APPLICATION USING A COMPUTER PACKAGE

As an illustration of the application of simple correlation and regression techniques, the administrator of a new paralegal program in a community and technical college was interested in determining the relationship between the high school grade point average of the students and their grade point

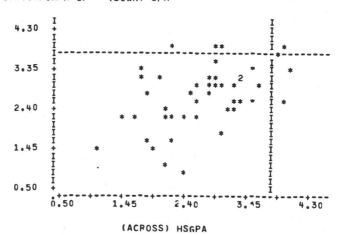

PARALEGAL PROGRAM ANALYSIS
SCATTERGRAM OF   (DOWN) GPA

(ACROSS) HSGPA

```
STATISTICS..
   CORRELATION (R)-          0.48526
   STD ERR OF EST -          0.65650
   PLOTTED VALUES -          45

   R SQUARED        -        0.23548
   INTERCEPT (A)    -        1.42329
   EXCLUDED VALUES-          0

   SIGNIFICANCE     -        0.00036
   SLOPE (B)        -        0.51208
```

Source: Plan Administrator, Community and Technical College, The University of Toledo, Ohio.

average in the second year of the program. The Statistical Package for the Social Sciences (SPSS) mentioned previously was used.

The scatter diagram on page 518 shows considerable scatter, indicating only a moderate degree of correlation. Pearson's r was computed to be about 0.49, thus verifying that observation. The coefficient of determination is about 0.24, signifying that only 24 percent of the variation in the paralegal grade point averages is explained by high school grade point average. The general conclusion was that high school GPA is not a reliable predictor of achievement in the paralegal program. (In the next chapter two other independent variables will be added in an attempt to improve the prediction.)

CHAPTER SUMMARY

Often a statistical investigation involves examining the relationship between two variables. As a first step, the regression equation, which relates one variable to the other, is determined, and the error in the estimate measured using the standard error of estimate. Then the degree of linear relationship between the two variables is calculated. One measure which describes the relationship is the coefficient of correlation. It can assume any value between -1.00 and $+1.00$. Coefficients near -1 and $+1$ are evidence that there is strong correlation between the two variables of interest. A coefficient near zero indicates weak correlation, and zero means there is no correlation.

A test of significance can be applied to find out if the correlation in the population from which the sample was selected is zero. One approach is used for small samples, another for large samples.

Two other measures of relationship are the coefficient of determination and the coefficient of nondetermination. The coefficient of determination is found by squaring r and is defined as the proportion of the variation in Y explained by X. A coefficient of determination of 0.74, for example, indicates that 74 percent of the variation in Y is explained by X. The coefficient of nondetermination is found by $1 - r^2$ and is the proportion of the variation in Y not explained by X.

CHAPTER OUTLINE

Simple regression and correlation analysis

I. Regression analysis.
    A. *Purpose.* To arrive at the regression equation in order to predict the value of one variable, designated by Y and called the dependent variable, based on another variable, denoted by X and called the independent variable.
    B. *Procedure.*
        1. Select a sample from the population and list the paired data (X and Y) for each observation.
        2. Draw a scatter diagram to give a visual portrayal of the relationship. It might appear as:

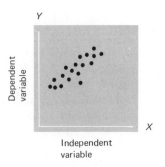

3. Determine the regression equation which has the form $\bar{Y}_p = a + bX$.

$\bar{Y}_p$ is the average predicted value of the Y variable for any X value.
a is the y intercept, or the estimated value of Y when $X = 0$.
b called the slope of the line, is the average change in $\bar{Y}_p$ for each change of one in X.
X is any value of X.

4. The computations for a and b can be accomplished by either solving two equations simultaneously or an equivalent shortcut method.

*Solving two
equations
simultaneously*

$\Sigma Y = na + b\Sigma X$
$\Sigma XY = a\Sigma X + b\Sigma X^2$

*Shortcut
method*

$$b = \frac{n\Sigma XY - (\Sigma X)(\Sigma Y)}{n\Sigma X^2 - (\Sigma X)^2}$$
$$a = \bar{Y} - b\bar{X}$$

5. Measure the error associated with predicting $\bar{Y}_p$ based on the regression equation. For large samples, two ways of determining this error, called the standard error of estimate, are:

$$S_{y \cdot x} = \sqrt{\frac{\Sigma Y^2 - a(\Sigma Y) - b(\Sigma XY)}{n - 2}} \qquad S_{y \cdot x} = \sqrt{\frac{\Sigma (Y - \bar{Y}_p)^2}{n - 2}}$$

6. The confidence limits for the mean value of Y for a given value of X are found by:

$$\bar{Y}_p \pm t(s_{y \cdot x}) \sqrt{\frac{1}{n} + \frac{(X - \bar{X})^2}{\Sigma (X - \bar{X})^2}}$$

To set confidence limits for an individual value of Y for a given value of X:

$$\bar{Y}_p \pm t(s_{y \cdot x}) \sqrt{1 + \frac{1}{n} + \frac{(X - \bar{X})^2}{\Sigma (X - \bar{X})^2}}$$

II. Correlation analysis.

    A. *Purpose.* To find the degree of association between the dependent and independent variables, and to determine the proportion of the dependent variable accounted for by the independent variable.

    B. *Measures.*

        1. Correlation coefficient r measures the degree of linear association between X and Y. Pearson's r can assume any value between -1 and $+1$. Formula:

$$r = \frac{n(\Sigma XY) - (\Sigma X)(\Sigma Y)}{\sqrt{[n(\Sigma X^2) - (\Sigma X)^2][n(\Sigma Y^2) - (\Sigma Y)^2]}}$$

        2. Coefficient of determination r^2 is the proportion of the variation in Y explained by X. It can assume any value between zero and one inclusive.

        3. Coefficient of nondetermination, $1 - r^2$, is the proportion of the variation in the dependent variable not accounted for by the independent variable.

    C. *Testing significance of r.* Is the correlation in the population zero? For small samples (less than 50) use the t-test. Select a level of significance.

$$t = \frac{r\sqrt{n - 2}}{\sqrt{1 - r^2}}$$

For large samples (50 or more) use the z-test. Select a level of significance.

$$z = \frac{r}{\dfrac{1}{\sqrt{n - 1}}}$$

CHAPTER EXERCISES

For questions 5 through 19, record the *letter* in front of the correct answer. Questions 5 through 7 are based on the following chart.

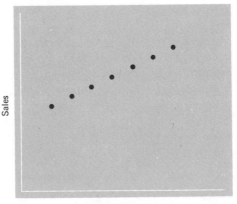

Length of service

5. The chart is called (*a*) a straight-line chart, (*b*) a shotgun pattern, (*c*) a scatter diagram, (*d*) a two-way graph, (*e*) none of these is correct.

6. To plot the points on the chart, the length of service of a sample of salespersons and their sales were paired. Each dot represents the length of service and the sales of one salesperson. The relationship between length of service and sales is (*a*) perfect, (*b*) negative, (*c*) about average, (*d*) about zero, (*e*) near infinity.

7. If the coefficient of correlation were computed it would be (*a*) 100.0, (*b*) −1.00, (*c*) about 0.50, (*d*) 1.00, (*e*) it cannot be estimated.

Questions 8 through 10 are based on the following chart.

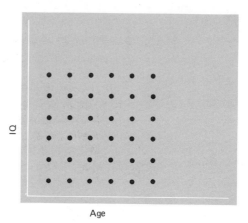

8. If the coefficient of correlation were computed, it would be about (*a*) 1.00, (*b*) 10.00, (*c*) 100.00, (*d*) 0.00, (*e*) −1.00.

9. The researcher is trying to predict (*a*) the IQ of a person based on the age of the person, (*b*) the age of a person based on his or her IQ, (*c*) cannot determine based on the chart.

10. If computed, the coefficient of nondetermination would be about (*a*) 0.50, (*b*) 0.00, (*c*) 1.00, (*d*) 1,000.00, (*e*) cannot determine based on the chart.

Questions 11 through 16 are based on the following chart.

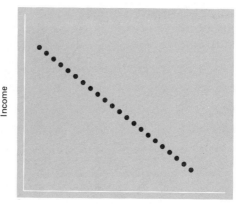

11. In this particular problem, the researcher is trying to predict (*a*) the test score of an individual based on his or her income, (*b*) the income of an individual based on his or her test score, (*c*) both income and test scores, (*d*) none of these is correct.

12. If computed, the coefficient of determination would be about (*a*) −1.00, (*b*) 100.0, (*c*) 1.00, (*d*) 50.00, (*e*) cannot be determined based on the chart.

13. Based on the chart, (*a*) a test score is of no value as a predictor of income, (*b*) income is of little or no value as a predictor of the test score of an individual, (*c*) a test score is a perfect predictor of income, (*d*) a test score is about a 50 percent predictor of income, (*e*) none of these is correct.

14. The equation for the line going through the dots would take the form of (*a*) $\bar{Y}_p = a + b + c$, (*b*) $\bar{Y}_p = a + bX$, (*c*) $\bar{Y}_p = X - 1$, (*d*) $\bar{Y}_p = a + bX^2$.

15. The independent variable is (*a*) test score, (*b*) income, (*c*) both income and test score, (*d*) none of these is correct.

16. If computed, the standard error of estimate would be about (*a*) 1.00, (*b*) −1.00, (*c*) 50.0 percent, (*d*) 0.00, (*e*) none of these is correct.

17. In a regression and correlation problem involving one dependent variable and one independent variable, the proportion of the variation in Y which is explained by X is called the (*a*) coefficient of correlation, (*b*) coefficient of determination, (*c*) coefficient of nondetermination, (*d*) standard error of estimate, (*e*) none of these is correct.

18. The primary use of a regression equation is to (*a*) predict a value of the dependent variable based on the independent variable, (*b*) predict a value of the independent variable based on the dependent variable, (*c*) none of these is correct.

19. A correlation coefficient of −1.00 indicates that the relationship between the dependent and independent variables is (*a*) about average, (*b*) practically zero, (*c*) perfect, (*d*) questionable, (*e*) cannot have a coefficient of −1.00.

20. The United Nations released these annual birth rates and suicide rates for selected countries.

Country	Birth rate (per 1,000 population)	Suicide rate (per 1,000 population)
Australia	15.7	11.1
Czechoslovakia	18.4	21.9
Finland	13.5	25.1
East Germany	13.9	30.5
Italy	12.5	5.8
Mexico	35.3	2.1
Poland	19.0	12.1
Singapore	17.0	11.3
Spain	17.2	4.0
United States	15.3	12.7

To explore the relationship between birth rate and suicide rate:
a. Draw a scatter diagram.
b. Determine the regression equation.
c. Plot the regression equation on the scatter diagram. (Suggestion: select three X values and compute the corresponding $\bar{Y}_p$ values.
d. Compute the coefficients of correlation, determination, and nondetermination.

e. Summarize your findings.

21. Recall that in the chapter the plan administrator of a new paralegal program in a community and technical college explored the possibility of predicting grade point averages in the program based on the high school grade point averages of the students. The correlations proved to be relatively low, indicating that high school achievement would not be a good predictor of success in the paralegal program.

In this problem the age of the students will be used in an effort to predict paralegal GPA. The paralegal program is career oriented and many of those enrolled are older persons considering the possibility of a new career. Did these older persons earn higher grades than the younger persons in the program? That is, is there a high correlation between age and GPA? The data on age (year of birth) and GPA follow.

Year of birth	Paralegal GPA	Year of birth	Paralegal GPA	Year of birth	Paralegal GPA
57	2.6	52	4.0	49	3.0
57	2.3	46	3.7	40	3.7
20	1.8	57	2.7	52	4.0
56	3.1	56	3.2	56	2.7
44	2.4	52	3.0	45	2.8
33	2.3	47	2.3	57	2.8
58	3.1	51	3.0	49	2.8
50	3.6	57	1.0	56	2.5
24	2.2	53	2.0	43	3.0
46	3.0	55	2.3	41	3.4
48	3.2	54	3.3	57	2.0
39	3.9	57	3.4	32	3.5
51	4.0	48	1.1	56	2.8
45	3.6	54	2.8	56	2.5
55	3.2	54	3.2	57	2.3

Source: Plan Administrator, Community and Technical College, The University of Toledo, Ohio.

a. Select a random 20 pairs of data (year of birth and GPA).
b. Draw a scatter diagram.
c. Determine the regression equation (to the nearest tenth, such as 5.6).
d. Based on the equation, predict the GPA of a person born in 1950.
e. Plot the line on the scatter diagram.
f. Determine the standard error of estimate.
g. Using the regression equation and the standard error of estimate, set confidence limits for those persons born in 1950.
h. Determine the coefficient of correlation, the coefficient of determination, and the coefficient of nondetermination.
i. Test the significance of the coefficient of correlation.
j. Write a brief summary of your findings.

22. If a computer is available, use all 45 paired observations given in Problem 21 and follow the same directions given in parts b through j.

CHAPTER SELF-REVIEW EXAMINATION

Do all of the problems and then check your answers against those given in Appendix A.

Score each problem 33 points.

Sales of toothpaste seem to be heavily dependent on the level of advertisement. In order to explore this observation further, the annual advertising expenditure for several well-known brands and their annual sales were obtained.

Brand	Annual advertising expenditures ($000,000)	Annual sales ($000,000)
Glint 2		5
Pearl One 4		7
Shine On 3		6
Number 1 1		2

1. *a.* Draw a scatter diagram.
   b. Compute the least squares regression equation.
   c. Based on the regression equation, an advertising expenditure of $1.9 million should produce what amount of sales on the average?
   d. Compute three points and plot the straight line on the scatter diagram.

2. *a.* Determine the standard error of estimate.
   b. Set the 95 percent confidence limits for the average sales you predicted in 1 *c.*
   c. Interpret these limits.

3. Assess the degree of correlation by computing:
   a. Pearson's product-moment correlation coefficient. Interpret.
   b. The coefficient of determination. Interpret.
   c. The coefficient of nondetermination. Interpret.

INTRODUCTION

Recall that the previous chapter dealt with regression and correlation involving *one* independent variable. In that chapter a test was devised to predict sales. In order to validate the test, a group of experienced salespersons was given the test, and their individual test scores were paired with their sales. The coefficient of correlation of 0.88 indicated a rather high degree of association between the test scores and weekly sales. And, the coefficient of determination (r^2) of 0.77 gave the variation in sales which is explained by the test scores. Based on the computed regression equation, $\overline{Y}_p = a + bX = 1.202 + 1.133X$, the average weekly sales of potential salesperson could be predicted based on the score earned on the test. The standard error measures the probable error in the prediction.

The use of only one independent variable, however, ignores the relationship of other variables to the dependent variable. Intuitively, it does seem logical that if more than one independent variable is included in the explanation of the dependent variable, the prediction process might be improved. For example, including the achievement rating each salesperson earned in Phase I of the initial training program is one independent variable which, when combined with his or her test score, might improve the sales prediction. When the problem is extended to include a second independent variable, the analysis is called **multiple regression and correlation analysis.**

Multiple regression and
correlation analysis

MULTIPLE REGRESSION ANALYSIS

Again recall from Chapter 20 that the simple linear regression equation encompassing one independent variable and one dependent variable has the form $\overline{Y}_p = a + bX$. The multiple regression case merely extends the equation to include the additional independent variables. For two independent variables, the **multiple regression equation** is:

$$\overline{Y}_p = a + b_1 X_1 + b_2 X_2$$

Continuing with the problem of predicting the weekly sales, we see that b_1 and X_1 would refer to the test scores examined in the foregoing chapter, and b_2 and X_2 are the achievement ratings earned in Phase I of the initial training program.

The scatter diagram for this three-variable problem coincides with a three-dimensional plane and is referred to as the *regression plane*. To put it another way, the dependent variable Y is related to the independent variables X_1 and X_2 by a plane and not be a straight line as was the case in simple regression. However, the usual reference is that the relationship is linear, and it is the linear multiple regression equation.

The interpretation of the regression coefficient a in the linear multiple regression equation is basically the same as it was in $\overline{Y}_p = a + bX$; that is, it is the Y-intercept. Recall that b in $\overline{Y}_p = a + bX$ was defined as the net change in $\overline{Y}_p$ for each change of one in the independent variable X. The interpretation of b_1 differs from the simple regression case in this respect: It is defined as the net change in $\overline{Y}_p$ for each change of one in X_1, *but X_2 is held constant*. Likewise, b_2 is defined as the net change in $\overline{Y}_p$ for each change of one in X_2, *but X_1 is held constant*. Since b_1 or b_2 only partially reveals the change in $\overline{Y}_p$ due to a change in X_1 or X_2 (because one or the other is being held at a constant value), b_1 and b_2 are usually called **partial regression coefficients.**

To illustrate the interpretation of a and the two partial regression coefficients, suppose that a vehicle's mileage per gallon of gasoline is directly related to the octane rating of the gasoline being used (X_1) and to the weight of the automobile (X_2). Assume that the multiple regression equation was computed to be $\overline{Y}_p = 6.3 + 0.2 X_1 + (-0.001) X_2$. The a value of 6.3 indicates that the regression plane intercepts the Y-axis at 6.3. The b_1 of 0.2 indicates that for each increase of one in the octane rating of the gasoline, the automobile would travel two tenths of a mile more per gallon, *regardless of the weight of the vehicle;* that is, the vehicle's weight is held constant. The b_2 value of -0.001 reveals that for each increase of one pound in the vehicle's weight, the number of miles traveled per gallon decreases 0.001 per mile, regardless of the octane of the gasoline being used.

As an example, an automobile with 92-octane gasoline in the tank and weighing 2,000 pounds would travel on the average 22.7 miles per gallon, found by

$$\overline{Y}_p = a + b_1 X_1 + b_2 X_2$$

$$= 6.3 + 0.2(92) + (-0.001)2,000$$

$$= 22.7 \text{ miles per gallon}$$

Solving for the multiple regression equation

In Chapter 20 the regression equation for the problem involving one dependent and one independent variable was reached by solving two normal equations simultaneously:

$$\Sigma Y = na + b\Sigma X$$
$$\Sigma XY = a\Sigma X + b\Sigma X^2$$

As was shown, the least squares method minimizes the sum of the squares of the vertical deviations about the straight line. The same applies to linear multiple regression. Three normal equations are solved simultaneously, namely:

$$\Sigma Y = na + b_1\Sigma X_1 + b_2\Sigma X_2$$
$$\Sigma X_1 Y = a\Sigma X_1 + b_1\Sigma X_1^2 + b_2\Sigma X_1 X_2$$
$$\Sigma X_2 Y = a\Sigma X_2 + b_1\Sigma X_1 X_2 + b_2\Sigma X_2^2$$

Solving for a, b_1, and b_2 using the three normal equations is a very laborious process, and for real-world problems the calculations are usually beyond the capacity of most electronic calculators. Instead, a simplified procedure will be applied.

A shortcut method

EXAMPLE

To illustrate the shortcut method, the sales prediction problem from the previous chapter is reintroduced. Remember that a small sample of experienced salespersons was given a test, and the test scores were paired with sales. A second independent variable will be introduced in this chapter in an effort to improve the predictive process. It is the achievement rating in Phase I of the initial training program (see Table 21–1).

**TABLE 21–1
Weekly sales, test scores, and achievement ratings for the sample of salespersons**

Salesperson	Weekly sales ($000) Y	Test score X_1	Achievement rating X_2
Mr. Amber	5	4	2
Mr. Archer	12	7	5
Ms. Smith	4	3	1
Mr. Malcolm	8	1	4
Ms. Goodwin	11	10	6

What is the multiple regression equation?

SOLUTION

The shortcut procedure reduces the three equations to two by eliminating the first normal equation.[1] The remaining two equations, using lowercase letters, are:

---

[1] In brief, this is accomplished by centering each variable or shifting its origin to the mean of each series. Exactly how this is done is beyond the scope of this introductory text.

$$\Sigma x_1 y = b_1 \Sigma x_1^2 + b_2 \Sigma x_1 x_2$$
$$\Sigma x_2 y = b_1 \Sigma x_1 x_2 + b_2 \Sigma x_2^2$$

where:

$$\Sigma x_1 y = \Sigma X_1 Y - n\bar{X}_1\bar{Y}$$
$$\Sigma x_1^2 = \Sigma X_1^2 - n\bar{X}_1^2$$
$$\Sigma x_1 x_2 = \Sigma X_1 X_2 - n\bar{X}_1\bar{X}^2$$
$$\Sigma x_2 y = \Sigma X_2 Y - n\bar{X}_2\bar{Y}$$
$$\Sigma x_2^2 = \Sigma X_2^2 - n\bar{X}_2^2$$
$$\Sigma y^2 = \Sigma Y^2 - n\bar{Y}^2$$

The calculations for $\Sigma X_1 Y$, ΣX_1^2, and so on are in Table 21–2.

TABLE 21–2
Calculations needed for the multiple regression equation

Weekly sales Y	Test score X_1	Achievement rating X_2	$X_1 Y$	X_1^2	$X_1 X_2$	$X_2 Y$	X_2^2	Y^2
$ 5	4	2	20	16	8	10	4	25
12	7	5	84	49	35	60	25	144
4	3	1	12	9	3	4	1	16
8	6	4	48	36	24	32	16	64
11	10	6	110	100	60	66	36	121
$40	30	18	274	210	130	172	82	370

Solving for $\bar{Y}$, $\bar{X}$, and $\bar{X}_2$:

$$n = 5; \quad \bar{Y} = \frac{\$40}{5} = \$8; \quad \bar{X}_1 = \frac{30}{5} = 6; \quad \bar{X}_2 = \frac{18}{5} = 3.6$$

Using the column sums and the means, we get:

$$\Sigma x_1 y = \Sigma X_1 Y - n\bar{X}_1\bar{Y}$$
$$= 274 - (5)(6)(8)$$
$$= 34$$
$$\Sigma x_1^2 = \Sigma X_1^2 - n\bar{X}_1^2$$
$$= 210 - 5(6)^2$$
$$= 30$$
$$\Sigma x_1 x_2 = \Sigma X_1 X_2 - n\bar{X}_1\bar{X}_2$$
$$= 130 - (5)(6)(3.6)$$
$$= 22$$
$$\Sigma x_2 y = \Sigma X_2 Y - n\bar{X}_2\bar{Y}$$
$$= 172 - (5)(3.6)(8)$$
$$= 28$$
$$\Sigma x_2^2 = \Sigma X_2^2 - n\bar{X}_2^2$$
$$= 82 - 5(3.6)^2$$
$$= 17.2$$
$$\Sigma y^2 = \Sigma Y^2 - n\bar{Y}^2$$
$$= 370 - 5(8)^2$$
$$= 50$$

Inserting these sums in the two equations and solving them simultaneously for b_2 (the first equation was multiplied by 11, the second by 15), we get:

$$\begin{aligned}
\text{I} \quad & \Sigma x_1 y = b_1 \Sigma x_1^2 + b_2 \Sigma x_1 x_2 \\
\text{II} \quad & \Sigma x_2 y = b_1 \Sigma x_1 x_2 + b_2 \Sigma x_2^2 \\
\text{I} \quad & 34 = 30 b_1 + 22 b_2 \\
\text{II} \quad & \underline{28 = 22 b_1 + 17.2 b_2} \\
& 374 = 330 b_1 + 242 b_2 \\
& \underline{420 = 330 b_1 + 258 b_2} \\
& 46 = 16 b_2 \\
& b_2 = 2.875
\end{aligned}$$

Substituting the value of b_2 in the first equation and solving for b_1, we get:

$$\begin{aligned}
34 &= 30 b_1 + 22 b_2 \\
34 &= 30 b_1 + 22(2.875) \\
b_1 &= -0.975
\end{aligned}$$

Referring back to the three normal equations and using the computed values of b_1 and b_2, we see that the constant a is computed to be 3.5, found by:

$$\begin{aligned}
\Sigma Y &= na + b_1 \Sigma X_1 + b_2 \Sigma X_2 \\
40 &= 5a + (-0.975)(30) + 2.875(18) \\
a &= 3.5
\end{aligned}$$

The multiple regression equation is, therefore:

$$\bar{Y}_p = 3.5 + (-0.975)X_1 + 2.875 X_2$$

An alternative shortcut procedure
As a check on the computations for b_1 and b_2, or if large numbers are involved, the following alternative procedure is usually preferred.

$$b_1 = \frac{\Sigma x_2^2 \, \Sigma x_1 y - \Sigma x_1 x_2 \, \Sigma x_2 y}{\Sigma x_1^2 \, \Sigma x_2 y - \Sigma x_1 x_2 \, \Sigma x_1 y}$$

$$b_2 = \frac{\Sigma x_1^2 \, \Sigma x_2 y - \Sigma x_1 x_2 \, \Sigma x_1 y}{\Sigma x_1^2 \, \Sigma x_2^2 - (\Sigma x_1 x_2)^2}$$

Solving for b_1 and b_2:

$$\begin{aligned}
b_1 &= \frac{\Sigma x_2^2 \, \Sigma x_1 y - \Sigma x_1 x_2 \, \Sigma x_2 y}{\Sigma x_1^2 \, \Sigma x_2^2 - (\Sigma x_1 x_2)^2} \\[2mm]
&= \frac{(17.2)(34) - (22)(28)}{(30)(17.2) - (22)^2} \\[2mm]
&= -0.975
\end{aligned}$$

$$b_2 = \frac{\Sigma x_1^2 \, \Sigma x_2 y - \Sigma x_1 x_2 \, \Sigma x_1 y}{\Sigma x_1^2 \, \Sigma x_2^2 - (\Sigma x_1 x_2)^2}$$

$$= \frac{(30)(28) - (22)(34)}{(30)(17.2) - (22)^2}$$

$$= 2.875$$

These b_1 and b_2 values are the same partial regression coefficients as were computed before.

Predicting Y

The main use of the multiple regression equation is, of course, to predict a value of the dependent variable based on values of the independent variables.

EXAMPLE

Suppose that an applicant for an opening in the sales department scored 6.0 on the test and earned an achievement rating of 3.8 in Phase I of the training program. What should the applicant sell per week on the average?

SOLUTION

On the average, the applicant should sell $8,575 weekly, found by:

$$\bar{Y}_p = 3.5 + (-0.975)6.0 + 2.875(3.8)$$
$$= 8.575 \text{ (in } \$000)$$

SELF-REVIEW 21–1

a. $\bar{Y}_p = -0.5 + 2X_1 + 1X_2$, found by

Outside diameter X_1	Molyb- denum X_2	Tensile strength Y	X_1X_2	X_1^2
3	6	11	18	9
2	5	9	10	4
4	8	16	32	16
3	8	12	21	9
12	26	48	81	38

X_2^2	X_1Y	X_2Y	Y^2
36	33	66	121
25	18	45	81
64	64	128	256
49	36	84	144
174	151	323	602

$$\Sigma x_1 y = 151 - 4\left(\frac{12}{4}\right)(12) = 7$$

(A reminder: Cover the answers in the left-hand column.)

The quality control engineer is interested in predicting the tensile strength of a steel wire based on its outside diameter and the amount of molybdenum in the steel. As an experiment, he selected four pieces of wire, measured the outside diameter, and determined the molybdenum content. Then he measured the tensile strength of each piece. The results were:

Piece	Outside diameter (cm)	Amount of molybdenum (units)	Tensile strength (psi)
A	3	6	11
B	2	5	9
C	4	8	16
D	3	7	12

$$\Sigma x_1^2 = 38 - 4(3)^2 = 2$$
$$\Sigma x_1 x_2 = 81 - 4(3)(6.5) = 3$$
$$\Sigma x_2 y = 323 - 4(6.5)(12) = 11$$
$$\Sigma x^2 = 174 - 4(6.5)^2 = 5$$
$$\Sigma y^2 = 602 - 4(12)^2 = 26$$

Then:

$$b_1 = \frac{5(7) - 3(11)}{2(5) - 3^2} = 2$$

$$b_2 = \frac{2(11) - (3)(7)}{2(5) - 3^2} = 1$$

Using the first normal equation, we find $a = -0.5$, found by: $48 = 4a + 2(12) + 1(26)$.

b. The b_2 of 1 means that tensile strength will increase one pound per square inch for each increase of one unit of molybdenum, but outside diameter is held constant.

a. Determine the multiple regression equation.
b. Explain what the value of b_2 in the equation means.

Standard error of estimate

Returning to the sales problem, the applicant's estimated average weekly sales based on his test score and achievement rating was $8,575. Obviously, some weeks his sales will be more than this amount, and some weeks they will be less. The error in this estimate can be measured by the standard error of estimate, denoted by $S_{y \cdot 12}$. (The subscripts indicate that two independent variables are being used to predict Y).

Recall that the standard error of estimate in simple regression analysis measures the variation about the straight line. Likewise, the **standard error of estimate** in multiple regression analysis measures the error for values of Y about the regression plane. Note that the formula is almost the same as that used in the simple case where n is the number of observations and k is the number of parameters.

$$S_{y \cdot 12} = \sqrt{\frac{\Sigma(Y - \bar{Y}_p)^2}{n - k}}$$

The weekly sales problem is used again to show that the standard error of estimate does, in fact, measure the error in Y (sales) about the multiple regression plane ($\bar{Y}_p$ values). The first salesperson selected at random was Mr. Amber. His test score was 4; this is X_1. His achievement rating was 2; this is X_2. His predicted sales ($\bar{Y}_p$) are $5,350, found by $\bar{Y}_p = 3.5 + (-0.975)$ $4 + 2.875(2) = 5.35$ (in $000). The sales, predicted sales, and the calculations needed for the standard error are shown in Table 21–3 on the top of the next page.

In this problem, $n = 5$ (five salespersons), and $k = 3$ (three parameters, namely, one dependent and two independent variables).

534

TABLE 21-3
Calculations needed for the standard error of estimate

Salesperson	Weekly sales ($000) Y	Predicted sales ($000) Y_p	$Y - \bar{Y}_p$	$(Y - \bar{Y}_p)^2$
Mr. Amber	$ 5	$ 5.35	$-0.35	0.1225
Mr. Archer	12	11.05	0.95	0.9025
Ms. Smith	4	3.45	0.55	0.3025
Mr. Malcolm	8	9.15	−1.15	1.3225
Ms. Goodwin	11	11.00	0.00	0.0000
			$ 0.00*	2.6500

*Must equal 0.

Solving for the standard error of estimate:

$$S_{y \cdot 12} = \sqrt{\frac{\Sigma(Y - \bar{Y}_p)^2}{n - k}} = \sqrt{\frac{2.65}{5 - 3}} = 1.151 \text{ (in \$000)}$$

The standard error of estimate computed in Chapter 20 involving only sales and test scores was $1,954. Adding one additional independent variable (achievement rating) reduced the error in making a prediction to $1,151. This, of course, signifies that adding a second independent variable made the sales predictions more precise.

The foregoing procedure to find the standard error of estimate was applied mainly to show that it measures the variation in Y about the multiple regression plane. It required additional work, namely, that the squared deviations be computed. Instead, a more convenient formula using various measures already on hand is show below. (Note that it is also quite similar to the one in Chapter 20.)

$$S_{y \cdot 12} = \sqrt{\frac{\Sigma y^2 - b_1 \Sigma x_1 y - b_2 \Sigma x_2 y}{n - k}}$$

Inserting the appropriate sums and b_1 and b_2 from the weekly sales problem, we have:

$$S_{y \cdot 12} = \sqrt{\frac{50 - (-0.975)(34) - 2.875(28)}{5 - 3}}$$

$$= 1.151 \text{ (in \$000)}$$

This is the same answer as was found before.

Interpretation. If the weekly sales are distributed normally about the multiple regression plane, approximately **68 percent** of the sales would fall within $1,151 of their estimated $\bar{Y}_p$ value. And, 95 percent of the weekly sales would be with $1.96 S_{y \cdot 12}$, that is, 1.96($1,151), of the $\bar{Y}_p$ value predicted by the equation. Further, approximately 99.7 percent of the sales would lie within $\pm 3 S_{y \cdot 12}$.

In Chapter 20 we used the standard error of estimate to construct confidence limits of small samples for both the mean value of Y given a value of

X_1 and for an individual value of Y given a value of X. The procedure for constructing these limits in the multiple regression case is somewhat similar to that followed in simple regression and will not be repeated here.

MULTIPLE CORRELATION ANALYSIS

The same three coefficients cited in simple correlation analysis to describe the relationship between the dependent and independent variables are used in multiple correlation analysis. They are the **coefficients of determination, nondetermination,** and **correlation.**

Coefficient of multiple determination

The **coefficient of multiple determination** is the ratio of the explained variation to the total variation in Y. To put it another way, it is one minus the unexplained variation over the total variation in Y. A capital R^2 represents it, with $_{y \cdot 12}$ indicating that Y is the dependent variable and X_1 and X_2 are the two independent variables.

$$R^2_{y \cdot 12} = 1 - \frac{S^2_{y \cdot 12}}{s^2_y}$$

It can assume any value between 0 and 1 inclusive.

EXAMPLE

What is the coefficient of multiple determination for the weekly sales prediction problem?

SOLUTION

The numerator is simply the standard error of estimate squared. The standard error in the sales prediction problem was computed to be $1.151 thousand, so $S^2_{y \cdot 12} = (1.151)^2$. The denominator s^2_y is the total variation in Y, found by

$$s^2_y = \frac{\Sigma y^2}{n - 1}$$

Σy^2 was computed in the multiple regression section to be 50. The total variance $s^2_{y'}$, therefore, is 12.5, found by $50/5 - 1$. Inserting these values and solving for the multiple coefficient of determination:

$$R^2_{y \cdot 12} = 1 - \frac{S^2_{y \cdot 12}}{s^2_y}$$

$$= 1 - \frac{(1.151)^2}{12.5}$$

$$= 0.894$$

Interpreting, about 89 percent of the variation in weekly sales is explained by the two independent variables, test scores and achievement ratings.[2]

Coefficient of multiple nondetermination

The *coefficient of multiple nondetermination*, $1 - R_{y \cdot 12}^2$, is defined as *the variation in Y which is not accounted for by the independent variables*. In the sales problem it is 0.106, found by $1 - 0.894$. About 11 percent of the variation in weekly sales is not explained by the test scores and achievement ratings. It can also assume any value between zero and one inclusive.

Coefficient of multiple correlation

The **coefficient of multiple correlation**, $R_{y \cdot 12}$ is defined as the square root of the coefficient of multiple determination. It can have any value between zero and one inclusive. It gives the degree of association between the dependent variable Y and the independent variables. In the sales problem, $R_{y \cdot 12} = 0.97314$ or 0.97 rounded, found in this case by using the unadjusted coefficient of determination of 0.947. Then $\sqrt{0.947} = 0.97314$. This indicates a very strong relationship between weekly sales and the two independent variables—test scores and achievement ratings.

AN APPLICATION USING A COMPUTER PACKAGE

A number of computer packages are available which can be applied to problems involving regression and correlation. These packages are used extensively in business, the social sciences, education, and other areas; they require very little knowledge of computer programming. As noted previously, one of the more widely used is called the Statistical Package for the Social Sciences (SPSS). Developed at the University of Chicago, it incorporates what is termed a "stepwise" multiple regression procedure.

To illustrate, the previous problem involving two independent variables (a test score and an achievement rating) and weekly sales as the dependent variable is used. The first output is a **correlation matrix** giving all possible simple correlation coefficients. DEP is the abbreviation for the dependent variable, IND1 is one of the independent variables (test scores), and IND2 represents achievement ratings. Note, for example, that the simple coefficient of correlation between sales and test scores is 0.87788 (the same as computed in Chapter 20).

---

[2] The coefficient of multiple determination, as computed, is said to be adjusted for the number of degrees of freedom. As will be shown shortly, computer printouts usually give both the adjusted and unadjusted coefficients. For small samples the adjusted coefficient is much less than the unadjusted one and, being more conservative, it should probably be used to reveal what proportion of Y is explained by the independent variables. The unadjusted coefficient can be found by:

$$1 - \frac{S_{y \cdot 12}^2}{s_y^2} \left(\frac{n - k}{n - 1} \right)$$

where again k is the total number of parameters. In the sales problem the coefficient of determination adjusted for the number of degrees of freedom was computed to be 0.894; the unadjusted coefficient would be 0.947. For large samples the two values are about equal.

```
                          DEP        IND1        IND2
           DEP          1.00000    0.87788     0.95479
           IND1         0.87788    1.00000     0.96850
           IND2         0.95479    0.96850     1.00000
```

An analysis of the simple correlation coefficients reveals that independent variable 2 (achievement ratings) is more highly correlated with the dependent variable (sales), because 0.95479 is greater than 0.87788. This variable is entered first and designated STEP NUMBER 1. Measures such as the multiple correlation coefficient are then computed. MULTIPLE R is really a simple correlation coefficient because it is measuring only the degree of relationship between one dependent and one independent variable (see the following output). Only the essential measures are shown. Later a full output will be given.

```
DEPENDENT VARIABLE..     DEP

VARIABLE(S) ENTERED ON STEP NUMBER   1..      IND2

MULTIPLE R              0.95479
R SQUARE               0.91163
ADJUSTED R SQUARE      0.88217
STANDARD ERROR         1.21362

----------------- VARIABLES IN THE EQUATION --------

VARIABLE               B            BETA      STD ERROR B

IND2                 1.62791      0.95479       0.29263
(CONSTANT)           2.13953
```

The values for the regression equation using just the one independent variable are at the bottom of the computer output. It would be $\overline{Y}_p = a + bX_2 = 2.13953 + 1.62791X_2$. The standard error for the estimate of weekly sales is 1.12362, or $1,123.62.

In STEP NUMBER 2, the other variable (test scores) is brought in (see the following output). Note that the multiple coefficient of determination (R SQUARE) and the other values are the same as computed previously.

```
VARIABLE(S) ENTERED ON STEP NUMBER   2..      IND1

MULTIPLE R              0.97314
R SQUARE               0.94700
ADJUSTED R SQUARE      0.89400
STANDARD ERROR         1.15109

----------------- VARIABLES IN THE EQUATION ------

VARIABLE               B            BETA      STD ERROR B

IND2                 2.87500      1.68623       1.11453
IND1                -0.97500     -0.75523       0.84391
(CONSTANT)           3.50000
```

538

a. $\overline{Y}_p = 3.5 + (-0.975)X_1 + 2.875X_2$. *Note:* This is the same equation computed previously by hand.

b. $8,575, found by $\overline{Y}_p = 3.5 + (-0.975)6.0 + 2.875(3.8)$.

a. Inserting the appropriate values, state the multiple regression equation in the form of

$$\overline{Y}_p = a + b_2X_2 + b_1X_1$$

b. Based on the equation, suppose that a person earned an achievement rating of 3.8 in the training program and had a test score of 6.0. What is his or her predicted weekly sales?

Finally, some summary figures are printed. As expected, the inclusion of a second independent variable increased the multiple coefficient of correlation from 0.95479 to 0.97314. Likewise the unadjusted coefficient of determination (R SQUARE) increased from 0.91163 for one independent variable to 0.94700, meaning that the two independent variables combined account for 94.7 percent of the variation in weekly sales.

SUMMARY TABLE

VARIABLE	MULTIPLE R	R SQUARE	RSQ CHANGE	SIMPLE R
IND2	0.95479	0.91163	0.91163	0.95479
IND1	0.97314	0.94700	0.03537	0.87788

It should be also noted that the error in the estimate *decreased,* as expected, with the inclusion of the second variable. It went from 1.21362 down to 1.15109 (the same value as computed by hand).

A SALARY-PREDICTION PROBLEM

To cite another example of the use of multiple regression and correlation, and to show the universal application of the computer in problem solving, suppose that the president of the university received the annual salary report published by the American Association of University Professors and wants to know how the salary structure at his university compares with those of other universities. The president is also interested in what factors, such as academic rank, age, and year of appointment, are important in establishing the annual salary of a faculty member. Finally, he is wondering which of these factors, if any, could be used in estimating faculty salaries for the next few years.

As an experiment, the research assistant to the president collected data on a sample of 30 faculty. To show the type of data collected, pertinent information on four faculty members follows. (The actual salaries and other data are from the files of a midwestern state university.)

Salary (9 months)	Year of birth	Rank	Year of appointment	Tenure	Degree	Merit Rating
$18,429	1942	Assistant	1974	No	Ph.D.	42
26,674	1920	Professor	1946	Yes	CPA, JD	16
21,524	1938	Associate	1967	Yes	Ph.D.	42
12,229	1943	Instructor	1976	No	MBA	38

In order to prepare for computer analysis, the last two digits of the faculty member's year of birth and year of appointment were keypunched on a punch card. The rank of professor was coded 1, an associate 2, an assistant 3, and an instructor 4. If the person had achieved tenure a 1 was keypunched; if not, a 2. A bachelor's degree was coded 1, a master's 2, post master's training but no doctorate 3, and a doctorate 4.

Thus, there are six independent variables, including academic rank, and the annual merit rating the faculty member received from all the members of the department, and one dependent variable (salary). In order to visualize the relationship between some of the independent variables and the dependent variable (salary), scatter diagrams have been drawn.

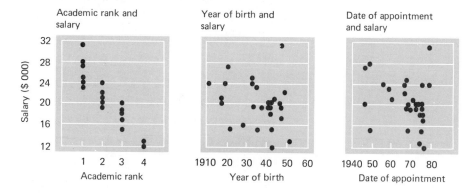

Of the three independent variables shown, it does appear that the highest degree of correlation exists between academic rank and salary. And, observing the wide scatter, one might conclude that there is practically no correlation between salary and the year the person joined the faculty.

The initial output is a correlation matrix showing all possible simple correlation coefficients. Referring to the following matrix and reading across the top line, the correlation between salary and salary is logically 1.00000. The correlation coefficient for salary and year of birth is −0.46573, and so on. One other coefficient; the correlation between academic rank and degree held, is −0.34310.

FACULTY SALARY ANALYSIS

FILE   (CREATION DATE = 03/09/

CORRELATION COEFFICIENTS

A VALUE OF 99.00000 IS PRINTED
IF A COEFFICIENT CANNOT BE COMPLIED.

	SALARY	MERIT	RANK	BIRTH	APPT	TENURE	DEGREE
SALARY	1.00000	-0.25935	-0.87996	-0.46573	-0.36891	-0.47468	0.45193
MERIT	-0.25935	1.00000	0.41905	0.73234	0.56946	0.42705	0.25739
RANK	-0.87996	0.41905	1.00000	0.60127	0.53010	0.69062	-0.34310
BIRTH	-0.46573	0.73234	0.60127	1.00000	0.79065	0.63833	0.07576
APPT	-0.36891	0.56946	0.53010	0.79065	1.00000	0.67977	0.10464
TENURE	-0.47468	0.42705	0.69062	0.63833	0.67977	1.00000	0.04946
DEGREE	0.45193	0.25739	-0.34310	0.07576	0.10464	0.04946	1.00000

SELF-REVIEW 21-3
---

a. Based on the above correlation matrix, which independent variable is the most highly correlated with salary?

b. What is the correlation between date of birth and degree held?

As before, the independent variable having the highest correlation with the dependent variable is brought in first as STEP NUMBER 1. That variable is academic rank, with a coefficient of correlation of −0.87996. In brief, academic rank accounts for about 77 percent of the variation in faculty salary, and if just this one independent variable were to be used for predictive purposes, the equation would be $\overline{Y}_p = 29.53728 + (-4.00460)X_1$. The error in the prediction would be $2,077.91 (see the following output).

```
FACULTY SALARY ANALYSIS
FILE                 (CREATION DATE = 03/09

* * * * * * * * * * * * * * * * * * * * * *

DEPENDENT VARIABLE..    SALARY
VARIABLE(S) ENTERED ON STEP NUMBER   1..    RANK

MULTIPLE R              0.87996
R SQUARE               0.77433
ADJUSTED R SQUARE      0.76627
STANDARD ERROR         2.07791

        -------- VARIABLES IN THE EQUATION --------

  VARIABLE          B         BETA     STD ERROR B

  RANK          -4.00460    -0.87996     0.40856
  (CONSTANT)    29.53728
```

The question now arises: Which independent variable should be brought in as STEP NUMBER 2? Logically, it should be the independent variable which when included with academic rank results in the greatest *proportional reduction in the unexplained variation*. To put it another way, the independent variable that results in the largest *increase* in explained variation will enter in STEP NUMBER 2. In order to arrive at a decision, all possible *coefficients of partial correlation*, (marked PARTIAL in the following output) are computed. Basically, a **coefficient of partial correlation**, is an index of association. At this stage in the analysis, it reveals the relationship between the dependent variable (salary) and an independent variable not as yet considered (such as year of birth), while the independent variable rank already in the equation is *considered but held constant*. The highest partial coefficient of correlation is 0.38723, associated with the independent variable tenure.

```
------------ VARIABLES NOT IN THE EQUATION --------------
VARIABLE     BETA IN    PARTIAL    TOLERANCE       F
  MERIT      0.13270    0.25364    0.82440      1.856
  BIRTH      0.09924    0.16692    0.63848      0.774
  APPT       0.13569    0.24220    0.71899      1.683
  TENURE     0.25435    0.38723    0.52304      4.763
  DEGRFE     0.17003    0.33619    0.88228      3.441
```

Following is the computer output for STEP NUMBER 2.

```
DEPENDENT VARIABLE..      SALARY
VARIABLE(S) ENTERED ON STEP NUMBER  2..     TENURE

MULTIPLE R              0.89898
R SQUARE                0.80817
ADJUSTED R SQUARE       0.79396
STANDARD ERROR          1.95095

          -------- VARIABLES IN THE EQUATION --------

   VARIABLE            B           BETA       STD ERROR B

   RANK           -4.80402     -1.05562        0.53040
   TENURE          2.16905      0.25435        0.99390
   (CONSTANT)     28.24032
```

Comparing the measures in STEP NUMBER 1 and STEP NUMBER 2 we see that the addition of the second independent variable (1) increased the degree of correlation from 0.87996 to 0.89898; (2) increased the explained variation from 76.627 percent to 79.396 percent; (3) decreased the unexplained variation, found by $1 - R^2$, from 23.373 percent to 20.604 percent; and (4) decreased the error in the estimate from $2,077.91 to $1,950.05.

The multiple regression equation for the two independent variables is:

$$\overline{Y}_p = a + b_1X_1 + b_2X_2 = 28.24032 + (-4.80402)X_1 + 2.16905X_2$$

If an associate professor (coded 2) had tenure (coded 1), then his estimated salary would be $20,801.44, found by $\overline{Y}_p = 28.24032 + (-4.80402)2 + 2.16905(1)$. The error in this prediction is $1,950.95, meaning that about 68 percent of the associate professors with tenure will have an income of $20,801.33 ± $1,950.95, or between $18,850.38 and $22,752.28. And, about 95 percent of the associate professors with tenure will have incomes of $20,801.33 ± 1.96($1,950.95).

As before, the variables not in the multiple regression equation in STEP NUMBER 2 are listed next along with their PARTIALS.

```
         ------------- VARIABLES NOT IN THE EQUATION -------------
   VARIABLE       BETA IN      PARTIAL     TOLERANCE          F

   MERIT          0.09438      0.19131      0.78817        0.988
   BIRTH          0.01218      0.02051      0.54333        0.011
   APPT           0.03349      0.05571      0.53088        0.081
   DEGREE         0.10637      0.20684      0.72545        1.162
```

SELF-REVIEW 21-4

a. The partial coefficient of correlation.
b. Degree, because 0.20684 is the largest partial.

Refer to the above computer output:

a. What does PARTIAL stand for?
b. Based on the variables not in the equation, which independent variable will be brought in next as STEP NUMBER 3?

To further explain the function of the partial correlation coefficient, had the computer brought in the faculty members' dates of birth instead of degree as the third variable, the partial coefficient would be only 0.02051 compared with 0.20684 for degree held. To put it another way, the inclusion of date of birth as the third variable would have reduced the unexplained variation in Y by only about 2 percent (compared with over 20 percent for degree held). The output for STEP NUMBER 3 follows.

```
VARIABLE(S) ENTERED ON STEP NUMBER   3..      DEGREE


MULTIPLE R              0.90353
R SQUARE                0.81637
ADJUSTED R SQUARE       0.79519
STANDARD ERROR          1.94512

---------------- VARIABLES IN THE EQUATION ---------

VARIABLE              B              BETA         STD ERROR B

RANK               -4.45487       -0.57290         0.62012
TENURE              1.67236        0.15811         1.09280
DEGREE              0.49569        0.10637         0.45982
(CONSTANT)         26.50854


------------ VARIABLES NOT IN THE EQUATION --------------

VARIABLE      BETA IN       PARTIAL     TOLERANCE          r

MERIT         0.06191       0.11574      0.64186        0.335
BIRTH        -0.02044      -0.03401      0.50809        0.025
APPT          0.01087       0.01816      0.51273        0.006
```

Although this process is not shown, the other variables were entered step by step: merit rating, date of birth, and year of appointment, in turn. Finally, a summary table was printed out:

```
DEPENDENT VARIABLE..     SALARY



                        SUMMARY TABLE
VARIABLE      MULTIPLE R   R SQUARE   RSQ CHANGE    SIMPLE R

RANK           0.87996     0.77433     0.77433     -0.87996
TENURE         0.89898     0.80817     0.03384     -0.47468
DEGREE         0.90353     0.81637     0.00821      0.45193
MERIT          0.90469     0.81883     0.00246     -0.25935
BIRTH          0.90668     0.82207     0.00324     -0.46573
APPT           0.90694     0.82254     0.00047     -0.36891
```

Referring back to the summary table, note that the degree of relationship (MULTIPLE R) increased from 0.87996 for X_1 and Y to 0.90694 for all six independent variables and salary. And, the proportion of the variation in Y explained by the X variable increased from about 0.77 for one independent variable to about 0.82 for all six. Also note that there was an extremely small change in the proportion explained after the second independent variable was brought in; that is, the first independent variable (rank) accounted for over 77 percent of the variation in Y (salary). The second independent variation by 3 percent, but thereafter the change was extremely small (less than 1 percent).

CHAPTER SUMMARY

Simple correlation and regression, discussed in Chapter 20, dealt with the relationship between two variables—a dependent variable and an independent variable. This chapter expanded the discussion to include the relationship between a dependent variable and two or more independent variables. This relationship is aptly called multiple correlation and regression.

The concepts and formulas for the simple case and the multiple case are quite similar. For example, the regression equation for simple regression is $\overline{Y}_p = a + bX$. In multiple regression the formula for any number of independent variables is $\overline{Y}_p = a + b_1X_1 + b_2X_2 + b_3X_3 + \cdots b_kX_k$.

The purpose of the multiple regression equation is to predict a value for the dependent variable based on two or more independent variables. The error in the prediction is measured by the multiple standard error of estimate.

The strength of the relationship between the dependent variable and the independent variables is measured by the multiple coefficient of correlation R. An R of zero indicates no correlation; values near zero show weak correlation; and values near one mean strong correlation. An R of 1.00 signifies perfect correlation.

The coefficient of determination R^2 is the proportion of the variation in Y explained by the independent variables. The coefficient of nondetermination, $1 - R^2$, is the proportion not explained.

CHAPTER OUTLINE

Multiple regression and correlation analysis

I. Multiple regression analysis.
   A. *Purpose.* To arrive at a multiple regression equation whereby two or more independent variables can be used to estimate the value of a dependent variable. For two independent variables denoted X_1 and X_2, the general form of the equation is

   $$\overline{Y}_p = a + b_1X_1 + b_2X_2$$

   a is the Y-intercept, that is, the value of Y where the regression plane intercepts the Y-axis.

   b_1 is defined as the net change in Y for each change of one in X_1, but X_2 is held at a constant value. It is usually called a partial regression coefficient.

   b_2 is the net change in Y for each change of one in X_2, but X_1 is held constant.

   B. *Predicting Y.* Example: Suppose the purpose is to predict sales, based on advertising expenditures, X_1, and number of retail outlets, X_2. The equation was computed to be $\overline{Y}_p = a + b_1X_1 + b_2X_2 = 3 + (-2)X_1 + 0.05X_2$ (in \$000,000). If \$4 million were spent on advertising, and the item were carried in 600 retail outlets, estimated sales would be \$25 million, found by $\overline{Y}_p = 3 + (-2)4 + 0.05$ (600).

   C. *Standard error of the estimate.* Measures the error for values of Y about the regression plane. Formula (for two independent variables):

$$S_{y \cdot 12} = \sqrt{\frac{\Sigma(Y - \bar{Y}_p)^2}{n - k}} \quad \text{or} \quad \sqrt{\frac{\Sigma y^2 - b_1 \Sigma x_1 y - b_2 \Sigma x_2 y}{n - k}}$$

II. Multiple correlation analysis.
   A. *Purpose.* To measure the explained variation, the unexplained variation, and the degree of relationship.
      1. *Coefficient of multiple determination.* It is the variation in Y explained by the independent variables. Formula (for two independent variables):

$$R^2_{y \cdot 12} = 1 - \frac{S^2_{y \cdot 12}}{s^2_y}$$

      2. *Coefficient of multiple nondetermination.* It is the variation in Y not explained by the independent variables. Found by one minus coefficient of multiple determination.
      3. *Coefficient of multiple correlation.* It is defined as the square root of the coefficient of multiple determination. It gives the degree of association between the dependent variable Y and the independent variables.

CHAPTER EXERCISES

1. A large distributor of such items as laundry detergent and toothpaste wanted to assess the effect of a planned coupon advertising campaign on sales. Nineteen retail outlets in the test market area were selected for the experiment. The two-week sales, the number of outlets carrying the item, and the advertising expenditures follow.

Item	Sales ($000)	Number of outlets	Advertising expenditures ($000)
Presoak	$30	19	$15
Smell Nice Detergent	20	14	16
Snow White Bleach	22	17	14
Glim Toothpaste	14	15	12
Brace After-Shave	5	12	10
Smoothie Shave Cream	9	13	13

   a. Determine the regression equation.
   b. Compute the standard error of estimate.
   c. Based on the regression equation, if $13,000 was spent on an item and 12 outlets carried it, what are the predicted sales? Set the 95 percent confidence limits for the sales. Interpret.
   d. What percent of the variation in sales can be explained by the number of outlets and advertising expenditures?
   e. What is the coefficient of nondetermination? Interpret.
   f. What is the coefficient of multiple correlation?
   g. Write a brief summary paragraph explaining your findings.
2. If a computer is available, verify the various measures computed in Problem 1.
3. If a computer is available:

a. Select a dependent variable which you think can be predicted by several independent variables. One suggested problem might involve predicting sales, another might be the tensile strength of a wire based on the outside diameter, and so on. Stock prices, the gross national product, employment, production, and grade point average in college are other possible dependent variables. Sports enthusiasts might be interested in predicting the American League division baseball champions based on runs batted in, home runs, and so on, for each team as early as the All-Star break in July. Hockey, football, and basketball are other possibilities where past history is available.

b. Collect the data and prepare them for the computer.

c. Analyze the computer printout and write a summary of the findings. Include in your discussion such measures as the multiple correlation coefficient, the multiple regression equation, and the standard error of estimate.

4. If a computer is not available, do the following problem.

Suppose that the sales manager of a large automotive parts distributor wants to develop an objective tool to predict as early as April the total annual sales of a region. Based on regional sales, the total sales for the company can also be estimated. If based on past experience it is found that the April estimates of annual sales are reasonably accurate, then in future years the April forecast could be used to revise production schedules and maintain the correct inventory at the retail outlets.

Several factors appear to be related to sales, including the number of retail outlets in the region stocking the company's parts, the number of automobiles in the region registered as of April 1, and the total personal income for the first quarter of the year. A total of six independent variables was finally selected as being the most important (according to the sales manager). Then the number of automobiles registered for each region as of April 1, data on the personal income, by region, and so on were gathered for a recent year. The total annual sales for that year for each region was also recorded. Note that for region no. 1 there were 1,739 retail outlets stocking the company's automotive parts, there were 9,270,000 registered automobiles in the region as of April 1, and (in the extreme right column) sales for the region that year were $37,702,000.

Number of retail outlets X_1	Number of automobiles registered (millions) X_2	Interest rate (percent) X_3	Personal income ($ billions) X_4	Average age of automobiles (years) X_5	Number of supervisors X_6	Annual sales ($ millions) X_7 or Y
1739	9.27	7.0	85.4	3.5	9.0	37.702
1221	5.86	7.0	60.7	5.0	5.0	24.196
1846	8.81	7.0	68.1	4.4	7.0	32.055
120	3.81	7.0	20.2	4.0	5.0	3.611
1096	10.31	7.0	33.8	3.5	7.0	17.625
2290	11.62	7.0	95.1	4.1	13.0	45.919
1687	8.96	7.0	69.3	4.1	15.0	29.600
241	6.28	7.0	16.3	5.9	11.0	8.114
649	7.77	7.0	34.9	5.5	16.0	20.116
1427	10.92	7.0	15.1	4.1	10.0	12.994

The Statistical Package for the Social Sciences (SPSS) was used to generate the following output. To shorten the analysis, only the first three steps are included. Specifically:

a. Explain the first output entitled CORRELATION COEFFICIENTS.
b. Why was personal income entered as STEP NUMBER 1?
c. In STEP NUMBER 1, explain R SQUARE.
d. If only the personal income of a region was used to predict the annual regional sales, what would be the predicting regression equation?
e. Why did the number of automobiles registered come in as STEP NUMBER 2?
f. Explain the various measures in STEP NUMBER 3 as they relate to this problem.
g. If only the independent variables in STEP NUMBERS 1, 2, and 3 were used to predict sales, what would be the multiple regression equation? Using some hypothetical data, show how this equation could be used to predict sales.

```
CORRELATION COEFFICIENTS

A VALUE OF 99.00000 IS PRINTED
IF A COEFFICIENT CANNOT BE COMPUTED.


            SALES     OUTLET    REGIS     INT       INCOME    AGE       SUPV

SALES       1.00000   0.89942   0.60476   99.00000  0.96469  -0.32266   0.28576
OUTLET      0.89942   1.00000   0.77525   99.00000  0.82583  -0.48935   0.18332
REGIS       0.60476   0.77525   1.00000   99.00000  0.40918  -0.44651   0.39507
INT         99.00000  99.00000  99.00000  1.00000   99.00000  99.00000  99.00000
INCOME      0.96469   0.82583   0.40918   99.00000  1.00000  -0.34708   0.15592
AGE        -0.32266  -0.48935  -0.44651   99.00000 -0.34708   1.00000   0.29067
SUPV        0.28576   0.18332   0.39507   99.00000  0.15592   0.29067   1.00000


        DEPENDENT VARIABLE..    SALES

        VARIABLE(S) ENTERED ON STEP NUMBER  1..     INCOME


        MULTIPLE R            0.96469
        R SQUARE             0.93062
        ADJUSTED R SQUARE    0.92195
        STANDARD ERROR       3.72840


---------------- VARIABLES IN THE EQUATION ------------------

        VARIABLE         B          BETA      STD ERROR B      F

        INCOME        0.43814     0.96469      0.04230      107.308
        (CONSTANT)    1.37396


------------- VARIABLES NOT IN THE EQUATION --------------

        VARIABLE      BETA IN     PARTIAL    TOLERANCE       F

        OUTLET        0.32313     0.69179     0.31801       6.435
        REGIS         0.25227     0.87389     0.83257      22.622
        INT           0.0         0.0         1.00000       0.0
        AGE           0.01382     0.04921     0.87954       0.011
        SUPV          0.13872     0.52020     0.97569       2.591


        DEPENDENT VARIABLE..    SALES

        VARIABLE(S) ENTERED ON STEP NUMBER  2..     REGIS


        MULTIPLE R            0.99177
        R SQUARE             0.98361
        ADJUSTED R SQUARE    0.97892
        STANDARD ERROR       1.93757
```

```
---------------- VARIABLES IN THE EQUATION -------------------

VARIABLF          B          BETA      STD ERROR B         F

INCOME        0.39126     0.86146       0.02409        263.807
REGIS         1.37440     0.25227       0.28896         22.622
(CONSTANT)   -7.78271


------------ VARIABLES NOT IN THE EQUATION -------------.

VARIABLE      BETA IN     PARTIAL     TOLERANCE           F

OUTLFT       -0.08574    -0.19895      0.08828         0.2"?
INT           0.0         0.0          1.00000         0.0
AGE           0.11582     0.79280      0.76817        10.1":
SUPV          0.06135     0.44018      0.84388         1.4":



VARIABLE(S) ENTERED ON STEP NUMBER  3..      AGE


MULTIPLE R             0.99695
R SQUARE               0.99391
ADJUSTED R SQUARF      0.99086
STANDARD ERROR         1.27553


---------------- VARIABLES IN THE EQUATION -------------------

VARIABLE          B          BETA      STD ERROR B         F

INCOME        0.40164     0.88433       0.01619        615.465
REGIS         1.60518     0.25463       0.20355         62.187
AGE           1.91407     0.11582       0.60073         10.152
(CONSTANT)  -18.67052


------------ VARIABLES NOT IN THE EQUATION -------------.

VARIABLE      BETA IN     PARTIAL     TOLERANCE           F

OUTLFT       -0.03043    -0.11430      0.08590         0.0"?
INT           0.0         0.0          1.00000         0.0
SUPV         -0.00390    -0.03747      0.56126         0.0"?
```

5. If a computer is not available, do this problem. Recall from the previous chapter that the administrator of a new paralegal program at a community and technical college thought that high school grade point average would be a good predictor of student success in the paralegal program. However, it was found that only 24 percent of the variation in the paralegal grade point averages was explained by high school achievement. As a further experiment, the administrator recorded the Scholastic Aptitude Test (SAT) scores on the verbal and mathematics parts for nine students. The results follow.

Student	High school GPA	SAT verbal	SAT math	Paralegal GPA
1	3.25	480	410	3.21
2	1.80	290	270	1.68
3	2.89	420	410	3.58
4	3.81	500	600	3.92
5	3.13	500	490	3.00
6	2.81	430	460	2.82
7	2.20	320	490	1.65
8	2.14	530	480	2.30
9	2.63	469	440	2.33

Source: Plan Administrator, Community and Technical College, University of Toledo, Ohio.

Using this experimental group, select any two independent variables (the dependent variable is paralegal GPA) and:

a. Determine the multiple regression equation.

b. Find the standard error of estimate.

c. Compute the coefficient of determination, the coefficient of nondetermination, and the multiple coefficient of correlation.

d. Write an analysis of your findings.

6. If a computer is available, use all three independent variables in an effort to predict paralegal grade point average. Write an analysis of your findings based on the computer output.

CHAPTER SELF-REVIEW EXAMINATION

Do all of the problems and then check your answers against those given in Appendix A.

Score each problem 12½ points.

1. What is the general form of a multiple regression equation having two independent and one dependent variable?

Questions 2 through 5 are based on the following problem.

The multiple regression equation for a problem involving the prediction of automobiles sales in the United States by month is $Y_p = 6 + 0.7X_1 + (-9)X_2 + 5X_3$ (in $000,000), where X_1 is the number of automobile dealerships, X_2 is the number of persons unemployed, and X_3 is the average age of U.S. automobiles.

2. R SQUARE was computed to be 0.81. Explain in terms of this problem what it indicates.

3. What is the multiple coefficient of correlation?

4. What percent of the sales is not accounted for by the three independent variables?

5. Explain what the 5 is in front of X_3 and what it indicates.

6. The computer output for the foregoing automobile sales prediction problem showed the following correlation matrix:

	Sales	Dealerships	Unemployment	Average age
Sales	1.00000	0.34165	−0.71390	0.16233
Dealerships	0.34165	1.00000	0.00891	0.078962
Unemployment	−0.71390	0.00891	1.00000	0.23489
Average age	0.16233	0.078962	0.23489	1.00000

Which independent variable is entered as STEP NUMBER 1? Why?

7. Referring to the correlation matrix in Problem 6:

a. Explain the 1.00000 in the row labeled "Dealerships."

b. What is the correlation between the average age of the automobiles on the road and unemployment?

8. After STEP NUMBER 1 came the following computer output of variables not in the equation.

	Partial
Dealerships	0.20061
Average age	0.34838

a. What does the word *Partial* stand for?

b. What do the two figures indicate about the next step (STEP NUMBER 2)?

22

INTRODUCTION

The Pearson product-moment correlation coefficient r discussed in Chapter 20 is the most commonly used measure of association for two sets of *parametric* data, that is, data which are interval level of measurement. There are a number of business problems, however, which are concerned with the relationship between two or more sets of *nonparametric* data, that is, data which are either nominal scaled or ordinal scaled. As an illustration from the area of marketing research, suppose that a manufacturer of cake toppings has developed four new toppings. A group of consumers has been selected at random to test them. Each consumer is asked to indicate which topping he or she likes best (ranked 1), next best (ranked 2), and so on. Suppose that the results were:

Consumer	Toppings			
	A	B	C	D
1	1	3	4	2
2	4	2	1	3
3	2	1	3	4
4	3	4	2	1
5	2	3	1	4

A superficial examination of the rankings seems to indicate that there is practically no agreement among the consumers. A measure has been designed to measure the degree of relationship among these rankings. It will be discussed in detail shortly.

Some of the nonparametric measures of correlation available include the coefficient of contingency C, the phi coefficient, Spearman's Rho, and Kendall's coefficient of concordance W. The latter two are especially useful in business research and are the only ones presented in this chapter.

Nonparametric measures
of association

THE SPEARMAN RANK-ORDER CORRELATION COEFFICIENT

Spearman's rank-order correlation coefficient is usually designated as Rho. As the name implies, paired observations are ranked, thus requiring at least ordinal data. Rho, symbolized by ρ, measures the degree of relationship between two sets of ranked observations—i.e., it indicates the degree of effectiveness in predicting one ranked variable based on another ranked variable.

Like Pearson's r, Rho can assume any value from -1 to $+1$ inclusive, with -1 and $+1$ indicating perfect correlation and 0 no relationship.

The formula for Rho is:

$$\rho = 1 - \frac{6\Sigma d^2}{N^3 - N}$$

EXAMPLE

The paired data in Table 22–1 and the accompanying scatter diagram illustrate the case of perfect correlation between the rank a worker has within the sample group of workers on a finger dexterity test and his or her rank with respect to weekly production. Both finger dexterity scores and production level have been ranked from high (1) to low (5). However, as long as both groups are treated the same, there is no reason why the scores and production cannot be ranked from high (5) to low (1). Rho will be the same ($+1.00$) in either case. Note from the table that Joe had the highest test score, and he also ranked first with respect to production. Sue's performances ranked 2 and 2, respectively, within the group, and so on.

**TABLE 22–1
Finger dexterity test scores and weekly production**

Name of worker	Finger dexterity test score	Weekly production index	Rank Dexterity	Rank Production
Pete	62	800	4	4
Joe	92	900	1	1
Dee	70	840	3	3
Sam	50	775	5	5
Sue	86	875	2	2

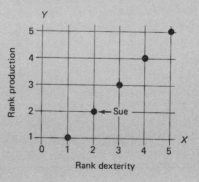

It should be emphasized that Rho is being used as a measure of correlation in this problem (instead of Pearson's r) because there is interest in the degree of relationship between sets of *ranked* data.

For the data in the Table 22–1 what is Spearman's rank-order correlation coefficient?

SOLUTION

N in this problem is the total number of workers in the sample or 5, and d is the deviation between ranks for each pair. In part, the formula merely directs one to square each deviation and then sum them.

The calculations for Rho are in Table 22–2.

TABLE 22–2
Calculations needed for Spearman's Rho

Worker	Finger dexterity	Weekly production	d	d^2
Pete 4		4	0	0
Joe 1		1	0	0
Dee 3		3	0	0
Sam 5		5	0	0
Sue 2		2	0	0
Total				0

Spearman's Rho is 1, found by:

$$\rho = 1 - \frac{6\Sigma d^2}{N^3 - N}$$

$$= 1 - \frac{6(0)}{5^3 - 5}$$

$$= 1 - 0$$

$$= 1$$

As expected, there is perfect (positive) correlation between the ranks.

EXAMPLE

Now to a case involving less than perfect correlation. The problem involves a composite rating given by executives to each college graduate joining a plastic-manufacturing firm. The executive rating is an expression of the future potential of the college graduate. (The ratings are, of course, ordinal level of measurement.) The recent college graduate then enters an in-plant training program and is given another composite rating (based on tests, opinions of foremen, training officers, and so on). The executive ratings and the in-plant training ratings are given in Table 22–3 on the top of the next page.

The problem is to determine the relationship between the ratings

TABLE 22–3
Executive ratings and in-plant training ratings for a selected group of college graduates

Graduate	Executive rating X	Training rating Y
A	8	4
B	10	4
C	9	4
D	4	3
E	12	6
F	11	9
G	11	9
H	7	6
I	8	6
J	13	9
K	10	5
L	12	9

college graduates received from the executives before they entered the in-plant training program (X) and the ratings they received in the training program (Y). That is, what is Rho?

SOLUTION

It was decided to rank the variables from low (1) to high. The lowest rating given by the executives was 4, so it was ranked 1. The next lowest was 7 and was ranked 2. Then there were two graduates rated 8. The tie is resolved by giving each a mean rank of 3.5. The same procedure is followed when there are more than two ratings tied. This is illustrated along with the necessary calculations for Rho in Table 22–4.

TABLE 22–4
Calculations needed for Rho

Graduate	Executive rating X	Training rating Y	Rank Executive	Rank Training	Difference between ranks d	Difference squared d²
A	8	4	3.5	3.0	0.5	0.25
B	10	4	6.5	3.0	3.5	12.25
C	9	4	5.0	3.0	2.0	4.00
D	4	3	1.0	1.0	0	0
E	12	6	10.5	7.0	3.5	12.25
F	11	9	8.5	10.5	−2.0	4.00
G	11	9	8.5	10.5	−2.0	4.00
H	7	6	2.0	7.0	−5.0	25.00
I	8	6	3.5	7.0	−3.5	12.25
J	13	9	12.0	10.5	1.5	2.25
K	10	5	6.5	5.0	1.5	2.25
L	12	9	10.5	10.5	0	0
					0.0*	78.50

* Sum of deviations must equal 0.

Rho was computed to be 0.7255, found by:

$$\rho = 1 - \frac{6\Sigma d^2}{N^3 - N} = 1 - \frac{6(78.50)}{(12)^3 - 12} = 1 - 0.27447552 = 0.7255$$

The usual practice is to record it as 0.73.

There is a large number of ties in the preceding problem. The following computer output contains a correction factor to correct for these ties. The resulting value of Rho, however, is very close to the uncorrected coefficient. There is a negligible difference in this problem (0.7255 uncorrected, 0.7148 corrected for ties). Usually the difference is only 2 percentage points. Therefore, the correction procedure will be disregarded.

TEST 1	TEST 2
8.00	4.00
10.00	4.00
9.00	4.00
4.00	3.00
12.00	6.00
11.00	9.00
11.00	9.00
7.00	6.00
8.00	6.00
13.00	9.00
10.00	5.00
12.00	9.00

NUMBER OF OBSERVATIONS 12

SPEARMAN RANK CORRELATION COEFFICIENT= 0.7148

SELF-REVIEW 22-1

---

a.

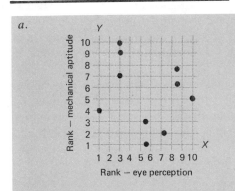

Rank — eye perception

b. There seems to be a rather low correlation between the two sets of ranks—perhaps negative.

c. Rho $= 1 - \dfrac{6\Sigma d^2}{N^3 - N} = 1 - \dfrac{6(193)}{(10)^3 - 10}$

$= 1 - 1.17 = -0.17.$

(A reminder: Cover the answers in the left-hand column.)

A small sample of individuals revealed the following scores on an eye perception test (X) and a mechanical aptitude test (Y).

Subject	Eye perception	Mechanical aptitude
001	805	23
002	777	62
003	820	60
004	682	40
005 ·...........	777	70
006	810	28
007	805	30
008	840	42
009	777	55
010	820	51

a. Draw a scatter diagram (using ranks).
b. Based on the scatter diagram, what can be said

		Rank			
X	Y	X	Y	d	d²
805	23	5.5	1	4.5	20.25
777	62	3.0	9	−6.0	36.00
820	60	8.5	8	0.5	0.25
682	40	1.0	4	−3.0	9.00
777	70	3.0	10	−7.0	49.00
810	28	7.0	2	5.0	25.00
805	30	5.5	3	2.5	6.25
840	42	10.0	5	5.0	25.00
777	55	3.0	7	−4.0	16.00
820	51	8.5	6	2.5	6.25
				0	193.00

about the correlation between the two variables?

c. Compute Rho.
d. Interpret Rho.

d. As expected, the correlation of −0.17 is quite low.

Testing the significance of Rho

H_0: The null hypothesis to be tested is, Rho in the population is zero.

H_1: The alternate hypothesis states that Rho in the population is greater than zero. Since the words *greater than* predict a direction, the test of significance is one-tailed.

Small samples. For a sample of less than 10, the critical value is determined by referring to Appendix M. If, based on the sample results, the computed value of Rho is less than the critical value, the null hypothesis is accepted. Otherwise, it is rejected and H_1 accepted.

Note that Appendix M actually extends from an N of 4 to 30, indicating that it may be used for any sample size in that range. As an example, in Self-Review 22–1 involving eye perception and mechanical aptitude, Rho was computed to be −0.17; $N = 10$. The critical value at the 0.05 level is 0.564. Since the 0.17 is less than 0.564, the null hypothesis is accepted. There is no relationship between eye perception and mechanical aptitude in the population; that is, the magnitude of the sample Rho (0.17) is due to chance.

Large samples. For $N \geq 10$, the significance of Rho may be determined by either (1) referring to Appendix M for the critical value or (2) computing Student's t. In this regard, the sampling distribution of Rho follows the t distribution with $N - 2$ degrees of freedom. The computed value of t is found by:

$$t = \rho \sqrt{\frac{N - 2}{1 - \rho^2}}$$

with $N - 2$ degrees of freedom.

Both methods will be applied to the Rho of 0.73 computed in the problem involving executive ratings and in-plant training ratings (Table 22–4). First, using Appendix M the critical value for an N of 12 and the 0.05 level is 0.506.

Since the computed value of Rho (0.73) falls beyond this critical value, the null hypothesis is rejected at the 0.05 level, and H_1 is accepted. This means that Rho in the population is greater than zero.

The decision rule for the second method using Student's t calls for accepting H_0 if the computed value of t is less than the critical value of 1.812 (Appendix E, 0.05 level, one-tailed test, and 10 df, found by $N - 2 = 12 - 2 = 10$ df).

The computed value of t is 3.38, found by:

$$t = \rho \sqrt{\frac{N - 2}{1 - \rho^2}} = 0.73 \sqrt{\frac{12 - 2}{1 - (0.73)^2}} = 3.38$$

The decision is the same as before, namely, the null hypothesis is rejected at the 0.05 level (because 3.38 is beyond the critical value of 1.812). To repeat, it is highly unlikely that the relationship between the two variables in the population is zero.

EXERCISES

(A reminder: The answer and method of solution for selected exercises are given in Appendix A.)

1. A series of questions on sports and world events was asked a randomly selected group of male senior citizens. The results were translated into a "knowledge" score. The scores were:

Citizen	Sports	World events
Mr. J. C. McCarthy	47	49
Mr. A. N. Baker	12	10
Mr. B. B. Beebe	62	76
Mr. L. D. Gaucet	81	92
Mr. C. A. Jones	90	86
Mr. J. N. Narko	35	42
Mr. A. F. Nissen	61	61
Mr. L. M. Zaugg	87	75
Mr. J. B. Simon	59	86
Mr. J. Goulden	40	61
Mr. A. A. Davis	87	18
Mr. A. M. Carbo	16	75
Mr. A. O. Smithy	50	51
Mr. J. J. Pascal	60	61

a. Determine the degree of association between how the senior citizens ranked with respect to knowledge of sports and how they ranked on world events.
b. Is the correlation in the population with respect to sports knowledge and knowledge of world events zero?

2. The average nine-month salaries of full-time faculty for the 1968–69 and 1975–76 academic years in Ohio institutions of higher learning follow.

(handwritten margin notes:)

$$R = 1 - \frac{6(138)}{(12)^2 - 12} = 1 - \frac{828}{1716} = 1 - 0.5175$$

Rank difference

measure the difference

square the difference

University	1968–69	1975–76
Akron	$11,320	$17,570
Bowling Green	11,760	17,581
Central State	10,593	14,577
Cincinnati	12,084	17,812
Cleveland State	11,392	18,299
Kent State	11,251	16,544
Miami	12,332	16,989
Ohio State	12,295	20,552
Ohio	11,716	16,931
Toledo	11,277	17,860
Wright State	10,959	16,250
Youngstown	10,012	17,143

Source: Douglas A. Lind, "Faculty Compensation Study for the State Universities of Ohio," Institutional and Resource Analysis, The University of Toledo, January 1977, p. 2.

a. Determine the degree of correlation between the rank the universities had in 1968–69 with respect to average faculty salaries and the rank in 1975–76. Interpret.

b. Is Rho significant? Cite evidence.

THE KENDALL COEFFICIENT OF CONCORDANCE: *W*

Spearman's Rho, discussed in the previous section, was designed to measure the degree of relationship between *two* sets of ordinal-level observations. Similarly, **Kendall's coefficient of concordance**, designated by *W*, measures the degree of agreement among *many* ordinal-scaled variables when ranked. It can assume any value between 0 and 1 inclusive.

EXAMPLE

Suppose that several persons in the 18–21-year age group were asked to rank six mockup models of a proposed new automobile. They were instructed to rank the model they liked best 1, the next 2, and so on. The rankings are in Table 22–5.

TABLE 22–5
Rankings given six mock-up models

	Proposed model					
Name of person	A	B	C	D	E	F
Mr. Jones	2	6	1	5	4	3
Ms. Smith	1	5	3	4	6	2
Mr. Angel	5	1	4	2	3	6
Sum R^j	8	12	8	11	13	11

A cursory examination of the rankings of the six proposed models seems to indicate that there is practically no agreement, or "concordance," among the persons doing the rankings. There appears to be no relationship among the rankings and, when computed, *W* will probably be close to zero.

What is Kendall's coefficient of concordance *W*?

SOLUTION

The formula for Kendall's statistic W is:

$$W = \left(\frac{12 \sum_j R_j^2}{k^2 N(N^2 - 1)} \right) - \frac{3(N + 1)}{N - 1}$$

where in this case:

N is the number of models being judged, or 6, i.e., the number of columns.

k is the number of persons judging the mock-up models, or 3 (number of rows).

R_j is the sum of the ranks for each model, namely, 8, 12, 8, 11, 13, and 11, respectively.

$\sum_j R_j^2$ directs one to square each rank sum and total them, i.e., $(8)^2 + (12)^2 + (8)^2 + (11)^2 + (13)^2 + (11)^2 = 683$.

Solving for W, we get

$$W = \left(\frac{12 \sum_j R_j^2}{k^2 N(N^2 - 1)} \right) - \frac{3(N + 1)}{N - 1}$$

$$= \left(\frac{12[(8)^2 + (12)^2 + (8)^2 + (11)^2 + (13)^2 + (11)^2]}{(3)^2(6)[(6)^2 - 1]} \right) - \frac{3(6 + 1)}{6 - 1}$$

$$= 4.337 - 4.200 = 0.137$$

As expected, there is very little concordance among the persons ranking the mock-up models. Had the sample size been much larger (and the coefficient of concordance been 0.137), from a practical standpoint it might indicate either that persons in the 18–21–year age group disagree among themselves regarding what constitutes the "best" style, or that none of the styles presented for judging was outstanding.

Ties. There were no ties in the previous problem. The person judging the mockup models, for example, was not allowed to rank his two favorite models 1.5 and 1.5—assuming that the was not sure which to rank 1 and which to rank 2. If ties are present in the data, a formula corrected for ties can be applied. But since the difference between W's computed with and without applying the correction factor for ties is negligible, the correction procedure will not be presented. Had the 18–21–year–olds been permitted to express ties when viewing the mock-up models, their rankings might have appeared as follows (see Table 22–6).

TABLE 22–6
Rankings given six mock-up models with ties permitted

Name of person	Proposed model					
	A	B	C	D	E	F
Mr. Jones	1.5	6.0	1.5	5.0	3.5	3.5
Ms. Smith	1.0	5.0	3.5	3.5	6.0	2.0
Mr. Angel	5.5	1.5	3.5	1.5	3.5	5.5

The W computed corrected for ties is 0.141; without being corrected, 0.133; and previously the W was 0.137 (no ties permitted). Again, this reaffirms that the effect of ties is insignificant.

──────────────────── **SELF-REVIEW 22-2** ────────────────────

Refer back to Table 22–6. Verify that W is 0.133.

$$W = \left(\frac{12[(8.0)^2 + (12.5)^2 + (8.5)^2 + (10.0)^2 + (13)^2 + (11.0)^2]}{3^2(6)[(6)^2 - 1]} \right)$$

$$- \frac{3(6 + 1)}{6 - 1}$$

$$= \frac{12(682.5)}{1890} - \frac{21}{5}$$

$$= \frac{8190}{1890} - 4.2$$

$$= 0.133$$

Testing the significance of W

Small samples. If N (the number of mock-up models to be ranked in this case) is equal to or less than seven, the sample is considered small. To test the significance of W:

H_0: W in the population $= 0$.
H_1: W in the population > 0.

A value designated by s is needed. It is the sum of the squared deviations of the column sums from the mean of the column sums. It can be computed either by:

$$\Sigma(R_j - \bar{R}_j)^2 \quad \text{or} \quad N\left[\frac{\Sigma R_j^2}{N} - \left(\frac{\Sigma R_j}{N}\right)^2\right]$$

Illustrating both using the problem from Table 22–5 and the accompanying calculations, we get:

For $s = \Sigma(R_j - \bar{R}_j)^2$			
R_j	$\bar{R}_j$	$R_j - \bar{R}_j$	$(R_j - \bar{R}_j)^2$
8	10.5	−2.5	6.25
12	10.5	1.5	2.25
8	10.5	−2.5	6.25
11	10.5	0.5	.25
13	10.5	2.5	6.25
11	10.5	0.5	0.25
63		0.0	21.50

For $s = N\left[\frac{\Sigma R_j^2}{N} - \left(\frac{\Sigma R_j}{N}\right)^2\right]$

$$= 6\left[\frac{683}{6} - \left(\frac{63}{6}\right)^2\right]$$

$$= 21.5$$

where: ΣR_j^2 is the total of each rank sum squared; that is, $(8)^2 + (12)^2 + (8)^2 + (11)^2 + (13)^2 + (11)^2 = 68.3$

Thus: $\Sigma(R_j - \bar{R}_j)^2 = 21.5$.

Referring to Appendix N, the 0.05 level, an N of 6, and a k of 3, we see that the critical value of $s = 103.9$. Using the usual decision procedure, the null hypothesis is accepted because the computed value of s (21.5) is less than the critical value (103.9). In essence, this indicates that there is no agreement in the population of 18–21–year–olds regarding the best styling of the six proposed automobiles. Further, although the computed W was only 0.137, it can be attributed to chance.

Large samples. If N is greater than seven the sampling distribution of the statistic s approximates the chi-square distribution with $N - 1$ degrees of freedom. For illustration, suppose that several consumers were asked to rank the impact of eight different advertising posters from 1 to 8. N therefore is 8. The results of the rankings are in Table 22–7.

TABLE 22–7
Rankings of the impact of eight advertising posters

Consumers	A	B	C	D	E	F	G	H
Ms. Susie	1	4	8	7	6	3	5	2
Ms. Green	3	7	8	1	2	6	4	5
Ms. Ankra	8	1	2	3	4	5	7	6
Ms. Silly	5	3	1	4	7	6	2	8

Kendall's coefficient of concordance was computed to be 0.05. To test whether the women in the population almost completely disagree regarding the impact of the eight advertising posters, χ^2 must be computed and compared with the value from the table of critical values of chi-square (Appendix H):

$$\chi^2 = k(N - 1)W, \text{ with } N - 1 \text{ } df$$

At the 0.01 level of significance, the null hupothesis that $W = 0$ in the population will be rejected if the computed value is equal to or greater than the critical value of 18.48 (Appendix H). Shown schematically:

Distribution of chi-square for 7 degrees of freedom, $\alpha = 0.01$

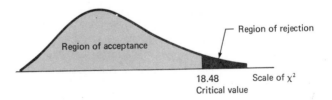

Computing chi-square, we get:

$$\chi^2 = k(N - 1)W = 4(8 - 1)(0.05) = 1.4$$

Since the computed value of chi-square (1.4) does not exceed the critical value (18.48), the null hypothesis is accepted. This means that in the population from which this sample was drawn there is no concordance regarding which advertising poster has the most impact, which poster is ranked second in impact, and so on.

a. Kendall's coefficient of concordance: W.

b. The column sums are 17, 15, 19, 15, 19, 20, 18, and 21 respectively. The sum of each of these squared is 2,626. Then:

$$W = \frac{12[2,626]}{(4)^2(8)(8^2 - 1)} - \frac{3(8 + 1)}{8 - 1}$$

$$= \frac{31,512}{8,064} - \frac{27}{7} = 3.908 - 3.857$$

$$= 0.05$$

Refer back to Table 22–7. In this problem involving the rankings of eight advertisements by a group of consumers, W was computed to be 0.05.

a. What is this measure called?

b. Verify that W does equal 0.05.

Finally, it should be noted that in the previous illustrations k identified the set in the left vertical margin (rows). N designated the ranks (columns). $k = 2$ and $N = 5$ in the following format. This same format *must* be maintained in order to compute Kendall's W using the formulas given.

k ↓	N							
	A	B	C	D	E			
X	2	3	4	1	5	← ← ←	ranks of 1,2,3 . . .
Z	3	1	2	5	4	← ← ←	ranks of 1,2,3 . . .

EXERCISES

3. Four different pension plans have been developed. In order to get the initial reaction of the union members over 50 years of age to the plans, a sample of size 12 was selected at random, and the plans were explained to the group. They were then asked to rank the plans from 1 to 4. The results were:

Union member	A	B	C	D
842	1	2	4	3
007	2	1	3	4
954	2	1	3	4
731	1	2	4	3
003	2	1	3	4
548	3	1	2	4
490	1	2	3	4
307	2	1	4	3
900	1	2	4	3
333	4	1	3	2
676	1	2	4	3
718	2	1	3	4

a. Determine the degree of concordance among the union members over 50 years of age with respect to the four pension plans.

b. Test the significance of W.

c. Interpret your findings.

4. Three applicants were interviewed for the job of computer manager. Each applicant worked with the computer department for a day and met all the key person-

nel. At the end of the interview period, each key person ranked the applicants 1, 2, or 3 in order of preference. The rankings are:

Key personnel	Applicant		
	John Lopez	Jean Neter	Joseph Fazio
A	1	2	3
B	2	3	1
C	2	1	3
D	3	1	2
E	1	3	2
F	1	2	3
G	3	2	1
H	2	3	1

a. Determine the degree of relationship among the ranks.
b. Test the significance of W.
c. Interpret your findings.

CHAPTER SUMMARY

Fortunately, several measures of correlation are available for nonparametric data, that is, nominal and ordinal level of measurement. As the name implies, Spearman's rank-order correlation coefficient, designated by Rho, measures the degree of association between two sets of data which have been ranked from low to high, or vice versa. Its value can range from -1 to $+1$ inclusive, with -1 and $+1$ indicating perfect correlation between the ranks and 0 indicating no correlation.

A test is available to evaluate the hypothesis that Rho in the population from which the sample was selected is zero. A small-sample procedure is used for samples of less than 10, and a large-sample approach for samples of size 10 or more.

Kendall's coefficient of concordance, designated by W, can be used to measure the degree of association between two or more sets of data which have been ranked. It can assume a value between zero and one inclusive, with zero indicating no correlation and one perfect correlation.

There is a test to evaluate the hypothesis that the correlation W in the population is zero. There is one procedure for small samples of seven or less and another for samples of more than seven.

CHAPTER OUTLINE

Nonparametric measures of association

I. Spearman rank-order correlation coefficient.
   A. *Purpose.* To explain the degree of relationship between two sets of data which are at least ordinal-level measurement. Rank coefficient is called Rho and symbolized by ρ.
   B. *Formula.*

   $$\text{Rho} = 1 - \frac{6\Sigma d^2}{N^3 - N}$$

   C. *Example:* What is the correlation between the rank on job rating and IQ?

Person	Rating on job	IQ	Rank Job	Rank IQ	d	d²
Gert	Fair	121	3	2	1	1
Sam	Excellent	130	1	1	0	0
Jean	Good	106	2	3	−1	1
						2

$$\text{Rho} = \rho = 1 - \frac{6\Sigma d^2}{N^3 - N} = 1 - \frac{6(2)}{3^3 - 3} = 1 - \frac{12}{24} = 0.50$$

Spearman's Rho can assume any value between -1 and $+1$. A -1 or a $+1$ indicates perfect correlation between the ranks. The 0.50 result reveals that there is a moderate degree of correlation.

D. *Testing the significance of Rho.*
   1. *State null and alternative hypotheses.*

       H_0: Rho in population is 0.
       H_1: Rho in population is not 0.

   2. *Small samples.* For N of less than 10, refer to Appendix M for the critical value. If Rho is less than the critical value, accept H_0; otherwise reject it.
   3. *Large samples.* If N is between 10 and 30, either use Appendix M for critical value, or use Student's t and Appendix E. For sample size over 30, use t.

$$t = \rho \sqrt{\frac{N-2}{1-\rho^2}}$$

II. Kendall coefficient of concordance: W.
  A. *Purpose.* To determine the degree of agreement (concordance) among many ordinal-scaled variables when ranked.
  B. *Formula.*

$$W = \left(\frac{12 \sum_j R_j^2}{k^2 N(N^2 - 1)} \right) - \frac{3(N+1)}{N-1}$$

where:

    N is the number of items being ranked. In the following example there are four sweaters ranked.
    k is the number of persons in the sample; $k = 3$ in the example.
    R_j is the sum of the ranks for each item.

  C. *Example.* Four different sweaters were ranked from 1 to 4 by three fashion designers. Ms. James, for instance, liked the shawl-collared sweater the best, the V-neck the least.

Fashion designer	Rank			
	Turtle-neck	V neck	Crew neck	Shawl collared
Ms. James	3	4	2	1
Mr. Dunn	4	1	3	2
Ms. Pierre	1	3	2	4
Total	8	8	7	7

$$W = \left(\frac{12 \sum_j R_j^2}{k^2 N(N^2 - 1)}\right) - \frac{3(N + 1)}{N - 1}$$

$$= \frac{12(8^2 + 8^2 + 7^2 + 7^2)}{3^2(4)(4^2 - 1)} - \frac{3(4 + 1)}{4 - 1}$$

$$= 0.02$$

W can assume a value between 0 and $+1$. As expected, W of 0.02 indicates practically no agreement among the fashion designers with respect to the four sweaters.

D. *Testing the significance of W.*
1. *State null and alternative hypotheses.*

   H_0: *W* in population $= 0$.
   H_1: *W* in population > 0.

2. *Small samples.* If $N \leq 7$, compute s either by $\Sigma(R_j - \bar{R}_j)^2$ or

$$N\left[\frac{\Sigma R_j^2}{N} - \left(\frac{\Sigma R_j}{N}\right)^2\right]$$

   Refer to Appendix N for the critical value. If W is less than the critical value, accept H_0; otherwise reject H_0 at the level of significance selected and accept H_1.
3. *Large samples.* If $N > 7$, s approximates chi-square. $\chi^2 = k(N - 1)W$ with $N - 1$ degrees of freedom. Refer to Appendix H for the critical value.

CHAPTER EXERCISES

5. A randomly selected group of fashion models was asked to try several newly developed waterproof makeups especially designed for use in photographic and television studios. They were requested to rate each from 1 to 50, with a low rating representing the most desirable makeup and a high number the least desirable. The rating results were:

Name of model	Makeup				
	A	B	C	D	E
Sue	41	10	6	48	1
Sami	9	40	50	37	16
Jean	48	40	20	10	25
Pei	40	6	10	48	45
Gladys	30	40	5	10	50
Fifi	2	20	45	40	10

a. Determine the degree of concordance with respect to the responses to the makeups.

b. Test the significance of the coefficient of concordance.

c. Interpret your findings.

6. Posto Pedic, a manufacturer of chairs for secretaries, telephone operators, and others who sit for long periods of time, has designed four new chairs. In order to determine customer reaction, a small group of secretaries and telephone operators was asked to try each of the chairs over a period of several hours and then rate them. Each chair was rated on a scale of 1 to 100, with 100 being a perfect score. The results were:

Name of person	Ratings of new chairs			
	Posto	Pedic	Comfy	Dreamy
Ms. Z.	26	19	5	82
Ms. C.	8	88	42	16
Mr. Z.	21	18	38	30
Ms. R.	91	68	62	86
Sgt. T.	52	19	38	5

The question to be explored is whether or not there is any agreement (concordance) among the group with regard to the four chairs.

a. Compute *W*.

b. Test whether *W* in the population is zero.

c. Interpret your findings.

7. A very brief explanation of the problem follows.

A physical inventory accounting program was conducted at an ordnance depot containing about 186,000 different items.[1] One objective was to determine how accurate the inventory data stored in the computer were. If, for example, the inventory figure on a certain size snow tire indicated that 1,000 were on hand, but an actual count revealed only 800, obviously the record would be 20 percent inaccurate. (The discrepancies were due to paperwork errors, stealing, and so on.)

The question to be examined here is: Are the active warehouses more inaccurate than the less active warehouses? A warehouse containing hardware such as nuts, bolts, and cotter pins would be considered as being an "active" warehouse because these items are always being shipped out to military installations. A warehouse containing antifreeze and similar slow-moving items would be considered an "inactive" one.

In order to measure the degree of activity, an *activity score* was computed for each warehouse. The *error rate* for each warehouse was also calculated. Note on the next page that warehouse number 2 was the most active, with an activity score of 328.6. The error rate for that warehouse was 42.3 percent, meaning that on the average there was a discrepancy of 42.3 percent between the computer records and the actual inventory for the items in that warehouse.

Specifically, the problem involves determining the relationship (correlation) between the *ranking* the warehouses have on the activity score and the corresponding *ranking* with respect to error rate. That is, do the warehouses which

[1] Source: Marion R. Bryson and Robert D. Mason, Office of Ordnance Research, *Physical Inventory Accounting Program,* Technical Report no. 1.

rank high in activity also have a high error rate? Conversely, are the inactive warehouses ranked low in error rate?

Warehouse number	Activity score	Error rate	Warehouse number	Activity score	Error rate
2	328.6	42.3	9	181.5	28.8
3	324.5	45.6	8	180.3	30.9
26	288.4	45.3	10	178.2	29.2
24	281.3	33.2	20	174.5	20.5
14	238.5	41.4	6	169.1	15.9
23	230.7	44.3	18	166.9	19.6
19	209.5	31.3	27	166.4	20.6
5	207.1	33.2	21	164.4	16.6
25	193.7	16.9	17	160.7	33.3
4	192.0	41.3	7	158.1	26.4
1	188.3	35.6	11	150.4	29.9
15	188.2	29.2	12	140.0	23.2
16	184.6	31.3	13	124.2	27.1
22	183.5	21.4			

a. Rank the activity scores. Then rank the error rates. (Watch the ties.)
b. Plot the paired rankings in the form of a scatter diagram. (Use the graph paper provided in the back of the manual.) The Y-variable is the ranking, error rate, and the X-variable is the ranking, activity score.
c. Interpret the scatter diagram.
d. Compute Spearman's rank correlation coefficient Rho.
e. Is Rho significant?
f. Interpret your findings.

CHAPTER SELF-REVIEW EXAMINATION

Do both problems and then check your answers against those given in Appendix A.

Score each problem 50 points.

1. The football coaches rate the performance of the players on a scale of 0 to 100 both during the weekly practice and during the game on Saturday. A sample of the players who played in the big game against Sociable University revealed that:

Player	Rating In practice	During game
Art	80	80
Bob	20	10
Jim	100	90
Abe	65	50
Arch	50	35
John	40	30
Dean	90	95
Jimmie	60	35

a. Determine the degree of relationship between how the players ranked in performance during the practice and how they ranked during the game.

b. Using the 0.01 level, test whether or not Rho is significantly different from zero.

c. Interpret.

2. The division managers of a large manufacturing firm act on all major promotions by ranking the applicants 1,2,3 . . . in order of preference. A new job has been created in the area of international sales, and there are three applicants. The preferences of the division managers are:

Division manager	Mr. Maisson	Mr. York	Ms. Thomas
A	1	3	2
B	2	3	1
C	2	3	1
D	3	2	1
E	2	3	1
F	2	3	1
G	2	3	1

Determine the degree of relationship among the ranks.

23

INTRODUCTION

Earlier chapters dealt with statistical inference and tests of hypotheses. In the chapter on inference, a decision to market a product was based on sample data. In the chapter on hypothesis testing, a decision to accept or reject several carloads of steel wire from a supplier was based on the sample results of tensile strength tests. This approach to decision making is often referred to as the *traditional approach.*

Another facet of decision making, called **statistical decision theory**, had its beginning in the latter part of the 1940s. It may be loosely defined as the collection of techniques which the decision maker can apply in certain situations in order to choose the best alternative action. Finding the best alternative usually includes factors other than quantitative evidence. For example, a firm with six plants seeking the most profitable course of action might reject the alternative that would result in the maximum level of profit, namely, to shut down the plant in Billings, Montana, and add a shift in two other plants. Management might be unwilling to disrupt the economy of Billings merely to satisfy a few shareholders. Other decisions involving nonquantitative matters might be the psychological and sociological effects of demoting or retiring key personnel or shifting from a high-priced, handcrafted product to a mass-produced, low-cost product.

Deciding among alternatives is not unique to business. A personal decision may be which pair of shoes to wear, whether to staple the pages of a homework assignment or use a paper clip, whether to have toast or a sweet roll for breakfast, which if any of three proposals of marriage to accept, and which common stock or home to purchase. Similarly, business decisions might include which brand of staples, paper clips, or cutting oil to purchase, how many portable 11-inch television sets to manufacture, or whether to move the finished product by truck or rail to its destination. Another problem might require a decision to either buy the assets of a small competitor or build a new plant to gain the needed additional output.

Many personal and business decisions are the result of personal preference at that moment and are made somewhat automatically. The selection of a sweet roll for breakfast is an illustration. However, the person interested in purchasing a new automobile would no doubt heavily weigh the price in making a decision. If the quotation from one dealer was $200 less than the quotations of others for the same model and equipment, the consumer would

An introduction to decision making under uncertainty

probably purchase it from that dealer (assuming that other intangibles such as service are equal among the dealers). Since all the facts are known, it can be said that the decision was made under conditions of *certainty.* Other personal decisions must be made under conditions of *uncertainty.* The family decision maker, for example, might decide to buy the house at 10 Gulf View Lane based on the observation that more-expensive homes are being built in that area. It would seem that the house will appreciate in value more in the long run than identical houses at 945 Ridge Crest Road and 19431 East Courvelle Drive, but one cannot be sure this will actually happen. Uncertainty of outcome also exists in common stock buying, marriage, and so on.

The purchasing agent will probably buy paper clips, steel ingots, and the like from the supplier offering the lowest price, assuming the quality and service are satisfactory. Again, since there are no unknown factors, the decision can be considered as being made under *conditions of certainty.* However, most decision problems are not as simple as purchasing paper clips. There is usually more than one unknown factor. For example, the manufacturer of a new toy is not sure what the future demand will be. In decision making under *conditions of uncertainty* a term has evolved to describe this uncertain condition. It is said that the actual **state of nature** (future demand) is unknown. The decision maker must decide to produce, buy, or sell far in advance of the actual purchase by the consumer. A department store buyer, for example, must decide during the summer how many heavy wool plaid shirts to order for the Christmas selling season. Past experience indicates that if the weather is extremely cold the six weeks before Christmas, shoppers will buy more heavy wool shirts than they will during a mild period. The buyer does not know what the weather will be and also does not know what competitors plan to offer. The local economic situation also has an effect on sales. The buyer can read and evaluate various forecasts by the federal government and others, but there is still an element of uncertainty concerning the actual conditions that will occur during the selling season—i.e., the state of nature is uncertain.

The actual demand for plaid wool shirts is called an **event**. If 3,142 plaid shirts were actually sold during the Christmas selling season, this demand (3,142) is the event. However, the buyer is not sure of the actual state of nature (demand) when ordering the shirts the preceding summer, but still must decide among several alternatives. Should 3,000 shirts in assorted sizes be ordered? 4,200? 5,500? or 10,000? Under these conditions of uncertainty it is said that the decision maker has a choice among several alternative **acts**. For each of these alternative acts there are many possible results called **outcomes**, **consequences**, or **payoffs**. If the buyer ordered 4,000 assorted shirts and 3,000 were sold during the selling season, 700 during the January clearance, and the remaining ones at 50 percent off on a bargain table, the payoff (outcome or consequence) might be a profit of $10,425. Had the buyer ordered 10,000 and only 200 were sold during the Christmas selling season and the remaining ones at reductions up to 60 percent, the consequence of this act might be a loss of $75.

The main elements of the decision problem under conditions of uncertainty are identified schematically.

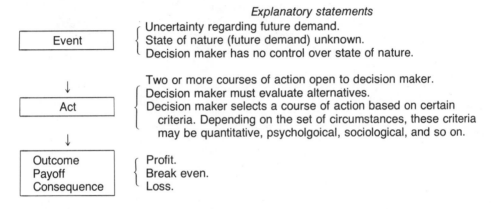

Explanatory statements

Event
- Uncertainty regarding future demand.
- State of nature (future demand) unknown.
- Decision maker has no control over state of nature.

Act
- Two or more courses of action open to decision maker.
- Decision maker must evaluate alternatives.
- Decision maker selects a course of action based on certain criteria. Depending on the set of circumstances, these criteria may be quantitative, psycholgoical, sociological, and so on.

Outcome Payoff Consequence
- Profit.
- Break even.
- Loss.

AN ILLUSTRATIVE CASE OF DECISION MAKING UNDER UNCERTAINTY

At the outset it should be emphasized that this case description includes only the fundamental concepts found in a decision-making problem. The purpose of examining the case is to explain the logical procedure which might be followed in the simplest of problems. In most real-world problems there would be many other variables which would be considered.

Payoff table

A small investor, Bob Hill, studied the performance of several common stocks and narrowed his choice to three, namely, Kayser Chemicals, Rim Homes, and Texas Electronics. He reasoned that if his $1,100 was invested in Kayser Chemicals and a strong bull market developed by the end of the year (that is, stock prices increased drastically), the value of his Kayser stock would more than double to $2,400. However, if there was a bear market (i.e., stock prices declined), the value of his Kayser stock could conceivably drop to $1,000 by the end of the year. His predictions regarding the value of his $1,100 investment for the three stocks for a bull market and a bear market are shown in Table 23–1. This table is usually referred to as a **payoff table**.

**TABLE 23–1
Payoff table for three common stocks under two market conditions**

Purchase	Value under bull market	Value under bear market
Kayser Chemicals	$2,400	$1,000
Rim Homes	2,200	1,100
Texas Electronics	1,900	1,150

Expected payoff

If the payoff table were the only information available, the investor might take a conservative action and buy Texas Electronics in order to be assured of at least $1,150 at the end of the year (a slight profit). A speculative venture, however, might be to buy Kayser Chemicals with the possibility of more than doubling his $1,100 investment.

Any decision regarding the purchase of one of the three common stocks made solely on the information in the payoff table would ignore the valuable historical records kept by Moody's, Value Line, and other investment services relative to the stock price movements over a long period of time. A study of these records, for example, revealed that during the past 10 years stock market prices increased six times and declined only four times. Thus, it can be said that the probability of a market rise in 0.60 and the probability of a market decline is 0.40.

Assuming that these historical frequencies are somewhat typical, we see that the payoff table and the probability estimates (0.60 and 0.40) can be combined to arrive at the **expected payoff** of buying each of the three stocks. Expected payoff is alternatively called **expected monetary value**. The calculations needed to arrive at the expected payoff for the act of purchasing Kayser Chemical are shown in Table 23–2.

To explain one calculation, note that if the investor had purchased Kayser Chemicals and the market prices declined, the value of the stock would be only $1,000 at the end of the year (from Table 23–1). Past experience, how-

TABLE 23–2
Expected payoff for the act of buying Kayser Chemicals

| Event | Payoff | Probability of event | Expected value |
X	Y	P(X)	P(X) · Y
Market rise $2,400		0.60	$1,440
Market decline 1,000		0.40	400
			$1,840

ever, revealed that this event (a market decline) occurred only 40 percent of the time. In the long run, therefore, a market decline would contribute $400 to the total expected payoff from the stock, found by $1,000 × 0.40. Adding the $400 to the $1,440 expected under rising market conditions gives $1,840, the total payoff in the long run.

Purchasing Kayser Chemicals stock is only one possible choice. The expected payoff in the long run for the acts of buying Rim Homes and Texas Electronics are given in Table 23–3.

TABLE 23–3
Expected payoff for three stocks

Purchase	Expected payoff
Kayser Chemicals	$1,840
Rim Homes	1,760
Texas Electronics	1,600

An analysis of the expected payoffs in the foregoing table indicates that purchasing Kayser Chemicals would yield the greatest expected profit. This outcome is based upon (1) the investor's estimated future value of the stocks, and (2) historical experience with respect to the rise and decline of stock prices. It should be emphasized that although the purchase of Kayser stock represents the best action under the expected value criterion, the investor might decide to buy Texas Electronics stock in order to minimize the risk of losing some of his $1,100 investment.

─────── **SELF-REVIEW 23–1** ───────

| Event | Payoff | Probability of event | Expected value |
X	Y	P(X)	P(X) · Y
Market rise $2,200		0.60	$1,320
Market decline ... 1,100		0.40	400
			$1,760

(A reminder: Cover the answers in the left-hand column.)

Verify the conclusion, shown in Table 23–3, that the expected payoff for the act of purchasing Rim Homes stock is $1,760.

Opportunity loss

Another way of arriving at a decision regarding which common stock to purchase is to determine the profit that might be lost because the exact state of nature (the market behavior) was not known at the time the investor bought the stock. This potential loss is called **opportunity loss** or **regret**. To illustrate, suppose that the investor had purchased the common stock of Rim Homes and a bull market developed. Further, suppose the value of his Rim Homes stock increased from $1,100 to $2,200 as anticipated. But had the investor bought Kayser Chemicals stock and market values increased, the value of his Kayser stock would be $2,400 (from Table 23–1). Thus, the investor missed making an extra profit of $200 by buying Rim Homes instead of Kayser Chemicals. To put it another way, the $200 represents the opportunity loss for not knowing the correct state of nature. If market prices did increase, the investor would have *regretted* buying Rim Homes. However, had the investor bought Kayser Chemicals and market prices increased, he would have had no regret—i.e., no opportunity loss.

The opportunity losses corresponding to this example are given in Table 23–4. Each amount is the outcome (opportunity loss) of a particular combination of acts and events, that is, stock purchase and market reaction.

TABLE 23–4
Opportunity losses for various combinations of stock purchase and market movement

	Opportunity loss	
Purchase	Market rise	Market decline
Kayser Chemicals	$ 0	$150
Rim Homes	200	50
Texas Electronics	500	0

It is apparent that the stock of Kayser Chemicals would be a good investment choice in a rising (bull) market, Texas Electronics in a declining (bear) market, and Rim Homes somewhat of a compromise choice.

──────────────── **SELF-REVIEW 23–2** ────────────────

a. Suppose that the investor purchased Rim Homes stock and the value of the stock in a bear market dropped to $1,100 as anticipated (Table 23–1). Instead, had the investor purchased Texas Electronics and the market declined, the value of his Texas Electronics stock would be $1,150. The difference of $50, found by $1,150 − $1,100, represents the investor's regret for buying Rim Homes stock.

b. Suppose that the investor purchased Texas Electronics stock and then a bull market developed. The stock rose to $1,900, as anticipated (Table 23–1). But, had the investor bought Kayser Chemicals stock and the market value increased to $2,400 as anticipated, the difference of $500 represents the extra profit the investor could have made by purchasing Kayser Chemicals stock.

Refer back to Table 23–4. Verify that:

a. The opportunity loss for Rim Homes given a market decline is $50.

b. The opportunity loss for Texas Electronics given a market rise is $500.

Expected opportunity loss

The opportunity losses in Table 23–4 again ignore the historical experience of market movements. Recall that the probability of a market rise was 0.60 and that of a market decline, 0.40. These probabilities and the opportunity losses are combined to determine the **expected opportunity loss**. The essential calculations are shown in Table 23–5 for the decision to purchase Rim Homes. The expected opportunity loss was found to be $140.

TABLE 23–5
Expected opportunity loss for the act of buying Rim Homes stock

Event X	Opportunity loss OL	Probability of event P(X)	Expected opportunity loss P(X) · OL
Market rise	$200	0.60	$120
Market decline	50	0.40	20
			$140

Interpreting, we see that the expected opportunity loss of $140 means that in the long run the investor would lose the opportunity to make an additional profit of $140 if he decided to buy Rim Homes stock. This expected loss would be incurred because the investor was unable to accurately predict the trend of the stock market. In a bull market he could earn an additional $200 by purchasing the common stock of Kayser Chemicals, but in a bear market the investor could earn an additional $50 by buying Texas Electronics stock. When weighted by the probability of the event, the opportunity loss is $140.

The expected opportunity loss for each of the three stocks is given in Table 23–6. The lowest expected opportunity loss is $60, meaning that the investor would experience the least regret in the long run if he purchased Kayser Chemicals.

TABLE 23–6
Expected opportunity loss for the three stocks

Purchase	Expected opportunity loss
Kayser Chemicals	$ 60
Rim Homes	140
Texas Electronics	300

Incidentally, note that the decision to purchase Kayser Chemicals stock based on the fact that it offers the lowest expected opportunity loss reinforces the decision made previously that Kayser stock would ultimately result in the highest payoff ($1,840). These two approaches (lowest expected opportunity loss and highest expected payoff) will always lead to the same decision concerning a course of action to follow.

Event X	Opportunity loss OL	Probability of event P(X)	Expected opportunity loss P(X) · OL
Market rise	$500	0.60	$300
Market decline . . .	0	0.40	0
			$300

Referring back to Table 23-6, verify that the expected opportunity loss for the act of purchasing Texas Electronics is $300.

MAXIMIN, MAXIMAX, AND MINIMAX REGRET STRATEGIES

Several financial advisors consider the purchase of Kayser Chemicals stock too risky. They note that the payoff might not be $1,840 but only $1,000 (from Table 23-1). Arguing that the stock market is too unpredictable, they urge the investor to take a more conservative position and recommend buying Texas Electronics. This is called a **maximin strategy**. It maximizes the minimum gain. To explain, based on the payoff table (Table 23-1) they reason that the investor would be assured of at least a $1,150 return, that is, a small profit. Those who subscribe to this somewhat pessimistic maximin strategy are sometimes called **maximiners.**

At the other extreme are the optimistic *maximaxers*. If their **maximax strategy** were followed, the investor would purchase Kayser Chemicals stock. These extreme optimists note that there is a possibility of selling the stock in the future for $2,400 instead of only $1,150 as being advocated by the maximiners.

Another possible strategy is called the **minimax regret strategy**. Financial advisors advocating this would scan the opportunity losses in Table 23-4 and select the stock that minimizes the maximum regret. In this example it would be Kayser Chemicals stock, with a maximum opportunity loss of $150.

VALUE OF PERFECT INFORMATION

Before deciding on a stock and purchasing it, the investor might want to consider ways of predicting the movement of the stock market in the near future. If he know precisely what the market would do, profit could be maximized by always purchasing the correct stock. The question is: What is this advance information worth? The dollar value of this information is called the **value of perfect information**. In this problem, it would mean knowing beforehand whether the stock market will rise or decline in the near future.

An acquaintance who is an analyst with a large brokerage firm said that he would be willing to supply information which the investor might find quite valuable in predicting market rises and declines. Of course, there would be a fee, as yet undetermined, for this information regardless of whether the investor used it. What should the maximum amount paid for this special service—$10, $100, $500?

The value of the information from the analyst is in essence the value of perfect information, because the investor would then be assured of buying the most profitable stock. The value of perfect information is defined as *the difference between the maximum payoff under conditions of certainty and the maximum payoff under uncertainty*. In this problem it is the difference between the maximum values of the stock at the end of the year under conditions of certainty and uncertainty. From a practical standpoint, the maximum expected value under conditions of certainty means that the investor would buy Kayser Chemicals if a market rise was predicted and Texas Electronics if a market decline was imminent. The expected payoff in the long run under conditions of *certainty* is $1,900 (see Table 23-7).

**TABLE 23-7
Calculations for the
expected payoff
under conditions of
certainty**

Event X	Payoff Y	Probability of event P(X)	Expected payoff $P(X) \cdot Y$
Market rise	$2,400	0.60	$1,440
Market decline	1,150	0.40	460
			$1,900

Recall that if the actual behavior of the stock market were unknown (conditions of uncertainty) the stock to buy was Kayser Chemicals, and its expected value at the end of the period was computed to be $1,840 (from Table 23-3). The value of perfect information is therefore $60, found by:

$1,900   Expected value of stock purchases under conditions
          of certainty
−1,840   Expected value of purchase (Kayser) under conditions
          of uncertainty
$ 60   Value of perfect information

It would be worth up to $60 for the information the stock analyst might supply. In essence, the analyst would be "guaranteeing" a selling price in the long run of $1,900, and if the analyst asked $40 for the information, the investor would be assured of a $1,860 payoff, found by $1,900 − $40. Thus, it would be worthwhile for the investor to agree to this fee ($40) because the expected outcome ($1,860) would be greater than the expected value under conditions of uncertainty ($1,840). If, however, his acquaintance wanted a fee of $100 for the service, the investor would realize only $1,800 in the long run, found by $1,900 − $100. Logically, it would not be worth $100 because the investor could expect $1,840 in the long run without agreeing to this financial arrangement.

It should be noted that the value of perfect information ($60) is the same as the minimum of the expected regrets (Table 23-6).

**SENSITIVITY
ANALYSIS**

Recall that in the foregoing stock selection problem the set of probabilities applied to the payoff values was derived from historical experience with similar market conditions. Objections may be voiced, however, that future market behavior may be different from past experiences. Despite these differences, *the expected payoffs are not highly sensitive to any changes within a plausible range*. As an example, suppose the investor's brother believes that instead of a 60 percent chance of a market rise and a 40 percent chance of a decline, the reverse is true—that is, there is a 0.40 probability that the stock market will rise and a 0.60 probability of a decline. Further, the investor's cousin thinks that the probability of a market rise is 0.50 and that of a decline, 0.50. A comparison of the original expected payoffs (left column), the expected payoffs for the set of probabilities suggested by the investor's brother (center column), and those cited by the cousin (right column) is shown in Table 23–8.

TABLE 23–8
Expected payoff for three sets of probabilities

	Expected payoffs		
Purchase	Historical experience* (probability–0.60 rise, 0.40 decline)	Brother's estimate (probability–0.40 rise, 0.60 decline)	Cousin's estimate (probability–0.50 rise, 0.50 decline)
Kayser Chemicals	$1,840	$1,560	12,700
Rim Homes	1,760	1,540	1,650
Texas Electronics	1,600	1,450	1,525

* From Table 20–3.

A comparison of the three sets of expected payoffs reveals that the best alternative would still be to purchase Kayser Chemicals. As might be expected, there are some differences in the expected future values for each of the three stocks.

─────────────── **SELF-REVIEW 23–4** ───────────────

Event X	Payoff Y	Probability of event P(X)	Expected value P(X) · Y
a.			
Market rise	$1,900	0.40	$ 760
Market decline	1,150	0.60	690
			$1,450
b.			
Market rise	$2,400	0.50	$1,200
Market decline	1,000	0.50	500
			$1,700

Referring back to Table 23–8, verify that:

a. The expected payoff for Texas Electronics for the brother's set of probabilities is $1,450.

b. The expected payoff for Kayser Chemicals for the cousin's set of probabilities is $1,700.

If there are any drastic changes in the assigned probabilities, the expected values and the optimal decison may in fact change. As an example, suppose that the prognostication for a market rise was 0.20 and a market decline 0.80. The expected payoffs would be as shown in Table 23–9. In the long run the best alternative would be to buy Rim Homes stocks.

TABLE 23–9
Expected values for
purchasing the three
stocks

Purchase	Expected payoff
Kayser Chemicals	$1,280
Rim Homes	1,320
Texas Electronics	1,300

------------------------------ **SELF-REVIEW 23–5** ------------------------------

Either by trial and error or algebraically, for probabilities of a market rise (or decline) down to 0.333, Kayser Chemicals stock would provide the largest expected profit in the long run. For probabilities 0.333 to 0.143, Rim Homes would be the best buy, and for 0.143 and below Texas Electronics would give largest expected profit. Algebraic solutions:

Kayser: $2,400P + (1 - P)1,000$
Rim: $2,200P + (1 - P)1,100$
$$\overline{1,400P + 1,000 = 1,100P + 1,100}$$
$$P = 0.333$$

Rim: $2,200P + (1 - P)1,100$
Texas: $1,900P + (1 - P)1,150$
$$\overline{1,100P + 1,100 = 750P + 1,150}$$
$$P = 0.143$$

Is there any choice of probabilities for which the best alternative would be to purchase Texas Electronics stock? *Hint*: This can be arrived at algebraically or using a trail-and-error method (try a somewhat extreme probability for a market rise).

DECISION TREES

Another analytic tool introduced in Chapter 9 which is very useful when studying a decision situation is a **decision tree**. Basically, it is a picture of all the possible courses of action and the consequent possible outcomes. A box is used to indicate the point at which a decision must be made, and the branches going out from the box indicate the alternatives under consideration. Referring to Chart 23–1 which follows, we see that on the left is the box with three branches radiating from it representing the acts of purchasing Kayser Chemicals, Rim Homes, and Texas Electronics.

The three circled nodes, numbered 1, 2, and 3, represent the expected payoff of each of the three stocks. The branches going out to the right of the nodes show the chance events (market rise or decline) and their corresponding probabilities in parentheses. The numbers at the extreme ends of the branches are the estimated future values of stopping the decision process at those points. This is sometimes called the *conditional* payoff to denote that the payoff depends on a particular choice of action and a particular chance

**CHART 23–1
Decision tree for the
investor's decision**

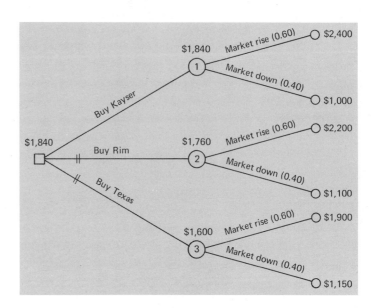

outcome. Thus, if the investor purchases Rim Homes stock and the market rises, the estimated value of the stock would be $2,200.

After the decision tree has been constructed, the optimal decision strategy can be found by what is termed *backward induction*. Suppose, for example, that the investor is considering the act of purchasing Texas Electronics. Starting at the lower right in Chart 23–1 with the anticipated payoff given a market rise ($1,900) and given a market decline ($1,150), going backwards (moving left) the appropriate probabilities are applied to give the expected payoff of $1,600 [found by 0.60($1,900) + 0.40($1,150)]. The investor would mark the expected value of $1,600 above the circled node No. 3 as shown in Chart 23–1. Similarly, the investor would determine the expected values for Rim Homes and Kayser Chemicals.

Assuming that the investor wants to maximize the expected future value of his stock purchase, $1,840 would be preferred to $1,760 or $1,600. Continuing moving to the left toward the box, the investor would draw a double bar across branches representing the two alternatives he rejected (numbers 2 and 3 representing Rim Homes and Texas Electronics). The unmarked branch that leads to the box is clearly the best action to follow, namely, the one to buy Kayser Chemicals stock.

The expected value under *conditions of certainty* can also be portrayed via a decision tree analysis (see Chart 23–2). Recall that under conditions of certainty the investor would know *before* the stock is purchased whether the stock market will rise or decline in the near future. Hence he would purchase Kayser Chemicals in a rising market and Texas Electronics in a falling market, and in the long run the expected payoff would be $1,900. Again, backward induction would be used to arrive at the expected payoff of $1,900.

CHART 23–2
Decision tree given perfect information

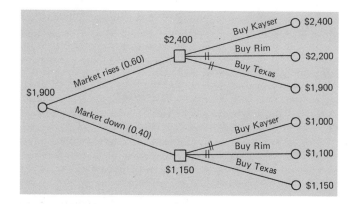

The monetary difference based on the perfect information in Chart 23–2 and the decision based on imperfect information in Chart 23–1 is $60, found by $1,900 − $1,840. Recall that the $60 is the value of perfect information.

Decision tree analysis merely provides an alternative way to perform the same calculations presented earlier in the chapter. Some managers find that these graphic sketches are helpful in following the decision path.

CHAPTER SUMMARY

Statistical decision theory is a relatively recent innovation. This introductory chapter examines some of the techniques which the decision maker can apply in certain situations in order to choose the best action to take.

For many businesses, such as clothing and automobile manufacturing, future demand, called the state of nature, is unknown. Given these conditions of uncertainty, the decision maker has a choice between several alternative acts. The clothing manufacturer, for example, can produce 50 or 60 or 70 gross of a sweater. The consequence of the decision makers action may be a profit or a loss, or the firm might break even.

To evaluate alternatives, a payoff table is set up and the expected payoff under various market conditions is computed. A second method of looking at the problem requires that a set of opportunity loss and expected opportunity loss figures be determined.

The decision maker may want to consider ways of predicting future conditions or demand. The worth of this information is called the "value of perfect information."

CHAPTER OUTLINE

An introduction to decision making under uncertainty

I. Decision making under uncertainty.
   A. *Purpose.* To explore some of the basic techniques which the decision maker can apply in order to choose the best alternative action.
   B. *Explanatory statements.*
      1. *Event.* The actual demand for a product or service. Uncertainty

regarding future demand. Decision maker has no control over future demand.

2. *Act.* A course of action open to decision maker. Decision maker must decide after assessing several courses of action.

3. *Payoff.* Consequence of act. Act may result in a profit, a loss, or no change.

C. *Steps in arriving at a decision.*
    1. Construct payoff table.
    2. Determine the expected payoffs.

D. *Opportunity loss.*
    1. *Definition.* Profit lost because the exact state of nature was not known. Also called *regret*.
    2. *Procedure.* Construct opportunity loss table and then calculate expected opportunity losses.

E. *Value of perfect information.*
    1. *Definition.* The difference between the maximum payoff under conditions of certainty and uncertainty.

F. *Sensitivity analysis.* Expected payoffs are not highly sensitive to any changes in probability within a plausible range. Example: A change in probabilities from 0.55 for a mild winter to 0.60 for a mild winter would probably not change the decision.

G. *Decision trees.* A graphic portrayal of the decision path.

CHAPTER EXERCISES

1. Dude Ranches Incorporated was founded on the idea that many families in the eastern and southern areas of the United States do not have a sufficient amount of vacation time to drive to the dude ranches in the Southwest and Rocky Mountain areas for their vacations. Various surveys indicated, however, that there was considerable interest in this type of family vacation including horseback riding, cattle drives, swimming, fishing, and the like. Dude Ranches Incorporated bought a large farm near several eastern cities and constructed a lake, a swimming pool, and other facilities. However, to build a number of family cottages on the ranch would have required a considerable amount of investment. Further, they reasoned that most of this investment would be lost should the ranch-farm complex be a financial failure. Instead, they decided to enter into an agreement with the Mobile Homes Manufacturing Company to supply a very attractive authentic ranch-type mobile home. Mobile Homes agreed to deliver a mobile home on Saturday for $300 a week. Mobile Homes must know early Saturday morning how many mobile homes Dude Ranches Incorporated wants for the forthcoming week. They have other customers to supply and can only deliver the homes on Saturday. This presents a problem. Dude Ranches will have some reservations by Saturday, but indications are that many families do not make them. Instead, they prefer to examine the facilities before making a decision. An analysis of the various costs involved indicated that $350 a week should be charged for a ranch home, including all privileges. The basic problem is, how many mobile ranch homes should be ordered from Mobile Homes each week? Should Dude Ranches Incorporated order 10 (considered the minimum), 11, 12, 13, or 14 (considered the maximum)?

a. Construct a payoff table.

Any decision made solely on the information in the payoff table would ignore, however, the valuable experience that Dude Ranches Incorporated has had in the past four years (about 200 weeks) actually operating a dude ranch in the Southwest. Their records showed that they always had nine advance reservations. Also, they never had a demand for 15 or more cottages. The occupancy of 10, 11, 12, 13, or 14 ranch cottages, in part, represented families that drove in and inspected the facilities before renting. A frequency distribution showing the number of weeks 10, 11 . . . 14 ranch cottages were rented during the 200-week period is found in the following table.

Number of cottages rented	Number of weeks
10	26
11	50
12	60
13	44
14	20
	200

b. Determine the expected payoffs and arrive at a decision.
c. Set up an opportunity loss table.
d. Compute the expected opportunity losses and arrive at a decision.
e. Determine the value of perfect information.

2. The proprietor of the newly built Ski and Swim Lodge has been considering the purchase or lease of several snowmobiles for the use of guests. The owner found that other financial obligations made it impossible to purchase the machines. Snowmobiles Incorporated (SI) will lease a machine for $20 a week, including any needed maintenance. According to SI, the usual rental to the guests of the lodge is $25 a week. Gasoline and oil are extra. Snowmobiles Incorporated only leases a machine for the full season. The proprietor of Ski and Swim could sustain a loss by leasing an excessive number of snowmobiles and therefore investigated. The combined experience at several other lodges was found to be:

Number of snowmobiles demanded by guests	Number of weeks
7	10
8	25
9	45
10	20

a. Design a payoff table.
b. Compute the expected profits for leasing 7, 8, 9, or 10 snowmobiles based on the cost of leasing of $20, a rental charge of $25, and the experience at other lodges.
c. Which act appears to be most profitable?
d. Now design an opportunity loss table.
e. Find the expected opportunity loss for leasing 7, 8, 9, and 10 snowmobiles.
f. Which act would give the least expected opportunity loss?

g. Determine the value of perfect information.

h. Suggest a course of action to the proprietor of the Ski and Swim Lodge and include in your explanation the various figures, such as expected profit.

3. A furniture store has had numerous inquiries regarding the availability of furniture and equipment which could be rented for large outdoor summer parties. This includes such items as folding chairs and tables, a deluxe grill, propane gas, lights, and so on. No rental equipment of this nature is available locally, and the management of the furniture store is considering forming a subsidiary to handle rentals.

An investigation revealed that most persons interested in renting wanted a complete group of party essentials (about 12 chairs, 4 tables, a deluxe grill, a bottle of propane gas, tongs, etc.). Management decided not to buy a large number of complete sets because of the financial risk involved. That is, if the demand for the rental groups was not as large as anticipated, a large financial loss might be incurred. Further, outright purchase would mean that the equipment would have to be stored during the off-season.

It was then discovered that a firm in Boston leased a complete party set for $560 for the summer season. This amounts to about $5 a day. In the promotional literature from the Boston firm a rental fee of $15 was suggested. Thus, for each set rented, a profit of $10 would be earned. It was then decided to lease from the Boston firm, at least for the first season.

The Boston firm suggested that, based on the combined experience of similar rental firms in other cities, either 41, 42, 43, 44, 45, or 46 complete sets be leased for the season. Based on this suggestion, management must now decide on the most profitable number of complete sets to lease for the season.

a. Construct a payoff table (As a check figure, for the act of having 41 complete sets available and the event of renting 41, the payoff is $410.)

The leasing firm in Boston also made available some additional information gathered from several rental firms similar to the newly formed subsidiary. Note in the following table (which is based on the experience of other rental firms) that 360 days out of the total of 6,000 days' experience—or about 6 percent of the days—these rental firms rented out 41 complete party sets. And on 10 percent of the days during a typical summer they rented 42 complete sets, and so on.

Number of sets rented	Number of days out of the total (6,000 days)
40	0
41	360
42	600
43	840
44	2400
45	1500
46	300
47	0

b. The expected daily profit for leasing 43 complete sets from the Boston firm is $426.70, for 45 sets $431.70, and for 46 sets $427.45. Organize these expected daily profits into a table, and complete the table by finding the expected daily profit for leasing 41, 42, and 44 sets from the Boston firm.

c. Based on the expected daily profit, what is the most profitable action to take?

d. The expected opportunity loss for leasing 43 party sets from the Boston firm is $11.60, for 45 sets $6.60, and for 46 sets $10.85. Organize these into an expected opportunity loss table, and complete the table by computing the expected opportunity loss for 41, 42, and 44.

e. Based on the expected opportunity loss table, what is the most profitable course of action to take? Does this agree with your decision in Question c?

f. Determine the value of perfect information. Explain what it indicates in this problem.

CHAPTER SELF-REVIEW EXAMINATION

Do all the problems and then check your answers against those given in Appendix A.

Score each problem 20 points.

A manufacturer has $100,000 available to make either lightweight or heavy jackets for winter wear. A decision must be made in the summer in order to have the jackets available for early fall shipments. Of course the manufacturer is unable to predict whether the winter will be mild or severe. If lightweight jackets are manufactured and the winter is mild, the payoff would be $120,000, but if it is severe the payoff will only be $105,000 (because consumers will purchase heavy jackets from competitors). If heavy jackets are produced, the payoffs for mild and severe winters are $110,000 and $125,000, respectively.

1. Construct a payoff table.

   Continuing with the problem, past records showed that 55 percent of the winters were mild and 45 percent were severe.

2. Determine the two expected payoffs and arrive at a decision.

3. Construct an opportunity loss table and determine the expected opportunity losses.

4. Compute the value of perfect information.

5. Design a decision tree for this problem.

INTRODUCTION

An English clergyman, the Reverend Thomas Bayes, developed a theorem in the 1700s which has become extremely useful in decision making. *Decision making* in this context refers to the body of techniques that have been developed since the 1940s to assist the decision maker in choosing from among several alternatives the best course of action. His theorem is referred to as the **rule of Bayes**, **Bayes' rule**, or **Bayes' theorem**.

A simple example is used to illustrate the concept and computations. Suppose that a thin flat part is precision ground on both sides but one side is color coded to denote the thickness. Red indicates that the piece is 0.02 inches thick, yellow means that the piece is 0.33 inches thick, and so on. One side is color coded and the other side is not; that is, it is left polished. The operator wraps each machined piece in a special paper to protect it and packs five like-colored pieces in a box.

During the lunch period the machine operator making red pieces suddenly realized he forgot to color code one of the pieces he packed in the last box; that is, one of the pieces has two polished sides. One might ask: What is the probability that if one of the five pieces were selected at random from the box and then unwrapped, it would be the defective piece, that is, not color coded? Since one out of the five is defective, the probability is 1/5, or 0.20, that the one selected at random is defective. This is called the **prior probability**.

Now suppose the machine operator unwraps all five pieces and none of the five sides facing upward is coded red. Then as an experiment he plans to toss the piece on the extreme right in the air. If it lands with red facing upward, the operator would know it was not the defective piece. If it lands with a polished face upward, however, he cannot be sure that it is a defective piece or a correctly prepared piece. What is the probability that, if it did land with a polished side facing up, it is the defective piece? To solve the problem, assume that each of the five machined pieces were tossed in the air 200 times. If a piece was finished correctly, theoretically a polished side would appear face up 100 times and the color-coded face 100 times. However, if the piece were defective, a polished side would appear face up on all 200 tosses. Shown schematically:

Number of tosses	200	200	200	200	200 = 1,000 total
	□	□	□	□	□
If piece is	Perfect	Perfect	Perfect	Perfect	Defective
Number of polished faces	100	100	100	100	200 = 600 total

Bayes' theorem
and decision making

Note that in the long run, out of 600 polished sides facing up, 200 would be attributed to the defective piece (assumed to be on the extreme right). Thus, the probability is 200/600 = 1/3, or 0.33, that the piece on the extreme right is defective. It is called the **posterior probability** because it was determined after the machine operator conducted an experiment.

In summary, initially one of five matched pieces was known to be defective (not color coded). The prior probability is 1/5, or 0.20, that if the wrapped piece on the extreme right were picked at random it would be the defective piece. When it was unwrapped, a polished face was observed. The machine operator then tossed it in the air, and it landed with a polished side facing up. After this experiment the prior probability of 0.20 was revised upward to 0.33. The 0.33 is the posterior probability.

SELF-REVIEW 24-1

a. 1/4 or 0.25 is the prior probability (one out of four is two headed).

b. 0.40 is the posterior probability. It could be reasoned that if each of the four coins were tossed, say, 200 times, theoretically out of the 500 heads which would appear face up, 200, or 40 percent, would be attributed to the two-headed coin.

c. 0.57+. If the two headed coin were tossed, say, another 200 times, then 400 out of the 700 heads appearing face up would be attributed to the defective (two-headed) coin.

(A reminder: Cover the answers.)

Determine the prior and posterior probabilities in the following problem. One of four coins hidden under a piece of paper is known to have two heads, instead of the usual head on one side and a tail on the other.

a. What is the probability that if one of the coins was selected at random it would be the two-headed coin?

b. The paper covering the coins was removed, and all four coins had a head showing face up. The coin on the extreme left was tossed in the air and it landed with a head facing up. Now what is the probability that it is the two-headed coin?

c. If that same coin were tossed in the air a second time and again it landed with a head facing up, what is the probability that it is the two-headed coin?

THE RULE OF BAYES

Returning to the problem involving the five machined pieces, we will use Bayes' theorem to find the probability that the piece on the extreme right is defective (not color coded on one side) after the operator tossed it in the air and it landed with a polished side facing up. Abbreviations such as Def (standing for defective) will be used in order to make it easier to follow the application of Bayes' theorem to this problem. Other abbreviations are: Pol = polished face and OK = piece satisfactory (color coded on one side, polished on the other side). Bayes' theorem then becomes:

$$P(\text{Def}|\text{Pol}) = \frac{P(\text{Def}) \cdot P(\text{Pol}|\text{Def})}{P(\text{Def}) \cdot P(\text{Pol}|\text{Def}) + P(\text{OK}) \cdot P(\text{Pol}|\text{OK})}$$

To explain each of the terms:

$P(\text{Def}|\text{Pol})$ is the probability to be determined. In this problem it is the probability that the piece on the extreme right is defective (Def), given (|) the experimental results of a polished side (Pol) face up after the operator had tossed it in the air. It is a posterior probability because it is determined *after* experimental results have been observed.

$P(\text{Def})$ is the probability of choosing one of the five machined pieces *prior* to the experiment and finding it defective. $P(\text{Def}) = 1/5 = 0.20$.

$P(\text{Pol}|\text{Def})$ is the probability that a polished side (Pol) will appear face up after the piece has been tossed in the air, *assuming that a defective piece* (Def) *is being tossed in the air*. (This is the same as asking what is the probability that a head will appear on the toss of a coin knowing that the coin is two headed.) Logically, $P(\text{Pol}|\text{Def}) = 1.00$.

$P(\text{OK})$ is the probability of choosing one of the five machined pieces *prior* to any experiment and finding it satisfactory (color coded on one side and polished on the other side). $P(\text{OK}) =$ 4/5, or 0.80 (because four out of the five pieces are satisfactory).

$P(\text{Pol}|\text{OK})$ is the probability that outcome Pol (a polished face) will appear after the machined piece on the extreme right has been tossed in the air, *assuming the piece is satisfactory* (OK).

$P(\text{Pol}|\text{OK}) = \frac{1}{2}$, or 0.50 (because one face of an OK piece is color coded and the other face is polished).

The posterior probability that the piece on the extreme right is defective after is was observed that it landed with a polished face up is 0.33, found by:

$$P(\text{Def}|\text{Pol}) = \frac{P(\text{Def}) \cdot P(\text{Pol}|\text{Def})}{P(\text{Def}) \cdot P(\text{Pol}|\text{Def}) + P(\text{OK}) \cdot P(\text{Pol}|\text{OK})}$$

$$= \frac{(0.20)(1.00)}{(0.20)(1.00) + (0.80)(0.50)} = \frac{0.20}{0.60} = 0.33$$

Note that this is the same answer as found previously using a logical approach.

SELF-REVIEW 24–2

0.40 is also the posterior probability using Bayes' rule. To find the posterior probability that the coin on the extreme left is the two-headed one, given that a head was observed after the coin was tossed:

$P(\text{two-headed}|A) =$

$$\frac{P(\text{two-headed})P(A|\text{two-headed})}{P(\text{two-headed})P(A|\text{two-headed}) + P(\text{OK})P(A|\text{OK})}$$

$$= \frac{1/4(1.00)}{1/4(1.00) + 3/4(1/2)} = \frac{1/4}{5/8} = 8/20 = 0.40$$

Recall from Self-Review 24–1 that one of four coins was known to be two headed. When unwrapped, all four coins had heads showing face up. The coin on the extreme left was tossed in the air, and it landed with a head facing up. You computed the posterior probability that it is the two-headed coin to be 2/5, or 0.40. Now verify your answer by applying Bayes' rule.

In the foregoing paragraphs the Bayes' formula was applied to a simple problem using OK, Def, and other such abbreviations. Now these abbreviations will be changed to the more commonly accepted letters, such as A and B, so that the Bayes' formula can be made applicable for a wide variety of problems. To effect this conversion, A_1 replaces Def and denotes a defective, A_2 represents a satisfactorily machined piece, and B a polished face.

So, $P(A_1)$ would be the prior probability of a defective, and so on. Thus, the same formula designed to determine the probability of a defective given that a polished face was observed after the operator tossed the piece in the air would be:

$$P(A_1|B) = \frac{P(A_1) \cdot P(B|A_1)}{P(A_1) \cdot P(B|A_1) + P(A_2) \cdot P(B|A_2)}$$

This form of the Bayes' rule includes only two mutually exclusive events, namely, a defective A_1 and a good piece A_2. The one observed result B was the polished face facing up. If there are more than two mutually exclusive events (such as the ratings excellent, good, fair, and unsatisfactory that trainees receive in a management training program), the corresponding letters would be A_1, A_2, A_3, and A_4, respectively.

Thus, in general it can be said that if A_1, A_2, A_3 . . . A_k are a set of mutually exclusive events that cover all possible outcomes, then for any particular result B, the posterior probability of event A_1 for a particular result B can be found using Bayes' theorem, namely:

$$P(A_1|B) = \frac{P(A_1) \cdot P(B|A_1)}{\begin{array}{c} P(A_1) \cdot P(B|A_1) + P(A_2) \cdot P(B|A_2) + P(A_3) \\ \cdot P(B|A_3) + \cdots + P(A_k) \cdot P(B|A_k) \end{array}}$$

The posterior probability of event A_2 would be found by:

$$P(A_2|B) = \frac{P(A_2) \cdot P(B|A_2)}{\begin{array}{c} P(A_1) \cdot P(B|A_1) + P(A_2) \cdot P(B|A_2) + P(A_3) \\ \cdot P(B|A_3) + \cdots + P(A_k) \cdot P(B|A_k) \end{array}}$$

The posterior probability of $P(A_3|B)$ and so on would be determined in a like manner. Note again that when computing each posterior probability, the denominator remains the same.

A CASE INVOLVING THE BEST LEVEL OF PRODUCTION FOR GIGGLE DOLLS

The United Specialty Corporation manufactures toys, dolls, games, puzzles, and the like. The actual number of each item manufactured is governed by the most convenient shipping size, such as 400 gross of a teddy bear, 100,000 puzzles, and so on. They have developed a doll that giggles and aptly named it Giggles. The decision problem involves how many to manufacture. The case illustrates how the decision-making procedure discussed in the previous chapter and Bayes' theorem can be combined to arrive at the best level of production.

It has been decided that a minimum of 60,000 Giggle dolls will be manufactured, and the most convenient number will be 60,000, 70,000, 80,000, or 90,000. The cost of manufacturing Giggles is estimated to be $2, and the selling price has been set at $6. Thus, if they manufacture 60,000 and all 60,000 are sold, the total profit would be $240,000 (found by 60,000 × $4 profit on each doll). However, if 90,000 dolls are manufactured and only 60,000 are sold, the profit would be $200,000, found by (60,000 × $6) − (90,000 × $2). Recall from Chapter 23 that these profits (and possibly losses) can be organized into a **payoff table** (Table 24–1).

TABLE 24–1
Profit (payoff) for various quantities of Giggle dolls manufactured and demanded (in $000)

Number manufactured	Number of Giggle dolls demanded			
	60,000	70,000	80,000	90,000
60,000	$240	$240	$240	$240
70,000	220	280	280	280
80,000	200	260	320	320
90,000	180	240	300	360

SELF-REVIEW 24–3

$320,000 profit (payoff), found by:

$6 selling price ×
  80,000 sold   = $480,000
$2 cost of mfg. ×
  80,000 manufactured = −160,000
                        $320,000 profit

You may want to review the construction of a payoff table by verifying the payoff in Table 24–1 of $320,000 for manufacturing 80,000 Giggle dolls when there were orders for 90,000 dolls. (Of course, any orders in excess of 80,000 dolls could not be filled.)

To continue with the Giggle doll problem, based on long experience manufacturing dolls and other similar specialties, the management of United Specialty assigns probabilities to each possible level of production. In a sense, the probabilities represent their judgment regarding the future demand for Giggles. A perusal of Table 24–2 reveals that management envisions rather high sales for the doll. According to their judgment, there is a 55 percent chance that sales will be 80,000 or over, with the most probable level being 80,000.

TABLE 24–2
Probability of demand for Giggle dolls

Number demanded	Probability of demand
60,000	0.20
70,000	0.25
80,000	0.40
90,000	0.15
	1.00

The payoffs (Table 24–1) and the prior probabilities (Table 24–2) are combined to arrive at the **expected payoff** of an act. Table 24–3 shows the necessary calculations to find the expected payoff for the act of producing 70,000 Giggle dolls. It is $268,000.

TABLE 24–3
Expected payoff for the act of manufacturing 70,000 dolls

| | | (1) | (2) Probability | Expected profit |
Demand		Payoff*	of payoff†	(1) × (2)
60,000		$220,000	0.20	$ 44,000
70,000		280,000	0.25	70,000
80,000		280,000	0.40	112,000
90,000		280,000	0.15	42,000
				$268,000

All the expected payoffs are given in Table 24–4.

TABLE 24–4
Expected payoffs for all possible levels of production

Number produced	Expected profit
60,000	$240,000
70,000	268,000
80,000	281,000
90,000	270,000

It is apparent that based on the *prior* probabilities assigned by management, a $2 manufacturing cost, and a $6 selling price, the best profit alternative would be to manufacture 80,000 giggle dolls. The expected profit would be $281,000.

─────────────────────── **SELF-REVIEW 24–4** ───────────────────────

| | | (1) | (2) | (3) Expected |
| | | | Probability | profit |
Demand		Payoff	of payoff	(1) × (2)
60,000		$180,000	0.20	$ 36,000
70,000		240,000	0.25	60,000
80,000		300,000	0.40	120,000
90,000		360,000	0.15	54,000
				$270,000

Referring to Table 24–4, you may want to verify that the expected payoff for the act of manufacturing 90,000 Giggle dolls is $270,000.

Immediately after management assesses the sales potential of a proposed new product, a few samples are handmade. The salespersons show these to buyers in key retail and wholesale outlets, and they either solicit an order or have the buyer give an evaluation of the sales potential of the product. In a sense, the selection of key outlets by management can be considered a judgment sample, and the sample results as possible **additional information** which could be used to revise the prior probabilities assigned by management.

The demand D for a newly developed product is rated from a low of D_6 (representing 60,000 dolls) to a high of D_9 (90,000). The advance orders and opinions are then evaluated in the home office, and one demand figure is derived. For example, level D_6 would indicate that based on the opinions and advance orders of key buyers, a clown, a puzzle, or a mechanical toy probably would have a low level of sales. Conversely, a composite of D_8 would suggest that the newly developed specialty has a very favorable sales outlook.

United Specialty made a study of the relationship between the judgment of the management of United Specialty and the judgment of the buyers in key outlets on 3,000 toys, puzzles, dolls, and so on which had previously been manufactured and marketed. Various ways of determining the level of production to be used were evaluated. It was finally agreed to produce the level associated with the *maximum expected profit*. Thus, for example, if the prior maximum expected profit figures for a mechanical dump truck indicated that 60,000 (L_6) should be manufactured, but the key outlets were very enthusiastic about it and their composite rating was 90,000 (D_9), then this truck would be one of the 20 such specialties (L_6 and D_9) noted in Table 24–5.

TABLE 24–5
Suggested level of production and anticipated demand for 3,000 specialites

Suggested production	Anticipated demand				
	D_6	D_7	D_8	D_9	Total
L_6	400	110	170	20	700
L_7	640	320	160	80	1,200
L_8	180	240	200	180	800
L_9	20	40	100	140	300
					3,000

Referring back to Table 24–5, note that the study of past experience revealed that for the most part, the prior judgment of the management of United Specialty regarding a proposed product and the judgment of the buyers at the key outlets tended to coincide. For example, if management thought a newly developed product would have a low level of sales (L_6), it was highly likely that the key outlets would rate it low (D_6). Conversely, if management initially thought a new toy, doll, or puzzle would require a high level of production (L_8 or L_9), the buyers, having no knowledge of this prior rating, would also indicate that it would have a high level of sales by rating it, say, D_8 or D_9 for the most part.

This past experience consisting of the prior judgment of management regarding a newly developed product cross-classified with the judgment of key buyers represents *additional information* which management could use in the future to revise its initial (prior) probabilities. However, in order to insert this additional information in Bayes' theorem, the data must first be converted to probabilities. As an example of the conversion, refer back to Table 24–5. Note that management thought that a total of 700 newly developed products warranted the lowest level of production (L_6). In 400 out of 700 cases, or 57 percent, the key outlets (not knowing management's evaluation) agreed completely and thought that the products would have a very low level of sales (D_6). The probability for the figure in the lower right-hand corner of the table (0.47) is found by 140/300. The additional information converted to probabilities is in Table 24–6.

TABLE 24–6
Probabilities for suggested level of production and anticipated demand*

Suggested production	Anticipated demand				
	D_6	D_7	D_8	D_9	Total
L_6	0.57	0.16	0.24	0.03	1.00
L_7	0.53	0.27	0.13	0.07	1.00
L_8	0.23	0.30	0.25	0.22	1.00
L_9	0.07	0.13	0.33	0.47	1.00

*From Table 24–5.

Using this additional information, which essentially represents 3,000 different judgment samples, we can revise the prior probabilities assigned by management to the newly developed Giggle doll.

The handmade samples of Giggles were shown to buyers at key outlets. Some advance orders were received. The home office evaluated these orders and the opinion of the key buyers, and indications are that *the sales of Giggles will be about 60,000 (D_6).*

Note that the reaction of the buyers to Giggles is not nearly as enthusiastic as that of the management of United Specialty, who thought of producing 80,000 dolls. Investigation revealed that salespersons from another company recently showed samples of a similar doll which laughs instead of giggles. The key outlets plan to stock both dolls for the Christmas selling season but think that the strong competition will affect the sales of Giggles.

The Bayes' rule will now be used to revise the prior probability of 0.40 assigned by management to the production level of 80,000 dolls (L_8). It is apparent that based on the rather discouraging sample results of D_6 (potential sales of only 60,000 dolls), the prior probability L_8 of 0.40 will be revised downward.

In the Bayes' formula which follows, $P(L_8|D_6)$ indicates the *conditional* probability assigned to L_8 given the sample results D_6. As before, $P(L_8)$ is the *prior* probability assigned by management to the sales level of 80,000 dolls. Interpreting one other probability, we see that $P(D_6|D_8)$ is the conditional probability that key outlets will report potential sales to be 60,000 given an earlier estimate of sales by management of 80,000.

The additional information from the key buyers of only a 60,000 sales potential for Giggles, that is, D_6, dictates that only the probabilities conditional on D_6 will be used in the Bayes' theorem. To revise management's prior probability of L_8 given a D_6 sales potential by the key outlets:

$$p(L_8|D_6) = \frac{P(L_8)P(D_6|L_8)}{P(L_6)P(D_6|L_6) + P(L_7)P(D_6|L_7) + P(L_8)P(D_6|L_8) + P(L_9)P(D_6|L_9)}$$

$$= \frac{(0.40)(0.23)}{(0.20)(0.57) + (0.25)(0.53) + (0.40)(0.23) + (0.15)(0.07)}$$

$$= \frac{0.092}{0.349} = 0.264$$

Thus, the prior probability that management assigned to a sales level of 80,000 dolls (0.40) should be revised downward to 0.26 (because of the rather discouraging additional information from the key buyers that retail sales of Giggle dolls will probably reach only 60,000).

───────────────────────────── SELF-REVIEW 24–5 ─────────────────────────────

$$P(L_9|D_6) = \frac{P(L_9)P(D_6|L_9)}{\text{Denominator remains the same}}$$

$$= \frac{(0.15)(0.07)}{0.349} = 0.03$$

Revise the prior probability assigned to the manufacturing level of 90,000 dolls, assuming the same additional information—that is, the key outlets indicated sales of 60,000.

The prior probabilities and the posterior probabilities are shown in Table 24–7.

TABLE 24–7
Prior probabilities and posterior probabilities for various levels of demand

Number demanded	Prior probabilities*	Posterior probabilities
60,000	0.20	0.33
70,000	0.25	0.38
80,000	0.40	0.26
90,000	0.15	0.03
	1.00	1.00

*From Table 24–2.

Using the posterior probabilities (Table 24–7) and the payoffs from Table 24–1, we can compute a new set of expected profits. Both the original set and those resulting from the posterior probabilities are given in Table 24–8.

TABLE 24–8
Expected profit based on prior probabilities and posterior probabilities

Number produced	Expected profit based on	
	Prior probabilities*	Posterior probabilities
60,000	$240,000	$240,000
70,000	268,000	260,200
80,000	281,000	257,600
90,000	270,000	239,400

*From Table 24–4.

Interpreting Table 24–8, management initially thought that producing 80,000 Giggle dolls would yield the maximum expected profit ($281,000). However, after assessing the opinions from key buyers and using Bayes' rule, they concluded that a production run of only 70,000 dolls would probably result in the highest expected profit ($260,200).

	(1)		(2)	(3)
				Expected
			Probability	profit
Demand	Payoff		of payoff	(1) × (2)
60,000	.....	$220,000	0.33	$ 72,600
70,000	.....	280,000	0.38	106,400
80,000	.....	280,000	0.27	72,800
90,000	.....	280,000	0.03	8,400
				$260,200

Referring back to Table 24–8, you may want to verify that the expected profit using the posterior probabilities is $260,200 for the act of producing 70,000 Giggle dolls.

CHAPTER SUMMARY

Thomas Bayes developed a theorem which is very useful in decision making. It allows the decision maker to revise prior probabilities based on additional information. These revised probabilities are referred to as posterior probabilities. To illustrate the use of Bayes' theorem, a problem involving the production of Giggle dolls was examined. As a first step, a payoff table was set up based on selected levels of production and anticipated demand. Then, based on the set of payoffs and the probability of various levels of demand assigned by management, the expected payoff for 60,000, 70,000, 80,000 and 90,000 dolls was determined. Additional information on Giggles in the form of the opinions of buyers of toys and dolls allowed the prior probabilities of management to be revised using Bayes' theorem. The new set of probabilities is called posterior probabilities and used to develop a new set of expected profit figures for Giggle dolls.

CHAPTER OUTLINE

Bayes' theorem and decision making

I. Bayes' theorem.
   A. *Purpose.* For use in decision making to revise prior probabilities based on additional information. The revised probabilities are called *posterior* probabilities.
   B. *Formula.* For $P(A_1|B)$:

   $$P(A_1|B) = \frac{P(A_1) \cdot P(B|A_1)}{P(A_1) \cdot P(B|A_1) + P(A_2) \cdot P(B|A_2) + \cdots + P(A_k) \cdot P(B|A_k)}$$

   and finally:

   $$P(A_k|B) = \frac{P(A_k) \cdot P(B|A_k)}{P(A_1) \cdot P(B|A_1) + P(A_2) \cdot P(B|A_2) + \cdots + P(A_k) \cdot P(B|A_k)}$$

   where $A_1, A_2, \ldots, A_k$ are a set of mutually exclusive events which cover all possible outcomes; B is a particular result; $P(A_1), P(A_2)$, ... are prior probabilities; and $P(A_1|B)$ and like terms are conditional probabilities. In this particular case it means "the probability that event A_1 will occur given that result B was observed."

II. Bayes' theorem and decision making.
  A. *Procedure*.
    1. Set up a payoff table (discussed in Chapter 23).
    2. List the set of prior probabilities.
    3. Compute expected payoffs based on payoffs and prior probabilities.
    4. Collect additional information and convert to probabilities.
    5. Revise prior probabilities based on additional information using Bayes' rule. This new set is called posterior probabilities.
    6. Recompute expected payoffs based on posterior probabilities.

CHAPTER EXERCISES

1. The Fur Shoppe wants to concentrate its promotional efforts on families in political precinct no. 4 whose incomes exceed $25,000. It has been estimated that in this precinct 25 percent of the families earn more than $25,000 a year and only 5 percent have incomes of less than $10,000. With respect to ownership of automobiles in the precinct, census data revealed:

	Number of families		
Family income	No car	One car	Two or more cars
Less than $10,000	50	80	20
$10,000–$25,000	300	350	400
Over $25,000	0	150	150

   In addition, the local motor vehicle registrar has a list of names and addresses of all families, by precinct, who own two or more automobiles. Unfortunately for the Fur Shoppe, the incomes of the families on the list are not given.
   a. If the Fur Shoppe selected a family from the list of families who reside in precinct No. 4 and who own two or more automobiles, what is the likelihood that the family's income will exceed $25,000?
   b. What is the probability it will not exceed $25,000?

2. Management wishes to have a projection of summer sales made as early as the preceding January. As chief forecaster you are to report the forecast in terms of probabilities, such as, the probability of *excellent* summer sales is 0.70, of *average* summer sales is 0.20, and of *low* summer sales is 0.10 (just an illustration). Further, management wants you to consider giving a revised summer forecast in March, April, or May should any additional information become available. Fortunately, the Federal Reserve Board issues its general forecast of national sales for the summer on April 1 of each year. In order to assess the relationship between your January forecasts and the FRB forecasts in April, a study of past relationships is conducted. It was discovered that in the years you forecasted *excellent* summer sales (in January), the FRB forecasted on April 1 (note they use slightly different terminology):

Prediction	Frequency
High sales	70 percent of the years
Median sales	20 percent of the years
Sluggish sales	10 percent of the years

When you forecasted *average* summer sales (in January), the FRB (in April) said summer sales would be:

Prediction	Frequency
High sales	20 percent of the years
Median sales	60 percent of the years
Sluggish sales	20 percent of the years

And when you forecasted in January that sales would be *low,* the FRB in April forecasted:

Prediction	Frequency
High sales	15 percent of the years
Median sales	25 percent of the years
Sluggish sales	60 percent of the years

There does appear to be considerable agreement between your January forecasts and the April forecasts of the FRB.

This past January you issued the summer forecast:

Sales	Probability
Excellent	0.85
Average	0.10
Low	0.05

The FRB has just released their April forecast. They said, "The forecast for the coming summer is for *high* sales."

a. Revise your January forecast (excellent, 0.85; average, 0.10; and low, 0.05) based on this additional information using Bayes' theorem.

b. Interpret.

CHAPTER SELF-REVIEW EXAMINATION

Do the problem and then check your answer against the one given in Appendix A. Score the problem 100 points.

1. Michael McGee's old automobile has just failed him, and he is confronted with the classic problem of deciding whether to repair or replace the vehicle. He has narrowed the source of the fatal breakdown to either the automatic transmission or the carburetor. He is not a mechanic, but he guesses that the odds are two to one that the automatic transmission is the source of failure. The costs of repairing or replacing the automobile are as follows.

	Defective part	
Action	Automatic transmission	Carburetor
Repair	$600	$100
Replace	300	300

a. Based on this information, what would you advise McGee to do?

Michael suddenly remembered that he has a cousin who is an automotive specialist, and he telephoned him for advice. His cousin asked Michael if there were a black grease mark inside the engine compartment. He noted that when a transmission fails there is a 10 percent chance of that kind of mark appearing. Further, when a carburetor fails, 80 percent of the time a black grease mark appears.

Being familiar with probability, Bayes' rule, and other statistical techniques, Michael wants to use this additional information to revise his prior estimates regarding the source of the trouble and to reconsider his decision with respect to repairing or replacing the car.

b.   Based on this additional information and assuming that there is a black grease mark inside the engine compartment, reevaluate Michael's earlier decision.

Appendixes

Appendix A

ANSWERS TO SELECTED EXERCISES AND THE CHAPTER SELF-REVIEW EXAMINATIONS

Note: There are no exercises or self-review examinations in Chapters 1 and 2.

Chapter 3.   Describing data—frequency distributions

Answers to selected exercises

1. *a.*

Percents		Percents		Percents	
0		17	//	34	
1	//	18		35	//
2		19		36	
3	//	20	/	37	
4	/	21		38	/
5	/	22	/	39	
6	//	23		40	
7	////	24	/	41	
8	州 /	25	/	42	
9	//	26	/	43	/
10	////	27	//	44	
11	州 /	28	/	45	
12	////	29		46	
13	州 //	30	/	47	
14	//	31		48	
15	//	32		49	
16	/	33			

b. Suggested class interval is 6.2 or 6, found by

$$\frac{44 - 1}{1 + 3.322 (\log \text{ of } 61)} = \frac{43}{1 + 3.322(1.7853)}$$

$$= \frac{43}{1 + 5.9307666}$$

$$= \frac{43}{6.9307666}$$

c. Using the suggested class interval of 6:

Annual percent increase	Number
0– 5	6
6–11	24
12–17	18
18–23	2
24–29	6
30–35	3
36–41	1
42–47	1
Total	61

d. Based on the frequency distribution, the percent increases in the consumer prices ranged from 0 percent to 47 percent (actually from about 1 percent to about 44 percent). Most of the percent increases in prices from one year to the next year ranged from 6 percent to 17 percent, with the most increases in the 6-to-11 class.

3.

True limits	f
− 0.5– 5.5	6
5.5–11.5	24
11.5–17.5	18
17.5–23.5	2
23.5–29.5	6
29.5–35.5	3
35.5–41.5	1
41.5–47.5	1
Total	61

Histogram

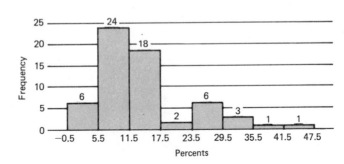

5.

Midpoints (percents)	f
2.5	6
8.5	24
14.5	18
20.5	2
26.5	6
32.5	3
38.5	1
44.5	1

Frequency polygon

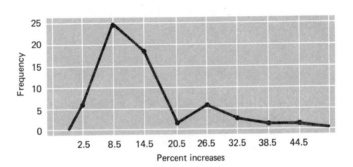

7. a.

Stated limits	Upper true limit	CF
0– 5	5.5	6
6–11	11.5	30
12–17	17.5	48
18–23	23.5	50
24–29	29.5	56
30–35	35.5	59
36–41	41.5	60
42–47	47.5	61

Less − than cumulative frequency polygon

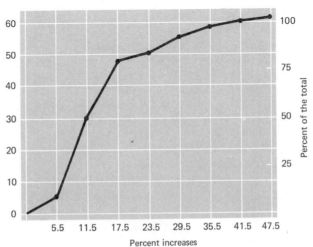

  c. About 11.5 percent.

Chapter 4. Describing data—measures of central tendency

Answers to selected exercises
2. *a.* $1.34.
    b. $1.36, found by ($1.34 + $1.38)/2.
    c. $1.658, found by $33.16/20.

4. *a.* 290.
    b. 289.
    c. 15, 15.
    d. 287.35, found by 8908/31.

6. $39.77, found by $10,341.25/260.

9. *a.* 38.60714, found by 3243/84.
    b. 38.60714, found by:

$$37 + \frac{5(27)}{84} = 37 + 1.60714$$

Ages	f	X	fX	d	fd
20–24	3	22	66	−3	−9
25–29	9	27	243	−2	−18
30–34	15	32	480	−1	−15
35–39	26	37	962	0	0
40–44	12	42	504	1	12
45–49	8	47	376	2	16
50–54	5	52	260	3	15
55–59	4	57	228	4	16
60–64	2	62	124	5	10
	84		3,243		27

12. $61,687.50, found by:

True lower limits	Cumulative frequencies
$29,500	16
39,500	46
49,500	91
59,500	171
69,500	203
79,500	217

$n/2 = 217/2 = 108.5$. Median is in the $60,000–$69,000 class.

$$\text{Median} = L + \frac{\dfrac{n}{2} - CF}{f} \quad (i)$$

$$= \$59,500 + \frac{\dfrac{217}{2} - 91}{80} \; (\$10,000)$$

$$= \$59,500 + \frac{17.5}{80} \; (\$10,000)$$

$$= \$59,500 + \$2,187.50$$

$$= \$61,687.50$$

15. *a.* \$64,500 which is the midpoint of the \$60,000–\$69,000 class.
    b. (Optional.) \$63,716.87, found by:

$$\$59,500 + \frac{35}{35 + 48}(\$10,000) = \$59,500 + \frac{\$350,000}{85}$$

$$= \$59,500 + \$4,216.87$$

18. *a.* 52, found by:

$$\frac{3(\text{median}) - \text{mode}}{2} = \frac{3(48) - 40}{2} = 52$$

   b. Positively skewed, because mean is the highest average, mode is the lowest.
20. 6.22 percent, found by:

Rates	
X	Log of X
6.3%	0.7993
5.4	0.7324
4.9	0.6902
6.4	0.8062
8.1	0.9085
7.7	0.8865
5.4	0.7324
	5.5555

$$\text{Log of G.M.} = \frac{5.5555}{7} = 0.7936$$

$$\text{Antilog of } 0.7936 \cong 6.22$$

23. 28 percent, found by:

$$\left[\sqrt[6-1]{\frac{\$1.50}{\$0.4375}} \right] - 1 = [\sqrt[5]{3.43}] - 1$$

Then,

$$\frac{\log \text{ of } 3.43}{5} = \frac{0.5353}{5} = 0.1071$$

$$\text{Antilog of } 0.1071 \cong 1.28$$

Subtracting one (1), $1.28 - 1 = 0.28 = 28$ percent.

Answers to the chapter self-review examination

1. B.
2. A.
3. K.
4. E.
5. C.
6. J.
7. H.
8. D.
9. C.
10. A.
11. 21 years, found by 105/5.
12. 22 years, found by arranging the lengths of service from low to high (13, 19, 22, 24, 27) and selecting the middle observation.
13. The median is $164,500, found by $159.5 + 4/16 of $20 (in $000).
14. The arithmetic mean sales is $160,700, found by $8,035,000/50.
15. The crude mode is $169,500 (which is the midpoint of the class containing the largest number of frequencies.
16. Negatively skewed because the mode is the highest of the three averages ($169,500), the median is the next highest ($164,500), and the arithmetic mean is the lowest ($160,700). Shown schematically, it looks like this:

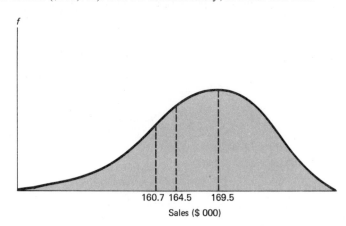

17. About 72 percent per year on the average, found by $\left[\sqrt[5]{15.2} \right] - 1$.

$$\frac{\log \text{ of } 15.2}{5} = \frac{1.1818}{5} = 0.2364.$$ The antilog of 0.2364 if about 1.72. Then,

$1.72 - 1 = 72$ percent.

18. The arithmetic mean. The midpoint of the two open-end classes cannot be determined.

19. Arithmetic mean, because for its construction all of the values are summed.
20. About 220. The median is about 2/3 of the distance between the mode and mean. Or, the formula [2(Mean) + Mode]/3 can be used.

Bonus: Computed mode is $170,269, found by $159.5 + \dfrac{7}{7 + 6}$ ($20) in thousands of dollars.

Chapter 5.   Measures of dispersion and skewness

Answers to selected exercises.

3. *a.*   10 days, found by 10 − 0.
   b.   3.5 days, found by 28/8.
   c.   2.375 days, found by 19/8.

X	X − X̄		Absolute deviations
2	|− 1.5|	=	1.5
0	|− 3.5|	=	3.5
6	|− 2.5|	=	2.5
3	|− 0.5|	=	0.5
10	|− 6.5|	=	6.5
4	|− 0.5|	=	0.5
1	|− 2.5|	=	2.5
2	|− 1.5|	=	1.5
			19

   The average of days absent due to illness deviates 2.375 days from the mean of 3.5.
   d.   The means, the ranges, and the average deviations are about the same. There is practically no difference between the two groups with respect to days lost due to illness.

4. *a.*   Range is 7 grams, found by 127 − 120.
   b.   124 grams, found by 1,240/10.
   c.   Population variance is 4.2, found by either:

X	X − μ	(X − μ)²	
124	0	0	$\sigma^2 = \dfrac{(X - \mu)^2}{N}$
125	1	1	
125	1	1	$= \dfrac{42}{10}$
123	−1	1	
120	−4	16	$= 4.2$
124	0	0	
127	3	9	
125	1	1	
126	2	4	
121	−3	9	
1,240	0	42	

or

X	X²
124 ...	15,376
125 ...	15,625
125 ...	15,625
123 ...	15,129
120 ...	14,400
124 ...	15,376
127 ...	16,129
125 ...	15,625
126 ...	15,876
121 ...	14,641
1,240	153,802

$$\sigma^2 = \frac{\Sigma X^2}{N} - \left(\frac{\Sigma X}{N}\right)^2$$

$$= \frac{153,802}{10} - \left(\frac{1,240}{10}\right)^2$$

$$= 1,5380.2 - 15,376.0$$

$$= 4.2, \text{ same as above}$$

d. 2.05 grams, found by $\sqrt{4.2}$.
e. Fatso 1B, because $1.20 < 2.05$.

6. 1.3 units, found by $(\overline{X} = 9.5)$.

X	$X - \overline{X}$	$(X - \overline{X})^2$	X²
8....	−1.5	2.25	64
9....	−0.5	0.25	81
8....	−1.5	2.25	64
10....	0.5	0.25	100
9....	−0.5	0.25	81
10....	0.5	0.25	100
12....	2.5	6.25	144
10....	0.5	0.25	100
76	0.0	12.00	734

$$s = \sqrt{\frac{\Sigma(X - \overline{X})^2}{n - 1}}$$

$$= \sqrt{\frac{12}{8 - 1}}$$

$$= 1.3 \text{ units}$$

$$s = \sqrt{\frac{\Sigma X^2 - \frac{(\Sigma X)^2}{n}}{n - 1}}$$

$$= \sqrt{\frac{734 - \frac{(76)^2}{8}}{8 - 1}}$$

$$= 1.3 \text{ units}$$

8. a. Either 18 minutes, using the true class limits $(18.5 - 0.5 = 18)$, or 15 minutes, using the class midpoints of 2 and 17 $(17 - 2 = 15)$.
    b. 3.89 minutes. Using the direct method:

Time (minutes)	f	Midpoint X	fX	fX²
1- 3	4	2	8	16
4- 6	8	5	40	200
7- 9	14	8	112	896
10-12	9	11	99	1089
13-15	5	14	70	980
16-18	2	17	34	578
	42		363	3759

$$s = \sqrt{\frac{\Sigma fX^2 - \frac{(\Sigma fX)^2}{n}}{n - 1}}$$

$$= \sqrt{\frac{3,759 - \frac{(363)^2}{42}}{42 - 1}}$$

$$= \sqrt{\frac{3,759 - 3,137.3571}{41}}$$

$$= \sqrt{15.162021}$$

$$= 3.89 \text{ minutes}$$

Using the coded method:

Time (minutes)	f	d	fd	fd²
1- 3	4	-2	-8	16
4- 6	8	-1	-8	8
7- 9	14	0	0	0
10-12	9	1	9	9
13-15	5	2	10	20
16-18	2	3	6	18
	42		+9	71

$$s = i\sqrt{\frac{\Sigma fd^2 - \frac{(\Sigma fd)^2}{n}}{n - 1}}$$

$$= 3\sqrt{\frac{71 - \frac{9^2}{42}}{42 - 1}}$$

$$= 3\sqrt{\frac{71 - 1.9285714}{41}}$$

$$= 3\sqrt{1.684669}$$

$$= 3.89 \text{ minutes}$$

    c.   15.162021. It is the value under the radical in the direct method.

13. *a.*   About 85.

    b.   About 18 or 19, found by dividing the range of 110 by 6.

    c.   Using 18, $\bar{X} \pm 1(s) = 85 + 1(18) = 67$ and 103.

    d.   Using 18, $\bar{X} \pm 2(s) = 85 + 2(18) = 49$ and 121.

14.

Weekly incomes	Number	Cumulative number
$ 0-$ 49	8	8
50- 59	16	24
60- 69	24	48
70- 79	48	96
80- 89	22	118
90- 99	14	132
100- 109	11	143
110- 119	7	150

a. $Q_1 = \$65.13$, found by:

$$L + \frac{\frac{n}{4} - CF}{f}\,(i) = \$59.50 + \frac{\frac{150}{4} - 24}{24}\,(\$10)$$

$$= \$59.50 + \$5.625$$
$$= \$65.125$$
$$= \$65.13$$

b. $87.00 found by:

$$\$79.50 + \frac{\frac{3(150)}{4} - 96}{22}\,(\$10) = \$79.50 + \$7.50$$

c. $21.87. The distance between the first and third quartiles is $21.87.
d. $10.94. Half the range between Q_1 and Q_3 is $10.94.
e. $48.35, found by $102.23 − $53.88 where:

$$\text{10th percentile} = \$49.50 + \frac{\frac{10(150)}{100} - 8}{16}\,(\$10)$$

$$= \$49.50 + \$4.38$$

$$\text{90th percentile} = \$99.50 + \frac{\frac{90(150)}{100} - 132}{11}\,(\$10)$$

$$= \$99.50 + \$2.73$$

The middle 80 percent of the weekly incomes lie between $53.88 and $102.23 (approximately).

16. No. Cannot compare the two distributions directly because the measurements are in different units.

Weight

$$\text{C.V.} = \frac{2}{87}\,(100) = 2.2989\%$$

Outside diameter

$$\text{C.V.} = \frac{0.25}{2.54}\,(100) = 9.8425\%$$

Greater relative dispersion in outside diameters.

Answers to the chapter self-review examination.

1. About 420 and 580, found by $\bar{X} \pm 2(s) = 500 \pm 2(40)$.
2. About 475 and 525, found by Median $\pm$ $Q.D.$ = 500 ± 25.
3. 8 percent, found by $(s/\bar{X})100 = (40/500)100$.
4. Doma. The range of 240 is greater than the range of 120. Standard deviation of $40 > 20$. $C.V.$ of 8 percent for Doma is greater than 3.3 percent for Betz.
5. 1,600, found by $(40)^2$.

X	$X - \bar{X}$	$(X - \bar{X})^2$
7	−1	1
9	+1	1
11	+3	9
9	+1	1
4	−4	16
40		10		28

6. $A.D. = 10/5 = 2$.

7. Variance $s^2 = 28/5 - 1 = 7$. Standard deviation $s = \sqrt{7} = 2.65$ pounds per square inch.

8. Either 28, found by $29.5 - 1.5$, or 24, found by $27.5 - 3.5$.

9.

	f	CF
2- 5	7	7
6- 9	11	18
10-13	20	38
14-17	30	68
18-21	14	82
22-25	10	92
26-29	8	100

10th percentile = 6.6, found by

$$5.5 + \frac{\frac{10(100)}{100} - 7}{11} (4) = 5.5 + 1.09 = 6.59 = 6.6$$

90th percentile = 24.7, found by

$$21.5 + \frac{\frac{90(100)}{100} - 82}{10} (4) = 21.5 + 3.2 = 24.7$$

Range = 18.1, found by $24.7 - 6.6$.

10. It appears to be about symmetrical.

Chapter 6. Index numbers *(answers to selected exercises)*.

1. *a.* 244.7, found by ($246.96/$100.93)(100). Earnings increased 144.7 percent from 1967 to 1980.

   b. 79.4, found by ($80.11/$100.93)(100). Earnings in 1960 were 20.6 percent below those in 1967.

   c. 135.3, found by ($246.96/$182.56)(100).

3. *a.* 121.0, found by ($97.71/$80.75)100.

Fruit	Price 1973 p_0	Amount consumed q_0	$p_0 q_0$	Price 1981 p_n	$p_n q_0$
Bananas ...	$0.23	100	$23.00	$0.35	$35.00
Grapefruit ..	0.29	50	14.50	0.27	13.50
Apples	0.35	85	29.75	0.35	29.75
Strawberries	1.02	8	8.16	1.69	13.52
Oranges ...	0.89	6	5.34	0.99	5.94
			$80.75		$97.71

612

b. Price of fruits in 1981 was 21.0 percent more than the price in 1973.

Answers to the chapter self-review examination.

1. *a.* 1982 price index is 161.3 (1967 = 100), found by ($80.65/$50.00)(100).
    b. Price of aluminum scrap increased 61.3 percent from 1967 to 1982.

Questions 2–5 are based on the following sums.

	p_0q_0	p_nq_0	p_0q_n	p_nq_n
Corn	$20	$40	$ 24	$ 48
Wheat	18	6	24	8
Oats	14	10	63	45
	$52	$56	$111	$101

2. 107.7, found by ($56/$52)(100).
3. 213.5, found by ($111/$52)(100).
4. 194.2, found by ($101/$52)(100).
5. *a.* 91.0, found by ($101/$111)(100).
    b. The difference is explained by the two different weighting systems. The Laspeyres system is used extensively.
6. $0.38, found by ($1/263.2)(100).
7. *a.* $600 in 1967, found by ($600/100.0)(100).
        $577 in 1971, found by ($700/121.3)(100).
        $380 in 1981, found by ($1,000/263.2)(100).
    b. Although his take-home pay increased from 1967 to 1981, the prices he paid for food, services, transportation, and other items increased at a more rapid rate. Thus, his purchasing power (real income) decreased.
8. *a.* Based on 1976 = 100, real sales for 1969 were $2 million, found by ($2,400,000/120)(100).
        For 1982 they were $1,316,284, found by ($3,500,000/265.9)(100).
    b. Both the actual sales and the prices Nogood paid for raw materials increased from 1969 to 1982. However, sales increased less rapidly than raw material prices. Therefore, the company's sales deflated for price changes were less in 1982 than in 1969.

Chapter 7. Time series analysis

Answers to selected exercises

2. *a.* $\bar{Y}_p = a + bX = 900 - 33.3X$. Freehand line went from 900 in 1966 to 400 in 1981. Then (400 − 900)/15 = −33.3.
    b. − 33.3 units.
    c. 234 units, found by $\bar{Y}_p = 900 - 33.3(20)$. The year 1986 is time period 20.
3. *a.*

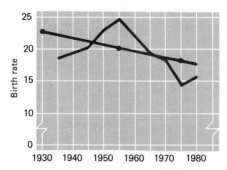

b. $\bar{Y}_p = a + bX = 20.03 - 0.47x$.

Year	Birth rate Y	x	xY	x²
1930	21.3	−5	−106.5	25
1935	18.7	−4	− 74.8	16
1940	19.4	−3	− 58.2	9
1945	20.5	−2	− 41.0	4
1950	23.9	−1	− 23.9	1
1955	24.9	0	0	0
1960	23.8	1	23.8	1
1965	19.6	2	39.2	4
1970	18.2	3	54.6	9
1975	14.7	4	58.8	16
1980	15.3	5	76.5	25
	220.3		− 51.5	110

$$a = \frac{\Sigma Y}{n} = \frac{220.3}{11} = 20.03$$

$$b = \frac{\Sigma xy}{\Sigma x^2} = \frac{-51.5}{110} = -0.47$$

c.

Year	$\bar{Y}_p$	Found by
1930	22.38	$\bar{Y}_p = 20.03 - 0.47(-5)$
1955	20.03	$\bar{Y}_p = 20.03 - 0.47(0)$
1975	18.15	$\bar{Y}_p = 20.03 - 0.47(4)$

d. 16.74, found by $\bar{Y}_p = 20.03 - 0.47(7)$. It indicates that, based on the birth rate since 1930, the birth rate in 1990 should be 16.7 per 1,000 population.

5. a. (See sales chart on next page.)

b. Log $\bar{Y}_p = \log a + \log b (x) = 1.4724 + 0.1137x$.

Year	Sales ($ millions) Y	Log of Y	x	x(log Y)	x²
1972 ...$	8.0	0.9031	−5	−4.5155	25
1973 ...	10.4	1.0170	−4	−4.0680	16
1974 ...	13.5	1.1303	−3	−3.3909	9
1975 ...	17.6	1.2455	−2	−2.4910	4
1976 ...	22.8	1.3579	−1	−1.3579	1
1977 ...	29.3	1.4669	0	0	0
1978 ...	39.4	1.5955	1	1.5955	1
1979 ...	50.5	1.7016	2	3.4032	4
1980 ...	65.0	1.8162	3	5.4486	9
1981 ...	84.1	1.9248	4	7.6992	16
1982 ...	109.0	2.0374	5	10.1870	25
		16.1962		12.5102	110

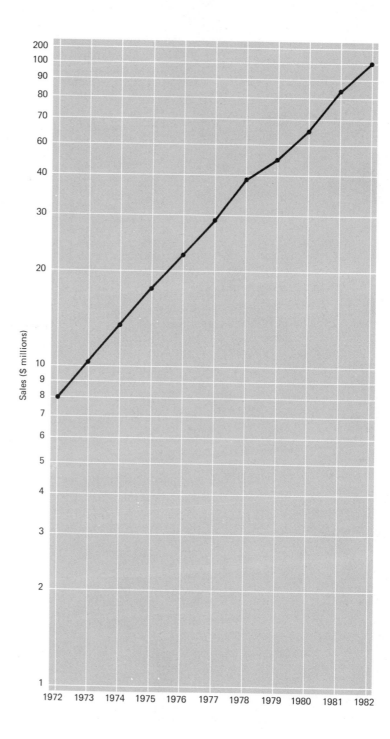

$$\log a = \frac{\Sigma \log Y}{n} \qquad \log b = \frac{\Sigma(x \log Y)}{\Sigma x^2}$$

$$= \frac{16.1962}{11} \qquad = \frac{12.5102}{110}$$

$$= 1.4724 \qquad = 0.1137$$

c.

Year	x	Log $\bar{Y}_p$	$\bar{Y}_p$	Found by
1973	−4	1.0176	$10.4	Log $\bar{Y}_p$ = 1.4724 + 0.1137(−4)
1982	5	2.0409	$111.0	Log $\bar{Y}_p$ = 1.4724 + 0.1137(5)

d. About 30 percent, found by $1 - $ (antilog of 0.1137) $= 1 - 1.30$.
e. $313 million, found by log $\bar{Y}_p$ = 1.4724 + 0.1137(9) = 2.4957. Antilog of 2.4957 = 313.

Answers to the chapter self-review examination

1. *a* and *b*.

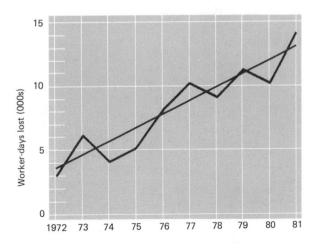

c. Your line may not be exactly the same as the freehand line drawn through the data. The line drawn on the chart goes through the points (1972, 3.5) and (1981, 13.0). Worker-days lost increased from 3.5 to 13.0, or 9.5 in nine years. So, $b = 1.056$, found by 9.5/9. Letting 1972 be the origin, or zero year, $a = 3.5$. Thus the equation is $\bar{Y}_p = a + bX = 3.5 + 1.056X$, where worker-days lost are in thousands, the origin or zero year is 1972, and X increases by one unit for each year.

2. The equation using the direct method is $\bar{Y}_p = a + bX = 3.203 + 1.066X$. The equation using the coded method is $\bar{Y}_p = a + bx = 8.000 + 0.533x$. The essential calculations for both methods are:

Year	Worker-days lost (000) Y	Long method			Coded method		
		X	XY	X²	x	xY	x²
1972	3	0	0	0	−9	−27	81
1973	6	1	6	1	−7	−42	49
1974	4	2	8	4	−5	−20	25
1975	5	3	15	9	−3	−15	9
1976	8	4	32	16	−1	−8	1
1977	10	5	50	25	+1	+10	1
1978	9	6	54	36	+3	+27	9
1979	11	7	77	49	+5	+55	25
1980	10	8	80	64	+7	+70	49
1981	14	9	126	81	+9	+126	81
	80	45	448	285	0	+176	330

Long method

$$\text{I} \quad \Sigma Y = na + b\Sigma X$$
$$\text{II} \quad \Sigma XY = a\Sigma X + b\Sigma X^2$$

$$\text{I} \quad 80 = 10a + 45b$$
$$\text{II} \quad 448 = 45a + 285b$$

Multiply I by 9 and II by 2:

$$\text{I} \quad 720 = 90a + 405b$$
$$\text{II} \quad 896 = 90a + 570b$$

Subtracting I from II, we get:

$$176 = 165b$$
$$b = 1.066$$

To find a:

$$80 = 10a + 45b$$
$$80 = 10a + 45(1.066)$$
$$a = 3.203$$

So, $\overline{Y}_p = a + bX = 3.203 + 1.066X$

where:

Worker-days lost are in thousands.
1972 is the origin, or zero.
X increases one unit for each year.

Coded method

$$a = \frac{\Sigma Y}{n} = \frac{80}{10} = 8$$

$$b = \frac{\Sigma xY}{\Sigma x^2} = \frac{176}{330} = 0.533$$

So, $\overline{Y}_p = a + bx = 8 + 0.533x$

where:

Worker-days lost are in thousands.
Origin is January 1, 1977, i.e., halfway between July 1, 1976, and July 1, 1977.
x increases by *two* units for each year.

3. *a.* For the long method, the *b* value of 1.066 really means that on the average, worker-days lost increased by 1,066 days every year.
For the coded method, the *b* value of 0.533 means that on the average, worker-days lost increased by 533 every six months (or 1,066 every year).

b. All the points are (regardless of whether the long or coded method was used):

Year	$\overline{Y}_p$ (000)	Year	$\overline{Y}_p$ (000)
1972	3.203	1977	8.533
1973	4.269	1978	9.599
1974	5.335	1979	10.665
1975	6.401	1980	11.731
1976	7.467	1981	12.797

c. With the direct method, 1987 = year 15. Then $\overline{Y}_p$ = 19.193 (really 19,193 worker-days lost), found by $\overline{Y}_p$ = 3.203 + 1.066(15).

With the coded method, 1987 = year + 21. Then $\overline{Y}_p$ = 19.193 (same answer), found by $\overline{Y}_p$ = 8 + 0.533(21).

4. a.

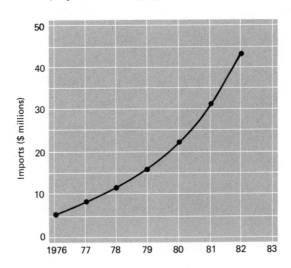

b.

Year	Imports (million tons) Y	x	Log of Y	x(log Y)	x^2
1976	6.00	−3	0.7782	−2.3346	9
1977	8.44	−2	0.9263	−1.8526	4
1978	11.70	−1	1.0682	−1.0682	1
1979	15.50	0	1.1903	0	0
1980	21.90	+1	1.3404	+1.3404	1
1981	30.80	+2	1.4886	+2.9772	4
1982	43.00	+3	1.6336	+4.9008	9
			8.4256	+3.9630	28

$$a = \frac{\Sigma \log Y}{n} = \frac{8.4256}{7} = 1.2037$$

$$b = \frac{\Sigma(x \log Y)}{\Sigma x^2} = \frac{3.9630}{28} = 0.1415$$

The equation is: $\log \overline{Y}_p = 1.2037 + 0.1415x$.

c. The coordinate of the point on the line for 1982 is approximately 42.5 (in millions of tons), found by finding the antilogarithm of 1.6282. The 1.6282 was found by log $\bar{Y}_p = 1.2037 + 0.1415(3)$.

d. About 416 million tons. To explain: year 1989 is coded 10. Then, log $\bar{Y}_p = 1.2037 + 0.1415(10) = 2.6187$. The antilog of 2.6187 is about 416.

e. About 38.5 percent, found by finding the antilogarithm of 0.1415.

Chapter 8. Seasonal analyses

Answers to the chapter self-review examination

1. a. The computations for the specific seasonals are:

Month	Sales (000)	12-month moving total	12-month moving average	Centered 12-month moving average	Specific seasonals
1978 Jan.	$ 2				
Feb.	1				
Mar.	3				
Apr.	5				
May	4				
June	3				
		$56	$4.67		
July	3			$4.63	64.8
		55	4.58		
Aug.	4			4.67	85.7
		57	4.75		
Sept.	5			4.79	104.4
		58	4.83		
Oct.	6			4.88	123.0
		59	4.92		
Nov.	8			4.88	163.9
		58	4.83		
Dec.	12			4.88	245.9
		59	4.92		
1979 Jan.	1			5.00	20.0
		61	5.08		
Feb.	3			5.25	57.1
		65	5.42		
Mar.	4			5.55	72.1
		68	5.67		
Apr.	6			5.80	103.4
		71	5.92		
May	3			6.05	49.6
		74	6.17		
June	4			6.25	64.0
		76	6.33		
July	5			6.46	77.4
		79	6.58		
Aug.	8			6.54	122.3
Sept.	8				
Oct.	9				
Nov.	11				
Dec.	14				
1980 Jan.	4				
Feb.	2				

b. The complete table of specific seasonals follows. The modified mean was used (high and low values for each month were deleted). The correction factor applied to the modified means is 1.00376, found by 1,200.0/1,195.5

	Jan	Feb	Mar	Apr	May	June	July	Aug	Sept	Oct	Nov	Dec
1978	—	—	—	—	—	—	64.8	85.7	104.4	123.0	163.9	245.9
1979	20.0	57.1	72.1	103.4	49.6	64.0	77.4	122.3	106.4	126.2	160.7	240.6
1980	22.8	58.2	77.1	102.9	49.7	64.1	68.2	120.6	105.9	124.7	161.6	249.9
1981	46.1	41.6	73.9	101.6	49.4	60.0	65.6	118.6	109.7	113.6	162.8	250.0
1982	26.8	55.5	71.6	104.7	41.2	40.6	—	—	—	—	—	—

	Jan	Feb	Mar	Apr	May	June	July	Aug	Sept	Oct	Nov	Dec	Total
Modified means	24.8	56.3	73.0	103.2	49.5	62.0	66.9	119.6	106.2	123.9	162.2	247.9	1,195.5
Typical seasonal indexes	24.9	56.5	73.3	103.6	49.7	62.2	67.2	120.0	106.6	124.4	162.8	248.8	1,200.0

c. This particular drug and proprietary store has unusually low sales during January, February, and March, and from May until August. April sales, however, are slightly above the average for the year. Sales climb steadily beginning in August, and they peak in December. December sales, for example, are typically 148.8 percent above the average for the year (which in terms of an index is 100.0).

Chapter 9. A survey of probability concepts

Answers to selected exercises

5. $\frac{3}{6}$ or $\frac{1}{2}$, or 0.50, found by $\frac{1}{6} + \frac{1}{6} + \frac{1}{6}$.

10. 119/123 or 0.9675, found by either $1 - 4/123$ or $1 - 0.0325$.

13. a. $\frac{1}{16}$ or 0.0625, found by $\frac{1}{2} \times \frac{1}{2} \times \frac{1}{2} \times \frac{1}{2}$.

   b. $P(A \text{ and } B \text{ and } C \text{ and } D) = P(A) \cdot P(B) \cdot P(C) \cdot P(D)$.

   c. $\frac{1}{2}$.

17. a. 0.08, found by 0.80×0.10.

   b.

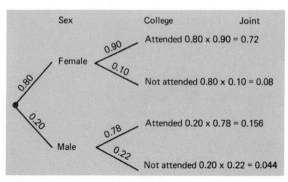

   c. Yes, because all possible outcomes are shown on the tree diagram.

18. *a.* 360 units, found by $\dfrac{6!}{(6-4)!}$

   b. 1296 units, found by 6^4.

Answers to the chapter self-review examination

1. A Venn diagram.
2. Sample space.
3. The complement rule.
4. 1.
5. 0.99, found by $0.57 + 0.40 + 0.02$.
6. *a.* $P(A \text{ and } B) = P(A) \cdot P(A|B)$.
   b. 6/2,450 or 0.0024, found by (3/50)(2/49).
7. 1/625 or 0.0016, found by (1/5)(1/5)(1/5)(1/5).

8. 190 matches, found by $\dfrac{20!}{2!(20-2)!}$.

9. 24, found by $\dfrac{4!}{(4-4)!}$.

10. 0.70, found by $P(A \text{ or } B) = P(A) + P(B) - P(A \text{ and } B) = 0.60 + 0.40 - 0.30 = 0.70$.

Chapter 10. Discrete probability distributions

Answers to selected exercises.

1. *a.* 0.5905, from Appendix I.
   b.   *c.*

Number absent r	Probability of occurrence $P(r)$
0	0.5905
1	0.3280
2	0.0729
3	0.0081
4	0.0004
5	0.0000

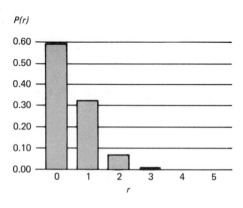

   d. Discrete because the outcomes can only be 0, 1, 2, 3, 4, or 5.

7. *a.* About 6,065. The probability for zero blemishes from Appendix J is 0.606531.
   b. About 902, found by $1 - (0.606531 + 0.303265) = 0.090204$. This is about 902 per 10,000.

Answers to the chapter self-review examination

1. True.
2. True.
3. False. It is a discrete distribution.
4. True.
5. False. It is referred to as being a continuous random variable.
6. True.
7. False. Only about 7 percent of the samples will contain either zero or one near sighted person, found by referring to Appendix I and $n = 20, p = 0.20$. Adding $P(0) + P(1) = 0.0115 + 0.0576 \cong 0.07$, or 7 percent.
8. True. ($\mu = np = 100(0.001) = 0.1$. Then referring to Appendix J and a μ of 0.1, the probability of zero defectives of 0.9048374, or about 0.90.)
9. True.
10. True. (Referring to Appendix I, an n of 10, a p of 0.50, and an r of 10, the probability is 0.0010, which is the same as 1 in 1,000.)

Chapter 11. The normal probability distribution

Answers to selected exercises

2. *a.* 0.47725, found by:

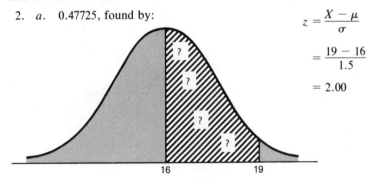

$$z = \frac{X - \mu}{\sigma}$$

$$= \frac{19 - 16}{1.5}$$

$$= 2.00$$

    The z-score for a z of 2.00 is 0.47725.
  b. 0.02275, found by $0.50000 - 0.47725$.
  c. 0.97725, found by $0.50000 + 0.47725$.

4. 0.60062, found by:

$$z = \frac{X - \mu}{\sigma}$$

$$= \frac{\$42,000 - \$40,000}{\$5,000}$$

$$= 0.4$$

The area for a z of 0.4 is 0.15542.

$32,000 $40,000 $42,000

The area for a z of 1.6 is 0.44520. Adding: $0.15542 + 0.44520 = 0.60062$.

6. *a.*   0.00820, found by $(320 - 500)/75 = -2.4$. Area under curve for a z of -2.4 is 0.49180. Then $0.50000 - 0.49180 = 0.00820$.

   b.   About 563, found by $0.84 = \dfrac{X - 500}{75}$. Then $63 = X - 500$ and $X = 563$.

11. *a.*   0.95053, found by $\mu = np = 100(0.38) = 38$ and $\sigma^2 = np(1 - p) = 100(0.38)(1 - 0.38) = 23.56$. $\sigma = \sqrt{23.56} = 4.85$. Then: $z = \dfrac{X - \mu}{\sigma} = \dfrac{30 - 38}{4.85} = -1.65$. Area under curve for -1.65 is 0.45093. Adding: $0.45093 + 0.50000 = 0.95053$.

   b.

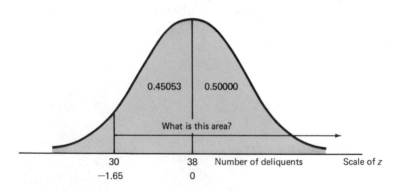

0.45053   0.50000

What is this area?

| 30 | 38 | Number of deliquents | Scale of z |
| -1.65 | 0 | | |

Answers to the chapter self-review examination

1. *a.*   (1) There are only two mutually exclusive outcomes—the answer is correct, or it is wrong.
        (2) The distribution results from counting the number of correct answers.
        (3) The answer to each question is independent.
        (4) The probability p remains the same from question to question. It is 1/4 or 0.25.

   b.   0.00027, indicating that the probability of guessing 40 or more is rather remote. $\mu = np = 100(0.25) = 25$ and $\sigma^2 = np(1 - p) = 100(0.25)(1 - 0.25) = 18.75$. Then $\sigma = \sqrt{18.75} = 4.33$. $z = \dfrac{X - \mu}{\sigma} = \dfrac{40 - 25}{4.33} = 3.46$. The area, from Appendix G, is 0.49973. Subtracting: $0.50000 - 0.49973 = 0.00027$.

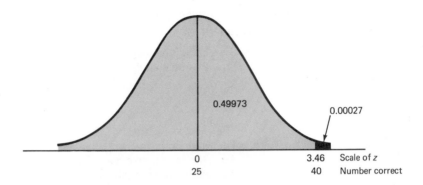

2. 6/10 of 1 percent, found by $z = \dfrac{1{,}250 - 1{,}200}{20} = 2.5$. Area under curve for a z of 2.5 is 0.49379. Subtracting from 0.50000 gives 0.00621, or 6/10 of 1 percent.

3. *a.* Slightly below average on history test.
   b. In the top 1 percent with respect to the science test.

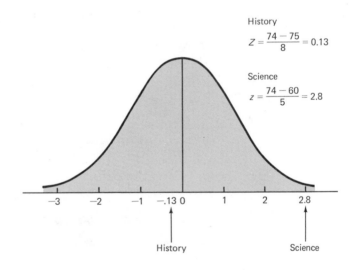

History

$Z = \dfrac{74 - 75}{8} = 0.13$

Science

$z = \dfrac{74 - 60}{5} = 2.8$

4. About 118, found by:

$$z = \frac{13 - 15}{1.75} = -1.14.$$ Area under curve is 0.37286.

$$z = \frac{16 - 15}{1.75} = 0.57.$$ Area under curve is 0.21566.

Adding: $0.37286 + 0.21566 = 0.58852$. Then, $0.58852 \times 200 = 117.7$.

Chapter 12. An introduction to sampling

Answers to selected exercises

2. *a.* Systematic sampling.
   b. Stratified random sampling.

6. *a.* $29.69 to $30.31, found by:

$$\$30 \pm 1.96 \left(\frac{\$5}{\sqrt{1,000}} \right)$$

b. The width of the interval is based on the standard error of the mean, $s/\sqrt{n}$. As n, the sample size, increases, the standard error decreases and so does the confidence interval.

7. 553, found by:

$$n = \left(\frac{z \cdot s}{E} \right)^2 = \left(\frac{1.96 \cdot 3}{0.25} \right)^2 = 553$$

10. *a.* 5,683, found by:

$$n = p(1 - p)\left[\frac{z}{E} \right]^2$$

$$= 0.30(1 - 0.30)\left[\frac{1.645}{0.01} \right]^2 = 5,683$$

b. By relaxing the preciseness of the estimate from 1 percent to 3 percent. Then,

$$n = 0.30(1 - 0.30)\left[\frac{1.645}{0.03} \right]^2 = 631$$

Answers to the chapter self-review examination

1. Between 34.3 and 45.7 percent, found by:

$$0.40 \pm 1.645 \sqrt{\frac{0.40(1 - 0.40)}{200}}$$

$$= 0.40 \pm 1.645 \sqrt{0.0012}$$

2. Between 106 and 114 minutes, found by:

$$110 \pm 1.96 \left(\frac{30}{\sqrt{200}} \right) = 110 \pm 1.96(2.12)$$

3. Between 65.2 and 74.8 percent, found by:

$$0.70 \pm 2.33 \sqrt{\frac{0.70(1 - 0.70)}{500}}$$

4. About 96, found by:

$$n = \left(\frac{1.96 \cdot \$500}{\$100} \right)^2$$

Chapter 13. Tests of hypotheses: Large samples

Answers to selected exercises

1. *a.* H_0: $\mu = \$20,000$.
        H_1: $\mu \neq \$20,000$.

    b. 0.10.

    c. Accept the null hypothesis if the computed value of z falls in the region between -1.645 and $+1.645$. Otherwise, reject H_0 and accept H_1.

    d. Computed z is 2.74, found by:

$$\frac{\$20,500 - \$20,000}{\dfrac{\$2,000}{\sqrt{120}}} = \frac{\$500}{\$182.57418} = 2.74$$

    Reject H_0. For tack welders in shipbuilding, the mean is not $20,000.

3. *a.* H_0: $\mu_1 = \mu_2$.
        H_1: $\mu_1 \neq \mu_2$.

    b. $z = 34.20$, found by:

$$\frac{2,175 - 2,050}{\sqrt{\left(\dfrac{12}{\sqrt{64}}\right)^2 + \left(\dfrac{20}{\sqrt{36}}\right)^2}}$$

    c. Reject null hypothesis at 0.10 level since 34.20 falls in the tail beyond 1.645. We recommend an investigation to find out the reason for the wide discrepancies between the two shifts.

Answers to chapter self-review examination

1. *a.* H_0: $\mu \leq 40,000$.
        H_1: $\mu > 40,000$.

    b. One-tailed, because the alternate hypothesis states a direction.

    c. 1.28.

    d. $z = 15$, found by:

$$\frac{43,000 - 40,000}{\dfrac{2,000}{\sqrt{100}}}$$

    Reject null hypothesis (since 15 exceeds 1.28). It is highly unlikely that the mean mileage is 40,000. We can conclude that the newly developed tire does last longer, on the average, than the previous tires.

2. *a.* The test is two-tailed because H_1 does not state a direction (such as, The average age of the presidents of large manufacturing firms is *greater than* the mean for presidents of medium-sized firms).

    b. Plus or minus 1.96, found by determining the z-value for the area under the curve associated with 0.4750.

    c. Accept the null hypothesis at the 0.05 level. Computed z is about 1.25, found by:

$$z = \frac{47 - 45}{\sqrt{\dfrac{(15)^2}{100} + \dfrac{(5)^2}{80}}} = \frac{2}{1.6} = 1.25$$

The computed z of 1.25 falls in the area of acceptance, which is defined as being between ± 1.96.

    d. Yes.

Chapter 14.   Tests of hypotheses about proportions

Answers to selected exercises

1.   The null hypothesis is: There is no significant statistical difference between the two proportions (0.48 and 0.50). The null hypothesis is not rejected. The computed value of z of -0.40 falls in the area of acceptance between 0 and -1.645. The calculations for z are:

$$z = \frac{\dfrac{48}{100} - 0.50}{\sqrt{\dfrac{0.50(1 - 0.50)}{100}}} = \frac{-0.02}{0.05} = -0.40$$

3. *a.* Yes, For New Go-Away $np = 200(0.90) = 180$, and $n(1 - p) = 200(0.10) = 20$. For the old Go-Away, $np = 300(0.87) = 261$, and $n(1 - p) = 300(0.13) = 39$.

    b. New Go-Away is 0.90, found by 180/200.
        Old Go-Away is 0.87, found by 261/300.

    c. $H_0: p_1 \le p_2$ and $H_1: p_1 > p_2$.

    d. 1.645.

    e.

$$\bar{p} = \frac{X_1 + X_2}{n_1 + n_2} = \frac{180 + 261}{200 + 300} = \frac{441}{500} = 0.882$$

$$z = \frac{0.90 - 0.87}{\sqrt{\dfrac{0.882(0.118)}{200} + \dfrac{0.882(0.118)}{300}}}$$

$$= \frac{0.03}{\sqrt{0.0005203 + 0.0003469}}$$

$$= \frac{0.03}{\sqrt{0.0008672}} = \frac{0.03}{0.0294482} = 1.02$$

Do not reject the null hypothesis. There is no statistically significant difference between the effectiveness of the new and old Go-Away.

Answers to the chapter self-review examination

1.   The boss is correct in his observation that there is no significant statistical change in production. That is, the 72 percent can be attributed to sampling. The critical value for this one-tailed test is about 2.05. The computed z-value is 0.44. Since the computed value of z lies between 0 and 2.05, the null hypothesis is not rejected.

$$z = \frac{0.72 - 0.70}{\sqrt{\dfrac{(0.70)(0.30)}{100}}} = \frac{0.02}{\sqrt{0.0021}} = 0.44$$

2. $H_0: p_1 \leq p_2.$
    $H_1: p_1 > p_2.$

    Do not reject H_0. Computed z is 1.48, which falls in the acceptance region between 0 and 1.645.

$$z = \frac{\dfrac{78}{120} - \dfrac{90}{160}}{\sqrt{\dfrac{0.60(1 - 0.60)}{120} + \dfrac{0.60(1 - 0.60)}{160}}}$$

where:

$$\bar{p} = \frac{78 + 90}{120 + 160} = 0.60$$

Chapter 15. Students t test: Small samples

Answers to selected exercises

1. Yes. The critical value of t for $n - 1 = 18 - 1 = 17$ degrees of freedom, a one-tailed test, and the 0.05 level is 1.740 (from Appendix E). Computing t:

$$t = \frac{\bar{X} - \mu}{\dfrac{\sigma}{\sqrt{n}}} = \frac{23,400 - 22,100}{\dfrac{1,500}{\sqrt{18}}}$$

$$= \frac{1,300}{\dfrac{1,500}{4.2426406}} = 3.677$$

Since 3.677 exceeds 1.740, the null hypothesis that $\mu = 22,100$ is rejected. H_1, which states that $\mu > 22,100$, is accepted.

5. $H_0: \mu_1 = \mu_2.$
    $H_1: \mu_1 \neq \mu_2.$

    Reject H_0. Computed t falls in the tail to the left of -2.052. (The -2.052 is from Appendix E, 27 df, a two-tailed test.) $t = -3.06$, found by:

$$t = \frac{300 - 305}{\sqrt{\dfrac{(16 - 1)(20) + (13 - 1)(18)}{16 + 13 - 2}\left(\dfrac{1}{16} + \dfrac{1}{13}\right)}}$$

$$= \frac{-5}{\sqrt{2.664528}}$$

$$= \frac{-5}{1.6323382} = -3.06$$

Answers to chapter self-review examination

1. T.
2. F. 21 degrees of freedom, found by $n - 1 = 22 - 1$.

3. T.

4. F. There are many t distributions, each with a mean of zero. The shapes of the t distributions vary with the sample size.

5. T.

6. T.

7. T.

8. T.

9. F. $t = 2.080$. There are $n_1 + n_2 - 2 = 12 + 11 - 2 = 21$ degrees of freedom. From Appendix E, two-tailed test, 0.05 level, 21 degrees of freedom, the critical value of t is 2.080.

10. T.

Chapter 16. Analysis of variance: One-way and two-way classifications

Answers to the chapter self-review examination

1. *a.* The tolerances maintained by the four machines are not all equal.
   b. Both null hypotheses are accepted. For the four machines:

$$F_{3,6} = \frac{0.888866}{1.8056} = 0.49$$

which is less than the critical value of F of 4.76.

For the three steels:

$$F_{2,6} = \frac{0.25}{1.8056} = 0.14$$

which is less than the critical value of F of 5.14. The two-way ANOVA table is:

Source	Sum of squares	Degrees of freedom	Mean square
Treatment (machines) .. $SST =$	2.6666	$4 - 1 = 3$	$2.6666/3 = 0.8889$
Treatment (steel) ......$SSB =$	0.05	$3 - 1 = 2$	$0.5/2 = 0.25$
Error ....$SSE =$	10.8334	$3 \times 2 = 6$	$10.8334/6 = 1.8056$
SS total	14.0000		

   c. The four machines perform equally well; that is, the tolerances maintained by the four machines are equal. And, there is no difference in the three steels being ground by the machines. They maintain the same tolerances on the four machines.

Chapter 17. Nonparametric tests of hypotheses: One-sample and two-sample tests

Answers to selected exercises

1. H_0: There is no difference among the opinions of the buyers.
   H_1: There is a difference.

   Computed chi-square is 3.400. The critical value from Appendix H is 15.09 ($k - 1 = 6 - 1 = 5df$). Do not reject H_0. 3.400 falls in the acceptance area.

f_0	f_e	$f_0 - f_e$	$(f_0 - f_e)^2$	$\dfrac{(f_0 - f_e)^2}{f_e}$
47	40	7	49	1.225
45	40	5	25	0.625
40	40	0	0	0
39	40	−1	1	0.025
35	40	−5	25	0.625
34	40	−6	36	0.900
240	240	0		3.400

6.

Usual steps		Group using experimental techniques	
Raw scores	Rank	Raw scores	Rank
41	14	21	3.5
36	10	27	7
42	15	36	10
39	12.5	20	2
29	8	19	1
36	10	21	3.5
48	16	39	12.5
	85.5	24	6
		22	5
			50.5

$$U = (7)(9) + \frac{7(7 + 1)}{2} - 85.5 = 5.5$$

$$U' = (7)(9) + \frac{9(9 + 1)}{2} - 50.5 = 57.5$$

As a check: $U' = n_1 n_2 - U = (7)(9) - 5.5 = 57.5$. Refer to Appendix L. This is a one-tailed test because the alternate hypothesis states that the experimental group required less time. Use the bottom table. The critical value is 15. Since 5.5 (the smaller value) is between 0 and 15, the null hypothesis is rejected at the 0.05 level. The experimental group required less time.

7. H_0: Associates with a bachelor's degree only and those with a master's degree remain with the company the same length of time.

H_1: Associates with a master's degree remain longer.

It is a one-tailed test using the Kolmogorov-Smirnov test. Computed value is 16.03, found by:

$$\chi^2 = (4)(0.3833)^2 \left[\frac{(60)(50)}{60 + 50} \right]$$

D is found by:

		Cumulative decimals		
B	M	B	M	Difference
15	1	0.2500	0.0200	0.2300
17	9	0.5333	0.2000	0.3333
15	10	0.7833	0.4000	0.3833
10	15	0.9500	0.7000	0.2500
3	15	1.0000	1.0000	0

Since the computed value of chi-square (16.03) is greater than the critical value (5.99), the null hypothesis is rejected.

Answers to the chapter self-review examination

1. Chi-square was computed to be 1.61. Since this computed value is less than the critical value of 11.34 for three degrees of freedom, the null hypothesis that there is no significant statistical difference is accepted. (*Note:* There are four categories, so $k - 1 = 4 - 1 = 3$ df.) The calculations for χ^2 are:

f_0	f_e	$f_0 - f_e$	$(f_0 - f_e)^2$	$\dfrac{(f_0 - f_e)^2}{f_e}$
7	10	−3	9	$\dfrac{9}{10} = 0.90$
34	30	+4	16	$\dfrac{16}{30} = 0.53$
48	50	−2	4	$\dfrac{4}{50} = 0.08$
11	10	$\dfrac{+1}{0}$	1	$\dfrac{1}{10} = \dfrac{0.10}{1.61}$

2. The computed value of D for the Kolmogorov-Smirnov two-sample test is 0.05. Since the alternative hypothesis merely states there is a difference, a two-tailed test is used. The critical value for the 0.01 level is 0.28. The null hypothesis, which states that there is no difference, is accepted at the 0.01 level because 0.05 < 0.28. The calculations for D are:

Offenders	Behavior				
	Exemplary	Very good	Good	Fair	Unsatisfactory
		Cumulative fractions			
First	$\dfrac{12}{60}$	$\dfrac{25}{60}$	$\dfrac{45}{60}$	$\dfrac{54}{60}$	$\dfrac{60}{60}$
Second	$\dfrac{14}{80}$	$\dfrac{34}{80}$	$\dfrac{64}{80}$	$\dfrac{76}{80}$	$\dfrac{80}{80}$
	Cumulative fractions expressed as decimals				
First	0.200	0.417	0.750	0.900	1.000
Second	0.175	0.425	0.800	0.950	1.000
Absolute difference	0.025	0.008	0.050	0.050	0

Chapter 18. Nonparametric tests of hypotheses: More than two samples.

Answers to selected exercises

1. Computed Q is 1.33. Since it is less than the critical value, 9.49, H_0 is accepted.

$$Q = \frac{(5 - 1)[5(7^2 + 5^2 + 6^2 + 6^2 + 5^2)] - (29)^2}{5(29) - 103}$$

$$= \frac{4(14)}{42} = 1.33$$

Sums are:

Very low	Low	Moderate	High	Very high	L	L²
7	5	6	6	5	29	103

3. H_0: There is no difference with respect to the overall ratings.
    H_1: There is a difference.

There are $k - 1 = 3 - 1 = 2$ degrees of freedom. The critical value is 5.99. Sum of ranks is: $A = 11, B = 16, C = 21$. $X_r^2 = 54.25$, found by:

$$\frac{12}{(8)(3)(3 + 1)} [(11)^2 + (16)^2 + (21)^2] - [3(8)(3 + 1)]$$

Since $54.25 > 5.99$, reject the null hypothesis and accept H_1.

6.

	Low		Medium		High		Total	
Age	f_o	f_e	f_o	f_e	f_o	f_e	Number	Percent
Under 25.....	20	20	18	20	22	21	60	12
25–39	50	45	46	48	44	47	140	28
40–59	58	58	63	61	59	60	180	36
60 and over ..	34	39	43	41	43	40	120	24
	162	162	170	170	168	168	500	100

$$\chi^2 = \frac{(20 - 20)^2}{20} + \frac{(50 - 45)^2}{45}$$

$$+ \cdots + \frac{(43 - 40)^2}{4} = 2.125$$

There are six degrees of freedom, found by $(4 - 1)(3 - 1)$. Table value of chi-square from Appendix H is 16.81. Accept the null hypothesis because $2.125 < 16.81$. There is no relationship between age and pressure.

Answers to the chapter self-review examination

1. Using the Friedman test, the computed value of χ_r^2 is 0.88. This is less than the critical value of chi-square of 9.49. (There are $k - 1 = 5 - 1 = 4\,df$. The critical value of chi-square for $4\,df$ and the 0.05 level is 9.49.) The null hypothesis, which stated that there is no difference in the overall ratings awarded by the panel of experts, is accepted at the 0.05 level. The calculations of ratings are:

Expert no.	A	B	C	D	E
1	3	5	1	4	2
2	4	2	5	3	1
3	1	2	3	4	5
4	5	4	1	2	3
5	3	5	2	1	4
6	4	1	5	2	3
7	1	4	2	3	5
8	3	1	5	4	2
9	4	5	2	3	1
10	4	3	2	1	5
	32	32	28	27	31

Computation:

$$\chi_r^2 = \frac{12}{(10)(5)(5+1)} \ [(32)^2 + (32)^2 + (28)^2$$

$$+ \ (27)^2 + (31)^2] - [3(10)(5+1)]$$

$$= 0.04[4,522] - 180$$

$$= 0.88$$

2. The computed value of chi-square is about 1.5, which is less than the critical value of 16.81. Thus, the null hypothesis, which states that there is no significant difference in the responses with regard to the level of management, is accepted. To put it another way, there is no relationship between the degree of concern about environmental issues and the level of management. The critical value of 16.81 was determined by (rows − 1)(col − 1) = (4 − 1) (3 − 1) = 6 df and then referring to Appendix H.

Level of management	No concern f_0	No concern f_e	Some concern f_0	Some concern f_e	Very concerned f_0	Very concerned f_e	Total Number	Total Percent
Top management ..	15	(14)	13	(12)	12	(14)	40	20
Middle management ..	20	(21)	19	(18)	21	(21)	60	30
Supervisor	7	(7)	6	(6)	6	(7)	20	10
Foreman	28	(28)	21	(24)	31	(28)	80	40
	70	(70)	60	(60)	70	(70)	200	100

$$\chi^2 = \frac{(15-14)^2}{14} + \frac{(13-12)^2}{12} + \frac{(12-14)^2}{14} + \frac{(20-21)^2}{21} + \cdots$$

$$\cong 1.5$$

Chapter 19. Statistical quality control

Answers to selected exercises

2. *a.* Ranges are: 16, 6, 6, 2, 9, and 1. The arithmetic mean range is 6.67.

$$UCL = D_4\bar{R} = 2.282(6.67) = 15.22$$
$$LCL = D_3\bar{R} = 0(6.67) = 0$$

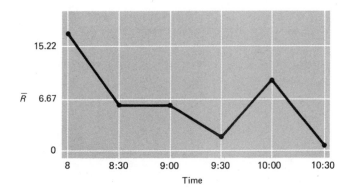

$\bar{R}$ 6.67

b.   The average range is 6.67 degrees. Based on the sample readings, about 99.7 percent of the ranges will fall between 0 and 15.22 degrees.

Answers to the chapter self-review examination

1. *a.*   *UCL* and *LCL* are 6.0531375 inches and 6.0098625 inches, respectively, found by $\bar{X} \pm A_2\bar{R} = 6.0315 \pm 0.577(0.0375)$.

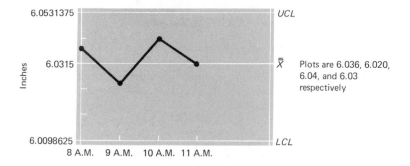

Plots are 6.036, 6.020, 6.04, and 6.03 respectively

b.   If the process is in control, over 99 percent of the means of the samples of five pieces will fall between 6.0531375 inches and 6.0098625 inches. The mean measurement is 6.0315 inches.

2. *a.*   The *UCL* and *LCL* for the range chart are 0.0793125 and 0, found by $D_4\bar{R} = (2.115)(0.0375)$ and $D_3\bar{R} = (0)(0.0375)$.

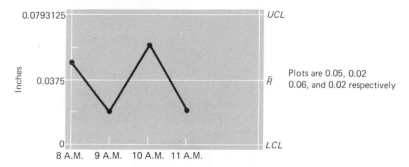

Plots are 0.05, 0.02 0.06, and 0.02 respectively

b. If the process is in control, over 99 percent of the ranges of the samples of five pieces will fall between 0.0793125 inch and 0 inch. The average range is 0.0375 inch.

3. a. The *UCL* and *LCL* are 3.1108 and 0 percent, found by

$$0.01 \pm 3 \sqrt{\frac{(0.01)(0.99)}{200}}.$$

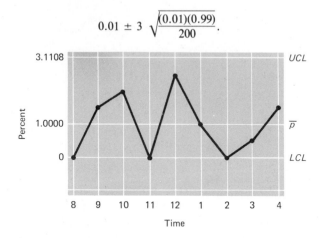

b. If production continues, as evidenced by the nine samples of 200 pieces selected at random, then the average percent defective will be 1.0 percent. Over 99 percent of the samples of 200 will contain between 0 percent and 3.1108 percent defectives.

4. a. The *UCL* and *LCL* for the *c* chart are 4.949648 and 0, respectively, found by $\bar{c} \pm 3 \sqrt{c} = 1.4 \pm 3 \sqrt{1.4}$.

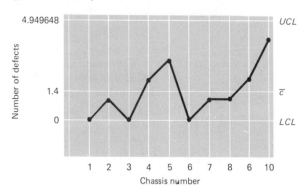

b. If the assembly process continues as evidenced by the first ten produced, over 99 percent of the chassis will have between 0 and 4.949648 defects. The average will be 1.4 defects per chassis.

Chapter 20. Simple regression and correlation analysis

Answers to selected exercises

1. a. Efficiency rating.

b.

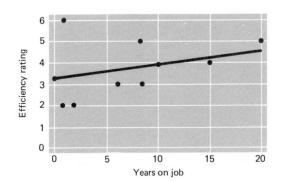

c. No.

d. $\bar{Y}_p = a + bX = 3.166352 + 0.076544X$

where:

$$b = \frac{8(254) - (61)(30)}{8(795) - (61)^2}$$

$$= \frac{202}{2639} = 0.076544$$

$$a = \frac{30}{8} - 0.076544 \left(\frac{61}{8}\right)$$

$$= 3.166352$$

e.

When X is:	$\bar{Y}_p$ is:
0	3.166352
6	3.625616
10	3.931792

f. found by:

$$= \sqrt{\frac{128 - 3.166352(30) - 0.076544(254)}{8 - 2}}$$

$$= \sqrt{\frac{13.567264}{6}} = 1.504$$

g. $\bar{Y}_p = 3.319$, found by $3.166352 + 0.076544(2)$. $t = 2.447$ from Appendix E. Confidence limits are 1.6 and 5.0, found by:

$$3.319 \pm 2.447(1.504) \sqrt{\frac{1}{8} + \frac{(2 - 7.625)^2}{329.875}}$$

$$= 3.319 \pm 2.447(1.504)(0.47)$$

$$= 3.319 \pm 1.730$$
$$1.589 \text{ and } 5.049$$

3. *a.* $r = 0.35$, found by:

$$r = \frac{8(254) - (61)(30)}{\sqrt{[8(795) - (61)^2][8(128) - (30)^2]}}$$

$$= \frac{202}{\sqrt{[2,639][124]}}$$

$$= \frac{202}{\sqrt{327,236}} = \frac{202}{572.04545} = 0.35$$

b. $r^2 = (0.35)^2 = 0.12.$

c. $1 - r^2 = 0.88.$ There is rather weak positive correlation. Only 12 percent of the variation in efficiency ratings is explained by years on the job; 88 percent is not.

Answers to the chapter self-review examination

1. a.

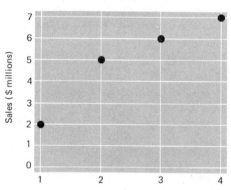

b. $\overline{Y}_p = a + bX = 1 + 1.6X$ (in millions of dollars).

As a check:

I:	$20 = 4a + 10b$	$b = \dfrac{4(58) - 10(20)}{4(30) - (10)^2}$
II:	$58 = 10a + 30b$	
I × 3:	$60 = 12a + 30b$	$= \dfrac{32}{20} = 1.6$
II × 1:	$58 = 10a + 30b$	
Subtract	$2 = 2a$	
II from I:	$a = 1$	$a = \dfrac{20}{4} - 1.6\left(\dfrac{10}{4}\right)$
		$= 5 - 4 = 1$

Solving for b using I, we get

$$20 = 4(1) + 10b$$
$$16 = 10b$$
$$b = 1.6$$

c. An average of $4.04 million, found by $\overline{Y}_p = 1 + 1.6(1.9).$

d.

For an advertising expenditure of X	Estimated sales $\overline{Y}_p$	Found by
$1	$2.6	$\overline{Y}_p = 1 + 1.6(1)$
2	4.2	$\overline{Y}_p = 1 + 1.6(2)$
3	5.8	$\overline{Y}_p = 1 + 1.6(3)$
4	7.4	$\overline{Y}_p = 1 + 1.6(4)$

2. *a.* The standard error of the estimate is approximately 0.77 (in millions) found by:

$$\sqrt{\frac{114 - 1(20) - 1.6(58)}{4 - 2}} = \sqrt{\frac{1.2}{2}} = \sqrt{0.60} \cong 0.77$$

  b. About $2.53 million and $5.55 million, found by $4.04 \pm 1.96(0.77)$.
  c. The probability is 0.95 that for an advertising expenditure of $1.9 million, sales will be in the interval between $2.53 million and $5.55 million.

3. *a.* Pearson's r is about 0.96, indicating that there is almost perfect relationship between advertising expenditures and sales.

$$r = \frac{4(58) - (10)(20)}{\sqrt{[4(30) - (10)^2][4(114) - (20)^2]}}$$

$$= \frac{32}{\sqrt{1120}} \cong 0.96$$

  b. The coefficient of determination is about 0.92, found by $(0.96)^2$. About 92 percent of the variation in sales is explained by the advertising expenditures.
  c. The coefficient of nondetermination is 0.08, found by $1 - 0.92$. About 8 percent of the variation in sales is not explained by advertising expenditures.

Chapter 21. Multiple regression and correlation analysis

Answers to the chapter self-review examination

1. $\overline{Y}_p = a + b_1X_1 + b_2X_2$.
2. 0.81 indicates that 81 percent of the variation in automobile sales is explained by the number of automobile dealerships, the number of unemployed persons, and the average age of the automobiles on the road.
3. 0.90, found by $\sqrt{0.81}$.
4. 19 percent, found by $1 - 0.81$.
5. The 5 is the value of b_3 and is called a partial regression coefficient. Specifically, it indicates that for each change of one year in the average age of automobiles, automobile sales increase (or decrease) by $5 million, but dealerships and unemployment are held at a constant value.
6. Unemployment, because -0.71390 indicates that the highest simple correlation is between sales and number of unemployed.
7. *a.* The 1.00000 between the number of dealerships and the number of dealerships indicates that the degree of correlation between them is perfect (logically).

b. 0.23489 (indicating a rather low correlation).

8. a. Partial coefficient of correlation.

b. The average age of automobiles will enter as STEP NUMBER 2 because the partial coefficient is higher than that for dealerships.

Chapter 22. Nonparametric measures of association

Answers to selected exercises

1. a.

Rank			
Sports	World events	d	d²
10	11	−1	1.00
14	14	0	0.00
5	4	1	1.00
4	1	3	9.00
1	2.5	−1.5	2.25
12	12	0	0.00
6	8	−2	4.00
2.5	5.5	−3	9.00
8	2.5	5.5	30.25
11	8	3	9.00
2.5	13	−10.5	110.25
13	5.5	7.5	56.25
9	10	−1.0	1.00
7	8	−1.0	1.00
			234.00

Rho is 0.4857, found by:

$$1 - \frac{6(234)}{(14)^3 - 14}$$

b. Rho in population is not zero. Computed t is 1.92, found by:

$$0.4857\sqrt{\frac{14 - 2}{1 - (0.4857)^2}}$$

Since $1.92 > 1.782$, from Appendix E, the null hypothesis which states that Rho in the population is zero is rejected at the 0.05 level.

3. a. $\Sigma A = 22; \Sigma B = 17; \Sigma C = 40; \Sigma D = 41$.

$$W = \frac{12[(22)^2 + (17)^2 + (40)^2 + (41)^2]}{(12)^2(4)(4^2 - 1)}$$

b. H_0: W is 0.
H_1: $W > 0$.

Small sample, because N is less than seven.

$$s = 4\left[\frac{4,054}{4} - \left(\frac{120}{4}\right)^2\right] = 454$$

c. The critical value of s from Appendix N is 127.8. Since 454 > 127.8, the null hypothesis is rejected. W in the population is greater than zero.

Answers to the chapter self-review examination

1. a. Rho was computed to be about 0.97, found by:

	Rank		Difference	
	In	In		
Player	practice	game	d	d²
Art	6	6.0	0	0
Bob	1	1.0	0	0
Jim..............	8	7.0	+1.0	1.00
Abe	5	5.0	0	0
Arch.............	3	3.5	−0.5	0.25
John	2	2.0	0	0
Dean	7	8.0	−1.0	1.00
Jimmie	4	3.5	+0.5	0.25
			0	2.50

$$\text{Rho} = 1 - \frac{6\Sigma d^2}{N^3 - N} = 1 - \frac{6(2.50)}{8^3 - 8} \cong 0.97$$

b. At the 0.01 level, the null hypothesis that there is no relationship between the two rankings in the population is rejected. It is rejected because the computed value of Rho (0.97) is greater than the critical value of 0.833 (from Appendix M).

c. There is a very high degree of relationship between how the players ranked in performance during the practice and how they ranked in performance during the S.U. game. If all the players were included in this study, it is highly unlikely that Rho would be zero.

2. Kendall's coefficient of concordance W is 0.73, indicating a rather high degree of agreement (concordance) among the division managers with respect to the applicants.

$$W = \frac{12[(14)^2 + (20)^2 + (8)^2]}{(7)^2(3)(3^2 - 1)} - \frac{3(3 + 1)}{3 - 1}$$

$$= \frac{7,920}{1,176} - 6 = 0.73$$

Chapter 23. An introduction to decision making under uncertainty

Answers to the chapter self-review examination

1.

	Payoff	
	Mild	Severe
Manufacture	winter	winter
Lightweight jacket $120,000	$105,000
Heavy jacket 110,000	125,000

2. For lightweight jackets, $113,250; for heavy jackets, $116,750. Calculations for lightweight jackets are:

Winter	Payoff		Prob-ability		Expected payoff
Mild	$120,000	×	0.55	=	$ 66,000
Severe	105,000	×	0.45	=	47,250
Total					$113,250

3. Decision: Manufacture heavy jackets because the expected payoff in the long run is greater.

	Opportunity loss	
Manufacture	Mild winter	Severe winter
Lightweight jacket	$ 0	$20,000
Heavy jacket	10,000	0

The expected opportunity loss for lightweight jackets is $9,000, for heavy jackets, $5,500. Decision: Manufacture heavy jackets. Work for lightweight jackets is as follows:

Winter	OL		Prob-ability		Expected loss
Mild	$ 0	×	0.55	=	$ 0
Severe	20,000	×	0.45	=	9,000
Total					$9,000

4. The value of perfect information is $5,500, found by:

$122,250   Expected payoff under conditions of certainty
−116,750   Expected payoff under conditions of uncertainty
$ 5,500   Value of perfect information

Note: This is the same as the minimum expected opportunity loss. The expected payoff under certainty is $122,250, found by:

Winter	Expected payoff		Prob-ability		Expected payoff
Mild					
(lightweight) ...	$120,000	×	0.55	=	$ 66,000
Severe					
(heavy)	125,000	×	0.45	=	56,250
					$122,250

5. The decision tree is:

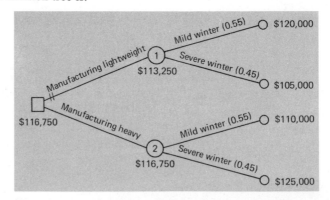

Chapter 24.   Bayes' theorem and decision making

Answers to the chapter self-review examination

1. *a.*   Replace the automobile. The expected repair cost of $433 is greater than the replacement cost of $300.

	Repair cost		Prob- ability		Expected cost
Transmission	$600	×	$\frac{2}{3}$	=	$400
Carburetor	100	×	$\frac{1}{3}$	=	$\underline{\quad 33}$
					$433

b.   Now the decision is to repair the automobile. The expected repair cost of $200 is less than the replacement cost of $300. To explain: Let T = failure in transmission, C = failure in carburetor, and M = black grease mark appearing. Using these letters, we can write the Bayes' formula and solution as (recall that the prior probabilities are 2/3 and 1/3):

$$P(T|M) = \frac{P(T) \cdot P(M|T)}{P(T) \cdot P(M|T) + P(C) \cdot P(M|C)}$$

$$= \frac{\frac{2}{3}\left(\frac{1}{10}\right)}{\frac{1}{2}\left(\frac{1}{10}\right) + \frac{1}{3}\left(\frac{8}{10}\right)}$$

$$= \frac{1}{5}$$

Then:

	Repair cost		Prob- ability		Expected cost
Transmission	$600	×	$\frac{1}{5}$	=	$120
Carburetor	100	×	$\frac{4}{5}$	=	$\underline{\quad 80}$
					$200

Appendix B

LOGARITHMS

 base 10 →

N	0	1	2	3	4	5	6	7	8	9
10	0000	0043	0086	0128	0170	0212	0253	0294	0334	0374
11	0414	0453	0492	0531	0569	0607	0645	0682	0719	0755
12	0792	0828	0864	0899	0934	0969	1004	1038	1072	1106
13	1139	1173	1206	1239	1271	1303	1335	1367	1399	1430
14	1461	1492	1523	1553	1584	1614	1644	1673	1703	1732
15	1761	1790	1818	1847	1875	1903	1931	1959	1987	2014
16	2041	2068	2095	2122	2148	2175	2201	2227	2253	2279
17	2304	2330	2355	2380	2405	2430	2455	2480	2504	2529
18	2553	2577	2601	2625	2648	2672	2695	2718	2742	2765
19	2788	2810	2833	2856	2878	2900	2923	2945	2967	2989
20	3010	3032	3054	3075	3096	3118	3139	3160	3181	3201
21	3222	3243	3263	3284	3304	3324	3345	3365	3385	3404
22	3424	3444	3464	3483	3502	3522	3541	3560	3579	3598
23	3617	3636	3655	3674	3692	3711	3729	3747	3766	3784
24	3802	3820	3838	3856	3874	3892	3909	3927	3945	3962
25	3979	3997	4014	4031	4048	4065	4082	4099	4116	4133
26	4150	4166	4183	4200	4216	4232	4249	4265	4281	4298
27	4314	4330	4346	4362	4378	4393	4409	4425	4440	4456
28	4472	4487	4502	4518	4533	4548	4564	4579	4594	4609
29	4624	4639	4654	4669	4683	4698	4713	4728	4742	4757
30	4771	4786	4800	4814	4829	4843	4857	4871	4886	4900
31	4914	4928	4942	4955	4969	4983	4997	5011	5024	5038
32	5051	5065	5079	5092	5105	5119	5132	5145	5159	5172
33	5185	5198	5211	5224	5237	5250	5263	5276	5289	5302
34	5315	5328	5340	5353	5366	5378	5391	5403	5416	5428
35	5441	5453	5465	5478	5490	5502	5514	5527	5539	5551
36	5563	5575	5587	5599	5611	5623	5635	5647	5658	5670
37	5682	5694	5705	5717	5729	5740	5752	5763	5775	5786
38	5798	5809	5821	5832	5843	5855	5866	5877	5888	5899
39	5911	5922	5933	5944	5955	5966	5977	5988	5999	6010
40	6021	6031	6042	6053	6064	6075	6085	6096	6107	6117
41	6128	6138	6149	6160	6170	6180	6191	6201	6212	6222
42	6232	6243	6253	6263	6274	6284	6294	6304	6314	6325
43	6335	6345	6355	6365	6375	6385	6395	6405	6415	6425
44	6435	6444	6454	6464	6474	6484	6493	6503	6513	6522
45	6532	6542	6551	6561	6571	6580	6590	6599	6609	6618
46	6628	6637	6646	6656	6665	6675	6684	6693	6702	6712
47	6721	6730	6739	6749	6758	6767	6776	6785	6794	6803
48	6812	6821	6830	6839	6848	6857	6866	6875	6884	6893
49	6902	6911	6920	6928	6937	6946	6955	6964	6972	6981
50	6990	6998	7007	7016	7024	7033	7042	7050	7059	7067
51	7076	7084	7093	7101	7110	7118	7126	7135	7143	7152
52	7160	7168	7177	7185	7193	7202	7210	7218	7226	7235
53	7243	7251	7259	7267	7275	7284	7292	7300	7308	7316
54	7324	7332	7340	7348	7356	7364	7372	7380	7388	7396

Logarithms (*continued*)

N	0	1	2	3	4	5	6	7	8	9
55	7404	7412	7419	7427	7435	7443	7451	7459	7466	7474
56	7482	7490	7497	7505	7513	7520	7528	7536	7543	7551
57	7559	7566	7574	7582	7589	7597	7604	7612	7619	7627
58	7634	7642	7649	7657	7664	7672	7679	7686	7694	7701
59	7709	7716	7723	7731	7738	7745	7752	7760	7767	7774
60	7782	7789	7796	7803	7810	7818	7825	7832	7839	7846
61	7853	7860	7868	7875	7882	7889	7896	7903	7910	7917
62	7924	7931	7938	7945	7952	7959	7966	7973	7980	7987
63	7993	8000	8007	8014	8021	8028	8035	8041	8048	8055
64	8062	8069	8075	8082	8089	8096	8102	8109	8116	8122
65	8129	8136	8142	8149	8156	8162	8169	8176	8182	8189
66	8195	8202	8209	8215	8222	8228	8235	8241	8248	8254
67	8261	8267	8274	8280	8287	8293	8299	8306	8312	8319
68	8325	8331	8338	8344	8351	8357	8363	8370	8376	8382
69	8388	8395	8401	8407	8414	8420	8426	8432	8439	8445
70	8451	8457	8463	8470	8476	8482	8488	8494	8500	8506
71	8513	8519	8525	8531	8537	8543	8549	8555	8561	8567
72	8573	8579	8585	8591	8597	8603	8609	8615	8621	8627
73	8633	8639	8645	8651	8657	8663	8669	8675	8681	8686
74	8692	8698	8704	8710	8716	8722	8727	8733	8739	8745
75	8751	8756	8762	8768	8774	8779	8785	8791	8797	8802
76	8808	8814	8820	8825	8831	8837	8842	8848	8854	8859
77	8865	8871	8876	8882	8887	8893	8899	8904	8910	8915
78	8921	8927	8932	8938	8943	8949	8954	8960	8965	8971
79	8976	8982	8987	8993	8998	9004	9009	9015	9020	9025
80	9031	9036	9042	9047	9053	9058	9063	9069	9074	9079
81	9085	9090	9096	9101	9106	9112	9117	9122	9128	9133
82	9138	9143	9149	9154	9159	9165	9170	9175	9180	9186
83	9191	9196	9201	9206	9212	9217	9222	9227	9232	9238
84	9243	9248	9253	9258	9263	9269	9274	9279	9284	9289
85	9294	9299	9304	9309	9315	9320	9325	9330	9335	9340
86	9345	9350	9355	9360	9365	9370	9375	9380	9385	9390
87	9395	9400	9405	9410	9415	9420	9425	9430	9435	9440
88	9445	9450	9455	9460	9465	9469	9474	9479	9484	9489
89	9494	9499	9504	9509	9513	9518	9523	9528	9533	9538
90	9542	9547	9552	9557	9562	9566	9571	9576	9581	9586
91	9590	9595	9600	9605	9609	9614	9619	9624	9628	9633
92	9638	9643	9647	9652	9657	9661	9666	9671	9675	9680
93	9685	9689	9694	9699	9703	9708	9713	9717	9722	9727
94	9731	9736	9741	9745	9750	9754	9759	9763	9768	9773
95	9777	9782	9786	9791	9795	9800	9805	9809	9814	9818
96	9823	9827	9832	9836	9841	9845	9850	9854	9859	9863
97	9868	9872	9877	9881	9886	9890	9894	9899	9903	9908
98	9912	9917	9921	9926	9930	9934	9939	9943	9948	9952
99	9956	9961	9965	9969	9974	9978	9983	9987	9991	9996

Appendix C

SQUARES AND SQUARE ROOTS

N	N²	√N	√10N	1/N
1	1	1.000 000	3.162 278	1.0000000
2	4	1.414 214	4.472 136	.5000000
3	9	1.732 051	5.477 226	.3333333
4	16	2.000 000	6.324 555	.2500000
5	25	2.236 068	7.071 068	.2000000
6	36	2.449 490	7.745 967	.1666667
7	49	2.645 751	8.366 600	.1428571
8	64	2.828 427	8.944 272	.1250000
9	81	3.000 000	9.486 833	.1111111
10	100	3.162 278	10.00000	.1000000
11	121	3.316 625	10.48809	.09090909
12	144	3.464 102	10.95445	.08333333
13	169	3.605 551	11.40175	.07692308
14	196	3.741 657	11.83216	.07142857
15	225	3.872 983	12.24745	.06666667
16	256	4.000 000	12.64911	.06250000
17	289	4.123 106	13.03840	.05882353
18	324	4.242 641	13.41641	.05555556
19	361	4.358 899	13.78405	.05263158
20	400	4.472 136	14.14214	.05000000
21	441	4.582 576	14.49138	.04761905
22	484	4.690 416	14.83240	.04545455
23	529	4.795 832	15.16575	.04347826
24	576	4.898 979	15.49193	.04166667
25	625	5.000 000	15.81139	.04000000
26	676	5.099 020	16.12452	.03846154
27	729	5.196 152	16.43168	.03703704
28	784	5.291 503	16.73320	.03571429
29	841	5.385 165	17.02939	.03448276
30	900	5.477 226	17.32051	.03333333
31	961	5.567 764	17.60682	.03225806
32	1 024	5.656 854	17.88854	.03125000
33	1 089	5.744 563	18.16590	.03030303
34	1 156	5.830 952	18.43909	.02941176
35	1 225	5.916 080	18.70829	.02857143
36	1 296	6.000 000	18.97367	.02777778
37	1 369	6.082 763	19.23538	.02702703
38	1 444	6.164 414	19.49359	.02631579
39	1 521	6.244 998	19.74842	.02564103
40	1 600	6.324 555	20.00000	.02500000
41	1 681	6.403 124	20.24846	.02439024
42	1 764	6.480 741	20.49390	.02380952
43	1 849	6.557 439	20.73644	.02325581
44	1 936	6.633 250	20.97618	.02272727
45	2 025	6.708 204	21.21320	.02222222
46	2 116	6.782 330	21.44761	.02173913
47	2 209	6.855 655	21.67948	.02127660
48	2 304	6.928 203	21.90890	.02083333
49	2 401	7.000 000	22.13594	.02040816
50	2 500	7.071 068	22.36068	.02000000

N	N²	√N	√10N	1/N .0
50	2 500	7.071 068	22.36068	2000000
51	2 601	7.141 428	22.58318	1960784
52	2 704	7.211 103	22.80351	1923077
53	2 809	7.280 110	23.02173	1886792
54	2 916	7.348 469	23.23790	1851852
55	3 025	7.416 198	23.45208	1818182
56	3 136	7.483 315	23.66432	1785714
57	3 249	7.549 834	23.87467	1754386
58	3 364	7.615 773	24.08319	1724138
59	3 481	7.681 146	24.28992	1694915
60	3 600	7.745 967	24.49490	1666667
61	3 721	7.810 250	24.69818	1639344
62	3 844	7.874 008	24.89980	1612903
63	3 969	7.937 254	25.09980	1587302
64	4 096	8.000 000	25.29822	1562500
65	4 225	8.062 258	25.49510	1538462
66	4 356	8.124 038	25.69047	1515152
67	4 489	8.185 353	25.88436	1492537
68	4 624	8.246 211	26.07681	1470588
69	4 761	8.306 624	26.26785	1449275
70	4 900	8.366 600	26.45751	1428571
71	5 041	8.426 150	26.64583	1408451
72	5 184	8.485 281	26.83282	1388889
73	5 329	8.544 004	27.01851	1369863
74	5 476	8.602 325	27.20294	1351351
75	5 625	8.660 254	27.38613	1333333
76	5 776	8.717 798	27.56810	1315789
77	5 929	8.774 964	27.74887	1298701
78	6 084	8.831 761	27.92848	1282051
79	6 241	8.888 194	28.10694	1265823
80	6 400	8.944 272	28.28427	1250000
81	6 561	9.000 000	28.46050	1234568
82	6 724	9.055 385	28.63564	1219512
83	6 889	9.110 434	28.80972	1204819
84	7 056	9.165 151	28.98275	1190476
85	7 225	9.219 544	29.15476	1176471
86	7 396	9.273 618	29.32576	1162791
87	7 569	9.327 379	29.49576	1149425
88	7 744	9.380 832	29.66479	1136364
89	7 921	9.433 981	29.83287	1123596
90	8 100	9.486 833	30.00000	1111111
91	8 281	9.539 392	30.16621	1098901
92	8 464	9.591 663	30.33150	1086957
93	8 649	9.643 651	30.49590	1075269
94	8 836	9.695 360	30.65942	1063830
95	9 025	9.746 794	30.82207	1052632
96	9 216	9.797 959	30.98387	1041667
97	9 409	9.848 858	31.14482	1030928
98	9 604	9.899 495	31.30495	1020408
99	9 801	9.949 874	31.46427	1010101
100	10 000	10.00000	31.62278	1000000

Squares and square roots (*continued*)

N	N²	$\sqrt{N}$	$\sqrt{10N}$	1/N .0	N	N²	$\sqrt{N}$	$\sqrt{10N}$	1/N .00
100	10 000	10.00000	31.62278	10000000	150	22 500	12.24745	38.72983	6666667
101	10 201	10.04988	31.78050	09900990	151	22 801	12.28821	38.85872	6622517
102	10 404	10.09950	31.93744	09803922	152	23 104	12.32883	38.98718	6578947
103	10 609	10.14889	32.09361	09708738	153	23 409	12.36932	39.11521	6535948
104	10 816	10.19804	32.24903	09615385	154	23 716	12.40967	39.24283	6493506
105	11 025	10.24695	32.40370	09523810	155	24 025	12.44990	39.37004	6451613
106	11 236	10.29563	32.55764	09433962	156	24 336	12.49000	39.49684	6410256
107	11 449	10.34408	32.71085	09345794	157	24 649	12.52996	39.62323	6369427
108	11 664	10.39230	32.86335	09259259	158	24 964	12.56981	39.74921	6329114
109	11 881	10.44031	33.01515	09174312	159	25 281	12.60952	39.87480	6289308
110	12 100	10.48809	33.16625	09090909	160	25 600	12.64911	40.00000	6250000
111	12 321	10.53565	33.31666	09009009	161	25 921	12.68858	40.12481	6211180
112	12 544	10.58301	33.46640	08928571	162	26 244	12.72792	40.24922	6172840
113	12 769	10.63015	33.61547	08849558	163	26 569	12.76715	40.37326	6134969
114	12 996	10.67708	33.76389	08771930	164	26 896	12.80625	40.49691	6097561
115	13 225	10.72381	33.91165	08695652	165	27 225	12.84523	40.62019	6060606
116	13 456	10.77033	34.05877	08620690	166	27 556	12.88410	40.74310	6024096
117	13 689	10.81665	34.20526	08547009	167	27 889	12.92285	40.86563	5988024
118	13 924	10.86278	34.35113	08474576	168	28 224	12.96148	40.98780	5952381
119	14 161	10.90871	34.49638	08403361	169	28 561	13.00000	41.10961	5917160
120	14 400	10.95445	34.64102	08333333	170	28 900	13.03840	41.23106	5882353
121	14 641	11.00000	34.78505	08264463	171	29 241	13.07670	41.35215	5847953
122	14 884	11.04536	34.92850	08196721	172	29 584	13.11488	41.47288	5813953
123	15 129	11.09054	35.07136	08130081	173	29 929	13.15295	41.59327	5780347
124	15 376	11.13553	35.21363	08064516	174	30 276	13.19091	41.71331	5747126
125	15 625	11.18034	35.35534	08000000	175	30 625	13.22876	41.83300	5714286
126	15 876	11.22497	35.49648	07936508	176	30 976	13.26650	41.95235	5681818
127	16 129	11.26943	35.63706	07874016	177	31 329	13.30413	42.07137	5649718
128	16 384	11.31371	35.77709	07812500	178	31 684	13.34166	42.19005	5617978
129	16 641	11.35782	35.91657	07751938	179	32 041	13.37909	42.30839	5586592
130	16 900	11.40175	36.05551	07692308	180	32 400	13.41641	42.42641	5555556
131	17 161	11.44552	36.19392	07633588	181	32 761	13.45362	42.54409	5524862
132	17 424	11.48913	36.33180	07575758	182	33 124	13.49074	42.66146	5494505
133	17 689	11.53256	36.46917	07518797	183	33 489	13.52775	42.77850	5464481
134	17 956	11.57584	36.60601	07462687	184	33 856	13.56466	42.89522	5434783
135	18 225	11.61895	36.74235	07407407	185	34 225	13.60147	43.01163	5405405
136	18 496	11.66190	36.87818	07352941	186	34 596	13.63818	43.12772	5376344
137	18 769	11.70470	37.01351	07299270	187	34 969	13.67479	43.24350	5347594
138	19 044	11.74734	37.14835	07246377	188	35 344	13.71131	43.35897	5319149
139	19 321	11.78983	37.28270	07194245	189	35 721	13.74773	43.47413	5291005
140	19 600	11.83216	37.41657	07142857	190	36 100	13.78405	43.58899	5263158
141	19 881	11.87434	37.54997	07092199	191	36 481	13.82027	43.70355	5235602
142	20 164	11.91638	37.68289	07042254	192	36 864	13.85641	43.81780	5208333
143	20 449	11.95826	37.81534	06993007	193	37 249	13.89244	43.93177	5181347
144	20 736	12.00000	37.94733	06944444	194	37 636	13.92839	44.04543	5154639
145	21 025	12.04159	38.07887	06896552	195	38 025	13.96424	44.15880	5128205
146	21 316	12.08305	38.20995	06849315	196	38 416	14.00000	44.27189	5102041
147	21 609	12.12436	38.34058	06802721	197	38 809	14.03567	44.38468	5076142
148	21 904	12.16553	38.47077	06756757	198	39 204	14.07125	44.49719	5050505
149	22 201	12.20656	38.60052	06711409	199	39 601	14.10674	44.60942	5025126
150	22 500	12.24745	38.72983	06666667	200	40 000	14.14214	44.72136	5000000

Squares and square roots (*continued*)

N	N²	√N	√10N	1/N .00	N	N²	√N	√10N	1/N .00
200	40 000	14.14214	44.72136	5000000	250	62 500	15.81139	50.00000	4000000
201	40 401	14.17745	44.83302	4975124	251	63 001	15.84298	50.09990	3984064
202	40 804	14.21267	44.94441	4950495	252	63 504	15.87451	50.19960	3968254
203	41 209	14.24781	45.05552	4926108	253	64 009	15.90597	50.29911	3952569
204	41 616	14.28286	45.16636	4901961	254	64 516	15.93738	50.39841	3937008
205	42 025	14.31782	45.27693	4878049	255	65 025	15.96872	50.49752	3921569
206	42 436	14.35270	45.38722	4854369	256	65 536	16.00000	50.59644	3906250
207	42 849	14.38749	45.49725	4830918	257	66 049	16.03122	50.69517	3891051
208	43 264	14.42221	45.60702	4807692	258	66 564	16.06238	50.79370	3875969
209	43 681	14.45683	45.71652	4784689	259	67 081	16.09348	50.89204	3861004
210	44 100	14.49138	45.82576	4761905	260	67 600	16.12452	50.99020	3846154
211	44 521	14.52584	45.93474	4739336	261	68 121	16.15549	51.08816	3831418
212	44 944	14.56022	46.04346	4716981	262	68 644	16.18641	51.18594	3816794
213	45 369	14.59452	46.15192	4694836	263	69 169	16.21727	51.28353	3802281
214	45 796	14.62874	46.26013	4672897	264	69 696	16.24808	51.38093	3787879
215	46 225	14.66288	46.36809	4651163	265	70 225	16.27882	51.47815	3773585
216	46 656	14.69694	46.47580	4629630	266	70 756	16.30951	51.57519	3759398
217	47 089	14.73092	46.58326	4608295	267	71 289	16.34013	51.67204	3745318
218	47 524	14.76482	46.69047	4587156	268	71 824	16.37071	51.76872	3731343
219	47 961	14.79865	46.79744	4566210	269	72 361	16.40122	51.86521	3717472
220	48 400	14.83240	46.90416	4545455	270	72 900	16.43168	51.96152	3703704
221	48 841	14.86607	47.01064	4524887	271	73 441	16.46208	52.05766	3690037
222	49 284	14.89966	47.11688	4504505	272	73 984	16.49242	52.15362	3676471
223	49 729	14.93318	47.22288	4484305	273	74 529	16.52271	52.24940	3663004
224	50 176	14.96663	47.32864	4464286	274	75 076	16.55295	52.34501	3649635
225	50 625	15.00000	47.43416	4444444	275	75 625	16.58312	52.44044	3636364
226	51 076	15.03330	47.53946	4424779	276	76 176	16.61325	52.53570	3623188
227	51 529	15.06652	47.64452	4405286	277	76 729	16.64332	52.63079	3610108
228	51 984	15.09967	47.74935	4385965	278	77 284	16.67333	52.72571	3597122
229	52 441	15.13275	47.85394	4366812	279	77 841	16.70329	52.82045	3584229
230	52 900	15.16575	47.95832	4347826	280	78 400	16.73320	52.91503	3571429
231	53 361	15.19868	48.06246	4329004	281	78 961	16.76305	53.00943	3558719
232	53 824	15.23155	48.16638	4310345	282	79 524	16.79286	53.10367	3546099
233	54 289	15.26434	48.27007	4291845	283	80 089	16.82260	53.19774	3533569
234	54 756	15.29706	48.37355	4273504	284	80 656	16.85230	53.29165	3521127
235	55 225	15.32971	48.47680	4255319	285	81 225	16.88194	53.38539	3508772
236	55 696	15.36229	48.57983	4237288	286	81 796	16.91153	53.47897	3496503
237	56 169	15.39480	48.68265	4219409	287	82 369	16.94107	53.57238	3484321
238	56 644	15.42725	48.78524	4201681	288	82 944	16.97056	53.66563	3472222
239	57 121	15.45962	48.88763	4184100	289	83 521	17.00000	53.75872	3460208
240	57 600	15.49193	48.98979	4166667	290	84 100	17.02939	53.85165	3448276
241	58 081	15.52417	49.09175	4149378	291	84 681	17.05872	53.94442	3436426
242	58 564	15.55635	49.19350	4132231	292	85 264	17.08801	54.03702	3424658
243	59 049	15.58846	49.29503	4115226	293	85 849	17.11724	54.12947	3412969
244	59 536	15.62050	49.39636	4098361	294	86 436	17.14643	54.22177	3401361
245	60 025	15.65248	49.49747	4081633	295	87 025	17.17556	54.31390	3389831
246	60 516	15.68439	49.59839	4065041	296	87 616	17.20465	54.40588	3378378
247	61 009	15.71623	49.69909	4048583	297	88 209	17.23369	54.49771	3367003
248	61 504	15.74802	49.79960	4032258	298	88 804	17.26268	54.58938	3355705
249	62 001	15.77973	49.89990	4016064	299	89 401	17.29162	54.68089	3344482
250	62 500	15.81139	50.00000	4000000	300	90 000	17.32051	54.77226	3333333

Squares and square roots (*continued*)

N	N²	√N	√10N	1/N .00	N	N²	√N	√10N	1/N .00
300	90 000	17.32051	54.77226	3333333	350	122 500	18.70829	59.16080	2857143
301	90 601	17.34935	54.86347	3322259	351	123 201	18.73499	59.24525	2849003
302	91 204	17.37815	54.95453	3311258	352	123 904	18.76166	59.32959	2840909
303	91 809	17.40690	55.04544	3300330	353	124 609	18.78829	59.41380	2832861
304	92 416	17.43560	55.13620	3289474	354	125 316	18.81489	59.49790	2824859
305	93 025	17.46425	55.22681	3278689	355	126 025	18.84144	59.58188	2816901
306	93 636	17.49286	55.31727	3267974	356	126 736	18.86796	59.66574	2808989
307	94 249	17.52142	55.40758	3257329	357	127 449	18.89444	59.74948	2801120
308	94 864	17.54993	55.49775	3246753	358	128 164	18.92089	59.83310	2793296
309	95 481	17.57840	55.58777	3236246	359	128 881	18.94730	59.91661	2785515
310	96 100	17.60682	55.67764	3225806	360	129 600	18.97367	60.00000	2777778
311	96 721	17.63519	55.76737	3215434	361	130 321	19.00000	60.08328	2770083
312	97 344	17.66352	55.85696	3205128	362	131 044	19.02630	60.16644	2762431
313	97 969	17.69181	55.94640	3194888·	363	131 769	19.05256	60.24948	2754821
314	98 596	17.72005	56.03570	3184713	364	132 496	19.07878	60.33241	2747253
315	99 225	17.74824	56.12486	3174603	365	133 225	19.10497	60.41523	2739726
316	99 856	17.77639	56.21388	3164557	366	133 956	19.13113	60.49793	2732240
317	100 489	17.80449	56.30275	3154574	367	134 689	19.15724	60.58052	2724796
318	101 124	17.83255	56.39149	3144654	368	135 424	19.18333	60.66300	2717391
319	101 761	17.86057	56.48008	3134796	369	136 161	19.20937	60.74537	2710027
320	102 400	17.88854	56.56854	3125000	370	136 900	19.23538	60.82763	2702703
321	103 041	17.91647	56.65686	3115265	371	137 641	19.26136	60.90977	2695418
322	103 684	17.94436	56.74504	3105590	372	138 384	19.28730	60.99180	2688172
323	104 329	17.97220	56.83309	3095975	373	139 129	19.31321	61.07373	2680965
324	104 976	18.00000	56.92100	3086420	374	139 876	19.33908	61.15554	2673797
325	105 625	18.02776	57.00877	3076923	375	140 625	19.36492	61.23724	2666667
326	106 276	18.05547	57.09641	3067485	376	141 376	19.39072	61.31884	2659574
327	106 929	18.08314	57.18391	3058104	377	142 129	19.41649	61.40033	2652520
328	107 584	18.11077	57.27128	3048780	378	142 884	19.44222	61.48170	2645503
329	108 241	18.13836	57.35852	3039514	379	143 641	19.46792	61.56298	2638522
330	108 900	18.16590	57.44563	3030303	380	144 400	19.49359	61.64414	2631579
331	109 561	18.19341	57.53260	3021148	381	145 161	19.51922	61.72520	2624672
332	110 224	18 22087	57.61944	3012048	382	145 924	19.54483	61.80615	2617801
333	110 889	18.24829	57.70615	3003003	383	146 689	19.57039	61.88699	2610966
334	111 556	18.27567	57.79273	2994012	384	147 456	19.59592	61.96773	2604167
335	112 225	18.30301	57.87918	2985075	385	148 225	19.62142	62.04837	2597403
336	112 896	18.33030	57.96551	2976190	386	148 996	19.64688	62.12890	2590674
337	113 569	18.35756	58.05170	2967359	387	149 769	19.67232	62.20932	2583979
338	114 244	18.38478	58.13777	2958580	388	150 544	19.69772	62.28965	2577320
339	114 921	18.41195	58.22371	2949853	389	151 321	19.72308	62.36986	2570694
340	115 600	18.43909	58.30952	2941176	390	152 100	19.74842	62.44998	2564103
341	116 281	18.46619	58.39521	2932551	391	152 881	19.77372	62.52999	2557545
342	116 964	18.49324	58.48077	2923977	392	153 664	19.79899	62.60990	2551020
343	117 649	18.52026	58.56620	2915452	393	154 449	19.82423	62.68971	2544529
344	118 336	18.54724	58.65151	2906977	394	155 236	19.84943	62.76942	2538071
345	119 025	18.57418	58.73670	2898551	395	156 025	19.87461	62.84903	2531646
346	119 716	18.60108	58.82176	2890173	396	156 816	19.89975	62.92853	2525253
347	120 409	18.62794	58.90671	2881844	397	157 609	19.92486	63.00794	2518892
348	121 104	18.65476	58.99152	2873563	398	158 404	19.94994	63.08724	2512563
349	121 801	18.68154	59.07622	2865330	399	159 201	19.97498	63.16645	2506266
350	122 500	18.70829	59.16080	2857143	400	160 000	20.00000	63.24555	2500000

Squares and square roots (continued)

N	N²	√N	√10N	1/N .00	N	N²	√N	√10N	1/N .00
400	160 000	20.00000	63.24555	2500000	450	202 500	21.21320	67.08204	2222222
401	160 801	20.02498	63.32456	2493766	451	203 401	21.23676	67.15653	2217295
402	161 604	20.04994	63.40347	2487562	452	204 304	21.26029	67.23095	2212389
403	162 409	20.07486	63.48228	2481390	453	205 209	21.28380	67.30527	2207506
404	163 216	20.09975	63.56099	2475248	454	206 116	21.30728	67.37952	2202643
405	164 025	20.12461	63.63961	2469136	455	207 025	21.33073	67.45369	2197802
406	164 836	20.14944	63.71813	2463054	456	207 936	21.35416	67.52777	2192982
407	165 649	20.17424	63.79655	2457002	457	208 849	21.37756	67.60178	2188184
408	166 464	20.19901	63.87488	2450980	458	209 764	21.40093	67.67570	2183406
409	167 281	20.22375	63.95311	2444988	459	210 681	21.42429	67.74954	2178649
410	168 100	20.24846	64.03124	2439024	460	211 600	21.44761	67.82330	2173913
411	168 921	20.27313	64.10928	2433090	461	212 521	21.47091	67.89698	2169197
412	169 744	20.29778	64.18723	2427184	462	213 444	21.49419	67.97058	2164502
413	170 569	20.32240	64.26508	2421308	463	214 369	21.51743	68.04410	2159827
414	171 396	20.34699	64.34283	2415459	464	215 296	21.54066	68.11755	2155172
415	172 225	20.37155	64.42049	2409639	465	216 225	21.56386	68.19091	2150538
416	173 056	20.39608	64.49806	2403846	466	217 156	21.58703	68.26419	2145923
417	173 889	20.42058	64.57554	2398082	467	218 089	21.61018	68.33740	2141328
418	174 724	20.44505	64.65292	2392344	468	219 024	21.63331	68.41053	2136752
419	175 561	20.46949	64.73021	2386635	469	219 961	21.65641	68.48357	2132196
420	176 400	20.49390	64.80741	2380952	470	220 900	21.67948	68.55655	2127660
421	177 241	20.51828	64.88451	2375297	471	221 841	21.70253	68.62944	2123142
422	178 084	20.54264	64.96153	2369668	472	222 784	21.72556	68.70226	2118644
423	178 929	20.56696	65.03845	2364066	473	223 729	21.74856	68.77500	2114165
424	179 776	20.59126	65.11528	2358491	474	224 676	21.77154	68.84766	2109705
425	180 625	20.61553	65.19202	2352941	475	225 625	21.79449	68.92024	2105263
426	181 476	20.63977	65.26868	2347418	476	226 576	21.81742	68.99275	2100840
427	182 329	20.66398	65.34524	2341920	477	227 529	21.84033	69.06519	2096436
428	183 184	20.68816	65.42171	2336449	478	228 484	21.86321	69.13754	2092050
429	184 041	20.71232	65.49809	2331002	479	229 441	21.88607	69.20983	2087683
430	184 900	20.73644	65.57439	2325581	480	230 400	21.90890	69.28203	2083333
431	185 761	20.76054	65.65059	2320186	481	231 361	21.93171	69.35416	2079002
432	186 624	20.78461	65.72671	7314815	482	232 324	21.95450	69.42622	2074689
433	187 489	20.80865	65.80274	2309469	483	233 289	21.97726	69.49820	2070393
434	188 356	20.83267	65.87868	2304147	484	234 256	22.00000	69.57011	2066116
435	189 225	20.85665	65.95453	2298851	485	235 225	22.02272	69.64194	2061856
436	190 096	20.88061	66.03030	2293578	486	236 196	22.04541	69.71370	2057613
437	190 969	20.90454	66.10598	2288330	487	237 169	22.06808	69.78539	2053388
438	191 844	20.92845	66.18157	2283105	488	238 144	22.09072	69.85700	2049180
439	192 721	20.95233	66.25708	2277904	489	239 121	22.11334	69.92853	2044990
440	193 600	20.97618	66.33250	2272727	490	240 100	22.13594	70.00000	2040816
441	194 481	21.00000	66.40783	2267574	491	241 081	22.15852	70.07139	2036660
442	195 364	21.02380	66.48308	2262443	492	242 064	22.18107	70.14271	2032520
443	196 249	21.04757	66.55825	2257336	493	243 049	22.20360	70.21396	2028398
444	197 136	21.07131	66.63332	2252252	494	244 036	22.22611	70.28513	2024291
445	198 025	21.09502	66.70832	2247191	495	245 025	22.24860	70.35624	2020202
446	198 916	21.11871	66.78323	2242152	496	246 016	22.27106	70.42727	2016129
447	199 809	21.14237	66.85806	2237136	497	247 009	22.29350	70.49823	2012072
448	200 704	21.16601	66.93280	2232143	498	248 004	22.31591	70.56912	2008032
449	201 601	21.18962	67.00746	2227171	499	249 001	22.33831	70.63993	2004008
450	202 500	21.21320	67.08204	2222222	500	250 000	22.36068	70.71068	2000000

Squares and square roots (continued)

N	N²	√N	√10N	1/N .00	N	N²	√N	√10N	1/N .00
500	250 000	22.36068	70.71068	2000000	550	302 500	23.45208	74.16198	1818182
501	251 001	22.38303	70.78135	1996008	551	303 601	23.47339	74.22937	1814882
502	252 004	22.40536	70.85196	1992032	552	304 704	23.49468	74.29670	1811594
503	253 009	22.42766	70.92249	1988072	553	305 809	23.51595	74.36397	1808318
504	254 016	22.44994	70.99296	1984127	554	306 916	23.53720	74.43118	1805054
505	255 025	22.47221	71.06335	1980198	555	308 025	23.55844	74.49832	1801802
506	256 036	22.49444	71.13368	1976285	556	309 136	23.57965	74.56541	1798561
507	257 049	22.51666	71.20393	1972387	557	310 249	23.60085	74.63243	1795332
508	258 064	22.53886	71.27412	1968504	558	311 364	23.62202	74.69940	1792115
509	259 081	22.56103	71.34424	1964637	559	312 481	23.64318	74.76630	1788909
510	260 100	22.58318	71.41428	1960784	560	313 600	23.66432	74.83315	1785714
511	261 121	22.60531	71.48426	1956947	561	314 721	23.68544	74.89993	1782531
512	262 144	22.62742	71.55418	1953125	562	315 844	23.70654	74.96666	1779359
513	263 169	22.64950	71.62402	1949318	563	316 969	23.72762	75.03333	1776199
514	264 196	22.67157	71.69379	1945525	564	318 096	23.74868	75.09993	1773050
515	265 225	22.69361	71.76350	1941748	565	319 225	23.76973	75.16648	1769912
516	266 256	22.71563	71.83314	1937984	566	320 356	23.79075	75.23297	1766784
517	267 289	22.73763	71.90271	1934236	567	321 489	23.81176	75.29940	1763668
518	268 324	22.75961	71.97222	1930502	568	322 624	23.83275	75.36577	1760563
519	269 361	22.78157	72.04165	1926782	569	323 761	23.85372	75.43209	1757469
520	270 400	22.80351	72.11103	1923077	570	324 900	23.87467	75.49834	1754386
521	271 441	22.82542	72.18033	1919386	571	326 041	23.89561	75.56454	1751313
522	272 484	22.84732	72.24957	1915709	572	327 184	23.91652	75.63068	1748252
523	273 529	22.86919	72.31874	1912046	573	328 329	23.93742	75.69676	1745201
524	274 576	22.89105	72.38784	1908397	574	329 476	23.95830	75.76279	1742160
525	275 625	22.91288	72.45688	1904762	575	330 625	23.97916	75.82875	1739130
526	276 676	22.93469	72.52586	1901141	576	331 776	24.00000	75.89466	1736111
527	277 729	22.95648	72.59477	1897533	577	332 929	24.02082	75.96052	1733102
528	278 784	22.97825	72.66361	1893939	578	334 084	24.04163	76.02631	1730104
529	279 841	23.00000	72.73239	1890359	579	335 241	24.06242	76.09205	1727116
530	280 900	23.02173	72.80110	1886792	580	336 400	24.08319	76.15773	1724138
531	281 961	23.04344	72.86975	1883239	581	337 561	24.10394	76.22336	1721170
532	283 024	23.06513	72.93833	1879699	582	338 724	24.12468	76.28892	1718213
533	284 089	23.08679	73.00685	1876173	583	339 889	24.14539	76.35444	1715266
534	285 156	23.10844	73.07530	1872659	584	341 056	24.16609	76.41989	1712329
535	286 225	23.13007	73.14369	1869159	585	342 225	24.18677	76.48529	1709402
536	287 296	23.15167	73.21202	1865672	586	343 396	24.20744	76.55064	1706485
537	288 369	23.17326	73.28028	1862197	587	344 569	24.22808	76.61593	1703578
538	289 444	23.19483	73.34848	1858736	588	345 744	24.24871	76.68116	1700680
539	290 521	23.21637	73.41662	1855288	589	346 921	24.26932	76.74634	1697793
540	291 600	23.23790	73.48469	1851852	590	348 100	24.28992	76.81146	1694915
541	292 681	23.25941	73.55270	1848429	591	349 281	24.31049	76.87652	1692047
542	293 764	23.28089	73.62065	1845018	592	350 464	24.33105	76.94154	1689189
543	294 849	23.30236	73.68853	1841621	593	351 649	24.35159	77.00649	1686341
544	295 936	23.32381	73.75636	1838235	594	352 836	24.37212	77.07140	1683502
545	297 025	23.34524	73.82412	1834862	595	354 025	24.39262	77.13624	1680672
546	298 116	23.36664	73.89181	1831502	596	355 216	24.41311	77.20104	1677852
547	299 209	23.38803	73.95945	1828154	597	356 409	24.43358	77.26578	1675042
548	300 304	23.40940	74.02702	1824818	598	357 604	24.45404	77.33046	1672241
549	301 401	23.43075	74.09453	1821494	599	358 801	24.47448	77.39509	1669449
550	302 500	23.45208	74.16198	1818182	600	360 000	24.49490	77.45967	1666667

Squares and square roots (*continued*)

N	N²	√N	√10N	1/N .00	N	N²	√N	√10N	1/N .00
600	360 000	24.49490	77.45967	1666667	650	422 500	25.49510	80.62258	1538462
601	361 201	24.51530	77.52419	1663894	651	423 801	25.51470	80.68457	1536098
602	362 404	24.53569	77.58866	1661130	652	425 104	25.53429	80.74652	1533742
603	363 609	24.55606	77.65307	1658375	653	426 409	25.55386	80.80842	1531394
604	364 816	24.57641	77.71744	1655629	654	427 716	25.57342	80.87027	1529052
605	366 025	24.59675	77.78175	1652893	655	429 025	25.59297	80.93207	1526718
606	367 236	24.61707	77.84600	1650165	656	430 336	25.61250	80.99383	1524390
607	368 449	24.63737	77.91020	1647446	657	431 649	25.63201	81.05554	1522070
608	369 664	24.65766	77.97435	1644737	658	432 964	25.65151	81.11720	1519757
609	370 881	24.67793	78.03845	1642036	659	434 281	25.67100	81.17881	1517451
610	372 100	24.69818	78.10250	1639344	660	435 600	25.69047	81.24038	1515152
611	373 321	24.71841	78.16649	1636661	661	436 921	25.70992	81.30191	1512859
612	374 544	24.73863	78.23043	1633987	662	438 244	25.72936	81.36338	1510574
613	375 769	24.75884	78.29432	1631321	663	439 569	25.74879	81.42481	1508296
614	376 996	24.77902	78.35815	1628664	664	440 896	25.76820	81.48620	1506024
615	378 225	24.79919	78.42194	1626016	665	442 225	25.78759	81.54753	1503759
616	379 456	24.81935	78.48567	1623377	666	443 556	25.80698	81.60882	1501502
617	380 689	24.83948	78.54935	1620746	667	444 889	25.82634	81.67007	1499250
618	381 924	24.85961	78.61298	1618123	668	446 224	25.84570	81.73127	1497006
619	383 161	24.87971	78.67655	1615509	669	447 561	25.86503	81.79242	1494768
620	384 400	24.89980	78.74008	1612903	670	448 900	25.88436	81.85353	1492537
621	385 641	24.91987	78.80355	1610306	671	450 241	25.90367	81.91459	1490313
622	386 884	24.93993	78.86698	1607717	672	451 584	25.92296	81.97561	1488095
623	388 129	24.95997	78.93035	1605136	673	452 929	25.94224	82.03658	1485884
624	389 376	24.97999	78.99367	1602564	674	454 276	25.96151	82.09750	1483680
625	390 625	25.00000	79.05694	1600000	675	455 625	25.98076	82.15838	1481481
626	391 876	25.01999	79.12016	1597444	676	456 976	26.00000	82.21922	1479290
627	393 129	25.03997	79.18333	1594896	677	458 329	26.01922	82.28001	1477105
628	394 384	25.05993	79.24645	1592357	678	459 684	26.03843	82.34076	1474926
629	395 641	25.07987	79.30952	1589825	679	461 041	26.05763	82.40146	1472754
630	396 900	25.09980	79.37254	1587302	680	462 400	26.07681	82.46211	1470588
631	398 161	25.11971	79.43551	1584786	681	463 761	26.09598	82.42272	1468429
632	399 424	25.13961	79.49843	1582278	682	465 124	26.11513	82.58329	1466276
633	400 689	25.15949	79.56130	1579779	683	466 489	26.13427	82.64381	1464129
634	401 956	25.17936	79.62412	1577287	684	467 856	26.15339	82.70429	1461988
635	403 225	25.19921	79.68689	1574803	685	469 225	26.17250	82.76473	1459854
636	404 496	25.21904	79.74961	1572327	686	470 596	26.19160	82.82512	1457726
637	405 769	25.23886	79.81228	1569859	687	471 969	26.21068	82.88546	1455604
638	407 044	25.25866	79.87490	1567398	688	473 344	26.22975	82.94577	1453488
639	408 321	25.27845	79.93748	1564945	689	474 721	26.24881	83.00602	1451379
640	409 600	25.29822	80.00000	1562500	690	476 100	26.26785	83.06624	1449275
641	410 881	25.31798	80.06248	1560062	691	477 481	26.28688	83.12641	1447178
642	412 164	25.33772	80.12490	1557632	692	478 864	26.30589	83.18654	1445087
643	413 449	25.35744	80.18728	1555210	693	480 249	26.32489	83.24662	1443001
644	414 736	25.37716	80.24961	1552795	694	481 636	26.34388	83.30666	1440922
645	416 025	25.39685	80.31189	1550388	695	483 025	26.36285	83.36666	1438849
646	417 316	25.41653	80.37413	1547988	696	484 416	26.38181	83.42661	1436782
647	418 609	25.43619	80.43631	1545595	697	485 809	26.40076	83.48653	1434720
648	419 904	25.45584	80.49845	1543210	698	487 204	26.41969	83.54639	1432665
649	421 201	25.47548	80.56054	1540832	699	488 601	26.43861	83.60622	1430615
650	422 500	25.49510	80.62258	1538462	700	490 000	26.45751	83.66600	1428571

Squares and square roots (*continued*)

N	N²	√N	√10N	1/N .00	N	N²	√N	√10N	1/N .00
700	490 000	26.45751	83.66600	1428571	750	562 500	27.38613	86.60254	1333333
701	491 401	26.47640	83.72574	1426534	751	564 001	27.40438	86.66026	1331558
702	492 804	26.49528	83.78544	1424501	752	565 504	27.42262	86.71793	1329787
703	494 209	26.51415	83.84510	1422475	753	567 009	27.44085	86.77557	1328021
704	495 616	26.53300	83.90471	1420455	754	568 516	27.45906	86.83317	1326260
705	497 025	26.55184	83.96428	1418440	755	570 025	27.47726	86.89074	1324503
706	498 436	26.57066	84.02381	1416431	756	571 536	27.49545	86.94826	1322751
707	499 849	26.58947	84.08329	1414427	757	573 049	27.51363	87.00575	1321004
708	501 264	26.60827	84.14274	1412429	758	574 564	27.53180	87.06320	1319261
709	502 681	26.62705	84.20214	1410437	759	576 081	27.54995	87.12061	1317523
710	504 100	26.64583	84.26150	1408451	760	577 600	27.56810	87.17798	1315789
711	505 521	26.66458	84.32082	1406470	761	579 121	27.58623	87.23531	1314060
712	506 944	26.68333	84.38009	1404494	762	580 644	27.60435	87.29261	1312336
713	508 369	26.70206	84.43933	1402525	763	582 169	27.62245	87.34987	1310616
714	509 796	26.72078	84.49852	1400560	764	583 696	27.64055	87.40709	1308901
715	511 225	26.73948	84.55767	1398601	765	585 225	27.65863	87.46428	1307190
716	512 656	26.75818	84.61678	1396648	766	586 756	27.67671	87.52143	1305483
717	514 089	26.77686	84.67585	1394700	767	588 289	27.69476	87.57854	1303781
718	515 524	26.79552	84.73488	1392758	768	589 824	27.71281	87.63561	1302083
719	516 961	26.81418	84.79387	1390821	769	591 361	27.73085	87.69265	1300390
720	518 400	26.83282	84.85281	1388889	770	592 900	27.74887	87.74964	1298701
721	519 841	26.85144	84.91172	1386963	771	594 441	27.76689	87.80661	1297017
722	521 284	26.87006	84.97058	1385042	772	595 984	27.78489	87.86353	1295337
723	522 729	26.88866	85.02941	1383126	773	597 529	27.80288	87.92042	1293661
724	524 176	26.90725	85.08819	1381215	774	599 076	27.82086	87.97727	1291990
725	525 625	26.92582	85.14693	1379310	775	600 625	27.83882	88.03408	1290323
726	527 076	26.94439	85.20563	1377410	776	602 176	27.85678	88.09086	1288660
727	528 529	26.96294	85.26429	1375516	777	603 729	27.87472	88.14760	1287001
728	529 984	26.98148	85.32292	1373626	778	605 284	27.89265	88.20431	1285347
729	531 441	27.00000	85.38150	1371742	779	606 841	27.91057	88.26098	1283697
730	532 900	27.01851	85.44004	1369863	780	608 400	27.92848	88.31761	1282051
731	534 361	27.03701	85.49854	1367989	781	609 961	27.94638	88.37420	1280410
732	535 824	27.05550	85.55700	1366120	782	611 524	27.96426	88.43076	1278772
733	537 289	27.07397	85.61542	1364256	783	613 089	27.98214	88.48729	1277139
734	538 756	27.09243	85.67380	1362398	784	614 656	28.00000	88.54377	1275510
735	540 225	27.11088	85.73214	1360544	785	616 225	28.01785	88.60023	1273885
736	541 696	27.12932	85.79044	1358696	786	617 796	28.03569	88.65664	1272265
737	543 169	27.14774	85.84870	1356852	787	619 369	28.05352	88.71302	1270648
738	544 644	27.16616	85.90693	1355014	788	620 944	28.07134	88.76936	1269036
739	546 121	27.18455	85.96511	1353180	789	622 521	28.08914	88.82567	1267427
740	547 600	27.20294	86.02325	1351351	790	624 100	28.10694	88.88194	1265823
741	549 081	27.22132	86.08136	1349528	791	625 681	28.12472	88.93818	1264223
742	550 564	27.23968	86.13942	1347709	792	627 264	28.14249	88.99438	1262626
743	552 049	27.25803	86.19745	1345895	793	628 849	28.16026	89.05055	1261034
744	553 536	27.27636	86.25543	1344086	794	630 436	28.17801	89.10668	1259446
745	555 025	27.29469	86.31338	1342282	795	632 025	28.19574	89.16277	1257862
746	556 516	27.31300	86.37129	1340483	796	633 616	28.21347	89.21883	1256281
747	558 009	27.33130	86.42916	1338688	797	635 209	28.23119	89.27486	1254705
748	559 504	27.34959	86.48699	1336898	798	636 804	28.24889	89.33085	1253133
749	561 001	27.36786	86.54479	1335113	799	638 401	28.26659	89.38680	1251564
750	562 500	27.38613	86.60254	1333333	800	640 000	28.28427	89.44272	1250000

Squares and square roots (*continued*)

N	N²	√N	√10N	1/N .00	N	N²	√N	√10N	1/N .00
800	640 000	28.28427	89.44272	1250000	850	722 500	29.15476	92.19544	1176471
801	641 601	28.30194	89.49860	1248439	851	724 201	29.17190	92.24966	1175088
802	643 204	28.31960	89.55445	1246883	852	725 904	29.18904	92.30385	1173709
803	644 809	28.33725	89.61027	1245330	853	727 609	29.20616	92.35800	1172333
804	646 416	28.35489	89.66605	1243781	854	729 316	29.22328	92.41212	1170960
805	648 025	28.37252	89.72179	1242236	855	731 025	29.24038	92.46621	1169591
806	649 636	28.39014	89.77750	1240695	856	732 736	29.25748	92.52027	1168224
807	651 249	28.40775	89.83318	1239157	857	734 449	29.27456	92.57429	1166861
808	652 864	28.42534	89.88882	1237624	858	736 164	29.29164	92.62829	1165501
809	654 481	28.44293	89.94443	1236094	859	737 881	29.30870	92.68225	1164144
810	656 100	28.46050	90.00000	1234568	860	739 600	29.32576	92.73618	1162791
811	657 721	28.47806	90.05554	1233046	861	741 321	29.34280	92.79009	1161440
812	659 344	28.49561	90.11104	1231527	862	743 044	29.35984	92.84396	1160093
813	660 969	28.51315	90.16651	1230012	863	744 769	29.37686	92.89779	1158749
814	662 596	28.53069	90.22195	1228501	864	746 496	29.39388	92.95160	1157407
815	664 225	28.54820	90.27735	1226994	865	748 225	29.41088	93.00538	1156069
816	665 856	28.56571	90.33272	1225490	866	749 956	29.42788	93.05912	1154734
817	667 489	28.58321	90.38805	1223990	867	751 689	29.44486	93.11283	1153403
818	669 124	28.60070	90.44335	1222494	868	753 424	29.46184	93.16652	1152074
819	670 761	28.61818	90.49862	1221001	869	755 161	29.47881	93.22017	1150748
820	672 400	28.63564	90.55385	1219512	870	756 900	29.49576	93.27379	1149425
821	674 041	28.65310	90.60905	1218027	871	758 641	29.51271	93.32738	1148106
822	675 684	28.67054	90.66422	1216545	872	760 384	29.52965	93.38094	1146789
823	677 329	28.68798	90.71935	1215067	873	762 129	29.54657	93.43447	1145475
824	678 976	28.70540	90.77445	1213592	874	763 876	29.56349	93.48797	1144165
825	680 625	28.72281	90.82951	1212121	875	765 625	29.58040	93.54143	1142857
826	682 276	28.74022	90.88454	1210654	876	767 376	29.59730	93.59487	1141553
827	683 929	28.75761	90.93954	1209190	877	769 129	29.61419	93.64828	1140251
828	685 584	28.77499	90.99451	1207729	878	770 884	29.63106	93.70165	1138952
829	687 241	28.79236	91.04944	1206273	879	772 641	29.64793	93.75500	1137656
830	688 900	28.80972	91.10434	1204819	880	774 400	29.66479	93.80832	1136364
831	690 561	28.82707	91.15920	1203369	881	776 161	29.68164	93.86160	1135074
832	692 224	28.84441	91.21403	1201923	882	777 924	29.69848	93.91486	1133787
833	693 889	28.86174	91.26883	1200480	883	779 689	29.71532	93.96808	1132503
834	695 556	28.87906	91.32360	1199041	884	781 456	29.73214	94.02127	1131222
835	697 225	28.89637	91.37833	1197605	885	783 225	29.74895	94.07444	1129944
836	698 896	28.91366	91.43304	1196172	886	784 996	29.76575	94.12757	1128668
837	700 569	28.93095	91.48770	1194743	887	786 769	29.78255	94.18068	1127396
838	702 244	28.94823	91.54234	1193317	888	788 544	29.79933	94.23375	1126126
839	703 921	28.96550	91.59694	1191895	889	790 321	29.81610	94.28680	1124859
840	705 600	28.98275	91.65151	1190476	890	792 100	29.83287	94.33981	1123596
841	707 281	29.00000	91.70605	1189061	891	793 881	29.84962	94.39280	1122334
842	708 964	29.01724	91.76056	1187648	892	795 664	29.86637	94.44575	1121076
843	710 649	29.03446	91.81503	1186240	893	797 449	29.88311	94.49868	1119821
844	712 336	29.05168	91.86947	1184834	894	799 236	29.89983	94.55157	1118568
845	714 025	29.06888	91.92388	1183432	895	801 025	29.91655	94.60444	1117318
846	715 716	29.08608	91.97826	1182033	896	802 816	29.93326	94.65728	1116071
847	717 409	29.10326	92.03260	1180638	897	804 609	29.94996	94.71008	1114827
848	719 104	29.12044	92.08692	1179245	898	806 404	29.96665	94.76286	1113586
849	720 801	29.13760	92.14120	1177856	899	808 201	29.98333	94.81561	1112347
850	722 500	29.15476	92.19544	1176471	900	810 000	30.00000	94.86833	1111111

Squares and square roots (*concluded*)

N	N^2	$\sqrt{N}$	$\sqrt{10N}$	$1/N$ .00	N	N^2	$\sqrt{N}$	$\sqrt{10N}$	$1/N$ .00
900	810 000	30.00000	94.86833	1111111	950	902 500	30.82207	97.46794	1052632
901	811 801	30.01666	94.92102	1109878	951	904 401	30.83829	97.51923	1051525
902	813 604	30.03331	94.97368	1108647	952	906 304	30.85450	97.57049	1050420
903	815 409	30.04996	95.02631	1107420	953	908 209	30.87070	97.62172	1049318
904	817 216	30.06659	95.07891	1106195	954	910.116	30.88689	97.67292	1048218
905	819 025	30.08322	95.13149	1104972	955	912 025	30.90307	97.72410	1047120
906	820 836	30.09983	95.18403	1103753	956	913 936	30.91925	97.77525	1046025
907	822 649	30.11644	95.23655	1102536	957	915 849	30.93542	97.82638	1044932
908	824 464	30.13304	95.28903	1101322	958	917 764	30.95158	97.87747	1043841
909	826 281	30.14963	95.34149	1100110	959	919 681	30.96773	97.92855	1042753
910	828 100	30.16621	95.39392	1098901	960	921 600	30.98387	97.97959	1041667
911	829 921	30.18278	95.44632	1097695	961	923 521	31.00000	98.03061	1040583
912	831 744	30.19934	95.49869	1096491	962	925 444	31.01612	98.08160	1039501
913	833 569	30.21589	95.55103	1095290	963	927 369	31.03224	98.13256	1038422
914	835 396	30.23243	95.60335	1094092	964	929 296	31.04835	98.18350	1037344
915	837 225	30.24897	95.65563	1092896	965	931 225	31.06445	98.23441	1036269
916	839 056	30.26549	95.70789	1091703	966	933 156	31.08054	98.28530	1035197
917	840 889	30.28201	95.76012	1090513	967	935 089	31.09662	98.33616	1034126
918	842 724	30.29851	95.81232	1089325	968	937 024	31.11270	98.38699	1033058
919	844 561	30.31501	95.86449	1088139	969	938 961	31.12876	98.43780	1031992
920	846 400	30.33150	95.91663	1086957	970	940 900	31.14482	98.48858	1030928
921	848 241	30.34798	95.96874	1085776	971	942 841	31.16087	98.53933	1029866
922	850 084	30.36445	96.02083	1084599	972	944 784	31.17691	98.59006	1028807
923	851 729	30.38092	96.07289	1083424	973	946 729	31.19295	98.64076	1027749
924	853 776	30.39737	96.12492	1082251	974	948 676	31.20897	98.69144	1026694
925	855 625	30.41381	96.17692	1081081	975	950 625	31.22499	98.74209	1025641
926	857 476	30.43025	96.22889	1079914	976	952 576	31.24100	98.79271	1024590
927	859 329	30.44667	96.28084	1078749	977	954 529	31.25700	98.84331	1023541
928	861 184	30.46309	96.33276	1077586	978	956 484	31.27299	98.89388	1022495
929	863 041	30.47950	96.38465	1076426	979	958 441	31.28898	98.94443	1021450
930	864 900	30.49590	96.43651	1075269	980	960 400	31.30495	98.99495	1020408
931	866 761	30.51229	96.48834	1074114	981	962 361	31.32092	99.04544	1019368
932	868 624	30.52868	96.54015	1072961	982	964 324	31.33688	99.09591	1018330
933	870 489	30.54505	96.59193	1071811	983	966 289	31.35283	99.14636	1017294
934	872 356	30.56141	96.64368	1070664	984	968 256	31.36877	99.19677	1016260
935	874 225	30.57777	96.69540	1069519	985	970 225	31.38471	99.24717	1015228
936	876 096	30.59412	96.74709	1068376	986	972 196	31.40064	99.29753	1014199
937	877 969	30.61046	96.79876	1067236	987	974 169	31.41656	99.34787	1013171
938	879 844	30.62679	96.85040	1066098	988	976 144	31.43247	99.39819	1012146
939	881 721	30.64311	96.90201	1064963	989	978 121	31.44837	99.44848	1011122
940	883 600	30.65942	96.95360	1063830	990	980 100	31.46427	99.49874	1010101
941	885 481	30.67572	97.00515	1062699	991	982 081	31.48015	99.54898	1009082
942	887 364	30.69202	97.05668	1061571	992	984 064	31.49603	99.59920	1008065
943	889 249	30.70831	97.10819	1060445	993	986 049	31.51190	99.64939	1007049
944	891 136	30.72458	97.15966	1059322	994	988 036	31.52777	99.69955	1006036
945	893 025	30.74085	97.21111	1058201	995	990 025	31.54362	99.74969	1005025
946	894 916	30.75711	97.26253	1057082	996	992 016	31.55947	99.79980	1004016
947	896 809	30.77337	97.31393	1055966	997	994 009	31.57531	99.84989	1003009
948	898 704	30.78961	97.36529	1054852	998	996 004	31.59114	99.89995	1002004
949	900 601	30.80584	97.41663	1053741	999	998 001	31.60696	99.94999	1001001
950	902 500	30.82207	97.46794	1052632	1000	1 000 000	31.62278	100.00000	1000000

Appendix D

TABLE OF RANDOM NUMBERS

```
 694 5965 7212 5888 5434 4983 4609 6026 8599 7791 9200 1605 6935 9527
9121 9791 5207 9769 4703 8188 8328 1545 5541 7449 1327  541 2451 6390
6970  319 7338 8785 2063 7467 1758  451  383 8819 2844 3421 4694 7975
3426 8805 2534 8295  794 8264   94 2168 9879 7222 6123  844 9423 6739
5010 5246  667 5349 3034 9794 5275 1337  770 7720 7579 4326 9512 8796
2311 3155 2566 9022 7506 2646  859 9758 4441 2151 9479 8027 4639 6704
4197 6549  647 4900 2722 2618  223 5130 8000 4016 2368 4469 2802 4467
2742 3066  528 2159 9667 2343 3903 9787 5101 7338 8779 1927 4321 9391
6013 8302  967 2253 1824 1973 5399 4189 6359 6269 4197 6534  295 6789
6152 1508 4696 8027 4635 6626 2419 5637 9654 2054 7247 6684 3750 6260
3992 1825 1990 5784 3045   55 1283 9519 8952 5911 5957 7024 1553 5738
1993 5859 4767 9648 1914 4023 2534 8287  612 4079 3828 8066 5533 7280
7456 1497 4435 2014 6327 5534 7290 7685 6772 5774 2812 4688 7833  168
3886 9385 5870 5013 5302 1950 4851 1592 6638 2695 1999 5980 7561 3925
 286 6579 1324  461  616 4169 5894 5565 8005 4119 4757 9426 6816 6784
6042 8974 6407 7365 9404 6296 4830 1104 5407 4365  415 9547 9598  757
7426  817 8805 2529 8173 7989 3761 6517 9896 7621 5296 1808 1586 6489
9264 3081  876  154 3551 1692 8929 5369 3497  448  318 7335 8717  495
1396 2114 8625 8387 2917 7103 3380 7761 8506 5644 9828 6052 9207 1779
 917 1105 5428 4857 1725 9687 2822 4918 3130 2006 6158 1636 7640 5733
1867 2944 7722 7612 5089 7068 2578 9310 4137 5154 8554 6742 5077 6772
5766 2634  596 3722 5626 9417 6599 1783 1020 3469 9795 5299 1880 3247
4697 8049 5129 7973 3398 8170 7923 2234 1389 1967 5255  885  358 8242
9581  363 8353 2123 8832 3157 2612   93 2161 9715 3464 9680 2658 1137
6169 1899 3684 4737 8966 6231 3326 6507 9682 2708 2299 2896 6626 2398
5171 8951 5878 5196 9514 8834 3197 3548 1607 6976  457  520 1975 5447
5288 1640 7723 7630 5501 6538  378 8716  468  773 7788 9140  237 5463
5662  233 5361 3311 6169 1887 3421 8702  165 3805 7526 3103 1372 1556
5805 3525 1082 4907 2861 5808 3593 2655 1079 4828 1055 4287 8608 7991
3809 7624 5358 3244 4630 6509 9728 3748 6215 2952 7901 1739    3   80
1846 2465 6701 4124 4854 1656 8094 6174 2009 6222 3110 1531 5230  300
6909 8910 4931 3424 8752 1306   57 1311  156 3602 2867 5958 7036 1833
2172 9973 9397 6144 1326  516 1880 3248 4714 8425 3776 6856 7707 7275
7344 8916 5090 7089 3064  493 1339  797 8338 1779  929 1368 1480 4050
3162 2738 2982 8607 7983 3620 3269 5203 9677 2586 9494 8376 2657 1115
5663  268 6184 2237 1461 3619 3244 4632 6551  694 5967 7260 7001 1039
3908 9893 7551 3681 4667 7343 8909 4914 3026 9598  754 7352 9109 9515
8866 3934  501 1538 5376 3663 4251 7775 8832 3150 2454 6464 8684 9754
4359  260 5982 7596 4713 8406 3346 6969  308 7103 3382 7786 9087 9021
7485 2167 9862 6838 7274 7316 8271  238 5487 6221 3085  957 2020 6477
8971 6346 5980 7554 3757 6415 7561 3923  245 5652    0   12  281 6472
8875 4134 5092 7119 3752 6316 5272 1261 9009 7229 6268 4177 6079 9821
5902 5748 2216  981 2571 9152  517 1896 3630 3491  302 6954 9946 8760
1492 4330 9592  628 4450 2356 4196 6514 9841 6356 6188 2344 3923  236
5429 4867 1947 4788  131 3033 9774 4819  859 9771 4742 9073 8681 9663
2255 1881 3278 5409 4417 1599 6786 6078 9798 5368 3469 9801 5424 4754
9346 4961 4125 4891 2512 7781 8985 6656 3091 1110 5547 7599 4783   19
 457  512 1798 1364 1374 1603 6879 8221 9104 9395 6105  431 9927 8333
1668 8385 2861 5809 3608 2990 8775 1827 2042 6986  682 5686  792 8234
9395 6099  293 6744 5127 7921 2197  533 2264 2081 7871 1042 3968 1285
9557 9830 6110  549 2640  734 6889 8457 4517 3904 9802 5459 5575 8231
9331 4617 6196 2518 7919 2150 9459 7576 4255 7887 1422 2723 2640  730
6801 6424 7756 8391 3005 9133   65 1511 4754 9345 4937 3570 2131 9015
7345 8946 5763 2550 8658 9153  541 2449 6339 5813 3706 5242  572 3167
2842 5366 3430 8891 4494 3371 7549 3628 3450 9358 5247  681 5681  665
```

Courtesy: University of Toledo Computation Center.

Appendix E

CRITICAL VALUES OF t^*

df	Level of significance for one-tailed test					
	.10	.05	.025	.01	.005	.0005
	Level of significance for two-tailed test					
	.20	.10	.05	.02	.01	.001
1	3.078	6.314	12.706	31.821	63.657	636.619
2	1.886	2.920	4.303	6.965	9.925	31.598
3	1.638	2.353	3.182	4.541	5.841	12.941
4	1.533	2.132	2.776	3.747	4.604	8.610
5	1.476	2.015	2.571	3.365	4.032	6.859
6	1.440	1.943	2.447	3.143	3.707	5.959
7	1.415	1.895	2.365	2.998	3.499	5.405
8	1.397	1.860	2.306	2.896	3.355	5.041
9	1.383	1.833	2.262	2.821	3.250	4.781
10	1.372	1.812	2.228	2.764	3.169	4.587
11	1.363	1.796	2.201	2.718	3.106	4.437
12	1.356	1.782	2.179	2.681	3.055	4.318
13	1.350	1.771	2.160	2.650	3.012	4.221
14	1.345	1.761	2.145	2.624	2.977	4.140
15	1.341	1.753	2.131	2.602	2.947	4.073
16	1.337	1.746	2.120	2.583	2.921	4.015
17	1.333	1.740	2.110	2.567	2.898	3.965
18	1.330	1.734	2.101	2.552	2.878	3.922
19	1.328	1.729	2.093	2.539	2.861	3.883
20	1.325	1.725	2.086	2.528	2.845	3.850
21	1.323	1.721	2.080	2.518	2.831	3.819
22	1.321	1.717	2.074	2.508	2.819	3.792
23	1.319	1.714	2.069	2.500	2.807	3.767
24	1.318	1.711	2.064	2.492	2.797	3.745
25	1.316	1.708	2.060	2.485	2.787	3.725
26	1.315	1.706	2.056	2.479	2.779	3.707
27	1.314	1.703	2.052	2.473	2.771	3.690
28	1.313	1.701	2.048	2.467	2.763	3.674
29	1.311	1.699	2.045	2.462	2.756	3.659
30	1.310	1.697	2.042	2.457	2.750	3.646
40	1.303	1.684	2.021	2.423	2.704	3.551
60	1.296	1.671	2.000	2.390	2.660	3.460
120	1.289	1.658	1.980	2.358	2.617	3.373
∞	1.282	1.645	1.960	2.326	2.576	3.291

*This table is abridged from Table III of Fisher and Yates: *Statistical Tables for Biological, Agricultural, and Medical Research,* published by Oliver and Boyd Ltd., Edinburgh, by permission of the authors and publishers.

Appendix F

WILCOXON *T* VALUES

Critical values of *T*, the Wilcoxon signed rank statistic, where *T*
is the largest integer such that $Pr(T \leq t/N) \leq \alpha$
the cumulative one-tail probability

N	2 α .15 / α.075	.10 / .050	.05 / .025	.04 / .020	.03 / .015	.02 / .010	.01 / .005
4	0						
5	1	0					
6	2	2	0	0			
7	4	3	2	1	0	0	
8	7	5	3	3	2	1	0
9	9	8	5	5	4	3	1
10	12	10	8	7	6	5	3
11	16	13	10	9	8	7	5
12	19	17	13	12	11	9	7
13	24	21	17	16	14	12	9
14	28	25	21	19	18	15	12
15	33	30	25	23	21	19	15
16	39	35	29	28	26	23	19
17	45	41	34	33	30	27	23
18	51	47	40	38	35	32	27
19	58	53	46	43	41	37	32
20	65	60	52	50	47	43	37
21	73	67	58	56	53	49	42
22	81	75	65	63	59	55	48
23	89	83	73	70	66	62	54
24	98	91	81	78	74	69	61
25	108	100	89	86	82	76	68
26	118	110	98	94	90	84	75
27	128	119	107	103	99	92	83
28	138	130	116	112	108	101	91
29	150	140	126	122	117	110	100
30	161	151	137	132	127	120	109
31	173	163	147	143	137	130	118
32	186	175	159	154	148	140	128
33	199	187	170	165	159	151	138
34	212	200	182	177	171	162	148
35	226	213	195	189	182	173	159
40	302	286	264	257	249	238	220
50	487	466	434	425	413	397	373
60	718	690	648	636	620	600	567
70	995	960	907	891	872	846	805
80	1318	1276	1211	1192	1168	1136	1086
90	1688	1638	1560	1537	1509	1471	1410
100	2105	2045	1955	1928	1894	1850	1779

Source: Abridged from Robert L. McCormack, "Extended Tables of the Wilcoxon Matched Pair Signed Rank Statistic," *Journal of the American Statistical Association*, September 1965, pp. 866–67.

Appendix G

TABLE OF AREAS AND ORDINATES OF THE NORMAL CURVE*

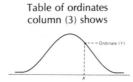

Table of areas column (2) shows	Table of ordinates column (3) shows

$z = \dfrac{X-\mu}{\sigma}$	Area Under the Curve between μ and X	Ordinate (Y) of the curve at X	$z = \dfrac{X-\mu}{\sigma}$	Area Under the Curve between μ and X	Ordinate (Y) of the curve at X
(1)	(2)	(3)	(1)	(2)	(3)
.00	.00000	.39894	.20	.07926	.39104
.01	.00399	.39892	.21	.08317	.39024
.02	.00798	.39886	.22	.08706	.38940
.03	.01197	.39876	.23	.09095	.38853
.04	.01595	.39862	.24	.09483	.38762
.05	.01994	.39844	.25	.09871	.38667
.06	.02392	.39822	.26	.10257	.38568
.07	.02790	.39797	.27	.10642	.38466
.08	.03188	.39767	.28	.11026	.38361
.09	.03586	.39733	.29	.11409	.38251
.10	.03983	.39695	.30	.11791	.38139
.11	.04380	.39654	.31	.12172	.38023
.12	.04776	.39608	.32	.12552	.37903
.13	.05172	.39559	.33	.12930	.37780
.14	.05567	.39505	.34	.13307	.37654
.15	.05962	.39448	.35	.13683	.37524
.16	.06356	.39387	.36	.14058	.37391
.17	.06749	.39322	.37	.14431	.37255
.18	.07142	.39253	.38	.14803	.37115
.19	.07535	.39181	.39	.15173	.36973

*From: J. F. Kenney and E. S. Keeping, *Mathematics of Statistics* (Princeton, N.J.: D. Van Nostrand Company, Inc., 1954).

Table of areas and ordinates of the normal curve (*continued*)

$z = \dfrac{X-\mu}{\sigma}$	Area Under the Curve between μ and X	Ordinate (Y) of the curve at X	$z = \dfrac{X-\mu}{\sigma}$	Area Under the Curve between μ and X	Ordinate (Y) of the curve at X
(1)	(2)	(3)	(1)	(2)	(3)
.40	.15542	.36827	.90	.31594	.26609
.41	.15910	.36678	.91	.31819	.26369
.42	.16276	.36526	.92	.32121	.26129
.43	.16640	.36371	.93	.32381	.25888
.44	.17003	.36213	.94	.32639	.25647
.45	.17364	.36053	.95	.32894	.25406
.46	.17724	.35889	.96	.33147	.25164
.47	.18082	.35723	.97	.33398	.24923
.48	.18439	.35553	.98	.33646	.24681
.49	.18793	.35381	.99	.33891	.24439
.50	.19146	.35207	1.00	.34134	.24197
.51	.19497	.35029	1.01	.34375	.23955
.52	.19847	.34849	1.02	.34614	.23713
.53	.20194	.34667	1.03	.34850	.23471
.54	.20540	.34482	1.04	.35083	.23230
.55	.20884	.34294	1.05	.35314	.22988
.56	.21226	.34105	1.06	.35543	.22747
.57	.21566	.33912	1.07	.35769	.22506
.58	.21904	.33718	1.08	.35993	.22265
.59	.22240	.33521	1.09	.36214	.22025
.60	.22575	.33322	1.10	.36433	.21785
.61	.22907	.33121	1.11	.36650	.21546
.62	.23237	.32918	1.12	.36864	.21307
.63	.23565	.32713	1.13	.37076	.21069
.64	.23891	.32506	1.14	.37286	.20831
.65	.24215	.32297	1.15	.37493	.20594
.66	.24537	.32086	1.16	.37698	.20357
.67	.24857	.31874	1.17	.37900	.20121
.68	.25175	.31659	1.18	.38100	.19886
.69	.25490	.31443	1.19	.38298	.19652
.70	.25804	.31225	1.20	.38493	.19419
.71	.26115	.31006	1.21	.38686	.19186
.72	.26424	.30785	1.22	.38877	.18954
.73	.26730	.30563	1.23	.39065	.18724
.74	.27035	.30339	1.24	.39251	.18494
.75	.27337	.30114	1.25	.39435	.18265
.76	.27637	.29887	1.26	.39617	.18037
.77	.27935	.29659	1.27	.39796	.17810
.78	.28230	.29431	1.28	.39973	.17585
.79	.28524	.29200	1.29	.40147	.17360
.80	.28814	.28969	1.30	.40320	.17137
.81	.29103	.28737	1.31	.40490	.16915
.82	.29389	.28504	1.32	.40658	.16694
.83	.29673	.28269	1.33	.40824	.16474
.84	.29955	.28034	1.34	.40988	.16256
.85	.30234	.27798	1.35	.41149	.16038
.86	.30511	.27562	1.36	.41309	.15822
.87	.30785	.27324	1.37	.41466	.15608
.88	.31057	.27086	1.38	.41621	.15395
.89	.31327	.26848	1.39	.41774	.15183

Table of areas and ordinates of the normal curve (*continued*)

$z = \dfrac{X-\mu}{\sigma}$	Area Under the Curve between μ and X	Ordinate (Y) of the curve at X	$z = \dfrac{X-\mu}{\sigma}$	Area Under the Curve between μ and X	Ordinate (Y) of the curve at X
(1)	(2)	(3)	(1)	(2)	(3)
1.40	.41924	.14973	1.90	.47128	.06562
1.41	.42073	.14764	1.91	.47193	.06438
1.42	.42220	.14556	1.92	.47257	.06316
1.43	.42364	.14350	1.93	.47320	.06195
1.44	.42507	.14146	1.94	.47381	.06077
1.45	.42647	.13943	1.95	.47441	.05959
1.46	.42786	.13742	1.96	.47500	.05844
1.47	.42922	.13542	1.97	.47558	.05730
1.48	.43056	.13344	1.98	.47615	.05618
1.49	.43189	.13147	1.99	.47670	.05508
1.50	.43319	.12952	2.00	.47725	.05399
1.51	.43448	.12758	2.01	.47778	.05292
1.52	.43574	.1256€	2.02	.47831	.05186
1.53	.43699	.12376	2.03	.47882	.05082
1.54	.43822	.12188	2.04	.47932	.04980
1.55	.43943	.12001	2.05	.47982	.04879
1.56	.44062	.11816	2.06	.48030	.04780
1.57	.44179	.11632	2.07	.48077	.04682
1.58	.44295	.11450	2.08	.48124	.04586
1.59	.44408	.11270	2.09	.48169	.04491
1.60	.44520	.11092	2.10	.48214	.04398
1.61	.44630	.10915	2.11	.48257	.04307
1.62	.44738	.10741	2.12	.48300	.04217
1.63	.44845	.10567	2.13	.48341	.04128
1.64	.44950	.10396	2.14	.48382	.04041
1.65	.45053	.10226	2.15	.48422	.03955
1.66	.45154	.10059	2.16	.484€1	.03871
1.67	.45254	.09893	2.17	.48500	.03788
1.68	.45352	.09728	2.18	.48537	.03706
1.69	.45449	.09566	2.19	.48574	.03626
1.70	.45543	.09405	2.20	.48610	.03547
1.71	.45637	.09246	2.21	.48645	.03470
1.72	.45728	.09089	2.22	.48679	.03394
1.73	.45818	.08933	2.23	.48713	.03319
1.74	.45907	.08780	2.24	.48745	.03246
1.75	.45994	.08628	2.25	.48778	.03174
1.76	.46080	.08478	2.26	.48809	.03103
1.77	.46164	.0&329	2.27	.48840	.03034
1.78	.46246	.06183	2.28	.48870	.02965
1.79	.46327	.08038	2.29	.48899	.02898
1.80	.46407	.07895	2.30	.48928	.02833
1.81	.46485	.07754	2.31	.48956	.02768
1.82	.46562	.07614	2.32	.48983	.02705
1.83	.46638	.07477	2.33	.49010	.02643
1.84	.46712	.07341	2.34	.49036	.02582
1.85	.46784	.07206	2.35	.49064	.02522
1.86	.46856	.07074	2.36	.49086	.02463
1.87	.46926	.06943	2.37	.49111	.02406
1.88	.46995	.06814	2.38	.49134	.02349
1.89	.47062	.06687	2.39	.49158	.02294

Table of areas and ordinates of the normal curve (*continued*)

$z = \dfrac{X-\mu}{\sigma}$	Area Under the Curve between μ and X	Ordinate (Y) of the curve at X	$z = \dfrac{X-\mu}{\sigma}$	Area Under the Curve between μ and X	Ordinate (Y) of the curve at X
(1)	(2)	(3)	(1)	(2)	(3)
2.40	.49180	.02239	2.90	.49813	.00595
2.41	.49202	.02186	2.91	.49819	.00578
2.42	.49224	.02134	2.92	.49825	.00562
2.43	.49245	.02083	2.93	.49831	.00545
2.44	.49266	.02033	2.94	.49836	.00530
2.45	.49286	.01984	2.95	.49841	.00514
2.46	.49305	.01936	2.96	.49846	.00499
2.47	.49324	.01889	2.97	.49851	.00485
2.48	.49343	.01842	2.98	.49856	.00471
2.49	.49361	.01797	2.99	.49861	.00457
2.50	.49379	.01753	3.00	.49865	.00443
2.51	.49396	.01709	3.01	.49869	.00430
2.52	.49413	.01667	3.02	.49874	.00417
2.53	.49430	.01625	3.03	.49878	.00405
2.54	.49446	.01585	3.04	.49882	.00393
2.55	.49461	.01545	3.05	.49886	.00381
2.56	.49477	.01506	3.06	.49889	.00370
2.57	.49492	.01468	3.07	.49893	.00358
2.58	.49506	.01431	3.08	.49897	.00348
2.59	.49520	.01394	3.09	.49900	.00337
2.60	.49534	.01358	3.10	.49903	.00327
2.61	.49547	.01323	3.11	.49906	.00317
2.62	.49560	.01289	3.12	.49910	.00307
2.63	.49573	.01256	3.13	.49913	.00298
2.64	.49585	.01223	3.14	.49916	.00288
2.65	.49598	.01191	3.15	.49918	.00279
2.66	.49609	.01160	3.16	.49921	.00271
2.67	.49621	.01130	3.17	.49924	.00262
2.68	.49632	.01100	3.18	.49926	.00254
2.69	.49643	.01071	3.19	.49929	.00246
2.70	.49653	.01042	3.20	.49931	.00238
2.71	.49664	.01014	3.21	.49934	.00231
2.72	.49674	.00987	3.22	.49936	.00224
2.73	.49683	.00961	3.23	.49938	.00216
2.74	.49693	.00935	3.24	.49940	.00210
2.75	.49702	.00909	3.25	.49942	.00203
2.76	.49711	.00885	3.26	.49944	.00196
2.77	.49720	.00861	3.27	.49946	.00190
2.78	.49728	.00837	3.28	.49948	.00184
2.79	.49736	.00814	3.29	.49950	.00178
2.80	.49744	.00792	3.30	.49952	.00172
2.81	.49752	.00770	3.31	.49953	.00167
2.82	.49760	.00748	3.32	.49955	.00161
2.83	.49767	.00727	3.33	.49957	.00156
2.84	.49774	.00707	3.34	.49958	.00151
2.85	.49781	.00687	3.35	.43960	.00146
2.86	.49788	.00668	3.36	.49961	.00141
2.87	.49795	.00649	3.37	.49962	.00136
2.88	.49801	.00631	3.38	.49964	.00132
2.89	.49807	.00613	3.39	.49965	.00127

Table of areas and ordinates of the normal curve (*concluded*)

$z = \dfrac{X-\mu}{\sigma}$	Area Under the Curve between μ and X	Ordinate (Y) of the curve at X	$z = \dfrac{X-\mu}{\sigma}$	Area Under the Curve between μ and X	Ordinate (Y) of the curve at X
(1)	(2)	(3)	(1)	(2)	(3)
3.40	.49966	.00123	3.70	.49989	.00042
3.41	.49968	.00119	3.71	.49990	.00041
3.42	.49969	.00115	3.72	.49990	.00039
3.43	.49970	.00111	3.73	.49990	.00038
3.44	.49971	.00107	3.74	.49991	.00037
3.45	.49972	.00104	3.75	.49991	.00035
3.46	.49973	.00100	3.76	.49992	.00034
3.47	.49974	.00097	3.77	.49992	.00033
3.48	.49975	.00094	3.78	.49992	.00031
3.49	.49976	.00090	3.79	.49992	.00030
3.50	.49977	.00087	3.80	.49993	.00029
3.51	.49978	.00084	3.81	.49993	.00028
3.52	.49978	.00081	3.82	.49993	.00027
3.53	.49979	.00079	3.83	.49994	.00026
3.54	.49980	.00076	3.84	.49994	.00025
3.55	.49981	.00073	3.85	.49994	.00024
3.56	.49981	.00071	3.86	.49994	.00023
3.57	.49982	.00068	3.87	.49995	.00022
3.58	.49983	.00066	3.88	.49995	.00021
3.59	.49983	.00063	3.89	.49995	.00021
3.60	.49984	.00061	3.90	.49995	.00020
3.61	.49985	.00059	3.91	.49995	.00019
3.62	.49985	.00057	3.92	.49996	.00018
3.63	.49986	.00055	3.93	.49996	.00018
3.64	.49986	.00053	3.94	.49996	.00017
3.65	.49987	.00051	3.95	.49996	.00016
3.66	.49987	.00049	3.96	.49996	.00016
3.67	.49988	.00047	3.97	.49996	.00015
3.68	.49988	.00046	3.98	.49997	.00014
3.69	.49989	.00044	3.99	.49997	.00014

Appendix H

CRITICAL VALUES OF CHI-SQUARE

Percentages represent areas in right-hand end of distribution. Example:

For 9 degrees of freedom:
$P[x^2 > 16.92] = 0.05$

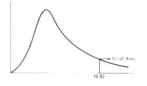

Degrees of freedom	Probability that chi-square value will be exceeded									
	0.995	0.990	0.975	0.950	0.900	0.100	0.050	0.025	0.010	0.005
1	0.0^4393	0.0^3157	0.0^3982	0.0^2393	0.0158	2.71	3.84	5.02	6.63	7.88
2	0.0100	0.0201	0.0506	0.103	0.211	4.61	5.99	7.38	9.21	10.60
3	0.072	0.115	0.216	0.352	0.584	6.25	7.81	9.35	11.34	12.84
4	0.207	0.297	0.484	0.711	1.064	7.78	9.49	11.14	13.28	14.86
5	0.412	0.554	0.831	1.145	1.61	9.24	11.07	12.83	15.09	16.75
6	0.676	0.872	1.24	1.64	2.20	10.64	12.59	14.45	16.81	18.55
7	0.989	1.24	1.69	2.17	2.83	12.02	14.07	16.01	18.48	20.28
8	1.34	1.65	2.18	2.73	3.49	13.36	15.51	17.53	20.09	21.96
9	1.73	2.09	2.70	3.33	4.17	14.68	16.92	19.02	21.67	23.59
10	2.16	2.56	3.25	3.94	4.87	15.99	18.31	20.48	23.21	25.19
11	2.60	3.05	3.82	4.57	5.58	17.28	19.68	21.92	24.72	26.76
12	3.07	3.57	4.40	5.23	6.30	18.55	21.03	23.34	26.22	28.30
13	3.57	4.11	5.01	5.89	7.04	19.81	22.36	24.74	27.69	29.82
14	4.07	4.66	5.63	6.57	7.79	21.06	23.68	26.12	29.14	31.32
15	4.60	5.23	6.26	7.26	8.55	22.31	25.00	27.49	30.58	32.80
16	5.14	5.81	6.91	7.96	9.31	23.54	26.30	28.85	32.00	34.27
17	5.70	6.41	7.56	8.67	10.09	24.77	27.59	30.19	33.41	35.72
18	6.26	7.01	8.23	9.39	10.86	25.99	28.87	31.53	34.81	37.16
19	6.84	7.63	8.91	10.12	11.65	27.20	30.14	32.85	36.19	38.58
20	7.43	8.26	9.59	10.85	12.44	28.41	31.41	34.17	37.57	40.00
21	8.03	8.90	10.28	11.59	13.24	29.62	32.67	35.48	38.93	41.40
22	8.64	9.54	10.98	12.34	14.04	30.81	33.92	36.78	40.29	42.80
23	9.26	10.20	11.69	13.09	14.85	32.01	35.17	38.08	41.64	44.18
24	9.89	10.86	12.40	13.85	15.66	33.20	36.42	39.36	42.98	45.56
25	10.52	11.52	13.12	14.61	16.47	34.38	37.65	40.65	44.31	46.93
26	11.16	12.20	13.84	15.38	17.29	35.56	38.89	41.92	45.64	48.29
27	11.81	12.88	14.57	16.15	18.11	36.74	40.11	43.19	46.96	49.64
28	12.46	13.56	15.31	16.93	18.94	37.92	41.34	44.46	48.28	50.99
29	13.12	14.26	16.05	17.71	19.77	39.09	42.56	45.72	49.59	52.34
30	13.79	14.95	16.79	18.49	20.60	40.26	43.77	46.98	50.89	53.67
40	20.71	22.16	24.43	26.51	29.05	51.80	55.76	59.34	63.69	66.77
50	27.99	29.71	32.36	34.76	37.69	63.17	67.50	71.42	76.15	79.49
60	35.53	37.48	40.48	43.19	46.46	74.40	79.08	83.30	88.38	91.95
70	43.28	45.44	48.76	51.74	55.33	85.53	90.53	95.02	100.4	104.22
80	51.17	53.54	57.15	60.39	64.28	96.58	101.9	106.6	112.3	116.32
90	59.20	61.75	65.65	69.13	73.29	107.6	113.1	118.1	124.1	128.3
100	67.33	70.06	74.22	77.93	82.36	118.5	124.3	129.6	135.8	140.2
z_α	-2.58	-2.33	-1.96	-1.64	-1.28	$+1.28$	$+1.64$	$+1.96$	$+2.33$	$+2.58$

Source: Adapted from E. S. Pearson and H. O. Hartley, eds., *Biometrika Tables for Statisticians,* vol. I, Table 18, pp. 160–63, published for the Biometrika trustees by Cambridge University, 1954, by permission of Professor Pearson and the trustees of Biometrika.

Appendix I

BINOMIAL DISTRIBUTION

$$P\{r\} = \frac{n!}{r!\,(n-r)!}\,p^r q^{n-r}$$

n	r	.05	.10	.15	.20	.25	p .30	.35	.40	.45	.50
1	0	.9500	.9000	.8500	.8000	.7500	.7000	.6500	.6000	.5500	.5000
	1	.0500	.1000	.1500	.2000	.2500	.3000	.3500	.4000	.4500	.5000
2	0	.9025	.8100	.7225	.6400	.5625	.4900	.4225	.3600	.3025	.2500
	1	.0950	.1800	.2550	.3200	.3750	.4200	.4550	.4800	.4950	.5000
	2	.0025	.0100	.0225	.0400	.0625	.0900	.1225	.1600	.2025	.2500
3	0	.8574	.7290	.6141	.5120	.4219	.3430	.2746	.2160	.1664	.1250
	1	.1354	.2430	.3251	.3840	.4219	.4410	.4436	.4320	.4084	.3750
	2	.0071	.0270	.0574	.0960	.1406	.1890	.2389	.2880	.3341	.3750
	3	.0001	.0010	.0034	.0080	.0156	.0270	.0429	.0640	.0911	.1250
4	0	.8145	.6561	.5220	.4096	.3164	.2401	.1785	.1296	.0915	.0625
	1	.1715	.2916	.3685	.4096	.4219	.4116	.3845	.3456	.2995	.2500
	2	.0135	.0486	.0975	.1536	.2109	.2646	.3105	.3456	.3675	.3750
	3	.0005	.0036	.0115	.0256	.0469	.0756	.1115	.1536	.2005	.2500
	4	.0000	.0001	.0005	.0016	.0039	.0081	.0150	.0256	.0410	.0625
5	0	.7738	.5905	.4437	.3277	.2373	.1681	.1160	.0778	.0503	.0312
	1	.2036	.3280	.3915	.4096	.3955	.3602	.3124	.2592	.2059	.1562
	2	.0214	.0729	.1382	.2048	.2637	.3087	.3364	.3456	.3369	.3125
	3	.0011	.0081	.0244	.0512	.0879	.1323	.1811	.2304	.2757	.3125
	4	.0000	.0004	.0022	.0064	.0146	.0284	.0488	.0768	.1128	.1562
	5	.0000	.0000	.0001	.0003	.0010	.0024	.0053	.0102	.0185	.0312
6	0	.7351	.5314	.3771	.2621	.1780	.1176	.0754	.0467	.0277	.0156
	1	.2321	.3543	.3993	.3932	.3560	.3025	.2437	.1866	.1359	.0938
	2	.0305	.0984	.1762	.2458	.2966	.3241	.3280	.3110	.2780	.2344
	3	.0021	.0146	.0415	.0819	.1318	.1852	.2355	.2765	.3032	.3125
	4	.0001	.0012	.0055	.0154	.0330	.0595	.0951	.1382	.1861	.2344
	5	.0000	.0001	.0004	.0015	.0044	.0102	.0205	.0369	.0609	.0938
	6	.0000	.0000	.0000	.0001	.0002	.0007	.0018	.0041	.0083	.0156
7	0	.6983	.4783	.3206	.2097	.1335	.0824	.0490	.0280	.0152	.0078
	1	.2573	.3720	.3960	.3670	.3115	.2471	.1848	.1306	.0872	.0547
	2	.0406	.1240	.2097	.2753	.3115	.3177	.2985	.2613	.2140	.1641
	3	.0036	.0230	.0617	.1147	.1730	.2269	.2679	.2903	.2918	.2734
	4	.0002	.0026	.0109	.0287	.0577	.0972	.1442	.1935	.2388	.2734
	5	.0000	.0002	.0012	.0043	.0115	.0250	.0466	.0774	.1172	.1641
	6	.0000	.0000	.0001	.0004	.0013	.0036	.0084	.0172	.0320	.0547
	7	.0000	.0000	.0000	.0000	.0001	.0002	.0006	.0016	.0037	.0078
8	0	.6634	.4305	.2725	.1678	.1002	.0576	.0319	.0168	.0084	.0039
	1	.2793	.3826	.3847	.3355	.2670	.1977	.1373	.0896	.0548	.0312
	2	.0515	.1488	.2376	.2936	.3115	.2065	.2587	.2090	.1569	.1094

Source: Extracted from "Tables of the Binomial Probability Distribution," U.S. Department of Commerce, National Bureau of Standards, Applied Mathematics Series 6, 1952.

Binomial distribution (*continued*)

n	r	.05	.10	.15	.20	.25	p .30	.35	.40	.45	.50
8	3	.0054	.0331	.0839	.1468	.2076	.2541	.2786	.2787	.2568	.2188
	4	.0004	.0046	.0185	.0459	.0865	.1361	.1875	.2322	.2627	.2734
	5	.0000	.0004	.0026	.0092	.0231	.0467	.0808	.1239	.1719	.2188
	6	.0000	.0000	.0002	.0011	.0038	.0100	.0217	.0413	.0403	.1094
	7	.0000	.0000	.0000	.0001	.0004	.0012	.0033	.0079	.0164	.0312
	8	.0000	.0000	.0000	.0000	.0000	.0001	.0002	.0007	.0017	.0039
9	0	.6302	.3874	.2316	.1342	.0751	.0404	.0207	.0101	.0046	.0020
	1	.2985	.3874	.3679	.3020	.2253	.1556	.1004	.0605	.0339	.0176
	2	.0629	.1722	.2597	.3020	.3003	.2668	.2162	.1612	.1110	.0703
	3	.0077	.0446	.1069	.1762	.2336	.2668	.2716	.2508	.2119	.1641
	4	.0006	.0074	.0283	.0661	.1168	.1715	.2194	.2508	.2600	.2461
	5	.0000	.0008	.0050	.0165	.0389	.0735	.1181	.1672	.2128	.2461
	6	.0000	.0001	.0006	.0028	.0087	.0210	.0424	.0743	.1160	.1641
	7	.0000	.0000	.0000	.0003	.0012	.0039	.0098	.0212	.0407	.0703
	8	.0000	.0000	.0000	.0000	.0001	.0004	.0013	.0035	.0083	.0176
	9	.0000	0000	0000	0000	0000	0000	0001	.0003	.0008	.0020
10	0	.5987	.3487	.1969	.1074	.0563	.0282	.0135	.0060	.0025	.0010
	1	.3151	.3874	.3474	.2684	.1877	.1211	.0725	.0403	.0207	.0098
	2	.0746	.1937	.2759	.3020	.2816	.2335	.1757	.1209	.0763	.0439
	3	.0105	.0574	.1298	.2013	.2503	.2668	.2522	.2150	.1665	.1172
	4	.0010	.0112	.0401	.0881	.1460	.2001	.2377	.2508	.2384	.2051
	5	.0001	.0015	.0085	.0264	.0584	.1029	.1536	.2007	.2340	.2461
	6	.0000	.0001	.0012	.0055	.0162	.0368	.0689	.1115	.1596	.2051
	7	.0000	.0000	.0001	.0008	.0031	.0090	.0212	.0425	.0746	.1172
	8	.0000	.0000	.0000	.0001	.0004	.0014	.0043	.0106	.0229	.0439
	9	.0000	.0000	.0000	.0000	.0000	.0001	.0005	.0016	.0042	.0098
	10	.0000	.0000	.0000	.0000	.0000	.0000	.0000	.0001	.0003	.0010
11	0	.5688	.3138	.1673	.0859	.0422	.0198	.0088	.0036	.0014	.0005
	1	.3293	.3835	.3248	.2362	.1549	.0932	.0518	.0266	.0125	.0054
	2	.0867	.2131	.2866	.2953	.2581	.1998	.1395	.0887	.0513	.0269
	3	.0137	.0710	.1517	.2215	.2581	.2568	.2254	.1774	.1259	.0806
	4	.0014	.0158	.0536	.1107	.1721	.2201	.2428	.2365	.2060	.1611
	5	.0001	.0025	.0132	.0388	.0803	.1321	.1830	.2207	.2360	.2256
	6	.0000	.0003	.0023	.0097	.0268	.0566	.0985	.1471	.1931	.2256
	7	.0000	.0000	.0003	.0017	.0064	.0173	.0379	.0701	.1128	.1611
	8	.0000	.0000	.0000	.0002	.0011	.0037	.0102	.0234	.0462	.0806
	9	.0000	.0000	.0000	.0000	.0001	.0005	.0018	.0052	.0126	.0269
	10	.0000	.0000	.0000	.0000	.0000	.0000	.0002	.0007	.0021	.0054
	11	.0000	.0000	.0000	.0000	.0000	.0000	.0000	.0000	.0002	.0005
12	0	.5404	.2824	.1422	.0687	.0317	.0138	.0057	.0022	.0008	.0002
	1	.3413	.3766	.3012	.2062	.1267	.0712	.0368	.0174	.0075	.0029

Binomial distribution (*continued*)

n	r	.05	.10	.15	.20	.25	.30	.35	.40	.45	.50
12	2	.0988	.2301	.2924	.2835	.2323	.1678	.1088	.0639	.0339	.0161
	3	.0173	.0852	.1720	.2362	.2581	.2397	.1954	.1419	.0923	.0537
	4	.0021	.0213	.0683	.1329	.1936	.2311	.2367	.2128	.1700	.1208
	5	.0002	.0038	.0193	.0532	.1032	.1585	.2039	.2270	.2225	.1934
	6	.0000	.0005	.0040	.0155	.0401	.0792	.1281	.1766	.2124	.2256
	7	.0000	.0000	.0006	.0033	.0115	.0291	.0591	.1009	.1489	.1934
	8	.0000	.0000	.0001	.0005	.0024	.0078	.0199	.0420	.0762	.1208
	9	.0000	.0000	.0000	.0001	.0004	.0015	.0048	.0125	.0277	.0537
	10	.0000	.0000	.0000	.0000	.0000	.0002	.0008	.0025	.0068	.0161
	11	.0000	.0000	.0000	.0000	.0000	.0000	.0001	.0003	.0010	.0029
	12	.0000	.0000	.0000	.0000	.0000	.0000	.0000	.0000	.0001	.0002
13	0	.5133	.2542	.1209	.0550	.0238	.0097	.0037	.0013	.0004	.0001
	1	.3512	.3672	.2774	.1787	.1029	.0540	.0259	.0113	.0045	.0016
	2	.1109	.2448	.2937	.2680	.2059	.1388	.0836	.0453	.0220	.0095
	3	.0214	.0997	.1900	.2457	.2517	.2181	.1651	.1107	.0660	.0349
	4	.0028	.0277	.0838	.1535	.2097	.2337	.2222	.1845	.1350	.0873
	5	.0003	.0055	.0266	.0691	.1258	.1803	.2154	.2214	.1989	.1571
	6	.0000	.0008	.0063	.0230	.0559	.1030	.1546	.1968	.2169	.2095
	7	.0000	.0001	.0011	.0058	.0186	.0442	.0833	.1312	.1775	.2095
	8	.0000	.0001	.0001	.0011	.0047	.0142	.0336	.0656	.1089	.1571
	9	.0000	.0000	.0000	.0001	.0009	.0034	.0101	.0243	.0495	.0873
	10	.0000	.0000	.0000	.0000	.0001	.0006	.0022	.0065	.0162	.0349
	11	.0000	.0000	.0000	.0000	.0000	.0001	.0003	.0012	.0036	.0095
	12	.0000	.0000	.0000	.0000	.0000	.0000	.0000	.0001	.0005	.0016
	13	.0000	.0000	.0000	.0000	.0000	.0000	.0000	.0000	.0000	.0001
14	0	.4877	.2288	.1028	.0440	.0178	.0068	.0024	.0008	.0002	.0001
	1	.3593	.3559	.2539	.1539	.0832	.0407	.0181	.0073	.0027	.0009
	2	.1229	.2570	.2912	.2501	.1802	.1134	.0634	.0317	.0141	.0056
	3	.0259	.1142	.2056	.2501	.2402	.1943	.1366	.0845	.0462	.0222
	4	.0037	.0349	.0998	.1720	.2202	.2290	.2022	.1549	.1040	.0611
	5	.0004	.0078	.0352	.0860	.1468	.1963	.2178	.2066	.1701	.1222
	6	.0000	.0013	.0093	.0322	.0734	.1262	.1759	.2086	.2088	.1833
	7	.0000	.0002	.0019	.0092	.0280	.0618	.1082	.1574	.1952	.2095
	8	.0000	.0000	.0003	.0020	.0082	.0232	.0510	.0918	.1398	.1833
	9	.0000	.0000	.0000	.0003	.0018	.0066	.0183	.0408	.0762	.1222
	10	.0000	.0000	.0000	.0000	.0003	.0014	.0049	.0136	.0312	.0611
	11	.0000	.0000	.0000	.0000	.0000	.0002	.0010	.0033	.0093	.0222
	12	.0000	.0000	.0000	.0000	.0000	.0000	.0001	.0005	.0019	.0056
	13	.0000	.0000	.0000	.0000	.0000	.0000	.0000	.0001	.0002	.0009
	14	.0000	.0000	.0000	.0000	.0000	.0000	.0000	.0000	.0000	.0001
15	0	.4633	.2059	.0874	.0352	.0134	.0047	.0016	.0005	.0001	.0000
	1	.3658	.3432	.2312	.1319	.0668	.0305	.0126	.0047	.0016	.0005
	2	.1348	.2669	.2856	.2309	.1559	.0916	.0476	.0219	.0090	.0032

Binomial distribution (*continued*)

15	3	.0307	.1285	.2184	.2501	.2252	.1700	.1110	.0634	.0318	.0139
	4	.0049	.0428	.1156	.1876	.2252	.2186	.1792	.1268	.0780	.0417
	5	.0006	.0105	.0449	.1032	.1651	.2061	.2123	.1859	.1404	.0916
	6	.0000	.0019	.0132	.0430	.0917	.1472	.1906	.2066	.1914	.1527
	7	.0000	.0003	.0030	.0138	.0393	.0811	.1319	.1771	.2013	.1964
	8	.0000	.0000	.0005	.0035	.0131	.0348	.0710	.1181	.1647	.1964
	9	.0000	.0000	.0001	.0007	.0034	.0116	.0298	.0612	.1048	.1527
	10	.0000	.0000	.0000	.0001	.0007	.0030	.0096	.0245	.0515	.0916
	11	.0000	.0000	.0000	.0000	.0001	.0006	.0024	.0074	.0191	.0417
	12	.0000	.0000	.0000	.0000	.0000	.0001	.0004	.0016	.0052	.0139
	13	.0000	.0000	.0000	.0000	.0000	.0000	.0001	.0003	.0010	.0032
	14	.0000	.0000	.0000	.0000	.0000	.0000	.0000	.0000	.0001	.0005
	15	.0000	.0000	.0000	.0000	.0000	.0000	.0000	.0000	.0000	.0000
16	0	.4401	.1853	.0743	.0281	.0100	.0033	.0010	.0003	.0001	.0000
	1	.3706	.3294	.2097	.1126	.0535	.0228	.0087	.0030	.0009	.0002
	2	.1463	.2745	.2775	.2111	.1336	.0732	.0353	.0150	.0056	.0018
	3	.0359	.1423	.2285	.2463	.2079	.1465	.0888	.0468	.0215	.0085
	4	.0061	.0514	.1311	.2001	.2252	.2040	.1553	.1014	.0572	.0278
	5	.0008	.0137	.0555	.1201	.1802	.2099	.2008	.1623	.1123	.0667
	6	.0001	.0028	.0180	.0550	.1101	.1649	.1982	.1983	.1684	.1222
	7	.0000	.0004	.0045	.0197	.0524	.1010	.1524	.1889	.1969	.1746
	8	.0000	.0001	.0009	.0055	.0197	.0487	.0923	.1417	.1812	.1964
	9	.0000	.0000	.0001	.0012	.0058	.0185	.0442	.0840	.1318	.1746
	10	.0000	.0000	.0000	.0002	.0014	.0056	.0167	.0392	.0755	.1222
	11	.0000	.0000	.0000	.0000	.0002	.0013	.0049	.0142	.0337	.0667
	12	.0000	.0000	.0000	.0000	.0000	.0002	.0011	.0040	.0115	.0278
	13	.0000	.0000	.0000	.0000	.0000	.0000	.0002	.0008	.0029	.0085
	14	.0000	.0000	.0000	.0000	.0000	.0000	.0000	.0001	.0005	.0018
	15	.0000	.0000	.0000	.0000	.0000	.0000	.0000	.0000	.0001	.0002
	16	.0000	.0000	.0000	.0000	.0000	.0000	.0000	.0000	.0000	.0000
17	0	.4181	.1668	.0631	.0225	.0075	.0023	.0007	.0002	.0000	.0000
	1	.3741	.3150	.1893	.0957	.0426	.0169	.0060	.0019	.0005	.0001
	2	.1575	.2800	.2673	.1914	.1136	.0581	.0260	.0102	.0035	.0010
	3	.0415	.1556	.2359	.2393	.1893	.1245	.0701	.0341	.0144	.0052
	4	.0076	.0605	.1457	.2093	.2209	.1868	.1320	.0796	.0411	.0182
	5	.0010	.0175	.0668	.1361	.1914	.2081	.1849	.1379	.0875	.0472
	6	.0001	.0039	.0236	.0680	.1276	.1784	.1991	.1839	.1432	.0944
	7	.0000	.0007	.0065	.0267	.0668	.1201	.1685	.1927	.1841	.1484
	8	.0000	.0001	.0014	.0084	.0279	.0644	.1134	.1606	.1883	.1855
	9	.0000	.0000	.0003	.0021	.0093	.0276	.0611	.1070	.1540	.1855

Binomial distribution (*continued*)

n	r	.05	.10	.15	.20	.25	p .30	.35	.40	.45	.50
17	10	.0000	.0000	.0000	.0004	.0025	.0095	.0263	.0571	.1008	.1484
	11	.0000	.0000	.0000	.0001	.0005	.0026	.0090	.0242	.0525	.0944
	12	.0000	.0000	.0000	.0000	.0001	.0006	.0024	.0081	.0215	.0472
	13	.0000	.0000	.0000	.0000	.0000	.0001	.0005	.0021	.0066	.0182
	14	.0000	.0000	.0000	.0000	.0000	.0000	.0001	.0004	.0016	.0052
	15	.0000	.0000	.0000	.0000	.0000	.0000	.0000	.0001	.0003	.0010
	16	.0000	.0000	.0000	.0000	.0000	.0000	.0000	.0000	.0000	.0001
	17	.0000	.0000	.0000	.0000	.0000	.0000	.0000	.0000	.0000	.0000
18	0	.3972	.1501	.0536	.0180	.0056	.0016	.0004	.0001	.0000	.0000
	1	.3763	.3002	.1704	.0811	.0338	.0126	.0042	.0012	.0003	.0001
	2	.1683	.2835	.2556	.1723	.0958	.0458	.0190	.0069	.0022	.0006
	3	.0473	.1680	.2406	.2297	.1704	.1046	.0547	.0246	.0095	.0031
	4	.0093	.0700	.1592	.2153	.2130	.1681	.1104	.0614	.0291	.0117
	5	.0014	.0218	.0787	.1507	.1988	.2017	.1664	.1146	.0666	.0327
	6	.0002	.0052	.0301	.0816	.1436	.1873	.1941	.1655	.1181	.0708
	7	.0000	.0010	.0091	.0350	.0820	.1376	.1792	.1892	.1657	.1214
	8	.0000	.0002	.0022	.0120	.0376	.0811	.1327	.1734	.1864	.1669
	9	.0000	.0000	.0004	.0033	.0139	.0386	.0794	.1284	.1694	.1855
	10	.0000	.0000	.0001	.0008	.0042	.0149	.0385	.0771	.1248	.1669
	11	.0000	.0000	.0000	.0001	.0010	.0046	.0151	.0374	.0742	.1214
	12	.0000	.0000	.0000	.0000	.0002	.0012	.0047	.0145	.0354	.0708
	13	.0000	.0000	.0000	.0000	.0000	.0002	.0012	.0045	.0134	.0327
	14	.0000	.0000	.0000	.0000	.0000	.0000	.0002	.0011	.0039	.0117
	15	.0000	.0000	.0000	.0000	.0000	.0000	.0000	.0002	.0009	.0031
	16	.0000	.0000	.0000	.0000	.0000	.0000	.0000	.0000	.0001	.0006
	17	.0000	.0000	.0000	.0000	.0000	.0000	.0000	.0000	.0000	.0001
	18	.0000	.0000	.0000	.0000	.0000	.0000	.0000	.0000	.0000	.0000
19	0	.3774	.1351	.0456	.0144	.0042	.0011	.0003	.0001	.0000	.0000
	1	.3774	.2852	.1529	.0685	.0268	.0093	.0029	.0008	.0002	.0000
	2	.1787	.2852	.2428	.1540	.0803	.0358	.0138	.0046	.0013	.0003
	3	.0533	.1796	.2428	.2182	.1517	.0869	.0422	.0175	.0062	.0018
	4	.0112	.0798	.1714	.2182	.2023	.1491	.0909	.0467	.0203	.0074
	5	.0018	.0266	.0907	.1636	.2023	.1916	.1468	.0933	.0497	.0222
	6	.0002	.0069	.0374	.0955	.1574	.1916	.1844	.1451	.0949	.0518
	7	.0000	.0014	.0122	.0443	.0974	.1525	.1844	.1797	.1443	.0961
	8	.0000	.0002	.0032	.0166	.0487	.0981	.1489	.1797	.1771	.1442
	9	.0000	.0000	.0007	.0051	.0198	.0514	.0980	.1464	.1771	.1762
	10	.0000	.0000	.0001	.0013	.0066	.0220	.0528	.0976	.1449	.1762
	11	.0000	.0000	.0000	.0003	.0018	.0077	.0233	.0532	.0970	.1442
	12	.0000	.0000	.0000	.0000	.0004	.0022	.0083	.0237	.0529	.0961
	13	.0000	.0000	.0000	.0000	.0001	.0005	.0024	.0085	.0233	.0518
	14	.0000	.0000	.0000	.0000	.0000	.0001	.0006	.0024	.0082	.0222

Binomial distribution (*concluded*)

n	r	.05	.10	.15	.20	.25	.30	.35	.40	.45	.50
19	15	.0000	.0000	.0000	.0000	.0000	.0000	.0001	.0005	.0022	.0074
	16	.0000	.0000	.0000	.0000	.0000	.0000	.0000	.0001	.0005	.0018
	17	.0000	.0000	.0000	.0000	.0000	.0000	.0000	.0000	.0001	.0003
	18	.0000	.0000	.0000	.0000	.0000	.0000	.0000	.0000	.0000	.0000
	19	.0000	.0000	.0000	.0000	.0000	.0000	.0000	.0000	.0000	.0000
20	0	.3585	.1216	.0388	.0115	.0032	.0008	.0002	.0000	.0000	.0000
	1	.3774	.2702	.1368	.0576	.0211	.0068	.0020	.0005	.0001	.0000
	2	.1887	.2852	.2293	.1369	.0669	.0278	.0100	.0031	.0008	.0002
	3	.0596	.1901	.2428	.2054	.1339	.0718	.0323	.0123	.0040	.0011
	4	.0133	.0898	.1821	.2182	.1897	.1304	.0738	.0350	.0139	.0046
	5	.0022	.0319	.1028	.1746	.2023	.1789	.1272	.0746	.0365	.0148
	6	.0003	.0089	.0454	.1091	.1686	.1916	.1712	.1244	.0746	.0370
	7	.0000	.0020	.0160	.0545	.1124	.1643	.1844	.1659	.1221	.0739
	8	.0000	.0004	.0046	.0222	.0609	.1144	.1614	.1797	.1623	.1201
	9	.0000	.0001	.0011	.0074	.0271	.0654	.1158	.1597	.1771	.1602
	10	.0000	.0000	.0002	.0020	.0099	.0308	.0686	.1171	.1593	.1762
	11	.0000	.0000	.0000	.0005	.0030	.0120	.0336	.0710	.1185	.1602
	12	.0000	.0000	.0000	.0001	.0008	.0039	.0136	.0355	.0727	.1201
	13	.0000	.0000	.0000	.0000	.0002	.0010	.0045	.0146	.0366	.0739
	14	.0000	.0000	.0000	.0000	.0000	.0002	.0012	.0049	.0150	.0370
	15	.0000	.0000	.0000	.0000	.0000	.0000	.0003	.0013	.0049	.0148
	16	.0000	.0000	.0000	.0000	.0000	.0000	.0000	.0003	.0013	.0046
	17	.0000	.0000	.0000	.0000	.0000	.0000	.0000	.0000	.0002	.0011
	18	.0000	.0000	.0000	.0000	.0000	.0000	.0000	.0000	.0000	.0002
	19	.0000	.0000	.0000	.0000	.0000	.0000	.0000	.0000	.0000	.0000
	20	.0000	.0000	.0000	.0000	.0000	.0000	.0000	.0000	.0000	.0000

Appendix J

POISSON DISTRIBUTION FOR SELECTED VALUES OF MU

Values in the table are for the function:

$$P(x) = \frac{\mu^x e^{-\mu}}{x(x-1)(x-2)\cdots 1}$$

P(x) for specified values of μ

x	$\mu = 0.1$	$\mu = 0.2$	$\mu = 0.3$	$\mu = 0.4$	$\mu = 0.5$	$\mu = 0.6$	$\mu = 0.7$	$\mu = 0.8$	$\mu = 0.9$	$\mu = 1.0$
0	.9048374	.8187308	.7408182	.6703200	.606531	.548812	.496585	.449329	.406570	.367879
1	.0904837	.1637462	.2222455	.2681280	.303265	.329287	347610	.359463	.365913	.367879
2	.0045242	.0163746	.0333368	.0536256	.075816	.098786	.121663	.143785	.164661	.183940
3	.0001508	.0010916	.0033337	.0071501	.012636	.019757	.028388	.038343	.049398	.061313
4	.0000038	.0000546	.0002500	.0007150	.001580	.002964	004968	.007669	.011115	.015328
5	.0000001	.0000022	.0000150	.0000572	.000158	.000356	000696	.001227	.002001	.003066
6		.0000001	.0000008	.0000038	.000013	.000036	.000081	.000164	.000300	.000511
7				.0000002	.000001	.000003	.000008	.000019	.000039	.000073
8							.000001	.000002	.000004	.000009
9										.000001

x	$\mu = 2.0$	$\mu = 3.0$	$\mu = 4.0$	$\mu = 5.0$	$\mu = 6.0$	$\mu = 7.0$	$\mu = 8.0$	$\mu = 9.0$	$\mu = 10.0$
0	.135335	.049787	.018316	.006738	.002479	.000912	.000335	.000123	.000045
1	.270671	.149361	.073263	.033690	.014873	.006383	.002684	.001111	.000454
2	.270671	.224042	.146525	.084224	.044618	.022341	.010735	.004998	.002270
3	.180447	.224042	.195367	.140374	.089235	.052129	.028626	.014994	.007567
4	.090224	.168031	.195367	.175467	.133853	.091226	.057252	.033737	.018917
5	.036089	.100819	.156293	.175467	.160623	.127717	.091604	.060727	.037833
6	.012030	.050409	.104196	.146223	.160623	.149003	.122138	.091090	.063055
7	.003437	.021604	.059540	.104445	.137677	.149003	.139587	.117116	.090079
8	000859	.008102	.029770	.065278	.103258	.130377	.139587	.131756	.112599
9	.000191	.002701	.013231	.036266	.068838	.101405	.124077	.131756	.125110
10	.000038	.000810	.005292	.018133	.041303	.070983	.099262	.118580	.125110
11	.000007	.000221	.001925	.008242	.022529	.045171	.072190	.097020	.113736
12	.000001	.000055	.000642	.003434	.011264	.026350	.048127	.072765	.094780
13		.000013	.000197	.001321	.005199	.014188	.029616	.050376	.072908
14		.000003	.000056	.000472	.002228	.007094	.016924	.032384	.052077
15		.000001	.000015	.000157	.000891	.003311	.009026	.019431	.034718
16			.000004	.000049	.000334	.001448	.004513	.010930	.021699
17			.000001	.000014	.000118	.000596	.002124	.005786	.012764
18				.000004	.000039	.000232	.000944	.002893	.007091
19				.000001	.000012	.000085	.000397	.001370	.003732
20					.000004	.000030	.000159	.000617	.001866
21					.000001	.000010	.000061	.000264	.000889
22						.000003	.000022	.000108	.000404
23						.000001	.000008	.000042	.000176
24							.000003	.000016	.000073
25							.000001	.000006	.000029
26								.000002	.000011
27								.000001	.000004
28									.000001
29									.000001

Source: E. C. Molina, *Poisson's Exponential Binomial Limit* (Princeton, N.J.: D. Van Nostrand Co., 1942). Reprinted by permission.

Appendix K

FACTORS FOR CONTROL CHARTS

Number of Items in Sample, n	Chart for Averages	Chart for Ranges		
	Factors for Control Limits	Factors for Central Line	Factors for Control Limits	
	A_2	d_2	D_3	D_4
2	1.880	1.128	0	3.267
3	1.023	1.693	0	2.575
4	.729	2.059	0	2.282
5	.577	2.326	0	2.115
6	.483	2.534	0	2.004
7	.419	2.704	.076	1.924
8	.373	2.847	.136	1.864
9	.337	2.970	.184	1.816
10	.308	3.078	.223	1.777
11	.285	3.173	.256	1.744
12	.266	3.258	.284	1.716
13	.249	3.336	.308	1.692
14	.235	3.407	.329	1.671
15	.223	3.472	.348	1.652

Source: Adapted from American Society for Testing and Materials, *Manual on Quality Control of Materials,* 1951, Table B2, p. 115. For a more detailed table and explanation, see Acheson J. Duncan, *Quality Control and Industrial Statistics,* 3d ed. (Homewood, Ill.: Richard D. Irwin, 1974), Table M, p. 927.

Appendix L

CRITICAL VALUES OF U IN THE MANN-WHITNEY TEST

In the first table the entries are the critical values of U for a one-tailed test at 0.025 or for a two-tailed test at 0.05; in the second, for a one-tailed test at 0.05 or for a two-tailed test at 0.10.

n_2 \ n_1	1	2	3	4	5	6	7	8	9	10	11	12	13	14	15	16	17	18	19	20
1																				
2								0	0	0	0	1	1	1	1	1	2	2	2	2
3					0	1	1	2	2	3	3	4	4	5	5	6	6	7	7	8
4			0	1	2	3	4	4	5	6	7	8	9	10	11	11	12	13	13	13
5		0	1	2	3	5	6	7	8	9	11	12	13	14	15	17	18	19	20	
6		1	2	3	5	6	8	10	11	13	14	16	17	19	21	22	24	25	27	
7		1	3	5	6	8	10	12	14	16	18	20	22	24	26	28	30	32	34	
8	0	2	4	6	8	10	13	15	17	19	22	24	26	29	31	34	36	38	41	
9	0	2	4	7	10	12	15	17	20	23	26	28	31	34	37	39	42	45	48	
10	0	3	5	8	11	14	17	20	23	26	29	33	36	39	42	45	48	52	55	
11	0	3	6	9	13	16	19	23	26	30	33	37	40	44	47	51	55	58	62	
12	1	4	7	11	14	18	22	26	29	33	37	41	45	49	53	57	61	65	69	
13	1	4	8	12	16	20	24	28	33	37	41	45	50	54	59	63	67	72	76	
14	1	5	9	13	17	22	26	31	36	40	45	50	55	59	64	67	74	78	83	
15	1	5	10	14	19	24	29	34	39	44	49	54	59	64	70	75	80	85	90	
16	1	6	11	15	21	26	31	37	42	47	53	59	64	70	75	81	86	92	98	
17	2	6	11	17	22	28	34	39	45	51	57	63	67	75	81	87	93	99	105	
18	2	7	12	18	24	30	36	42	48	55	61	67	74	80	86	93	99	106	112	
19	2	7	13	19	25	32	38	45	52	58	65	72	78	85	92	99	106	113	119	
20	2	8	13	20	27	34	41	48	55	62	69	76	83	90	98	105	112	119	127	

n_2 \ n_1	1	2	3	4	5	6	7	8	9	10	11	12	13	14	15	16	17	18	19	20
1																			0	0
2				0	0	0	1	1	1	1	2	2	2	3	3	3	4	4	4	
3		0	0	1	2	2	3	3	4	5	5	6	7	7	8	9	9	10	11	11
4		0	1	2	3	4	5	6	7	8	9	10	11	12	14	15	16	17	18	
5	0	1	2	4	5	6	8	9	11	12	13	15	16	18	19	20	22	23	25	
6	0	2	3	5	7	8	10	12	14	16	17	19	21	23	25	26	28	30	32	
7	0	2	4	6	8	11	13	15	17	19	21	24	26	28	30	33	35	37	39	
8	1	3	5	8	10	13	15	18	20	23	26	28	31	33	36	39	41	44	47	
9	1	3	6	9	12	15	18	21	24	27	30	33	36	39	42	45	48	51	54	
10	1	4	7	11	14	17	20	24	27	31	34	37	41	44	48	51	55	58	62	
11	1	5	8	12	16	19	23	27	31	34	38	42	46	50	54	57	61	65	69	
12	2	5	9	13	17	21	26	30	34	38	42	47	51	55	60	64	68	72	77	
13	2	6	10	15	19	24	28	33	37	42	47	51	56	61	65	70	75	80	84	
14	2	7	11	16	21	26	31	36	41	46	51	56	61	66	71	77	82	87	92	
15	3	7	12	18	23	28	33	39	44	50	55	61	66	72	77	83	88	94	100	
16	3	8	14	19	25	30	36	42	48	54	60	65	71	77	83	89	95	101	107	
17	3	9	15	20	26	33	39	45	51	57	64	70	77	83	89	96	102	109	115	
18	4	9	16	22	28	35	41	48	55	61	68	75	82	88	95	102	109	116	123	
19	0	4	10	17	23	30	37	44	51	58	65	72	80	87	94	101	109	116	123	130
20	0	4	11	18	25	32	39	47	54	62	69	77	84	92	100	107	115	123	130	138

Reproduced from the *Bulletin of the Institute of Educational Research at Indiana University*, vol. 1, no. 2; with the permission of the author and the publisher.

Appendix M

CRITICAL VALUES OF RHO, THE SPEARMAN RANK CORRELATION COEFFICIENT

N	Significance level (one-tailed test)	
	.05	.01
4	1.000	
5	.900	1.000
6	.829	.943
7	.714	.893
8	.643	.833
9	.600	.783
10	.564	.746
12	.506	.712
14	.456	.645
16	.425	.601
18	.399	.564
20	.377	.534
22	359	.508
24	.343	.485
26	.329	.465
28	.317	.448
30	.306	.432

Adapted from E. G. Olds, "Distributions of Sums of Squares of Rank Differences for Small Numbers of Individuals," *Annals of Mathematical Statistics* 9 (1938), pp. 133–48; and from E. G. Olds, "The 5% Significance Levels for Sums of Squares of Rank Differences and a Correction," *Annals of Mathematical Statistics* 20 (1949), pp. 117–18, with the kind permission of the author and publisher.

Appendix N

CRITICAL VALUES OF s IN THE KENDALL COEFFICIENT OF CONCORDANCE: W*

k	N					Additional values for N = 3	
	3†	4	5	6	7	k	s
Values at the .05 level of significance							
3			64.4	103.9	157.3	9	54.0
4		49.5	88.4	143.3	217.0	12	71.9
5		62.6	112.3	182.4	276.2	14	83.8
6		75.7	136.1	221.4	335.2	16	95.8
8	48.1	101.7	183.7	299.0	453.1	18	107.7
10	60.0	127.8	231.2	376.7	571.0		
15	89.8	192.9	349.8	570.5	864.9		
20	119.7	258.0	468.5	764.4	1,158.7		
Values at the .01 level of significance							
3			75.6	122.8	185.6	9	75.9
4		61.4	109.3	176.2	265.0	12	103.5
5		80.5	142.8	229.4	343.8	14	121.9
6		99.5	176.1	282.4	422.6	16	140.2
8	66.8	137.4	242.7	388.3	579.9	18	158.6
10	85.1	175.3	309.1	494.0	737.0		
15	131.0	269.8	475.2	758.2	1,129.5		
20	177.0	364.2	641.2	1,022.2	1,521.9		

*Adapted from M. Friedman, "A Comparison of Alternative Tests of Significance for the Problem of m Rankings," *Annals of Mathematical Statistics* 11 (1940), pp. 86–92, with the kind permission of the author and the publisher.
†Notice that additional critical values of x for N = 3 are given in the right-hand column of this table.

Appendix O

CRITICAL VALUES OF THE F DISTRIBUTION AT A 5 PERCENT LEVEL OF SIGNIFICANCE, α = 0.05

Degrees of freedom for numerator

Degrees of freedom for denominator	1	2	3	4	5	6	7	8	9	10	12	15	20	24	30	40	60	120	∞
1	161	200	216	225	230	234	237	239	241	242	244	246	248	249	250	251	252	253	254
2	18.5	19.0	19.2	19.2	19.3	19.3	19.4	19.4	19.4	19.4	19.4	19.4	19.4	19.5	19.5	19.5	19.5	19.5	19.5
3	10.1	9.55	9.28	9.12	9.01	8.94	8.89	8.85	8.81	8.79	8.74	8.70	8.66	8.64	8.62	8.59	8.57	8.55	8.53
4	7.71	6.94	6.59	6.39	6.26	6.16	6.09	6.04	6.00	5.96	5.91	5.86	5.80	5.77	5.75	5.72	5.69	5.66	5.63
5	6.61	5.79	5.41	5.19	5.05	4.95	4.88	4.82	4.77	4.74	4.68	4.62	4.56	4.53	4.50	4.46	4.43	4.40	4.37
6	5.99	5.14	4.76	4.53	4.39	4.28	4.21	4.15	4.10	4.06	4.00	3.94	3.87	3.84	3.81	3.77	3.74	3.70	3.67
7	5.59	4.74	4.35	4.12	3.97	3.87	3.79	3.73	3.68	3.64	3.57	3.51	3.44	3.41	3.38	3.34	3.30	3.27	3.23
8	5.32	4.46	4.07	3.84	3.69	3.58	3.50	3.44	3.39	3.35	3.28	3.22	3.15	3.12	3.08	3.04	3.01	2.97	2.93
9	5.12	4.26	3.86	3.63	3.48	3.37	3.29	3.23	3.18	3.14	3.07	3.01	2.94	2.90	2.86	2.83	2.79	2.75	2.71
10	4.96	4.10	3.71	3.48	3.33	3.22	3.14	3.07	3.02	2.98	2.91	2.85	2.77	2.74	2.70	2.66	2.62	2.58	2.54
11	4.84	3.98	3.59	3.36	3.20	3.09	3.01	2.95	2.90	2.85	2.79	2.72	2.65	2.61	2.57	2.53	2.49	2.45	2.40
12	4.75	3.89	3.49	3.26	3.11	3.00	2.91	2.85	2.80	2.75	2.69	2.62	2.54	2.51	2.47	2.43	2.38	2.34	2.30
13	4.67	3.81	3.41	3.18	3.03	2.92	2.83	2.77	2.71	2.67	2.60	2.53	2.46	2.42	2.38	2.34	2.30	2.25	2.21
14	4.60	3.74	3.34	3.11	2.96	2.85	2.76	2.70	2.65	2.60	2.53	2.46	2.39	2.35	2.31	2.27	2.22	2.18	2.13
15	4.54	3.68	3.29	3.06	2.90	2.79	2.71	2.64	2.59	2.54	2.48	2.40	2.33	2.29	2.25	2.20	2.16	2.11	2.07
16	4.49	3.63	3.24	3.01	2.85	2.74	2.66	2.59	2.54	2.49	2.42	2.35	2.28	2.24	2.19	2.15	2.11	2.06	2.01
17	4.45	3.59	3.20	2.96	2.81	2.70	2.61	2.55	2.49	2.45	2.38	2.31	2.23	2.19	2.15	2.10	2.06	2.01	1.96
18	4.41	3.55	3.16	2.93	2.77	2.66	2.58	2.51	2.46	2.41	2.34	2.27	2.19	2.15	2.11	2.06	2.02	1.97	1.92
19	4.38	3.52	3.13	2.90	2.74	2.63	2.54	2.48	2.42	2.38	2.31	2.23	2.16	2.11	2.07	2.03	1.98	1.93	1.88
20	4.35	3.49	3.10	2.87	2.71	2.60	2.51	2.45	2.39	2.35	2.28	2.20	2.12	2.08	2.04	1.99	1.95	1.90	1.84
21	4.32	3.47	3.07	2.84	2.68	2.57	2.49	2.42	2.37	2.32	2.25	2.18	2.10	2.05	2.01	1.96	1.92	1.87	1.81
22	4.30	3.44	3.05	2.82	2.66	2.55	2.46	2.40	2.34	2.30	2.23	2.15	2.07	2.03	1.98	1.94	1.89	1.84	1.78
23	4.28	3.42	3.03	2.80	2.64	2.53	2.44	2.37	2.32	2.27	2.20	2.13	2.05	2.01	1.96	1.91	1.86	1.81	1.76
24	4.26	3.40	3.01	2.78	2.62	2.51	2.42	2.36	2.30	2.25	2.18	2.11	2.03	1.98	1.94	1.89	1.84	1.79	1.73
25	4.24	3.39	2.99	2.76	2.60	2.49	2.40	2.34	2.28	2.24	2.16	2.09	2.01	1.96	1.92	1.87	1.82	1.77	1.71
30	4.17	3.32	2.92	2.69	2.53	2.42	2.33	2.27	2.21	2.16	2.09	2.01	1.93	1.89	1.84	1.79	1.74	1.68	1.62
40	4.08	3.23	2.84	2.61	2.45	2.34	2.25	2.18	2.12	2.08	2.00	1.92	1.84	1.79	1.74	1.69	1.64	1.58	1.51
60	4.00	3.15	2.76	2.53	2.37	2.25	2.17	2.10	2.04	1.99	1.92	1.84	1.75	1.70	1.65	1.59	1.53	1.47	1.39
120	3.92	3.07	2.68	2.45	2.29	2.18	2.09	2.02	1.96	1.91	1.83	1.75	1.66	1.61	1.55	1.50	1.43	1.35	1.25
∞	3.84	3.00	2.60	2.37	2.21	2.10	2.01	1.94	1.88	1.83	1.75	1.67	1.57	1.52	1.46	1.39	1.32	1.22	1.00

Critical values of the F distribution at a 1 percent level of significance, $\alpha = 0.01$ (continued)

Degrees of freedom for numerator

Degrees of freedom for denominator	1	2	3	4	5	6	7	8	9	10	12	15	20	24	30	40	60	120	∞
1	4,052	5,000	5,403	5,625	5,764	5,859	5,928	5,982	6,023	6,056	6,106	6,157	6,209	6,235	6,261	6,287	6,313	6,339	6,366
2	98.5	99.0	99.2	99.2	99.3	99.3	99.4	99.4	99.4	99.4	99.4	99.4	99.4	99.5	99.5	99.5	99.5	99.5	99.5
3	34.1	30.8	29.5	28.7	28.2	27.9	27.7	27.5	27.3	27.2	27.1	26.9	26.7	26.6	26.5	26.4	26.3	26.2	26.1
4	21.2	18.0	16.7	16.0	15.5	15.2	15.0	14.8	14.7	14.5	14.4	14.2	14.0	13.9	13.8	13.7	13.7	13.6	13.5
5	16.3	13.3	12.1	11.4	11.0	10.7	10.5	10.3	10.2	10.1	9.89	9.72	9.55	9.47	9.38	9.29	9.20	9.11	9.02
6	13.7	10.9	9.78	9.15	8.75	8.47	8.26	8.10	7.98	7.87	7.72	7.56	7.40	7.31	7.23	7.14	7.06	6.97	6.88
7	12.2	9.55	8.45	7.85	7.46	7.19	6.99	6.84	6.72	6.62	6.47	6.31	6.16	6.07	5.99	5.91	5.82	5.74	5.65
8	11.3	8.65	7.59	7.01	6.63	6.37	6.18	6.03	5.91	5.81	5.67	5.52	5.36	5.28	5.20	5.12	5.03	4.95	4.86
9	10.6	8.02	6.99	6.42	6.06	5.80	5.61	5.47	5.35	5.26	5.11	4.96	4.81	4.73	4.65	4.57	4.48	4.40	4.31
10	10.0	7.56	6.55	5.99	5.64	5.39	5.20	5.06	4.94	4.85	4.71	4.56	4.41	4.33	4.25	4.17	4.08	4.00	3.91
11	9.65	7.21	6.22	5.67	5.32	5.07	4.89	4.74	4.63	4.54	4.40	4.25	4.10	4.02	3.94	3.86	3.78	3.69	3.60
12	9.33	6.93	5.95	5.41	5.06	4.82	4.64	4.50	4.39	4.30	4.16	4.01	3.86	3.78	3.70	3.62	3.54	3.45	3.36
13	9.07	6.70	5.74	5.21	4.86	4.62	4.44	4.30	4.19	4.10	3.96	3.82	3.66	3.59	3.51	3.43	3.34	3.25	3.17
14	8.86	6.51	5.56	5.04	4.70	4.46	4.28	4.14	4.03	3.94	3.80	3.66	3.51	3.43	3.35	3.27	3.18	3.09	3.00
15	8.68	6.36	5.42	4.89	4.56	4.32	4.14	4.00	3.89	3.80	3.67	3.52	3.37	3.29	3.21	3.13	3.05	2.96	2.87
16	8.53	6.23	5.29	4.77	4.44	4.20	4.03	3.89	3.78	3.69	3.55	3.41	3.26	3.18	3.10	3.02	2.93	2.84	2.75
17	8.40	6.11	5.19	4.67	4.34	4.10	3.93	3.79	3.68	3.59	3.46	3.31	3.16	3.08	3.00	2.92	2.83	2.75	2.65
18	8.29	6.01	5.09	4.58	4.25	4.01	3.84	3.71	3.60	3.51	3.37	3.23	3.08	3.00	2.92	2.84	2.75	2.66	2.57
19	8.19	5.93	5.01	4.50	4.17	3.94	3.77	3.63	3.52	3.43	3.30	3.15	3.00	2.92	2.84	2.76	2.67	2.58	2.49
20	8.10	5.85	4.94	4.43	4.10	3.87	3.70	3.56	3.46	3.37	3.23	3.09	2.94	2.86	2.78	2.69	2.61	2.52	2.42
21	8.02	5.78	4.87	4.37	4.04	3.81	3.64	3.51	3.40	3.31	3.17	3.03	2.88	2.80	2.72	2.64	2.55	2.46	2.36
22	7.95	5.72	4.82	4.31	3.99	3.76	3.59	3.45	3.35	3.26	3.12	2.98	2.83	2.75	2.67	2.58	2.50	2.40	2.31
23	7.88	5.66	4.76	4.26	3.94	3.71	3.54	3.41	3.30	3.21	3.07	2.93	2.78	2.70	2.62	2.54	2.45	2.35	2.26
24	7.82	5.61	4.72	4.22	3.90	3.67	3.50	3.36	3.26	3.17	3.03	2.89	2.74	2.66	2.58	2.49	2.40	2.31	2.21
25	7.77	5.57	4.68	4.18	3.86	3.63	3.46	3.32	3.22	3.13	2.99	2.85	2.70	2.62	2.53	2.45	2.36	2.27	2.17
30	7.56	5.39	4.51	4.02	3.70	3.47	3.30	3.17	3.07	2.98	2.84	2.70	2.55	2.47	2.39	2.30	2.21	2.11	2.01
40	7.31	5.18	4.31	3.83	3.51	3.29	3.12	2.99	2.89	2.80	2.66	2.52	2.37	2.29	2.20	2.11	2.02	1.92	1.80
60	7.08	4.98	4.13	3.65	3.34	3.12	2.95	2.82	2.72	2.63	2.50	2.35	2.20	2.12	2.03	1.94	1.84	1.73	1.60
120	6.85	4.79	3.95	3.48	3.17	2.96	2.79	2.66	2.56	2.47	2.34	2.19	2.03	1.95	1.86	1.76	1.66	1.53	1.38
∞	6.63	4.61	3.78	3.32	3.02	2.80	2.64	2.51	2.41	2.32	2.18	2.04	1.88	1.79	1.70	1.59	1.47	1.32	1.00

Source: This table is reproduced from M. Merrington and C.M. Thompson, "Tables of Percentage Points of the Inverted Beta (F) Distribution," *Biometrika*, vol. 33 (1943), by permission of the Biometrika trustees.

Appendix P

CRITICAL VALUES OF D IN THE KOLMOGOROV-SMIRNOV TWO-SAMPLE TEST large samples, two-tailed test

Level of significance	Value of D so large as to call for rejection of H_0 at the indicated level of significance, where $D = \text{maximum} \left\| S_{n_1}(X) - S_{n_2}(X) \right\|$
.10	$1.22 \sqrt{\dfrac{n_1 + n_2}{n_1 n_2}}$
.05	$1.36 \sqrt{\dfrac{n_1 + n_2}{n_1 n_2}}$
.025	$1.48 \sqrt{\dfrac{n_1 + n_2}{n_1 n_2}}$
.01	$1.63 \sqrt{\dfrac{n_1 + n_2}{n_1 n_2}}$
.005	$1.73 \sqrt{\dfrac{n_1 + n_2}{n_1 n_2}}$
.001	$1.95 \sqrt{\dfrac{n_1 + n_2}{n_1 n_2}}$

Adapted from N. Smirnov, "Tables for Estimating the Goodness of Fit of Empirical Distributions," *Annals of Mathematical Statistics* 19 (1948), pp. 280–281, with the kind permission of the publisher.

Index

This book has been set VIP in 10 and 9 point Times Roman, leaded 2 points. Chapter numbers are 56 point Helvetica Bold and chapter titles are 20 point Helvetica Demi-Bold. The size of the text area is 28 by 48 picas.